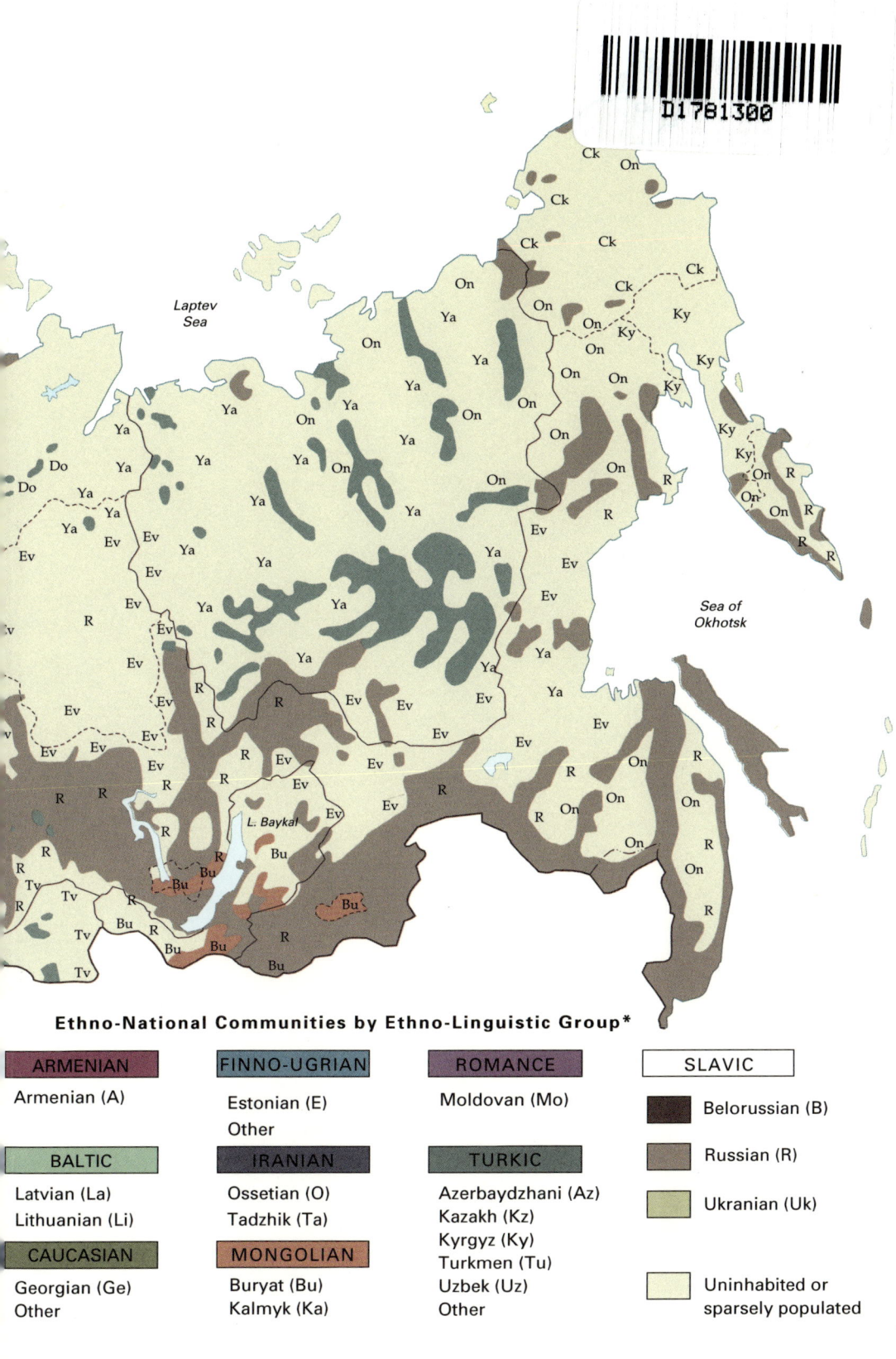

The Geography of Nationalism
in Russia and the USSR

The Geography of Nationalism in Russia and the USSR

Robert J. Kaiser

PRINCETON UNIVERSITY PRESS
PRINCETON, NEW JERSEY

Copyright © 1994 by Princeton University Press
Published by Princeton University Press, 41 William Street,
Princeton, New Jersey 08540
In the United Kingdom: Princeton University Press,
Chichester, West Sussex

All Rights Reserved

Library of Congress Cartaloging-in-Publication Data

Kaiser, Robert John.
    The geography of nationalism in Russia and the USSR / Robert J. Kaiser.
      p. cm.
    Includes bibliographical references and index.
    ISBN 0-691-03254-8 (alk. paper)
    1. Nationalism—Russia. 2. Nationalism and socialism—Soviet Union. 3. Self-determination, National—Russia. 4. Self-determination, National—Soviet Union. 5. Indigenous peoples—Russia. 6. Indigenous peoples—Soviet Union. I. Title.
JN6520.R43K37   1994
320.5'33'0947—dc20   93-34899
                                                                         CIP

Publication of this book has been aided by
a grant from the University of Missouri

This book has been composed in Times Roman

Princeton University Press books are printed on acid-free paper and meet the guidelines for permanence and durability of the Committee on Production Guidelines for Book Longevity of the Council on Library Resources

Printed in the United States of America

10 9 8 7 6 5 4 3 2

To Anne Marie

Contents

Full Key to Map "Ethnonational Communities of the USSR" (endpapers)	ix
List of Maps	xi
List of Tables	xiii
Preface	xvii
Acknowledgments	xix

PART ONE: *Theoretical and Historical Framework*

CHAPTER ONE
The Meaning of Homeland in the Study of Nationalism — 3
- *The Significance of Place* — 4
- *Defining the Nation* — 5
- *National Territoriality and Its Activation* — 22
- *Indigenization as Territorial Response* — 28

CHAPTER TWO
The Making of Nations in Tsarist Russia — 33
- *The Nationalization of the Elite* — 34
- *The Nationalization of the Masses, 1861–1914* — 43
- *The Development of a Sense of Homeland* — 83

CHAPTER THREE
National Consolidation and Territoriality during the Interwar Period — 94
- *Lenin on the National and Territorial Questions* — 96
- *Stalin on the National Question* — 102
- *The Formation of the USSR* — 107
- *Geographic Mobilization, 1917–1939* — 113
- *Korenizatsiya, Social Mobilization, and National Territoriality* — 124
- *National Consolidation and National Territoriality* — 135
- *International Integration and Russification during the 1930s* — 138

PART TWO: *National Territoriality in the Postwar USSR*

CHAPTER FOUR
Population Redistribution and National Territoriality, 1959–1989 — 151

National "Gravitation" to the Homeland   158
Interhomeland Mobility and Its Consequences   170

CHAPTER FIVE
Social Mobilization and National Territoriality   191

Social Mobilization and National Identity   192
Social Mobilization in the Postwar USSR   198
Social Mobilization and International Attitudes   243

CHAPTER SIX
The Ethnocultural Transformation of Soviet Society: Russification versus Indigenization   250

Language Usage Trends   253
International Marriage   295
Natural Assimilation   317

CHAPTER SEVEN
Political Indigenization and the Disintegration of the USSR   325

Political Indigenization and Totalitarianism   326
Economic Decentralization and the Problem of Regional Autarky   330
Political Indigenization and the Dissolution of the USSR   340

CHAPTER EIGHT
Conclusions and Implications   378

The Making of Nations and Homelands in Russia and the USSR   380
National Territoriality during the Postwar Period   385
The Significance of National Territoriality in Comparative Studies of Nationalism   400

Appendix A: Evolution of the Soviet Federal System   409

Appendix B: Native Language Instruction in the USSR   414

Bibliography   417

Index   447

Key to Map "Ethnonational Communities of the USSR"

Ethnolinguistic Group	National Community
ARMENIAN	Armenian (A)[a]
BALTIC	Latvian (La)
	Lithuanian (Li)
CAUCASIAN	Georgian (Ge)
	Abkhazian (Ab)
	Adygey (Ad)
	Avar (Aa)
	Chechen (Cc)
	Cherkess (Ce)
	Dargin (Da)
	Ingush (In)
	Kabardin (Kb)
	Lak (La)
	Lezgin (Le)
FINNO-UGRIAN	Estonian (E)
	Hungarian (H)
	Karelian (Ka)
	Khanty (Kh)
	Komi (Ko)
	Komi-Permyak (KP)
	Mansi (Mn)
	Mari (Ma)
	Mordvin (Mr)
	Udmurt (Ud)
IRANIAN	Tadzhik (Ta)
	Ossetian (O)
MONGOLIAN	Buryat (Bu)
	Kalmyk (Kl)
ROMANCE	Moldovan (Romanian) (Mo)
SLAVIC	Russian (R)
	Ukrainian (Uk)
	Belarusian (B)
	Bulgarian (Bl)
	Polish (P)

Key to Map of the USSR

TURKIC
    Uzbek (Uz)
    Kazakh (Kz)
    Azerbaydzhani (Az)
    Kyrgyz (Ky)
    Turkmen (Tu)
    Altay (Al)
    Balkar (Bk)
    Bashkir (Ba)
    Chuvash (Ch)
    Dolgan (Do)
    Gagauz (Ga)
    Karachay (Kc)
    Karakalpak (Kr)
    Khakass (Ks)
    Kumyk (Ku)
    Tatar (Tr)
    Tuvin (Tv)
    Uygur (Uy)
    Yakut (Ya)

OTHER
    German (G)
    Jewish (J)
    Korean (Ke)
    Chukchi (Ck)
    Evenk (Ev)
    Koryak (Ky)
    Nenets (Ne)
    Other peoples of the North (On)

[a]Initials are used to identify concentrated settlements of members of national communities outside their home republics (e.g., Armenians outside Armenia), and also to identify concentrations of indigenes whose homelands are located in sparsely populated regions of the country (e.g., Evenks in the Evenk Autonomous Okrug, Turkmen in sparsely settled regions of Turkmenistan). Colors for ethnolinguistic groupings are used to identify the regions of the homeland populated primarily by the indigenous national community (e.g., the color for the Baltic ethnolinguistic group represents Latvians in Latvia, and Lithuanians in Lithuania).

Maps

	Ethnonational Communities of the USSR	*Endpapers*
2.1	Rural Immobility by *Guberniya*, 1897	54
2.2	Urban Population by *Guberniya*, 1914	61
2.3	Literacy Rates by *Guberniya*, 1897	68
2.4	Primary Education by *Guberniya*, 1910	73
2.5	Industrial Work Force by *Guberniya*, 1897	77
3.1	Federal Structure of the USSR, 1926	111
3.2	Federal Structure of the USSR, 1939	114
4.1	Federal Structure of the USSR, 1989	155
4.2	Proportion of the National Community Residing in Its Home Republic, 1989	160
4.3	Change in Indigenous National Concentration, 1959–1989	163
4.4	Indigenous Percent of the Total Population by Federal Unit, 1989	172
4.5	Change in the Indigenous Proportion of the Total Population, 1959–1989	173
4.6	Russian Percent of the Total Population in the Non-Russian Homelands, 1989	179
4.7	Change in the Russian Proportion of the Total Population in the Non-Russian Homelands, 1959–1989	180
5.1	Urban Percent of the Total Population, 1989	205
5.2	Rate of Urbanization, 1959–1989	206
5.3	Indigenous Percent of the Urban Population, 1989	210
5.4	Indigenization of the Urban Population, 1959–1989	211
5.5	Russian Percent of the Urban Population, 1989	218
5.6	Derussification of the Urban Population, 1959–1989	219
6.1	Percent of Indigenes Claiming Russian as their Native Language, 1989	263
6.2	Linguistic Russification of Indigenes, 1959–1989	264
6.3	Native Language Retention among Indigenes, 1989	270
6.4	Change in Native Language Retention among Indigenes, 1959–1989	271
7.1	Ethnoterritorial Conflicts, 1992	359
7.2	Border Disputes and Territorial Conflicts, Moldova	366

Tables

2.1	Railroad Network by Gross Region, 1911	52
2.2	Rural Population by Place of Birth and Gross Region, 1897	55
2.3	Number of Voluntary and Involuntary Migrants into Asiatic Russia, 1801–1914	56
2.4	Urbanization by Gross Region, 1858–1914	62
2.5	Urban Population by Place of Birth and Gross Region, 1897	63
2.6	Ethnolinguistic Composition of the Total and Urban Population, 1897	64
2.7	Literacy Rates for the Total, Urban, and Rural Population, by Gross Region	69
2.8	Literacy and Education Rates by Language, Sex, and Ethnolinguistic Community, 1897	70
2.9	Level of Educational Attainment by Gross Region, 1911	74
2.10	Ethnolinguistic Groups and Their Change, 1897–1917	90
3.1	Geographic Distribution of Nations in the USSR, by Republic, 1926–1939	116
3.2	Distribution of Russians by Union and Autonomous Republics, 1917–1939	118
3.3	Urbanization in the USSR by Union Republic and Nation, 1926–1939	122
3.4	Indigenous and Russian Composition of the Urban Population by Union Republic, 1926–1959	123
3.5	Book Publication in the USSR, 1913–1937	128
3.6	Literacy Rates by Republic, 1897–1939	130
3.7	Education Rates by Indigenous Nation, Russians and Republic, 1939	131
3.8	Employment in Mental and Physical Labor Outside Agriculture, 1926–1939	133
3.9	National Consolidation of Ethnographic Groups, 1926–1959	136
3.10	Native Language Retention, 1926–1959	140
3.11	International Marriage Rates by Republic and Indigenous Nation, 1936	141
4.1	The Concentration of National Members in Their Home Republics, 1959–1989	161
4.2	Total and Russian Net Migration, 1979–1991	167
4.3	Nations as a Percentage of Their Respective Home Republic Populations, 1959–1989	174
4.4	Relative Change in the National Composition of the Population by Republic, 1959–1989	176
4.5	Population Born in the Republic of Current Residence, 1989	186
5.1	Urban Population of the USSR, by Nation and Home Republic, 1926–1959	201

xiv · Tables

5.2	Urban Population of the USSR, by Nation and Home Republic, 1959–1989	203
5.3	Urbanization in the USSR, by Nation and Home Republic, 1959–1989	207
5.4	The Location of National Members in Their Home Republics, 1959–1989	212
5.5	Location of National Members Outside Their Respective Home Republics, 1959–1989	215
5.6	National Composition of the Urban Population by Republic, 1959–1989	220
5.7	Urban Migration by Nation and Republic, 1989	224
5.8	Higher and Secondary Education (Complete and Incomplete) in the USSR	227
5.9	Higher Education Rates (Complete and Incomplete) by Nation, 1959–1979	229
5.10	Students in Higher Educational Institutions at the Beginning of School Years 1974–1975 and 1989–1990, by Nation	232
5.11	Indigenous Proportion of Students Entering Higher Education, by Republic	233
5.12	Class Composition of Soviet Nations, 1959–1979	237
5.13	Specialists with a Higher or Specialized Secondary Education by Nation	239
5.14	Proportional Representation of Indigenes in Blue- and White-Collar Work Force, 1967–1987; Proportional Representation of Indigenes among Directors of Enterprises and Organizations, 1989	241
5.15	International Attitudes among Male Tatars, 1967	245
6.1	Number of Pupils with Russian and Native Language Instruction, 1965–1972	256
6.2	Language of Instruction Preferred by Parents	256
6.3	Language of Publication by Republic, 1970–1988	259
6.4	Native Language Retention and Linguistic Russification by Nation, 1959–1989	266
6.5	Native Language Retention Rates by Nation and Location Inside and Outside of the Home Republic, 1959–1989	273
6.6	Linguistic Russification of Indigenes in Homeland Urban and Rural Locations, 1959–1989	276
6.7	Linguistic Russification of Nonindigenes in Urban and Rural Locations, 1959–1989	279
6.8	Russian as a Second Language by Nation and Location Inside and Outside the Home Republic, 1970–1989	290
6.9	Nonindigenes Claiming Fluency in the Indigenous Language as a First or Second Language, 1970–1989	294
6.10	Comparison of Positive Attitudes to International Marriage (mid-1970s) with Actual Rates for Selective Nations, 1978	297
6.11	International Family Proportions in the USSR by Republic, 1959–1989	298

6.12	Average Annual Percentage Point Change in the Proportion of International Families by Republic for Total, Urban, and Rural Populations, 1959–1989	299
6.13	International Marriage Rates by Nation and Sex, 1978–1988	302
6.14	International Marriage Rates by Age and Nation, 1978–1988	306
6.15	Intermarriage Rates for Lithuanians and Russians in Vilnius and Kaunas, 1947 and 1980	308
6.16	Indigenous Change in International Marriage Rates, 1978–1988	309
7.1	National Income and Trade Balances, and Potential Debt Burden, 1988	337
7.2	National Composition of Total Population, and Delegates to Congress of Peoples Deputies, Republican Supreme Soviets, and Local Soviets	349

Preface

THE RESEARCH for this book began as an investigation into the reasons why nations formed such strong emotional attachments to specific land areas, and how this sense of homeland influenced international relations in multinational, multihomeland states. The absence of such a geographic focus in the study of nations and nationalism has been especially pronounced in the United States, where the immigrant roots of the population has biased research into the nature of ethnonational group formation and international interaction. As an example of this bias, when I began giving lectures on the importance of homelands in the study of nations and nationalism, the term *homeland* itself was nearly incomprehensible to the general audience. It conjured up images of aboriginal peoples isolated from the forces of "modernization" or the artificial political geographic contrivances of Grand Apartheid in South Africa. It was only after 1989, when nationalists in the USSR increasingly began to speak of their emotional attachment to the homeland and to demand control over it, that this geographic aspect of nations and nationalism became a more frequently discussed (if no better understood) concept.

The limited appreciation of the geography of nationalism in general has also been apparent in studies of the so-called national problem in Russia and the USSR. The focus of much of this research was on nationality policy initiatives developed in Moscow by the Communist party elites and the impact of these policies on the national communities in the state. At best, these studies acknowledged the variable impact of nationality policies on different nations in the USSR, but few if any noted the geographic variability of these policies' effectiveness within the same national community. Furthermore, nations themselves were frequently equated with cultural communities (i.e., communities of language, religion, etc.), and the focus of empirical investigations often simply traced the changing strength of linguistic or religious affiliation over time. A national sense of homeland and the implications that this has had on national formation and international relations in the USSR was almost completely missing from this body of literature.

A final source of bias in the study of nationalism comes from nationalist historians, political scientists, sociologists, and so forth, who begin with the assumption that their nations are primordial organisms that have suffered from the "denationalization" policies emanating from Moscow, and that have only now reawakened to reclaim their glorious heritage and to fulfill their destiny as masters of their primordial homelands. These treatments of the "national question" in Russia and the USSR do not accord with the historical record, which indicates that the making of nations and homelands in Russia and the USSR, and indeed in the rest of the world, are relatively recent social processes. Far from a seventy-five-year period of denationalization, the Soviet period was the time during which most of the nations in the state became mass-based, and the national challenge to Soviet legitimacy was much more formidable in the post-World War II era than it had been at the time of the bolshevik revolution.

This book is a preliminary attempt to explore the dynamic societal processes that restructured human communities as nations, and geographic places as homelands. The focus here is not on political structures and institutions per se; as I noted above, policy and political elites have been overemphasized, if anything, in studies of the national question in the USSR. In particular, the book is an exploration into the nature of national territoriality and the degree to which national homelands, once created in the imaginations of the indigenous masses, have influenced their attitudes about themselves, their futures, and about ethnic "outsiders."

I say preliminary here because as I researched this topic, it became increasingly obvious that each chapter could easily form the basis of a volume in its own right. This is truly only a beginning point in the elaboration of the geography of nationalism in Russia and the USSR, and in multinational, multihomeland states more generally. It is hoped that this research will stimulate others working in the field of nationality studies to add a geographic dimension to their work, in order that the meaning of homeland in the study of nations and international relations may be explored from a multidisciplinary perspective.

The results of this research clearly have relevance that reaches far beyond the borders of the former Soviet Union. The increasing frequency of demands by nationalists for self-determination in regions proclaimed to be the ancestral homelands of their ethnonational communities in the First and Third Worlds indicates that a better understanding of the geography of nationalism is more critical than ever. The experience of the Soviet Union is certainly not unique in this regard. The very fact that successful independence drives by nations in the USSR struck a responsive chord leading to renewed calls for independence by nations in multinational, multihomeland states around the world provides convincing evidence of that. The development of a sense of homeland along with the formation of a national self-consciousness appears to be a nearly ubiquitous phenomenon of the twentieth-century world, and a deeper understanding of this general interrelationship is clearly warranted.

Acknowledgments

ANY RESEARCH effort of this magnitude and scope would be impossible without the encouragement, assistance, and critical guidance of numerous scholars and research institutes. I would like to take this opportunity to acknowledge my indebtedness to Robert Lewis, Walker Connor, and Ralph Clem for their helpful critiques of the manuscript; to the Kennan Institute of Advanced Russian Studies for providing me with financial support and a stimulating intellectual climate, and especially to Blair Ruble and Ted Taranowski for their critical comments on several chapters; to Duke University's East-West Center both for financial support and for providing me with the opportunity to research this subject at the USSR Academy of Science in Moscow; and to the Institute of Ethnology and Anthropology and the Institute of Geography in Moscow. I would like to offer special thanks to Nikolay Petrov, Vladimir Kolosov, Andrey Berezkin, Alexander Susokolov, Mikhail Guboglo, and Leokadia Drobizheva for their gracious hospitality and personal assistance in this research endeavor. I am also indebted to the Geographic Resource Center, University of Missouri-Columbia, and especially to Robin Kelly-Goss, for their work on the maps produced for this volume. Finally, I must acknowledge my profound gratitude to my wife, Anne Marie, who has been a steadfast supporter during the research and writing of this book.

PART ONE

Theoretical and Historical Framework

CHAPTER ONE

The Meaning of Homeland in the Study of Nationalism

THE AGE OF NATIONALISM, long thought to have reached its apex in the romanticism of the nineteenth century, has resurfaced to take ideological pride of place in the late twentieth century. Indeed, in many ways nationalism as a mass-based ideology is a new and more potent force for change today than it was in the past. The legitimacy of multinational states new and old has been increasingly challenged by smaller and smaller ethnic groups whose members proclaim their communities nations deserving of their own independent states. This centrifugal force is behind much of the ethnic and territorial conflict in the underdeveloped South following formal decolonization (e.g., India, Pakistan, Sri Lanka, Ethiopia, Uganda, Iraq, Sudan, Zaire, Zambia). It has clearly been the principal cause of disintegration of the multinational states in the socialist world (e.g., USSR, Yugoslavia, Czechoslovakia). Multinational states in the developed "core" have also faced national separatist challenges (Spain, Great Britain, Belgium, France, Canada), despite the European Community states forming a more confederal relationship with one another.

While it is true that the threat posed to multinational states by national separatism has varied over time and political geographic space, the nationalistic demand that nations be masters of their own homelands has strained to the breaking point the ties that supposedly bind nations together in these states. Political elites in multinational states have been successful in managing the separatist challenges confronting them for a time through the use of both accommodative (provision of cultural or territorial autonomy) and coercive (repression, ethnocide or forced acculturation/assimilation, genocide) policies. However, they have ultimately been unsuccessful in solving their national separatist problems, and policies designed to defuse the nationalist challenge have often proved counterproductive. In addition, although few national separatist movements have been successful in accomplishing their ultimate objective—secession and the establishment of an independent and ethnically homogeneous nation-state—they have been more successful in the political mobilization of the indigenous masses and in winning a degree of territorial autonomy over their homelands.

Nationalism has been defined as loyalty to the nation and its continued survival, and as "politicized ethnicity." Both these definitions highlight the political dimension of nationalism, but each begs the question: What is a nation? Or what is ethnicity? A more complete definition of nationalism is offered by Breuilly (1982, 3):

> The term 'nationalism' is used to refer to political movements seeking or exercising state power and justifying such actions with nationalist arguments.
> A nationalist argument is a political doctrine built upon three basic assertions:
> a) There exists a nation with an explicit and peculiar character.
> b) The interests and values of this nation take priority over all other interests and values.
> c) The nation must be as independent as possible. This usually requires at least the attainment of political sovereignty.

Ideally, most nationalist movements envision the construction of ethnically homogeneous nation-states within which the national membership will be able to determine its own future. This nation-state ideal is also often depicted as economically and politically independent of all other states, and as a place where the indigenous nation's cultural attributes (i.e., language, religion, way of life, etc.) are predominant. This idealized objective means that nationalism is not only a political movement for national independence but also has a demographic, sociocultural and economic agenda for change. This nationalistic ideal is clearly at odds with the multinational character of most states in the world today. It also runs counter to the economic and sociocultural trends toward globalization during the twentieth century, but this has not apparently dampened the nationalistic appeal of autarchy and absolute sovereignty, particularly for subordinate national communities in multinational states.

Nationalism is at heart a political geographic doctrine, since it has as its objective the congruence between political and ethnonational borders (Gellner 1983, 1; Williams 1986). The geographic centrality of nationalism is also identified in the work of Anthony Smith (1986, 163): "the need for a 'homeland', a national space of one's own, is a central tenet of nationalism. Indeed, nationalism is always, whatever other aims it may have, about the possession and retention of land." Geography is clearly a critical dimension of nationalism, although it has often been ignored in political and sociological studies on the subject. The purpose of the present work is to bring geography back into the study of nations and nationalism.

The definition of nationalism offered above still raises two crucial questions that this chapter seeks to address in a general way, and that the remainder of this book is devoted to in a case study of Russia and the USSR. The first of these two questions is: What is a nation? The second is: What is homeland, and what is the meaning of homeland in the study of nations and nationalism?

THE SIGNIFICANCE OF PLACE

With a few notable exceptions (e.g., Connor 1986; Smith 1981, 1986; Williams and Smith 1983), political and sociological studies of nations and nationalism, as with political sociology more generally, have tended to treat *place* as an insignificant explanatory variable (Agnew 1987).[1] If not ignored altogether, it is often seen as an empty container—meaningless in and of itself—within which individuals and groups live out their lives. During the 1980s, political geographers have increasingly been engaged in the study of nationalism, and as a consequence questions about the importance of place have been raised, if not definitively answered (e.g., Knight 1982; Johnston et al. 1988; Williams 1982, 1986; Williams and Kofman 1989; Agnew 1984, 1987). Nevertheless, even political geographic studies of nationalism have tended to treat "regions as little more than locational referents for particular peoples or groups," and have not looked into the creation of national places and their impact on national and international processes (Murphy 1991, 24). Specifically, the importance of *homeland*, both in the formation of national self-consciousness and as the place where international relations are played out, has rarely served as a focus of research in political geography.

A strong argument may be made for such a focus: the national homeland is a powerful geographic mediator of sociopolitical behavior and serves as a strong case in support of the place-based theory of political sociology recently elaborated by Agnew (1987). According to this thesis, the study of place has three dimensions (ibid., 28, 230–231): *locale*, *location*, and *sense of place*. Each dimension may be related to a place-based theory of nationalism. Locale, defined as "the setting in which social relations are constituted," may be equated with the objective or tangible land serving as the resource or political power base of the nation. Location, defined as "the geographical area encompassing the settings for social interaction as defined by social and economic processes operating at a wider scale," may be thought of as the external (i.e., international and interhomeland) geopolitical and socioeconomic environment within which national communities interact. Sense of place, defined as "the local 'structure of feeling,' " may be viewed as the subjective dimension through which a given national community identifies with a certain area as its ancestral homeland. The presence of an emotional attachment to the ethnonational homeland has been noted by several analysts (e.g., Connor 1986; Smith 1981; Tuan 1977; Anderson 1988; Williams and Smith 1983). The development of a "sense of homeland" along with a national self-consciousness, and its impact on international relations in the USSR, are central themes of this study.

Defining the Nation

The question "What is a nation?" is by no means simple, and this issue alone has been the subject of numerous publications both in the West (e.g., White 1985;

---

[1] As used in this book, nation is not synonymous with state. The meaning of nation and its derivatives (i.e., international, nationalism, etc.) are explored in this chapter.

1985; Symmons-Symonolewicz 1985; Connor 1978; Smith 1986; Armstrong 1982; Gellner 1983; Tiryakian and Rogowski 1985; Blaut 1987), and also in the former USSR (e.g., Stalin 1913; Hodnett 1967a; Shanin 1989; Zeymal' 1988; Bromley 1981, 1983a; Drobizheva 1985; Kryukov 1986).[2] Terminological confusion over the use of nation, state, nationality, and ethnic group is a serious problem which has contributed to the failure of social scientists to explain and predict the occurrence of nationalism (Connor 1978). As used in this study, nation refers to a self-defining community of belonging and interest whose members share a sense of common origins and a belief in a common destiny or future together. It is a primary form of group identity which includes both a "modern" or "instrumentalist" dimension (i.e., a community of interest), and also a "primordial" dimension (i.e., a shared perception of common origins), though the nation itself is decidedly modern.[3] This distinguishes the nation both from the state and also from ethnic groups or *ethnie*, the latter of which are defined by Smith (1986, 32) as "named human populations with shared ancestry myths, histories and cultures, having an association with a specific territory and a sense of solidarity." In this study, the term *ethnie* is used to refer to protonations, that is, ethnic communities of belonging that have not yet developed into future-oriented politicized communities of interest.

Nations are normally defined as having two dimensions—a set of objective characteristics that members of the nation share in common, and a more subjective sense of belonging, a national self-consciousness (Shafer 1972). Each of these dimensions is discussed in greater detail below. The importance of place as both a tangible attribute of national communities and also a critical element in the development of a national self-consciousness is highlighted in the following sections.

The Objective Dimension

Members of a nation normally share a number of tangible or objective characteristics, including a common language, land, religion, customs, rituals, dress,

[2] Hodnett 1967a and Shanin 1989 provide surveys of Soviet writing on the subject. Hodnett's in particular is worthwhile, since it details a debate on the meaning of nation conducted during the 1960s. Two decades later, Kryukov's 1986 article set off a new round of debate on the definition of "ethnic communities" conducted on the pages of *Sovetskaya Etnografiya* (1986, nos. 3–5: section "Diskussii i Obsuzhdeniya"). The definition of nation in Russia and the USSR changed over time, and is in some sense the main subject of the remaining chapters in the book. For this reason, the Soviet view of national identity is not elaborated in this chapter, which is meant to provide a more general, comparative context within which to assess the evolving "national question" in the USSR.

[3] Smith (1986, 6–13) provides a good discussion of these two approaches to the study of nations and their limitations, along with his own "perennial" approach. This approach is further elaborated in Smith (1988), and is rebutted in Zubaida (1989). See also Hobsbawm (1990) and Connor (1990), the latter of which asks the related question: "When is a nation?"

diet, and so on. These objective features are important in that they provide individuals with more or less readily identifiable "markers" of ethnonational belonging. These markers serve as one of the ways in which the sociocultural boundaries of ethnonational communities may be delimited and maintained (van den Berghe 1981).

The tangible characteristics of the nation are often treated as essentially timeless and unchanging elements around which the national community is structured, and this is particularly true of the nationalist literature on the subject. However, an assessment of social history in Europe and the Russian Empire as late as the mid-nineteenth century indicates that most of these objective criteria varied from locality to locality within the proclaimed nations that had been created (e.g., Weber 1976; Hobsbawm 1990; Hroch 1985; Connor 1990; Brooks 1985; Raun 1987). Standardized "national" languages were being created only during the late nineteenth and early twentieth centuries (Anderson 1983), at a time when mass-based nations themselves were actively being constructed (Hroch 1985). Homeland itself most often meant the local village or region in which one was born, and only changed with the broadening of the conceptualization of "nation" beyond locality to encompass much larger "imagined communities" (Hobsbawm 1990, 15–16; Anderson 1983; Weber 1976). Even though objective characteristics were given a primordial appearance by nationalists, they were for the most part new creations that coincided with the growing interaction among localities; with increasing communication and transportation; and frequently with the creation of states themselves which fostered linguistic standardization and a geographically more expansive perception of homeland.

The national land in its objective dimension (i.e., locale) may be viewed as the physical resource base of the nation. Land in this regard is, along with capital and labor, one of the three inputs into the nation's economic life. As a second dimension to the objective geographic base of the nation, land also serves as the place where the nation exercises political control (Blaut 1987, 62). From this objective perspective, the nation need not be sited in any particular place, and as a community of interest should favor land that is well endowed with natural resources, geostrategic location, and so forth. However, while it is true that nationalists normally lay claim to the most expansive homelands possible, nations have clearly not been as footloose as this objective depiction would suggest. The development of a sense of homeland, along with a sense of national belonging has served to attach nations to specific places during the last century or so.

A tendency both in the West and in the former USSR has been to equate the nation with the tangible attributes that its members share in common. For example, the international conflict in Northern Ireland between the Irish and Orange nations is often portrayed as a religious conflict between Catholics and Protestants, just as the conflict between the Flemish and Walloonian nations in

Belgium or between the Quebecois and British Canadians is said to be a linguistic dispute. Nationalists themselves often promote the idea that the nation is strictly bounded by its objective characteristics, and that the loss of the national religion, language, and so on, are harbingers of the nation's demise (e.g., Dzyuba 1970).

This tendency to equate the nation with a community of shared characteristics has resulted not only in an overly simplistic view of the nation, but also in an overly optimistic assessment of the prospects for resolving the "national problem" through international integration, i.e., the assimilation of nations into one statewide community (e.g., a Soviet People). The loss of ethnocultural characteristics by members of one nation and their replacement by those of another through a process of acculturation has been viewed as a preliminary stage which necessarily results in the eventual assimilation of members from one nation to that of another (e.g., Gans 1979). For Stalin (1913, 8), who defined the nation as "a historically evolved, stable community of language, territory, economic life, and psychological make-up manifested in a community of culture," it was deemed "sufficient for a single one of these characteristics to be absent and the nation ceases to be a nation."

While acculturation does normally precede assimilation, the former is not a sufficient condition for the occurrence of the latter. In a comparative study of the relationship between these two "stages of assimilation," Connor (1972, 341–342) found that "an individual (or an entire national group) can shed all of the overt cultural manifestations customarily attributed to his ethnic group and yet maintain his fundamental identity as a member of that nation. Cultural assimilation need not mean psychological assimilation." Of course, this statement also applies to land as a tangible attribute of the nation. A nation can exist without possessing land or dictating the economic uses to which that land is put, as the Basques and Catalans under Franco, the Jews prior to the creation of Israel, and indeed most nations living in a multihomeland setting demonstrate. However, it does appear that for a nation to exist, it must have some place that it can claim as its own, whether or not it has political or economic control of that geographic space at a given time.

The lack of coincidence between the tangible attributes and the essence of national identity has presented a dilemma not only for empiricists studying nations and nationalism but also for policymakers seeking to integrate a state's disparate national communities into a more unified whole. For example, centralizing authorities in multinational states have often promoted the adoption of statewide, ethnocultural traits (e.g., an official state language or *lingua franca*) in part as an attempt to create the conditions for the erasure of national identity and its replacement by a closer affiliation with a statewide identity.[4] However,

---

[4] A multinational state's attempts to integrate its population is rarely without bias in favor of a "dominant" nation within the state. For example, "Sovietization" in the USSR had a strong element

even when these policies are successful, they rarely have the desired assimilative effect. On the contrary, state attempts to force the pace of acculturation and assimilation have generally proven counterproductive (Connor 1972). This had been recognized by Soviet ethnographers and policymakers for much of the state's history, although actual policies often failed to live up to the voluntaristic tenets of a Marxist-Leninist approach to solving the "national problem" (Connor 1984a). Consequently, national self-consciousness may actually rise with the loss of the nation's objective characteristics, particularly when this acculturation is viewed as an attack on the nation by "foreigners." For example, state-sponsored "Russification" during the late nineteenth century was at least partially responsible for rising national self-consciousness in the non-Russian periphery. More recently, the main purpose of national front organizations formed in the USSR since 1985 is said to be to ensure the rebirth of the nation after a long period of forced "denationalization" (e.g., RUKH 1989, 9–11).

To conclude that the nation is not merely the sum of its objective parts is not to argue that these tangible features are unimportant. Objective characteristics become part of a subjective "myth-symbol complex" which is central to the evolving national sense of self (Smith 1986). For example, language was seen by Herder, the father of German cultural nationalism, as "a gift from God" that distinguished the German nation from all others, rather than "an artificial instrument" (Kohn 1945, 431), and the same can of course be said for the national religion and the belief that the nation itself is favored as the "chosen people." In addition, land often devoid of economic or geopolitical value is perceived by nationalists as priceless, sacred soil (Connor 1986; Anderson 1988; Williams and Smith 1983). Objective characteristics often become part of the nation's iconography, and along with a flag, anthem, monuments, and so on, function as symbols of the nation's uniqueness.[5]

Beyond this symbolic function, the objective national characteristics have an instrumental value. Language in particular can and has been used as an instrument by nationalists seeking to gain an edge in international competition for scarce resources, including high-status occupations. Having one's native language declared the lingua franca of the entire state or a region therein clearly provides strategic advantages to the "native" speakers, and this is undoubtedly one reason why the status of the indigenous language was one of the first items on the nationalists' political agenda in the USSR during the late 1980s.

Nevertheless, the retention of a distinct national language, religion, and so forth, is not necessary for a nation's continued existence. First, as is becoming increasingly clear with the growing number of historical studies on the making of nations, the idea that objective characteristics have existed "from time imme-

---

of "Russification" inherent in it, which was particularly apparent in the adoption of Russian as the state's lingua franca (Aspaturian 1968).

[5] See Gottmann (1973) on the importance of the use of iconography to state- or nation-building.

morial" essentially unchanged (except for the attacks launched against them by "foreigners") is a self-serving nationalistic concept that has little basis in reality.[6] The national idea did not depend on or derive from a preexistent primordial language; rather, national languages were created only after nations were conceived. In general, the same is true of the process of constructing a national homeland. Second, the loss of one's native language, religion, customs, and so forth, does not necessarily signify the loss of one's sense of national belonging. For example, the Irish nation is undoubtedly a viable entity, even though the Irish have for all intents and purposes acculturated to the English language. More generally, ethnospecific religious affiliation, rites, rituals, customs, dress, diet, and so on, are often undermined during the course of sociocultural and economic development, even while national self-consciousness has tended to grow stronger and to become mass-based over time with "modernization." In defining the nation, we need to go beyond the objective characteristics that may or may not be shared by its members, and examine the more subjective sense of belonging that binds the membership together.[7]

National Self-Consciousness

The more subjective dimension of national self-consciousness derives its strength from both a backward-looking sense of common origins and a forward-looking sense of common destiny (Emerson 1960, 95). The former promotes the perception that the nation is a "primordial organism," while the latter lends the nation a more "instrumentalist" appearance. Both of these temporal aspects of national self-consciousness are fused together in the nationalist's imagination by a "myth-symbol complex," which tells the nation where it has been and indicates a "trajectory" along which the nation will travel (Smith 1986). Each of these two temporal dimensions is discussed below.

As with the definition of nation in general, the importance of place cannot be understood without a consideration of a subjective sense of homeland which develops along with national self-consciousness. In essence, the subjective sense of homeland is founded on the perception held by members that a given place is both the geographic cradle of the nation and also the "natural" place where the nation is to fulfill its destiny. The national homeland itself is a "social construct" created during the past century or two along with the emerging national idea. Once created, the sense of homeland has in turn exerted a powerful influence on the nationalization process.[8]

---

[6] The invention of traditions was an integral part of the construction of a "myth-symbol complex." For a fascinating study of this topic, see Hobsbawm and Ranger (1983).

[7] The USSR made a clear distinction between sense of national belonging and objective attributes. For example, a question on language and a question on national identity were asked in each of the Soviet censuses. See Silver (1986).

[8] Alexander Murphy (1991) provides an excellent discussion of the importance of understanding

A SENSE OF COMMON ORIGINS—SHARED ANCESTRY

A sense of common origins normally involves a belief in shared ancestry, which is for the most part mythical. While certain authors have taken the view that nations *are* biological entities (e.g., Ardrey 1966; van den Berghe 1981; Gumilev 1990), the belief in a common ancestry cannot (and need not) be objectively verified. Contemporary nations most often consist of several subnational ethnographic groups whose members have undergone a process of horizontal (i.e., interethnic) consolidation in the recent past. Even in the USSR under "developed socialism," when the process of national consolidation was said to have been essentially complete (Bromley 1983b, 9), the nationalization process was still underway in the North Caucasus, Central Asia, Siberia, and the Far East.

In addition to horizontal consolidation, vertical incorporation into the national community is also something essentially new. Indeed, throughout feudal Europe before the nineteenth century, there was little sense among elites that the peasantry was part of the same species, let alone part of the same nation (Weber 1976; Pearson 1983; Breuilly 1982; Hobsbawm 1990). As discussed in chapter 2, the Russian peasants before the mid-nineteenth century were similarly viewed by the gentry and government as at best children needing strict guidance (Eklof 1986), and at worst subhumans in need of evolution (Riasanovsky 1968). Active attempts to integrate the masses into the emerging nations, and thus provide these collectivities with a mass base, occurred only during the late nineteenth and early twentieth centuries in Europe and Russia (Hroch 1985).

While the processes of horizontal and vertical consolidation were to some extent unique historical processes for each nation, a number of common elements can be identified. In a discussion of national consolidation in Western Europe, Smith (1986, 130–134) cites as critical the "triple Western revolution" of (1) capitalism, resulting in a much higher degree of economic integration; (2) the "rise of the bureaucratic state" and the increasing centralization of political power; and (3) a "cultural and educational revolution" and the increasing standardization of each. The critical importance of all three of these "revolutions" is that they had the effect of lowering the geographic, socioeconomic, cultural, and political barriers to integration. Specifically, the three revolutions meant improvements in transportation and communication; the development of a capitalist market economy linking urban center with rural hinterland and elites with masses; and the promotion of mass literacy, the standardization of languages, and innovations that allowed for communication with the masses. These "revolutions" were of great importance in that they created the preconditions within which members of the nation who had never met one another could

---

"regions as social constructs." The subsequent impact of these "social constructs" may be seen as a feedback effect which, in turn, helps to reconstruct social relations in the future.

imagine themselves as belonging to the same extended family (Anderson 1983).

Although the processes outlined above are referred to as revolutions, their impact on the masses was neither immediate nor universal. Change penetrated into the countryside only slowly. For example, it was not until the period from 1870 to 1920 that localized peasants in France were consolidated into a French nation (Weber 1976). And, as the contemporary rise in national self-consciousness among Bretons, Corsicans, Basques, and other ethnonational communities in France reveals, all regions and ethnic groups have still not been successfully nationalized (e.g., Tiryakian and Nevitte 1985, 76–77). While the "three revolutions" played a crucial role in dramatically increasing the potential for national consolidation, they were in and of themselves insufficient for the formation of national self-consciousness. This may be seen as one of the critical flaws in the so-called diffusionist theory, which posits that national consolidation is solely a response to the spread of "modernization" (e.g., Deutsch 1966).

It was not only the diffusion of socioeconomic development that was important but also the message of shared ancestry that was being diffused. On the surface the myth of common descent appears to be at odds with the process of modernization and nationalization and yet, paradoxically perhaps, the shared ancestry myth provided an essential glue binding the more expansive national community together. The most important function of the common origins myth is that it creates an image of the nation as a "primordial organism," as something both " 'natural' and 'eternal' " (Portugali 1988, 155). The nation becomes an extended family in the perception of its members, and this in itself is a strong argument for internal cohesion, particularly in an era of relatively dramatic change.

Nationalist intellectuals began promoting the idea of a "primordial" nation in earnest during the nineteenth century, a period during which the spread of education, communication networks, and particularly innovations such as the printing press greatly facilitated the diffusion of this mythology to an increasingly literate population (Hobsbawm 1983; Anderson 1983). Thus, the nineteenth century throughout Europe was proclaimed as a period of national "rebirth" or "reawakening," even though this was in reality the first time the lower strata of society were considered by the elite, or indeed considered themselves, to be part of such a large, internally cohesive community (Weber 1976; Pearson 1983; Hobsbawm 1990).

There is a question as to the motivations of the nationalist intelligentsia in reconstructing "history" in such a way. A Marxist approach argues that the bourgeoisie created its own nation in order to secure for itself a loyal work force and market (Connor 1984a, 7; Salikov et al. 1987, 24). However, such a direct economic argument does not appear valid, since the most active promoters of the nation's ancient lineage and glorious past were educators, historians, sociologists, archeologists, and so forth, and not "captains of industry" (Hroch 1985). And, while these constructors and purveyors of the national myth-symbol complex may have benefited in the long run from this activity, there was little immediate economic incentive, and often a number of strong disincentives to becoming proselytizers of the national idea, ranging from loss of work to loss of life. This was particularly true for members of subordinate ethnic groups. The nationalist intelligentsias appear to have been motivated more by a romantic desire to end their own sense of alienation and to merge with the masses than they were by material interests alone. Insecurity among the indigenous lower middle class ("the lesser examination-passing classes") was also apparently instrumental in the rise of xenophobic, often anti-Semitic nationalism during the period from 1870 to 1918 (Hobsbawm 1990, 118).

Whatever the motivations of the nationalist elites, in order to understand how nations became mass-based entities, one needs to consider why the masses themselves took part in the process. For Connor (1984b, 357), nationalism is at heart a "mass sentiment to which elites appeal" rather than a creation of the intelligentsia. At minimum, nationalization has been an interactive process through which elites and masses came to see each other as part of the same extended family.

National consolidation was most successful within a region of places sharing ethnocultural attributes; for this process the objective characteristics of the communities involved in the nationalization process did serve to facilitate or inhibit the spread of the national idea (Nielsen 1985). The ancestry myth was clearly easier to construct and promote among ethnoculturally similar communities that shared in the legends and mythical histories of the region. Thus, the masses "went along" with the myth because it was grounded in the local "legends and landscapes" (Smith 1986, 200–208) that were familiar to them, or were a part of their own folklore. This grounding of the myth-symbol complex in the rural folkways of the region also upgraded the status of the peasantry and other low socioeconomic strata in the process, relocating them in ideological terms from the sociocultural "periphery" of society to its sociocultural—if not its socioeconomic—"core."

Beyond this, the nation promised a brighter socioeconomic and political future for its members. A new golden age was said to be just over the horizon, that is, after the nation took charge of its own destiny (Smith 1988, 2). And, in Europe at least, modernization provided vast improvements over the local conditions of life that had previously existed (e.g., Weber 1976). In sum, the nation offered "status superiority" over "outsiders" for the lower strata of society, and promised "economic as well as psychological rewards" (Anderson 1988, 36). At the same time, the masses were made to feel both a part of something eternal and a part of the noble quest for future greatness. The nationalist message of a primordial organism reawakening to fulfill its destiny (the reconstruction of a national golden age) clearly struck a responsive chord among the masses, or at least those who could identify closely with the nation that was being "reborn."[9]

The grounding of the nation's mythical past in the local "legends and landscapes" limited the geographic and ethnographic range of the nationalization process. The localized myth of common ancestry, with its legendary heroes and glorious past, was unlikely to find a receptive audience outside the locality around which the myth-symbol complex was constructed. In each of the European states that had expanded through the conquest of ethnically distinct peripheral regions (i.e., Great Britain, France, Spain, and Russia/USSR), the outlying ethnic communities were not successfully consolidated into the dominant nations of each state. This is not surprising, since the past glories for the core nation were likely to be the past defeats for those in the periphery. In addition, conquest normally meant continued subordination of the peripheral *ethnies*. For example, "an English national idea had implicit implications of subordination for those who were not defined or did not wish to define themselves as English within the British Isles" (Breuilly 1982, 57). During the twentieth century we have witnessed the growth of a national self-consciousness within each of these unconsolidated communities, rather than their integration into the dominant nations of each state. Indigenous elites from these "peripheral" nations have elaborated their own myth-symbol complexes of localized common origins and a glorious past (e.g., Linz 1985, 204). Thus, although nationalization did occur with modernization and the political socialization of the masses by a nationalistic intelligentsia, the majority of states in Europe—where this process has had the longest time to work itself out—have not become nation-states.[10]

A Territorial versus an Ethnic Nationalism? The comparability of the "national problem" in Western Europe on the one hand and the USSR and Eastern Europe on the other has been the subject of serious debate. According to Hans Kohn, who made perhaps the most well known statement in this regard (1945, 329–351), essentially two types of nationalism—a "Western territorialism" based on political nation-states and an "Eastern ethnicism" founded on a folk

---

[9] This same message of rebirth has reemerged as a central theme of the national front organizations created in the USSR after 1985. For Belorussia's *Adradzhen'ne* ("Revival"), the very name of the organization is borrowed from the earlier period of Belorussian national "reawakening" (Vakar 1956, 91–92).

[10] According to nationality data provided in Bruk (1986), only in Denmark is more than 90 percent of the population Danish and more than 90 percent of all Danes live in the state. Austria, Greece, Germany, Ireland, Iceland, Italy, Malta, Norway, Portugal, Finland, and Sweden are states with more than 90 percent of the population comprised of one nation, but with a larger proportion of that nation living outside the state. Even since reunification, Germany does not qualify as a nation-state using these criteria, though that event brought the state much closer to nation-state status (85 percent of all Germans now live in Germany).

community or ethnonation—have emerged since the eighteenth century.[11] While undoubtedly some degree of variation existed between the nation idea as it emerged in Western Europe and the way in which peoples outside Western Europe adapted this idea to the local setting, the above depiction of political nation-states in the West as opposed to folk nations in the East is clearly overdrawn.[12] Nations in Western states, such as the English, Scottish, Welsh, Irish, French, Castilian, Basque, Catalan, Flemish, and Walloonian, also claim to have an ancient ethnographic basis. According to Smith (1986, 148), "most nationalisms after 1789 became increasingly influenced by an 'ethnic model' of the nation. . . . To achieve integration and legitimate a set of borders and a 'homeland,' myths of descent were needed, not only for external consumption, but for internal mobilization and co-ordination."

Also, while a sense of British, Spanish, or Belgian identity certainly exists at some level, it has clearly not overcome the "ethnonational" identities that continue to command primary loyalty from the vast majority of the population of these states (e.g., English, Scottish, Welsh, Irish, Orange; Castilian, Basque, Catalan, Galician; Flemish, Waloonian). Indeed, a resurgent nationalism has occurred among these "ethnic" communities during the postwar period. On the other hand, few of the Eastern "ethnic" nations emerged as mass-based entities before the establishment of some form of territorial autonomy, whether in the form of independent national states or "sovereign" republics in multinational, multihomeland states. Furthermore, as discussed in chapters 2 and 3, a territorial "sense of homeland" arose with national self-consciousness in Russia during the nineteenth and early twentieth centuries. In both East and West, the territorial dimension of the national idea coincided not with the boundaries of the state but rather with the imagined borders of an ancestral homeland.

A SENSE OF COMMON ORIGINS—SHARED BIRTHPLACE

The backward-looking aspect of national self-consciousness refers not only to a mythical common ancestry but also to a common geographic birthplace— the national homeland. The terms for the national land themselves tend to denote a strong perceptual bond between ancestry and place (Connor 1986, 16): "As evidenced by the near universal use of such emotionally charged terms as the motherland, the fatherland, the native land, the ancestral land, land where

---

[11] As discussed in chapter 6, a new east-west national dichotomy supposedly emerged after the October Revolution: that of brotherly, nonantagonistic socialist nations in the East and hostile, conflictual capitalist nations in the West.

[12] The overdichotomization into eastern and western national types may be more a reflection of a sense of superiority among those doing the defining than it is a reflection of actual differences in the way national members perceive themselves and their communities. For a discussion of this problem in the defining of nations, see Seton-Watson (1977, 3–5).

my fathers died and, not least, the homeland, the territory so identified becomes imbued with an emotional, almost reverential dimension."

According to Murphy (1990, 532), the concept "territory cannot be understood as a collection of objective attributes." This echoes the work of Knight (1982, 517), who asserted that "territory is not; it becomes, for territory itself is passive, and it is human beliefs and actions that give territory meaning." National "territory" clearly fits within this more subjective conceptual framework. It is perceived by members of the nation as much more than a tangible or objective geographical region (i.e., locale) for "history has nationalized a strip of land, and endowed its most ordinary features with mythical content and hallowed sentiments." (Williams and Smith 1983, 509). Anderson (1988, 24) views the importance of territory in similar subjective terms: "Associations with the past are central to nationalism's territoriality, for territory is the receptacle of the past in the present. The nation's unique history is embodied in the nation's unique piece of territory—its 'homeland,' the primeval land of its ancestors, older than any state, the same land which saw its greatest moments, perhaps its mythical origins."

As with the nation's genealogical bond, much about the ancestral homeland is mythical. In much of Europe prior to the nineteenth century, the "sense of place" was spatially limited to the local village, where a relatively isolated population lived out the majority of its existence (e.g., Hobsbawm 1990, 15–16; Weber 1976). Even by the turn of the nineteenth century in Germany, the use of the term *fatherland* by intellectuals referred more often than not to the local state (e.g., Bavaria) than to a larger German homeland (Kohn 1945, 388), indicating that the nationalization of the elite itself had barely begun by this time. This localism was also clearly apparent in rural France throughout much of the nineteenth century (Weber 1976, 45–47):

> "The least of our villages," wrote a local historian of the Var, "considers itself a *pays* in its language, legends, customs, ways." The awkward and untranslatable term *pays* has the fundamental significance of "native land" and applies more properly to local than to national territory.
>
> "Every valley," wrote an economist in 1837 about the central Pyrenees, "is still a little world that differs from the neighboring world as Mercury does from Uranus. Every village is a clan, a sort of state with its own patriotism."

As discussed in chapter 2, life in rural Russia, at least to the time of World War I, was similarly localized (e.g., Kingston-Mann 1991, 15–16).

At least some evidence suggests that the local place continues to exert a great deal of influence over sociopolitical behavior (Agnew 1987). In the former Soviet Union, favoritism was often shown not only to members of the indigenous nation but also to members of one's own local village or extended family. Localism continues to be relatively strong not only in the less developed non-Russian periphery (i.e., Central Asia, North Caucasus, and Transcaucasia (e.g., Atkin 1992; 1993; Carlisle 1991; Nissman 1993) but also in Russia itself. Nevertheless, it is also apparent that where places are similar, a region of places may emerge (Agnew 1987, 28): "In this situation the sense of place can be projected onto the region or a 'nation' and give rise to regionalism or nationalism."

With nationalization there emerged a broader geographic perception of home. The homeland myth developed along with the ancestry myth as part of an attempt to foster "internal solidarity and a sense of territorial 'rootedness' " (Smith 1986, 148). However, this expansive view of national belonging and territorial homeland occurred only slowly, and in the main only among localities whose populations could identify with the genealogical and geographical myths around which national consolidation was occurring. Attempts to expand the borders of the perceptual homeland were not always and everywhere successful. For example, as discussed in chapter 2, during the nineteenth century Siberia was perceived by many Russians migrating east as a Russian Utopia, but this myth was soon dispelled, at least for those who had "gone east" and suffered the hardships of a Siberian winter. This resulted in a large return migration stream westward.[13] Today the question "What is Russia?" remains a lively topic of debate.

During the nineteenth and twentieth centuries, and in conjunction with the promotion of the idea of a primordial nation, nationalists have laid claim to an ancestral homeland.[14] During this period, the literary imagery of blood and soil mixing through the ages to produce a unique nation in its special place has been a common theme certain to evoke strong emotions. This theme of the special historic role played by the homeland in creating the nation has apparently not lost its potency over the years. Even in the Soviet Union at the height of "developed socialism," it was not difficult to find evidence of this. For example, Russian nationalists such as Yuri Bondarev spoke out against the scheme to divert water from Russian rivers for use in Central Asia using just such emotive terms (as quoted in Petro 1987, 248): "From the first hour of our birth to the last second [of our lives] we are beholden to the earth which gave birth to us, and to the national culture that transmitted to us all that is good, solid, [and] moral—that which is called the warmth of patriotism. This priceless quality can be measured only in terms of returning this spiritual debt to our ancestral home."

---

[13] Judging by the difficulty that the USSR/Russia has had in holding the eastern migrants in place, it remains questionable whether Siberia has yet been adopted as part of Russia's perceptual homeland.

[14] According to Kozlov (1971, 94), the development of claims to an ancestral land occurred as human communities became less nomadic and more sedentary, at which time "territorial ties" replaced "blood ties." However, in Tuan's study of peoples' "attachment to homeland" (1977, 156–157), nomadic groups also exhibit a strong "sentiment for the nurturing earth." In addition, as a broader national self-consciousness develops, "blood ties" are not so much replaced as they are made mythical, as are territorial ties themselves.

Similar sentiments have been espoused by non-Russians in the state as well. For example, the Kirgiz poet Kozhomberdiyev exhorted his fellow Kirgiz in 1971 to "Remember, even before your mother's milk / You drank the milk of the homeland" (as quoted in Allworth 1973, 16).

The belief in an ancestral homeland reinforces the perception that the nation is a primordial organism, and one that is rooted to a particular place. For members of the indigenous nation, this is reflected in a strong emotional attachment to the homeland, in a belief among members that they belong only there and nowhere else. In its role as a crucial element of the common origins mythology, the homeland-as-birthplace myth may also be seen as an underlying ingredient of national territoriality. This accords with Soja (1971, 34), who identified a "sense of spatial identity" as the first of three major elements of human group territoriality.[15]

Since this dimension of territoriality serves to enhance the perception of the nation as a primordial organism, it has been mistaken for an innate response to the need for "survival, stimulation, and identity" found in other species (e.g., Ardrey 1966; Gumilev 1990). However, motivations for behavior in this regard appear to derive more from nationalistic perceptions of reality than from reality itself. Nationally self-conscious individuals behave (in part) according to perceptions of the nation as an extended family and of the homeland as the geographic birthplace, and not according to a "territorial imperative" dictated by the survival instincts of a "biological nation."

Since the nation (as perceived by members) is not only an extended family but also an organism that needs its ancestral soil in order to thrive, the sense of spatial identity felt by members of the nation toward their homeland provides a foundation for legitimizing nationalist claims to territory. For example, RUKH's program (1989) repeatedly bases the Ukrainian nation's claim to Ukraine on the "fact" that this territory has belonged to the Ukrainian people "from time immemorial." This claim to primordial connectivity between nation and homeland was made with increasing frequency and intensity in the USSR after 1985. However, since in reality nations and before them ethnic communities have not remained stationary and geographically isolated throughout the history of their formation, each nation's claim to an ancestral homeland is not incontrovertible. Nationalist historians, of course, choose the historic period most beneficial to their own nations. Pearson (1983, 17) certainly found this to be the case in Eastern Europe: "What does the 'historic' claim mean? The *longest* chronological span of ownership? The *earliest* significant period of ownership? The *latest* or the most *beneficial* period of ownership? In practice, claimants select the criteria favouring their own case, transforming past history into present politics in the process."

---

[15] The other two elements are "a sense of exclusiveness" and "the compartmentalization or channeling of human interaction in space" (Soja 1971, 34). These are discussed below.

There were and continue to be serious conflicts between neighboring nations as to the geographic extent of "ancestral" homelands. On both the interstate and intrastate scales, international conflicts over the delimitation of homelands are a nearly ubiquitous feature of the geopolitical landscape. National self-determination through the use of plebiscites in the disputed regions has often been proposed as a potential solution to these conflicts. However, self-determination based on contemporary ethnodemographic settlement patterns is not likely to satisfy the nationalist whose claim to a region as part of the homeland is grounded in the "primordial" past. Indeed, the emphasis on contemporary ethnic demography enhances the likelihood that indigenous nationalists in a demographically tenuous position will pursue a strategy of ethnoterritorial purification in order to solidify their claim to their "ancestral" homeland (e.g., the ethnic "cleansing" programs conducted by Serbs in Croatia and Bosnia and Hercegovina, as well as the removal of Armenians and Azeris from border regions between the two republics). The changing demography of nations may have diminished the relative weight of the primordial nation in certain parts of the perceived homeland (e.g., Serbs versus Albanians in Kosovo), but this has not necessarily diminished the resolve of indigenous nationalists to regain or maintain control of these regions. For example, Estonians now comprise only 61.5 percent of Estonia's population (Goskomstat SSSR 1991a, 140) due to the in-migration of Russians and other nonindigenes during the past fifty years. Estonian nationalists seeking to gain independence from the USSR called for national self-determination by the population of "pre-Occupation" Estonia, that is, the population (and its descendants) of Estonia prior to 1940, at which time Estonians were demographically (and otherwise) dominant.[16] Latvians, who comprised only 52 percent of Latvia's population in 1989 (Goskomstat SSSR 1991a, 124), have called for similarly restrictive definitions of citizenship in independent Latvia.

Of course, in addition to the lack of coincidence between ethnic demography and ethnic geography, it is also true that the principle of national self-determination itself has rarely been used as the primary basis for intra- or interstate border delimitation. In his survey of the ethnopolitical landscape, Connor (1986, 20) found that "political borders of states have been superimposed upon the ethnic map with cavalier disregard for ethnic homelands." Since members view their nations and homelands as more ancient than any state, their claim to the homeland is perceived as more legitimate than any claim a state may make.

To conclude, a backward-looking sense of common origins is a crucial dimension of national self-consciousness, in that it provides a deep-seated

---

[16] T. Kelam, a leader of the Estonian National Independence Party, discussed these issues during a meeting at the Kennan Institute for Advanced Russian Studies, Washington, D.C., 1 December 1989.

emotional rationale for national consolidation. Basing nationalization on a common ancestry myth helped promote the image of the nation as a primordial organism, but was only successful within a limited ethnocultural and geographic range. As part of the sense of common origins, a sense of spatial identity formed around the idea that the nation had a common geographic birthplace, the national homeland. This ancestral homeland myth has served to enhance the perception of primordialism surrounding the nation, helping to make the nation appear both eternal and natural. Given this intimate connection between nation and homeland, it should not be surprising that the nation's future well-being, indeed its very survival, is frequently said to be tied to its obtaining or retaining control over the ancestral homeland.

A SENSE OF COMMON DESTINY

The forward-looking nation, whose members share a sense of destiny, has been viewed as a goal-oriented community of interest (e.g., Nielsen 1985; Hechter et al. 1982; Breuilly 1982). Here the nation is seen as the community most capable of articulating and satisfying the needs of its members. This is a more instrumentalist answer to the question "What is a nation?" and it is often presented as an alternative to primordialism. The instrumentalist nation is also often defined as a modern nation without a past, created by the "three revolutions" briefly described above.

This view of the "modern" nation is a reasonably accurate depiction, so far as it goes. However, the nation must be viewed as a distinctly different sort of interest group. The reason for this has to do with the perceptual linkage between the primordial and instrumental aspects of national self-consciousness. Even if national elites are unsuccessful in attaining benefits for their members, the masses are unlikely to abandon the nation. Indeed, the very idea of voluntary "denationalization" probably would not occur to most members, who perceive their membership as being conferred by birth. This is a distinct advantage that the nation enjoys over other communities of interest (e.g., class).

The national destiny is often perceived as the reconstruction of a modern golden age. To accomplish this objective, the nation must at minimum survive. Any loss of membership through international integration or assimilation is often viewed as a direct threat to the nation's future viability. Horowitz (1985, 263) found that this loss was a recurrent theme underlying separatist movements in the Third World. Even "natural" population decline resulting from a decreasing rate of birth has been perceived as a threat to the nation (e.g., the Baltic nations, France, Rumania), while rapid population growth has been interpreted as a sign of national vitality (e.g., Soviet Central Asia) (Carrere d'Encausse 1978, 70).

Of course, national survival means more than demographic growth or stability, for the nation in reality is not a natural and eternal organism. Each succeeding generation must become nationally self-conscious, and this in turn means that national consciousness itself is a dynamic process. The nation's history is reinterpreted and rewritten by each successive generation, incorporating new events and selecting from among alternative myths and symbols. This may be seen as one of the major reasons why the perceived relative importance of the nation's objective attributes (i.e., language, religion, etc.) waxes and wanes over time. This will have an impact on the nation's perceived destiny, since the future "trajectory" is at least partially set in the past (Smith 1986). Conversely, a reassessment of the national destiny may serve as an impetus for reconstructing the nation's history. In this way, national self-consciousness becomes a dialogue between past and future conducted in the present, and with the nationalization of the masses it is a dialogue engaged in not only by an elite few, but by the national membership generally. The nation should thus be viewed as a flexibly delimited community of interest. This flexibility is clearly a strength, for the nation is easily able to incorporate recent events into its myth-symbol complex. For example, Estonian, Latvian, and Lithuanian nationalists justify their present claim to an independent political existence not only on the claim to Estonia, Latvia, and Lithuania as their ancestral homelands but also on the fact that they were independent during the interwar period. In the same way, Georgian nationalists point to their independence during the period from 1918 to 1921 as historic justification for the reestablishment of a new independent "Republic of Georgia," and have adopted the flag, anthem, name, and other state symbols from the period of independence. Even more recently the April 19, 1989, demonstrations in Tbilisi and the harsh reaction by Soviet troops quickly became part of the historic dialogue reorienting Georgians toward a future outside the Soviet Union.

As a means of establishing the conditions for the future prosperity of the national community (i.e., a new golden age), national self-determination, however defined, becomes a dominant objective among nations large and small (Knight 1988; Connor 1967). A central belief is that the nation must control its own destiny, and cannot leave its future in the hands of "outsiders" who have their own parochial national interests at heart. If a sense of common origins serves to enhance intranational cohesion, a sense of common destiny tends to encourage if not demand international separation. In this way the multinational, multihomeland state is perceived (at least by subordinate nationalists) as anachronistic.

Just as a sense of common destiny is intimately connected across time with a myth of common descent, the claim to homeland as a place for the nation exclusively to control its destiny is founded on the belief that this area is the geographic birthplace of the nation, or at least the place where the historic community experienced a glorious past. In other words, the nation's sense of spatial identity provides the historic justification for the development of a nationalistic "sense of exclusiveness" regarding the indigenous nation's standing in its own homeland. This sense of exclusiveness may thus be seen as the present-future aspect of a nation's sense of homeland and is also the second major ingredient of human group territoriality identified by Soja (1971, 34). The homeland is not only the place where indigenes feel most "at home." It is also the place that indigenes believe they alone should control (Connor 1986; Shibutani and Kwan 1972). Fundamentally, nationalists demand that they be "masters of their own land."[17]

The two temporal dimensions of a developing sense of homeland, as noted above, may be identified as key ingredients of national territoriality. However, this territoriality may be latent (Soja 1971), in that members of the nation may feel a sense of spatial identity and exclusiveness regarding their status in the perceived homeland without necessarily acting on these feelings. National territoriality as an active strategy, and the sociocultural, economic, and political factors serving as catalysts in its activation, are examined below.

NATIONAL TERRITORIALITY AND ITS ACTIVATION

Territoriality at both the individual and group levels has been a topic of serious debate between those who view human territorial behavior as little more than animal instinct (e.g., Ardrey 1966), and those who argue "that territoriality represents a culturally derived and transmitted answer to particular human problems, not the blind operation of instinct" (Gold 1982, 48). This disagreement is as fundamental and nearly as old as the "nature versus nurture" debate. The definition of national territoriality as a latent sense of homeland that becomes activated whenever the nation-homeland bond is seriously threatened may appear to correspond more closely with an innate reaction comparable to that found in other (though not in all) species. However, as we have already discussed above, the motivation for territorial behavior among indigenes derives not so much from instinctual need as from a desire to control their own lives in order to fulfill their national destiny (i.e., to create a new golden age for members of the nation). This desire to satisfy "higher needs" clearly accords more with the second depiction of human territoriality as a problem-solving strategy.

According to Sack (1986, 19), human territoriality represents "the attempt by an individual or group to affect, influence, or control people, phenomena, and relationships, by delimiting and asserting control over a geographic area." An activated national territoriality may be viewed as a special case of this, as a strategy used by members of the nation to control their own destiny (according to the dictates of the nation's historic mission) by gaining control over their perceived homeland. Viewed in this way, activated national territoriality becomes the essential equivalent of nationalism. This is certainly implied by

---

[17] This phrase has been heard and seen with increasing regularity in the former USSR since 1989.

Gellner (1983, 1), who defines nationalism as "a political principle, which holds that the political and the national unit should be congruent," and as "a theory of political legitimacy, which requires that ethnic boundaries should not cut across political ones."[18]

According to Sack (1983, 1986), territoriality is always a means to an end, though it may appear as an end in itself. The appearance of national territoriality as an end rather than as a means to an end is closely linked to the backward-looking sense of homeland, to the perception that the nation-homeland bond is something both organic and primordial, and that the nation cannot exist without the homeland. The nation's sovereignty over its perceived homeland is often portrayed as the fulfillment of the national destiny itself; the new golden age becomes synonymous with indigenous territorial control. The "Magyar Creed," a Hungarian lament to the loss of territory following World War I, provides an excellent example of this (Pearson 1983, 176):

> I believe in one God,
> I believe in one Fatherland,
> I believe in one divine, eternal Truth,
> I believe in the resurrection of Hungary.
> Hungary dismembered is no country,
> Hungary united is Heaven. Amen.

This subjective rationalization for the use of national territoriality provides a potent additional dimension to the more objective reasons for using territoriality identified by Sack (1986, 32–34), including the ease of "classification, communication and enforcement of control."

Under what conditions does national territoriality become an activated strategy to gain control of the perceived homeland? Primarily, this conversion takes place whenever the indigenes' sense of homeland is challenged by nonindigenes. This perceived threat to the nation-homeland bond may arise in a number of ways in a multihomeland state. The factors serving to activate national territoriality should be viewed as catalysts rather than causes, since the reason for a territorial response by nationalists lies in the sense of homeland that has evolved along with national self-consciousness.[19] An understanding of these catalytic agents likely to activate national territoriality is essential to the study of contemporary national problems in multihomeland states such as the USSR. Part 2 of this book examines four of the most commonly cited catalysts and the way they have affected international relations in the postwar USSR: the geographic mobility of national members across homeland borders; the social

---

[18] See also Colin Williams (1986).

[19] The confusion of catalysts with causes has led to mistaken nationality policies, as well as overly optimistic assessments of the potential for recasting the population in a new national or "anational" mold (Connor 1972, 1984b).

mobilization of indigenes and their increasing contact and competition with nonindigenes for the resources of the homeland; state-sponsored international integration (i.e., Sovietization) and the perceived threat of "denationalization;" and the centralized nature of economic and political decision making in the former USSR. These catalysts are certainly not unique to the former Soviet Union. A generalized discussion of each of these catalysts is presented below.

Geographic Mobilization and Demographic Indigenization

There is abundant evidence that the immigration of nonindigenes to another nation's homeland has served to heighten the perception among indigenes that the nation and its primordial claim to homeland is under attack (i.e., that interhomeland migration functions as a catalyst activating national territoriality). In his general discussion of societal territoriality, Soja (1971, 34) states that the "sense of exclusiveness" remains latent until it is activated by some sort of "invasion" by "aliens." Shibutani and Kwan (1972, 445) also found that "the national land is often regarded as a group possession on which foreigners are interlopers." Similarly, Weiner (1978) described the rise of "nativism" among the "sons of the soil" that occurred with the in-migration of nonindigenes in India. The rise of Le Pen's National Front party in France was primarily a response to the perceived threat to the French nation represented by an increased immigration of non-French into the country. Fear of massive immigration from the East has resulted in a similar rise in popularity of ultranationalist parties in Germany and Austria, as well as a rise in antiforeigner acts of violence. Even the *Gastarbeiter* (guestworkers) invited into West European states have caused a nationalistic reaction among indigenous nations, who perceive this foreign presence as a threat to the nation's status in its homeland and to national "purity" (e.g., Kramer 1972). Indeed, Connor (1986) appears correct in regarding all nonindigenes as essentially living in diaspora. Even if welcomed by indigenes at one time, nonindigenes are likely to serve as a catalyst for rising indigenous nationalism eventually—particularly during times of economic recession or uncertainty. They are unlikely ever to be made to feel "at home."

Chapter 4 examines interhomeland migration, the more general changes in ethnodemographic status of indigenes in their home republics, and the role of these demographic trends in activating national territoriality among members of the indigenous nations during the postwar period. While greater interhomeland migration has been encouraged by policymakers and ethnographers as a way to break national territorial ties and facilitate international integration, it has tended to result in the opposite effect (i.e., rising national self-consciousness and a more assertive territoriality among members of the indigenous nations). A rising *nativism*—the growth of anti-outsider sentiments that often results in a violent reaction among indigenes—has been an increasingly disturbing feature of the national problem in the USSR and its successor states since 1985. As a result of this much more active national territoriality, a trend toward the demographic indigenization of each homeland is in evidence, as nonindigenes leave for "home."

Social Mobilization and Sociocultural Indigenization

The social mobilization of indigenes is one of the most potent catalysts serving to activate national territoriality, since this process of "modernization" not only brings indigenes into closer contact with nonindigenes but also intensifies the competition between them for the resources of the homeland. This response is certainly implicit in the theoretical works elaborating a "competition theory" of nationalism in modernized and modernizing states (e.g., Nielsen 1980, 1985; Nagel and Olzak 1982, 1986), and helps to explain the failure of the "diffusionist thesis" which predicted the demise of national identity with modernization (e.g., Deutsch 1966).

Most models designed to examine the relationship between socioeconomic development and national identity treat social mobilization as an independent variable causing changes in national self-consciousness. However, a growing number of studies in the past decade have raised serious questions regarding the validity of this causal model (e.g., Connor 1984b; Orridge and Williams 1982; Smith 1988). In line with the competition theory, in several multihomeland states, including Spain, Yugoslavia, the Soviet Union, and India, the most developed or socially mobilized nations are also among the most nationalistic. On the other hand, Horowitz in his study of ethnic separatism in the Third World (1981, 173) found that "by far the largest number of secessionists can be characterized as backward groups living in backward regions." Furthermore, the development of "relative deprivation" among indigenes, that is, a condition in which the rate of social mobility experienced does not meet or exceed expectations (Gurr 1970), is also an important factor in the determination of whether social mobilization or the lack thereof will serve as a catalyst in the activation of national territoriality in multihomeland states.

Chapter 5 examines the relationship between social mobilization and national territoriality in the postwar Soviet Union. The research in this study indicates that social mobility alone is not a sufficient condition either for the creation of national self-consciousness or for its erasure from the collective memory. In addition to knowing whether or not social mobility is occurring, we need to know the geographic context in which modernization is taking place. The homeland and indigenous status are particularly important in mediating the effect of social mobilization on national self-consciousness. In general, increasing social mobility has served as a catalyst activating national territoriality among indigenes even while it has tended to erode a sense of national self-consciousness and facilitate international integration among nonindigenes.

International Integration and Ethnocultural Indigenization

In multinational states such as the former USSR, a desire often exists on the part of central authorities to internationalize or denationalize the population of the state. In Soviet terms, a goal of creating a "new Soviet people" from the numerous ethnonational communities has existed for much of the state's history (e.g., Konstantinov 1985). This objective was to be attained by the voluntary drawing together (*sblizheniye*) and merging (*sliyaniye*) of the nations in the state into an anational community of "Soviet people." However, a degree of coercion has been involved in the drawing together or acculturation process (Connor 1984a), which placed the Russian nation and its cultural attributes (particularly language) in a preferential position. The favored status of Russians as "first among equals" raises questions concerning the equality of peoples and the anational character of the Soviet people supposedly being created (Aspaturian 1968; Dzyuba 1970; Clem 1980; Connor 1984a; Silver 1974b, 1978). This officially endorsed process of international integration, and the consequent state support for Russification, have also served as catalysts in the activation of national territoriality among non-Russians. This "forced denationalization" was one of the major complaints lodged against central authorities by national front organizations (e.g., RUKH 1989). This was not so different from nationalist reactions against programs of "Bulgarization," "Magyarization," "Czechization" or even "re-Slovakization" in Eastern Europe, or against the cultural dominance of the French, English, or Castilian nations in France, Great Britain, or Spain.

On the other hand, the non-Russian languages and cultures were also officially supported, as part of a dialectical approach to solving the national problem in the state. The state-sponsored "flowering" (*rastsvet*) of national cultures was geographically limited for the most part to the home republic of each national community. As the state progressed toward communism, the flowering of national communities was to give way to their drawing together and eventual merger. This desired outcome obviously did not occur. The support for indigenes and their cultural attributes in their own homelands but not outside converged with the indigenes' sense of homeland to ensure both the continued survival of the nations and their cultural attributes, and even to raise them to a level that challenged the dominant status of Russians.

Chapter 6 explores the processes of acculturation and assimilation as they occurred during the postwar period in the USSR. While the Russian nation and culture retained a position of dominance throughout the state (at least up to the late 1980s), a second tier in the national stratification system emerged that favored the indigenous nation in its own homeland. This ethnocultural indigenization was one more element in the developing national separatism within the country during the past thirty years, and it accelerated greatly after 1985.

The Centralization of Decision-making Authority and Political Indigenization

Each of the catalysts discussed above has a political dimension, since the external forces perceived as threatening to the viability of the nation and its sense of homeland often emanate from policies made at the center, as well as from neighboring nations or global trends. For example, few multihomeland states allow each indigenous nation to control migration into and out of its homeland, and central policies that encourage the interhomeland movement of peoples, in addition to the migration streams themselves, may help to activate national territoriality (e.g., Weiner 1978). Similarly, the adoption of a lingua franca by the state and its attempts to acculturate all national communities to this language are likely to increase the perception among indigenes that the nation itself is under siege. As a final example, social and economic policies rarely have a geographically even effect, and the "lumpiness" or uneven development that occurs as a result provides proof to nationalists that their nations are not well served by the center (Nielsen 1985; Nairn 1977; Hechter 1975). Policies that result in uneven development are likely to activate national territoriality among those nations adversely affected, and this holds not only for less developed nations but also for relatively more developed nations (e.g., Slovenes, Estonians, Catalans) whose members feel that they contribute more than their fair share to statewide development. Such policies encourage the development of an indigenous perception of relative deprivation, which was cited above as a catalyst activating national territoriality. For example, during the 1960s Slovaks charged that investment decisions made in Prague did not allow for adequate development in Slovakia. As a consequence, Slovaks were "forced" to migrate to the Czech Socialist Republic in search of work, where they were said to be subjected to acculturation and assimilation (i.e., Czechization) pressures. This was one of the issues that Slovak nationalists cited in their demand for federalization of the state (Steiner 1973). In general, political subordination is likely to be viewed by indigenes as inherently undesirable, since the destiny of the nation and homeland is in the hands of outsiders who are likely to act in ways that promote their own national interests over those of the indigenous nation.

The political system in the USSR also reflected a dialectical approach to solving the "national problem." The federal structure of the Soviet government itself encouraged indigenes to think of themselves as the rightful owners of the republics named after them, since it was based for the most part on the geographic extent of national homelands. Attempts to do away with this special relationship, which was based not only on the Soviet constitution but on each nation's own sense of homeland, have resulted in sharp reactions by the indigenous communities who feel their own status is likely to be negatively affected.

Chapter 7, examines the political dimension of national territoriality in the

USSR. Particularly important in this analysis is the contemporary economic and political decentralization of decision-making authority from the center to the national leaders in each republic, who have tended to base their claim to legitimacy on their ability to represent the will of the indigenous nation. National territoriality expressed by these national communities has become more overtly political since 1985, leading first to a confederalization of center-periphery relations, with the members of each nation gaining greater control over their own homelands, and later to outright independence.

INDIGENIZATION AS TERRITORIAL RESPONSE

How do nationalists behave once territoriality becomes activated? This of course depends on a number of variables, including the seriousness of the perceived external threat, the penalties (both real and perceived) and expected benefits for acting, and also the degree to which the national membership can be mobilized to support nationalist goals (Hechter et al. 1982). At its core, an activated national territoriality is a strategy through which nationalists seek to bring about a beneficial "compartmentalization or channeling of human interaction in space," Soja's third and final ingredient of human group territoriality (1971, 34). It represents an attempt to construct and enforce political, economic, social, and ethnocultural barriers to any international interaction perceived as threatening to the indigenous nation's standing in its own homeland. Once activated, national territoriality becomes a politically mobilizing strategy to gain greater sovereignty for the nation in its perceived homeland.

How successfully has this strategy been employed? At first glance, it appears that nationalists have been relatively ineffective in attaining what may be viewed as the ultimate goal of national territoriality—the creation of independent nation-states. While the number of recognized sovereign states in the world political system has increased from about 130 in 1971 to nearly 200 at present, this increase has not coincided with an increase in the proportion that are nation-states (Bruk 1986; Connor 1978). Multinational, multihomeland states continue to represent the norm. And, since there are some two to three thousand nations and protonations (i.e., ethnic communities or *ethnies* that could provide the basis for the making of nations) in the world at present, this situation is unlikely to change dramatically in the near future, even with the successful national separatist movements that accompanied the collapse of the Second World.

The use of this measure—the establishment of nation-states—is an extremely restrictive and misleading way to assess the success or failure of national territoriality. Few national communities are actively secessionist at any given time, for a variety of intra- and international reasons. A more complex and meaningful examination of national territoriality must incorporate a broader definition of national separatism as a process that includes the sociocultural and economic as well as the political indigenization of life in the national homeland. Judged by this more sensitive measure, it is evident that national territoriality has been employed with a great deal of success, at least in the First and Second Worlds. The Quebecois and northern peoples of Canada have gained greater cultural and political autonomy from Ottawa. Basques and Catalans have won greater autonomy in Spain, as have Flemings and Walloonians in a more confederal Belgium. Yugoslavia became a confederation of essentially sovereign nation-states during the 1970s, though this did not solve its national problems. Greater indigenous national autonomy was also apparent during the postwar period in Czechoslovakia. As discussed in part 2, indigenization in the USSR has been an ongoing process for at least the entire post-World War II period, and the pressure for greater degrees of indigenization, particularly in the economic and political spheres, increased dramatically after 1985. Since 1990, national separatism has resulted in the disintegration of Yugoslavia, the USSR, and Czechoslovakia.

The successful use of national territoriality (i.e., indigenization) by one nation has itself served as a catalyst activating national territoriality elsewhere. This accords with Sack's tenth tendency of territoriality: "territoriality can help engender more territoriality" (Sack 1986, 34). This was clearly the case in the USSR, where the successful push for greater political sovereignty in one republic sparked similar demands elsewhere. Thus, while each nation is unique, the behavior of members from one nation is influenced by the experiences of members from another. This should not be thought of solely as a narrow reaction by neighbors to border provocations, since nationalist demands for certain rights and privileges are often founded on the success of nationalists in other world regions. This territoriality-engendering function has become increasingly global in scale. For example, the 1989 upheavals in Eastern Europe found resonance among the Chamorros of Guam, who called on the U.S. administration to respect their right to self-determination, as it did with regard to Eastern Europe (Borg 1989). Similarly, the pulling down of the Berlin Wall and the reunification of Germany appears to have struck a responsive chord in the Soviet republic of Azerbaydzhan, where Azerbaydzhanis attempted to open the Soviet-Iran border that dissects the Azerbaydzhani nation and homeland; and in Moldova, where nationalist elites have spoken favorably of eventual reunification with Rumania. For this reason, in order to explain the contemporary "national problem" confronting the USSR and to predict where it might lead, a comparative understanding of nationalism and territoriality is essential.

As defined in this study, the nation is a flexibly delimited, self-conscious community of belonging and interest founded on a myth-symbol complex that combines a sense of common origins with a sense of mission or destiny. The making of nations is an extremely complex process, involving not only the influence of a *location* dimension (i.e., the external environment and particularly the revolutionary changes in the social, economic, cultural, and political way of life beginning in Europe in the eighteenth century) on *locale* but also the influence of *locale* and *sense of place* on the ethnographic and geographic delimitation of nations and homelands, and of course on the process of modernization (i.e., the *location* dimension) itself.

The vast size and ethnonational diversity of the former USSR add to the difficulty presented by the subjective nature of the phenomena being studied. The Soviet Union encompassed approximately one-sixth of the earth's land surface, and its interstate borders incorporated in part or in *toto* the population and homelands of more than a hundred "nations and nationalities." In 1989 twenty-two of these nations had more than 1,000,000 members each, and fifty-five nations had more than 100,000 members living in the USSR (Goskomstat SSSR 1991a). In this world region there have been (and continue to be) great regional differences in levels of development, international interaction, and intranational cohesiveness.

Beyond this, it should be restated that the nation, though in mythological or perceptual terms a primordial and neverending entity, in reality became mass-based only recently, and cannot be taken for granted. A population's national self-consciousness must be reconstructed with each generation. For example, Suny (1989, 317) writes of his research on the making of the Georgian nation: "If there is any conclusion to be derived from such a study of the *longue duree* of a small nation, it might be that a nation is never fully 'made.' It is always in the process of being made. At any particular moment Georgia was in part formed by its prior history and its underlying deep structure and culture, and in part was being transformed by its present experience and the imperatives of an imperial imposition."

It must also be said that the intensity of national self-consciousness can and does vary among individual members, and within each individual member over time. This variance depends both on external conditions (i.e., international relations) and also on intranational cohesiveness, and has been discussed as levels of "marginality" by a number of authors (e.g., Gordon 1978; Germani 1980; Burkhardt 1983; Edwards 1986). Nevertheless, it is also apparent that once a mass-based national consciousness is attained, the nation is unlikely to be deconstructed. Indeed, it is the nation that has become the predominant community of interest during the twentieth century, the collectivity able to outcompete other groups that may lay primary claim to a member's time, resources, and loyalty. For Emerson (1960, 95–96), this relative preeminence is an essential ingredient in the very definition of nation: "The nation is today the largest community which, when the chips are down, effectively commands men's loyalty, overriding the claims both of the lesser communities within it and those which cut across it or potentially enfold it within a still greater society."

This definition also points to one of the complicating factors surrounding the issue of nationalization—the existence of numerous communities of interest to which individuals belong. Members of a subnational ethnographic community who become "nationalized" do not necessarily lose their sense of belonging to that subnational ethnographic group. As an example of this, a glossary of more than five hundred ethnonyms that people may have used in response to the question on national identity in the latest Soviet census (Goskomstat SSSR 1988a) varied little from earlier ethnic glossaries (TsSU SSSR 1959; TsSU SSSR 1969). The use of the glossaries by census tabulators to help construct the more than one hundred national categories listed in the censuses indicates that ethnonational identity continues to be a dynamic issue rather than a static and unchanging "primordial" affiliation.[20] Individuals may also belong to supranational collectivities, for example, a "Soviet People," a "European Community," the world of Islam, and so on. National self-consciousness can and does exist alongside affiliation with several other communities of interest, and it may be difficult to determine whether an individual has attained a national self-consciousness until he or she is put to the test (i.e., "when the chips are down").

The complex reality within which nations have been and are being formed makes the task of assessing the process of nationalization extremely difficult. And, because this did not happen at the same time or in response to the same set of factors for each and every national community in Russia and the USSR, a detailed examination of national consolidation occurring over the past two centuries is clearly beyond the scope of this or any one study. More research of this type, however, is critically needed; to date there has been an inadequate comparative assessment of the nationalization process as it has occurred in Russia and the Soviet Union. While this has not been a topic that has attracted much attention in the West, in the USSR itself Marxist-Leninist ideology in the past seriously biased Soviet ethnographic research into the nature of the nationalization process. Much as nationalist historians have re-created history in an effort to "prove" the ancient and noble lineage of their people, Soviet historians and ethnographers reconstructed events to "prove" the evils of bourgeois nationalism and the brotherly relations that existed between "socialist nations." This of course only makes the task at hand more difficult, though it is a fascinating aspect of the "national question" in the Soviet Union.[21]

As stated above, a developing sense of homeland is a central feature in the

---

[20] The total number of ethnonational categories enumerated in the 1989 census (128) also increased substantially over the 104 groups listed in 1979. However, this was less a real increase in the number of nations created during the decade than it was a reflection of the end to state-sponsored sovietization. Between 1959 and 1979 the number of national communities listed in the censuses steadily decreased in an effort by the state to show that the national communities of the USSR were "drawing together" into one Soviet people. This artificial contraction of census categories ended with the end of the "sovietization" myth.

[21] See, for example, Tillett (1969), who examined the way in which Soviet historians treated the "friendship of the peoples" (*druzhba narodov*) myth over time.

making of nations, since it is the mythical geographic birthplace of the nation, as well as the place where the nation's destiny is to be fulfilled. The two dimensions of this sense of place—a backward-looking "sense of spatial identity" and a present-future oriented "sense of exclusiveness"—describe the dimensions of a latent national territoriality, which may be activated by a number of (primarily) external (i.e., location) factors or catalysts. Once activated, national territoriality becomes a strategy used by nationalists to gain control over the destiny of the nation by gaining control over the national homeland (i.e., indigenization).

The remaining chapters of this book provide an examination of the nation-homeland relationship and national territoriality in Russia and the Soviet Union. Chapter 2 discusses the formation of nations and homelands before the October Revolution. Chapter 3 examines the continuation of this process during the interwar period, and the effect of Leninist nationality policy as well as the continuing impact of societal forces in the making of nations and homelands before World War II. As discussed above, the chapters of part 2 focus on the catalysts activating national territoriality in the USSR during the postwar period, and the processes of indigenization or "national separatism" that resulted.

The failure to recognize the meaning of homeland in the study of nationalism, both by policymakers in the Soviet Union and by analysts in the West more generally, resulted in serious misconceptions about the nature of nationalism in the USSR and the prospects for solving or at least managing the "national problem." This study, which emphasizes a neglected though extremely important topic, is one of the first serious steps in an effort to bring geography back into the study of nations and nationalism through an exploration of the meaning of territory to nationalists themselves. A better understanding of the nation-homeland bond and national territoriality is critical, for as events in the former Soviet Union since the late 1980s have demonstrated, the desire to control life in the homeland is one of the most powerful motivating forces driving nationalists in the region today. More generally, it has become increasingly clear that place has lost none of its significance in the contemporary world of multinational, multihomeland states.

CHAPTER TWO

The Making of Nations in Tsarist Russia

As was noted in chapter 1, the image of nations promoted by nationalists is one of ancient, even primordial communities of belonging whose members share genealogical and geographic roots. However, the idea that nations have existed as self-conscious, mass-based entities essentially unchanged "from time immemorial" is not supported by a closer examination of societal change in Russia before the October Revolution. The making of nations and homelands was a process that began in the nineteenth century, and was by no means completed by 1917. This chapter cannot explore the nationalization process during this period in all its complexity. However, it can offer a general examination of the critical factors involved in the rise of a national self-consciousness and sense of homeland during this period.

The making of nations in Russia (and the USSR) is best thought of as a process of both vertical (i.e., interclass) incorporation and horizontal (i.e., interethnic) consolidation occurring over the past two hundred years.[1] According to Hroch (1985, 23), "nationalization" in general proceeds through a series of stages, from a "period of scholarly interest" (Phase A) to a "period of patriotic agitation" (Phase B) to "the rise of a mass national movement" (Phase C). The first phase describes the "ethnicization" of elites as they "rediscover" their ethnocultural roots. The second phase marks the nationalization of the elites, and with it the rise of political nationalism. The final phase may be thought of as the "nationalization of the masses."[2] The third phase of this process certainly began no earlier than 1861 with the emancipation of serfs, and continued through the remainder of the prewar period. This is not to say that ethnic distinctions were unimportant to the masses in preemancipation Russia, nor is it to deny that these differences could lead to intercommunal conflict. However, it is true that mass-based group loyalties were by-and-large limited to

---

[1] Vertical incorporation does not necessarily mean that everyone in society becomes part of a classless society but rather that everyone perceives a connection among members of the nation across classes. This is quite different from conditions under slavery and feudalism, where there was little sense that the lower strata of society were in any way related to their masters. In Russia, this attitude began to change within the bulk of the population only after the emancipation of serfs, even though the Russian intellectuals had debated the so-called peasant question for decades before 1861.

[2] This is a phrase used by Mosse (1975) in his study of mass mobilization in Germany.

locality at this time, and that membership in the more extensive (ethnographically and geographically) nations could not yet be, in the words of Anderson (1983), "imagined" by the vast majority of people in the state.

Hroch's typology for national formation, which was derived from an examination of subordinate *ethnies* in the multiethnic states and empires of Europe, is well suited to the study of national consolidation in the Russian Empire. Russia's expansion through the conquest of non-Russian *ethnies*, and the establishment of an ethnic stratification system that placed Russians in a dominant "core" position and non-Russians in a subordinate "peripheral" position played a crucial role in the nationalization process for Russians and non-Russians alike. As discussed below, this was particularly critical at the end of the nineteenth century, when imperialistic Russification coincided with rising national self-consciousness among non-Russians (Rogger 1983, 182–207; Raeff 1971).

Most studies of nationalism in Russia have tended to focus almost exclusively on the nationalization of elites, often assuming that what the intelligentsia wrote and felt about its nation and homeland expressed the sentiments of the masses as well. A radically different approach is taken in this chapter. After a brief summary of the nationalization of elites, attention is focused on the process of national consolidation among the peasantry, and the relationship of this process to the geographic and social mobilization of the masses. This view of nationalization from the bottom up rather than from the top down provides a better gauge of the degree to which national sentiments had replaced localism in prerevolutionary Russia.

The Nationalization of the Elite

Phase A: Enlightened Patriotism

In the Russian Empire, though the timing of this phase varied from *ethnie* to *ethnie*, a "period of scholarly interest" can be dated roughly to the first half of the nineteenth century.[3] Nationalization entered what Hroch (1985, 22–23) refers to as Phase A, which in general was "marked by a passionate concern on the part of a group of individuals, usually intellectuals, for the study of the language, the culture, the history of the. . . . nationality. Their interest was motivated by a patriotism of the Enlightenment type, namely an active affection for the region in which they lived, associated with a thirst for knowledge of every new and insufficiently investigated phenomenon."

---

[3] An interest in the history of the land and people was apparent for a number of western *ethnies* during the sixteenth and seventeenth centuries, and a number of analysts have seen in this "historical consciousness" the makings of a national consciousness. However, both the land and the people were vaguely defined and shifting with time, and self-identification among the elites was often religious rather than national (Banac and Sysyn 1986; Longworth 1990). While it may be said that some "scholarly interest" in the history of one's land and people existed before the late eighteenth century, it was not motivated by enlightenment or by nationalism as a secular ideology.

Early Phase A intellectual interests focused on the history of the ethnic community and the region, on local folklore and folkways, language, and so on. This early "enlightened patriotism," intimately connected with an emotional attachment to homeland, was evident in the works of Alexandre Radishchev, particularly in his "What It Means to Be a Son of the Fatherland" (1789), as well as in the articles and books by Nicholas Karamzin, particularly his "On the Love of the Fatherland and National Pride" (1802) and his "Memoir on Ancient and Modern Russia" (1811).[4] In these works, love of fatherland is expressed as a motivating force in the study of, and concern for the nation.

Still, during the period of enlightened patriotism, the definitions of nation and homeland were not identical to those provided in chapter 1. For example, Alexandre Radishchev "had a wholly rationalist and nominalist view of the nation as 'a collection of citizens' rather than a supra-individual whole endowed with a 'collective soul' " (Walicki 1979, 40). The masses could not become part of the nation until they were emancipated and sufficiently "civilized." Beyond this, the state's definition of nation under the rubric of "Official Nationality" beginning with Nicholas I (1825–1855) equated Russian-ness with loyalty to the tsar and the Orthodox faith, rather than to ethnicity and geography (Riasanovsky 1969; Brooks 1985, 214). Furthermore, the "fatherland" (*otechestvo*) for enlightened patriots was for the most part equal to the state as a whole, or even enlightened Europe, and not to the ancestral homeland of the Russian people (*rodina*). Nonetheless, a scholarly interest in one's roots—both genealogical and geographic—led over time to a developing "ethnicization" of the enlightened elites, along with a growing "sense of spatial identity" with their ancestral homeland. This marks the first stage in the development of a national territoriality.[5]

An interest in the Russian "native" language led to a debate over whether the Russian literary language was to preserve a "high" style centered around the old Church Slavonic, or develop from a "low" style, utilizing the vernacular. During the late-eighteenth and early-nineteenth centuries, even "high style" Russian had to overcome its status as an inferior language—to Latin in the classroom and to French among polite society. Karamzin's advocacy of a "new style" that would adopt the conventions of "the speech practice of the salons of

---

[4] For a discussion of these works by Karamzin, see Pipes (1974). As the dominant group in an ethnically stratified empire, the Russians do not fully conform to Hroch's typology, which was modeled after the nationalization processes experienced by subordinate *ethnies*. Its dominant status and imperial past were themselves part of the Russian nationalization process. Nevertheless, the national consolidation of Russians does appear to be more similar to than different from that experienced by the subordinate *ethnies* of the Russian Empire, and the three phases identified by Hroch are clearly visible in the history of Russian nationalization. For this reason, the same typology is used to explore this process for both dominant Russians and subordinate non-Russians. The distinctions between the two are highlighted in separate discussions of each.

[5] A more detailed discussion of the evolution of a "sense of homeland" is given at the end of chapter 2.

the capitals" while abandoning the archaic Church Slavonic was a step in the direction of vernacularization (Rogger 1960, 85–125). This Russian language debate was a central feature of enlightened patriotism (Whittaker 1984, 32): "Scholars began to enshrine language as the essential vehicle of literature, the reflection of its speakers' entire cultural heritage, and the standard by which a nation's level of enlightenment is judged. Therefore, upon the development of language hinged the development of a national culture." The resolution of the language debate, which generally rejected the "high style" Church Slavonic and opted for a literary language more akin to the vernacular, can itself be seen as evidence that the Russian elites were undergoing a transition from Phase A to Phase B in the nationalization process. The development over time of a literary language closer to the spoken language of the peasantry helped create a needed link between elite and masses, through which the newly nationalized elites could reach "their people." Ultimately, the vernacularization of the Russian language, and particularly of the popular press, represented a clear victory for the nationalized elites such as the Slavophiles who sought to recenter the nation around the people (*narod*) rather than around "faith and tsar," and to redefine the meaning of Russian-ness in the process (Walicki 1975). The vernacularization of languages was a nearly universal aspect of nationalization during this time, not only in Russia but throughout Europe. According to Anderson (1983, 69), "the nineteenth century was, in Europe and its immediate peripheries, a golden age of vernacularizing lexicographers, grammarians, philologists, and litterateurs."

For the non-Russian *ethnies* in the Empire, a "period of scholarly interest" in the exploration of their ethnocultural roots varied in time and intensity. For the Ukrainians, a period of "enlightened patriotism" began in the 1820s "under the stimulus of the ideas of Western romanticism transmitted through Russia" (Pipes 1968, 10). Evidence of Lithuanian and Estonian scholarly interest in the history, customs, and language of "their people" is also found during the 1820s (Hroch 1985, 76–86; Raun 1987, 56). Suny (1989, 123–125) finds some evidence for an earlier beginning to a period of enlightened patriotism among Armenian and Georgian intellectuals. However, the onset of an Armenian national "revival" occurred in Venice among the Mekhitarist fathers, not in Yerevan, and indigenous intellectual interest in Georgian history, language, and literature does not appear to predate the nineteenth century. For the Turkic-Muslims in the state, a Phase A enlightened patriotism can be seen relatively early among the Kazan' Tatars as this intellectual current diffused from the nearby Russian core, and somewhat later among the Crimean Tatars, Kazakhs, and Azerbaydzhanis. The ethnicization of elites in Central Asia was impeded by the relative strength of conservative Islam, under which the elites tended to reject a particularistic ethnonational identity in favor of a more general Islamic one (Braker 1971, 190–197). Phase A nationalization in this region barely predated World War I and the October Revolution (e.g., Hanaway 1973).

One interesting aspect of the early nationalization process among non-Russian intellectuals in the state was the influence of life in St. Petersburg. The non-Russian intellectuals in St. Petersburg were exposed not only to the latest intellectual currents but also to an alien sociocultural environment, making their experience in the Russian capital particularly significant for their further nationalization. The capital, and particularly the university, served as one important core from which the new idea of nation was diffused to the non-Russian periphery. For example, Georgian students at St. Petersburg University in the 1860s were influenced by the populism of those times, which quickened the pace of the Georgian nationalization process (Suny 1989, 126–130). Lithuanians coming to the Russian capital at the turn of the twentieth century, once away from the Polonization pressures placed on them at home, quickly "reclaimed" their Lithuanian language and national identity (Yukhneva 1984, 30).

The early nationalization period for many subordinate groups in the Russian Empire developed as the result of "outsider" interests, which were frequently motivated more by geopolitical concerns than by "scholarly interests." For example, early research into the Belorussian language and folklore was conducted by Poles and Russians in an effort to prove that the Slavs of the region were a part of each group's respective *ethnie* in order to strengthen their territorial claims to Belorussia (Vakar 1956, 73–82). These outsider interests could also originate from the locally dominant, nonindigenous elites (Raun 1987, 56): "By the second half of the eighteenth century, as Enlightenment thinking reached the Baltic area, Estophiles—as these German literati came to be called—had begun to take a much more serious interest in the Estonian language. . . . The study and development of the Estonian language and culture remained in the hands of German or Germanized intellectuals before the 1840s."

The very existence of a Phase A among the so-called peoples of the north (*narody severa*) and other indigenous nationalities of the East is questionable, and certainly did not begin until the twentieth century. For several of these *ethnies*, a period of scholarly interest and even patriotic agitation (i.e., Phase B) appear to have been as much a part of the Stalinist indigenization (*korenizatsiya*) policies of the 1920s and 1930s, as they were an indigenous process of elite nationalization. Chapter 3 explores this topic further.

Phase B: Patriotic Agitation

After 1825 a number of nationalist movements mark the Russian intelligentsia's entry into a more romantic age, and with it a transition from a period of scholarly interest to Phase B nationalization, a "period of patriotic agitation" (Hroch 1985, 23). If during the enlightenment intellectuals took a scholarly interest in the history, language, and culture of their ancestors, during the age of romantic nationalism these ethnocultural elements were transformed into revered icons by nationalist poets and writers, historians, anthropologists, archaeologists, and so forth. The "nation's" past, as well as its impoverished rural members and their folkways, were seen through gold-colored glasses. The "nation's" history was necessarily glorious; its conquests as well as its defeats became "national" events for remembrance and veneration. The unadulterated "national" essence was perceived to be bound up in both the genes of the peasantry and the soil of the fatherland, waiting to be reawakened, at which time the "nation" would be "reborn" and arise once again to greatness. As an oversimplification, it may be said that enlightenment scholars were driven by a desire to comprehend the universe and their place in it. In contrast to this outlook, it may be said that nationalistic intellectuals of the romantic era that followed had found their place in the universe, and it was not in the rational pursuit of knowledge but in bonding with the masses and creating a new organic community—the nation.[6]

The Slavophile movement developed during the late 1830s in opposition to enlightenment and Westernism. The destiny of the Russian nation according to the Slavophiles—to eject Westernization and reconstruct Russia's organic past in the future—was the essential equivalent of the romantic nationalism that was sweeping Europe at the time (Riasanovsky 1976, 150). This parallel was not coincidental, of course. Russian intellectual life from Peter the Great on (at least) patterned itself after the dominant intellectual trends in Europe, and particularly in France and Germany. It is nonetheless highly ironic that romantic nationalism, which to Slavophiles meant an inward and backward orientation and a rejection of Western influences, was actually at heart a European intellectual current.

The contrast between romantic Slavophiles and enlightened "Westernizers" was particularly stark regarding their respective ideas on the nation. For Westernizers such as Belinsky (as quoted in Walicki 1975, 401), "Before Peter the Great Russia was merely a people (*narod*); she became a nation (*natsiya*) thanks to the changes initiated by the reformer." The Slavophiles, in contrast to this more Westernist and modernist conception of the Russian nation with Peter I as its patron saint, held that it was the Westernized Russian elite that had alienated itself from the nation, which was viewed as an ancient organism consisting of intimately connected and internally unified village communes. According to Slavophiles, before Peter I Russian communal life represented an "organic unity" (Riasanovsky 1976, 189): "Thus lived Russia, homogeneous, harmonious, and organic, without Western class divisions, without aristocracy and democracy, without enmity and compulsion. Russian society and Russian life

---

[6] As a note of caution, it must be stated that this more nationalistic orientation was not the only movement of the romantic era. This period in Russian intellectual history saw the development of organizations that spanned the right-left spectrum of political philosophy.

were distinguished by simplicity, by a complete absence of theatrical effects, so prevalent in the West." Peter the Great, and Westernism generally, were seen as threatening to this organic unity of the Russian nation. According to the Slavophiles, in order for the nation to be whole once again, the intelligentsia must reject the West and return to "a cultivation of the native . . . elements in the social life and culture of ancient Russia" (Walicki 1979, 92).[7]

Slavophilism, like so much of romantic nationalism, attempted to reduce the influence of external (i.e., location) factors while reinforcing the perceptual significance of locale and sense of place in the life of the nation. These two dimensions are clearly central to the conceptualization of the nation, with locale the equivalent of the organic unity of people with soil in the village commune, and sense of place the idea that a Russian homeland existed as an organism made up of all these interconnected localities. This organic image of Russia was more closely associated with ancient Muscovy or Novgorod and Pskov than with St. Petersburg, the window on the West (Kristof 1967b).

The transition to Phase B nationalism among the non-Russian *ethnies* in the empire was in part a response to the subordinate position in which indigenous intellectuals found themselves. Most of the indigenous *ethnies* in Russia were second-class citizens in what their own particularistic historical, anthropological, and so forth, studies identified as their ancestral homelands. Socially mobilized Latvians and Estonians migrating to local cities found Germans in a dominant position. Similarly, Lithuanians found themselves subordinate to Poles; Georgians and Azerbaydzhanis to Armenians and Russians; Ukrainians and Belorussians to Jews, Russians, and Poles; and later, Central Asians and dozens of *ethnies* in the contemporary Russian republic found themselves in a subordinate position to the dominant Russians. This subordinate position delayed for a time the onset of nationalization among these *ethnies*. Indeed, it was often the case that these indigenous groups had developed no effective intelligentsia of their own. For example, in his studies of Latvians in Riga, Henriksson (1986, 180) found that before the middle of the nineteenth century "upwardly mobile Latvians had Germanized as a matter of course. Hence there had been no Latvian upper or middle class; to be Latvian was to be lower class."[8] Vakar (1956, 74) notes a similar Russification of the Belorussian elites

---

[7] In an interesting comparison, Greenfeld (1990) saw Gorbachev as a new Russian Westernizer, while the nationalistic and anti-Semitic works of Igor Shafarevich, and particularly "Russophobia" (1989), was characterized as follows: "Reading this essay, one gets an eerie feeling of traveling 150 years backward in time. Shafarevich's Slavophilism is so authentic it could be mistaken for the original." A revival of the Westernizer versus Slavophile debate is clearly visible in Russia since 1991.

[8] A certain amount of caution must be exercised regarding this conclusion, for the "Germanization" found by Henriksson was undoubtedly measured by the linguistic assimilation of Latvians to the German language. As noted above, an individual may attain or retain national self-consciousness in spite of, and often in reaction to, linguistic assimilation toward another national community.

throughout the nineteenth century, while the common folk of Belorussia thought of themselves more as locals ("tutejsi" or "tutasni") than as Belorussians. Krawchenko (1985, 21) also found that "before the revolution [of 1861] and for decades after, Ukrainian was synonymous with peasant."

The inferior status of indigenes and the acculturation pressures that accompanied upward mobility became increasingly intolerable with their increasing geographic and social mobilization. A "reactive ethnicity" brought on by a growing perception of relative deprivation among non-Russian indigenous elites relegated to subordinate status in their own homelands became increasingly apparent during the last decades of the Russian Empire's existence, as indigenes became more urbanized, literate, educated, and upwardly mobile. For example, "Shevchenko's 'historicism' is perceived almost exclusively as assertion and glorification of Ukrainian freedom and nationhood in battle against foreign, especially Russian, domination" (Grabowicz 1982, 17). From an enlightened sense of spatial identity with the ancestral homeland, the nationalized elites increasingly felt a sense of exclusiveness regarding their status in the homeland relative to the position of nonindigenous outsiders. The anti-outsider localism that had been apparent earlier in the villages was not abandoned as indigenes became more "modern," but was adapted to fit their new surroundings and expanded to encompass "their cities" and ultimately "their homelands." In this more expansive national territoriality, "we" had been redefined as members of the indigenous *ethnie* and not just members of the elite or of the local community, while "they" became the members of all nonindigenous *ethnies* rather than all nonlocals regardless of ethnic background.

The Russian language debate was replicated for other *ethnies* in the state, though in general these debates occurred closer to the end of the nineteenth century. For example, a feud between Georgian intellectuals developed in the 1860s over attempts by the younger, more romantic generation to elevate the vernacular (i.e., "low style") to the status of a literary language, while the older, more "enlightened" generation argued in favor of the retention of the language of the church (i.e., "high style"). The same debate was occurring in Armenia at around the same time (Suny 1989, 129). The adoption of the "low style" allowed for the more rapid expansion of literacy and with it print capitalism, which Anderson (1983) has identified as the critical turning point in the creation of mass-based national communities. In a reversal of this typical formula, the more nationalistic Zionists in Congress Poland advocated the use of Hebrew as the standard language, while more moderate Jews opted for the development of Yiddish, which was closer to the local vernacular (Corrsin 1990, 83).

In addition to this type of linguistic debate, the intellectuals of several subordinate *ethnies* in the state had to contend with the fact that their own native languages had no "high style" or literary form, since the language of the locally dominant *ethnie* performed this function (e.g., German in Latvia and Estonia;

Polish in Lithuania; Russian or Polish in Belorussia and Ukraine). Under these conditions, it is not surprising that the early nationalist writings of the indigenous "enlightened patriots" were in the locally dominant language, and that only later was the native language developed as a literary language. As examples of this, both Raun (1987) in the case of Estonians and Myl'nikov (1989) in the case of Czechs note that the early nationalist elites of both subordinate *ethnies* wrote their anti-German, romantic nationalist tracts in German. That the early nationalists of subordinate *ethnies* were frequently linguistically assimilated provides a strong argument against the notion that linguistic assimilation (i.e., acculturation) is the same as, or must lead to, psychological assimilation, and supports the contention that acculturation itself often served as a catalyst in the activation of national territoriality.

One problem that several *ethnies* had to overcome was the stigma attached to the vernacular, and to peasant life itself. For example, Vakar (1956, 78–79) recounts an early negative treatment of the vernacular in Belorussia: "One may go back to the eighteenth century and find a few short plays written for schools, where the text was in Latin or in Polish, but the rural characters, stupid and uncouth, spoke in Belorussian to amuse the audience. . . . At the beginning of the nineteenth century the first work written entirely in the vernacular appeared, and its purpose also was to make fun of the language rather than to promote it as a literary medium." Grabowicz (1989, 123), Kohut (1986, 570–571) and Seton-Watson (1977, 186) note a similar treatment of Ukrainian in the early nineteenth century, as does Suny (1989, 129) regarding Georgian. This attitude changed slowly during the first half of the nineteenth century, so that by the 1860s "the spoken idiom received recognition as a literary medium, and now was used as such by the very people who ignored it only a decade or two before" (Vakar 1956, 79–80). This corresponded with the recentering of the "national idea" around the peasant masses (e.g., Conolly 1971, 161).

In the West, the vernacularization of the literary languages proceeded after the 1860s but was hampered by Russification policies as well as by the dominance of German and Polish in the region (e.g., Raun 1985, 17–18). At first, Russification diminished the status of these locally dominant languages, and was welcomed by the Estonians, Latvians, and Lithuanians. However, Russification quickly replaced Germanization and Polonization as a threat to indigenous nationalization in the Baltics, and although it slowed the pace of linguistic standardization, it had the unintended effect of stimulating nationalist sentiments, and was not generally effective in acculturating, let alone assimilating, the indigenes in the region (Raun 1987; Conolly 1971, 171–173). The effectiveness of replacing the local languages with Russian (i.e., linguistic Russification) also appears to have been overstated. An examination of linguistic standardization and language development during the period from 1880 to 1914 reveals that even national communities, such as the Estonians who were subjected to relatively oppressive Russification policies, experienced great progress in the development of their languages during this time (e.g., Raun 1985).

The Belorussian and Ukrainian languages were treated as branches of the Russian language, just as *Malorossiya* (Little Russia) and Belorussia (White Russia, also referred to as the *zapadno-russkoy kray* or the West-Russian region) were viewed as parts of the Russian Motherland. This clearly had a detrimental effect on the development of a Ukrainian and Belorussian literary language, as did the more concerted Russification effort in Ukraine after 1863. The Ukrainian language was finally recognized as a separate language by the St. Petersburg Academy of Sciences in March 1905 (Seton-Watson 1956, 234) but was still banned from use in schools throughout the remainder of the prerevolutionary period. Belorussian was not accepted as an independent language by the local elites themselves until late in the nineteenth century, and almost no attempt was made to develop a literary language from the vernacular before World War I (Vakar 1956, 77–82). The same appears to have been true in the case of Rumanians/Moldavians in Bessarabia (Seton-Watson 1956, 235).

Before the 1860s, the literary languages used by Muslim elites were Arabic, Persian, and Chagatay. Vernacularization among the Muslim *ethnies* in the Russian Empire began around 1870 with the Kazan' Tatars as part of the reformist *jadid* movement (Rorlich 1986, 66–67). Attempts to develop a standard literary language from the local vernacular were also made in Azerbaydzhan (1870s) and Kazakhstan (1880s) (Swietochowski 1991, 56; Olcott 1985, 185–189; Braker 1971, 188–190). As nationalist currents diffused to the southern tier, national particularism among the Muslim elites spread, and with it went more concerted efforts to develop literary languages from the local vernaculars. However, two forces impeded the progress of vernacularization and the nationalization of elites more generally in this region before World War I. First, conservative religious elites were relatively antipathetic to nationalization, and often refused to consider themselves as members of any particular national community (Braker 1971, 197). These conservatives were relatively strong in Central Asia, and this appears to be one of the main reasons why vernacularization was only beginning by the end of the tsarist era. Second, a movement spearheaded by Ismail Bey Gaspraly, a Crimean Tatar, sought to unify all Turks in the state through a common language, and urged Turkic-Muslim elites throughout Russia to promote this language over the development of the local vernacular. However, Gaspraly's pan-Turkic language was itself based in large part on the local Crimean Tatar vernacular, toward which all Turkic peoples were expected to acculturate. Not surprisingly, this caused resentment among a number of nationalized elites in Russia, and on the whole was not terribly effective in consolidating the Turkic-Muslim elites. According to Lazzerini (1985, 112–113), "linguistic particularism" (i.e., the development of literary vernaculars) among Turkic-Muslim elites during the last two decades of the tsarist era "rapidly overshadowed the notion of a pan-Turkic literary language." This linguistic particularism was particularly apparent after the 1905 Revolution (Swietochowski 1991, 60).

Opting for the development of the vernacular under conditions in which Russian stood as the official language, and another language often occupied a locally preferential status (e.g., German in the Baltics, Polish in Belorussia and Lithuania, etc.) was a conscious nationalistic act. Because it was also an act that symbolized the centrality of the masses to the life and destiny of the national community, vernacularization was clearly intended to further the process of national consolidation. For this reason, the development of a literary language from the vernacular—particularly for the subordinate *ethnies* in the state—provides a good measure of the degree to which the nationalized elites had entered a period of patriotic agitation.

A period of patriotic agitation (Phase B) assumed major importance during the last fifty years of the Russian Empire. Two types of "patriotic agitators" may be identified during this period—a nationalized elite and a "conscious" peasantry.[9] As outsiders, the nationalized elites participating in the "Go to the People" and other populist movements after 1870 were by-and-large rejected by the peasant masses. On the other hand, the development of a conscious peasantry among those members of the local community who had become more geographically and socially mobilized after 1861 greatly facilitated the process of diffusing the national idea to the masses. As insiders, these conscious peasants were much more capable of functioning as transmitters of nationalism to the localized and suspicious peasantry than were their elite counterparts, no matter how sympathetic the latter may have been to the plight of the rural "folk." As an example of this, both Seregny (1991) and Perrie (1990) note the importance of these rural intelligentsia in the successful mobilization of the peasantry during the 1905–1907 Revolution. This distinction of a conscious peasant elite as successful patriotic agitators accords well with the findings of Hroch (1985, 76–96), who identified the rural intelligentsia (i.e., school teachers, local clergy, etc.) and the educated "sons of peasants" as the most active and successful patriotic agitators in Estonia and Lithuania. The emergence and expansion of a conscious peasantry marks the entry into the third phase in the national consolidation process—the nationalization of the masses.

The Nationalization of the Masses, 1861–1914

The idea of nation and debates about it revolved around the elite's perception of the peasantry throughout the prewar period, and indeed beyond it. Throughout much of this period, the peasant masses were not considered, nor did they consider themselves to be, part of the nation. Radishchev (1789) described the masses as "beasts of burden" or "cattle," unable to be citizens of the state and

---

[9] The development of the latter is discussed in Seregny (1991).

therefore not "sons of the fatherland" so long as they were enslaved by serfdom. Pogodin, a proponent of "Official Nationality," also reflected the sense that an evolutionary gap existed between the masses and the elites when he stated in 1826 that (as quoted in Riasanovsky 1969, 99): "The Russian people is marvelous, but marvelous so far only in potentiality. In actuality, it is low, horrid, and beastly . . . [Russian peasants] will not become human beings until they are forced into it."

A massive chasm existed between peasantry and gentry in Russia as in other feudal societies; the educated elite may have perceived of itself as a "nation" of citizens (e.g., Walicki 1979; Riasanovsky 1976), but peasants were viewed either as children or as "toys to be manipulated at will" (Eklof 1986, 1). This "modernist" or "enlightened" view of the peasantry was typical of Westernizers throughout the nineteenth century, and was the *principal* outlook of the urban elite (Kingston-Mann 1991, 5–6; quoting Netting 1967): "The folk would become truly Russian only when they became human, human only as they acquired one by one enlightenment and the fruits of Western culture."

The idea that the "dark masses" were hardly part of the same species, let alone part of the same nation, was by no means unique to the Russian Empire. For example, Weber (1976, 5) found that as late as the 1870s a sense of Frenchness was limited to the urbanized, educated elite within the state, and that the peasants were seen by these Frenchmen as "savages" who "were intellectually several centuries behind the enlightened part of the country." Similarly, " 'Magyar,' 'Pole' and 'Croat' were initially at least as much labels denoting class privilege as ethnic affiliation. It was said that a Croat aristocrat would sooner admit his horse to membership of the Croat 'nation' than a peasant" (Pearson 1983, 32).

For their part, the peasant masses remained suspicious of "outsiders," and these anti-outsider sentiments were set primarily at the scale of the local village.[10] While the nationalized elite may have defined their communities of belonging and homelands in more expansive terms, it appears that the peasantry for the most part did not. As noted above, Belorussian peasants most frequently referred to themselves as locals, rather than Belorussians, and the same appears to have been true in Ukraine, and among local Russians living dispersed throughout the Russian Empire. The population in ethnographically mixed locales frequently intermarried, and over several generations came to see themselves, and were seen by others, as distinct *ethnies*. Of course, among the nomadic groups of Siberia and Central Asia, the internal ethnographic divisions were even more apparent. The Kazakhs, for example, were said to include representatives from all the Turkic tribes in the Empire, and at the turn of the

---

[10] Caution must be exercised in assessing the sentiments of the peasant masses, since they were primarily illiterate and left little in the way of a written record. For a variety of obvious reasons, the sentiments assigned to peasants by elites during this period were likely to be seriously biased.

century were internally divided into four hordes, eight tribes, two alliances, and more than sixty kinship groups (Semenov' Tyan'-Shanskiy 1903, 18:199–200). More generally, great intranational ethnographic variation across guberniyas is depicted in the major ethnogeographic study of this period, and this undoubtedly reinforced a sense of localism (Semenov' Tyan'-Shanskiy 1899–1914). Kingston-Mann (1991, 15) also finds that what the rural masses thought of as native (*rodnoy*) was much more localized than nation and homeland: "The language of the peasants was filled with words, phrases, and proverbs describing the uniqueness of one's own "place," where, as it was said, "birds sing differently and flowers bloom more brightly." Equally rich was the peasant store of epithets to describe those who were not *rodnoi*—the "white-eyed fools" from Perm, and the "big-ears" from Iaroslavl—the outsiders." A contemporary dictionary defined *rodina* (native land) broadly as the equivalent of *otechestvo* (fatherland), which might mean homeland or state, and narrowly as the rural area or city in which one was born and raised (Dal' 1881). It seems reasonable to suggest that the broad definition pertained to the nationalized elites, while the vast majority of the rural population understood *rodina* to mean locality.

For the peasantry, "we" was narrowly defined as locals while "they" were all outsiders, whether or not they were from the same nominal *ethnie*. The strength of this localism was still apparent in the 1870s and 1880s, as the nationalized elites who sought to 'Go to the People' quickly discovered. Even by the time of the 1897 census, group identities continued to be limited geographically, and even languages varied greatly from village to village. "In Dagestan, for example, many people reported as their native language the language of their village or town, making it difficult to allocate the population according to standard linguistic categories" (Silver 1986, 73). In large part because of the limited mass-based national consciousness at the time, this census did not attempt to gauge ethnonational affiliation or "tribal affiliation" (*plemennoy sostav'*), and used native language as a substitute for national identity. According to Troynitsky (1905, 2:I–II), even grouping village dialects into linguistic categories in the census was extremely difficult, and the great diversity rendered the ethnolinguistic results of this first empirewide census of limited utility.

The nationalization of the masses is often depicted as a unidirectional process with elites or the state mobilizing the otherwise inert masses to serve the purposes of the elites. This is certainly the way in which the enlightened Westernizers, as well as the tsarist regime and supporters of Official Nationality tended to view the relationship between the civilized elite and the "dark masses," and is typical of the modernization thesis generally.

On the other hand, the Slavophiles and other romantic nationalists held views diametrically opposed to the Westernizing modernists, seeing the peasant *narod* and its culture as the real core of the nation, which the elites had forsaken in favor of an alien Western culture (Walicki 1975, 396–422; Walicki 1979, 92; Conolly 1971, 161). From this perspective, it was not the peasant *narod* that needed civilizing but the elites themselves who needed "reawakening." This romantic nationalism was prominent during the transition from Phase A to Phase B.

Both the Westernist and the romantic images of the peasantry were undoubtedly mistaken. The masses themselves were not "inert," and during this period the impetus for change often came from below (e.g., Eklof 1990). On the other hand, the peasant's life was by no means ideal, and the romantic nationalist myth of a noble peasantry was kept alive only so long as the *narod* remained an abstraction for the intellectuals. The urbanized intellectuals for their part took almost no interest in the empirical study of the peasantry before the end of the nineteenth century (Yaney 1982; Kingston-Mann 1991, 25), and then it was primarily the romantic nationalists seeking out their national "roots" (Petrovich 1968). Once the rural *narod* became the subject of social scientific research and the object of attention from the more active patriotic agitators, disillusionment among the romanticists set in (e.g., Fanger 1968).

Rather than seeing the nationalization of the masses as a unidirectional process, it seems more reasonable to suggest that the final phase in the process of national consolidation in the Russian Empire and elsewhere was an interactive process of adaptation engaged in by both a primarily localized peasantry and a more nationally oriented elite. A greater sensitivity to the motivations of the masses in this process is certainly warranted, even though such a focus is made extremely difficult as the primarily illiterate countryside left behind little in the way of a written record. A comprehensive social history of the postemancipation period has yet to be written, but a number of more narrowly focused studies attempt to assess what the masses were thinking and doing during this time period (e.g., Eklof 1986; Eklof and Franks 1990; Brooks 1985; Kingston-Mann and Mixter 1991).[11]

For most of the nations in the Russian Empire, national consolidation was only beginning to enter a Phase C by the time of World War I and the October Revolution (e.g., Chistov 1977a).[12] The rural populace remained highly skeptical and suspicious of intellectual "outsiders" during the 1861–1914 period. This conforms with the general conclusions reached by Hroch in his investigation of "patriotic agitation" among several European *ethnies* (1985, 154): "In

---

[11] Unfortunately, most of these concentrate on the Russian or Slavic regions of the empire, and neglect the non-Slavic periphery. For these regions we rely on comparative data in the 1897 census and statistical yearbooks of the period, as well as on a number of nation-specific studies (e.g., Suny 1989; Raun 1987; Rorlich 1986; Vakar 1956; Olcott 1987; Swietochowski 1983, 1991; Krawchenko 1985).

[12] World War I itself had a mobilizing effect on the national communities being formed. The external threat coming first from Germany and the Ottoman Empire and later from famine, epidemics, and the Red Army served to enhance the internal cohesion of these national communities, and has since served as a critical historic episode in the lives of nations that continues to have significance, particularly for those nations who gained their independence—however briefly—during the interwar period. This period is examined in chapter 3.

the majority of the cases investigated the patriots identified themselves more enthusiastically with the peasantry and its life-style than the peasantry did with these very patriots and their national programme." The peasantry also remained highly localized in their orientation to life throughout this period, and began to respond to more broad-based national concerns only after emancipation and a degree of geographic and social mobility had begun to break down this localism. As noted above, the development of a nationally "conscious" peasantry that served as a transmitter was critically important in this process.

The period from 1861 to 1914 is significant as the beginning phase of a reorientation of the masses toward a national self-consciousness, and with it a sense of homeland that exceeded the bounds of locality.[13] The abolition of serfdom in 1861 and the subsequent increase in the rate of geographic and social mobilization among the peasantry were of critical importance in the nationalization process. Along with this, the development of transportation and communication began to shrink the sociocultural as well as physical distances separating town from country. Literacy and education rates were also on the rise throughout this period, and this increase was in large part a result of peasant initiative rather than an elite attempt to mobilize the "inert masses" (Eklof 1986). Along with urbanization and rising literacy and education went occupational mobility, though desires for better jobs clearly outpaced the ability of peasants to attain them, resulting in a growing sense of relative deprivation among the indigenous masses. With the geographic and social mobilization of the masses, the localism of the peasantry was beginning to break down by the end of the tsarist era, and mass-based national movements (i.e., Phase C) were beginning to emerge. In the following pages, these socio-cultural, economic, and political processes occurring between 1861 and 1914 are highlighted, and their impact on the nationalization of the masses is assessed.

The Abolition of Serfdom

The emancipation of serfs is viewed as a revolutionary turning point in the history of Russia, when feudalism gave way to the capitalist epoch.[14] For the nationalization of the masses to occur, emancipation was a necessary precondition (Hroch 1985, 153). It was certainly viewed this way by Russian romantic nationalists, who increasingly saw serfdom as a stumbling block in the pathway of Russia's "rebirth" (Riasanovsky 1976, 262). For the peasantry itself, however, change for the better after 1861 was less apparent, and improvements came only slowly to the countryside.

---

[13] The late timing of the nationalization of the masses in the Russian Empire is by no means atypical. For example, Weber (1976) provides convincing evidence that peasants in France did not begin to consider themselves part of the French nation until this same period (i.e., 1850–1917).

[14] This historic, even "revolutionary" change, coming as it did without a revolution, has posed difficulties for Marxist analysts. See Christian (1991, 261).

The so-called Great Reforms of February 19, 1861, ending formal serfdom in the Russian Empire were more a reflection of the center's concern that the Russian masses were becoming sufficiently politically mobilized to pose a serious revolutionary challenge to the regime than an indicator that the elites had radically altered their opinions regarding the peasantry.[15] Alexander II, in a statement to the Russian landed nobility in 1856 upon the conclusion of the Treaty of Paris ending the Crimean War, clearly reflected this attitude (as quoted in Emmons 1968, 41): "It is better to abolish serfdom from above than to await the day when it will begin to abolish itself from below." A strong desire for the abolition of serfdom existed among the peasant masses, even though under ordinary circumstances this desire was not overtly expressed, or took the form of "everyday resistance" rather than outright rebellion (Bohac 1991).[16]

The statutes themselves were complicated and often contradictory, and this led to a great deal of confusion in the illiterate countryside. For many peasants the problem was not with the statutes themselves, which the masses were convinced held the promised freedom within their clauses, but with the local messengers who read them—often members of the rural elite. When realization that the statutes did not contain full freedom, peasant uprisings occurred throughout the affected area (Emmons 1968, 54–61).

Expectations of complete emancipation among the serfs were certainly not met by these laws. One of the most important aspects of the promulgated statutes was their attempt to end the slavelike relationship between nobility and serfs while limiting and controlling the mobilization of the masses. The "emancipated" peasants were not given the option of accepting or rejecting the government's offer of land, and the land was not given freely to the former serfs. Rather, peasants were forced to accept land with redemption payments due, and since these payments were often higher than the value of the land itself, the peasants had little prospect of selling or even giving away this land.[17] The amount of land available to former serfs was also often insufficient for the family's needs, given the level of rural technology, capital available for investment, and the quality of the land. The combination of these factors, in addition to population growth in the countryside, led to the deterioration of economic conditions for the peasants, and the rapid increase in the number of adult male peasants taking part in temporary labor migration (*otkhod*). At least some evidence suggests that the impoverishment resulting from emancipation represented a deliberate attempt on the part of the state either to ensure an adequate supply of cheap labor to work the landowning elites' fields in the Central Black

---

[15] Serfs were often treated as virtual slaves, and were bought and sold practically up to the time of emancipation, even though laws restricting this practice were introduced as early as 1822 (Robinson 1932, 42; Zelnick 1968).

[16] As evidence of this desire, rumors that volunteers for the Crimean front would be set free literally emptied villages of their adult male population (Emmons 1968, 49).

[17] In 1905 redemption payments were finally canceled in response to rebellion from below.

Earth (*Chernozem*) region or to work in the growing nonagricultural sector in the non-*Chernozem* zone (Burds 1991).

The "Great Reforms" of 1861 primarily dealt with the Russian population in the empire, though emancipation at this time was also enacted (under different conditions) in Ukraine, Belorussia, Lithuania, and Transcaucasia (Robinson 1932, 85–86). In the East, serfdom was not practiced, and the reforms had no direct impact. The Baltic *guberniyas* (administrative districts) were emancipated earlier in the nineteenth century (Estland in 1816, Kurland in 1817, and Lifland in 1819), though the peasants were not freed with land and were restricted geographically to their areas of origin. An emancipation similar to this was granted in the Polish territory under tsarist rule in 1807. A more complete emancipation was enacted only with the great reforms and those that followed the 1863 Polish uprising (Yukhneva 1984, 29). In retaliation for the Polish uprising of 1863, which was led by the Polish landed elites, Polish peasants were granted much greater freedom, along with a reduction in the level of obligations. For much the same reason, the peasants in Belorussia, western Ukraine, and Lithuania, where the landed nobility was by-and-large of Polish descent, were in general treated more favorably than the peasants of Russia, in a clear attempt by the "Russian government to ally itself with the peasantry against the Polish nobles" (Robinson 1932, 85–86; Willetts 1971, 107). The reverse was true in Transcaucasia, where the nobility was favored over the peasantry (Suny 1989, 111).

In the Baltic *guberniyas*, Ukraine (western *guberniyas*), Belorussia, and Lithuania, indigenous peasants were under "foreign" control, and landowners were primarily either German or Polish. In Transcaucasia, Poland, and Russia, both peasants and landowners were primarily from the same *ethnie*. This regional difference did not seem an overwhelming factor in the timing of the nationalization of the masses, which occurred relatively early in the Baltic *guberniyas* and Poland; later in European Russia, Transcaucasia, and Ukraine; and still later in Belorussia. It is apparent that no simple formulation relating nationalization to conditions of "internal colonialism" may be made with regard to the history of national developments in the Russian Empire, though "foreign domination" undoubtedly played a role in a rising sense of exclusiveness among indigenes in the non-Russian periphery (e.g., Vakar 1956; Raun 1987; Henriksson 1986).

The emancipation of serfs in 1861 may be seen as a necessary precondition for the nationalization of the masses, since it upgraded the social status of the peasant *narod* and also opened the way for greater geographic and social mobilization. However, this potentiality was limited in Russia after 1861. The "Great Reforms" were designed to avert revolutionary change by formally freeing the serfs while attempting to restrict their social mobility and channel their geographic mobility in ways that benefited the state and its industrialization policy. The objective of the reforms was to avoid the great upheavals that the ruling elites perceived to be on the horizon, and in this the emancipation statutes were successful in the short term. However, it has also been argued that the revolutions of 1905 and 1917 were in large part the result of the government's failure to fully emancipate the peasantry in 1861 (Mironov 1990, 33).

Geographic Mobilization

It is one of the great paradoxes of Russian history that as the Russian Empire was expanding to become the largest state in the world, the peasantry was becoming increasingly immobilized and impoverished through the development of serfdom (Robinson 1932, 1–24). This of course is not to imply that no movement among even the enserfed population was occurring. Along with the "fight" option, which occasionally proved disruptive, individuals attempted to escape the constrictions of serfdom through "flight."[18] However, before 1861 the vast majority of the population in the state was both rural and geographically immobile. After emancipation, due to the inability of the former serfs to make ends meet on the land allotments provided them, the migration rate of peasants in search of new lands (i.e., rural to rural migration), of peasant families seeking to supplement their agricultural income (seasonal migration to the cities), and of those who migrated to the cities on a permanent basis increased substantially, particularly after the legal restrictions on their movement were lifted.

The following sections focus on three dimensions of this increasing geographic mobility. First, the development of a transportation network in the Russian Empire during this period is assessed. Second, rural-to-rural migration patterns—both local and interregional—are examined. Finally, the developing rural-to-urban migration stream and its impact on nationalization processes are analyzed.

TRANSPORTATION

According to Weber's study of national consolidation in France (1976, 218), "there could be no national unity before there was national circulation." If this generalization is valid, and it certainly appears to be, one factor in the limited degree of mass-based nationalization in the Russian Empire must have been the primitive state of its transportation network. The development of a railroad in the Russian Empire barely predated emancipation. The first rail line connecting St. Petersburg and Moscow was completed only in 1838, and by 1861, with around 1,600 kilometers of track in use, the rail network remained in its infancy. After that date there was a relatively dramatic increase in railroad construction. In 1910 nearly 68,000 kilometers of track were in use, serving a total of 187 million passengers traveling an average distance of 117 kilometers,

---

[18] Pearson (1983) uses this "fight versus flight" categorization in his study of national minorities in Eastern Europe.

and hauling more than 252 million tons of freight (Russia TsSK 1912, part 11: 1–12). Of course, this crucial "circulatory system" was not equally accessible to all (Table 2.1). In the northwest, and particularly the Baltic *guberniyas* of Estland, Lifland, and Kurland, the rail network was much more extensive than in the eastern and southern regions of the country.[19] Still, even in European Russia, the density of track and the population served remained relatively underdeveloped by European standards throughout the prerevolutionary period. As late as 1910 only Portugal and Montenegro had a less dense rail network than European Russia by territory, and only Serbia, Montenegro, and Turkey had a less dense rail network by population (Russia TsSK 1912, part 11: 23–26). At the same time, none relied more heavily on its railroad network than the Russian Empire (Thalheim 1971, 105). Thus, while this period was one of dramatic growth in the country's rail network, particularly in the European core, Russia remained far behind Europe in the development of its transportation infrastructure.

The Russian Empire also had a poorly developed system of roads. The vast majority of roads in existence were often little more than dirt cart tracks (*proselochnaya doroga*)—so much so that they were labeled "ordinary" or "commonplace" (*obyknovenaya doroga*). Even by 1910 more than 91 percent of all roads fell into this category (Russia TsSK 1912, part 11: 44–52). Clearly, legal restrictions on peasant migration were not the only reason for the relative geographic immobility of the rural population in the Russian Empire. The physical hardship associated with travel continued to restrict the geographic mobility of the population throughout the postemancipation period.

Overall, geographic mobility was becoming easier between 1861 and 1914 due in part to the development of a more sophisticated transportation network. However, growing regional disparities were emerging with the development of Russia's infrastructure, as with the modernization process in general. The Russian core around St. Petersburg and Moscow, Novorossiya with the importance of port facilities on the Black Sea, and the developed non-Russian northwest (the Baltic region, as well as Russia's Polish territory and Finland), were areas where geographic mobility was relatively easier than in the remaining parts of the country. This at least in part adds to the admittedly much more complex explanation for geographic differentials in the timing of mass-based nationalization in the waning years of the Russian Empire.

RURAL TO RURAL MIGRATION

Place of birth data provided in the first Russian census in 1897 indicate that the vast majority of the rural population lived in the same local area (*uyezd*) in

---

[19] However, since the population density was so low in Siberia, using the measure versts/100,000 population indicates that the inhabitants of this region were better served than those living in Moscow (Table 2.1). This, of course, is absurd.

TABLE 2.1
Railroad Network by Gross Region, 1911

Gross Region[a]	Versts[b]	Versts/100,000 Population	Versts/1,000 Square Versts
Russia			
Central Industrial	8989	41.5	16.7
Capitals	2384	38.7	34.8
North	1090	42.8	0.9
Central Agricultural	6853	40.6	26.1
Volga	5016	34.5	9.2
Urals	3790	30.0	5.4
Siberia/Far East	5317	61.0	0.5
Ukraine			
Novorossiya	6732	55.4	21.3
Left Bank	3298	33.2	23.9
Right Bank	3624	29.4	25.0
West			
Finland	3420	110.9	12.0
Poland	3172	25.4	28.4
Baltic	2101	78.2	25.9
Belorussia and Lithuania	5909	46.5	22.1
Bessarabia	800	32.1	20.5
Non-Slavic South			
North Caucasus	1530	28.6	7.6
Transcaucasus	2137	32.0	10.2
North Kazakhstan	1078	32.5	0.7
Central Asia	3059	45.1	2.0

Source: Russia TsSK (Tsentral'nyy Statisticheskiy Komitet) 1912, part 1:1–57; part 11:19–22.

[a] Gross Regions:
Central Industrial: Kaluzha, Kostroma, Moscow, Nizhni Novgorod, Novgorod, Pskov, St. Petersburg, Smolensk, Tver, Vladimir, Yaroslavl
  Capitals: Moscow, St. Petersburg
North: Arkhangel', Olonets, Vologda
Central Agricultural: Voronezh, Kursk, Orlov, Ryazan, Tambov, Tula
Volga: Astrakhan, Kazan', Penza, Samara, Saratov, Simbirsk
Urals: Vyatka, Orenburg, Perm, Ufa
Siberia/Far East: Amur, Irkutsk, Kamchatka, Primorya, Sakhalin, Tobolsk, Tomsk, Yakutiya, Yenisey, Zabaykal
Novorossiya: Don, Ekaterinoslav, Kherson, Tavrida
Left Bank Ukraine: Chernigov, Kharkov, Poltava
Right Bank Ukraine: Kiev, Podolsk, Volynsk
Finland: Eight guberniyas of Finland

TABLE 2.1 SOURCES (*Continued*)
Poland: Ten guberniyas of Poland
Baltic: Estland, Kurland, Lifland
Belorussia and Lithuania: Grodno, Kovno, Minsk, Mogilev, Vilno, Vitebsk
Bessarabia: Bessarabia
North Caucasus: Chernomorya, Kuban, Stavropol, Tersk
Transcaucasus: Baku, Batumi, Dagestan, Elisavetpol', Karsk, Kutaissi, Sukhumi, Tiflis, Yerevan, Zakatalsk
North Kazakhstan: Akmolinsk, Semipalatinsk, Turgay, Uralsk
Central Asia: Fergana, Samarkand, Semirechiye, Syr'-Darya, Zakaspisk

    Gross regions were constructed using Vodarskiy (1973) for comparability with urban data from 1858 (see Table 4) and are not identical to regions or republics in the USSR. For units more comparable to today's economic regions, see Leasure and Lewis (1966).

[b] Versts = 1.068 kilometers.

---

which they were born (Table 2.2; Map 2.1). The proportion was consistently more than 90 percent throughout the Russian Empire, with the highest rate (98 percent) registered in Central Asia. These data project an image of a rural population that was highly localized, with little geographic interaction not only across *guberniyas* but within them as well. Under these conditions of relative geographic immobility, what was *rodnoy* must have been defined within the parameters of locality, and it would be difficult to imagine that the rural population thought of itself in national, as opposed to local, terms, or that a sense of homeland was more extensive than place of residence.

There were two exceptions to the low level of rural mobility. First, in the Baltics and Poland, local (i.e., inter-*uyezd*) geographic interaction was relatively more intense (Table 2.2). This may reflect that this region had fewer legal restrictions on intercommunal movement for a longer period of time than was the case in much of the rest of European Russia. In addition, the relatively greater level of inter-*uyezd* mobility among the indigenous rural population is a signal that "what was *rodnoy*" for Estonians, Latvians, and Poles was becoming geographically more extensive than locality. This conclusion is supported by Hroch (1985, 63, 77), who found that national self-consciousness in Finland and Estonia was becoming mass-based during the 1870s and 1880s. Undoubtedly this was also occurring among Latvians and Poles.

Second, inter-*guberniya* migration was relatively high in Siberia and the Far East, Novorossiya, and Northern Caucasia (Table 2.2). This was not a reflection of increasing geographic mobility among indigenes but rather of the colonization of the non-European periphery by Slavic peasants (Bruk and Kabuzan 1980).[20] The migration from European to Asiatic Russia reached a peak during the first decade of the twentieth century. Indeed, voluntary migration between 1901 and 1910 exceeded the total rural eastward migration for the entire nine-

---

[20] Bruk and Kabuzan also describe the geographic mobility of Russians (1982) and Ukrainians (1981) during the prerevolutionary period.

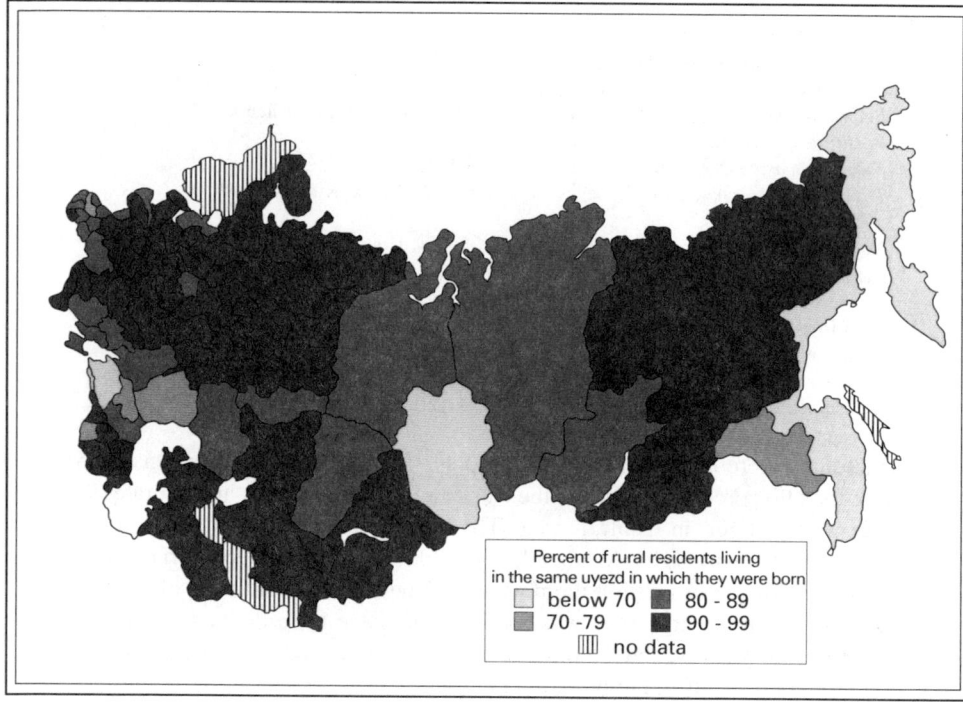

Map 2.1　Rural Immobility by Guberniya, 1897

teenth century, even though it was held down by the famine of 1901–1902 and by legal restrictions between 1904 and 1905.[21] The number leaving European Russia for the periphery after 1906 was particularly high, reflecting the impact that ending redemption payments and removing travel restrictions had on long distance migration (Table 2.3).

A number of factors explain the rapid increase in eastward migration during this period. First, the tsarist government reversed policies, ending the ban on migration to Siberia and elsewhere, and enacting legislation that lowered the barriers to and eventually even encouraged such migration. Between 1906 and 1915, approximately two million families were granted separation from their land allotments (Robinson 1932, 190). In addition to policy inducements, transportation was developing at the same time, lowering the obstacles to migration. Construction on the Trans-Siberian railroad began in 1891, and thirty-three hundred kilometers of track were laid by 1900. A rail line from European Russia to Tashkent also opened during the 1890s. By 1916 some

[21] Restrictions on eastward migration between 1904 and 1905 were due both to the Russo-Japanese War, which monopolized the limited transportation network (Demko 1969, 80), and also to the 1905 Revolution (Anderson 1980, 132–133).

TABLE 2.2
Rural Population by Place of Birth and Gross Region, 1897 (percent)

Gross Region[a]	Place of Birth[b]				
	Same Uyezd	Other Uyezd, Same Guberniya	Other Guberniya	Other State	Total
Russia					
Central Industrial	91.4	4.2	4.4	0.02	13,357,559
Capitals	81.9	7.6	10.5	0.1	1,986,479
North	95.4	2.1	2.4	0.01	1,932,057
Central Agricultural	95.5	2.5	2.0	0.01	11,638,460
Volga	93.5	2.7	3.9	0.02	10,295,326
Urals	91.2	3.4	5.4	0.01	9,287,034
Siberia/Far East	75.2	2.4	21.7	0.7	5,254,232
Ukraine					
Novorossiya	84.4	4.2	11.1	0.3	7,221,340
Left Bank	94.9	2.7	2.3	0.02	6,717,231
Right Bank	91.9	3.9	3.6	0.5	8,652,040
West					
Poland	83.8	8.6	6.5	1.2	7,243,592
Baltics	88.9	7.1	3.8	0.1	1,772,492
Belorussia and Lithuiana	92.5	3.8	3.6	0.1	8,879,018
Bessarabia	90.4	5.2	3.3	1.1	1,642,080
Non-Slavic South					
North Caucasus	72.6	3.2	23.5	0.7	3,339,674
Transcaucasus	92.2	3.1	3.0	1.7	4,749,434
North Kazakhstan	90.4	1.5	8.1	0.02	2,261,483
Central Asia	97.6	0.2	1.4	0.8	4,550,865

Source: Russia TsSK 1897, 89 vols.
[a] Gross Regions: See Table 2.1.
[b] Place of birth categories refer to the relationship of place of birth to place of current residence. An uyezd is the administrative unit within guberniyas, the first-order civil divisions of the state.

sixteen thousand kilometers of track had been laid in Siberia and Central Asia, compared to eighty-one thousand in European Russia (Lorimer 1946, 24–25). As a final factor serving to encourage movement eastward, peasants from the west viewed Siberia as a "kind of Utopia" (Robinson 1932, 251). The latter undoubtedly represented the idealized imagery that a vast, sparsely settled area must have created in the minds of the land-hungry Slavic peasants from the west. In addition, it may have reflected the utopian mythologies about Siberia as a promised land which entered the popular nationalist literature after the

TABLE 2.3
Number of Voluntary and Involuntary Migrants into Asiatic Russia,[a] 1801–1914 (total and average annual number, in thousands)

Period	Average Annual			Totals		
	Voluntary	Involuntary	Total	Voluntary	Involuntary	Total
1801–1850	3	5	8	125	250	375
1851–1860	9	10	19	91	100	191
1861–1870	11	14	25	114	140	254
1871–1880	7	18	25	68	180	248
1881–1890	28	14	42	279	140	419
1891–1900	108	13	121	1,078	130	1,208
1901–1910	226	3	229	2,257	25	2,282
1911–1914	174	6	180	696	27	723

Source: Lorimer 1946, 26.

Notes: Lorimer notes that "Illegal migrants in period prior to abolition of serfdom not included except in 1801–1850. Figures for 'Involuntary' are incomplete. The estimated total number of unreported migrants and those omitted from Table during the nineteenth century was 'not more than 700 thousand.'"

[a] Figures for Asiatic Russia include migration to Siberia, Turkestan, and the Asiatic steppe region (i.e., North Kazakhstan).

intellectual turn inward and eastward (i.e., away from Europe) during the 1860s (Kristof 1967a; Bassin 1991).

A relatively high rate of return migration occurred once peasants realized that their perceptions of the region as the new Russian paradise were not accurate. For example, in 1910 with a good harvest in the west, return migration reached 41 percent, while in 1911 with a particularly bad harvest in the east it reached 44.5 percent (Russia TsSK 1912, part 2: 9–11). However, in the more normal economic years of 1912 and 1913, the level of return migration decreased to 15–16 percent of the level of in-migration (Russia TsSK 1915, part 2: 19–21). An earlier survey taken in 1898 indicated that settlers "considered themselves to be better off in Siberia" and, in general, economic indicators suggest that this was the case (Poppe 1971, 145–146). If Siberia was not the Utopia that peasants had imagined, it was at least a relatively greater land of opportunity.

In addition to these positive factors "pulling" Slavic peasants eastward, negative factors such as population pressure (primarily in the Central *Chernozem* and in Ukraine)—resulting from population growth and reductions in the size of land allotments during the latter half of the nineteenth century— were "pushing" these peasants away from home. On the whole, "push factors" resulting from population pressure were the more telling (Anderson 1980, 122–139; Demko 1969, 51–63; Lorimer 1946, 18; Rashin 1956, 72–73). According to an official survey taken in Samara *Guberniya* in 1899, when asked why they had come, peasant in-migrants responded as follows (Robinson 1932, 106):

Rank	Response	Number of Respondents
1	Too little land	12,000
2	Bad harvest	10,000
3	Not enough work at home	8,000
4	Overburdened by debts	7,000

The size of the Slavic migration stream into a predominantly non-Slavic Asiatic Russia, and the rapid rate of increase in the number of in-migrants, was certain to be disruptive to the indigenes' primarily nomadic way of life.[22] According to Lorimer (1946, 27), by 1911:

> there were only about 400,000 Russians in Turkestan . . . in contrast to 1,500,000 in the Asiatic steppe region and 8,000,000 in Siberia. Russians formed 85 percent of the total population of Siberia at this time and were predominant in all major administrative districts, except Yakutia and Kamchatka. They formed 40 percent of the population of the steppe region, but were predominant only in the north-central area (Akmolinsk District). They formed 6 percent of the population of Turkestan, with the highest proportion (17 percent) in Semirechensk, which roughly corresponds to the present Soviet republic of Kirgiz.

Sedentary peasants from the west appropriated land that had served as vital pasturage for the Kazakhs and other nomadic groups, who were often viewed by the Russians as relatively primitive aborigines without a history and without a future. The nomadic peoples of Siberia, Central Asia, and North Caucasus had the legal status of *inorodtsy*, literally meaning "aliens" but officially used to differentiate the backward peoples of the empire as second-class citizens in comparison with the European "tribes." *Inorodtsy* was the designation given these groups in statistical yearbooks (e.g., Russia TsSK 1915), and these groups legally had fewer rights. In its broadest definition, *inorodtsy* referred not only to the "backward" peoples of the east but to all non-Slavs in the state (Inorodtsy 1894; Zhdanko 1977, 41).

In reaction to such encroachments by the flood of aliens after 1905, indigenes began to experience a growing national consciousness along with increasing hostility toward the newcomers to the region. As an example of this, Akiner (1983, 290) notes that what began as a relatively pro-Russian attitude among Kazakhs in the first half of the nineteenth century "did not survive the advent of the Russian settlers, who descended on the Kazakhs at the turn of the century and robbed them of their lands." The massive eastward movement into northern Kazakhstan and southern Siberia, as well as the southward movement into the Kuban and Stavropol' regions of the Caucasus, may have been positive as seen by the center, both in economic terms (in the sense that more agricultural output per acre would be produced by the sedentary in-migrants), in geopolitical terms

---

[22] The use of the term *Russian* should be read not as "Great Russians," but rather as predominantly Slavic in-migrants from the Russian core (i.e., nonindigenes to the region).

(the Slavic population being viewed as a more loyal group at a time of increasing insecurity, particularly after the loss to Japan), and in terms of reducing discontent within the European core (as in Europe, out-migration to the colonial holdings being viewed as a release valve for population pressure "at home"). However, from the vantage point of the non-Slavic indigenes being inundated by "outsiders," the migration streams that were developing could hardly be seen as anything other than imperialism, and their treatment as inferiors to the incoming Slavs began to awaken a national self-consciousness that was anti-Russian and antitsarist in orientation (Clem 1992; Olcott 1987, 101–112).

This "reactive ethnicity" was less apparent in Siberia, in part because it was more sparsely settled and the intensity of interaction between Russians and indigenes was lower than in the Northern Caucasus and Kazakhstan. Indeed, Semenov' Tyan'-Shanskiy (1907, 16:222–225) notes that not only was there little hostility between Russian in-migrants and the indigenous groups but also that they underwent extensive interethnic integration, with the indigenes becoming "Russianized" (*obruseniye*) and the Russian settlers becoming "indigenized." Nonetheless, once the in-migration became massive and disruptive (i.e., after 1905), indigenes such as the Yakuts and Buryats also experienced a rising national self-consciousness along with a rising sense of exclusiveness regarding their status in the homeland (eg. Kolarz 1969, 103; Seton-Watson 1956, 241).

The effect on the Russian nation of this geographic expansion has been the subject of serious debate for much of the twentieth century.[23] On the one hand, expansion through conquest of the non-Slavic periphery helped to promote the image of the Russian nation as an advanced people, and coincided with a more geographically expansive image of home (Kristof 1967b; Connor 1986). This resulted in a rising Russian chauvinism and with it a rising reactive nationalism among the non-Russians in the waning years of the Russian Empire. On the other hand, the expansion and dispersal of the Russian *narod* also resulted in greater intranational ethnographic diversity, as the Russians in non-Russian localities mixed with the indigenous peoples over the course of time (Semenov' Tyan'-Shanskiy 1899–1914). The great geographic extent of the Russian people has been blamed by some as one reason for the lack of a strong Russian national consciousness today (e.g., Starovoytova 1990). It is equally apparent today that few agree as to the geographic extent of "Mother Russia." While the expansion of the state and the interregional migration of Russians secured the empire's place as a major colonial power and the Russians' status as a dominant people, it also delayed the national consolidation of the Russian masses and the development of a strong sense of homeland.

[23] For a historical geography on the role of Asia and expansion eastward in the making of Russia, see Bassin (1991).

RURAL TO URBAN MIGRATION

Rural to urban migration was a more significant factor in the nationalization process than rural to rural migration, since it potentially represented not only the horizontal but also the vertical incorporation of the masses. The urban environment was not only a much more densely populated and ethnically diverse setting in which in-migrants were likely to experience a greatly intensified level of interethnic contact; it was also the place where a newly nationalized intelligentsia was emerging. The city was becoming a nationalistic as well as (or perhaps even in opposition to) a cosmopolitan environment, and it was into this increasingly nationalistic milieu that the rural indigenes were entering in increasing numbers between 1861 and 1914.

Prior to significant rural to urban migration, two developments appeared to be important. First, the economic opportunities in the cities had to be increasing relative to those in the rural areas, which could occur either through economic development in the cities or through the deterioration of conditions in the countryside. Both were occurring in European Russia during the latter half of the nineteenth century (Leasure and Lewis 1968, 380–383). Second, some minimal level of social mobilization in the countryside normally preceded this type of migration stream. According to Anderson (1980, 151–152), illiterate peasants under worsening local conditions chose rural to rural migration over movement to cities, even if the cities were relatively close by. This undoubtedly reflected the traditional suspicion and outright hostility with which the less socially mobilized peasantry regarded the city and its inhabitants (Vucinich 1968, xii; Krawchenko 1985, 18–70), as well as their lack of preparation for participation in the urban economy. On the other hand, higher literacy and especially education rates predisposed rural migrants toward urbanization (Anderson 1980; Eklof 1986).

Rural to urban migration absorbed an exceedingly small percentage of the natural increase of the rural population, and had no real impact before 1885 (Mironov 1990, 23–25). Even as late as 1901–1905, the equivalent of only about 1.5 percent of the rural population's natural increase in European Russia was absorbed by migration to cities (Rogger 1983, 127).[24] The Russian Empire remained overwhelmingly rural throughout the prerevolutionary period.

Nonetheless, urbanization increased relatively dramatically after emancipation. The cities of European Russia, having grown from 2.8 million (6.6 percent of the total) to 6.1 million (10 percent of the total) between 1811 and 1863, grew to 18.6 million (15.3 percent of the total) by 1914 (Rashin 1956, 98). This urbanization was clearly not occurring equally across the country; the northwest (the two capital *guberniyas* of St. Petersburg and Moscow, and the Baltic

---

[24] This refers only to permanent resettlement in cities. A much more substantial proportion of the rural population participated in temporary labor migration to the cities, particularly in the Central Industrial region (Burds 1991).

region) underwent a dramatic increase in the percentage of its population living in urban areas, while much of the rest of European Russia remained relatively stagnant in this regard (Table 2.4; Map 2.2). In addition, several of the "cities" included in the urban data at this time were little more than rural villages that also served as the administrative center of an *uyezd* (Rowland 1986, 115; Leasure and Lewis 1968, 376). This makes the relationship between urbanization and "modernization," not to mention nationalization, more tenuous. At the same time, the peasant "class" was becoming the largest sector in the rapidly growing cities. For example, in St. Petersburg the proportion of peasants increased from 31 percent in 1869 to 69 percent in 1910 (Yukhneva 1984, 38–39). The flood of peasants into the cities was so great that even large cities such as Moscow appeared in some ways to be little more than large rural villages (Bradley 1986).

After emancipation, the earliest peasant movement to the cities was often seasonal, the purpose of which was to supplement the income that could be earned on the family's land allotment. It was primarily adult males rather than entire families who engaged in this new form of nomadism, and the impact of urban life was undoubtedly more marginal for this group.[25] Beginning in the 1870s the level of temporary labor migration to the cities increased dramatically, and urban employment became permanent for a growing number of these "temporary" migrants. For example, during the 1890s in Vladimir *Guberniya* more than 50 percent of working-age men were engaged only in nonagricultural employment. This was true more generally for the entire rural population in the *guberniyas* of the Central Industrial region (Burds 1991).

Nonetheless, most urban peasants remained legally and otherwise tied to the commune until the first decade of the twentieth century, and since their children were normally raised in the countryside the rural connection was maintained even after two or three generations had gone to the factory. Johnson (1990, 90) concludes that contrary to popular beliefs that urban and rural occupy opposite ends of the modernity spectrum, in Russia "the village and factory were not opposites but were joined in a symbiotic relationship." Urbanization and industrialization in the Russian Empire continued to have a limited impact on the localist mentality of the peasant masses who were migrating to cities between 1861 and 1914, leading a contemporary demographer to conclude that (as quoted in Burds 1991, 94): "Even in migration a peasant remains a peasant." This "symbiotic relationship" was just beginning to break down by the onset of World War I (Eklof 1986, 482).

At least initially, rural migrants to cities attempted to transplant their local communities to the new urban setting. In a pattern that would be familiar to

---

[25] A similar finding regarding early temporary rural to urban migration in France was made by Weber (1976, 281): "part-time farmers with wife, mother, and family at home, their ambitions differed from those of city workers: their chief aim was to preserve or increase the family holding and to be treated with the respect and deference to which their role as the family breadwinner entitled them. Cultural integration on such divergent terms was hardly possible."

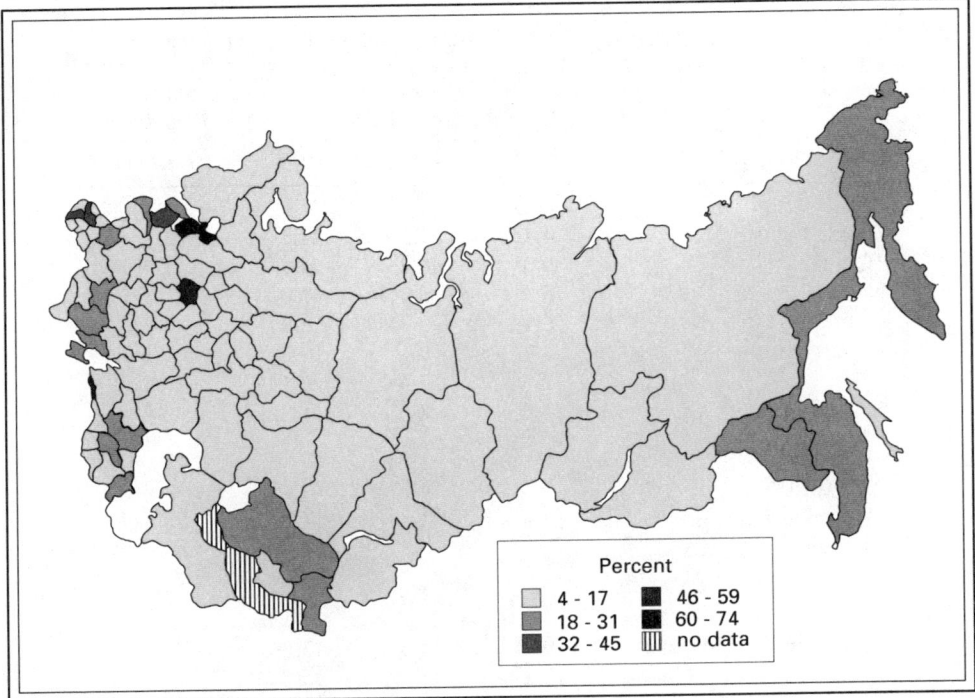

Map 2.2   Urban Population by Guberniya, 1914

demographers even today, migrants from the same village or locale tended to live and work together in the cities (Johnson 1990, 91–92; Burds 1991, 92–94). This retention of ties to one's fellow countrymen (*zemlyaki*), referred to as *zemlyachestvo*, made the transition to an urban life less disruptive, and tended to limit the impact of urbanization on the localism of the in-migrants. Of course, *zemlyachestvo* also impeded the process of national consolidation. Some evidence suggests that *zemlyachestvo* continued to serve as a buffer for rural in-migrants throughout the interwar period.[26]

Still, rural to urban migration was an extremely important dimension of the nationalization process. For the most part, rural migrants to urban areas came from the nearby countryside (Tables 2.5 and 2.6), and this was leading to the demographic indigenization of cities.[27] In the cities of Russia proper, this

---

[26] See chapter 3.

[27] The larger cities such as Moscow and St. Petersburg drew former peasants from much greater distances. The proportion of locally born migrants also declined over time as the cities and their economic activities grew, and as they became better connected with increasingly remote locales. For example, in 1869, 13.2 percent of the peasants living in St. Petersburg were born in Petersburg *Guberniya*. By 1910 this figure had dropped to 7.9 percent (Rashin 1956, 142–143).

TABLE 2.4
Urbanization by Gross Region, 1858–1914 (percent and percentage point change)

Region	Percent of Total Population			Percentage Point Change
	1858[a]	1897	1914	1867–1914
Russia				
Central Industrial	14.1	21.5	24.5	10.4
Capitals	39.3	56.2	62.9	23.6
North	5.9	5.9	7.0	1.1
Central Agricultural	6.9	9.4	8.7	1.8
Volga	7.4	9.1	10.3	2.9
Urals	3.5	5.4	6.4	2.9
Siberia/Far East[a]	7.3	8.4	11.9	4.6
Ukraine				
Novorossiya	14.7	18.5	19.2	4.5
Left Bank	9.5	11.2	12.3	2.8
Right Bank	8.3	9.6	12.1	3.8
West				
Baltic	10.9	25.7	33.1	22.2
Belorussia and Lithuania	9.2	11.8	13.0	3.8
Bessarabia	17.1	15.1	15.5	1.6
Non-Slavic South				
North Caucasus	9.7	11.7	11.1	1.4
Transcaucasus	6.8	13.7	17.3	10.5
North Kazakhstan[a]	6.9	8.3	10.2	3.3
Central Asia[a]	9.5	13.8	16.8	7.3

Source: Vodarskiy 1973, 132–150; Russia TsSK 1915, part 1:33–62.

[a] First column's figures for Siberia and the Far East, North Kazakhstan, and Central Asia are for 1867, not 1858.

migration resulted in a "Russification" of the masses over time. In addition to the various "Russian" groups entering the cities and becoming further Russified, Belorussians, Ukrainians, and non-Slavic peasants were also undergoing this process of acculturation toward the Russian *narod* during the latter half of the nineteenth and beginning of the twentieth centuries.[28] This was

---

[28] Of the Slavic groups migrating to St. Petersburg from the 1860s to World War I, the level of actual Russification is difficult to assess. At the turn of the century, ethnonational designations were often officially equated with the language spoken. "Russian" could alternatively mean all three Slavic languages or the Great Russian language alone. For this reason, Belorussians and Ukrainians could have declared themselves to be "Russian" without having undergone any psychological or indeed even linguistic assimilation (Yukhneva 1984, 129–130).

TABLE 2.5
Urban Population by Place of Birth and Gross Region, 1897 (percent)

Region	Place of Birth				
	Same Uyezd	Other Uyezd, Same Guberniya	Other Guberniya	Other State	Total
Russia					
Central Industrial	38.7	16.5	44.4	0.7	3,659,486
Capitals	30.1	14.0	54.9	0.9	2,556,135
North	64.2	23.8	11.9	0.2	120,420
Central Agricultural	68.0	17.9	14.0	0.1	1,203,285
Volga	53.6	22.2	23.9	0.2	1,034,368
Urals	52.6	22.1	25.2	0.1	534,885
Siberia/Far East	42.2	13.7	39.4	4.8	476,477
Ukraine					
Novorossiya	50.9	12.4	35.1	1.5	1,637,974
Left Bank	67.6	12.9	19.3	0.3	851,090
Right Bank	58.2	15.3	25.9	0.7	914,970
West					
Baltic	44.4	25.9	28.0	1.8	613,623
Belorussia and Lithuania	60.8	16.7	22.1	0.4	1,183,793
Bessarabia	69.7	9.4	19.4	1.4	293,332
Non-Slavic South					
North Caucasus	51.0	6.0	41.7	1.4	443,922
Transcaucasus	54.8	14.6	24.8	5.8	756,334
North Kazakhstan	48.3	9.6	41.9	0.2	204,252
Central Asia	80.6	1.8	14.3	3.3	730,118

Source: Russia TsSK 1897, 89 vols.

especially true in St. Petersburg, where most of the Finnic groups indigenous to the region were becoming culturally and linguistically Russified during this time (Semenov' Tyan'-Shanskiy 1900, 6:126). Similarly, Yukhneva (1984, 192–192) notes that while Estonian and Latvian peasants did not come to St. Petersburg already Russified, their descendants assimilated to the Russian nation by about the third generation born in the city.

The process of Russification appears to have been limited to the peasant population that came to the cities and whose ties to the rural village were broken down over the course of several generations. As noted above, non-Russian college students coming to St. Petersburg experienced a rising sense of national self-consciousness. This was undoubtedly related to the fact that as part of the

TABLE 2.6
Ethnolinguistic Composition of the Total and Urban Population, 1897 (percent)

Region	Total Population			Urban Population		
	% Ind.[a]	% of Ind.[b]	% Russ.[c]	% Ind.[d]	% of Ind.[e]	% Russ.[f]
European Russia	81.5	77.7	81.5	90.6	13.7	906
Siberia	11.0	99.5	76.8	1.3	1.1	835
Ukraine	68.2	79.2	17.2	28.1	5.4	385
Bessarabia	47.6	82.1	8.0	14.2	4.5	244
Belorussia and		72.5			2.6	
Lithuania	62.7	71.4	5.6	12.9	1.5	178
Latvia and		74.5			19.6	
Estonia	82.0	88.3	4.8	51.9	12.3	125
Congress Poland	71.8	85.2	2.8	48.8	15.6	80
North Caucasus	16.7	82.5	42.2	1.8	1.3	649
Dagestan	87.9	73.5	2.3	27.2	2.4	214
Georgia	55.7	98.8	5.0	33.1	8.9	191
Azerbaydzhan[g]	59.8	67.5	5.1	51.0	13.0	168
Armenia	53.2	37.6	1.6	58.5	12.2	84
North Kazakhstan	77.2	46.6	17.5	14.8	1.6	689
Central Asia	94.7	93.8	3.0	79.6	11.6	114

Source: Troynitsky 1905, vol. 2.

Notes: Indigenous language groups for Siberia = North Siberian Tribes, Yakuts, Buryats; for North Caucasus = Ossetians, Karachays, Kumyks, Nogays, Kabardins, Cherkess, Chechens, and Ingush; for Dagestan = Lezgin language groups, Kumyks, and Nogays; for North Kazakhstan = Kirgiz (Kazakhs); for Central Asia = Turkmen, Kirgiz, Kara-Kirgiz, Kara-Kalpaks, Kipchaks, Sarts, Uzbeks, Taranchi, Turks, Tadzhiks, and Kazhgars.
Georgia = Kars, Tiflis, Kutaissi guberniyas; Armenia = Yerevan guberniya; Azerbaydzhan = Baku and Elisavetpol' guberniyas; North Caucasus = Kuban, Stavropol', Tersk, and Chernomorya guberniyas; European Russia = 50 European Guberniyas, including Baltic, Ukraine (i.e., Novorossiya, Left Bank, Right Bank), Belorussia and Lithuania, Bessarabia. Other regions as in Table 2.1.

[a] % Ind. = the percent of the total population composed of the indigenous language group (e.g. Armenian language speakers as a percentage of the total population of Armenia).

[b] % of Ind. = the percent of the indigenous language group resident in the given region (separate figures given for Belorussians, Lithuanians, Latvians, and Estonians).

[c] % Russ. = the percent of Russian speakers in the total population of the region.

[d] % Ind. = the percent of indigenous language speakers in the urban population of the region.

[e] % of Ind. = percent of the indigenous language speakers in the region who lived in urban areas.

[f] % Russ. = the percent of Russian speakers in the urban population of the region.

[g] Azerbaydzhanis in 1897 = Tatars. Figure for column 2 = the percent of all "Tatar" speakers living in the Caucasus resident in Azerbaydzhan.

intelligentsia, these college-bound students had already experienced some degree of nationalization at home. This was certainly true by the end of the nineteenth century in the Baltic, Transcaucasian, and European Russian regions. Far from becoming "Russified," these nationalized elites became conduits for the diffusion of the national idea to their respective areas of origin on their return home.

In the non-Russian periphery, as the indigenous groups began to urbanize they often were confronted with an additional challenge—a nonindigenous elite already well entrenched in the urban political and economic power structure. As noted above, before the mid-nineteenth century the few indigenes who were upwardly mobile were likely to assimilate to the dominant ethnic community in the cities (i.e., German in the Baltic, Polish in Lithuania, and Polish or Russian in Belorussia). However, after this time an increasing number of mobilized indigenes, fueled by socioeconomic development and with it more intense interethnic contact and competition, led to rising national self-consciousness among the upwardly mobile indigenes. For example, Henriksson (1986, 180–181) found the following transition occurring in Riga:

> In the past upwardly mobile Latvians had Germanized as a matter of course. Hence there had been no Latvian upper or middle classes; to be Latvian was to be lower class. The growth of Latvian national consciousness, the sheer size of the Riga Latvian community and the increased opportunities for upward mobility created by industrialization, however, all worked against Germanization. Fewer and fewer Latvians were assimilated into the German community after the 1860s, and by the 1880s Riga had a small but growing Latvian bourgeoisie.

In the Baltic region in particular, which was experiencing the most rapid urbanization rate in the non-Russian borderlands during this period, the urban areas were quickly transformed from nonindigenous enclaves into indigenous cities (Table 2.6). Estonians comprised 52 percent of Tallin's population by 1871 and 72 percent by 1913, while in Riga Latvians increased rapidly from 24 percent of the population in 1867 to 64 percent by 1913 (Yukhneva 1984, 191; Raun 1987, 91). A similar urban "indigenization" was occurring in Georgia (Suny 1986; Suny 1989, 116) and Azerbaydzhan (Alstadt-Mirhadi 1986) at about the same time, though fairly extensive Russian in-migration also occurred, and the cities in each region had a large Armenian presence. This urbanization of indigenes in each case tended to heighten interethnic tensions and raise antioutsider sentiments. For Ukrainians (Liber 1989; Krawchenko 1985) and Belorussians (Vakar 1956; Guthier 1977), and the indigenous *ethnies* of Central Asia, urbanization and with it the extensive nationalization of the masses came only later, during the early Soviet period. The relative isolation of town from country was especially great in Central Asia, where 81 percent of the urban population were born in the city and only 2 percent were born in other *uyezds* of the same *guberniya* (Table 2.5). Finally, the cities of Siberia, Northern Kazakhstan, Novorossiya, and North Caucasus (i.e., the regions of extensive colonization during the latter years of this period), grew in large part as a result of inter-*guberniya* migration, and this undoubtedly resulted in their demographic Russification over time.

Rural to urban migration and the demographic indigenization of cities during the last decades of the tsarist era coincided with a rising national self-consciousness and a rising sense of exclusiveness regarding the indigenes' standing in their own cities. However, this nationalization with urbanization occurred only slowly, and was impeded to a great extent by the continued strong localist mentality or *zemlyachestvo* felt by peasants who were migrating to cities at the turn of the twentieth century. A more expansive nationalism was apparent among the urbanizing masses in the northwestern region of the country, and this was undoubtedly due to the relatively greater level of social mobility in this region of the empire. It is this topic on which the following section will focus.

Social Mobilization

Beyond emancipation and geographic mobility, a minimal level of social mobilization appears to be a necessary precondition for nationalization to become mass-based (Hroch 1985, 153). As the data on urbanization between 1861 and 1914 suggest, social mobility among the masses was quite limited. Prewar data on the development of a communications network that would help to integrate city and countryside also show that while the postal and telegraph networks in the Russian Empire were expanding, communication links between urban and rural localities, and across geographic space in general, remained relatively primitive before the October Revolution, particularly outside the more developed northwest (Russia TsSK 1915, part 11: 85–99). This provides additional evidence that the national "circulatory system" in Russia was not well developed, and this undoubtedly hampered the process of national consolidation.

This section assesses the degree of social mobilization among the masses in the Russian Empire, and attempts to draw some conclusions as to the development of a sense of national consciousness and a sense of homeland that had become apparent by the end of the tsarist era. The measures of social mobility used here include literacy, education, and occupational mobility.

LITERACY

According to Brooks (1985, 3), "for literacy to become a valued skill among peasants, Russia had to change, and the thinking of rural people had to change as well." As with geographic mobility, the social mobilization of the peasantry could come only after its emancipation.[29] Clearly, the greater independence of action, as well as the heightened responsibility of tending to their own economic and political interests, led the peasantry after 1861 to increasingly view literacy as essential (Brooks 1985, 3–34). The lack of literacy among peasants meant their continued dependence on the literate rural elites (nobles), whom the peasants viewed with a good deal of suspicion (Eklof 1990).

---

[29] This may in part help to explain the difference between the relatively high literacy rates in the Baltic *guberniyas*, where emancipation came in the 1810s, and the relatively lower rates elsewhere.

Literacy rates were rising during this period, though the Russian Empire remained the least literate European state before World War I. According to Rashin (1956, 295), "even though during the 45 years (from the mid-1860s to 1908) literacy of the rural population rose from 5–6 to 24–25 percent, nevertheless three-fourths of the population in the countryside remained illiterate." In the cities, literacy rates were relatively higher at the beginning of the period (e.g., 56 percent in St. Petersburg) but did not experience a rapid increase during the remainder of the nineteenth century due to the high rate of in-migration from the relatively illiterate countryside. Still, on the eve of World War I, literacy rates in the largest cities of the empire were close to 75 percent (Rashin 1956, 297–299), maintaining the literacy gap between city and country that had existed at the beginning of the period.

Literacy rates varied substantially across the empire (Table 2.7; Map 2.3).[30] The highest rates for the entire period were registered in the Baltic *guberniyas* of Estland and Lifland, while the lowest rates for the fifty *guberniyas* of European Russian were found in Bessarabia, the core region of present-day Moldova, and Ufa, one of the easternmost of the European *guberniyas* that is home to the Bashkirs. Outside European Russia, literacy rates were generally much lower, and the rates for indigenes were in general lower than for European in-migrants. For example, in Central Asia the literacy rate for the indigenous population was only 2.6 percent, while for Russians living there the figure was 26 percent (Rashin 1956, 305–308). A great literacy gap also existed between men and women in the empire, which was less pronounced in urban areas and in the northwestern part of the country.

At the turn of the century, literacy was primarily in the Russian language, and this was especially the case for Slavic language groups, Jews, and Moldavians, and was truer for men than for women (Table 2.8). Literacy rates were higher in the indigenous language for Latvians, Lithuanians, Georgians, and Germanic and Finnic language groups. Most of the remaining ethnolinguistic groups, and particularly those in the non-Slavic south and in East Asia, had exceedingly low rates of literacy in both the Russian language and the indigenous language. For many of these groups, a literary language had not yet been developed.

Along with the vernacularization of the written word, the publication of cheap, widely distributed popular literature greatly enhanced the ability of the nationalist message to reach a large audience. The Russian *lubok* (cheap popular print) stories by the end of the nineteenth century portrayed Russians—regardless of class affiliation—as superior to non-Russians in the state. According to Brooks (1985, 245), "this provided a sense of pride and status congruent psychologically with the other changes that were part of the greater geographic and economic mobility of common Great Russians at the end of the

---

[30] In the 1897 census, respondents were only asked if they could read, and writing skills were not required for the respondent to be considered literate (Liebowitz 1986, 167).

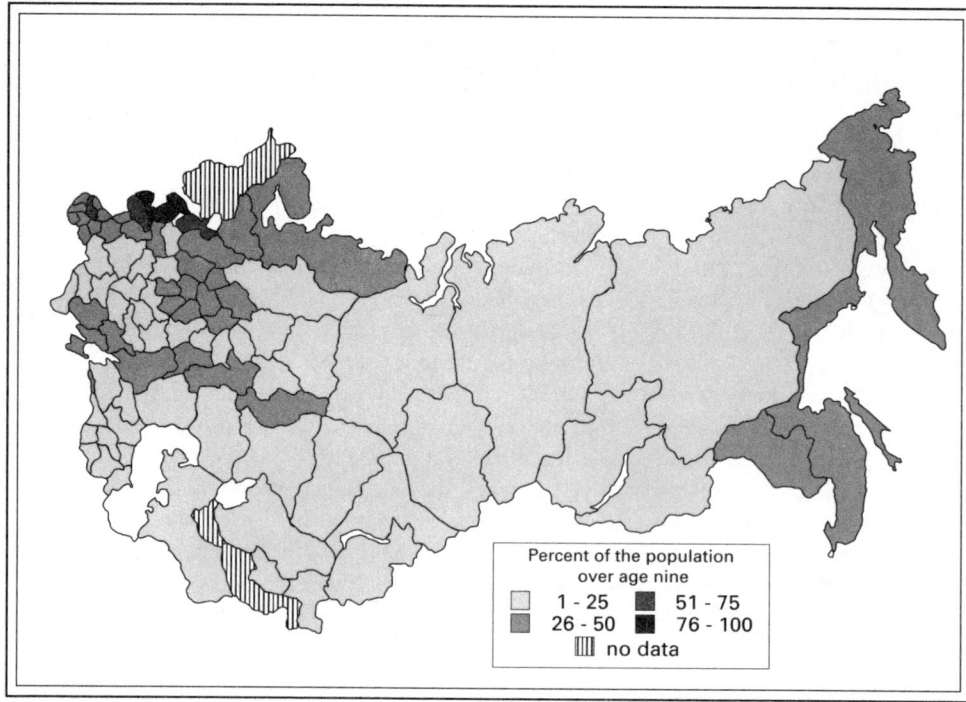

Map 2.3   Literacy Rates by Guberniya, 1897

nineteenth century." The orientation of the *lubok* stories changed during the course of the nineteenth century, with changing attitudes regarding the meaning of Russian-ness. In particular, "the emphasis on the tsar and Church as symbols of nationality declined, but the new treatment of nationality . . . was oriented more toward geography and ethnicity than toward culture" (Brooks 1985, 333). These *lubok* tales were the most popular reading material among the increasingly literate peasantry (Eklof 1990, 126). Thus, what Russians read as they became increasingly literate was almost certain to encourage them to think in more nationalistic, even chauvinistic terms about their past, their present status, and their destiny.

The two central messages being transmitted in non-Russian literature at the time were that the subordinate indigenes were every bit the nations that the dominant *ethnies* were, and that as indigenous nations they should be in control of their own destinies in their own homelands, rather than being the victims of "outsiders." This was certainly understandable, given that the social mobilization of indigenes brought them into more intense contact and competition with these "outsiders," in comparison with whom the indigenes found themselves at a disadvantage. These two themes were often combined in works that glorified

TABLE 2.7
Literacy Rates for the Total, Urban, and Rural Population, by Gross Region (percent of total, men, and women aged 10 years and older according to the 1897 census)

	Total			Urban			Rural		
Region	Men	Women	Total	Men	Women	Total	Men	Women	Total
Russia									
Central Industrial	56	21	38	76	52	65	48	14	29
Capitals	71	40	56	77	54	67	60	25	40
North	44	10	26	76	49	62	42	8	24
Central Agric	39	9	23	66	39	53	35	6	20
Volga	37	14	25	63	38	50	34	11	22
Urals	35	13	23	62	41	52	33	11	22
Siberia	25	6	16	56	34	47	21	4	13
Ukraine									
Novorossiya	46	18	33	65	39	53	42	13	27
Left Bank	38	9	24	63	35	49	34	6	20
Right Bank	34	11	23	62	38	51	30	9	19
West									
Poland	46	36	41	63	48	56	40	32	36
Baltic	91	90	91	87	84	86	92	92	92
Belorussia and Lithuania	43	26	35	67	48	58	39	23	31
Bessarabia	29	11	20	53	28	41	24	8	16
Non-Slavic South									
North Caucasus	33	9	21	55	26	42	30	7	19
Transcaucasus	20	8	14	50	30	42	13	5	9
North Kazakhstan	16	5	11	51	29	41	13	38	7
Central Asia	10	1	5	25	8	18	4	1	3

Source: Troynitsky 1905, vol. 1.

the "nation's" past prior to the arrival of the dominant *ethnies* (e.g., Suny 1989, 125, 133; Raun 1987, 77–78; Grabowicz 1982, 23; Grabowicz 1989, 129). It is not surprising, then, that the use of several of these languages in schools and in publications were severely restricted in the waning years of the Russian Empire, while a Russification of both language and message was promoted by the tsarist regime (Rogger 1983, 182–207; Isayev 1979, 33). While the Russification policy may have impeded the development of literacy in the local vernaculars for a time, it ultimately proved counterproductive, since it raised the level of anti-Russian and antisarist sentiments. This was especially true in those regions where nationalization had proceeded the farthest (e.g., Hroch 1985, 95; Raun 1987, 67; Conolly 1971; Corrsin 1990).

TABLE 2.8
Literacy and Education Rates by Language, Sex, and Ethnolinguistic Community, 1897 (percent)

Ethnolinguistic Group	Literacy				Education	
	Russian Language		Other Language		> Primary	
	Men	Women	Men	Women	Men	Women
Russian	29.0	8.2	0.1	0.2	1.5	1.0
Polish	18.9	9.3	13.0	19.0	2.9	1.2
Other Slavic	35.0	11.7	5.0	6.0	2.4	1.0
Lithuanian-Latvian	22.1	12.8	29.8	39.6	0.7	0.1
Romance	11.2	2.3	0.7	0.6	0.8	0.8
German	27.5	21.6	27.0	33.1	5.4	3.8
Other Germanic	30.6	36.2	32.8	35.1	18.9	11.1
Other Indo-European	7.2	2.9	7.2	1.8	1.5	0.6
Jewish	31.2	16.5	16.9	10.7	0.9	1.0
Georgian	6.3	2.1	10.1	8.1	1.6	0.5
North Caucasian	1.2	0.1	7.9	1.2	0.1	0.01
Finnic	19.2	8.5	15.8	18.4	0.3	0.1
Turko-Tatar	2.2	0.4	7.3	4.6	0.1	0.01
Mongol-Buryat	4.0	0.3	6.5	0.2	0.1	0.01
"Cultured Peoples of East Asia"	2.2	0.3	22.4	1.7	0.1	0.1
Other Northern "Tribes"	4.2	0.5	1.2	0.04	0.03	0.01
Other Groups	6.1	0.8	8.3	1.8	1.3	0.2
Group not indicated	17.3	10.1	3.9	4.9	2.8	2.2
Total (average)	23.6	7.9	4.3	4.4	1.4	0.9

Source: Troynitsky 1905, 2:xxxvi.

Notes: "Russians" = Russians, Ukrainians, and Belorussians; "Other Slavic" = Czechs, Bulgarians, Serbs, Croats, and Slovenes; "Other Germanic" = Swedes, Norwegians, Dutch, and English; "Romance" = Moldavians (Rumanians), French, Italians, and Spanish; "Cultured Peoples of East Asia" = Chinese, Japanese, and Koreans. For a complete listing of ethnolinguistic groups, see Troynitsky 1905, 2:vi–xxx.

Still, it was one thing for the nationalized elites to develop a standardized literary language and a nationalist message but quite another for the masses to become literate in it. If gaining literacy in a standardized language is seen as an important instrument in the nationalization of the masses, it is clear from the data available that outside the developed northwest, this instrument was barely in place. In addition, since linguistic standardization around the local vernacular was only beginning or had not yet begun in much of the state, it is easy to see why a localist sense of belonging continued to predominate throughout the tsarist era. According to contemporary surveys, even after attending primary school and becoming literate in the standardized language, Russian peasants often reverted to the local language after a few years, and this reflected the continued primacy of a local identity over a national consciousness (Eklof 1986, 403–407).

Throughout most of the prerevolutionary period, the majority of the population in each local area continued to speak and think primarily in its own patois.[31] The language situation was extremely complex, with literally hundreds of such patois being spoken (Zhdanko 1977, 44; Kreindler 1985). Lacking a standardized language reinforced the localist mentality in the countryside, since it was often difficult to communicate with outsiders. This was true not only for the geographically dispersed Russian *ethnie*; according to Semenov' Tyan'-Shanskiy (1901, 6:179), the linguistic differences were often so great between Mokshans and Erzyans (the two major ethnographic groups comprising the Mordvin *ethnie*) that they had to turn to Russian as a common language, unless the two individuals were from the same local area. This type of intranational communication gap across localities was found throughout turn-of-the-century Russia (Semenov' Tyan'-Shanskiy 1899–1914). The language and literacy map of Russia reinforces the image of a highly localized rural population that was only beginning to see itself in broader, national terms.

EDUCATION

As we noted above, literacy is only one aspect of social mobilization, important though it may be. Indeed, literacy by itself may not signify much in the way of "modernization" (Eklof 1986, 8): "Literacy is context-dependent and fits easily into a traditional matrix, but school-based learning fosters the 'transfer of conceptual rules' to tasks outside the classroom. . . . Thus schooling, rather than literacy, removes learning (both skills and values) from its traditional setting, and it is here that the first steps to 'becoming modern' may take place."

Throughout Europe, schooling was extremely important in the nationalization as well as the modernization process, for it was in the classroom that the masses came into intensive contact with the idea of nation. More than that, it appears that rural teachers themselves were often at the forefront of nationalist agitation that marked the height of Phase B nationalization, and even the beginnings of a Phase C (Hroch 1985). The vernacularization of the language that served as a medium for secondary education was particularly important, because this "linked social mobility to the vernacular, and in turn to linguistic nationalism" (Hobsbawm 1990, 118).

Before 1861 education rates in the Russian Empire were generally low, and this was particularly the case for serfs, who were prohibited from obtaining an education without the permission of the gentry. Even with permission, serfs

---

[31] This was true not only in relatively backward Russia but in West European countries such as France (Weber 1976, 70): "The Third Republic found a France in which French was a foreign language for half the citizens." See also Hobsbawm (1990).

were only legally eligible for a primary education. "To send a serf to a gymnasium or a university was forbidden in 1827, and again in 1843 (unless he was to be set free)" (Robinson 1932, 45). In part this reflected an ambivalent attitude toward education on the part of the tsarist regime. On the one hand, a universal education was favored in order that the masses become more productive or at least less "wild." On the other hand, fearing that too much education would prove disruptive to the social order, even Catherine the Great would not commit fully to educating the masses. Ironically, under Nicholas I, a more reactionary figure who made no pretense to being "enlightened," a basic system of education was developed to a greater extent. However, the purpose of these schools was not the social mobilization of the masses, which was opposed by Nicholas I, but rather the socialization of the peasants to the values espoused under the rubric of Official Nationality: "to impart to the peasants the rules of the faith and the duties of a subject, as the foundation of morality and order" (Eklof 1986, 20–33).

Between 1863 and 1914, the number of children attending state schools increased from 541,100 to 5,942,100, or more than a tenfold increase in fifty years, while those in church schools increased from 413,500 in 1863 to more than 2,000,000 in 1914. The increase was particularly great after 1890, when education began to be "treated as an important source of military strength, national integration, economic productivity, labor discipline, and political stability" (Eklof 1986, 472). Overall, about 51 percent of all school-aged children in European Russia were enrolled in some kind of school in 1915, while in Siberia a comparable figure was only about 39 percent, in the Caucasus about 37 percent, and in Central Asia and Kazakhstan about 14 percent (Rashin 1956, 312–317).

The regional variation in elementary and secondary school enrollments indicates that Finland, the Baltic *guberniyas*, the Central Industrial region, the Far East, including the Amur and Primorsk oblasts, and Novorossiya were the most socially mobilized regions in the country in 1911 (Table 2.9; Map 2.4). In general, the figures for the non-Russian periphery from Belorussia and Lithuania to the Caucasus, Central Asia, and Siberia, were much lower than in the industrial northwest, and this follows the development gradient noted above with regard to urbanization and literacy. Religious education figures do not follow those of the other categories. In European Russia, religious schooling had given way to a more secularized education, while in Central Asia Muslim primary schools remained dominant throughout the tsarist era. However, the continued predominance of religious schools does not necessarily imply a lack of "modernization." First, the continuing high percentage of pupils taught in *mektebs* (Muslim primary schools) after 1870 was at least in part due to the promotion of the Russian language in state schools.[32] Second, within the Mus-

---

[32] Education in these Central Asian religious schools was primarily conducted in Arabic, not in a local vernacular (Fierman 1985).

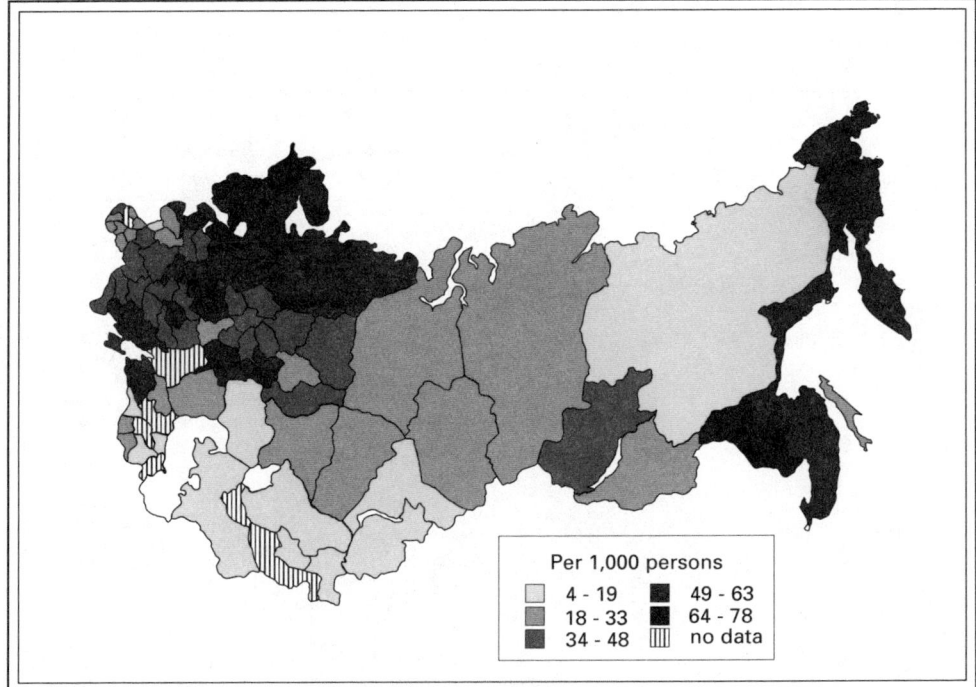

Map 2.4   Primary Education by Guberniya, 1910

lim regions of the empire, and particularly in Kazan', a movement toward the secularization of Islamic schools (i.e., jadidism) began during the last two decades of the nineteenth century. The Islamic schools by the end of the tsarist era began to function as agents of nationalization as well as Islamicization (Rorlich 1986, 86–91). However, except for the Kazan' Tatars, these *ethnies* had extremely low levels of educational attainment throughout the period, and the impact of education on the nationalization of the masses must have been limited.

The dramatic increase in school attendance for the country as a whole during this time reflected a strong upsurge in demand among peasants for basic language and math skills. Much of the school expansion prior to the 1890s was the state's incorporation of the literacy schools set up under peasant initiative. This social mobilization from below certainly does not conform to the elite depiction of "inert masses" incapable of civilizing themselves (Eklof 1990, 123).

The goals of the peasants were at odds with those of the tsarist regime, in that the masses wanted their children to gain "literacy without socialization" (Eklof 1990, 124). This struggle against socialization in the classroom indicates that the masses for the most part remained localists who were suspicious of the

TABLE 2.9
Level of Educational Attainment by Gross Region, 1911
(percent of students and per 1,000 population)

Region	Percent in Secondary Schools	Percent in Trade Schools	Percent in Primary Schools[a]	Per 1,000 Total Population[b]	Per 1,000 Aged 10–19
Russia					
Central Industrial[c]	7.2	4.9	88.2	50.7	290.2
Moscow	12.3	11.0	76.7	75.9	399.7
North	4.1	3.6	92.4	55.7	263.1
Central Agricultural	5.5	2.7	91.7	46.1	211.2
Volga	4.1	2.6	93.3	51.0	235.0
Urals	5.2	2.9	91.9	43.6	201.4
Siberia/FE	6.9	3.2	89.9	32.5	161.8
Ukraine					
Novorossiya[c]	7.4	3.8	88.9	62.7	297.4
Left Bank	6.3	2.2	91.5	46.4	210.6
Right Bank	5.4	3.7	90.9	42.5	188.4
West					
Finland	7.4	5.3	87.2	77.4	n.a.
Poland[c]	4.2	3.7	92.1	40.5	192.0
Baltics	7.3	2.1	90.5	74.0	390.8
Belorussia and Lithuania[c]	5.1	2.5	92.4	42.4	191.2
Bessarabia	6.4	2.8	90.8	48.2	212.3
Non-Slavic South					
North Caucasus[c]	4.9	2.2	92.9	47.4	226.5
Transcaucasus[c]	8.6	2.3	89.0	26.0	144.8
North Kazakhstan	7.0	7.0	86.1	20.3	104.3
Central Asia	4.5	0.8	94.7	22.2	51.5

Source: Russia TsSK 1912, part 1.

[a] Primary education figures include data on private schools, religious schools, and schools for the blind and deaf.
[b] Per 1,000 rates determined in the following manner: Total population, 1911; 10–19 using age data from 1897 census applied to totals from 1911.
[c] Data missing from St. Petersburg guberniya (Central Industrial); Don Oblast (Novorossiya); Warsaw guberniya, but data for Warsaw city included (Poland); Grodno guberniya (Belorussia/Lithuania); Tersk guberniya (North Caucasus); Tiflis guberniya and Baku city (Caucasus).

motives of the educated, nationalized elites. More important perhaps, peasants who sent their children to school recognized the desirability of a basic education but also saw the danger to patriarchal authority that a more extensive education represented (Eklof 1986, 476).

By 1914 the indigenous *ethnies* in the Russian Empire were not only becoming more urbanized and more literate over time, they were also gaining higher levels of education. The role of the classroom in the nationalization process was becoming more important as a larger segment of the younger generation attended for a longer period, and as the rural teachers of these young indigenes became more nationalistic. Still, the evidence at hand suggests that with the possible exception of the northwestern *ethnies* in the state (i.e., Estonians, Latvians, Poles, Finns), the masses entering the classroom after 1861 remained fundamentally localist in outlook. Introducing more advanced education may have even reinforced this localism in the countryside by siphoning off the most socially mobilized young, who frequently moved out to cities as they moved up (Eklof 1986, 442).[33] And, unlike the role that rural teachers played in nationalizing the countryside in Finland and Estonia (Hroch 1985), Eklof (1986, 480) finds almost no evidence of a similar function performed by rural teachers in the Slavic *guberniyas*. Clearly, by the onset of World War I and the revolutions that followed, mass-based education, and with it nationalization, were only beginning to penetrate the localized rural mentality in the vast majority of ethnic communities in the Russian Empire.

OCCUPATIONAL MOBILITY

Prior to 1861, at least for the enserfed population, occupational mobility was nearly impossible.[34] For those peasants who had been freed earlier (e.g., those in the Baltic region), laws limiting both their geographic movement from the villages and their ability to own land effectively stifled occupational mobility in the countryside. Even after emancipation, the possibility for greater occupational mobility for the vast majority of people in the country changed only slowly, and may have become even more remote in several rural regions during the latter half of the nineteenth century.

During the period from 1861 to 1914, and particularly after the turn of the century, urbanization and industrialization were expanding relatively rapidly. Industrial production in the Russian Empire grew at an average annual rate of 5 percent for that entire 1861 to 1914 period, and grew by nearly 6 percent per year between 1885 and 1914. This rate of growth was greater than that experienced by the United States, Britain, or Germany during this time, and as a result Russia advanced from the seventh largest industrial power in 1880 to the fifth largest by 1913 (Rogger 1983, 106–107; Thalheim 1971, 96). Nonetheless, the industrial work force remained a small segment of the population in the Russian

---

[33] However, these more nationally conscious peasants do appear to have been instrumental in the mobilization of the rural masses during the 1905 revolution, and more generally could be seen as a vital link in the development of mass-based national movements during the late nineteenth and early twentieth centuries. This topic is further discussed below.

[34] According to Zelnick (1968), during the eighteenth century it was legal for manufacturers to purchase entire villages for work in their factories, and while this practice was restricted over time, it continued in fact up to the time of emancipation itself.

Empire up to World War I. Industrial workers increased from 0.76 percent of the total population in 1860 to 1.4 percent by 1913, or using the broader industrial category which includes miners and railroad workers, about 2.6 percent by 1913 (Rogger 1983, 109).[35] Furthermore, when industrial production is measured per capita, the Russian Empire remained the least developed European power throughout the prewar period (Nove 1969, 14–17).

As in the case of urbanization, literacy, and education, the opportunity for upward mobility also varied regionally (Map 2.5). In the Baltic, Polish, and capital *guberniyas* (i.e., Moscow and St. Petersburg), the proportion of the industrial work force was much higher than the statewide average. Novorossiya was also relatively developed. Not surprisingly, the least industrialized regions were Siberia and Central Asia (Russia TsSK 1912, part 1: 85–87). The limited economic development that was occurring in these two regions resulted not in an indigenization of industry but benefited primarily Slavic in-migrants and resulted in a demographic Russification and more generally a Slavicization of the urban/industrial sector, as it did in the case of the North Caucasus and Novorossiya (Bruk and Kabuzan 1982a; Lewis et al. 1976, 132).

In addition to its small size, the nascent industrial proletariat retained strong ties to the rural village throughout the prewar period. As noted above, *zemlyachestvo* lessened the impact of urbanization and industrialization on the self-perception of the labor force in Russia, and raises serious questions about the "proletarianization" of the masses as well as their nationalization. A statistician writing in 1906 concluded (as quoted in Burds 1991, 100): "In the majority of cases, Russian workers, when questioned about their professional occupation, tend as a rule to label themselves peasant-farmers . . . even in those cases when *otkhodniki* had been working at the factory for a long time and were accustomed to continual outside work."

On the other hand, ties to the rural population began to cause concern among the St. Petersburg and Moscow police, who expressed the fear as early as the 1880s that these seasonal workers would serve as a conduit for diffusing revolutionary fervor to the "inert masses" in the countryside (Rogger 1983, 110). While during the 1880s this concern was undoubtedly exaggerated, during the 1905 Revolution strong evidence suggests that a "conscious" peasantry, which was literate and had spent time in the cities, was successful in mobilizing the rural masses (Seregny 1991, 375; Perrie 1990, 201–202). The ties that bound the industrial workers to their home villages were undoubtedly weakening over time, but they remained relatively strong up to 1914. These ties may be seen as impeding the pace of nationalization among the newly urbanized, indus-

---

[35] Of course, the use of the total population as the denominator is problematic, since in 1897 the population aged 0–9 accounted for 27.3 percent of the total population, and nearly half the population was younger than twenty years of age (Russia TsSK 1915, part 1: 92). As a proportion of the work force, the industrial sector accounted for 9.6 percent in 1897 (Russia TsSK 1906, 115–116).

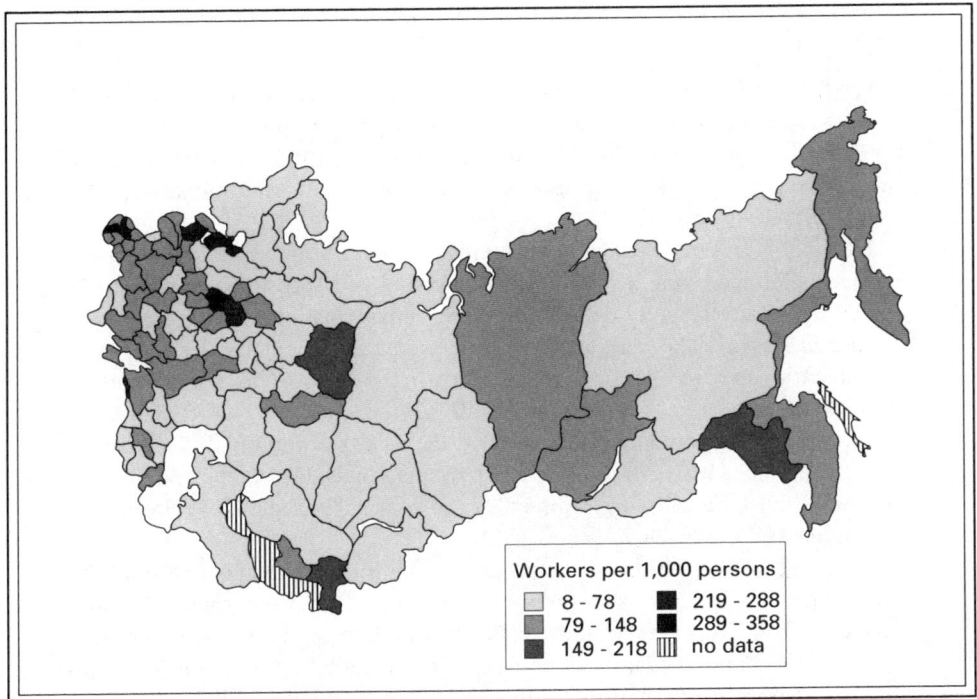

Map 2.5   Industrial Work Force by Guberniya, 1897

trialized segment of the *narod*, but they also facilitated the diffusion of a broader, national consciousness to the countryside.

A relatively large proportion of the industrial work force was motivated more by negative (i.e., push) factors in the countryside than by the attraction of the factory (e.g., Burds 1991). This is not to say that the desire for upward mobility was lacking in the countryside. Aspirations for a better life were stimulated during the latter half of the nineteenth century both in schools and in the books, newspapers, and other printed media that the increasingly literate peasants were reading. An education—even the limited formal schooling received in the Russian countryside—had a profound effect on the aspirations of young people (Brooks 1985, 55–56):

> Nearly half of the rural children questioned in an early twentieth century survey wanted to pursue an "educated profession," which usually meant teaching, clerical work, or, for some, the creative arts. Only 2 percent of the boys and 1 percent of the girls wanted to follow in the footsteps of their parents in the village. . . . Some observers complained that children who had been to school were less willing than

their uneducated peers to work hard and put up with the deprivations of rural and lower-class urban life.

Given the small size of the "educated professions" and the fact that only about 1 percent of peasant children advanced beyond primary school (Eklof 1986, 457), the widening gap between aspirations and capabilities of achieving them in the Russian countryside serves as a classic example of "aspirational deprivation" (Gurr 1970, 50–52).

Not only were employment opportunities not improving at a rate that would have satisfied the rising aspirations of the young rural peasants; conditions in the villages were actually deteriorating after emancipation in several parts of European Russia. The land area available per peasant actually declined with emancipation in several regions, particularly in the Central Chernozem, Volga, and Steppe *guberniyas* (Willetts 1971, 107; Wheatcroft 1991).[36] It decreased further with rural population growth, and increasing economic differentiation in the communes between wealthy and poor peasants added to the "population pressure" felt by a growing segment of the peasantry (e.g., Nove 1969, 21; Panyutich 1990, 279–347).[37]

As a measure of the deteriorating living conditions in the countryside, the proportion of military conscripts who were judged physically unfit for duty increased from 26 percent of those called up between 1874 and 1878 (and born between 1853 and 1857), to 38 percent of those called up between 1897 and 1901 (and born from 1876 to 1880). According to Rogger (1983, 79) in the famine year of 1891, 78 percent of the peasants called up for military service were rejected due to poor health. Mironov (1990, 29) concludes that these data reflect "the declining health of the peasants (who made up the lion's share of those drafted), which was the product of malnutrition caused by the deterioration in its economic circumstances." The size of the surplus labor pool in rural areas was also growing (Rogger 1983, 79), and unemployment was undoubtedly more severe among the young. The number of internal passports issued for work outside the commune increased throughout this period, though the purpose of this *otkhod* was to help pay the family's debts, which could not be met through production in the commune alone. Because there was a concern that

---

[36] As noted above, the peasants fared better in the northwestern *guberniyas* of European Russia (Willetts 1971, 107). This was particularly true in those areas where the landowning elites were mainly Polish (i.e., Poland, Lithuania, parts of Belorussia). After the 1863 Polish uprising, the tsarist government favored the peasantry over the gentry in these regions (Conolly 1971, 157). This also gives a strong indication that the main nationalist threat—at least as perceived by the center—came from the nationalized elite, and that it had little mass-based support.

[37] Mironov (1990, 25) notes that even though intracommunal economic differentiation was growing, the extreme rich and poor frequently left the commune for the city, the military, or for new lands. This helped to preserve a semblance of socioeconomic homogeneity in the rural communes for much of this period.

young unmarried men would break with village ties rather than contribute, their eligibility for passports was severely restricted (Burds 1991).

The relative deprivation experienced by a growing number of young peasants was in all likelihood becoming worse over time, and this was beginning to undermine the internal unity of the commune. This helps to explain why the peasantry was relatively more receptive to the revolutionaries in 1905 than they were to the populists a generation earlier. It also helps to explain the massive increase in out-migration from the Slavic agricultural core to the non-Slavic periphery after 1906. Still, one should not necessarily conclude that the growing gap between aspirations and capabilities was resulting in the nationalization of the masses. As noted above, peasant unrest during the 1905 Revolution was often sparked by those conscious peasants who had become more geographically and socially mobilized during the preceding thirty years or so, while the populists were more often "outsiders" drawn from the urban intelligentsia. The creation of a group of conscious peasants—patriotic agitators drawn from the peasantry—may be seen as the beginnings of mass-based nationalization. Nevertheless, in the Russian countryside, the peasants were not mobilized behind broad social goals but rather behind more localist, "sectional interests" (Perrie 1990, 214). The very success of the conscious peasants depended on their being perceived as local "insiders" (i.e., *rodnoy*), not on their sharing a national self-consciousness with the rural *narod*.

Along with education, urbanization, and industrialization, the military is often cited as an alternative agency for the mobilization and nationalization of the masses. By all accounts, the tsarist army did not function effectively in this regard. Before 1870 peasants were taken from the village for a period of twenty-five years, essentially a lifetime in a country where life expectancy at birth was less than thirty-two years (Goskomstat SSSR 1987, 409). Little wonder, then, that "when a man was taken for the army his family bewailed him as though he were already dead" (Curtiss 1968, 110). Under these conditions, the socialization that a peasant received in the army was not normally carried back to the village. In addition, before 1870 only Russians, Ukrainians, and Belorussians were conscripted (Jones 1985, 182).

After 1870 the reforms to the military made conscription more universal and the length of service was shortened to six years, but even the new Russian army had little impact on the nationalization process. First, because the army was expected to be essentially self-sufficient, the peasant soldiers were often used to grow food, make clothing, and were even hired out as wage laborers. The relationship between officer and soldier was comparable to that between master and serf, and it is reported that "Denikin remarked in 1903 that officers could not conceive of their soldiers as fellow men." Under these conditions little nationalization could be expected (Bushnell 1990), and this became evident in wartime (Seregny 1991, 341): "During World War I Russian peasant-soldiers failed to identify with national objectives, with the result that the Russian army found itself at a comparable disadvantage with armies that exhibited a greater degree of modern nationalism."

Beyond this, although the reformed military was to nurture a "sense of unity" between the nationalities in the empire (Baumann 1987), dozens of *ethnies* (i.e., the *inorodtsy*) were not conscripted. Those non-Slavs who were conscripted in an era of increasing Russian chauvinism may have experienced a rising sense of nationalism, but it was likely to be both anti-Russian and antitsarist in orientation. This successful nationalization could not have been what the state had in mind.

As noted above, the path to upward mobility for non-Russian indigenes in the state was often blocked by a locally dominant nonindigenous *ethnie* and those few who became socially mobile also often acculturated to the locally dominant *ethnie*. As a result, throughout much of the nineteenth century to be a member of the indigenous *ethnie* was to be a peasant. With the acceleration of economic development after 1861, an increasing number of young indigenes entered the cities in search of jobs. The rising pressure for upward mobility coincided with a rising perception of relative deprivation and a sense of exclusiveness. This rising indigenous territoriality was not new but rather was a transplanted anti-outsider sentiment from the village. With social and geographic mobilization, however, the question "Who was *rodnoy*?" was answered in more expansive, nationalist terms, such that "we" now became the indigenous *ethnie* rather than the local villagers, and "they" were not all those from outside the rural locality, but nonindigenes.

This transformation was occurring in cities throughout the non-Russian periphery, as indigenes migrated to them in greater numbers. The demographic indigenization of cities made the ethnic stratification that favored nonindigenes increasingly unbearable, particularly during a period when the indigenous elites that did exist had become patriotic agitators. Upward mobility and the expansion of an indigenous middle class was relatively more successful in Estonia and Latvia, and economic conditions in the countryside also improved (e.g., Raun 1987, 89). Nevertheless, Germans and Russians still occupied positions of authority, and upwardly mobile indigenes were undoubtedly reacting to that. Beyond this "reactive ethnicity," the national territoriality evidenced in the Baltic *guberniyas* during the last decades of the tsarist era also reflected a growing conviction among indigenes that a dominant sociocultural, economic, and political position rightfully belonged to Estonians and Latvians. This more nationally assertive "sense of exclusiveness" was undoubtedly also a mobilizing factor in Poland and Finland during the 1905 Revolution and after.

Throughout the remaining non-Russian periphery, a sense of exclusiveness was also increasing with upward mobility but was often a response to limited opportunities resulting from the system of ethnic stratification. In addition, the occupational mobility was relatively more restricted; therefore, this reactive ethnicity did not become mass-based prior to World War I. For Ukrainians and Belorussians, as with Russians more generally, a national self-consciousness among the rural masses was much more weakly developed (Rogger 1983, 184–185; Vakar 1956, 85). The urban/industrial sector remained relatively small and was dominated by nonindigenes, primarily Jews and Russians, throughout this period. Deterioration of economic conditions in the countryside resulted more often in rural to rural migration than in migration to cities, and this may have reflected the low level of social mobilization among the Ukrainian and Belorussian peasants (Anderson 1980). According to Conolly (1971, 164), in Ukraine between 1905 and 1914 "the nationalist movement extended its influence especially among country schoolmasters, lower local officials and the cooperative movement, but its nucleus remained a small urban intelligentsia." The lack of nationalization among the Ukrainian peasant masses was a source of frustration for the Ukrainian nationalists, as evidenced by this 1906 *Rada* article (as quoted in Krawchenko 1985, 28): "In our country peasants are only very little conscious when it comes to nationality. They know they are not Muscovites, but Little Russians as they call themselves. But what is a Little Russian? What are his needs and how does he differ from a Muscovite? This they cannot say." This limited urban/industrial indigenization restricted the emergence of a mass-based nationalization until the interwar years (Vakar 1956; Liber 1989). This appears to have been the case in Galicia among the Ruthenians as well (Magosci 1978).

The situation in Georgia was similar to that found in the Russian countryside but in the cities was overlaid by ethnic stratification with Armenians economically dominant and Russians dominant politically. During the period from 1860 to 1914, a demographic indigenization of the urban/industrial work force was occurring, though as in Russia the Georgian working class retained strong ties to the village and the extent of their nationalization or proletarianization was minimal before the turn of the twentieth century (Suny 1989, 152–156). Nevertheless, anti-Armenian and anti-Russian sentiments became more widespread during this period, particularly in Tiflis (Suny 1989, 139–140), and corresponded to a rising sense of exclusiveness among the indigenous working masses. Under these conditions of ethnic stratification, it is not surprising that Georgian socialists, who were able to unify both the ethnic and socioeconomic questions in a coherent program, were relatively more successful in mobilizing the masses.

In Armenia the potential for upward mobility was relatively restricted. This was not due so much to a system of ethnic stratification, though Russification in the last decades of the tsarist era occurred here as elsewhere. Rather, upward mobility was restricted by the lack of economic development in Armenia, where Yerevan remained relatively underdeveloped, "a sleepy oriental town of 30,000 in 1914" (Hovannisian 1983, 260). Socially mobilized Armenians were often found outside Russian Armenia (i.e., Yerevan *Guberniya*) and particularly in the major cities of Transcaucasia such as Tiflis and Baku. These Armenian elites had established "roots" outside the historic Armenian homeland, and to some extent had become aliens to the mass of Armenians living there (Libardian 1983, 186). During the last two decades of the tsarist period, the rural indigenous population of Armenia proper was only beginning to "awaken," and this awakening was primarily in reaction against the division of the homeland and the perceived threat of the Turks, including the Azerbaydzhanis.

According to Swietochowski (1983, 212), "Of all the ethnic groups in Transcaucasia, the Azerbaijanis remained the least revolutionized, and they were shaken from their docility only by intercommunal hostility." The Armenian-Azerbaydzhan War of 1905, which did serve to mobilize the Azerbaydzhani masses, also began as a reaction by Azerbaydzhanis migrating to Baku against the privileged status of Armenians in the city. The Azerbaydzhani reaction against Armenian privileges and a growing sense of relative deprivation among the Azerbaydzhanis moving to Baku were indicative of the rising sense of exclusiveness among socially and geographically mobilized indigenes as they came into closer contact and competition with nonindigenes in the growing urban/industrial complexes of "their homeland cities." At the same time, it is evident that neither a pan-Islamic nor a pan-Turkic sentiment "was capable of arousing the Muslims to mass action" (Swietochowski 1983, 212).

In Kazakhstan, as noted above, the disruption to the Kazakh way of life caused by the massive influx of Slavic settlers and increasingly oppressive tsarist policies at the turn of the century had a nationalizing effect on the Kazakh tribes (Olcott 1987, 112): "During the decades straddling the turn of the century, the Kazakhs increasingly thought and acted as a homogeneous community." In Turkestan, where the impact of Russian rule was less apparent to the vast majority of the population, where the geographic and social mobility of the population was for all intents and purposes nonexistent, and where the Islamic elites tended toward a more conservative stance, rejecting national identity in favor of a Muslim identity, the conditions for mass-based nationalization did not yet exist (Braker 1971; Rogger 1983, 197). It is evident that the cities in Central Asia were relatively isolated enclaves that drew almost none of their population from the surrounding equally isolated countryside (Tables 2.2 and 2.5). While an urbanized elite may have considered itself as part of a Muslim nation and its homeland as *Dar ul-Islam*, the rural masses in general looked with disdain on the sedentary urbanites, and identified more closely with family and locality. On the other hand, the Kazan' Tatars, with a more nationalized elite and relatively greater social and geographic mobilization of the masses, showed signs of a beginning mass-based national movement by the end of the tsarist era (Rorlich 1986).

Overall, the social mobilization and nationalization of the masses was relatively limited before World War I. For the most part, the peasantry remained highly localized in its orientation to life, and highly suspicious of outsiders. The degree of localism varied by region, with the northwest relatively more nationalized, and with some evidence that the same was true in the case of Georgians (Hroch 1985; Suny 1989). Elsewhere, the nationalization of the masses was just beginning before 1914.

The Development of a Sense of Homeland

The development of a national self-consciousness coincided with the evolution of a sense of homeland. As with the nationalization process, three phases in the development of national territoriality can be identified. During Phase A, the search for ethnogeographic roots emerged as a major scholarly interest. This interest in the native land evolved into an elite "sense of spatial identity" during the late eighteenth to early nineteenth centuries.[38] However, Russian "enlightened patriots" were likely to identify the entire state, or indeed all of enlightened Europe, as their true *otechestvo* or fatherland. Similarly for Poles, "up to the close of the eighteenth century, the notion of one's native country was identified with that of the state" (Tazbir 1986: 333). During Phase A it is clear that the intelligentsia in Russia and elsewhere was more taken with the "state idea" than the "national idea" (Kristof 1967a).

During the late enlightenment era, an elite sense of spatial identity became more closely associated with the homeland of one's *ethnie*, and the emergence of this sense of homeland became especially apparent during the age of romanticism. At that time nationalist historians, anthropologists, archaeologists, geographers, novelists, and poets actively sought to establish their nations' claims to a homeland in the distant, even "primordial" past (e.g., Smith 1986; Kristof 1967a, 1967b; Pearson 1983; Longworth 1990).[39]

As noted above, as late as the early nineteenth century the meaning of Russian "nationality" itself was limited to loyalty to tsar and Orthodoxy; the relatively weak sense of national consciousness coincided with a poorly developed sense of homeland. However, loyalty to the Russian "fatherland" was increasingly invoked during the course of the nineteenth century, such that by the middle of the century "a territorial view of Russianness . . . supplemented

---

[38] Chronicles written in the sixteenth and seventeenth centuries evidence a historical interest in the fatherlands of several western *ethnies*, and in these early works a "sense of spatial identity" was apparent (Banac and Sysyn 1986). However, as with the idea of nation, the bounds of fatherland were extremely vague in these early works, and a true sense of homeland crystallized only later. See Longworth (1990).

[39] As noted in chapter 1, the perception of a primordial nation-homeland bond has become prominent in the statements and programs of the new national front organizations today. For example, the program of RUKH (1989, 12) proclaims as one of its major objectives "to wage a relentless struggle against the policy of denationalization and demand the creation of all conditions necessary for the unfettered development and self-preservation of the Ukrainian people *on the territory which has been theirs from time immemorial*" (emphasis added).

the cultural symbols of tsar and Church in popular literature" (Brooks 1985, 241).

The Russian meaning of homeland varied geographically as it evolved during the course of the nineteenth century. Little consensus seems to have been reached among the various Russian elites over the geographic extent of "Mother Russia," and in this regard Russians appear similar to other dominant nations that expanded their territorial holdings through conquest (Clem 1992; Connor 1986). Each image of Russia "has mixed reality with idealization, embellished truth and invented myths; each has sought inspiration in a chapter from the past as well as in legends and folklore, and each has visualized a different variant of future civilization, as seen through the prisms of fact and its own imagination" (Kristof 1967b, 942).[40]

One image of Russia was more restrictive geographically, and included what may be considered the Eastern Slavic core area or ethnocultural heartland (i.e., Kievan Rus' or Muscovite Russia). While Kiev served as a more European symbol for those Russians who rejected both Westernism and Slavophilism, Muscovy—and Novgorod and Pskov even more so—was promoted by Slavophiles as the real "Mother Russia" (Kristof 1967b, 942). The latter most closely corresponded with the delimitation of the ancient, organic Russian nation as it was depicted by the Slavophiles, since this "heartland" was seen as the geographic extent of an "organically linked" village communal system which was declared to be the core of the nation. This uniquely Russian homeland centered around Moscow was at odds with the symbol of St. Petersburg and its Western orientation, much as Slavophilism opposed Westernism as an intellectual orientation.

However, as reflected in the popular literature of the later nineteenth century, the image of Russia expanded with the growth of empire. According to Kristof (1967b), during the latter half of the nineteenth century, as a series of catastrophes, such as the Crimean War and the Polish uprising, turned Russia away from Europe, the homeland image became oriented eastward, toward the Asiatic core. Siberia was viewed by Dostoevsky and others as a new utopian place that would revitalize Russia and make her the equal of Europe. By the turn of the twentieth century, the Russian "homeland" included the newly conquered lands as well as the cultural hearth (Brooks 1985, 242; Kristof 1967b). Expansion of the empire—at least into the southern and eastern frontiers—appeared as gradual and natural to Russians, and often occurred in response to the outward movement of peasants in search of additional land (Bassin 1991, 11). This led to a belief "that the new territory had to become part and parcel of the

---

[40] This depiction of the process involved in the creation of the homeland image fits the definition of nation and the process of a developing national self-consciousness (discussed in chapter 1) very well, in that it blends truth with fiction, the past with the future. The utility of what Smith (1986) refers to as a national "myth-symbol complex" is clearly apparent as well.

Russian land" (Raeff 1971, 30). This perception was particularly apparent in the case of Siberia, which "from the time of its entry 'became "Russian land," to be populated and assimilated by the Russian people' " (Ivanov 1989, 3). At least demographically, this goal was realized as early as the seventeenth century, during which time Russians attained majority status (Bruk and Kabuzan 1982a, 17).[41] Although a distinction was drawn between Russia—the ancestral homeland—and Rossiya—the geographic extent of the Russian Empire—this distinction lost clear meaning over the course of time. This was reflected by the overlapping usage of the words *otechestvo* and *rodina*, each of which could mean both national homeland and state (Dal' 1881).

Along with this expansive idea of homeland, a growing conviction emerged during the nineteenth century, at least among Russian nationalists, that the state could support only one nation—the Russians (Riasanovsky 1969, 77; Kristof 1967a, 246–247), and this reflected a more chauvinistic sense of exclusiveness in the way nationalists came to regard their homeland. This Russian nationalist vision of re-creating the Russian Empire as a Russian nation-state was clearly at odds with the process of national consolidation and growing sense of homeland evident among the non-Russian elites, at least in the western part of the state. Indeed, this emerging Russian nationalist sense of exclusiveness itself served over time as a catalyst helping to activate the national territoriality of several non-Russian indigenous elites who believed that their own proprietary rights in their "ancestral" homelands, not least of which was the right to their own independent national existence, had been trampled by the Russians. For example, similar to the case of Poland, partition and Russification in Ukraine in the early part of the nineteenth century "awakened the spirit of nationalism among the more enlightened Ukrainians," who "became aware of the past of their country" (Hrushevsky 1970, 476; Krawchenko 1985, 1). Belorussian nationalists seeking independence during the early twentieth century based their demands in part on Polonization as well as Russification efforts conducted in the past (as quoted in Vakar 1956, 64): "All in all, 'there was nothing in the glorious past of the Belorussian nation' which might suggest to modern Belorussia a feeling of sympathy or gratitude to either Poland or Russia: 'Bitter reminiscences of the past turn the Belorussian away from both, with an equal disgust.' "

There was a widespread emergence of a more activated sense of exclusiveness among the subordinate *ethnies* who were becoming more geographically and socially mobilized, and so interacting more intensely with locally dominant "outsiders" during the age of romanticism. For example, according to Henriksson (1986, 194), "one of the guiding principles of Latvian nationalism was the conviction that Riga was rightfully a Latvian city where the Germans

---

[41] On the other hand, it may be argued that Siberia has yet to be assimilated by the Russian people.

represented an alien element," even though Riga had been a German-dominated city for generations. Estonians moving to Tallinn, Georgians moving to Tiflis (Tbilisi), Azerbaydzhanis moving to Baku, Ukrainians moving to Kiev and Odessa, and so forth, all evidenced a rising national consciousness that was anti-outsider (e.g., Hroch 1986; Suny 1986, 1989; Alstadt-Mirhadi 1986; Liber 1989). With the activation of this sense of exclusiveness among ever-growing numbers of indigenes, a mass-based national consciousness, and with it an "international" struggle for control of the homeland (i.e., national territoriality) began in earnest.

A sense of homeland among the masses is more difficult to discern during the prerevolutionary period. As noted above, what was *rodnoy* to the rural population was narrowly defined as locality, and this implied that a more expansive sense of homeland was not of primary importance for the majority of the population. Perhaps reflecting this more localist orientation of the masses, *rodina* was also defined narrowly to mean the city or rural locale in which one was born and raised (Dal' 1881). This would accord with the localist mentality evident in the countryside.

Surveys at the time also indicated that the geographic awareness of pupils was extremely limited. In a study of lower-class children in Moscow, for example, more than half the pupils surveyed did not know that they lived in a city. A survey of rural children found that fewer than half knew the name of the *uyezd* in which they lived (Brooks 1985, 55–56). The result of all this was undoubtedly that a sense of homeland remained only weakly developed in the Russian countryside, while more localist sentiments continued to be dominant in the thinking of the Russian peasant. If a geographically more expansive image of homeland existed, it was more likely to be drawn from the legends and myths promoted in the popular *lubki* and *skazki* (fantasies) tales than from formal learning in the classroom.

The geographically restricted sense of homeland prominent among the masses obviously had an impact on the nationalization process. While patriotic agitators had redefined the nation to include the masses, and even to center the national idea around the peasant *narod*, the peasants defined themselves according to locality, and only secondarily felt themselves to be members of the nation. This was true not only in the less developed south and east but also in the relatively more developed northwest. Even in Congress Poland (Tazbir 1986, 334): "The sense of ethnic community extended over a much greater territory than did that of regional identity. But whereas the latter was common everywhere, a sense of ethnic identity existed only among parts of the population. The number of people having a strong sense of national identity was constantly increasing; yet, in about the year 1870, they were . . . not more than 30 to 35 percent of the Polish-speaking people."

The localism of the peasantry coincided with a more localized form of territoriality as well as a more localized form of identity. Anti-outsider sentiments, regardless of the national identity of these outsiders, remained evident throughout the prewar period. As peasants became more geographically and socially mobilized, they carried these anti-outsider sentiments with them to the cities, where they attempted to transplant their native life (Kingston-Mann 1991, 16). Only slowly did a more geographically expansive sense of spatial identity, and with it a sense of exclusiveness, replace the localism of the village. These more mobilized peasants—the nationally "conscious" peasantry discussed above—remained a small segment of the rural population throughout much of the prewar period. A sense of national self-consciousness, as well as a sense of homeland, continued to be elite constructs with which the masses were only beginning to identify.

As in much of Europe, the development of a national self-consciousness proceeded through a series of stages in the Russian Empire from the late eighteenth century to World War I. By the end of this period, the elites of most major *ethnies* in the state experienced a rising sense of "enlightened patriotism" and an "ethnicization" (Phase A), which gave way to "patriotic agitation" (Phase B) during the latter half of the nineteenth century. The nationalization of the masses (Phase C) during the prerevolutionary period was a complex process involving the geographic, social, cultural, and political mobilization of rural peoples. This nationalization process was most advanced in the industrial northwest, but in general was only beginning at the end of the tsarist period.

Geographic mobility and intercommunal interaction were extremely limited before the twentieth century. Local rural to rural mobility was almost nonexistent. Urbanization was also limited, though temporary labor migration to cities grew rapidly, particularly in the Central Industrial region of the country. However, this had little impact on the localist mentality of the rural migrants to the cities, and the practice of peasants from the same village working and living together (*zemlyachestvo*) reduced the influence of urban life still further.

Social mobility was also quite low among the masses for much of the prewar period. Literacy and education rates were increasing but remained among the lowest of any European state. The standardization of literary languages around the "low style" spoken vernacular was just beginning for most of the *ethnies* in the state. This process of linguistic standardization was impeded not only by the Russification of schools and the press during this period but also by the low level of education itself. Surveys showed that the local vernaculars retained a primacy in the lives of villagers even after they had gone to literacy schools and learned the standardized language. This is another measure of the strength of localism, and the limited nature of a national self-consciousness among even the more socially mobilized peasants before World War I. The limited geographic and social mobilization among localities that did occur tended to heighten localism and anti-outsider sentiments rather than to enhance national consolidation.

Localism was giving way to nationalism among the more upwardly mobile young peasants but only gradually. Even this more urbanized, industrialized, educated segment of the population continued to consider itself as part of the peasantry. Nevertheless, they were emerging as a more nationally "conscious" segment of the peasantry by the turn of the century, and this "conscious" peasantry played a vital role in diffusing the broader nationalist message to the more localist countryside, whose members continued to view outsiders with a good deal of suspicion. The conscious peasantry was larger in the industrial northwest, where one can speak of nationalization becoming mass-based by the last decade of the tsarist era. Elsewhere, Phase C was barely beginning by 1914.

The sense of homeland changed over time with nationalization, and these changes conform to some extent with the "elements of human group territoriality" identified by Soja (1971, 34). A "sense of spatial identity" with the homeland of one's *ethnie* emerged along with Phase A "ethnicization" of the elites, and this was transformed into a more assertive "sense of exclusiveness" regarding the indigenes' right to control the homeland during Phase B. For the masses, a "sense of exclusiveness" was also apparent but was restricted geographically to locality rather than the more expansive ethnonational homeland of the elites. The peasant sense of exclusiveness was manifested in antioutsider sentiments, which remained evident throughout the period from 1861 to 1914. Geographic and social mobilization did not mean an end to these anti-outsider sentiments. Rather, this localist territoriality was adapted to the new urban/industrial environment, and in the process the "outsiders" became redefined as members of nonindigenous *ethnies*, particularly those in positions of economic or political dominance (i.e., Germans in the Baltic, Jews in the cities of the "Pale of Settlement," Armenians in Tiflis and Baku, Russians throughout the non-Russian periphery). In this way, socioeconomic development led not to the end of localism but to its reorientation as ethnonationalism.

The idea of nation changed along with nationalization. An early definition of nation as the enlightened citizenry of the state gave way to a more romantic view of nation as the indigenous *narod* with the shift from Phase A to Phase B. As this occurred, the elite recentered the idea of nation around the peasantry, peripheralizing "faith and tsar" which had served as core criteria of the earlier national idea. Still, early efforts by the nationalized elites to spread the good word among the masses, such as the populist "Go to the People" movement of the 1870s, often ended in disaster, since the peasantry for the most part continued to define "community of belonging" in local rather than in national terms. This more localized self-consciousness among the masses retained primacy over a nationalized consciousness throughout the prewar period. The disillusionment among nationalized elites with the localist peasant *narod* was apparently an important factor for their rising interest in Marxism and its new *narod*—the proletariat (Rogger 1983, 144).

The nationalization process as it occurred in the waning decades of the Russian Empire was not leading to the creation of one Russian nation-state, but rather to the formation of numerous nations living in what they considered to be their ancestral homelands. Attempts by the tsarist government to dampen the rise of non-Russian nationalism and even to promote the development of a Russian nation-state through a Russification policy proved counterproductive. While Russification delayed the nationalization process among non-Russians for a time, it ultimately enhanced the likelihood of success, since it served as a catalyst in the activation of an indigenous sense of exclusiveness among non-Russians. Russification, a policy of forced acculturation pursued most intensely in areas where the indigenous nationalization process had proceeded furthest, was almost certain to produce a strong nationalistic reaction. Even where linguistic Russification was apparently successful, rising national self-consciousness and anti-Russian sentiments often developed (e.g., Kasperovich 1985, 33; Suny 1989, 140–141; Hroch 1985, 76–96; Raun 1987, 66–67; Corrsin 1990, 87). Russification was a centrist policy that had the unintended consequence of helping both to crystalize national self-consciousness and to activate a national territoriality that was anti-Russian and increasingly anti-Empire.

Given the data from the late tsarist period, one could even question the degree to which linguistic Russification was successful. From 1897 to 1917 the community of Russian speakers grew at a rate only slightly faster than that of the country as a whole, and even the Ukrainian- and Belorussian-speaking populations grew at a faster rate than the Russian-speaking community (Table 2.10).[42] A number of the Western ethnolinguistic groups were in decline during this period, but these were primarily small Finno-Ugrian language groups whose members have continued to assimilate to the Russian nation since 1917. Several of the northern Siberian ethnolinguistic groups were also undergoing decline, and linguistic Russification was the most likely cause.[43] For the most part, however, Russification, or even national consolidation, does not appear to have made much headway during this period.

The mass-based national awakening that began for several *ethnies* during the period from 1861 to 1914 continued into the Soviet period. World War I and the

---

[42] Caution must be exercised in using the 1917 data. They are a combination of census results and survey data collected in areas where the census was not taken, and the two types of data are not necessarily comparable. Furthermore, given the chaos of the period, the figures from 1917 are bound to be less reliable. For more complete information on the methodology used to collect these data, see Bruk and Kabuzan (1980, 85–90).

[43] As discussed in chapter 3, a number of these groups were revived in the 1920s and 1930s during a period of sociocultural indigenization (*korenizatsiya*).

TABLE 2.10
Ethnolinguistic Groups and Their Change, 1897–1917
(population in 1,000s, change in percent)

Ethnolinguistic Group	1897	1917	Change in Percent, 1917 ÷ 1897
Slavic			
Great Russian	83,933.6	114,467.2	136.4
Ukrainian	55,667.5	76,676.2	137.7
Belorussian	22,380.6	31,022.9	138.6
Polish	5,885.5	6,768.1	115.0
Bulgarian	172.7	169.5	98.1
Czech	50.4	34.7	68.8
Lithuanian-Latvian			
Lithuanian[a]	1,210.5	1,785.8	107.7
Zhmudian[a]	448.0		
Latvian	1,435.9	1,635.2	113.9
Romance			
Moldavian and Rumanian	1,121.7	1,216.5	108.5
Germanic			
Jewish	5,063.2	7,253.2	143.3
German	1,791.0	2,448.5	136.7
Other Indo-European			
Armenian	1,173.1	1,988.7	169.5
Tadzhik	350.4	488.0	139.3
Greek	186.9	261.1	139.7
Ossetian	171.7	237.2	138.1
Kurdish	99.9	117.8	117.9
Tat	95.1	51.5	54.2
Gypsy	44.6	52.4	117.5
Talysh	35.3	45.5	128.9
Persian	31.7	35.3	111.4
Kartvelian[b]	(1,352.5)	(1,748.2)	(129.3)
Georgian		824.0	
Imeretian		273.2	
Mingrelian		239.6	
Svan		15.7	
Cherkees			
Kabardin	98.6	102.9	104.4
Cherkess	46.3	58.6	126.6
Abkhaz	72.1	103.2	143.1

(*continued*)

TABLE 2.10 (Continued)

Ethnolinguistic Group	1897	1917	Change in Percent, 1917 ÷ 1897
Chechen			
Chechen	226.5	253.1	111.7
Ingush	47.4	57.5	121.3
Lezgin[b]	(600.1)	(772.2)	(128.7)
Avar-Andin	212.7		
Dargin	130.2		
Kyurin (Lezgin)	159.2		
Kazi-Kumykh (Lak)	90.9		
Udin	7.1		
Finno-Ugric			
Finnish	143.1	126.2	88.2
Votyak (Udmurt)	421.0	535.2	127.1
Karelian	208.1	145.1	69.7
Izhor	13.8	10.6	76.8
Chudin	25.8	17.9	69.4
Estonian	1,002.7	1,153.9	115.1
Loparin	1.8	1.9	105.6
Zyrian (Komi)	153.6	180.7	117.6
Permyak	104.7	125.6	120.0
Mordvin	1,023.8	1,187.9	116.0
Cheremiss (Mari)	375.4	458.8	122.2
Vogul' (Mansi)	7.6	6.0	78.9
Ostyak (Khanty)	19.7	24.3	123.4
Turko-Tatar			
Tatar	3,737.6	5,082.9	136.0
Bashkir	1,321.4	1,732.8	131.1
Meshcheryak	53.8	11.5	21.4
Teptyar	117.7	74.8	63.6
Chuvash	843.8	1,123.8	133.2
Karachay	27.2	55.0	202.2
Kumyk	83.4	95.0	113.9
Nogay	64.1	56.7	88.5
Turk	208.8	108.1	51.8
Karapapakh	29.9	43.3	144.8
Turkmen	281.4	360.8	128.2
Kirgiz-Kaysak (Kazakh)	4,084.1	4,697.7	115.0
Kara-Kirgiz (Kirgiz)	201.7	737.2	365.5
Kipchak	7.6	42.1	553.9
Karakalpak	104.3	107.9	103.5

(continued)

TABLE 2.10 (Continued)

Ethnolinguistic Group	1897	1917	Change in Percent, 1917 ÷ 1897
Sart[a]	968.7		
Uzbek[a]	726.5	1,963.7	115.8
Taranchin	56.5	78.7	139.3
Kashgar	14.9	35.6	238.9
Tyurk	440.4	—	—
Yakut	225.4	226.9	100.7
Mongol-Buryat			
Kalmyk	190.6	158.7	83.3
Buryat	288.7	278.8	96.6
North Siberian			
Samoyed	15.9	20.8	130.8
Tungus	66.3	83.8	126.4
Manchurian	3.4	5.1	150.0
Chukchi	11.8	11.4	96.6
Koryak	6.1	6.2	101.6
Kamchadal'	4.0	4.1	102.5
Yukagir	0.9	1.4	155.6
Chuvan	0.5	0.5	100.0
Eskimo	1.1	1.1	100.0
Gilyak (Nivkhi)	5.2	8.6	165.4
Aleut	0.6	0.6	100.0
Yenisey-Ostyak (Ket)	1.0	1.0	100.0
East Asian			
Chinese	57.4	78.1	136.1
Korean	26.0	60.3	231.9
Other, including those not indicating native language	64.9	907.2	1397.8
Total	125,635.2	168,828.5	134.4

Source: Bruk and Kabuzan 1980, 88–89. For alternative ethnolinguistic designations, see Wixman 1984.

Notes: Ethnolinguistic data for 1917 were drawn from the 1917 census, as well as population surveys conducted between 1914 and 1916 for regions not part of Russia at the time of the 1917 census. For a complete discussion of data sources and methods of estimation, see Bruk and Kabuzan 1980, 85–90.

[a] Zhmudi language group listed as Lithuanians after 1897. Sarts listed as Uzbeks after 1897.

[b] Kartvelian language groups listed together in 1917. In 1926, there were 242,484 Mingrelian speakers (232,990 who claimed Mingrelian as their nationality) and 13,154 Svan speakers (13,218 who claimed Svan as their nationality), in addition to 70,504 Adzhar speakers and 375 Laz speakers (TsSU SSSR 1929).

Lezgin language groups were not listed separately in 1917. In 1926, there were 157,593 Avar speakers (158,769 Avars by nationality), 7,691 Andin speakers (7,840 by nationality),

TABLE 2.10 SOURCES (*Continued*)
107,133 Dargin speakers (108,963 by nationality), 131,049 Lezgin speakers (134,529 by nationality), 40,141 Lak speakers (40,380 by nationality), and 2,377 Udin speakers (2,455 by nationality).

---

following revolutionary period in the newly created Union of Soviet Socialist Republics were also important catalysts in the further nationalization of *ethnies* in the state and also in the activation of national territoriality. The nations of the multiethnic empire were becoming mass-based precisely at a time of great political instability, and nationalists both contributed to and benefited from this unrest, at least for a time.

CHAPTER THREE

National Consolidation and Territoriality during the Interwar Period

As DISCUSSED in chapter 2, a mass-based national consciousness, and with it a sense of homeland more expansive than locality, were weakly developed throughout the Russian Empire before World War I and the internal revolutionary upheaval that ensued. As the nationalization process developed, along with geographic and social mobilization, the nationalist claims to a homeland in which members deserved exclusive control in order to fulfill the nation's destiny (i.e., national territoriality) began to mobilize an increasing number of indigenes. The national homeland, mythologized by indigenous elites as an organically and historically linked group of localities, provided the soil in which the nations of the Russian Empire could take root, and as this occurred it made for increasingly tenuous interethnic relations in the state. Nevertheless, on the eve of World War I, with the exception of the indigenous nations of the more developed northwest (Polish, Finnish, Estonian, Latvian, Lithuanian), mass-based perceptions of a national homeland were only beginning to take shape.

World War I certainly enhanced both the pace of nationalization in the state and the volume of nationalist demands for control over homelands. National communities whose leaders had previously espoused only the goal of greater autonomy for the nation in its homeland found independence thrust on them. It was the most developed nations (i.e., those that had become most strongly mass-based) that were also those which succeeded not only in gaining but in retaining their independence for at least the entire interwar period (Poland, Finland, Estonia, Latvia, Lithuania). In addition, the nations that experienced independence at this time—however briefly—used this period of national statehood as historical justification for their independence demands in the late 1980s. The brief period of independence—viewed by nationalists today as their nations' most recent golden age—was used to help legitimize the national self-determination movements not only by Estonians, Latvians, and Lithuanians but also by Georgians, Armenians, Azerbaydzhanis, and even Moldavians and Belorussians, whose degree of national self-consciousness during the 1910s was by all accounts minimal (e.g., Vakar 1956; Guthier 1977). The nationalist revision of this period of independence is an excellent contemporary example of the way in which past events are mythologized and utilized in the promotion of nationalist goals and objectives in the present. Even as early as the 1950s Vakar

(1956, 105) observed that "the ten-month period of symbolic independence has left an indelible impression on the Belorussian mind. A fact, historically accidental and trivial, has grown into a heroic legend."

Just before World War I, the national question began to assume growing importance for Russia's Marxists. The Balkan Wars and rising nationalism in Austria-Hungary and in Germany created an environment in which the Marxists of Russia and elsewhere devoted increasing attention to the question of nationalism and its resolution. The central issue of debate over the "national problem" at this time, particularly as it developed between the Austrian and Russian Marxists, was whether to use territorial or extraterritorial (i.e., "national-cultural") autonomy to solve the national problems faced by these two empires (Lenin [1913a] 1968, [1914] 1968; Stalin [1913] 1934).

The utilization of a territorial autonomy approach to "solve the national problem" in Russia had serious repercussions for the USSR. The reasons for choosing a federal form of government delimited according to the geographic extent of ethnonational communities are examined in this chapter. Of course, the consequences of this choice provide a dominant focus for the remainder of this work.

The other major nationality policy during the interwar period was *korenizatsiya* or the promotion of "indigenization" of social, cultural, and even economic and political institutions in each homeland of the state. Both federalization and *korenizatsiya* represented elements of the equalization aspect of Soviet nationality policy, which clearly accelerated the pace of nationalization and an emerging "sense of exclusiveness" regarding the indigenes' perceived standing in their own homelands. The move away from *korenizatsiya* and toward international integration through Russification in the latter part of the 1930s was in large part a reaction by central authorities against rising national territoriality and separatism. Like the Russification policies of the late tsarist period, the Russification promoted by Stalin during the late 1930s proved counterproductive. Along with a period of "national" independence, the "denationalization" promoted through Russification policies during the 1930s (and later) was cited by nationalists in the late 1980s as one of the primary justifications for demanding independence (e.g., RUKH 1989).

Beyond direct nationality policies, a truly revolutionary increase in the level of geographic and social mobilization of the masses occurred during the interwar period. Rural localism and isolation were undermined by the collectivization of agriculture, the concerted effort to spread literacy and education to the masses, and the industrialization drive which accelerated urbanization and the occupational mobility of the population. This rapid "modernization," coupled with national territorial autonomy and *korenizatsiya*, encouraged a heightened sense of national consciousness along with a developing "sense of homeland." The end result of the revolutionary changes taking place in the USSR during the interwar period was the more rapid nationalization of the masses throughout the state.

This chapter traces the developing relationship between nationality policies, socioeconomic development, and nationalization processes during the interwar period. This was a revolutionary period, and this environment of upheaval had an effect on, and was in turn affected by, the nationalization process and the developing sense of homeland. The major issues examined in this chapter include: Lenin's theses on the national question and the issue of territorial versus extraterritorial autonomy; Stalin's treatment of the same issues; the formation of the USSR during the 1920s and 1930s, the geographic mobility of national communities in the state, including their "gravitation" to the homeland and urbanization; *korenizatsiya*, social mobilization, and national consolidation of the population; and finally Russification and the international integration of the population.

LENIN ON THE NATIONAL AND TERRITORIAL QUESTIONS

Lenin's treatment of the national question indicated that he was a "strategic Marxist" whose support for or opposition to a particular "national liberation movement" depended more on the historical, socioeconomic, and political context in which it occurred than on strict adherence to dogmatic Marxism (Connor 1984a, 30). This flexibility was almost essential with regard to the national question as it existed in Russia, because the ethnic scene was so variegated, because Russia was not an advanced capitalist state, and also because Marx left little in the way of prescriptions for dealing with nationalism.

Lenin appeared to view nations as primarily backward-looking, traditional communities that the bourgeoisie were able to consolidate and mobilize under capitalism, but that disappeared as capitalism and the development of a global world economy advanced (Lenin [1913] 1968).[1] Lenin saw this denationalization with the advancement of capitalism as progressive, as the basis for solving national problems throughout the world. Turn-of-the-century New York City, a melting pot into which immigrants of different nationalities entered and from which Americans emerged, was cited by Lenin as evidence of this relationship between modernization and denationalization. Russian (and later Soviet) citizens would similarly be forged in the growing urban/industrial complex of the Russian Empire, and later the USSR.

However, this variant of the "modernization thesis" was modified for multinational states such as Russia, due to the additional problem of international inequality (i.e., ethnic stratification) resulting from a history of colonialism. In this sense Lenin was a proponent of the "reactive ethnicity" or "internal colonialism" model; inequality between peoples was viewed as a causal factor

---

[1] In defining the nation, Lenin and Marxists generally have come closer to the definition used in this volume than many Western analysts have. However, both Lenin and Stalin viewed nations as more dependent on objective characteristics (i.e., language, customs, etc.), while our definition emphasizes a more subjective national self-consciousness.

explaining continued ethnonational solidarity in modernized states.[2] International equalization was seen as a necessary precondition for the assimilation of nations into one anational communist people, the latter of which was the ultimate goal of Marxists. This international equality was necessary not only in the socioeconomic sphere but also in the cultural and political spheres.

The importance of international equality in all areas of life was derived at least in part from Lenin's reading of Marx regarding the national question. The one Marxist slogan that Lenin cited repeatedly throughout his works on the national question from 1913 to 1922 was that "no nation can be free if it oppresses other nations" (e.g., Lenin [1916] 1968, 116). This idea was undoubtedly central to Lenin's thinking on the national question, perhaps reflecting his own experiences as a member of the dominant Russian nation that had served as the "oppressor nation" in the Russian Empire. Before the national problem could be solved (i.e., before international integration and the disappearance of nations), both Russians and non-Russians would have to overcome this history of "ethnic stratification." This condition of inequality was seen as the primary reason why nations and international problems would continue to exist even after a successful socialist revolution. According to Lenin ([1916] 1968, 126–130), a socialist revolution alone was not enough to guarantee international integration, since a socialist victory only provided nations with legal equality. Actual equalization in the sociocultural, economic, and political spheres would take longer to achieve, perhaps even as much as a generation or more.

Lenin in all his writings on the national question drew a clear distinction between the role of socialist members of oppressor nations and oppressed nations. The former must espouse and fight for the right of national self-determination, which was equated in principle with the right of oppressed nations to secede and create their own independent nation-states. On the other hand, socialist members of oppressed nations were duty-bound to struggle for the international integration of all workers, their assimilation and the end of national distinctions. This dialectical approach to the national problem in Russia remained a central theme throughout the interwar period; it represents an early version of the national dialectic familiar to anyone who has studied the postwar "national question" in the former USSR: *thesis*—the flowering of nations (*rastsvet*), *antithesis*—their drawing together (*sblizheniye*), *synthesis*—their ultimate merger (*sliyaniye*) into one Soviet people (e.g., Tankayev 1985; Konstantinov 1985). This was also seen as a process intimately related to modernization, and was consistent with the generally accepted thesis that nations "awakened" during the early phase of capitalism and then underwent international integration or assimilation in more advanced stages of capitalism.

---

[2] For a more current argument in favor of this model, see Hechter (1975). These models, along with the competition thesis, are discussed at the beginning of chapter 5.

At least before World War I, solving the national problem appeared as a necessary precondition for the transition from capitalism to socialism (Lenin [1913] 1968, 21):

> Is there anything real left in the concept of assimilation, after all violence and all inequality have been eliminated?
>
> Yes, there undoubtedly is. What is left is capitalism's world-historical tendency to break down national barriers, obliterate national distinctions, and to *assimilate* nations—a tendency which manifests itself more and more powerfully with every passing decade, and is one of the greatest driving forces transforming capitalism into socialism.

For Lenin, support for the right of oppressed nations to self-determination (i.e., secession) as a principle was not the same as encouraging the division of the world political system into numerous nation-states. First, Lenin ([1914] 1968, 71) believed that once the suspicions of the oppressed peoples were overcome, the economic advantages of living in large, integrated states would outweigh the nationalistic desire for independence. In this way, and also dialectically, supporting the right of nations to self-determination should in and of itself reduce the likelihood of disintegration of the multinational empire through secession. Second, as noted above, Lenin was a "strategic Marxist" and above all else was concerned that support for actual movements should be in line with the goals of socialism (i.e., in the interests of the proletariat) and should be in the general interest rather than only in the interests of one nation, or the bourgeois elites of that nation. In addition, although nationalists today portray independence during the period from 1918 to 1922 as the result of mass movements (e.g., Georgia), no plebiscites or referendums were held in the regions declaring their independence. Lenin could legitimately claim that secession during World War I and the civil war period did not reflect the self-determination of the masses but rather the self-interests of the local political and economic elites. In this way his stance on national self-determination could be squared with the use of the Red Army in the early 1920s to recover lost territories for the new socialist state, since the secession of bourgeois nations from the more progressive socialist state being created in Russia was certainly neither in the interests of the world proletarian movement nor in the interests of the oppressed non-Russian masses in the periphery of the Russian Empire, at least as these interests were defined by Lenin.

The Territorial Question

The "territorial question" formed an integral part of Lenin's flexible, dialectical response to the national question. In principle, Lenin was in favor of the right of nations to control their own homelands. This is self-evident in his stance regarding the right of nations to political secession and the creation of independent nation-states. In addition, in an otherwise unitary state Lenin also spoke of the need for local national-territorial autonomy in order to make the centralism favored by the socialists truly democratic, and to overcome the tendency toward bureaucratism at the center (Lenin [1913] 1968, 39–42). In Russia, in particular, Lenin ([1913] 1968, 42) argued in favor of redrawing the internal administrative units (*guberniyas* and *uyezds*) so that they more closely matched national homelands:

> A uniform national population is undoubtedly one of the most reliable factors making for free, broad and really modern commercial intercourse. It is beyond doubt that not a single Marxist, and not even a single firm democrat, will stand up for the Austrian crown lands and the Russian *guberniyas* and *uezds*, or challenge the necessity of replacing these obsolete divisions by others that will conform as far as possible with the national composition of the population. Lastly, it is beyond doubt that in order to eliminate all national oppression it is very important to create autonomous areas, however small, with entirely homogeneous populations, towards which members of the respective nationalities scattered all over the country, or even all over the world, could gravitate, and with which they could enter into relations and free associations of every kind.

How the boundaries of these autonomous national units were to be delimited is a matter of some controversy. According to the above quote, national composition of the population would appear to be the decisive factor. However, Lenin also noted that other factors, such as economic and social considerations, must be taken into account in the creation of such units, and that "national composition" was "not the sole and not the most important factor" (Lenin [1913] 1968, 43). In the same article, Lenin notes that national composition is on an even plane with economic and other factors, and that delimitation is to be determined by the local populations themselves (Lenin [1913] 1968, 43). Finally, it is necessary to point out that this prescription for creating autonomous units in an otherwise unitary state was made with reference to how presocialist Russia and other *capitalist* states should deal with domestic national questions, and not necessarily how a multinational *socialist* state should restructure itself in order to solve its national problems.

Although approving of the creation of autonomous units, Lenin was, in principle, strongly opposed to federalism as a system that would undermine political and economic centralism, which were viewed as major achievements of capitalism and as necessary preconditions for the future success of socialism (Lenin [1913] 1968, 38): "But while, and insofar as, different nations constitute a single state, Marxists will never, under any circumstances, advocate either the federal principle or decentralisation. The great centralised state is a tremendous historical step forward from medieval disunity to the future socialist unity of the whole world, and only *via* such a state. . . . can there be any road to socialism."

This does not answer the question of whether or not federalism was acceptable in a socialist state, though it strongly suggests that socialist states—being more advanced—would be centralized. Nevertheless, while in principle federalism was opposed, Lenin was flexible enough to accept it as a compromise in Russia after the October Revolution (Connor 1984a, 218). This view is confirmed by Karpovich (1986, 16), who claims that Lenin's support for a "socialist type of federation" after 1917 flowed from his belief in the need for both international equality and local territorial autonomy, and represented a "creative application of Marxism to the revolutionary realities of Russia." For Lenin, the secession of nations from Russia which had already occurred or was in the process of occurring was clearly not in the interests of the proletariat of those nations or of socialism generally. At the same time, national territorial autonomy alone would not solve the ethnic stratification problem inherited from the colonial past, but rather would support the continued dominance of Great Russian chauvinists over the "oppressed nations" in the state (Lenin [1916] 1968, 148–149). A federation based on territorial "sovereignty" for the nations in a multinational state was seen as a necessary expedient that provided a middle ground between these two extremes (Lenin [1920], 622–623; Connor 1984a, 218).

In addition to this domestic reason for federation, the Soviet Union was to serve as a model for the colonies that would gain their independence from the imperialist powers now that the weakest link in the chain (Russia) had been broken. These new states as they formed must see not only that socialism offered an alternative to capitalism but also that it was in their interests to merge with the socialist fatherland—the USSR. In other words, the Soviet Union was to serve as a core area around which a new communist world would accumulate, and the federal nature of the state was a key element of this expansion. As seen from this interstate dimension, the federal USSR was not necessarily viewed as a short-term exigency. While the need for a federation among the nations in the original USSR would quickly diminish, the need for federal relations with new territories that would become part of the USSR would continue until ultimately a world socialist state was formed. This state over time would also lose the need for federation as it moved toward communism (Lenin [1920] 1975, 624).

This territorial question was of particular concern in the early 1920s, when the form that the state structure was to take was being debated. Stalin's attempt to promote the "autonomization" of the socialist state within one overarching Russian republic was rejected by Lenin out of concern that "Great Russian chauvinism" would be preserved in a unitary state that provided only autonomy for non-Russians (Lenin [1922] 1975). However, while Lenin argued vehemently against an autonomization that would subordinate non-Russians to an oppressive Russian nation, his support for federalism does not appear to have ever been more than lukewarm, as a necessary evil in accelerating the advancement of Russia toward communism. The main reason for this ambivalence was that federalization of the state undermined centralism, which was seen as an absolute requirement for the state's advancement. The structural separation of party and government in the USSR was an attempt to avoid this dilemma, but in essence it made of federalism a mere formality, while real political power was concentrated in the centralized Communist party (Pipes 1968, 242): "The existence of the Communist Party, with its unique internal organization and extraordinary rights with regard to the institutions of the state, made it possible for the rulers of the Soviet republic to retain all the important features of a unitary state in a state which was formally decentralized." On balance, the preservation of centralism was for Lenin more important than solving the territorial question in favor of the formerly oppressed nations of Russia. This being the case, Soviet federalism was to be the essential equivalent of territorial autonomy in practice, even though the two were quite different in principle.[3]

One compromise that Lenin would not make was support for "national-cultural autonomy" (i.e., extraterritoriality), which was promoted by the Austrian Marxists. The Austrian Marxists started from a position of how to preserve the Austro-Hungarian Empire, and rejected the political right to secession from the outset. This being the case, "extraterritoriality" was seen as a means of protecting the rights of national minorities without the risk of "Balkanization." This was diametrically opposed to Lenin's position on the right of nations to self-determination. According to Lenin, nations could be held together only through voluntary consent; the preservation of a multinational empire could not be the starting point. However, as we have already seen, this principle of voluntarism was sacrificed in the interests of "proletarian internationalism" during and after the civil war. In addition, Lenin was concerned that extraterritorial rights as discussed by its proponents would promote the nation to a position of primacy, even over class and the desire for international integration. This was apparent in two senses. First, since national-cultural autonomy would provide support for one's national identity no matter where one lived in the state, it would impede the process of assimilation which was expected to accelerate with heightened geographic and social mobilization of the masses. Second, and more fundamentally, national-cultural autonomy would lead to the national fragmentation of the Communist party. For Lenin this was particularly odious—Communists were to remain above nationalism and to work toward the internationalization of the population, toward its denationalization (Lenin

---

[3] This view is opposed by a number of Soviet analysts today, who see in Lenin's work "To the Question of Nationalities or 'Autonomization' " (1922) a major shift in favor of real confederalization of the USSR (e.g., Rodionov and Muntyan 1990). However, in this work Lenin stressed that what was important was that the Communist party leadership take into account the attitudes of the "proletarian" or class conscious element of each nation—who were expected to support internationalism and integration, not the attitudes of the majority of members or of the oppressed nation as a whole—who might be more inclined toward national separatism.

[1916] 1968, 151): "It is our duty to teach workers to be 'indifferent' to national distinctions. . . . To be an internationalist Social-Democrat one must *not* think of one's own nation, but place *above it* the interests of all nations, their common liberty and equality."

Lenin's nationality policy before and during World War I was clearly designed to erode further the already tenuous support for the tsarist government among the non-Russians who made up more than half the population in the state, while at the same time attempting to garner support for the Bolsheviks among the non-Russians. In particular, Lenin's position on the right to national self-determination was diametrically opposed both to the interests of the tsarist state and also to the policy of Russification then in force in much of the non-Russian periphery. Lenin's position on the national question, and especially his stance against "Great Russian Chauvinism" did appeal to the non-Russian nations who had been oppressed. The support gained from this stance was crucial in ensuring the victory of the Red Army over the loyalist Whites during the civil war (Connor 1984a, 46–47).

In presenting himself and his party as sympathetic to the wishes of the non-Russian nations, Lenin made the consolidation of territories formerly under the Russian Empire easier than it would have been had he taken the chauvinistic "Russians first" position both of the previous rulers and the leaders of the White Army. However, the use of the Red Army in the recovery of those territories over which nationalists had declared their independence at least in principle violated the right of nations to self-determination, up to and including secession. For Lenin, support for the principle of self-determination was important for strategic reasons, but the exercise of that principle by "bourgeois nationalists" was not in the interests of the proletariat, or its spokesman—the Bolshevik Party. Still, it is apparent that the lack of coincidence between theory and practice troubled the Communist party leadership. The creation of the "voluntary union" myth in the 1922 Union Treaty and the Soviet Constitutions, which was openly challenged only after 1989, provides evidence of this.

STALIN ON THE NATIONAL QUESTION

Stalin's first important thesis on the national question was written at the behest of Lenin in response to the "national-cultural" (i.e., extraterritorial) autonomy program of the Austrian Marxists.[4] In this article, Stalin ([1913] 1934, 8) begins with a definition of the nation as "a historically evolved, stable community of language, territory, economic life, *and* psychological make-up manifested in a community of culture" (emphasis added). The nation for Stalin was

---

[4] According to Wolfe (1964, 581) Lenin chose Stalin to write this article on the national question because Noah Zhordania, the leader of the Georgian Mensheviks, was a strong advocate of national-cultural autonomy. See also Suny (1989, 176–177) on the influence of Austrian Marxists on the Georgian Mensheviks.

primarily a community sharing common tangible characteristics, not a subjectively defined community of belonging and fate. Reflecting this position, Stalin added that communities lacking any one of the above characteristics could not be considered nations; by implication the loss of one's native language, customs, and so forth, would mean the loss of one's national self-consciousness (i.e., acculturation was seen as the essential equivalent of assimilation).

This emphasis on the objective ethnonational attributes extended not only to language but to territory. Jews were said not to comprise a nation, since they had no common territory. Indeed, the artificial creation of a Jewish Autonomous Oblast in a desolate corner of southern Siberia (Birobidzhan) in May 1934 was at least in part an effort to correct this shortcoming, though this was never a homeland toward which Jews "gravitated." However, as later writings make clear, Stalin did not understand the significance of the more subjective sense of homeland that indigenes were developing toward their perceived ancestral homelands. In arguing against the abolition of national territories in the USSR as a way of accelerating the process of assimilation, Stalin (1930, 259) stated "To abolish the national republics and regions now would mean to deprive vast masses of the peoples of the USSR of the opportunity of receiving education in their *native* language, to deprive them of the opportunity of having their schools, courts, administration, public and other organizations and institutions operating in their *native* language, and to deprive them of the possibility of partaking in socialist construction." Not one word is said about depriving indigenes of their native territory or homeland as itself something detrimental to the "blossoming" of nations under socialism. National territory was for Stalin merely an empty container within which nations were created or destroyed through the development or disappearance of their objective cultural features. This lack of understanding regarding the subjective sense of homeland almost certainly made the territorial solution to the national problem more acceptable to Stalin and to Bolsheviks more generally than it would otherwise have been.

In addition to defining the nation, Stalin in "Marxism and the National Question" ([1913] 1934) set out the bolshevik argument against extraterritoriality (i.e., national-cultural autonomy) and in favor of territorial autonomy. Stalin's response to the Austrian Marxists was somewhat different from Lenin's position. First, national-cultural autonomy was opposed primarily because it would artificially preserve nations that should be disappearing with socioeconomic development. In addition, in a statement that smacks of the "Great Russian chauvinism" of which this Georgian would later be accused, Stalin ([1913] 1934, 49) also argued that many peoples in Russia, and particularly in his own Caucasus region, were primitives whose cultures should not be preserved: "The national problem in the Caucasus can be solved only by drawing the backward nations and peoples into the common stream of a higher culture." Beyond this, national-cultural autonomy made the interests of the nation and national divisions the focal points of life in multinational states, even surpassing the interests of the proletariat (Stalin [1913] 1934, 34). According to Stalin, territorial autonomy rather than national-cultural autonomy was the only Marxist way of solving the national problem in Russia. Like the national dialectic regarding the right of nations to self-determination, Stalin ([1913] 1934, 57) claimed that territorial autonomy would serve to break down national barriers and encourage international integration. Of course, this national dialectic did not prove true in practice.

The "regional autonomy" supported by Stalin was not equal to national sovereignty. While affirming that nations had the right to self-determination, Stalin ([1913] 1934, 53) countered by stating that Social Democrats must agitate to influence nations to behave in a manner best suited to the interests of the proletariat. His three points to solving the national problem in Russia consisted of regional autonomy for "crystallized units," including "Poland, Lithuania, Ukraine, the Caucasus, and so on"; international equality; and "international solidarity of workers" (Stalin [1913] 1934, 57–61). Stalin's failure to grasp the importance of advocating the right to national self-determination (i.e., the right to secession) led to the publication of Lenin's "Critical Remarks on the National Question" later that same year.

Stalin was arrested and exiled to Siberia, and did not contribute to the growing number of articles on the national question in Russia until his return in 1917, at which time he was made the head of the "People's Commissariat for Nationality Affairs" (*Narkomnats*). *Narkomnats* was organized as a number of national commissariats (i.e., Armenian, Latvian, Turkmen, etc.), each of which was responsible for serving all members of that nation, regardless of where they lived (Bolmenkova 1988, 23). These sections were structured suspiciously like the national-cultural or extraterritorial organizations envisioned by the Austrian Marxists.

In April 1917, in his report on the national question to the Seventh All-Russian Conference of the Russian Social Democrats (RSDLP) and in the resolution adopted by the conference, the free right to secede was upheld and national-cultural autonomy was rejected. For those non-Russian regions choosing to remain in Russia (Transcaucasia, Turkestan, and Ukraine were mentioned specifically), regional autonomy was offered. As with Lenin, the delimitation of autonomous regions was to be the result of popular referendums held at the local level (Stalin [1917] 1934, 65): "The geographical boundaries of these autonomous regions shall be determined by the population itself with due regard for the exigencies of economic life, social life, etc." However, when the indigenous elites of these regions did not opt to remain in Russia or to rejoin after the October Revolution, the right to secession changed. By 1920, Stalin asserted ([1920] 1934, 79) that the demand for secession must be rejected, since it was undermining the socialist revolution and was therefore not in the proletariat's best interests. The demand for secession in a socialist context had become counterrevolutionary.

Territorial autonomy, which had always been favored by Stalin as the "only expedient form of alliance between the centre and the border regions" ([1920] 1934, 80), was developed further at this time into a hierarchy of regions ranging from the narrowest autonomy limited primarily to cultural questions for *ethnies* such as the Chuvash and Karelians, to the broadest autonomy over a wide range of sociocultural, economic, and even political issues for national communities such as the Azerbaydzhanis. The national communities mentioned specifically by Stalin included Volga Germans, Chuvash, Karelians—least autonomous; Bashkirs, Tatars, Kirgiz—lesser autonomy; Ukraine and Turkestan—more autonomy; and Azerbaydzhanis—most autonomy (Stalin [1920] 1934, 81). Russians, Belorussians, Georgians, and Armenians were not included in this schema; the latter three were still at least nominally independent at the time of this article's publication. In addition, Ukraine and Turkestan rather than Ukrainians and Central Asians were to be given regional autonomy. Finally, the proposed construction of a four-tiered system of autonomy is also noteworthy in that it is comparable to the Soviet federal system that ultimately emerged, including union republics, autonomous republics, autonomous oblasts, and nationality (autonomous) okrugs.

At this time, "soviet autonomy" was declared to be neither temporary nor artificial but rather essential for the sovietization of life in the non-Russian periphery. The primary means of achieving this goal was to be *korenizatsiya* or the indigenization of cadres in sociocultural, economic, and political institutions in each national territory in an effort to create indigenous elites who would be loyal to communism (Stalin [1920] 1934, 82–85). Territory in this regard, as was noted above, was to be the empty container within which this political socialization through indigenous national forms was to take place. However, since territory was not an "empty container" in reality but rather was increasingly perceived as the ancestral homeland claimed as an integral part of national identity, linking *korenizatsiya* to territorial autonomy for indigenous *ethnies* was likely and indeed did lead to a rising sense of exclusiveness among upwardly mobile indigenes. Rather than providing the basis on which a new Soviet people would be created, the territorial "solution" to the national problem selected by Stalin (and Lenin) helped to ensure that national consciousness would grow along with a national sense of homeland. In the end, this approach to "solving the national problem" inherited from the Russian Empire helped make the problem more intractable than ever.

In 1923 Stalin's "Report on National Factors in Party and State Development" laid out what was to become a central theme regarding the national question for the remainder of the interwar period. This report not only tied the national question in the USSR to the so-called colonial question but also began the debate between which form of nationalism—Great Russian or local (i.e., oppressor versus oppressed)—was the most harmful.[5] At this time and

---

[5] An additional point of interest in this report is that NEP is blamed for the rise in both "Great Russian chauvinism" and "local nationalism" (Stalin [1923] 1934, 153–157). This is a clear

throughout the 1920s, Great Russian chauvinism was cited as the greater threat; local nationalism was primarily—though not entirely—said to be a response to the system of ethnic stratification or "internal colonialism," which had placed Russians in a preferential position throughout the state. In addition, the relationship between Russians and non-Russians in the state was linked to class differences between the two, the Russians dominant in the proletariat and non-Russians overwhelmingly made up of peasants. Because the proletariat was the favored class of the Bolsheviks, non-Russians mistrusted not only Russians but also the Communist party as a Russian party (Stalin [1923] 1934, 150). This was declared to be the "class essence" of the national problem. To overcome this hinderance to the real amalgamation of nations (i.e., psychological assimilation), the non-Russians would have to become the sociocultural and economic equals of the formerly dominant Russians, and not just their politico-juridical equals (i.e., "legal" equality). This was to be done through the *korenizatsiya* or "indigenization" of local political apparatuses of party and state, operating commissariats of the republics to meet local needs, and creating a bicameral legislature with one house for national representation to deal with the national problems that arose (Stalin [1923] 1934, 163–164).

However, this report also points out that local nationalism was not solely a reaction against Great Russian chauvinism in the periphery. Georgian chauvinism in Georgia over Abkhazians, Ossetians, Armenians, and so forth, and Uzbek dominance over Turkmen in Bukhara and Khorezm were cited, indicating that for these nations at least a sense of exclusiveness was readily apparent and was directed against neighboring *ethnies*. In a more pointed reference to the homeland factor in the development of international hostilities on the periphery, Stalin ([1923] 1934, 157–158) noted: "Among a certain section of the Azerbaidjanians there is also a tendency, sometimes quite unconcealed, to think that the Azerbaidjanians are the native population of the country and the Armenians are intruders. . . . This is also chauvinism. It undermines that equality of nationalities on which the Soviet power is based." In this report, which was perhaps Stalin's most important written work on the national question, a discussion of the right of secession was nearly absent. From this point on, the right of nations to self-determination was retained primarily for foreign consumption, and was supported not for the nations of Russia and the USSR, but for the nations awakening in the colonies of the imperialist powers.

After Gorbachev's rise to power in the late 1980s, it became common practice among Soviet analysts to blame the recent national problems on Stalin's "deformation" of Lenin's nationality policies (e.g., Zotov 1989; Iskenderov 1989).[6] The move toward a more unitary "command-administrative system" at

---

foreshadowing of the demise of NEP after it had barely begun and almost a year before Lenin's death.

[6] This formula was increasingly challenged, and Lenin's policy statements themselves were increasingly attacked after 1989. This issue is further discussed in chapter 7.

the end of the 1920s and early 1930s, along with a shift over time away from international equalization and toward Russification, did not coincide with Lenin's nationality policies, at least in principle. On the other hand, the maintenance of centralized political power was clearly in line with Lenin on the priority of safeguarding proletarian interests. Beyond this, while it is undoubtedly true that Stalin was not as strong a believer in the need for international equalization in all spheres of life, it is also true that the *korenizatsiya* program implemented under Stalin did provide for the more rapid sociocultural, economic, and political development of the relatively underdeveloped national communities in their respective home republics. The continuing national problem—in the interwar period and after—was more a reflection of the failure of both Lenin and Stalin to recognize the meaning of homeland to the indigenes becoming more geographically and socially mobilized. Rather than encouraging international integration into a new Soviet people, territorial autonomy and *korenizatsiya* have not only encouraged further national consolidation among the numerous *ethnies* in the state but also enhanced the likelihood that national territoriality would become the principal mechanism through which both intranational and international relations in the state would be played out.

THE FORMATION OF THE USSR

Before the creation of the USSR, a number of national states, nominally independent, were tied to Russia through bilateral treaties. In December 1922 a "union treaty" amalgamated Ukraine, Transcaucasia, Belorussia, and the RSFSR into a "confederation" of equal Soviet republics.[7] This union was declared to be the prototype for a future world USSR (Stalin [1922] 1934, 120–136). Three reasons for the need for closer relations between republics were cited by Stalin at this time: (1) the economic situation, which included a need to pool resources, re-create the historical division of labor, and reunify the communication and transportation systems; (2) the military situation, which included the dangers of foreign intervention and economic and diplomatic boycotts; and (3) a natural striving among the entire population for amalgamation as part of a growing socialist internationalism.

The actual formation of the USSR and the delimitation of borders was a process that continued throughout the interwar period (Appendix A). As noted above, the process of delimitation was to be conducted according to the wishes of the local populace, in what should have amounted to a series of plebiscites of the sort being conducted at the same time in Eastern Europe. However, the process used to create the federal structure was much more centralized than

---

[7] The Transcaucasian "federated" republic (i.e., TCSFSR) included Georgia, Armenia, and Azerbaydzhan. At this time, Khorezm and Bukhara remained independent "peoples republics" because they were not yet socialist. Interestingly, this is the only time the USSR was termed a confederation, perhaps in an effort to enhance the myth that sovereign political entities had voluntarily united.

this. This is not to imply that the ethnodemographic composition of the population was irrelevant to the process of creating union republics and autonomous units within them. Data from censuses were used to construct the autonomous units in the Russian republic. For example, the 1926 census results provided a data base for the delimitation of nationality okrugs in order to maximize the number of indigenes in each (Gurvich 1980, 6). In addition, the ethnic subsections of *Narkomnats* (e.g., Mordvin, Komi, etc.) commissioned studies of the ethnographic, socioeconomic, and sociocultural characteristics of the prospective autonomous regions before the delimitation of borders (Makarova 1987, 107–118). In the case of Central Asia, a special expedition collected ethnographic data for the task of delimiting political borders (Zhdanko 1972).

According to Schwartz (1986, 1990), borders were generally delimited to conform with ethnodemographic settlement patterns. Of course, these settlement patterns in the 1920s did not necessarily conform to the ancestral homelands as perceived by nationalists themselves. Many of the interrepublican border disputes that have emerged since 1987 result not from present or even past ethnodemographic arguments but from conflicting nationalist images of the ancestral homeland that predate the Soviet period by decades if not centuries. Given the mythologization surrounding national homelands, it is not surprising that the borders delimited during the 1920s and 1930s do not correspond to the mental maps of indigenous nationalists.[8]

Allowing the people to decide their political geographic future directly posed two very different problems for the central authorities at the time. First, throughout the more isolated rural areas of the country, mass-based national consciousness was lacking, as was a corresponding sense of "class consciousness." As discussed in chapter 2, in most of the Russian Empire, and in practically all the territory that remained part of the USSR during the interwar period, a sense of national identity along with a sense of homeland were only beginning to become predominant among the masses before World War I. Although the war and the bolshevik rhetoric itself accelerated the nationalization process, by the 1920s most of the population—particularly in the east and south, but even in the west—had a stronger sense of affiliation with their subnational, ethnographic communities or localities than with more expansive nations and homelands. For example, according to the published results of the expedition sent to Central Asia mentioned above, ethnonational affiliation was often difficult to determine not only for the researchers but for the people in the region themselves (Zhdanko 1972). More important, these relatively localized communities were primarily composed of rural peasants to whom the Commu-

---

[8] Both the U.S. State Department's Office of the Geographer and Russian geographers have mapped the ethnoterritorial disputes that have emerged since 1987 (Dillon 1990; Kolosov 1992). This topic is further discussed in chapter 7.

nist party elites could not entrust the delimitation of federal borders in the new socialist USSR.

Second, in those areas where the population was more "modernized"' a sense of national consciousness was also stronger (i.e., was becoming mass-based). These more developed nations had become independent during the war and revolutionary upheaval, and they showed little interest in rejoining the newly created USSR. Of course a plebiscite was out of the question in Poland, Finland, Lithuania, Latvia, and Estonia, which had gained and retained their independence throughout the interwar period. In addition, the concern over renewed attempts at secession—particularly in Georgia—resulted in the formation of a Transcaucasian Federal Republic which then joined the RSFSR in 1922. This political geographic fusion of the Armenian, Azerbaydzhani, Georgian *ethnies* and homelands removed or reduced the threat of secession from any one of these groups since only the Transcaucasian Federated Republic had the right to self-determination. Given the international and interstate relations in the region, and the fact that the local Bolsheviks owed greater loyalty to the center than to the region (and were often Russians), central authorities in Moscow could be fairly certain that no officially sanctioned attempts at secession by the TCSFSR would be made. Over the vehement opposition of Georgian and other nationalist leaders, the TCSFSR was created and maintained until the Stalin Constitution of 1936.

Thus the masses in different regions of the state were judged by central decision-making authorities to be either too nationalistic or too primitive to be trusted to vote in a way conducive to the interests of "proletarian internationalism." Even though the ethnodemographic composition of the population was taken into account in the delimitation of intrastate political borders, the process itself was completed from above.

The USSR was constructed to provide varying degrees of autonomy, depending on the level of indigenous national consciousness. The USSR during the interwar period consisted of national territorial formations that ranged from the union republics for fully formed nations to nationality okrugs, rayons, and soviets, the latter of which numbered some fifty-three hundred by the early 1930s (Bolmenkova 1988, 58–70; Kozlov 1977a, 95).[9] The smaller nationality units were to provide territorial autonomy to what were considered more primitive *ethnies* and included not only "nationality soviets," but also "aboriginal or indigenous (*tuzemnyye*) soviets," "tribal (*rodovyye*) soviets," and even "no-

[9] The national village soviets and rayons were abolished during the 1930s along with the turn away from *korenizatsiya*. Interestingly, the platform adopted at the September 1989 party plenum on the national question allowed for the re-creation of new national village soviets and rayons to provide officially recognized homelands for national communities without them (*Pravda* 24 September 1989, 2). After 1989, a number of Soviet analysts advocated the widespread adoption of these more localized national territories as a way of managing the growing minority rights problem in the state (e.g., Kuznetsov 1991). See chapter 7.

madic (*kochevyye*) soviets" (Gurvich 1987, 63). Nationality rayons and soviets were also formed for Russians, Ukrainians, Belorussians, and others living in compact settlements outside their respective home republics. The creation of these units undoubtedly slowed the pace of both national consolidation among the peoples of the north and international integration in the West.

By the time of the 1922 Union Treaty, most of the autonomous regions (republics and oblasts) of the RSFSR had already been established, but most of the nationality okrugs were not formed until 1929 (Appendix A; Map 3.1). Few of these autonomous units had more than an indigenous plurality, due to decades of Russian in-migration and also to the geographic dispersal of the non-Russian *ethnies* themselves, particularly the Volga Tatars.[10]

The last area of the RSFSR to be "autonomized" was Central Asia. Between 1924 and 1936, the union republics of Central Asia were formed from the autonomous republic of Turkestan and the Peoples' Soviet Republics of Bukhara and Khorezm. All three were nationally mixed areas, with Uzbeks serving as the locally dominant *ethnie*. These three "republics" were abandoned in 1924–1925, and the region was reconstructed over time into a series of union and autonomous republics, each to provide autonomy for a major *ethnie* in the region.

The national territorial delimitation of Central Asia during the interwar period has frequently been portrayed as an attempt by the central authorities to "divide and rule" the Turkic or Muslim population in the region, which was thought to be developing a pan-Turkic or a pan-Islamic consciousness. This concern was one motivating factor in the center's decision to demarcate the republics of the region as it did, but it was not the only reason. First, the ethnographic differentiation of the population in Central Asia at the time was so great, and the process of national consolidation was so weakly developed, that a mass-based nationalist, let alone a pan-nationalist movement, posed almost no threat. Second, the behavior of the state in the delimitation process was not reflective of a center unconcerned with the ethnic composition of the population. The 1920 census—the ethnographic data base used for delimitation of autonomous units elsewhere in the state—was not conducted in nominally independent Bukhara and Khorezm. Lacking the ethnic data needed to construct national homelands, the USSR sent a special expedition to the two Peoples' Soviet Republics in 1924 to gather ethnographic information that could be used for this purpose (Zhdanko 1972). This was the first ethnographic data base collected for Central Asia, specifically for the purpose of delimiting ethnonational territories. While misperceptions about the degree of pan-Turkic or pan-Islamic sentiment in Central Asia may have motivated central authorities to think in terms of "divide and rule" at some level, both the painstaking process

---

[10] For a number of groups in the Volga-Urals region, their geographic dispersal eastward resulted, at least in part, from the Russian push to the east during the conquest of the region (Donnelly 1968, 14; Kreindler 1985, 238–239).

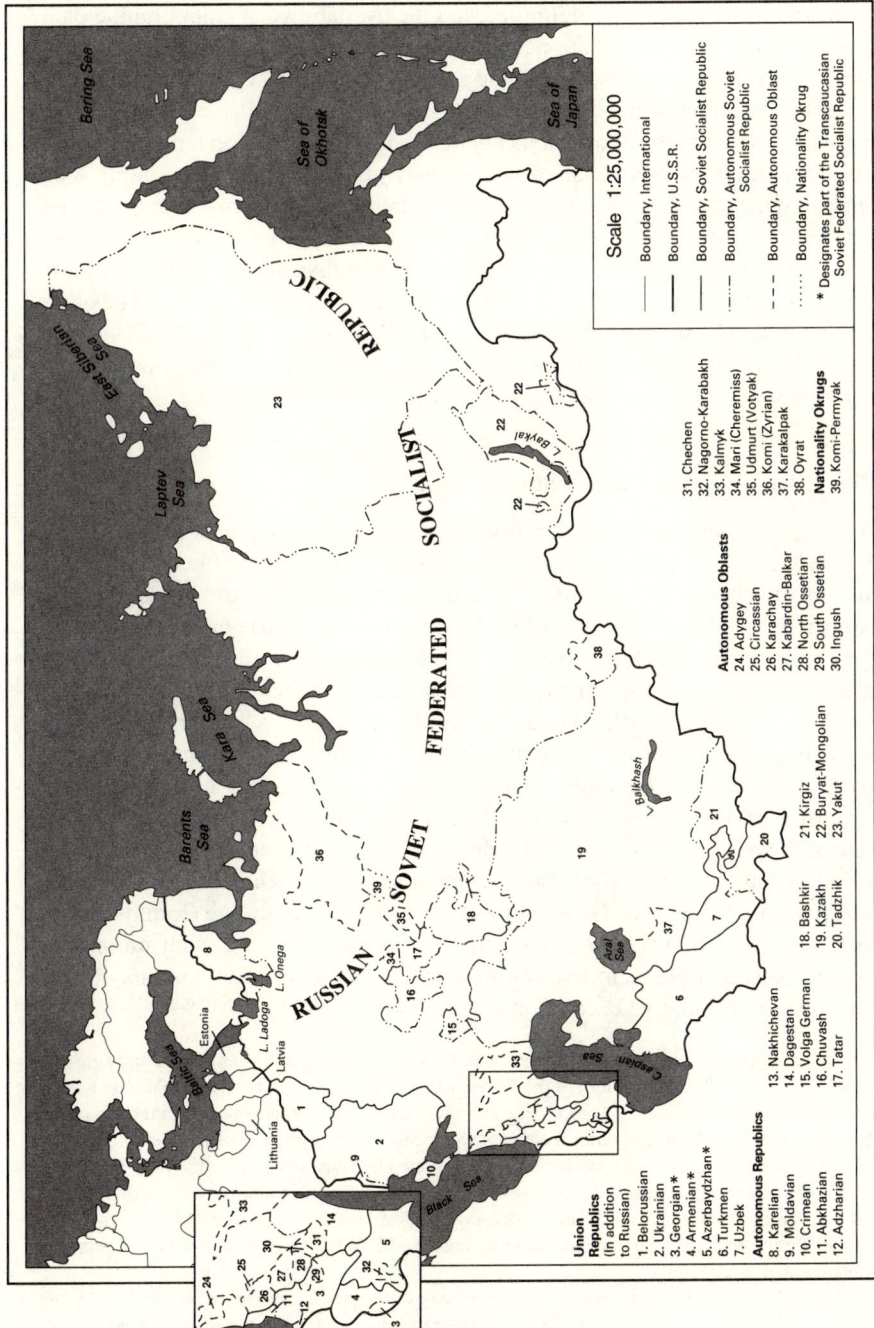

Map 3.1 Federal Structure of the USSR, 1926

by which the borders were delimited and the availability of ethnographic data that indicated little supranational or even national consciousness among the local masses argue against this as the sole or even primary factor.[11]

Union republics were supposedly created for advanced (i.e., mass-based) nations. Yet few of the eponymous *ethnies* provided with union republics could truly be called nations at this time. As was just indicated, the Central Asia *ethnies* at the union republic level were only beginning a process of mass-based national consolidation during the interwar period. Belorussians, and to an extent even Ukrainians, could not be considered fully formed nations yet they, like the Central Asian "nations," were provided with union republics. The other two members of the Soviet federation—the RSFSR and the TCSFSR—were themselves federated republics that encompassed numerous ethnonational communities at various stages in the nationalization process.

Confederal in Form, Unitary in Essence

Although declared a "confederation," the allocation of powers in the 1922 Union Treaty between center and republics was highly favorable to the center, and included not only control over interstate and military relations but also control over the economy, including the power to tax, utilize natural resources, formulate laws, develop principles of education (i.e., curriculum development), regulate labor, and annul decisions made by the republics (Stalin [1922] 1934, 132–136). The 1922 Union Treaty was in essence a "unitary" document allocating most of the social, economic, and political decision-making authority to the center.[12] This dialectical formula for the emerging center-periphery relationship, which could be described as confederal in form, unitary in essence, did not change substantially during the interwar period. The 1924 Constitution was essentially the same document as the 1922 Union Treaty, with the addition of a Council of Nationalities to the Central Executive Committee. In this new council, which replaced the *Narkomnats* system, each union and autonomous republic sent five representatives, while the autonomous oblasts sent one representative each (Conquest 1967, 42).[13]

---

[11] A stronger case can be made for the use of "divide and rule" in the case of the Tatar ASSR, which encompassed only one-third of the Tatars in the Volga region, and omitted adjoining *uyezds* with Tatar majorities in them. A good indicator that there were problems with the creation of the Tatar ASSR is that the neighboring Bashkir ASSR had a Tatar majority (Rorlich 1986, 138).

[12] This was not the way this document was presented by centrist figures supporting the Union Treaty proposed by Gorbachev. According to these analysts, who also tended to argue that today's national problems result from "Stalinist deformation" of Leninist nationality policies, the 1922 Union Treaty was truly confederal, and the only problem has been that it was not properly implemented. See chapter 7.

[13] The Council of Nationalities was the forerunner of the postwar Soviet of Nationalities in the bicameral Supreme Soviet. Equal representation for union and autonomous republics was meant to allay fears that nationalities with autonomous status would be oppressed by union republic nations.

By the time of the 1936 Constitution, there were eleven union republics, each with the right to self-determination up to and including secession from the USSR (Map 3.2). Unlike the 1922 Union Treaty, the state in 1936 was not referred to as a confederation, but rather as a "federal state." And, while the union republics retained a number of rights that gave the appearance of sovereignty, including the right to enter into foreign relations, to coin money, to create and maintain military units, and so forth, they actually lost rights between 1924 and 1936. The ministries of agriculture, health, justice, and internal affairs, previously under union republic authority with central guidance on "general principles," were reallocated to the Union-Republican level in 1936, a category designating joint supervision of these functions between center and union republic (Conquest 1967, 121–122). This loss of power may have been more apparent than real, since "central guidance" in the 1922 Union Treaty probably differed little in practice from joint supervision. Only education and social security remained at the republican level, and with regard to education, the curricula were set at the center, while the republics were in control only of the form (i.e., the language used), according to the familiar dictum "national in form, socialist in content."

The USSR thus became a mythical confederation of nation-states within a unitary political system, which became more centralized during the interwar period. Under these conditions the union republics were unable to function as the sovereign entities that the constitution declared them to be, nor were the indigenous nations able to exercise the right to secede from the USSR. This of course deprived the union republics, and the entire federal structure for that matter, of their *raison d'être*. Undoubtedly, the growing gap between the sovereign status of the union republics—which indigenous nationalists perceived as proper and just, even if the borders were in dispute—and the reality of the centralized USSR resulted in a rising sense of relative deprivation among the indigenous nationalists in the state. This national problem became more intractable during the interwar period as indigenes became more geographically and socially mobilized, and as the indigenous masses became more nationally self-conscious.

Geographic Mobilization, 1917–1939

During the interwar period, there was a dramatic increase in the disruption of rural localities, where the vast majority of each national community's population continued to live. In addition to the chaotic period of war and revolution from 1914 to 1922, collectivization and rapid industrialization beginning at the

---

Of course, since most of the autonomous units were in the RSFSR and since many of these had large numbers of Russians in them, an alternative reason would be to increase the weight of Russians in the Council, since representatives were not required to be members of the indigenous nation (Conquest 1967, 42).

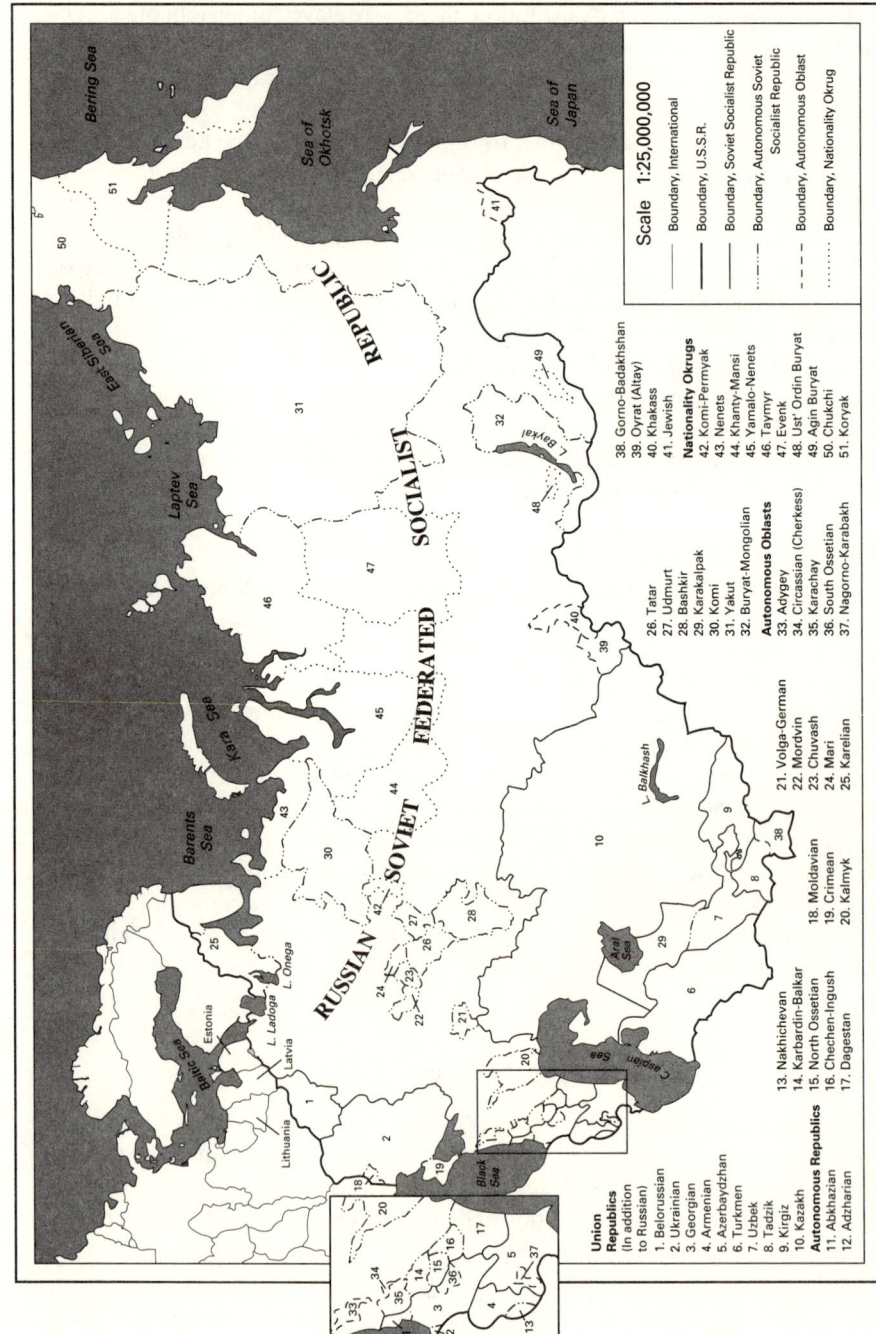

Map 3.2 Federal Structure of the USSR, 1939

close of the 1920s restructured rural society more fundamentally than had any previous reform effort. As a result of this disruption, the formerly isolated, localist peasantry was more quickly drawn into the larger society. Nationalism and sovietization were the chief contenders to replace localism as the primary sociocultural, economic, and even political orientation of the masses. The relative standing of each new ideology also varied geographically—nationalization had proceeded much farther in the Transcaucasus region and in the industrial northwest than it had further east, and sovietization coexisted much more easily with Russianization, or the national consolidation of the Russian nation, than it did with Ukrainization, Georgianization, and so forth. In addition, while nationalization and sovietization of the masses occurred between the wars, it is also apparent that localism continued to play a strong role in the countryside. Finally, all three orientations were blended together as the geographic and social mobilization of the masses progressed; peasants continued to respond to alien in-migration with anti-outsider nativism, but poor peasants also often supported regime efforts at *dekulakization*, even when the rich peasants were of the same *ethnie* and locality. Ethnic stratification as it developed also pitted privileged nonindigenes against upwardly aspiring indigenes, who often reacted with a combination of localism, nationalism, and socialism. Nevertheless, among most *ethnies* of the country this was primarily a period of national consolidation, which was enhanced not only by nationality policies but also by the geographic and social mobilization of the masses.

The following sections examine two aspects of geographic mobilization of the masses. First to be assessed is the degree to which the home republics, as delimited by the state, served as places toward which members of indigenous *ethnies* gravitated. Along with this, we examine the extent of increasing interethnic interaction in these "homelands." Next we discuss the urbanization process as a measure of the geographic and social mobilization of the masses.

Geographic Gravitation to the "Home" Republics

The national "home" republics were, at least according to earlier statements by Lenin ([1913] 1968), to serve as places toward which indigenes would tend to gravitate, and also were ideally to be nationally homogeneous. They were to serve as guarantors of international equality until they were no longer needed by the nations themselves (i.e., when the national membership voluntarily assimilated into a broader international or even world cultural community). In addition, for Stalin the home republics were to serve as empty containers within which nationality policies from above would be implemented and the national dialectic would play itself out.

For the ethnonational communities whose homelands were designated as union republics, there was a slight tendency toward greater concentration (Table 3.1). On average, the eleven national communities increased from 79.5

TABLE 3.1
Geographic Distribution of Nations in the USSR, by Republic, 1926–1939 (percent of indigenous population in "home" republic)

	Percent in Home Republic			Percent of Home Republic		
Republic	1926	1939	Percentage Point Change[a]	1926	1939	Percentage Point Change
RSFSR	93.4	90.7	−2.7	77.8	83.4	5.6
Ukraine	73.5	83.1	9.6	80.6	73.5	−7.1
Belorussia	84.8	87.5	2.7	80.6	82.9	2.3
Georgia	98.1	96.6	−1.5	67.0	61.4	−5.6
Armenia	47.4	49.3	1.9	84.4	82.8	−1.6
Azerbaydzhan	84.3	82.2	−2.1	62.1	58.4	−3.7
Kazakhstan	93.6	75.1	−18.5	57.1	38.2	−18.9
Uzbekistan	84.5	84.2	−0.3	74.2	64.4	−9.8
Turkmenistan	82.7	91.3	8.6	70.2	59.2	−11.0
Tadzhikistan	63.0	71.9	8.9	74.6	59.6	−15.0
Kyrgyzstan	86.7	85.3	−1.5	66.6	51.7	−14.9
ASSRs:						
Bashkir	87.7	79.6	−8.1	23.7	21.2	−2.5
Buryat	90.5	51.8	−38.7	43.8	21.3	−22.5
Kabardin-Balkar	89.9	93.3	3.4	76.3	53.7	−22.6
Kalmyk	81.1	79.8	−1.3	75.6	48.6	−27.0
Karelian	40.6	43.0	2.4	57.1	63.2	6.1
Komi	50.9	54.8	3.9	92.2	72.5	−19.7
Mari	57.9	56.7	−1.2	51.4	47.2	−4.2
North Ossetian	47.1	46.7	−0.4	84.2	50.3	−33.9
Tatar	39.9	33.0	−6.9	44.9	48.8	3.9
Udmurt	78.5	79.2	0.7	52.3	39.4	−12.9
Chechen-Ingush	92.0	90.3	−1.7	93.8	64.8	−29.0
Chuvash	59.8	56.7	−3.1	74.6	72.2	−2.4
Yakut	98.0	96.4	−1.6	81.6	56.5	−25.1
Abkhaz	98.1	95.2	−2.9	27.8	18.0	−9.8
Moldavia[b]	61.8	65.7	3.9	30.1	28.5	−1.6

Source: Kozlov 1977a, 98–103.

Notes: Figures are for USSR borders at the time of the censuses, and not contemporary borders. Komi figures include Komi and Komi-Permyaks ("Permyaks" in the 1926 census). ASSRs are the autonomous republics, the tier in the federation immediately below the union republics. Figures are not included for Lithuania, Latvia, or Estonia, nor for the Mordvin, Dagestan, Karakalpak, or Tuvin ASSRs, nor for any autonomous oblasts or nationality okrugs. For those nations with more than one "home" republic (e.g., Armenians in Armenia and Nagorno Karabakh Autonomous Oblast, Ossetians in the North Ossetian ASSR and South Ossetian Autonomous Oblast, etc.), only the largest is included above. The figures for the first two columns of those ASSRs with more than one indigenous nation (i.e., Kabardin-Balkar, Chechen-Ingush) were derived from Kozlov (1977b, 487–489).

[a] The percentage point change is that which occurred between 1926 and 1939.
[b] During the interwar period, Moldavia was constituted as an ASSR within Ukraine. Bessarabia was seized by Rumania and remained outside the USSR until 1940 (Chew 1970, 96–102).

percent of members in their respective home republics in 1926 to 80.2 percent in 1939. However, these *ethnies* were about evenly divided between those who "gravitated" to the home republic and those who became increasingly dispersed during this period. A number of demographic factors influenced the trends in evidence, including differential natural increase, migration, and ethnic reidentification. For the Russians this was a period of dispersal, both from the RSFSR and also from the European "heartland" to the eastern periphery of the RSFSR (Bruk and Kabuzan 1982b, 9). In most cases the declining proportion of indigenes in the non-Russian republic's total population was matched by an increase in the percent comprised by Russians. During the interwar period, it may be said that union and autonomous republics served as places toward which Russians gravitated. Still, the vast majority of Russians remained in the RSFSR throughout this period, and the only other two republics with a sizable proportion of the Russian national population were Kazakhstan and Ukraine (Table 3.2). These Russians lived in regions bordering the Russian republic, and these areas were undoubtedly perceived as part of the homeland by the Russians living there.[14]

At the same time that Russians were becoming more geographically dispersed throughout the country, their share in the total population of the RSFSR actually increased between 1926 and 1939, indicating that the Russian population was growing faster than the other national communities resident there. This increasing homogenization was probably not due so much to international differentials in the rate of natural increase (i.e., births over deaths), although this may have been a factor in comparing the Russian rate of growth with some of the indigenous national communities who suffered greater losses during collectivization. The rapid population growth of Russians in the RSFSR during the intercensal period was mainly the result of the reidentification of non-Russians, and especially Ukrainians living in the RSFSR, to the Russian nation (Lewis et al. 1976, 219).[15]

For the Ukrainians, greater concentration in Ukraine appears to have resulted from reidentification to the Russian nation by a large number of Ukrainians living outside the home republic, particularly in the North Caucasus region of the RSFSR (Bruk and Kabuzan 1982b, 15–16; Lewis et al. 1976, 219). This may help explain why their percent of Ukraine's total population actually declined—a result of famine in the early 1930s and Russian in-migration—at a time when they were becoming relatively more concentrated in their homeland. The decline among Ukrainians living outside Ukraine through reidentification was even more rapid than the decline within the republic.

Belorussia does appear to have served as a place toward which Belorussians gravitated during the interwar period, and as they became more concentrated in

---

[14] As discussed in chapter 7, these border regions have recently become zones of international tension between Ukrainians, Kazakhs, and Russians.

[15] The reasons for this dramatic increase are discussed in a later section on Russification.

TABLE 3.2
Distribution of Russians by Union and Autonomous Republics, 1917–1939 (percent of total population, percent of Russian population, and percentage point change)

Republic	Percent of Republic			Percentage Point Change	Percent of Russians			Percentage Point Change
	1917	1926	1939	1917–39	1917	1926	1939	1917–39
Percent of total population	46.8	47.0	52.4	5.6	100	100	100	—
Union Republics								
RSFSR	77.4	77.8	83.4	6.0	91.4	92.1	90.1	−1.3
Ukraine	9.9	8.6	10.4	0.5	4.7	4.2	4.3	−0.4
Belorussia	6.1	4.9	4.3	−1.8	0.6	0.5	0.4	−0.2
Estonia	2.8	3.5	4.8	2.0	0.1	0.1	0.1	0.0
Latvia	6.7	8.0	9.0	2.3	0.2	0.2	0.2	0.0
Lithuania	4.0	2.6	2.6	1.4	0.2	0.1	0.1	−0.1
Moldavia	5.9	8.2	7.7	1.8	0.2	0.2	0.2	0.0
Georgia	6.7	3.6	8.7	2.0	0.2	0.1	0.3	0.1
Armenia	1.2	2.3	4.0	2.8	0.0	0.0	0.1	0.1
Azerbaydzhan	8.7	9.6	16.5	7.8	0.3	0.3	0.5	0.2
Kazakhstan	20.5	21.2	40.3	19.8	1.6	1.6	2.4	0.8
Uzbekistan	2.8	5.2	11.5	8.7	0.2	0.3	0.7	0.4
Turkmenistan	3.9	7.4	18.6	14.7	0.1	0.1	0.2	0.1
Tadzhikistan	0.7	0.6	9.1	8.4	0.0	0.0	0.1	0.1
Kyrgyzstan	11.9	11.6	20.8	8.8	0.2	0.2	0.3	0.1
Autonomous Republics, RSFSR:					1926–39			1926–39
Bashkir	—	39.8	40.6	0.8	—	1.3	1.3	0.0
Buryat	—	52.7	72.0	19.3	—	0.3	0.4	0.1
Dagestan	—	12.5	14.3	1.8	—	0.1	0.1	0.0
Kabardin-Balkar	—	7.5	35.9	28.4	—	0.0	0.1	0.1
Kalmyk	—	10.7	45.7	35.0	—	0.0	0.1	0.1
Karelian	—	57.1	63.2	6.1	—	0.2	0.3	0.1
Komi	—	6.6	22.0	15.4	—	0.0	0.1	0.1
Mari	—	43.6	46.1	2.5	—	0.3	0.3	0.0
Mordvin	—	59.2	60.5	1.3	—	0.9	0.7	−0.2
North Ossetian	—	6.6	37.2	30.6	—	0.0	0.2	0.2
Tatar	—	43.1	42.9	−0.2	—	1.4	1.2	−0.2
Tuvin	—	20.0	17.2	−2.8	—	0.0	0.0	0.0
Udmurt	—	43.3	55.7	12.4	—	0.6	0.7	0.1
Chechen-Ingush	—	2.6	28.8	26.2	—	0.0	0.2	0.2
Chuvash	—	20.0	22.4	2.4	—	0.2	0.2	0.0
Yakut	—	10.4	35.5	25.1	—	0.0	0.2	0.2
Total ASSRs	—	35.8	41.4	5.6	—	5.5	6.1	0.5

Source: Bruk and Kabuzan 1982b.

Notes: Figures are comparable with the postwar territory of the USSR, and include areas outside the USSR during the interwar period: Baltic republics, western Ukraine, and Belorussia, Bessarabia, and Tuva. RSFSR totals include the ASSR figures.

Belorussia it, in turn, became more nationally homogeneous. This demographic "Belorussification" was enhanced by an absolute decrease in the number of Jews and Russians in the republic. For Belorussians living outside Belorussia, reidentification to the Russian nation also appears to have occurred between 1917 and 1939.

In Transcaucasia, Georgians and Azerbaydzhanis remained highly concentrated in their respective home republics, although Azerbaydzhanis did become more dispersed, and their homeland became more ethnically heterogeneous during the interwar period. Armenians became more highly concentrated in Armenia, in part as a result of the increasing favoritism shown Georgians and Azerbaydzhanis in "their" cities, which increased pressure on Armenians to leave (e.g., Suny 1989, 282). The growing anti-outsider sentiments apparent prior to 1917 among urbanizing indigenes against the formerly dominant (economically if not politically) Armenians continued and in all likelihood grew more intense during the interwar period. Still, Armenians remained one of the most dispersed national communities in the country in 1939. On the other hand, Armenia was the most nationally homogeneous of the Transcaucasian republics. In Azerbaydzhan, the other major national component was Armenians, not Russians (who were concentrated in the Baku oil industry). In Georgia, Armenians, Ossetians, and Abkhazians made up a relatively larger proportion of the population than Russians, though the Russian percentage nearly doubled during the intercensal period (Table 3.2).

In Central Asia, Tadzhiks and Turkmen "gravitated" to their respective home republics, and Uzbeks and Kirgiz remained at about the same level of concentration. However, Kazakhs experienced a massive dispersion from Kazakhstan during this period, and at the same time experienced an absolute decline in population. Kazakhs migrated from Kazakhstan to the Kazakh lands in western China after the 1916 revolt against the military draft and the oppressive Russian land policies that forced Kazakhs and Kirgiz from their traditional areas of settlements and onto more marginal land (Lewis et al. 1976, 232–233; Olcott 1987, 119–125). Between 1926 and 1939, a decrease of nearly 1.5 million Kazakhs overall (absolute decrease plus expected natural increase) occurred. While part of this decrease was caused by Kazakh emigration to western China and Kazakh reidentification to the Uzbek national community, it was also due to excess mortality resulting from collectivization.

All five Central Asian republics became less nationally homogeneous between 1926 and 1939 and, aside from Kazakhstan, this increasing "internationalization" cannot be explained by a decrease in the number of indigenes in their respective home republics. Rather, it indicates that a relatively large number of nonindigenes were migrating to the region during this period. Russian in-migration comprised the largest segment of this nonindigenous influx that accompanied the socioeconomic development of the region (Table 3.2).

A similar trend was occurring within the ASSRs (autonomous republics) of

Russia during the interwar period. Aside from the Buryats, who like the Kazakhs declined absolutely as some members migrated to their extended homeland in Mongolia and others to the two Buryat autonomous oblasts created around Lake Baykal, the indigenous nationalities did not experience much dispersion from the newly formed ASSRs. For some of the more dispersed national communities, such as the Tatars and Karelians, some gravitation to the home republic was in evidence. However, as in the case of Ukrainians, Karelian reconcentration resulted primarily from reidentification of Karelians living outside Karelia to the Russian nation. The same was occurring with Mordvins and several other smaller nationalities indigenous to the RSFSR, and had been occurring before the Revolution (Bruk and Kabuzan 1982a, 1982b). None of the indigenous *ethnies* declined precipitously in their own homelands. However, the ASSRs during the intercensal period became much less nationally homogeneous, indicating that nonindigenous in-migration exceeded indigenous population growth. Primary among the in-migrants were the Russians, who by 1939 comprised a majority in four ASSRs (Buryatia, Karelia, Mordvinia, and Udmurtia) and represented more than 40 percent of the population in another four (Bashkiria, Kalmykia, Mari, and Tatarstan) (Table 3.2). Russians were an even larger demographic component in the autonomous oblasts and nationality okrugs being created during this period.

The construction of national autonomous regions in the USSR fulfilled one of the principles of Leninist nationality policies. However, these home republics functioned only weakly as places toward which members of the indigenous nations gravitated and in which the population remained nationally homogeneous. The reasons for the failure of form to match function in this regard are many, and some have been noted above. In addition to the problems of delimiting home republics to match national homelands (whether defined in contemporary ethnodemographic or in more historical, mythical terms), in the relatively underdeveloped regions of the country there appeared to be greater interest in creating an industrial proletariat as quickly as possible than in ethnodemographic homogeneity and *korenizatsiya*. This was particularly true in Central Asia, Siberia, and the North Caucasus, where socioeconomic development resulted in increasing in-migration of Russians. In these areas, where the nationalization process had barely begun before World War I, national consolidation was further impeded by the ethnic stratification system that developed during the interwar period. In other regions of the USSR, greater interethnic interaction, coupled with collectivization that served to disrupt the localized lives of the peasants (Russians and non-Russians alike), accelerated the pace of nationalization and enhanced the growing sense a exclusiveness among indigenes regarding their status in the homeland. Of course, this national consolidation was encouraged not only by socioeconomic development but also by federalization on the basis of national territories, and by *korenizatsiya* policies.

It is difficult to find evidence that the central authorities encouraged indigenes to gravitate to their respective home republics in any direct sense, though the *korenizatsiya* policies of the 1920s indirectly made residence in the home republic much more appealing. Much of the gravitation that did occur resulted not from the positive "pull" of the homeland but rather from a negative "push" against the members of each national community living outside the homeland. In addition to this, reidentification of members of this outside segment—both to the indigenous nation and to the Russian nation—tended to result in a reconcentration of indigenes in their homelands, since higher losses were incurred outside.

Urbanization

During the interwar period, the USSR experienced one of the most rapid rates of urbanization recorded in human history (Lewis and Rowland 1979). All republics became more urbanized between 1926 and 1939, and according to the coefficients of variation (CVs), there was interrepublic equalization over time for this measure of geographic and social mobilization (Table 3.3).[16] In 1926 the CV equaled 31.5 percent, and decreased to 22.7 percent by 1939. By 1939 the RSFSR, Ukraine, Azerbaydzhan, and Turkmenistan had higher urban percents than the statewide average, and the rate of urbanization between 1926 and 1939 was higher than the USSR average in the RSFSR, Ukraine, Kazakhstan, and Turkmenistan.

The urbanization of national communities in the state offers a somewhat different picture. First, there was convergence or international equalization in the level of urbanization between 1926 and 1939, as the CV decreased from 72.4 percent to 52 percent. However, these figures indicate that international inequality was greater than interrepublic inequality. Second, only Russians and Armenians had higher urban percents than the USSR average in 1939. For Armenians the high urban percent was not a new phenomenon, as Armenians made up a large and economically dominant segment of the urban populations throughout Transcaucasia. For Russians, the relatively high urban percent did reflect the occurrence of rapid urbanization between 1926 and 1939. Indeed, the Russian rate of urbanization since 1926 was not only higher than all non-Russian nationalities in the state but was also among the highest rates of urbanization of any group in human history (Lewis et al. 1976, 141). In general, this meant that much of the urbanization experienced by different republics in the USSR between 1926 and 1939 came about as a result of Russians migrating to cities in these non-Russian homelands. Ukrainians and Kazakhs also equaled or exceeded the statewide average for urbanization between 1926 and 1939,

---

[16] The coefficient of variation, measured as the standard deviation divided by the mean, may be used as a measure of interregional or intergroup equality. A figure of 0 would mean complete equality, with every value identical to every other value. Decreasing CVs over time may be read as evidence of equalization.

TABLE 3.3
Urbanization in the USSR by Union Republic and Nation, 1926–1939 (percent)

	Republic			Nation		
Republic/Nation	1926	1939	Percentage Point Change	1926	1939	Percentage Point Change
USSR	18	32	14	18	32	14
Russian	18	33	15	21	38	17
Ukrainian	19	34	19	10	29	19
Belorussian	17	21	4	10	21	11
Georgian	22	30	8	17	25	8
Armenan	19	29	10	36	41	5
Azerbaydzhan	28	36	8	16	21	5
Kazakh	9	28	19	2	16	14
Uzbek	22	23	1	19	15	−4
Turkmen	14	33	19	2	10	8
Kirgiz	12	19	7	1	4	3
Tadzhik	10	17	7	15	12	−3
Coefficients of Variation	31.5	22.7		72.4	52.0	

Source: Arutyunyan 1972, 18.

Notes: Figures for USSR within the borders at the time of the censuses.

and the Ukrainian rate of increase actually surpassed that of the Russians. However, the latter was at least in part the result of excess rural mortality during the famine of 1932–1933, and was not the result of rural to urban migration alone (Wheatcroft 1990). Finally, unlike urbanization by republic, not all national communities experienced increasing rates of urbanization. Both the Uzbeks and Tadzhiks—the most urbanized Central Asian *ethnies* in 1926—experienced a decrease in the proportion of population living in cities between 1926 and 1939.

Unfortunately, 1939 urban figures for nationalities by republic were never published. However, a comparison of the demographic indigenization of cities between 1926 and 1959 is possible (Table 3.4). These data indicate that a demographic Russification of cities not only in the RSFSR but also in Uzbekistan, Tadzhikistan, Kyrgyzstan, and Georgia continued throughout the Stalinist period.[17] A stronger demographic indigenization of cities occurred in Ukraine, Belorussia, Azerbaydzhan, Armenia, and Turkmenistan.

Rural to urban migration among indigenous peasants—accelerated by collectivization and rapid industrialization—was quantitatively much higher than the urbanization occurring before World War I. However, the peasants migrat-

[17] In the latter republic, Georgians comprised more than half the urban population, and the Russian urban increase was only slightly higher than that of the Georgian increase.

TABLE 3.4
Indigenous and Russian Composition of the Urban Population by Union Republic, 1926–1959 (percent of urban population and percentage point change)

Republic[a]	Indigenous			Russian		
	1926	1959	Percentage Point Change	1926	1959	Percentage Point Change
RSFSR	84.9	87.2	2.3	—	—	—
Ukraine[b]	47.4	61.5	14.1	25.0	29.9	4.9
Belorussia[b]	39.3	67.0	27.7	15.6	19.4	3.8
Moldavia[b]	7.6	28.2	20.6	23.3	30.4	7.1
Georgia	48.2	52.9	4.7	11.8	18.8	7.0
Armenia	89.3	91.9	2.6	3.2	4.5	1.3
Azerbaydzhan	37.6	51.3	13.7	27.0	24.8	−2.2
Kazakhstan	14.4	16.7	2.3	52.6	57.6	5.0
Uzbekistan	57.0	37.2	−19.8	19.2	33.4	14.2
Turkmenistan	7.0	34.7	24.7	46.4	35.4	−11.0
Tadzhikistan	73.6	31.8	−41.8	9.9	35.3	25.4
Kyrgyzstan	4.6	13.2	8.6	37.2	51.8	14.6

Source: Kozlov 1977a, 152–155.
[a] Republics in the borders as they existed at the time of the censuses.
[b] In Ukraine, Belorussia, and Moldavia, republics were significantly smaller in 1926 than in 1959, after the incorporation of western Ukraine, western Belorussia, and Bessarabia. A comparable set of regions would indicate a less dramatic rate of urban indigenization than in Table 3.4.

ing to cities during the 1920s and 1930s were similar to those of the late nineteenth century in a number of regards. First, the rich peasants were more likely to move to the cities, as was the case before the October Revolution. However, this tendency from the past was taken to extremes during the late 1920s, when in order to avoid the *dekulakization* drive aimed at the wealthier peasants, a large number of these peasants fled to the cities (Hoffmann 1992). The practice of *otkhodnichestvo* (temporary labor migration to cities) and *zemlyachestvo* (peasant in-migrants from the same villages or regions living in the same urban neighborhoods and working in the same factories) also continued through much of the interwar period (Suny 1989, 254; Hoffmann 1990). As in the prewar period, these practices undoubtedly impeded the processes of nationalization and sovietization, though by the end of the 1930s peasant in-migrants were coming on a more permanent basis and were becoming more fully integrated into the new socioeconomic environment (Straus 1990).

The movement of indigenes to cities in their own homelands during the 1920s and 1930s, the predominant rural to urban migration stream of the period, was undoubtedly leading to the more rapid nationalization of the masses. As with Latvians, Georgians, and others a few decades earlier, urbanization was particularly rapid for rural, agrarian indigenes, and quickly led to the Ukrainization, Belorussification, and so forth, of the urban populations in their respective home republics (e.g., Liber 1989; Guthier 1977). The USSR created an internal passport system in 1932 in an effort to gain control of this migration stream. Collective farmers were not issued passports, and in theory this eliminated their spontaneous geographic mobility (Zaslavsky and Luryi 1979).[18] However, the state was generally unsuccessful in controlling rural to urban migration directly, though the rapid industrialization policy coupled with preferential investment in the RSFSR certainly had the indirect effect of accelerating urbanization and of influencing its direction (Lewis et al. 1976, 133). Indigenization of cities was also impeded by the in-migration of Russians and other skilled workers from the European part of the USSR; this was particularly true in Central Asia. As urbanization proceeded, there was a nationalization of the incoming rural indigenes and even a partial reversal of the Russification of urban indigenes that had occurred earlier (e.g., Liber 1989, 587). This process of indigenous nationalization with urbanization was greatly enhanced by both the federalization of the state (e.g., Gardanov et al. 1961, 12) and also the *korenizatsiya* policy implemented during the 1920s and conducted throughout much of the 1930s.

KORENIZATSIYA, SOCIAL MOBILIZATION, AND NATIONAL TERRITORIALITY

As discussed above, international equalization was seen by Lenin as a key ingredient to solving the national problem inherited from tsarist Russia. The federalization of the state was viewed as a way of providing the major nations of the USSR legal equality with the formerly dominant Russians and with one another. However, this was not thought to be sufficient to overcome the system of ethnic stratification inherited from the past—equality under the law or "equal opportunity" was to be supplemented by a sort of "affirmative action" policy that targeted non-Russian indigenes for preferential treatment in their home republics.[19] Lenin even went so far as to assert that non-Russians would need to be given preference over Russians for a time, in order to overcome the legacy of Great Russian chauvinism. However, Stalin ([1923] 1934, 168) declared that for Lenin this was "merely a figure of speech," and that placing Russians in a subordinate position was absurd. The debate over the preferential treatment of non-Russians relative to Russians in the state was a major aspect of the "national question" throughout the interwar period.

Korenizatsiya, or indigenization of the sociocultural, economic, and political

---

[18] Zaslavsky and Luryi (1979, 147) note that "the registration of nationality in documents originated simultaneously with the introduction of the passport system." This, too, has tended to reinforce a national consciousness in the population.

[19] The term *affirmative action* was never used by officials in the former USSR to describe *korenizatsiya* or other international equalization policies.

sectors and cadres of each national territory, was to provide for the more rapid advancement of the relatively backward indigenes in the state, which would result in real as well as legal international equality. However, rather than promote equality among members of different nations regardless of where they lived (i.e., extraterritoriality), *korenizatsiya* favored indigenes over nonindigenes in each home republic. With the overlay of national territorial autonomy, *korenizatsiya* helped to ensure that an indigenous "sense of exclusiveness" would grow along with socioeconomic development. In this way, nationality policies designed to promote international equalization in the USSR served not to "draw together" the national communities in the state as their members became more socially and geographically mobilized, but on the contrary encouraged both a rising national self-consciousness among upwardly mobile indigenes and the continued geographic segregation of national communities, each in its own respective homeland with its own national territorial agenda. Under these circumstances, even international equalization was likely to heighten national consciousness and the indigene's sense of exclusiveness in the homeland, since it brought a greater number of upwardly mobile indigenes into more intense contact and competition with nonindigenes. International equality, even if it could be achieved through these means, was unlikely to solve the national problem.

For those groups whose national consciousness had become mass-based, *korenizatsiya* policies "from above" converged with efforts at *korenizatsiya* "from below" (i.e., national territoriality), while for those whose national consciousness was only just becoming or had not yet become mass-based, *korenizatsiya* from above helped to accelerate the nationalization process and to ensure that the territorial dimension of national self-consciousness would become of paramount importance. The rising national territoriality in evidence among non-Russians during the late 1920s and early 1930s led to a policy reversal in favor of Russification by the mid-1930s, although *korenizatsiya* was never openly rejected, and at least in the sociocultural sector continued to the eve of World War II.[20]

Korenizatsiya had a number of dimensions, including the promotion of indigenous cultural forms (especially language), and affirmative action-type programs providing easier access to higher education and elite positions in the socioeconomic and political institutions for the indigene in his or her own home republic. The development of national cultural forms, along with a rapid increase in literacy and educational attainment in the indigenous language, were the major achievements of this period of *korenizatsiya*. Written languages were developed where none existed before, and these in turn were used as languages

---

[20] *Korenizatsiya* policies reappeared after World War II, and continued into the 1980s. However, in the postwar period, as discussed in part 2, *korenizatsiya* from below became a relatively more important reason for the continued indigenization than it had ever been during the interwar period.

of instruction to educate the indigenous masses. The strategic use of national forms to promote socialism in the relatively backward Soviet state was a clear priority at the time. According to Connor (1984a, 205), Lenin held that "the nationalist form is not to be restricted to language but is to incorporate whatever aspects of traditional attire are apt to prove effective at making the socialist content appear less exotic, more familiar, and therefore more compatible with a group's predispositions." Thus *korenizatsiya* was seen as a dialectical facilitator of sovietization and ultimately international integration.

The period of *korenizatsiya* was also marked by the "vernacularization" of indigenous languages throughout the country. More than forty written languages were created during the interwar period (Izmaylov and Kolmakova 1980, 146). In the period from 1932 to 1933 alone, written languages were constructed from the vernacular for sixteen of the largest *ethnies* of the northeastern region of the country (Balabanov and Shvetsova 1987, 30). This vernacularization and linguistic standardization was most frequently the result of research conducted and policies implemented from outside, often under the auspices of the center, and were not the result of "patriotic agitation" on the part of a nationalized indigenous elite. In a sense, the center in these cases acted as a surrogate national elite, attempting to assist relatively "backward" indigenes to leap directly to mass-based national consolidation, omitting Phase A and Phase B nationalization, just as they in theory were to leap over a capitalist stage of development directly to socialism. This leap was not made without problems. First, by 1931 only five of twenty-six peoples of Siberia had literary languages, and a concerted effort to expand this number did not truly begin until 1932 (Rozyeva 1980, 335). One of the greatest impediments was that the dialects spoken by the ethnographic segments of each group were so different from the dialect chosen for the literary language that "vernacularization" is hardly a proper term for the process of adopting these "foreign" tongues (e.g., Fierman 1985, 210–211; Kreindler 1985, 248; Gurvich and Taksami 1985, 57). In addition, indigenous teachers were rarely available, since indigenous rates of education were so low. To use the newly created literary languages as media of instruction, the nonindigenous teachers first had to be taught the native languages (e.g., Khomich 1980, 70).

Even among the more established literary languages in the USSR, linguistic standardization and consolidation occurred only during the interwar period. Of course, Estonian, Latvian, and Lithuanian became state languages after independence and this greatly expanded their standardization and utilization. Ukrainian was declared the equal of Russian in Ukraine in 1920, although the promotion of the Ukrainian language was resisted and Ukrainization truly began only in 1923 (Solchanyk 1985, 67–69). Belorussian was also declared the official language of Belorussia during the early 1920s, and vernacularization and "purification" of the Belorussian language occurred throughout the remainder of the decade (Wexler 1985, 39–42). Even Georgian continued to undergo consolidation during the interwar period (Hewitt 1985, 175). In the east, the first decade after the October Revolution produced limited results, and only after 1927 was there a more concerted effort to bring about *korenizatsiya*.

During the period of the *korenizatsiya* of languages, which lasted from the early 1920s until the end of the 1930s, in addition to questions of vernacularization and linguistic standardization of literary languages, the choice of script also became a topic of heated debate. During this time, the Latin script was promoted by the central authorities, and also supported by indigenous elites among several *ethnies*, as a revolutionary break with the past. There was even discussion of the 'Latinization' of Russian in the 1920s (Isayev 1979, 58). Between 1925 and 1938, eighteen Turkic languages were Latinized, along with several of the non-Turkic languages of the east whose literary languages were being created at this time. The Latin script was seen as progressive and, in the case of the Turkic-Muslims, easier to learn than Arabic. Arabic was the language of Islam, and this was reason enough for the center to oppose it. In addition, the Arabic script was not developed for the Turkic vernaculars, and was known by relatively few in the region, where literacy rates remained extremely low, even by 1926. During the early 1920s, an effort to reform Arabic so that it more closely conformed to the needs of the Central Asian vernaculars were attempted, but this gave way to Latinization by the mid- to late 1920s. Some evidence suggests that popular support for Latinization existed, at least among indigenous elites, and that it was not solely a means of manipulating language development by the center (Smith 1991). However, this indigenous elite support varied by group. Latinization was apparently seen as an anti-*korenizatsiya* element among Crimean Tatars (Lazzerini 1985, 116–117) and Kazakhs (Olcott 1985, 193), but was seen as facilitating *korenizatsiya* in Uzbekistan (Fierman 1985, 210) and in Azerbaydzhan (Smith 1991). By the end of the 1930s, the use of a Latin script was abruptly curtailed and replaced by Cyrillic. Nevertheless, even after the conversion to a Cyrillic script, the development of indigenous languages continued, particularly in the east. For example, during the second half of the 1930s, the "social function of native languages of the nationalities of the taiga and tundra expanded sharply" as means of communication in the sociopolitical sphere, in terms of greater numbers of publications, and in expanded use in elementary schools (Gurvich and Taksami 1985, 57). This continued expansion of native language use during a period of ostensible Russification appears to have been the case in much of the non-Russian periphery.

The spread of these newly formed vernacular languages, and of non-Russian languages generally, was greatly facilitated by the creation of a central state publishing house for the peoples of the USSR in 1924. That same year literature was published in twenty-five languages of the peoples of the USSR, and by 1931 the number had expanded to seventy-six (Izmaylov and Kolmakova 1980, 147). The expansion of non-Russian publications during the *korenizatsiya* pe-

TABLE 3.5
Book Publication in the USSR, 1913–1937 (percent by language of publication)

Language	Number of Titles			Number of Copies		
	1913	1928–32	1933–37	1913	1928–32	1933–37
Russian	90.9	65.2	70.2	91.9	77.2	76.6
Non-Russian	6.0	32.0	26.9	4.9	21.8	22.1
Foreign	3.1	2.8	2.9	1.7	1.0	1.3

Source: Guboglo 1972, 124.
Notes: "Non-Russian" = languages of other indigenous peoples of the USSR. "Foreign" = languages of nonindigenous peoples.

riod was greater than the growth of the number of Russian titles and copies (*tirazh*), though there was a slight reduction in the proportion of non-Russian titles relative to Russian titles during the mid-1930s (Table 3.5). Even in Belorussia, where *korenizatsiya* was supposedly at an end early in the 1930s, Belorussian language newspapers made up 75 percent of all newspapers in the republic (149 of 199 titles) in 1938, and Belorussian language books comprised 84 percent of the total tirazh of books published (12.3 of 14.7 million) in the same year (Guthier 1977, 59).

The expansion of native language schools for indigenes was, if anything, even more impressive. During the 1920s in the RSFSR the number of native language schools and indigenous students grew twice as fast as the number of Russian schools and students (Guboglo 1977a, 264–265). The number of languages in which educational materials were published increased along with the increasing number of literary languages, growing from 70 in 1931 to 104 in 1934 (Rozyeva 1980, 335). The impact on indigenous school attendance was dramatic. In the 1925/26 school year, 30 percent of school-aged non-Russian children were enrolled in elementary schools, compared to 62.5 percent of school-aged Russian children. By the 1929/30 school year, 70 percent of non-Russian children were attending elementary school. Although language standardization problems continued, as well as a lack of indigenous teachers, and even transportation problems that impeded the expansion of education among the *ethnies* of the RSFSR up to the end of the 1930s (Izmaylov and Kolmakova 1980, 148–150), universal elementary education for non-Russian children in the RSFSR was essentially achieved by 1932 (Bolmenkova 1988, 153–155).[21]

Outside the RSFSR, the number of schools, as well as the number of students using the indigenous languages, grew markedly. For example, in Ukraine the

---

[21] An additional problem among the peoples of the North and the non-Slavic South was that many were still nomadic or seminomadic. Even though special boarding schools and mobile schools were created for their children, universal education for these *ethnies* continued to pose great difficulties.

proportion of Ukrainian elementary schools (i.e., where Ukrainian was the language of instruction) grew from 61 percent in 1923 to 80 percent by 1926. In 1927, 94 percent of Ukrainian pupils and even 66 percent of Russian pupils were taught in the Ukrainian language. The high percentage of Russian pupils learning in Ukrainian was used against Skrypnyk as evidence of Ukrainian national chauvinism in the political purges of the 1930s (Solchanyk 1985, 72). However, even though there was an apparent shift away from political *korenizatsiya* with the political purges of the early 1930s in Ukraine, this reversal did not immediately affect sociocultural *korenizatsiya*. By the 1935/36 school year 83 percent of all pupils in general education were taught in Ukrainian, a greater proportion than in 1927 (Solchanyk 1985, 69–73). By the 1931/32 school year, universal elementary education was essentially in place in Ukraine (Izmaylov and Kolmakova 1980, 152). The same landmark was achieved in the early 1930s in Armenia and Georgia, in the mid-1930s in Azerbaydzhan and Belorussia, during the 1940s in Kazakhstan and Central Asia, and in the 1949/50 school year in Turkmenistan (Drobizheva 1977, 337; Bolmenkova 1988, 161). In the Islamic regions of the southern tier, religious schools were closed and state schools in the native languages were opened during the 1920s and 1930s, and the expansion of school attendance was dramatic. For example, in Tadzhikistan in the 1924/25 school year, 31 schools were in operation with 904 pupils in attendance. In the 1929/30 school year, this had expanded to 417 schools with 22,590 pupils in attendance (Izmaylov and Kolmakova 1980, 165–166).

During the interwar period, interrepublic and international equalization occurred in the level of sociocultural development. As noted in chapter 2, literacy varied dramatically by region and ethnic group in the Russian Empire, and this situation had not changed significantly by 1926. In that year literacy for the country as a whole stood at 39.6 percent, and for the population aged nine to forty-nine it was 56.6 percent. However, for those nations with homelands in the European part of the country (except for the Belorussians), literacy rates were consistently above the all-union average, and for most of these nations significantly so. On the other hand, the national communities of Siberia and Central Asia often had literacy rates in the single digits (TsSU SSSR 1928). By 1939, at least according to official statements, more than 87 percent of the population aged nine to forty-nine was literate, and illiteracy was being "liquidated" throughout the country (e.g., Maksimov 1976, 182; Table 3.6). The most rapid rate of growth was in those regions where literacy had been the lowest. A contemporary studying the effects of native language schools in the north noted in 1934 in Koryak Okrug that after education in the Koryak language was introduced, "literacy began to spread literally as an epidemic—children instructed parents, men (instructed) women" (Gurvich and Taksami 1985, 56).

A similar equalization occurred in education rates. As noted above, the push

TABLE 3.6
Literacy Rates by Republic, 1897–1939 (percent of population aged 9–49 years)

Republic	Percent			Percentage Point Change	
	1897	1926	1939	1897–1926	1926–1939
USSR	28.4	56.6	87.4	28.2	30.8
RSFSR	29.6	60.9	89.7	31.3	28.8
Ukraine	27.9	63.6	88.2	35.7	24.6
Belorussia	32.0	59.7	80.8	27.7	21.1
Uzbekistan	3.6	11.6	78.7	8.0	67.1
Kazakhstan	8.1	25.2	83.6	17.1	58.4
Georgia	23.6	53.0	89.3	29.4	36.3
Azerbaydzhan	9.2	28.2	82.8	19.0	54.6
Lithuania	54.2	—	76.7	—	—
Moldavia	22.2	—	45.9	—	—
Latvia	79.7	—	92.7	—	—
Kyrgyzstan	3.1	16.5	79.8	13.4	63.3
Tadzhikistan	2.3	3.8	82.8	1.5	79.0
Armenia	9.2	38.7	83.9	29.5	45.2
Turkmenistan	7.8	14.0	77.7	6.2	63.7
Estonia	96.2	—	98.6	—	—

Source: TsSU SSSR 1977, 9–10.

Note: Some caution must be exercised in interpreting the literacy data, since the criteria used to establish whether or not a person was literate changed over time. For example, while in 1897 a person was considered literate if he or she claimed the ability to read, in 1926 literacy was based on the respondent's ability to sign his or her last name. See Liebowitz 1986, 167.

for universal elementary education led to the equalization of basic education rates during a relatively brief time. Of course, this more rapid growth in the educational system in the non-Russian periphery was also reflected in the dramatic increase in literacy in the outlying regions of the state. However, the international equality of literacy and elementary education during the interwar period was not matched by a similar equality at the level of secondary and higher education (Table 3.7). Nevertheless here, too, rapid interregional and international equalization, if not outright equality, was evident (e.g., Drobizheva 1977, 338; Rozyeva 1980; Bolmenkova 1988, 148–172).

The creation of an indigenous urban/industrial proletariat was also part of *korenizatsiya*, although the proletariat in the socialist USSR was to be a force for international integration, transcending national consciousness. As an example of this thinking Stalin, in a letter to Kaganovich in 1926, declared that while the proletariat of Ukraine may become more Ukrainian in composition as a result of social mobilization of indigenes in the republic, the "Ukrainization of the proletariat" must not be compelled from above (i.e., a policy of *korenizat-*

TABLE 3.7
Education Rates by Indigenous Nation, Russians and Republic, 1939 (per 1,000 population aged ten years and older with a higher or secondary education)

Republic	Total			Indigenes			Russians		
	Total	Urban	Rural	Total	Urban	Rural	Total	Urban	Rural
Total USSR	83	178	39	—	—	—	88	165	41
RSFSR	83	174	38	82	165	36	82	165	36
Ukraine	103	183	56	81	164	48	151	169	118
Belorussia	83	201	43	58	191	31	221	235	205
Uzbekistan	42	130	15	16	69	7	160	182	108
Kazakhstan	65	122	43	22	67	13	97	134	72
Georgia	124	276	59	137	351	69	167	210	92
Azerbaydzhan	80	164	32	52	146	25	142	160	76
Kyrgyzstan	34	112	17	10	115	6	92	135	58
Tadzhikistan	29	119	11	11	74	3	148	153	139
Turkmenistan	49	120	15	14	66	7	147	145	164
Armenia	87	204	40	92	207	41	131	176	87

Source: TsSU SSSR 1962, 16 vols., Table 57.

siya must not exist in this regard). Indeed, at about the same time Stalin ([1925] 1934, 210) declared that a universal human culture was forming that was "proletarian in content and national in form," a strong indication that the proletarianization of nations in the USSR was seen as a step toward the international integration of the population. This conformed with Lenin's stance on the need to ensure the internationalization of the proletariat. This objective formed the core of the dialectical relationship between *korenizatsiya* and national consolidation on the one hand, and proletarian internationalism on the other.

The desire to expand the size and international character of the proletariat through *korenizatsiya* was undoubtedly hampered to some degree by the decision to accelerate the pace of industrialization, which in the more backward regions of the state meant the in-migration of nonindigenous workers. However, the belief that on entering the proletariat the localist or nationalist indigenes would be transformed into internationalists encouraged the indigenization of the proletariat. In Ukraine, Ukrainians increased their share of the blue-collar work force from 50 percent in 1926 to 62 percent by the middle of the Second Five-Year Plan (Bolmenkova 1988, 104). Even in Soviet Central Asia, an indigenization of the blue-collar work force was evident from the mid-1920s to the mid-1930s. For example, the Kazakh share of the proletariat increased from 21 percent in 1925 to 42 percent in 1933. In Uzbekistan, the shift in favor of Uzbeks was even more dramatic, increasing from 29 percent to 52 percent between 1925 and 1929 (Ostapenko 1980, 96–97). According to

Fierman (1985, 208), the pressure on European (i.e., Slavic) directors of enterprises to hire indigenes increased after 1927, and this caused a chain reaction, with ill-prepared Uzbeks given preference in access to higher education and higher status employment. The growth of the indigenous work force, when compared to the republic as a whole, was quite impressive between 1926 and 1939 in the non-Russian periphery, though in Central Asia nonindigenous blue- and white-collar workers grew relatively more rapidly than the indigenous nonagricultural work force (Table 3.8).

In the RSFSR, a *korenizatsiya* of the proletariat was also occurring in the non-Russian homelands. For example, between 1926 and 1940, Mari industrial workers increased from 5.5 percent to 25 percent of the total industrial work force in the Mari ASSR; Chuvash industrial workers increased from 8.2 percent to 45 percent of the total in the Chuvash ASSR; and Tatars in the Tatar ASSR increased from 21 percent to 37.4 percent of all industrial workers over the same time period (Kuzeyev et al. 1988, 8). The indigenous share of the blue-collar work force for these and other non-Russians in the RSFSR was approaching their share of the population in their respective home republics. Nevertheless, upward occupational mobility continued to be limited in several autonomous units and for several indigenous *ethnies* due both to the lack of sociocultural development among the indigenes and also to the limited number of industrial enterprises constructed in these regions—especially in Siberia (Mitrofanova 1980; Alekseyev and Moskovskiy 1980).

In addition to accelerating the pace of forming indigenous proletariats loyal to the Communist party, the policy of *korenizatsiya* had the immediate objective of creating a cadre of indigenous intellectuals capable of governing their own home republics according to the tenets of Marxism-Leninism and the wishes of the central authorities. Rather than denying the political legitimacy of national identity and national territoriality, the Communist party recognized the importance of what Rothchild (1986) in his study of "hegemonial exchange" in Africa has referred to as "ethnoregional spokesmen" in enhancing the stability of the USSR as a multinational, multihomeland state. Communist party membership expanded rapidly during the 1920s to 1933, and this occurred along with a *korenizatsiya* of party and government cadres in the non-Russian federal units (Connor 1984a, 280). Political *korenizatsiya* as a method of coopting potential nationalist leaders was a major achievement of the interwar period, and was probably crucial to the survival of the USSR during this difficult phase of state-building.

Along with sociocultural and political *korenizatsiya* the Red Army was also restructured in accordance with the indigenization program through the creation of national-territorial units beginning in 1924. The major goal of this policy "was to extend the military service obligation to as many ethnic minority groups as possible" in a heavily Russified army (Jones 1985, 183–184). In this they appear to have been successful; the proportion of non-Russians increased

TABLE 3.8
Employment in Mental and Physical Labor Outside Agriculture, 1926–1939
(percent of total employed by indigenous nation and republic)

	Mental				Physical			
	Total Population		Indigenous		Total Population		Indigenous	
Republic	1926	1939	1926	1939	1926	1939	1926	1939
Ukraine	4.4	17.4	2.6	13.6	11.5	35.4	6.6	31.1
Belorussia	3.2	14.8	2.0	10.2	9.6	28.6	4.2	23.1
Georgia	6.6	17.8	5.9	18.4	15.2	23.1	10.8	14.9
Armenia	3.9	16.1	4.3	17.1	12.3	22.5	12.3	22.4
Azerbaydzhan	8.5	18.0	3.6	12.4	28.4	29.0	19.9	16.2
Kazakhstan	2.0	18.6	0.4	11.1	5.7	37.2	2.5	25.1
Uzbekistan	3.6	14.5	1.3	8.8	13.8	20.4	10.1	12.4
Turkmenistan	3.7	17.0	0.4	8.4	12.3	28.7	3.7	13.7
Kyrgyzstan	1.7	14.5	0.2	7.7	5.8	22.4	1.1	8.5

	Percentage Point Change, 1926–1939				Percentage Change, 1939 ÷ 1926			
	Mental				Physical			
Republic	Total	Indigenous	Total	Indigenous	Total	Indigenous	Total	Indigenous
Ukraine	13.0	11.0	23.9	24.5	331	385	255	364
Belorussia	11.6	8.2	19.0	18.9	390	430	258	465
Georgia	11.2	12.5	7.9	4.1	350	373	198	166
Armenia	12.2	12.8	10.2	10.1	456	418	199	190
Azerbaydzhan	9.5	8.8	0.6	−3.7	322	497	156	119
Kazakhstan	16.6	10.7	31.5	22.6	682	1547	479	498
Uzbekistan	10.9	7.5	6.6	2.3	523	817	190	153
Turkmenistan	13.3	8.0	16.7	10.0	522	1733	274	383
Kyrgyzstan	12.8	7.5	16.6	7.4	1009	3039	466	703

Source: Arutyunyan 1972, 4–8.
Notes: No data were provided for the RSFSR or Moldavia, or for Tadzhikistan in 1939.

from 21 percent in 1922 to 39 percent in 1925, at which time national-territorial units comprised ten percent of all units in the army (Jones 1985, 184). Of course, national and regional differences were evident in the rate of recruitment during the 1920s. One of the major problems appeared to be a resistance on the part of indigenes, particularly Central Asians, to serve in the army. There was also the question of Central Asian loyalty to the USSR at that time (Jones 1985, 184–186). In addition to this, a number of national communities did not have indigenous commanders (Conquest 1967, 52). By the mid-1930s, national-territorial units were phased out along with the rest of the *korenizatsiya* program, although they were reinstituted briefly during World War II.

Although Conquest (1967, 51–53) argues that the achievements of political *korenizatsiya* were modest in several autonomous republics and Uzbekistan, this does not present an accurate picture of political indigenization overall. According to Suny (1989, 235), by the end of the 1920s "Georgians dominated state as well as party institutions," and this trend worked to the detriment of Russians as well as Armenians. This may be viewed as particularly surprising, since it was Georgian nationalism that the central authorities feared most in Transcaucasia, and was the primary reason for the merger of the three republics into a Transcaucasian federated republic. Political indigenization was undoubtedly occurring during the 1920s in other union and autonomous republics throughout the state (e.g., Kaymarazov 1988, 70).

Indeed, if anything, political *korenizatsiya* proceeded too rapidly to ensure that those indigenes placed in charge of their home republics would be loyal first and foremost to the Soviet Union and the Communist party. In a competition for the hearts and minds of politically mobilized indigenes in the 1920s, nationalism was clearly winning out over communism. From 1934 to 1938, extensive party and governmental purges of indigenes in the union republics and autonomous units on "charges of 'nationalist deviation,' 'bourgeois nationalism,' 'separatism,' 'anti-state activity,' and the like" (Connor 1984a, 280) brought the period of political *korenizatsiya* to a decisive end. Political *korenizatsiya* may have helped stabilize the USSR during the 1920s, but it had not led the indigenous political elites created during that period to the proper internationalist conclusions.

Korenizatsiya represented a concerted effort on the part of the state to bring about international equalization, which would in theory result in the withering away of nations after a period of national consolidation. While a number of analysts have argued that *korenizatsiya* ended in 1928 with the onset of collectivization and the installation of a command-administrative system that was highly centralized, the data from the interwar period indicate that the process of indigenization, particularly though not exclusively in the sociocultural arena, continued up to the eve of World War II. It is more accurate to view *korenizatsiya* as an attempt to mobilize and sovietize the masses more quickly by using indigenous cultural forms, while at the same time undermining the position of the previously nationalized elites. The problem with this, as the purges of the 1930s suggest, was that the *korenizatsiya* process itself was creating new nationalized elites, not internationalists.

Korenizatsiya policies achieved impressive results, and international equalization, if not yet outright equality, occurred during the 1920s and 1930s. Because *korenizatsiya* coincided with the desires for geographic and social mobilization of the indigenous masses, and along with federalization accommodated their developing sense of national self-consciousness and their sense of exclusiveness regarding their standing in the homeland, it is not surprising that these policies were effective. The following sections examine the impact of *korenizatsiya* and development generally on national consolidation and international integration processes during the interwar period.

NATIONAL CONSOLIDATION AND NATIONAL TERRITORIALITY

As discussed in chapter 2, before the revolution the majority of the population's primary form of identity was more localist than nationalist, though this was changing with geographic and social mobilization. Even after 1917, a more localized subnational or ethnographic level of identity remained strongly felt, and this was particularly the case in the less developed eastern and southern regions of the country. For example, during the 1924 ethnographic expedition to Bukhara and Khorezm mentioned above, one of the problems that researchers faced was the indigenes' lack of a basic understanding of the question: "To what tribe or clan do you belong?" (Zhdanko 1972, 23). In the same region, analysts have noted that indigenous urban intellectuals were as likely to consider themselves Bukharans (Hanaway 1973, 147–148) or Turkestanis (Becker 1973, 164) as they were to claim an ethnonational self-name. Still, these regional forms of identity did not appear to be shared by the masses at the time. According to the 1926 census, there were only 12,012 self-declared "Bukhartsy" (TsSU SSSR 1929, vol. 7:10). This statistical finding is echoed by Matley (1973, 141), who concluded "that a combination of ethnic, social, and geographical factors militated against the formation of an overall national identity among the people of the state of Bukhara." Similarly, Becker (1973, 167) found that a "Turkistan national consciousness never did progress beyond the thin stratum of modernist intelligentsia." The population of Central Asia was not unique in this regard; great ethnographic diversity existed throughout the country at this time. Even the dominant Russians continued to be divided ethnographically into Pomors, Pustozers, Ust'tsilems, Kerzhaks, Polekhs, Kolymchans, Kamchadals, various Cossack groups, and others until after the revolution (Bruk and Kabuzan 1982b, 14; Gurvich 1972, 19–20).

Korenizatsiya policies had the effect of accelerating the national consolidation of *ethnies* around the state, as isolated localities were integrated socially, culturally, economically, and politically into broader nations and homelands. The creation of standardized literary languages coupled with the rapid expansion of the education network in these languages not only enhanced nationalization processes that were already occurring (e.g., Chistov 1977b); these policies also helped to slow and even reverse the linguistic Russification of non-Russians (e.g., Gurvich and Taksami 1985; Kreindler 1985; Guthier 1977, 61). By targeting indigenes for preferential treatment, *korenizatsiya* policies, along with the geographic and social mobilization of indigenes, encouraged nationalization. The federalization of the state along ethnonational lines also encouraged the formation of a more expansive sense of homeland that had previously been limited to locality. The creation of officially recognized national homelands within which indigenes were placed in a privileged position *because* they were indigenes clearly enhanced the national consolidation process (Gardanov et al. 1961, 12).

A number of analysts have cited the declining number of ethnonational communities from 192 in 1926 to 97 in the 1939 census as evidence that national consolidation was occurring (e.g., Kozlov 1977b, 484–485). However, there are problems with drawing this conclusion. First, the 1926 census used the term *narodnost'*, from the root *narod* (a people), in order to get a more detailed ethnographic picture of the population living in the USSR, while the 1939 and subsequent censuses have used the term *natsional'nost'*, from the root *natsiya* (nation), in an attempt to gauge the level of mass national identity. Second, the number of nationalities listed in the 1939 census was kept artificially low in an effort to show that the peoples of the USSR were "drawing together." A number of people still identified themselves as Kipchaks, Yagnobs, Adzhars, and so forth, but were presented in the census, respectively, as members of the Uzbek, Tadzhik, and Georgian nations (Silver 1986). For this reason, the census results cannot be accepted at face value as evidence that national consolidation was occurring.

Nevertheless, one study comparing the size of selective ethnographic groups in 1959 with their membership in 1926 indicated that real national consolidation was taking place (Table 3.9), even though many people no doubt continued

TABLE 3.9
National Consolidation of Ethnographic Groups, 1926–1959 (total population claiming ethnographic identity in each census year)

Nation	Ethnographic Group	1926	1959
Uzbek	Fergana Tyurks	24,000	4,000
Uzbek	Kuramas	50,000	0
Uzbek	Kipchaks[a]	33,500	100
Tadzhik	Yagnobs	1,800	600
Tadzhik	Pamir Tadzhiks[b]	38,000	0
Georgian	Megrels (Mingrels)[c]	120,907	10
Georgian	Svans[c]	6,331	10
Georgian	Laz[c]	347	318
Azerbaydzhan	Tats	28,000	11,000

Source: Gardanov et al. 1961.

[a] Kipchaks: The 1959 figure is for Kipchaks in the Fergana Valley only. The Kipchak *ethnie* is also considered a part of the Kazakh nation (e.g., TsSU SSSR 1969, 9), and in all likelihood was consolidating with it during this period as well.

[b] Pamir Tadzhiks consist of nine ethnographic groups. According to Vinogradov (1968, vol. 1), between 45,500 and 50,000 still claimed one of the languages of these groups as their native tongue in 1959. Monogarova (1980, 125) also provides information on the Pamir Tadzhiks.

[c] Georgian ethnographic groups: According to Gardanov et al. (1961, 14), about 720 individuals still claimed Mingrel, Svan, or Laz as their native language in 1959.

to think of themselves primarily or at least secondarily as members of these subnational ethnographic groups. The process of this intranational drawing together occurred as a result of relatively high rates of intermarriage between members of these ethnographic groups (e.g., Gantskaya 1977, 433). For example, 80 percent of all marriages involving Kipchaks in Uzbekistan in 1936 were interethnic, primarily with (non-Kipchak) Uzbeks and Kazakhs (Borzykh 1984, 111). Over the course of generations, this resulted in a national consolidation of Kipchaks toward the locally dominant Uzbeks and Kazakhs. Evidence also suggests a national consolidation in Dagestan of the twenty-nine ethnographic groups into six nationalities during the interwar period, though this nationalization process was by no means complete by 1940 (Kushner 1951, 62; Ikhilov 1965). On the other hand, for several small indigenous groups in the northeast, the formation of nationality okrugs, rayons, and soviets, in addition to sociocultural and political *korenizatsiya*, served as impediments to greater interethnic drawing together while raising the level of national consciousness among these smaller, more localized *ethnies*.

The national consolidation encouraged by *korenizatsiya* was, in theory, to result in the international integration of the population into one Soviet people as development and political socialization proceeded. However, this "sovietization" of indigenes as they became more geographically and socially mobilized was less apparent. Instead, *korenizatsiya* and federalization interacted with the mobilization of the masses to produce a heightened "sense of exclusiveness" among indigenes regarding their status in and claim to the national homeland. Thus, according to Suny (1989, 282–290):

> In each union republic the titular nationality used its position to develop its own version of great power chauvinism, limiting where it was able the expression of its minorities. Georgia became a protected area of privilege for Georgians. They received the bulk of the rewards of the society, the leading positions in the state, and the largest subsidies for cultural projects, while the Armenians, Abkhazians, Ossetians, Ajarians, Kurds, Jews, and others were at a considerable disadvantage in the competition for the budgetary pie.

As this national territorality among non-Russian indigenes increased during the course of the 1920s and 1930s, it became clear to the center that the costs of *korenizatsiya* were outweighing the benefits.

A shift in policy favoring a more concerted effort at sovietization of the population through Russification was ushered in during the 1930s. The move away from *korenizatsiya* was most apparent in the political sphere, where indigenous elites who had implemented indigenization too enthusiastically were purged and replaced with individuals more willing to promote internationalization. However, in the sociocultural sphere, the shift away from *korenizatsiya* was less dramatic, and in several regions of the country barely preceded World War II. In the sociocultural and economic sectors, *korenizatsiya* lost momentum as a result of "benign neglect" from the center, which diminished the pressure placed on local elites to educate, hire, and promote indigenes (Fierman 1985, 213–215). In regions where the elites remained nonindigenous, the hiring and promotion of indigenes and the expanded use of their languages were reduced as soon as this pressure from the center was removed. However, in regions where nationalized indigenous elites had been created, purges were required to effect real change.

Even with the end of state-sponsored *korenizatsiya* by the late 1930s, it was difficult, if not impossible, to reverse the process of national consolidation and the rise of national territoriality among the indigenous masses, since the nationalization process itself coincided with the geographic and social mobilization of the masses, which had been an ongoing process before the 1920s, albeit at a relatively low level. Substituting a socialist for a nationalist content had not proven successful in breaking the link between socioeconomic development and the nationalization of the masses. By the 1930s, the center attempted to accelerate the pace of international integration through the use of Russian forms, or Russianization, which over time became a more nationally assertive policy of Russification (e.g., Aspaturian 1968).

INTERNATIONAL INTEGRATION AND RUSSIFICATION DURING THE 1930S

International integration was always the ultimate goal of the Communist party, and as noted above, the national federal system and *korenizatsiya* were seen as necessary expedients that in theory would accelerate not only the processes of international equalization and national consolidation but also (and dialectically) internationalization, as the members of each nation were socialized into one Soviet people (e.g., Gardanov et al. 1961, 12). Just as nationalization was promoted through social engineering, international drawing together or sovietization was also encouraged through the adoption of Russian national forms. During the 1920s and into the 1930s, although the promotion of the Russian language as the state lingua franca improved the status of Russians, and in all likelihood accelerated the national consolidation of the Russian masses, it was done for the sake of sovietization, not Russification (Szporluk 1980, 45). Indeed, this internationalist appropriation may have more than counteracted the nationalization effects, since Russian symbols of nationhood were appropriated as Soviet socialist symbols or replaced by a more internationalist iconography, and efforts at Soviet state-building impeded Russian nation-building (Allworth 1980). The appropriation of the fatherland image by the Communists was indicative of this general tendency (Lenin [1918] 1975, 436): "We are for 'defense of the fatherland'; but that patriotic war towards which we are moving is a war for a socialist fatherland, for socialism as a fatherland, for the Soviet Republic as a *contingent* of the world army of socialism." At this time, the homeland image was employed not in the service of the developing Russian nation but rather in the interests of world socialism. With the failure of a world socialist revolution to materialize and the shift toward developing socialism in one country, the fatherland image also appears to have undergone a metamorphosis such that it approximated *Rossiya* (i.e., the multinational empire), if not "Mother Russia." By the end of the 1930s a shift in favor of the Russian nation occurred, and Russification became less a means of sovietization and more an end in itself. With this shift, and particularly during World War II, "Mother Russia" and not the "socialist fatherland" became the central homeland image for the state.

Already by the second half of the 1920s, the Russian language was being promoted among non-Russians as the language of "international communication," thus creating a dialectic of linguistic processes in the country. During this time the first Russian language programs began in non-Russian schools, and by the mid-1930s non-Russians increasingly found it necessary to learn Russian (Guboglo 1977a, 266). Russian was becoming the language of upward mobility not only in the RSFSR but in the non-Russian republics as well. It was particularly difficult for the *ethnies* whose languages were used for instruction only in primary school to compete if their members were not also fluent in Russian. This shift in favor of the Russian language, accompanied by the replacement of the Latin with the Cyrillic script, became law in March of 1938, when the Central Committee of the Communist party passed a resolution "On the obligatory study of the Russian language in the schools of the national republics and oblasts," which stated (as quoted in Guboglo 1977a, 267): "Students, having completed incomplete secondary school (7th grade), must be able freely and accurately to express in the Russian language their ideas both orally and in writing, to have the habit of independent usage of books, corresponding to their age, to obtain an understanding of basic Russian grammar and syntax, and to some extent to become acquainted with Russian literature."

Still, in the growing competition between the indigenization of languages and the linguistic Russification of non-Russians, the latter was not making much headway among indigenes residing in their respective home republics during the Stalin period (Table 3.10).[22] With the exception of Ukrainians and Belorussians, nearly 100 percent of indigenes living in urban and rural areas of their home republics claimed the indigenous language as their native language (*rodnoy yazyk*) in both 1926 and 1959. For Ukrainians and Belorussians, the percent claiming the indigenous language as their native language actually increased between these two censuses.[23] The high and even increasing degree

---

[22] The depiction of language trends as the result of competing processes appears most accurate for this period, because for most *ethnies* in the state the indigenous language was being standardized and learned by the masses for the first time. The more typical alternative depiction of indigenes struggling to "retain" their "native languages" in the face of rising pressure for linguistic Russification from the center does not appear particularly accurate for the interwar period.

[23] This was in large part due to the fact that the western regions of each republic, a more ethnically homogeneous area for each, was outside the USSR in 1926 but was part of the state in 1959.

TABLE 3.10
Native Language Retention, 1926–1959 (percent of national members living in homeland urban [HU], homeland rural [HR], outside urban [OU] and outside rural [OR] locations)

Nation	HU		HR		OU		OR	
	1926	1959	1926	1959	1926	1959	1926	1959
Armenian	99.6	98.6	99.7	99.9	83.7	69.3	87.6	92.5
Tadzhik	99.6	97.9	99.2	99.6	99.2	92.7	95.5	95.1
Kazakh	99.5	98.1	99.9	99.5	57.3	91.6	95.1	96.8
Turkmen	99.4	98.0	99.2	100	94.8	81.6	66.1	93.8
Uzbek	99.2	97.2	99.0	99.0	99.3	94.9	99.3	98.5
Kirgiz	99.2	98.5	99.9	99.9	92.9	89.6	92.7	92.5
Georgian	98.7	98.9	96.4	99.9	76.8	68.3	88.1	86.3
Azerbaydzhan	98.5	97.7	92.5	98.3	97.5	87.0	95.6	98.1
Ukrainian	74.5	84.7	96.5	98.6	3.6	45.9	7.4	57.8
Belorussian	49.4	77.5	84.9	98.5	12.1	37.7	16.2	49.8

Sources: 1926: Guboglo 1977b, 297; 1959: TsSU SSSR 1962, 16 vols., Table 53.

of "native language" affiliation among indigenes during this period of great geographic and social mobilization is impressive, and indicates that a *korenizatsiya* of languages was proceeding even through a period of concerted Russification.

Outside the home republics, nonindigenes acculturated to the indigenous languages, and more significantly to Russian. However, even among those members living outside their home republic, where there was greater pressure to learn either the local indigenous language or Russian, most nonindigenes retained their own national languages to a high degree. In the case of Turkmen in outside rural areas, and of Kazakhs, Ukrainians, and Belorussians living in urban and rural areas outside their national homelands, the percent claiming their own national languages as their native language increased dramatically between 1926 and 1959. This is less a reflection of a renativization among these nonindigenes than it is an indicator that the more linguistically assimilated members of these groups living outside the homeland in 1926 identified themselves as members of other national communities in 1959. The more linguistically assimilated Ukrainians and Belorussians living outside their home republics, in particular, reidentified as Russians by 1959. The Kazakhs living in cities outside Kazakhstan and rural Turkmen outside Turkmenistan were mainly in Uzbekistan, and those who were assimilating most likely reidentified as Uzbeks by 1959.

To analyze the process of national reidentification, international marriage rates are a better measure than language change (e.g., Clem 1980). Particularly important is the national identity of children from such marriages; their choice of national identity may result in what Soviet ethnographers refer to as "natural assimilation" if they lean more heavily in favor of the national community of one parent over the other (Gantskaya 1977, 433). International marriage rates increased substantially between 1926 and 1936 as the population in the USSR became more geographically mobile, more urbanized, and consequently as international interaction increased. This was particularly the case in Belorussia, where the rate of intermarriage increased from 6.4 percent in 1926 to 19.4 percent in 1936. This was the highest rate of any union republic in 1936 (Table 3.11). On the surface, at least, international integration processes also appear to have been accelerating between the wars.

A key distinction in international marriage during this period and later was that it was a major tendency only among nonindigenes. For example, while 12 percent of Belorussian men and 10 percent of Belorussian women who entered into marriage in Belorussia married a member of another national community in 1936, 69 percent of Russian men and 75 percent of Russian women in Belorussia intermarried. The rate of intermarriage for Belorussian men increased from 2.7 percent in 1927 to 12.0 percent in 1936; for Belorussian women it increased from 4.9 percent to 10.0 percent during the same period. Between 1927 and 1936, the rate of intermarriage for Russian men in Belorussia increased from 20.7 percent to 69.3 percent; for Russian women it increased from 25.7 percent to 75.2 percent (Borzykh 1984, 103–108). The tremendous rise in the rate of Russian intermarriage during this period of *korenizatsiya* was

TABLE 3.11
International Marriage Rates by Republic and Indigenous Nation, 1936 (percent)

Republic	Total Population			Indigenes	
	Total	Urban	Rural	Men	Women
RSFSR	10.2	14.7	7.0	7.7	11.5
Ukraine	17.3	32.6	8.1	10.1	11.2
Belorussia	19.4	30.3	11.6	12.0	10.0
Georgia	17.4	23.8	11.1	12.4	6.2
Azerbaydzhan	9.6	17.6	3.7	4.0	3.7
Armenia	4.6	8.4	1.5	3.8	1.2
Kazakhstan	13.1	17.6	11.4	4.5	0.8
Uzbekistan	11.9	17.3	9.6	6.3	3.3
Kyrgyzstan	16.4	25.0	13.9	6.0	1.2
Tadzhikistan	14.3	25.0	12.2	9.2	5.1
Turkmenistan	14.4	25.5	6.1	6.0	1.2
Total USSR	12.5	18.4	7.8	—	—

Source: Borzykh 1984, 104–105.

matched in other republics by Russians and other nonindigenes. The differential between indigenes and nonindigenes was at least as great in other republics, where the indigenous *ethnies* were not as closely related to the dominant Russians as were the Belorussians.

In regions such as Central Asia, two intermarriage patterns developed. First, closely related local *ethnies* (i.e., the ethnographic groups making up the indigenous population) intermarried with one another during this period, and this was bringing about the national consolidation of Uzbeks, Turkmen, and so forth, in their respective home republics. Here, international integration, such as the apparent Kazakh and Turkmen assimilation to the Uzbek nation, was more likely a process of national consolidation, where members of subnational ethnographic groups identified as part of the Kazakh nation but located in Uzbekistan intermarried with members of closely related ethnographic groups who were identified as part of the Uzbek nation. On the other hand, the Slavic in-migrants intermarried with one another at high rates, and this appears to have resulted in a Russification of the nonindigenous population over time.

These trends suggest that international integration was occurring through the assimilation of nonindigenes toward the indigenous *ethnies* or alternatively toward the Russian nation if the marriage was between two nonindigenes and one was Russian. During the period of *korenizatsiya*, children of indigenous-nonindigenous marriages most often identified as members of the indigenous group, and this occurred even among the indigenous peoples of Siberia. For example, a majority of children of intermarriages involving Khanty, Sel'kups, and Evenks chose the national identity of the parent who was indigenous, because indigenes enjoyed privileged status regarding education, health care, and even tax rates (Sokolova 1961, 50). International integration tended to result not in an anational drawing together of groups into one Soviet people but rather in the nationalization of nonindigenes toward the indigenous *ethnie*.

Still, according to census results, the period from 1926 to 1939 was a time of massive reidentification toward the Russian nation. Bruk and Kabuzan (1982b, 13) have estimated that Russification between 1926 and 1939 accounted for an unprecedented 45 percent of the growth of the Russian nation during this time, and involved nearly 10 million non-Russians. This level of "assimilation" was truly aberrant, compared to an estimated 300,000 non-Russians who reidentified as Russians between 1917 and 1926 (16 percent of Russian population growth), and even to the 4.7 million estimate between 1939 and 1959 (34 percent of Russian population growth) (Bruk and Kabuzan 1982b, 13). The rate of national reidentification between 1926 and 1939 was especially high among Ukrainians living in the RSFSR in general, and in the northern Caucasus region in particular (Dzyuba 1970, 188; Lewis et al. 1976, 219). Gurvich (1972, 20) estimates that around 3 million Ukrainians reidentified as Russians between 1926 and 1939. It is interesting that the Belorussians, whose national consciousness was certainly weaker than that of Ukrainians, were not a major component of those reidentifying as Russians during this period, though some Belorussians living outside their home republic and particularly in Siberia were apparently involved in this Russification (Lewis et al. 1976, 222). The reason for the relatively lower level of reidentification among Belorussians was undoubtedly the comparatively greater degree of concentration of Belorussians in their homeland and in a relatively more rural, nationally homogeneous environment. Belorussians outside Belorussia in the RSFSR declined precipitously between 1926 and 1939, and much of this was the result of reidentification to the Russian nation.

A relatively higher rate of ethnonational reidentification may have been expected during this time, since a national consciousness was only beginning to become mass-based for most of these groups. At least for those Slavic nonindigenes who migrated from their homelands before extensive nationalization (and this especially applies to rural out-migrants), the intermarriage and integration would appear more akin to national consolidation, since these individuals in all likelihood had developed no strong sense of national consciousness before their out-migration. The intermarriage rates with Russians for Ukrainians, Belorussians, Mordvinians, and so forth, living outside their respective home republics was particularly high, and the children of such intermarriages were more likely to choose Russian over another identity (e.g., Gurvich 1972, 20).

The probability of this reidentification occurring increased after the shift away from *korenizatsiya* and in favor of Russification. This change in nationality policy was undoubtedly partly responsible for the dramatic rise in reidentification to the Russian nation in the 1939 census. To the degree that this Russification was forced and not voluntary, it is highly questionable whether it corresponded with a true "drawing together" of nations in the state, and more likely resulted in just the opposite. For, as Connor (1972, 351–352) found in his path-breaking study of "nation-building" and "nation-destroying" in the contemporary world, attempts to forcibly accelerate the pace of assimilation have more often than not proved counterproductive. The harshness of penalties against displays of "local nationalism" during the 1930s may have been successful in dampening this sort of overt political behavior, and the growing favor shown Russians may have encouraged several non-Russians living in the RSFSR to identify themselves as Russians to census takers in 1939. However, the national problem was in all likelihood becoming more, not less severe as a consequence of these policy decisions, particularly since they came on the heals of *korenizatsiya*.

During the latter half of the 1930s, as noted above, purges of indigenous party and government officials in the republics on charges of fomenting "bourgeois nationalism," "localism," and so on, became commonplace, and culminated in the Great Purges of 1937–1938 (Conquest 1968; Connor 1984a, 280). In 1936 the nationality rayons and soviets were abolished (Kuznetsov 1990, 6).

By 1939 the national territorial units of the Red Army were abolished in favor of mixed nationality units in order to promote international integration. Each of these reversals was a signal that *korenizatsiya* and federalization, along with the accelerated geographic and social mobilization of indigenes, had encouraged both the further nationalization of indigenous elites, as well as a rising sense of exclusiveness among the increasingly nationalized indigenous masses.

Clearly, by the mid-1930s, Stalin had rejected the importance of international equalization in solving the national question and returned to the system of ethnic stratification and nationality policies favored during the late-nineteenth-century tsarist period (i.e., Russification). In this radical departure from the precepts of Leninism, Stalin appeared to signal his lack of faith that the national dialectical process leading to the merger and denationalization of the population was inevitable and would occur spontaneously with development and equalization. Rather, social engineering was now viewed as essential to the success of the dialectic. This Stalinist "deformation" undoubtedly had an effect on the evolution of the national question in the USSR. However, it is highly dubious whether international equalization, even if it had been continuously pursued and achieved, would have resulted in the denationalization of the population. On the contrary, the equalization and socioeconomic development that were occurring between the wars, coupled as they were with federalization and *korenizatsiya*, were working together to accelerate the nationalization of the masses and to raise their sense of exclusiveness regarding their own status within their nominal homelands.

After World War II the favoritism shown Russians continued. Even though several non-Russians suffered proportionally greater losses than the Russians during the war (Anderson and Silver 1983), the Russian nation was said to have sacrificed most in the defense of the socialist fatherland. According to Tillett (1969, 86), during the years 1946 to 1953 (i.e., postwar Stalinism):

> The doctrine of Great Russian leadership, which had been growing during the War, now knew no bounds. Stalin had inaugurated the unlimited celebration of Russian national greatness in his famous toast on May 24, 1945, in honor of Red Army commanders. He proposed a toast to the Russian people, not to the Soviet people in general, and stated his reasons: (1) "It is the leading nation of all the nations belonging to the Soviet Union"; (2) "it earned in this war general recognition as a guiding force of the Soviet Union"; and (3) "it has a clear mind, a firm character and patience."

The third reason, in treating the Russian nation as a living organism, harks back to the romantic nationalism of the nineteenth-century Slavophiles.

During the interwar period, the Communist party leadership attempted to solve the national problem through a complex set of policies. The use of territorial autonomy and the promotion of *korenizatsiya* or "indigenization" within each national homeland were critical to the development of a "sense of homeland" among the indigenous masses, who were only beginning to imagine themselves as members of something more ethnographically and geographically expansive than their local communities. These nationality policies also encouraged a "sense of exclusiveness" in the way indigenes perceived their status in their own respective home republics.

This is not to say that nationality policies during the interwar period created the nations that currently exist in the former USSR. The process of national consolidation had been occurring before the October Revolution, and with this process a sense of homeland was also developing. Nevertheless, for most nations the process of nationalization had involved only the elites by 1917, and the masses primarily lived rural, isolated, localized lives. The nationality policies, in addition to the collectivization of agriculture and the rapid industrialization of the country, disrupted this rural localism and promoted the nationalization of the masses in a much more extensive way.

The ultimate goal of international integration was promoted only indirectly for much of the interwar period. During the early 1920s, international integration was seen as an almost natural outcome of international equalization and socioeconomic development, or modernization. By the late 1920s to early 1930s, this Leninist position had given way to a more active attempt to socialize (i.e., "sovietize") the masses. During this second phase, the failure of international integration to occur spontaneously was blamed on the nationalized political elites, who were labeled "bourgeois nationalists," "localists," and so forth. During the 1930s, these indigenous political elites were increasingly purged. Finally, on the eve of World War II, a third phase was initiated, marking an end to sociocultural *korenizatsiya* and the more active promotion of Russification. Purges of the indigenous political elites were not enough to bring about internationalization, and the nationalization of the non-Russian masses was increasingly viewed as threatening to the state. Russification was promoted not only as a means to accelerate the pace of international integration but also as an end in itself. The anational state ideal of Lenin had been transformed into a Russian nation-state ideal by 1940.

None of these three policy sets solved the national problem, though the latter two raised the costs of nationalist behavior to the point that overt nationalism was no longer a threat to the Soviet state. Socioeconomic development was rapid during the interwar period, and international equalization was occurring across a broad spectrum of sociocultural, economic, and political arenas. Equality was achieved in the basics, such as literacy and elementary education, and this occurred along with the development of indigenous literary languages. Equalization, though not equality, was occurring in higher education and the development of a nonagricultural work force. Indigenes also gained positions of authority in the governmental and party organizations of their homelands. However, international equalization through *korenizatsiya* was leading not to a growing proletarian internationalism but to growing demands by indigenous nationalists for a dominant position within their own home republics. This national territoriality was an unintended consequence of Leninist-Stalinist nationality policies, and the growth of this territorial nationalism encouraged a shift away from *korenizatsiya* by the mid-1930s.

The drawing together (*sblizheniye*) of nations into one Soviet people was less apparent. The international integration or assimilation that was taking place during the interwar period was primarily occurring among nonindigenes. They were acculturating to and intermarrying with the indigenous or the Russian national community. The children of indigenous-nonindigenous parents identified themselves as members of the indigenous nation, and this was particularly strong when *korenizatsiya* was in full swing. Children of Russian-nonindigenous parents most often chose a Russian national identity. In either case, much of this apparent international integration was more akin to national consolidation, since the nonindigenes undergoing a process of assimilation in all likelihood had a weakly developed sense of national consciousness at the time.

The shift to support for Russification and away from *korenizatsiya* at the end of the period may be seen as an admission that the drawing together of nations would not occur as a "natural" consequence of development and equalization, and that this *sblizheniye* must be socially engineered. The Russification of nonindigenes, which reached a figure of more than ten million between 1926 and 1939, may have also reflected a nationalization of earlier Slavic outmigrants from Ukraine and Belorussia whose sense of national consciousness was only weakly developed. Finally, under conditions of coercion such as those that existed during 1939, it is likely that many of these Slavic nonindigenes chose a Russian national identity even if they did not feel themselves to be Russians.[24]

The use of a territorial solution to the national question in the multihomeland USSR by both Lenin and Stalin raises the question of whether either of these two Soviet leaders understood the desire of nationalists to control their own homelands (i.e., national territoriality). A number of reasons suggest that they did not. First, Lenin's use of turn-of-the-century Americanization in New York City as an analogy of what would occur in Russia with modernization and urbanization completely overlooked the difference between an immigrant population seeking to fit in on the one hand, and an indigenous population seeking to assert its proprietary claims to homeland on the other. As indigenes in Russia and the USSR became more educated, urbanized, and so forth, they also tended

---

[24] The Ukrainians and others "lost" to the Russian nation between 1926 and 1939 did not reappear in the 1959 census, which may be taken as an indication that at least a portion of this Russification did represent national consolidation of nonindigenes to the Russian nation. However, a definitive statement on this issue is not possible, since the period between 1939 and 1959 was one of massive demographic disruption, which has masked any reidentification to the Ukrainian nation that might have occurred between 1939 and 1959.

to assert their claims to territory more vehemently. National territoriality thus undermined the "drawing together" of nations that was to have occurred with development and equalization. Similarly, Stalin's view of the homeland as an empty container within which nations could be created and destroyed ignored the significance of the subjective "sense of place" that served as an integral element in the way indigenes defined themselves and viewed the world around them. If he had understood this, he should not have been surprised that *korenizatsiya* from above served as a catalyst activating an indigenous sense of exclusiveness rather than fostering greater international understanding and brotherhood. Indeed, if either had understood the territorial dimension of nationalism it is at least questionable whether they would have advocated a territorial solution to the national question as strongly as they did.

After the death of Stalin in 1953, the USSR renewed its *korenizatsiya* policies and retained its federal structure. The post-Stalin period has also been a time of rapid geographic and social mobilization of the population, but with each indigenous national community remaining concentrated in its own respective homeland. Nationalization of these indigenous masses, which began before the revolution and accelerated during the 1920s and 1930s, continued after the war. Indeed, it is in the postwar era that the USSR confronted a mass-based national problem for the first time. Attempts to solve this new national problem with old nationality policies—policies designed when national consciousness among the masses was relatively weak, and policies that had made international relations in the state more intractable, if anything, during the interwar period—served to heighten national territoriality among increasingly nationalistic indigenes. In part 2, the dimensions of this national territoriality in the postwar USSR are explored.

PART TWO

National Territoriality in the Postwar USSR

CHAPTER FOUR

Population Redistribution and National Territoriality, 1959–1989

As NOTED in chapter 3, the leaders of the Communist party displayed a great degree of ambivalence regarding both the creation of the USSR as a federation of national republics, as well as the role these republics were to play in the life of the multinational, multihomeland state. Lenin's early writings on the subject (e.g., [1913] 1968) supported the creation of autonomous units toward which members of the indigenous nations would "gravitate." The resulting national homogeneity of autonomous regions would, however, reduce the potential for international integration, which was said to be the primary objective of Communists with regard to the national question. Lenin's support in the 1920s for a federal, and even a confederal power-sharing system between central anational communist elites and peripheral indigenous elites was half-hearted at best; it was viewed as a necessary evil until the entire population could be successfully "sovietized."

This ambivalence regarding the national question and its territorial dimension continued during the interwar period. Stalin's support for "autonomization" coincided more with Lenin's early writings. The system that emerged during the 1920s and 1930s took on the appearance of a confederation of sovereign republics, but the real power structure in the state became increasingly unitary during the Stalin era. This does not mean that the "confederal form" was unimportant. This structuring of the state along national territorial lines had a real impact on the nationalization and political mobilization of the indigenous masses (Connor 1984a, 1986; Kaiser 1991).

In addition to the political geographic restructuring of the state, *korenizatsiya* policies, which provided for preferential treatment of indigenes within their homelands but not outside, tended to promote national segregation (i.e., gravitation and homogenization). This contradicted the desire for greater international mixing and integration, which were more actively supported later in the 1930s. The acceleration of assimilation through the Russification of the population was encouraged both through laws promoting the Russian language to a position of primacy and through an officially sponsored attitude that imparted to Russians the status of "first among equals," "elder brother," and so on. These "Russians first" policies were especially apparent during the postwar Stalin years (e.g., Tillett 1969; Connor 1984a).

During the post-Stalin era, central authorities, Soviet ethnographers, and others spoke and wrote favorably of the rising international contact that had come with socioeconomic development. It has been a central tenet of Marxist-Leninist theory regarding the national question that this increasing social and geographic mobilization corresponded with an international "drawing together" (*sblizheniye*) that would over time lead to greater international integration or merger (*sliyaniye*) into one Soviet people. As this occurred, the national connection to homeland itself was to have eroded to a point where there would be no need for the confederal structure. Thus, according to the 1961 Communist Party Program (*Programma KPSS* 1961, 84): "In the soviet republics people of many nationalities live and work together. The borders between union republics within the USSR are increasingly losing their former significance, since all nations have equal rights, their life is constructed on a unified socialistic basis and the material and spiritual needs of each people are satisfied to an equal degree, they all are united by common life interests in one family and in common go toward one goal—communism."

The official position regarding the rate at which this merging of nations was to have occurred varied over time (Connor 1984a). Khrushchev favored an accelerated pace for the attainment of communism in the USSR, which was slated for 1980. This implied that the rate of international drawing together would also accelerate, although like Lenin, Khrushchev envisioned complete merger (*sliyaniye*) only in the distant future (Smith 1990, 8). During the Brezhnev years, the emphasis was placed on a more gradual drawing together (*sblizheniye*) of nations into one Soviet people in a socioeconomic and political sense. Their actual *sliyaniye*, implying the loss of national self-consciousness, was pushed into the background in discussions about international integration during this time. However, the basic theoretical assumption that socioeconomic development, and with it rising geographic mobilization and international mixing, would lead to the erosion if not the complete eradication of national self-consciousness was retained throughout much of the postwar period. It is evident that Gorbachev began his tenure as leader of the Communist party believing not only that this theoretical relationship was accurate but also that the process of integration into one Soviet people had been by-and-large completed. This was evident from the beginning of his campaign for restructuring (*perestroyka*), which made the assumption that a Soviet people existed whose primary concern was to make the USSR work more efficiently in providing for the needs of its citizens. Even as late as 1988, Gorbachev (1988a, 122) continued to cling to this belief: "In my travels to the republics and national regions of the Soviet Union, meeting there with people, each time I am more and more convinced that they value and take pride in the fact that their peoples belong to one large international family, that they are an integral part of a large and great country, which occupies so significant a place in the progress of humankind. This is *soviet* patriotism." The perception that a Soviet identity had become primary in the lives of the peoples of the USSR was quickly proven wrong when people were given the freedoms of expression that they had lacked for so long. This misperception of successful "sovietization," perhaps more than anything else, doomed *perestroyka* as an effort to revitalize Soviet socialism.

Rising international tensions and hostilities resulting from a growing "sense of exclusiveness" among indigenes as they interacted more intensely with nonindigenes was not recognized as a potential outcome of greater international mixing per se. At most, incidents of "national chauvinism," "national exclusivity," "bourgeois nationalism," "localism," and so forth, were thought to be the result of mistakes made by local or central authorities, or alternatively the work of a deviant few, and at any rate as something outside the norm of behavior for "socialist nations" (e.g., Gardanov et al. 1961, 26–27). More recently, the lack of international harmony in the state has been blamed on a Stalinist deformation of Lenin's national policies, which tended to force the pace of international mixing (e.g., Iskenderov 1989, 3; Gorbachev 1988a, 121).

It has become increasingly apparent that rising international interaction in general, and interhomeland migration in particular, have served as catalysts activating national territoriality. More broadly, the dilution of the indigenous nation's demographic strength in the homeland has served as a symbol of the center's efforts to eradicate the nation and its claim to the ancestral homeland. Ethnodemographic processes in general, and interhomeland migration in particular, have become emotionally charged issues serving to rally the national membership behind the goals of national separatism.

This alternative outcome of greater international and interhomeland geographic mobility has been found in a number of studies conducted outside the USSR. For example, Weiner's study (1978, 274–281) of the appropriately labeled "sons of the soil" in India substantiates the hypothesis that in-migration of nonindigenes is one of the most important conditions contributing to rising "nativism," which Weiner defined as "intense opposition to minorities because of their foreign origin." This is the essential equivalent of an activated sense of exclusiveness. Similarly, Shibutani and Kwan (1965, 445), in a comparative study of ethnic stratification, found that "the national land is often regarded as a group possession (by indigenes) on which foreigners are interlopers." Other studies have found a similar relationship between increasing international mixing in a multihomeland context and rising "nativism," or a more overtly expressed sense of exclusiveness (e.g., Connor 1986; Horowitz 1985; Soja 1971).

In part 1, historic evidence was found of this sense of exclusiveness, expressed both as anti-outsider nativism in isolated rural localities, and also as a more expansive national territoriality among the more urbanized and socially mobilized indigenes. The activation of national territoriality has also been the dominant response to increasing international interaction in the postwar USSR. This chapter examines the degree of international mixing that occurred between 1959 and 1989, and provides an overview of the effects this has had on international relations in the state. The focus is on interhomeland mobility and international mixing within homelands generally. An additional dimension of geographic mobilization—urbanization—is dealt with in the following chapter, since it is also an important surrogate measure of social mobilization.[1]

Before beginning this analysis, however, a few methodological considerations must be discussed. The principle methodological issue concerns the dilemma over how to delimit national homelands in order that the behavior of indigenes and nonindigenes may be studied. In this study we use the officially delimited territories (ODTs) comprising the Soviet federation (Map 4.1) as surrogates for the national homelands, while recognizing that this approach has a number of problems. As noted in previous chapters, the ancestral homeland as perceived by nationalists is often not equivalent to these union republics and autonomous units. For several nations, a large proportion of the members living outside the home republic live in bordering oblasts, reflecting either poorly drawn borders, regions where international mixing of population was great at the time of delimitation, or movement of the national members since these borders were established.

The problem, of course, with using the current demographic extent of the nation to adjust the borders of the national homeland is that it ignores the historic argument for inclusion of certain lands as part of the national homeland. Adjacent regions may have recently become new places of settlement, as is apparently the case for the Komi-Permyaks, Khakass, and Ingush. This is also true of the dominant Russians, who have over the past century migrated outward from their traditional northwestern core area in large numbers. It is difficult to argue that current ethnodemographic dominance should dictate national homeland borders. For example, Russian nationalist perceptions of "Mother Russia" have expanded with the growth of the state through conquest and the designation of Russians as the core nation (Connor 1986; Drobizheva 1991a). However, although regions where Russians currently comprise a majority of the population may be claimed by these same Russian nationalists as part of their rightful homeland, this does not mean that the perceptions of homeland by members of the nations who have been demographically overtaken have also diminished. While Russians may claim the northern oblasts of Kazakhstan as a part of their contemporary homeland (e.g., V. Osipov 1990; Solzhenitsyn 1990; Olcott 1993, 315–317), it is nonetheless true that Kazakhs would argue vehemently against any change in their own homeland borders (Olcott 1990). The violent Kazakh demonstrations in 1986 sparked by the removal of Kunayev, the First Party Secretary of Kazakhstan and a Kazakh, and his replacement by the Russian Kolbin provided strong evidence of the indigenes' sense of exclusiveness regarding their status in the homeland vis-à-vis

[1] Of course, the relationship between geographic mobilization and international relations is not an isolated one but is connected with socioeconomic, sociocultural, and political developments as well. For this reason, this relationship will be discussed in each of the following chapters.

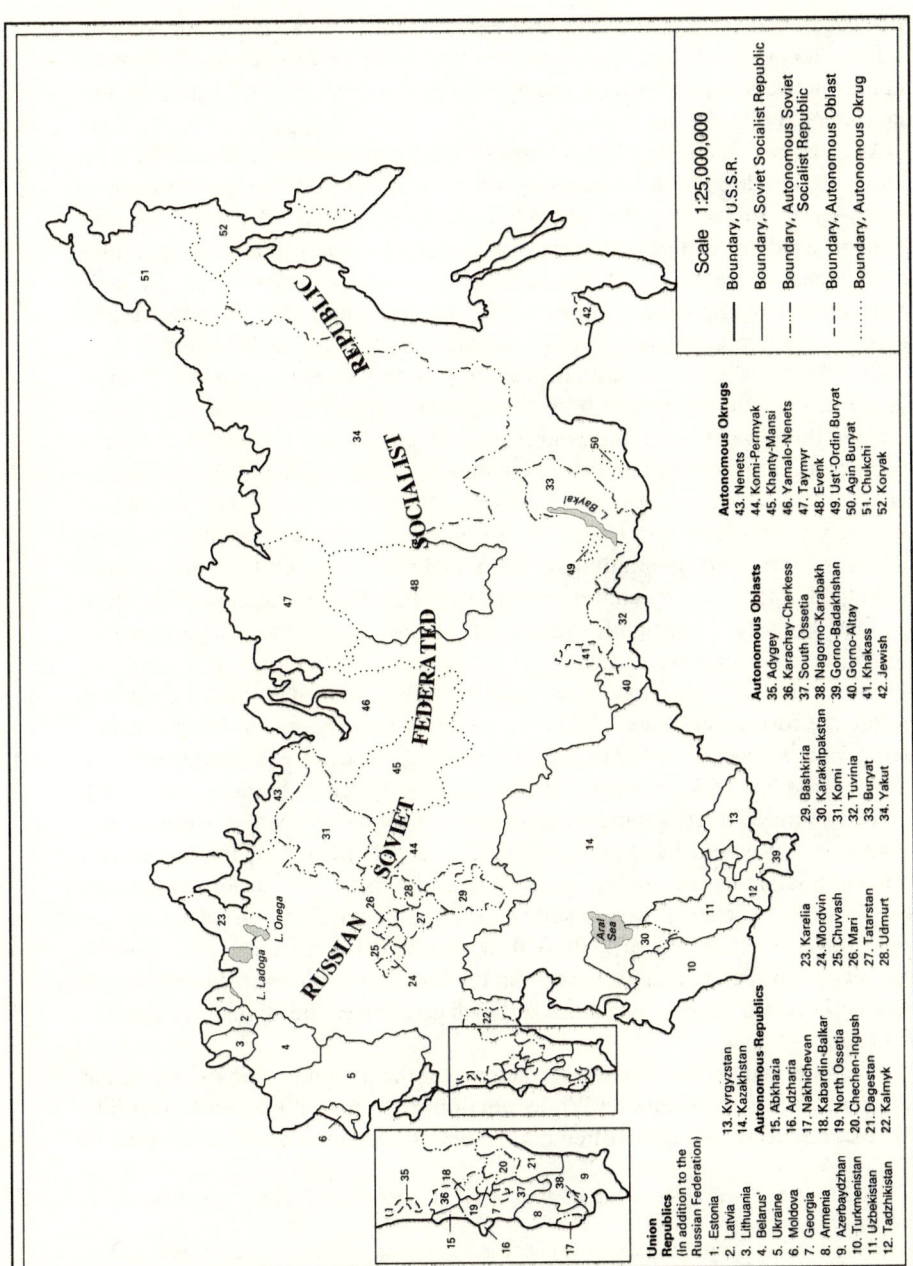

Map 4.1 Federal Structure of the USSR, 1989

Russians. More generally, as we have seen in Central Asia, Transcaucasia, the Baltics, Ukraine, Moldova, and increasingly within Russia itself, the border regions between republics have become the geographic focus of a great deal of international tension and conflict.[2]

As discussed in chapter 3, it is possible that the borders of some ODTs were poorly drawn due to the weakness of national identity in a given region. For example, the union republics of Soviet Central Asia and the autonomous regions in northern and eastern Russia were delimited at a time when the indigenes' sense of national self-consciousness was not well developed. In addition, several of the *ethnies* in these regions were nomadic, which certainly added to the confusion surrounding the question of homeland delimitation.

This does not, however, explain why the borders were not redrawn in areas where this would have been both possible and appropriate. One suggestion made in this regard is that the central government wanted to keep local border disputes alive in order to prevent the creation of regional alliances that might have weakened the center (e.g., Rakowska-Harmstone 1970, 27). While this may have some element of truth, it is also frequently the case that the members of each nation, while continuing to claim land beyond the ODT as part of their ancestral homeland, have come to perceive all the territory encompassed within the ODT as part of their rightful homeland. In other words, the official delimitation of national republics in the USSR has helped to structure or give form to a sense of homeland that was only vaguely perceived in most parts of the country before the formation of the USSR.[3] The ODT has thus come to be seen as the geographic *minimum* of the ancestral homeland. Under these conditions, any effort on the part of Moscow to "correct" the poorly drawn borders would have created as much international antagonism as it solved, since the nation losing almost surely would have perceived this as a loss of part of the homeland. Beyond this, adjusting borders for national reasons in one part of the country would almost certainly have resulted in rising demands for similar changes in dozens of other regions. Both these problems were clearly evident in the center's reluctance to use territorial reallocation in an effort to resolve the dispute between Armenians and Azerbaydzhanis over the status of Nagorno-Karabakh.

An additional problem arises in reference to the national composition of the adjacent oblasts themselves.[4] While a nation's population may spill over into these contiguous areas, it is often not the only or even the majority population

---

[2] These international tensions and conflicts along the interrepublic border are discussed in greater detail in chapter 7.

[3] For a broader, comparative discussion of "regions as social constructs," see Murphy (1991).

[4] Oblasts are the smallest units for which nationality data are normally available, and therefore are the smallest units available for adjusting the geographic dimensions of national homelands in this study.

there. Including these units in the homeland in this analysis would often result in the dilution of the eponymous nation as a percent of the total homeland population. For example, the adjacent oblasts for the Chukchi, Khanty, and Evenks are so vast and include so many other more numerous national populations that their inclusion in the autonomous okrugs of these nationalities would not provide a more accurate geographic delimitation of national homelands. The statistical "pollution" that such inclusions would create becomes a greater problem than the one that they are meant to overcome. For these reasons, residence in the home republics (ODTs) is used as a surrogate for homeland residence in this study.

In addition to the possibility that internal borders may not accurately reflect the demographic extent of the nation, it should also be noted that interstate borders often dissect nations and homelands (Connor 1986, 20): "The political borders of states have been superimposed upon the ethnic map with cavalier disregard for ethnic homelands." This general statement is certainly true of the interstate borders of the USSR. Throughout the southern tier, ethnonational communities and homelands were severed by the interstate border between the USSR and Turkey, Iran, Afghanistan, and China. This was also true for Belarus' and Ukraine before World War II. In this case the USSR used a combination of historic and demographic arguments to expand into Eastern Europe, thus reducing the irredentas to a minimum for these two nations. Finally, in the case of Moldova, the USSR sought to establish a separate nation in what was part of the Rumanian *ethnie* and homeland prior to its incorporation into the Russian Empire and then the USSR.[5]

One question often asked is this: Does the existence of a closed interstate border over time lead to the creation of two separate nations where there was one?[6] For the border *ethnies* in the former USSR, the boundary was often drawn before national consolidation. This was certainly the case in Central Asia and southern Siberia, as well as in Azerbaydzhan, Belarus', and Ukraine. However, the myth of a more expansive "natural" and "eternal" nation and homeland that was artificially severed by state borders has become important in the political mobilization of the masses since the late 1980s. In addition, external events, such as the reunification of Germany, have served as catalysts for rising irredentism, particularly in Azerbaydzhan and Moldova. Nationalists from the Moldovan People's Front have declared that the independence of the "Republic of

---

[5] The majority of Moldova was part of Rumania during the interwar period. Interestingly, that part which remained in the USSR—the left bank of the Dnestr River that is adjacent to Ukraine and was part of the Moldavian ASSR during the interwar period—declared its sovereignty as the Dnestr Republic on 2 September 1990. It is a region of Moldova populated primarily by Russians and Ukrainians that has become the scene of international conflict since 1991. See chapter 7.

[6] Pletsch (1979) offers an example of this in his assessment of whether or not an East German "socialist nation" had come into existence.

Moldova" is a preliminary stage in the eventual reunification with Rumania (FBIS 12 October 1990, 60).

The division of a nation and its homeland between two or more states often means that domestic attempts to manage national conflicts must take into account the interstate setting, and conversely that interstate relations may affect the status of a national community whose co-nationals are the dominant nation of another state. In Eastern Europe, the Magyars and Albanians outside Hungary and Albania have found themselves in this often unenviable position. In an effort to avoid this situation in its relations with Rumania, the USSR "created" the Moldavian nation; similarly, the appearance of a Macedonian nation was at least in part an attempt by Yugoslavia to dampen irredentist claims emanating from Bulgaria (King 1973; Shoup 1968). However, while a Macedonian and Moldavian national identity did not exist at the time of these attempts at nation-making, and although a general sense of belonging respectively to the Bulgarian and Rumanian ethnonational communities did exist, a localist or regional Macedonian and Moldavian identity—to some extent separate and distinct from their neighboring regions and *ethnies*—was also apparent (e.g., King 1973, 218; Semenov' Tyan'-Shanskiy 1910, 14:184–202).

The interstate dimension of the national question is beyond the scope of this study but will be considered when evidence suggests that the status as an irredenta has a significant effect on the strength of solidarity within a given nation. At this point it may be suggested that the Azerbaydzhanis and Moldavians in the former USSR are likely candidates in this regard. The focus in this chapter will be on the internal distribution and redistribution of each nation's population, with reference to the segment of the national homeland that lies within the former USSR.

NATIONAL "GRAVITATION" TO THE HOMELAND

The decision to migrate is complex, and is primarily related to "life-cycle events" such as the attainment of adulthood, marriage, change of employment, retirement, and so forth (Long 1988, 256–257). Where people move is determined by their assessment of economic and sociocultural conditions at given destinations, the distance of alternative destinations from the area of origin, as well as political factors such as borders and migration laws that facilitate or inhibit the development of migration streams. For the most part, people the world over move in response to geographic differentials in economic opportunity and standards of living, and this holds true for planned as well as for market economies (Lewis and Rowland 1979; Mitchneck 1991).

In any cursory examination of the national map of the USSR, or the world for that matter, it is readily apparent that nations have not been dispersed throughout states but are instead concentrated in what members perceive to be their national homelands (Table 4.1; Map 4.2).[7] While this population distribution pattern is certainly, in part, due to the force of inertia, the lack of a more thorough redistribution of nations as their members have become more socially mobilized and urbanized indicates that both the nation and its homeland have retained a degree of primacy that certainly would not have been predicted either by Marxism-Leninism or "developmentalism." The continued concentration of indigenes in their respective homelands appears to be the result of conscious decision making by an increasingly educated, upwardly mobilized populace, and not simply a reflection of the lack of mobility expected of a primarily rural, traditional society. This suggests that homelands have exerted a "pull" on members of the indigenous nations that has helped to hold them in place even while their members have become more socially mobilized. In addition, homelands appear to exert a "push" against nonindigenes.[8] Interhomeland migration in response to geographic differentials in economic opportunity occurred in the USSR but was tempered both by an attachment to homeland and also by the successful indigenization of life in the national homelands, which placed nonindigenes in a disadvantageous position vis-à-vis members of the indigenous nation (Rybakovskiy and Tarasova 1990, 39–40). Consequently, the interhomeland migration stream was much weaker than the intrahomeland movement.

Changes in the concentration of national communities in their respective home republics indicate that in general there was not a great degree of dispersal between 1959 and 1989 (Table 4.1; Map 4.3). The only nations to experience a major change were the Kalmyk, Chechen, and Ingush, three of the nations deported from their homelands after World War II and allowed to return after 1956. The period from 1959 to 1970 appears to have been one of relatively great interhomeland redistribution of national communities, at least compared to the later period from 1970 to 1989. This is an indication that a relatively greater degree of forced migration occurred during the Stalin period, and that in the years following Stalin's death a migratory readjustment took place. The population redistribution occurring between 1959 and 1970 resulted primarily in a reconcentration of indigenes in their respective home republics for nations whose ODTs were union or autonomous republics. This "gravitation" toward the homeland by nations in the USSR was taking place at the same time that the

---

[7] As noted above, homeland is often not synonymous with the officially delimited home republics that comprise the Soviet federation. For many national communities, including the Turkmen, Kirgiz, Tadzhiks, Uzbeks, Kazakhs, Azerbaydzhanis, and Armenians, more than half of the national members residing outside their home republic live in oblasts adjacent to it (Goskomstat SSSR 1991a; Statisticheskiy Komitet SNG 1993, vol. 7).

[8] A general discussion of migration as a response by the individual to "push" and "pull" factors at areas of origin and destination, as well as the need to overcome "intervening obstacles" (e.g., restrictive borders and laws), may be found in Lee (1966).

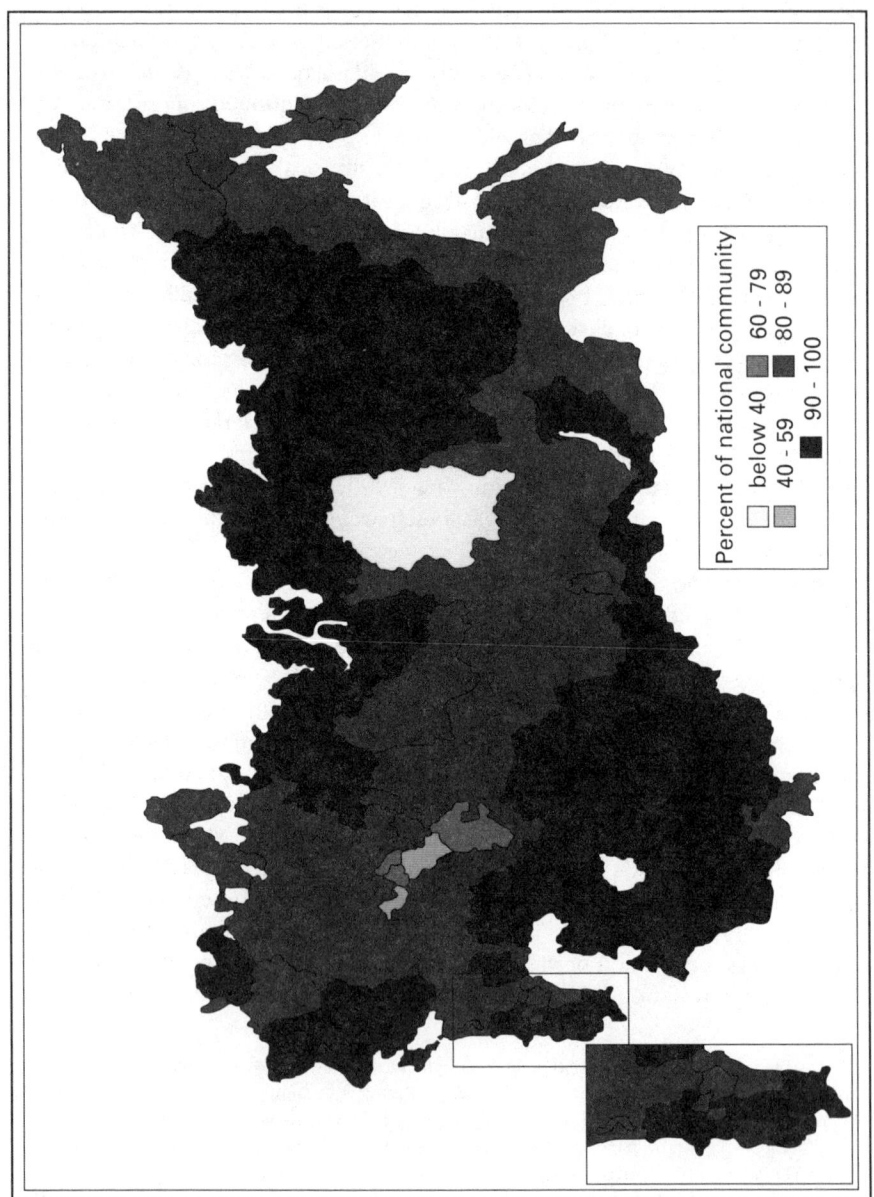

Map 4.2 Proportion of the National Community Residing in Its Home Republic, 1989

TABLE 4.1
The Concentration of National Members in Their Home Republics, 1959–1989
(percent of national members in republics, and percentage point change)

Nation	Percent				Percentage Point Change		
	1959	1970	1979	1989	1959–70	1970–79	1979–89
Union Republics							
Lithuanian	92.5	94.1	95.1	95.3	1.6	1.0	0.2
Latvian	92.7	93.8	93.4	95.1	1.1	−0.4	1.7
Georgian	96.6	96.5	96.1	95.1	−0.1	−0.4	−1.0
Estonian	90.3	91.9	92.9	93.8	1.6	1.0	0.9
Turkmen	92.2	92.9	93.3	93.0	0.7	0.4	−0.3
Kirgiz	86.4	88.5	88.5	88.2	2.1	0.0	−0.3
Azerbaydzhan	84.8	86.2	86.0	85.7	1.4	−0.2	−0.3
Ukrainian	86.3	86.6	86.2	84.7	0.3	−0.4	−1.5
Uzbek	83.8	84.0	84.9	84.7	0.2	0.9	−0.2
Moldavian	85.2	85.4	85.1	83.4	0.2	−0.3	−1.7
Russian	85.8	83.5	82.6	82.6	−2.3	−0.9	0.0
Kazakh	77.2	79.9	80.7	80.3	2.7	0.8	−0.4
Belorussian	82.5	80.5	80.0	78.8	−2.0	−0.5	−1.2
Tadzhik	75.2	76.3	77.2	75.3	1.1	0.9	−1.9
Armenian	55.7	62.1	65.6	66.7	6.4	3.5	1.1
Autonomous Republics							
Tuvin	97.9	97.1	97.5	96.0	−0.8	0.4	−1.5
Yakut	95.5	96.5	95.7	95.6	1.0	−0.8	−0.1
Kabardin	93.5	94.6	94.4	93.0	1.1	−0.2	−1.4
Karakalpak	90.4	92.2	92.9	91.9	1.8	0.7	−1.0
Abkhaz	93.5	92.9	91.4	88.6	−0.6	−1.5	−2.8
Komi	85.4	85.8	86.0	84.6	0.4	0.2	−1.4
Kalmyk	61.2	80.4	83.3	84.2	19.2	2.9	0.9
Kumyk	89.6	89.5	88.6	82.2	−0.1	−0.9	−6.4
Avar	88.5	88.1	86.7	82.0	−0.4	−1.4	−4.7
Buryat[a]	80.7	82.7	81.7	81.0	2.0	−1.0	−0.7
Balkar	80.4	86.3	90.0	83.2	5.9	3.7	−6.8
Dargin	93.7	90.0	85.9	76.8	−3.7	−4.1	−9.1
Chechen	58.2	83.0	80.9	76.8	24.8	−2.1	−4.1
Ingush	45.6	72.1	72.4	69.0	26.5	0.3	−3.4
Ossetian[a]	67.7	68.7	67.2	66.9	1.0	−1.5	−0.3
Udmurt	76.2	68.8	67.2	66.5	−7.4	−1.6	−0.7
Karelian	51.2	57.6	58.7	60.3	6.4	1.1	1.6
Bashkir	74.6	72.0	68.2	59.6	−2.6	−3.8	−8.6
Chuvash	52.4	50.5	50.7	49.2	−1.9	0.2	−1.5
Mari	55.4	50.0	49.3	48.3	−5.4	−0.7	−1.0
Lezgin	48.7	50.3	49.4	43.9	1.6	−0.9	−5.5

(*continued*)

TABLE 4.1 (*Continued*)

Nation	Percent				Percentage Point Change		
	1959	1970	1979	1989	1959–70	1970–79	1979–89
Mordvin	27.9	28.9	28.4	27.2	1.0	−0.5	−1.2
Tatar	27.1	25.9	26.0	26.6	−1.2	0.1	0.6
Autonomous Oblasts							
Altay	84.0	83.8	83.7	83.5	−0.2	−0.1	−0.2
Karachay	83.3	86.1	83.3	83.0	2.8	−2.8	−0.3
Khakass	85.8	82.0	80.9	78.3	−3.8	−1.1	−2.6
Cherkess	79.3	78.4	74.1	76.9	−0.9	−4.3	2.8
Adygey	82.8	81.6	79.5	76.5	−1.2	−2.1	−3.0
Autonomous Okrugs							
Nenets[a]	90.5	89.3	86.2	85.9	−1.2	−3.1	−0.3
Dolgan	—	89.1	85.9	71.2	—	−3.2	−14.7
Mansi	87.6	86.7	81.4	77.6	−0.9	−5.3	−3.8
Chukchi	85.0	81.0	80.7	78.5	−4.0	−0.3	−2.2
Koryak	81.1	78.8	71.8	71.1	−2.3	−7.0	−0.7
Komi-Permyak	87.5	80.6	70.0	62.7	−6.9	−10.6	−7.3
Khanty	58.9	57.8	53.6	52.8	−1.1	−4.2	−0.6
Evenk	14.1	12.7	11.8	11.5	−1.4	−0.9	−0.3

Sources: 1959: TsSU SSSR 1962, vols. 1–16, Tables 53 and 54; 1970: TsSU SSSR 1973, vol. 4:20–320; 1979: TsSU 1984, 71–137; 1989: Goskomstat SSSR 1991a.

Notes: Because the indigenous *ethnies* of the Adzhar and Gorno Badakhshan autonomous units are not listed in the census, and because the indigenous nation for Nakhichevan and Nagorno Karabakh also have union republics, they are not listed in this table.

[a] Nenets home republic = Nenets Autonomous Okrug, Yamalo Nenets Autonomous Okrug, and Taymyr Autonomous Okrug; Ossetian home republic = Severo-Ossetian ASSR and Yugo-Ossetian Autonomous Oblast; Buryat home republic = Buryat ASSR, Agin Buryat Autonomous Okrug, and Ust'-Ordyn Buryat Autonomous Okrug.

Communist party leadership was claiming that the national republics (i.e., homelands) had lost their significance. Reality was clearly out of step with the beliefs espoused by political elites during this period.

Overall, more than half the nations and nationalities became less concentrated in their home republics between 1979 and 1989 (Table 4.1). Further, this relative national dispersal affected a greater number of national communities between 1979 and 1989 than between 1970 and 1979, and the rate of dispersal during the 1970s was in turn relatively higher than during the 1960s. Among nations at the union-republic level, it was the Central Asians who caused this increasing dispersal during the 1980s, as a relatively larger number of indigenes began to migrate from their respective home republics. This out-migration was most likely the result of declining standards of living in the region, which fell

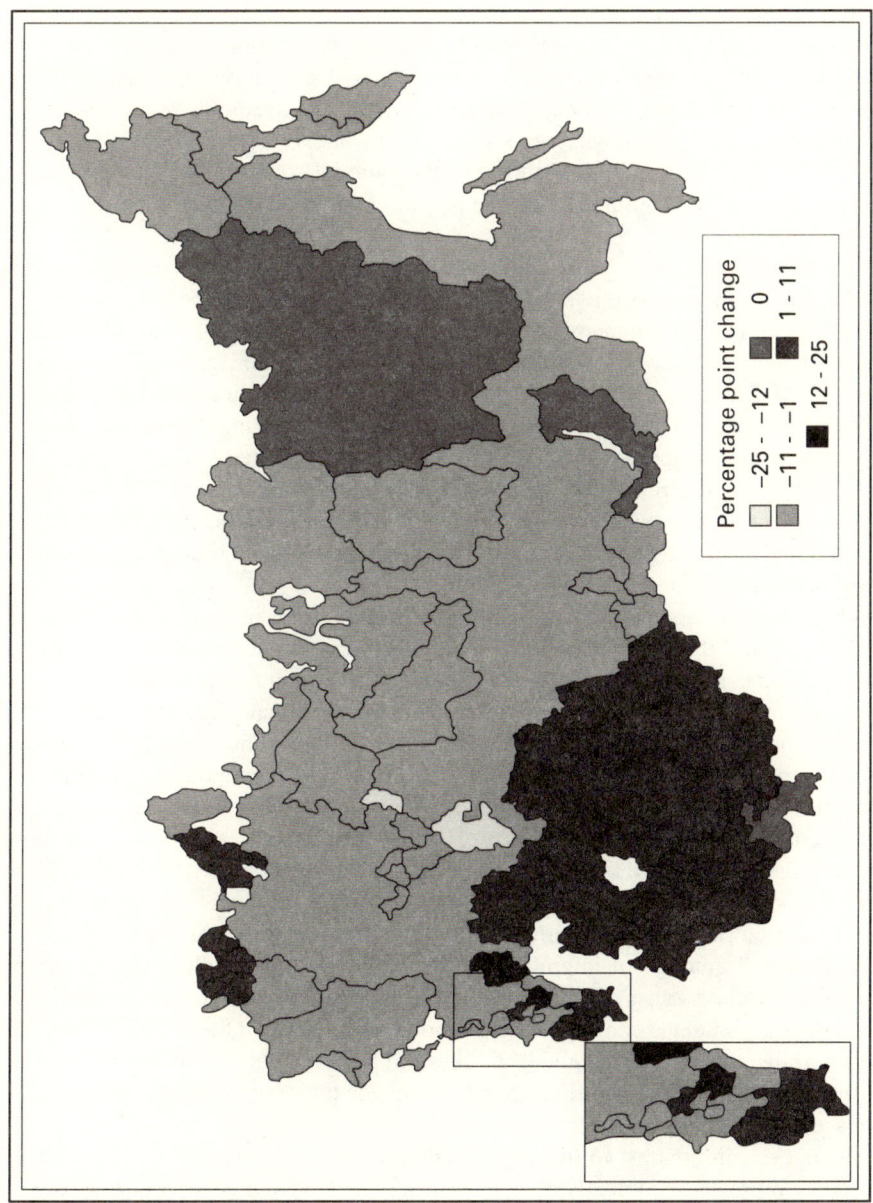

Map 4.3 Change in Indigenous National Concentration, 1959–1989

dramatically in the late 1980s (e.g., Gleason 1990b; Lewis et al. 1976, 354–381). However, thus far small numbers of indigenes have been involved in this out-migration stream.

On the other hand, during the 1980s the overall level of homeland concentration increased. For the nations whose homelands were union republics, 83.1 percent of the nations' members resided in their respective home republics, an increase of 1.8 percentage points over 1979 (Goskomstat SSSR 1991). In general, a high and stable percentage of the national community in its respective home republic continued to be the predominant trend during the 1970s and 1980s.

A number of factors have contributed to this continued concentration of indigenes in their respective homelands. First, natural increase (births minus deaths) among national members living in the homeland is normally higher than natural increase among co-nationals who live outside their respective home republics. The primary reason for this is that for most nations the homeland population is more rural and less educated than the outlying population, and these two "social mobilization" factors are inversely related to fertility levels (e.g., Jones and Grupp 1987). This has been particularly true in the case of Soviet Central Asia, where a more rapid natural increase among rural indigenes resulted in an increasing concentration of each nation's population in its respective homeland during the 1970s and early 1980s.

In addition to natural increase, geographic differentials in the rate of "natural assimilation," the intergenerational integration brought about as the result of international marriages, also tends to favor the continued concentration of nations in their respective home republics. International marriage rates are much higher outside the homeland than inside, and the children of such exogamous marriages most often assume the identity of the indigenous nation.[9] In a recent study of international marriage patterns, Susokolov found that a relatively high percentage of indigenes migrating from the homeland are married to nonindigenes before they leave. For example, 30 percent of the "planned" migration from Uzbekistan to Ivanov Oblast between 1983 and 1987 involved intermarried couples (Susokolov 1990, 130–133). This indicates that "national marginality" among out-migrating indigenes is relatively high, and that the relatively weaker sense of national self-consciousness among those voluntarily leaving the homeland enhances the likelihood for intergenerational assimilation outside the ancestral homeland. All other things being equal, this results over time in a relative loss of national members outside their respective home republics and a relative gain in the homeland.

However, in contrast to this typical situation, for a number of nations that became more geographically dispersed during the 1980s, it is possible that this

---

[9] Chapter 6, which examines cultural indigenization, discusses this international integration process in detail.

reflects a reversal of national reidentification among members living outside the home republic that had occurred previously. Balkars may be an example of this—while there was no absolute decline in the home republic, and actually a substantial increase, the population growth among Balkars living outside the home republic, and particularly in Central Asia, the North Caucasus region, and Ukraine, was extremely high. Unless these Balkars experienced a sharp rise in the level of fertility—an extremely unlikely event—then it is probable that a number of members who in the past had declared themselves to be members of some other national community decided to reclaim their Balkar identity in the 1989 census. This may have occurred among a number of other nonindigenes during the late 1980s, although the data needed to confirm this are not yet available. However, in a more nationally charged environment, and one in which claiming membership in the dominant Russian nation is no longer advisable in non-Russian homelands, it should not be surprising that this reverse reidentification occurred. This also indicates that international integration in the USSR, as expressed in the censuses, is at least for some more apparent than real, a matter of strategic choice made by subordinate nonindigenes seeking to gain an edge in international competition for resources, including high-status occupations, in an alien environment.

Finally, interhomeland migration has increased the level of international interaction but not to the extent that one would have expected. Studies of migration generally cite geographic differentials in economic opportunity as the critical factor in the decision to migrate. In the USSR, the prospects for this "natural" migration stream were enhanced by the official endorsement (made by both the Communist party leadership and by demographers and ethnographers) of people moving to areas of labor deficit, and from areas of labor surplus (Rybakovskiy 1987, 171–174). The wage differentials paid for labor in Siberia and the Far East were only one example of the instruments available to the Soviet leadership in its efforts to mobilize labor. Exhortations to do one's ideological duty, attempts to instill pride in being part of large projects (such as the Baykal-Amur Railroad [BAM]), as well as the ability to assign graduates to specific jobs and more generally the internal passport system were all additional methods with which the state could effect migration patterns.[10]

Although officials viewed increasing international mixing through interhomeland migration favorably, there is little evidence that migration policies were structured specifically to help bring this about. Rather, migration policies were designed to encourage greater geographic mobility toward areas of labor deficit primarily for economic reasons, not to increase international interaction and integration per se. Nonetheless, the latter effect was typically seen as a positive by-product of greater interhomeland movement in response to eco-

[10] The latter tended to keep migration lower than it otherwise would have been (Smith 1989; Zaslavsky and Luryi 1979).

nomic opportunity (e.g., Gardanov et al. 1961, 22–23). According to Kozlov (1977b, 139): "Settling in a new place of residence, migrants accommodate themselves to a new environment, i.e. adapt to it in social and cultural relations, become proficient in the language of this environment, if earlier they did not know it or knew it only poorly, gradually they move away from their former habits and customs, and finally, if not in the first, then in later generations they dissolve into this environment ethnically, they assimilate to it."

In theory at least, interhomeland migration should have been increasing throughout this period as nations drew closer together into one Soviet people and acted in ways that benefited society as a whole. However, limited migration of indigenes from their respective homelands, and on the contrary net migration toward the homeland, was evident in a number of cases, even before the nationalistic upheavals and the growing anti-outsider sentiments of the Gorbachev period. More generally, migration patterns in the former USSR did not conform to the policy goals enunciated by state officials. The depopulation of rural areas in the European part of the country, which has contributed to the inability of the USSR to bring in the harvest; the overpopulation and low level of out-migration in rural Central Asia; and the continued difficulty of holding the necessary labor in place in Siberia and the Far East were of greatest concern (Rybakovskiy and Tarasova 1989). Overall, the same article complained that for all the instruments at the disposal of the central authorities in the USSR, no "effective mechanism" for controlling migration existed (Rybakovskiy and Tarasova 1989, 76).

During the 1980s, and particularly in the latter half of the decade, a number of new migration patterns emerged. Most significant perhaps was the return migration of Russians to the RSFSR from the non-Slavic South, resulting in a reversal of the net out-migration among Russians to this region that had occurred throughout the entire Soviet period (Table 4.2). Russians were still migrating to the Baltic republics, Ukraine, and Belarus' through 1989, but this was reversed in the Baltic republics and Moldova during the 1989–91 period. The rate of Russian out-migration from the non-Slavic South increased particularly dramatically, and is indicative of the rising anti-Russian and anti-outsider nativism displayed by indigenes in the region.

Armenians, Latvians, Lithuanians, and Estonians continued to become more highly concentrated in their respective home republics, and this was primarily the result of return migration (Vishnevskiy and Zayonchkovskaya 1991, 9, 17). Although the census data for the entire decade do not show it, Azerbaydzhanis have also been returning by the hundreds of thousands from Armenia since 1987 (e.g., Goskomstat SSSR 1989b, 61–70; Goskomstat SSSR 1990a, 580–581; *Argumenty i Fakty* 1990c). On the other hand, the out-migration of Ukrainians and Belorussians from their respective home republics continued during the 1980s. Much of this appeared to be economically driven and directed toward the east, where resource development continued to attract labor. For

TABLE 4.2
Total and Russian Net Migration, 1979–1991

Republic	1979–88			1989–91		
	Total	Russian	% Russian	Total	Russian	% Russian
Russia	1,551,606	−69,916	—	299,000	376,400	126
Ukraine	47,774	292,334	612	271,000	142,300	53
Belarus'	−28,231	143,904	—	−19,000	17,400	—
Moldova	−63,917	27,765	—	−80,000	−13,500	17
Uzbekistan	−600,332	−106,290	18	−374,000	−100,300	27
Kazakhstan	−858,353	−102,159	12	−273,000	−87,000	32
Kyrgyzstan	−183,826	−46,656	25	−96,000	−31,900	33
Tadzhikistan	−125,482	−28,931	23	−108,000	−56,900	53
Turkmenistan	−98,976	−35,006	35	−17,000	−12,100	71
Georgia	−79,363	−51,432	65	−209,000	−39,400	19
Azerbaydzhan	−271,774	−109,803	40	−216,000	−138,100	64
Armenia	−291,326	−22,755	8	−3,000	−19,500	650
Lithuania	90,836	23,815	26	−12,690	−12,425	98
Latvia	97,172	37,638	39	−20,519	−9,806	48
Estonia	48,705	42,960	88	−8,601	−5,710	66
Northern Tier[a]	1,743,945	498,500	29	429,190	575,459	134
Southern Tier[b]	−2,509,432	−503,032	20	−1,296,000	−485,200	37

Source: 1979: Goskomstat SSSR 1989d, vol. 4, part 1, book 3, 206; 1989: Statisticheskiy Komitet SNG 1993, vol. 7; 1989–91 totals (except Baltic States): Statisticheskiy Komitet SNG 1992, 127; Russian proportions for all but the Baltic states were taken from estimates provided by Dr. Nicholas Petrov, Institute of Geography, Russian Academy of Science, July 1992. Baltic figures for total and Russian net migration were taken from Kirch et al. (1992,6).

Notes: Total migration was calculated using the residual of the intercensal population for each successor state and the natural increase for the republic registered between 1979 and 1988 inclusive (the 1989 census was taken on January 15). Russian migration was calculated using the residual of the intercensal population change for Russians in each of the successor states and the estimated natural increase of the Russian population in the USSR (.0565).

The difference between in-migration and out-migration (Total = −765,487; Russian = −4,532) represents the error of estimation and emigration. Between 1989 and 1991, emigration did increase substantially, and totaled 687,256 for 1989–90 alone (Goskomstat SSSR 1991b, 95). On the other hand, the net positive figure for Russians in column 5 obviously reflects the greater error involved in estimations of these figures, which were drawn from a variety of unofficial sources.

[a] Northern Tier = Russia, Ukraine, Belorussia, Moldova, Lithuania, Latvia, and Estonia.

[b] Southern Tier = Georgia, Azerbaydzhan, Armenia, Kazakhstan, Uzbekistan, Kyrgyzstan, Tadzhikistan, and Turkmenistan.

example, the number of Ukrainians and Belorussians more than tripled between 1979 and 1989 in Tyumen' Oblast, the site of intensive oil and gas exploration and extraction (TsSU SSSR 1984, 100; Goskomstat SSSR 1991, 74). However, data for 1989 migration to and from urban settlements indicate that both Ukrainians and Belorussians experienced a net migration toward their respective homelands overall, and even a positive net migration balance toward the homeland from Russia (Goskomstat SSSR 1990a: 580–623).[11] Thus, even for these two national communities, a migratory shift in favor of the homeland was apparent by the end of the decade (Vishnevskiy and Zayonchkovskaya 1991, 12).

The continued high concentration of indigenes in their respective homelands does not mean that interhomeland borders are impenetrable barriers to movement but rather that ODTs have served as "intervening obstacles" raising the threshold above which out-migration will occur. While the population became much more socially mobile in the postwar era, and while rural to urban migration increased dramatically between 1959 and 1989, the type of hypermobility across state borders apparent in the United States did not become prevalent in the USSR.[12] Two reasons for the limited degree of interhomeland migration may be suggested. First, as noted above, an emotional attachment to homeland is apparent among indigenes. Since the homeland is perceived as an intimate part of one's national identity, the decision to leave the homeland is undoubtedly a difficult one. Empirical evidence for this factor is difficult to find. Because territory was viewed by officials as an empty container that was unimportant in and of itself, it is not surprising that few surveys attempted to explore the nature of this more subjective "sense of homeland." However, in a recent questionnaire, residents of cities in Western Siberia were asked to state their preferences for Soviet economic regions and republics, and to give reasons for their selections (Korel' et al. 1988). Interestingly, preferences were not based primarily on socioeconomic factors but on more subjective emotional considerations. Overall, "favorable natural/climatic conditions" and "nearness to homeland" (*rodnoye mesto*) were ranked first and second, while "high wages" tied for last place with "low cost of living" (Korel' et al. 1988, 150). Only those who preferred the Far East ranked "high wages" above "nearness to homeland." In another survey, secondary school students from cities around the country expressed a clear regional preference for their native land, with the exception of students from cities in Siberia (Kostinskiy 1990). Although these surveys are not conclusive in and of themselves, and although much more work along these lines is needed, these studies indicate that the emotional attachment of indigenes to their homelands—over and above questions of socioeconomic privileges or other cost-benefit calculations—has a significant effect on the way people perceive the world around them and respond to it.

Beyond the subjective reasons for limited interhomeland migration, there were also more "rational" sociocultural, economic, and political reasons why indigenes chose to remain in their respective home republics. During the postwar period, a *korenizatsiya* (indigenization) of life was occurring, which pro-

---

[11] These migration data exclude rural to rural migration.

[12] Long (1988, 260) provides convincing evidence that long-distance migration is much higher in immigrant societies such as the United States than in states whose population claims a region or the entire state as its ancestral homeland.

vided indigenes with a preferential position vis-à-vis nonindigenes. Aside from the dominant Russians, who until recently were afforded a privileged status throughout the USSR, indigenes living in their own home republics were provided easier access to higher education, employment, upward mobility in the local party and government institutions, and greater utility of ethnocultural attributes (e.g., language). This meant that while geographic differentials in economic opportunity may have existed on paper, international differentials in access to societal rewards favored indigenes in practice, and nonindigenes placed themselves at a competitive disadvantage by leaving their homelands. Under these conditions, continued high levels of concentration of indigenes in their respective homelands are not surprising.[13]

This "rational choice model" may also help explain why national communities at different levels of autonomy in the Soviet federal structure varied in their degree of "gravitation" to the homeland. Members of nations whose homelands were designated union republics received greater privileges than the national communities whose homelands were located farther down the federal hierarchy (i.e., autonomous republics, autonomous oblasts, autonomous okrugs). This structure of differential indigenous privilege was found in all spheres of life, from the number of years of instruction in the native language to the number of representatives sent to the Soviet of Nationalities.[14] This hierarchy of privilege, which operated for all but perhaps the dominant Russians, made the home republic a much more attractive place for the upper echelon of nations than for those at the lower end, and was almost certainly a factor in explaining why members of national communities whose home republics were afforded only autonomous status showed a greater tendency toward geographic dispersion from the home republic.

The Russian nation has been mentioned as an exception to the rule. First, as noted in chapter 2, the Russian perception of homeland is variable. For most it is at least equal to the entire Russian republic (Connor 1986). For others (e.g., the "Russian patriots"), the Russian nation as the one that has sacrificed the most is said to have a right to the entire USSR (Hammer 1988, 13). According to surveys conducted by the Soviet Institute of Ethnography during the late 1970s and early 1980s, 70 percent or more of Russians in Moscow, Kishinev, and Tashkent considered the entire USSR to be their homeland (*rodina*) (Drobizheva 1991a, 5). Finally, for a core group of "Russophiles," the homeland

---

[13] This indigenization in social, cultural, economic, and political spheres and its consequences for international relations is the focus of the remaining chapters of this book.

[14] Indigenous students in the union republic could receive instruction in the native language up to and including postsecondary education, while those in the autonomous units were for the most part restricted to studying the native language as a subject after the first few years of schooling (Appendix B). In the Soviet of Nationalities, there were thirty-two representatives from each union republic, eleven from each autonomous republic, five from each autonomous oblast, and one from each autonomous okrug.

(*rodina*) cannot be reduced to less than the RSFSR, Ukraine, Belarus', and northern Kazakhstan (e.g., Solzhenitsyn 1990). All three versions of homeland are geographically extensive and no doubt have enhanced Russian mobility.

Second, in terms of a "rational choice model" in the decision to migrate, the Russians were less restricted than other nations, since they did not suffer the same decline in status upon leaving their nominal home republic. Even outside the RSFSR, Russians were not forced to accommodate themselves culturally to the indigenous nation, particularly in the urban/industrial environment. Indeed, the cities of many non-Russian republics became Russian enclaves in a sea of rural indigenes.

As indigenes became more socially mobilized, and in particular more urbanized, they came into increasing contact and competition with these dominant Russians. As we discuss in the following chapters, this international interaction not only failed to result in the sovietization or Russification of upwardly mobile indigenes but served as a powerful catalyst in the activation of indigenous national territoriality. In the late 1980s, the Russians living outside their own home republic increasingly found that their privileged status was being challenged by indigenes, and this newly charged nativistic environment, together with economic decline in Soviet Central Asia, were at the heart of the reversal of over a century of Russian out-migration from the Russian heartland.

INTERHOMELAND MOBILITY AND ITS CONSEQUENCES

Beyond the indigenous nations' continued concentration in their respective homelands, the demographic predominance of the indigenous nation in its homeland is also important, though perhaps for a different reason than is normally given in works related to the national question in the USSR. As noted above, greater international mixing was almost universally hailed by Soviet analysts as the primary means through which integration toward one Soviet people would occur. A number of Western analysts have also seen increasing international interaction as a stimulus for increasing assimilation (e.g., Deutsch 1966, 118–119). However, since the weakening of a nation's position in its homeland in numerical terms often signifies the in-migration of members of dominant or achiever nations who are able to out-compete the indigenes for the upper strata of occupations in a modernizing economy (e.g., Lewis et al. 1976), it is reasonable to hypothesize that such a trend will result in a more virulent form of national territoriality among the indigenous nation so affected. This nativistic reaction was clearly apparent in India (Weiner 1978: 274–294) and has become increasingly evident in the USSR, from Yakutia in Eastern Siberia to Nagorno Karabakh in Azerbaydzhan, and from Estonia and Latvia in the Baltics to Kyrgyzstan and Tadzhikistan in Central Asia. Far from creating the conditions in which the indigene's sense of national self-consciousness would be eroded—an assumption on which nationality policies of the USSR were based—such international interaction served as a catalyst in the mobilization of national communities behind the goals of self-determination.

Although the majority of members (for the most part) are concentrated in the home republic, the *ethnies* whose homelands have an autonomous designation are in a much weaker demographic position than those with homelands at the union republic level, and to a great extent this is a linear relationship (Table 4.3; Maps 4.4 and 4.5).[15] For example, of all *ethnies* with autonomous oblasts and okrugs (excluding the Armenians and Nagorno Karabakh), only Komi-Permyaks comprise a majority in their home republic. In addition, all autonomous okrug *ethnies* declined as a percent of the homeland population between 1970 and 1989, with the exception of the Komi-Permyaks (1970–1979) and the Koryaks (1979–1989) (Table 4.4). This is a reversal of the trend between 1959 and 1970 for three of the six groups. The percentage of the total population accounted for by the Khanty, Mansi, Nenets, and Chukchi declined precipitously during this period, which was primarily due to rapid in-migration with the development of natural resources. For example, the total population in the Khanty-Mansi Autonomous Okrug more than doubled between 1979 and 1989, while that of the Yamalo Nenets Autonomous Okrug more than tripled during the same period. These were regions where oil and gas exploration and development have been intensive since the mid-1970s, bringing an enormous influx of Russians, Ukrainians, Belorussians, and increasingly even Central Asians to these northern Siberian regions.

In the past at least, the interaction of these indigenes with Russians and others had brought about their assimilation even in the territory considered as their homeland. This assimilation of indigenes may be closer to a process of national consolidation than international integration, because these groups had not yet attained a national consciousness. Except for the Karelians, this pattern of indigenous assimilation and absolute decline in the homeland was not repeated for other national communities in the USSR during the postwar period.[16]

In contrast to this picture of demographic decline, three of the four autonomous oblast *ethnies* increased as a percentage of the total population between 1970 and 1989. All appear relatively stable in terms of this characteristic. However, at present all except the Armenians in Nagorno-Karabakh and Ossetians in South Ossetia comprise a fairly small percentage of the total population in these autonomous units, while Russians are a demographic majority or at least a plurality of those in the Russian Federation.

The indigenous nations in ten of eighteen autonomous republics increased as a percentage of the total population between 1970 and 1989, but this represented a decrease from the period between 1959 and 1970, when twelve

---

[15] The term *ethnie* is used here once again to denote that the indigenous groups whose homelands are designated Autonomous Oblasts and Autonomous Okrugs in the federal hierarchy had not attained a national self-consciousness even by the post-World War II period.

[16] This issue is considered in greater detail in chapter 6.

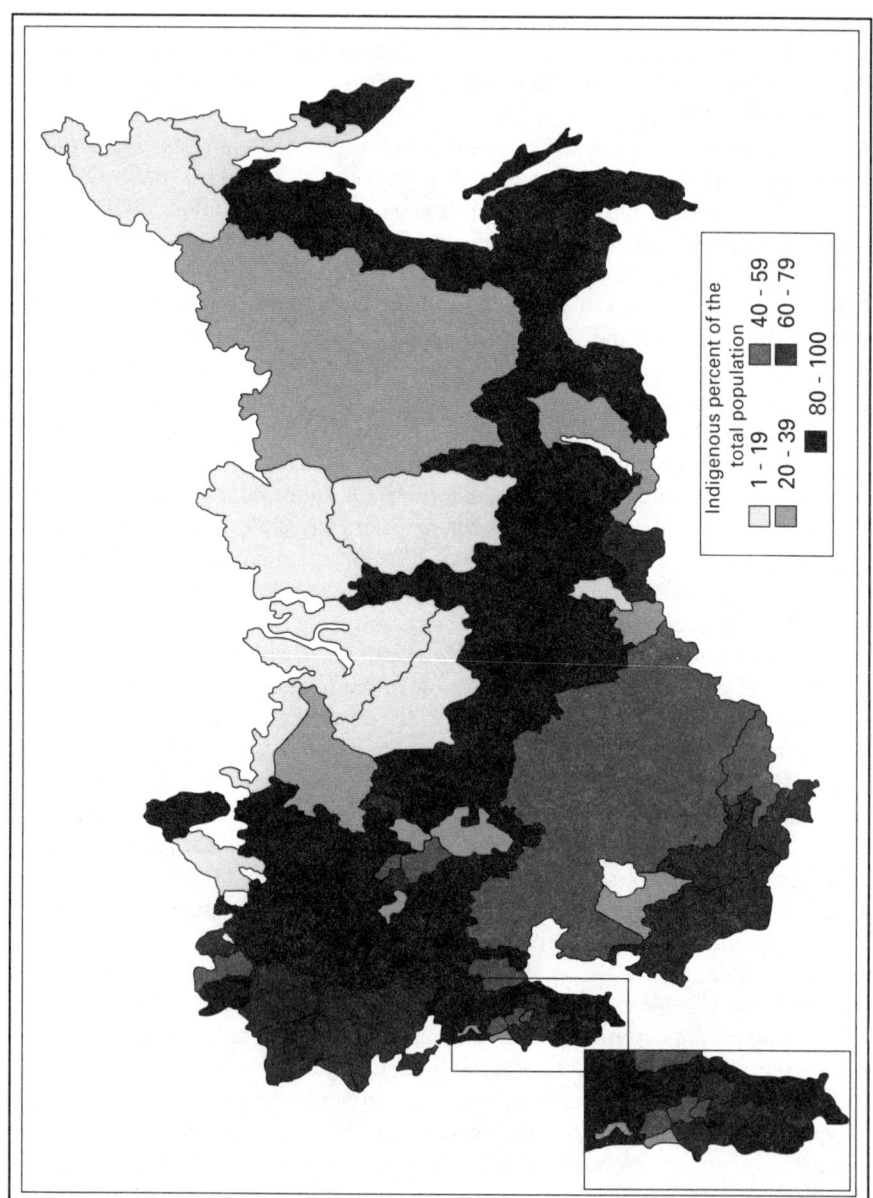

Map 4.4 Indigenous Percent of the Total Population by Federal Unit, 1989

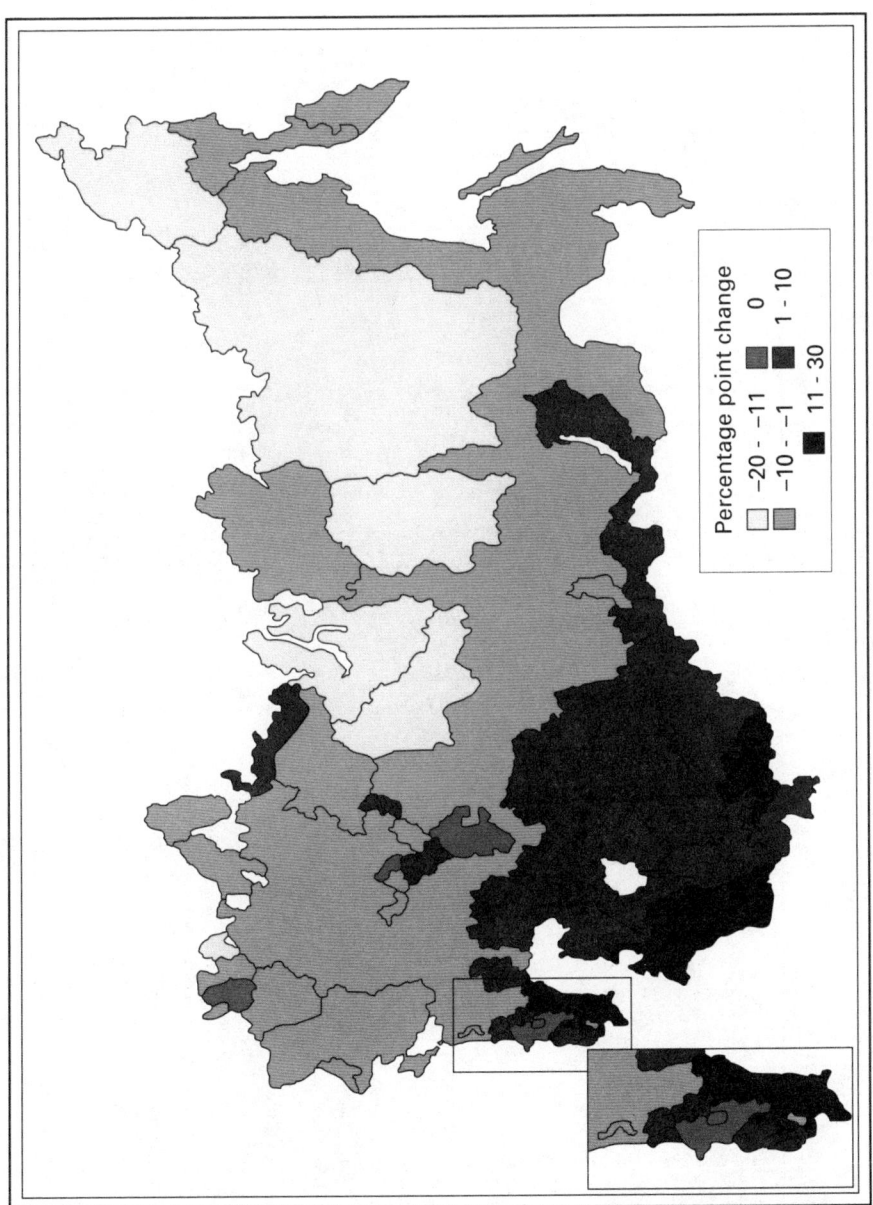

Map 4.5 Change in Indigenous Proportion of the Total Population, 1959–1989

TABLE 4.3
Nations as a Percentage of Their Respective Home Republic Populations, 1959–1989

Republic	1959 Indigene	1959 Russian	1970 Indigene	1970 Russian	1979 Indigene	1979 Russian	1989 Indigene	1989 Russian
Union Republics								
RSFSR	83.3	—	82.8	—	82.6	—	81.5	—
Ukraine	76.8	16.9	74.9	19.4	73.6	21.1	72.7	22.1
Belarus'	81.1	8.2	81.0	10.4	79.4	11.9	77.9	13.2
Uzbekistan	62.1	13.5	65.5	12.5	68.7	10.8	71.4	8.3
Kazakhstan	30.0	42.7	32.6	42.4	36.0	40.8	39.7	37.8
Georgia	64.3	10.1	66.8	8.5	68.8	7.4	70.1	6.3
Azerbaydzhan	67.5	13.6	73.8	10.0	78.1	7.9	82.7	5.6
Lithuania	79.3	8.5	80.1	8.6	80.0	8.9	79.6	9.4
Moldova	65.4	10.1	64.6	11.6	63.9	12.8	64.5	13.0
Latvia	62.0	26.6	56.8	29.8	53.7	32.8	52.0	34.0
Kyrgyzstan	40.5	30.2	43.8	29.2	47.9	25.9	52.4	21.5
Tadzhikistan	53.1	13.3	56.2	11.9	58.8	10.4	62.3	7.6
Armenia	88.0	3.2	88.6	2.7	89.7	2.3	93.3	1.6
Turkmenistan	60.9	17.3	65.6	14.5	68.4	12.6	72.0	9.5
Estonia	74.6	20.1	68.2	24.7	64.7	27.9	61.5	30.3
Autonomous Republics								
Bashkiria	22.1	42.4	23.4	40.5	24.3	40.3	21.9	39.3
Buryatia[a]	23.8	70.3	25.4	69.5	26.2	68.5	27.3	66.7
Dagestan[a]	69.3	20.1	74.3	14.7	77.8	11.6	80.2	9.2
Kabardin-Balkaria[a]	53.4	38.7	53.7	37.2	54.5	35.1	57.6	31.9
Kalmykia	35.1	55.9	41.1	45.8	41.5	42.6	45.4	37.8
Karelia	13.1	63.4	11.8	68.1	11.1	71.3	10.0	73.6
Komi	30.1	48.6	28.6	53.1	25.4	56.7	23.3	57.7
Mari	43.1	47.8	43.7	46.9	43.5	47.5	43.3	47.5
Mordvinia	35.7	59.1	35.4	58.9	34.2	59.7	32.5	60.8
North Ossetia	47.8	39.6	48.7	36.6	50.5	33.9	53.0	29.9

Tatarstan	47.2	43.9	49.1	42.4	47.6	44.0	48.5	43.3
Tuvinia	57.0	40.1	58.6	38.3	60.5	36.2	64.3	32.0
Udmurtia	35.6	56.8	34.2	57.1	32.1	58.3	30.9	58.9
Chechen-Ingushetia[a]	41.1	49.0	58.5	34.5	64.6	29.6	70.7	23.1
Chuvashia	70.2	24.0	70.0	24.5	68.4	26.0	67.8	26.7
Yakutia	46.4	44.2	43.0	47.3	36.9	50.4	33.4	50.3
Abkhazia[b]	15.1	39.1	15.9	41.0	17.1	43.9	17.8	45.7
Karakalpakstan[b]	30.6	28.8	31.0	30.3	31.1	31.5	32.1	32.8
Autonomous Oblasts								
Adygey	23.2	70.4	21.1	71.7	21.4	70.6	22.1	68.0
Gorno-Altay	24.2	69.8	27.8	65.6	29.2	63.2	31.0	60.4
Karachay-Cherkess[a]	33.1	51.0	37.2	47.1	39.1	45.1	40.9	42.4
Khakass	11.8	76.5	12.3	78.4	11.5	79.5	11.1	79.5
Nagorno-Karabakh	84.4	13.8	80.5	18.1	75.9	23.0	76.9	21.5
South Ossetia	65.8	27.5	66.5	28.3	66.4	28.8	66.2	29.0
Autonomous Okrugs								
Taymyr (Dolgan)	9.1	65.3	11.4	66.9	9.6	68.2	8.9	67.1
Nenets[a]	14.7	56.8	16.3	56.1	10.3	61.9	4.9	60.5
Evenk	33.7	57.9	25.3	61.1	20.3	65.1	14.0	67.5
Koryak	18.5	60.6	19.1	63.1	16.2	64.5	16.5	62.0
Chukchi	21.4	60.7	10.9	69.7	8.1	68.9	7.3	66.1
Komi-Permyak	58.0	32.9	58.3	36.0	61.4	34.7	60.2	36.1
Khanty-Mansi[a]	13.8	72.5	7.0	76.9	3.0	74.3	1.4	66.3

Sources: 1959: TsSU SSSR 1962, vols. 1–16, Tables 53 and 54; 1970: TsSU SSSR 1973, vol. 4, 20–320; 1979: TsSU 1984, 71–137; 1989: Goskomstat 1991a.

[a]The "indigene" category for home republics with a geographic name or the name of more than one *ethnie* is a combination of the national communities treated as indigenous to the region. For example, Kabardins and Balkars are summed to arrive at the indigenous percentage for the Kabardin-Balkar ASSR. For Dagestan, the indigene category consists of the "Peoples of Dagestan."

The homeland for the Buryats and Nenets is considered to be all national territories which bear their names.

[b]For Nagorno Karabakh, Abkhazia, South Ossetia, and Karakalpakia, figures for Azerbaydzhanis, Georgians, and Uzbeks, respectively, are given in place of Russians. The Armenians were treated as the indigenous population of Nagorno Karabakh for the first time in the 1989 census, where they were listed first (Goskomstat SSSR 1991a, 120). In all previous postwar censuses, Azerbaydzhanis had been listed first.

TABLE 4.4
Relative Change in the National Composition of the Population by Republic, 1959–1989 (percentage point change)

Republic	Indigenes			Russians		
	1959–70	1970–79	1979–89	1959–70	1970–79	1979–89
Union Republics						
RSFSR	−1.5	−0.4	−1.1	−1.5	−0.4	−1.1
Ukraine	−1.9	−1.3	−0.9	2.5	1.7	1.0
Belarus'	−0.1	−1.6	−1.5	2.2	1.5	1.3
Uzbekistan[a]	3.4	3.2	2.7	−1.0	−1.7	−2.5
Kazakhstan	2.6	3.4	3.7	−0.3	−1.6	−3.0
Georgia[a]	2.5	2.0	1.3	−1.6	−1.1	−1.1
Azerbaydzhan[a]	6.3	4.3	4.6	−3.6	−2.1	−2.3
Lithuania	0.8	−0.1	−0.4	0.1	0.3	0.5
Moldova	−0.8	−0.7	0.6	1.5	1.2	0.2
Latvia	−5.2	−3.1	−1.7	3.2	3.0	1.2
Kyrgyzstan	3.3	4.1	4.5	−1.0	−3.3	−4.4
Tadzhikistan[a]	3.1	2.6	3.5	−1.4	−1.5	−2.8
Armenia[a]	0.6	1.1	3.6	−0.5	−0.4	−0.7
Turkmenistan[a]	4.7	2.8	3.6	−2.8	−1.9	−3.1
Estonia	−6.4	−3.5	−3.2	4.6	3.2	2.4
Autonomous Republics						
Bashkiria[b]	1.3	0.9	−2.4	−1.9	−0.2	−1.0
Buryatia	1.6	0.8	1.1	−0.8	−1.0	−1.8
Dagestan[a]	5.0	3.5	2.4	−5.4	−3.1	−2.4
Kabardin-Balkaria	0.3	0.8	3.1	−1.5	−2.1	−3.2
Kalmykia[a]	6.0	0.4	3.9	−10.1	−3.2	−4.8
Karelia[b]	−1.3	−0.7	−1.1	4.7	3.2	2.3
Komi	−1.5	−3.2	−2.1	4.5	3.6	1.0
Mari	0.6	−0.2	−0.2	−0.9	0.6	0.0
Mordvinia[a,b]	−0.3	−1.2	−1.7	−0.2	0.8	1.1
North Ossetia[a]	0.9	1.8	2.5	−3.0	−2.7	−4.0
Tatarstan	1.9	−1.5	0.9	−1.5	1.6	−0.7
Tuvinia	1.6	1.9	3.8	−1.8	−2.1	−4.2
Udmurtia	−1.4	−2.1	−1.2	0.3	1.2	0.6
Chechen-Ingushetia[a]	17.4	6.4	5.9	−14.5	−4.9	−6.5
Chuvashia	−0.2	−1.6	−0.6	0.5	1.5	0.7
Yakutia	−3.4	−6.1	−3.5	3.1	3.1	−0.1
Abkhazia[c]	0.8	1.2	0.7	1.9	2.9	1.8
Karakalpakstan[c]	0.4	0.1	1.0	1.5	1.2	1.3

(*continued*)

TABLE 4.4
(Continued)

	Indigenes			Russians		
Republic	1959–70	1970–79	1979–89	1959–70	1970–79	1979–89
Autonomous Oblasts						
Adygey	−2.1	0.3	0.7	1.3	−1.1	−2.6
Altay	3.6	1.4	1.8	−4.2	−2.4	−2.8
Karachay-Cherkess	−4.1	1.9	1.8	−3.9	−2.0	−2.7
Khakass	0.5	−0.8	−0.4	1.9	1.1	0.0
Nagorno-Karabakh[c]	−3.9	−4.6	1.0	4.3	4.9	−1.5
South Ossetia[c]	0.7	−0.1	−0.2	0.8	0.5	0.2
Autonomous Okrugs						
Taymyr (Dolgan)	2.3	−1.8	−0.7	1.6	1.3	−1.1
Nenets	1.6	−6.0	−5.4	−0.7	5.8	−1.4
Evenk	−8.4	−5.0	−6.3	3.2	4.0	2.4
Koryak	0.6	−2.9	0.3	2.5	1.4	−2.5
Chukchi	−10.5	−2.8	−0.8	9.0	−0.8	−2.8
Komi-Permyak[a,b]	0.3	3.1	−1.2	3.1	−1.3	1.4
Khanty-Mansi	−6.8	−4.0	−1.6	4.4	−2.6	−8.0

Source: Table 4.3.
[a] Russian population experienced an absolute decline between 1979 and 1989.
[b] Indigenous population experienced an absolute decline between 1979 and 1989.
[c] For Nagorno Karabakh, Karakalpakia, South Ossetia, and Abkhazia, percentage point changes are given for Azerbaydzhanis, Uzbeks, and Georgians, respectively, in place of Russians.

of eighteen experienced an increase (Tables 4.3 and 4.4; Map 4.5). Also, ten of these indigenous nations comprised a greater percentage of the home republic than did the Russians. However, two of these ten—the Abkhaz and Karakalpaks—are nations whose homelands lie outside Russia, and they are increasingly dominated by Georgians and Uzbeks (i.e., the locally dominant nations). Additionally, in three other autonomous republics, more than one national community is treated as the indigenous population.[17] Six of the indigenous nations at this level comprised an absolute demographic majority in their home republics in 1989 and 1979, an increase of one from 1959. The added homeland was the Chechen-Ingush ASSR, and this was due to return migration of members from these two deported nations during this thirty-year period. Two other indigenous nations comprised pluralities in their ASSRs. Russians were

[17] In the Chechen-Ingush and Kabardin-Balkar ASSRs, the first-named nations outnumber the Russians but the second-named nations do not. In the Dagestan ASSR, each of the four major indigenous nations (Avars, Dargins, Kumyks, and Lezgins) outnumber the Russians (Goskomstat SSSR 1991a).

an absolute majority in six of the autonomous republics in 1989, and gained this status in the Komi and Yakut ASSRs in 1979. However, they lost majority status in the Kalmyk ASSR, due again to return migration by members of this formerly deported nation. In two other ASSRs Russians comprised a plurality. In the remaining two autonomous republics—Abkhazia and Karakalpakia—the locally dominant nation (i.e., Georgians and Uzbeks, respectively) made up a plurality of the population.

Overall, the higher the homeland is within the federal hierarchy, the stronger is the demographic position of the indigenous nation (Maps 4.3–4.7). The autonomous okrug *ethnies* averaged 16.1 percent of the total population of their homelands in 1989 (a decrease of 2.3 percentage points for the decade), while the Russians averaged 60.8 percent (a decrease of 1.7 percentage points since 1979). The autonomous oblast *ethnies* (excluding Nagorno-Karabakh and South Ossetia) comprised an average of 26.2 percent of their home republics in 1989, an increase of 0.9 percentage points over 1979, while the Russians averaged 62.6 percent in 1989, a decrease of 2 percentage points since 1979. The nations with autonomous republics averaged 42.3 percent of their home republics' population (up 0.7 percentage points since 1979), while the Russians averaged 38.9 percent (down 1.4 percentage points).[18] Finally, the nations with union republic status were in the strongest demographic position, comprising on average 68.0 percent of the total population in their home republics in 1989 (up 0.4 percentage points since 1979). The Russians averaged only 15.7 percent of the population in the union republics in 1989, a decrease of 1 percentage point since 1979, and lost plurality status in Kazakhstan during the 1980s (Table 4.4).[19]

The relative shifts apparent in these data were the result of a combination of international differentials in the rate of natural increase as well as interhomeland migration. As an example of the first demographic cause, throughout the postwar period the indigenous nations of Soviet Central Asia became increasingly dominant in their respective home republics due to a high rate of natural increase. This national homogenization was occurring even though the Central Asian nations were becoming more geographically dispersed through outmigration during the 1980s.

Some analysts have equated international differentials in the rate of natural increase with a nation's "biological vitality," which provides the demographic dimension of the "nation as primordial organism" argument. For example, according to Carrere d'Encausse (1978, 70): "A new geography is emerging in the USSR, in which the divisions seem almost biological. On the one hand, the western part of the country seems to have had its vitality sapped by its repeated

---

[18] The Russian percentage would have been higher without the inclusion of the Abkhaz and Karakalpak ASSRs, as well as the inclusion of the South Ossetian Autonomous Oblast as part of the Ossetian homeland, since all three of these units lie outside Russia.

[19] The averages presented here are unweighted.

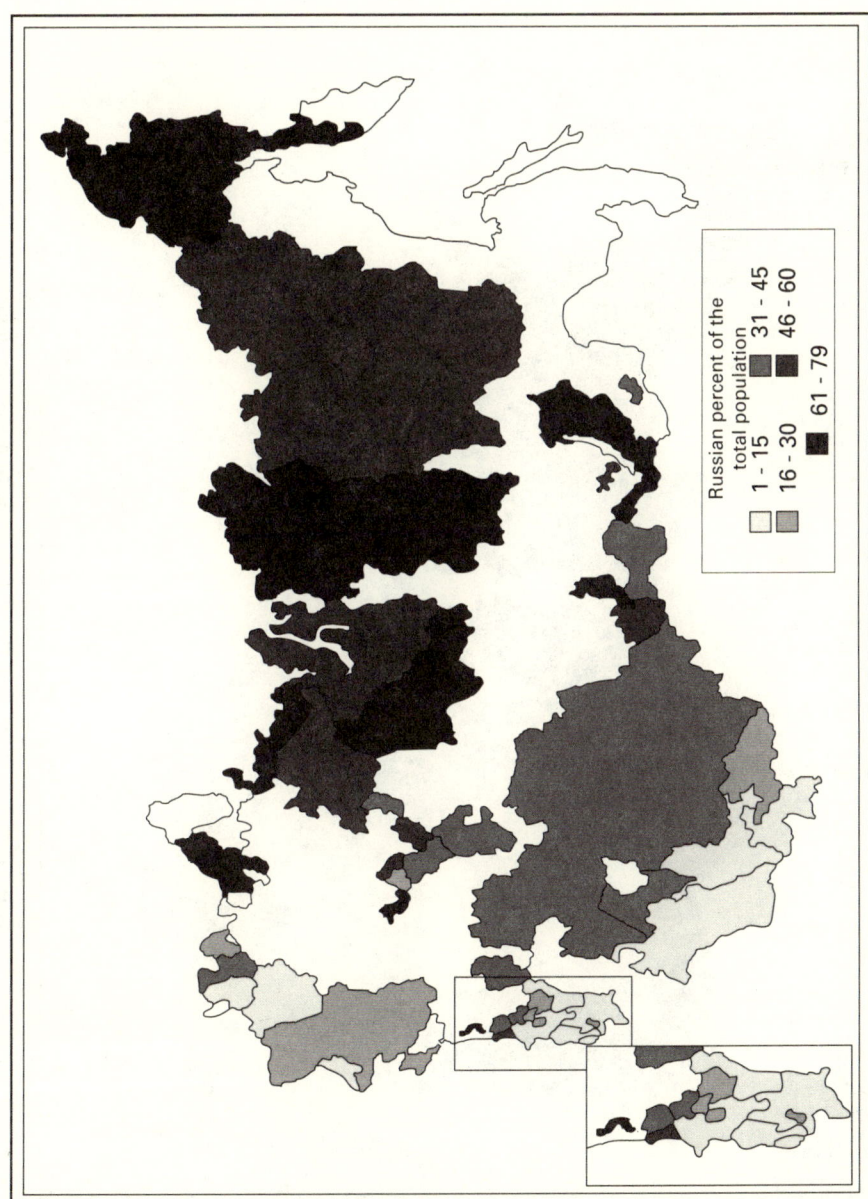

Map 4.6 Russian Percent of the Total Population in the Non-Russian Homelands, 1989

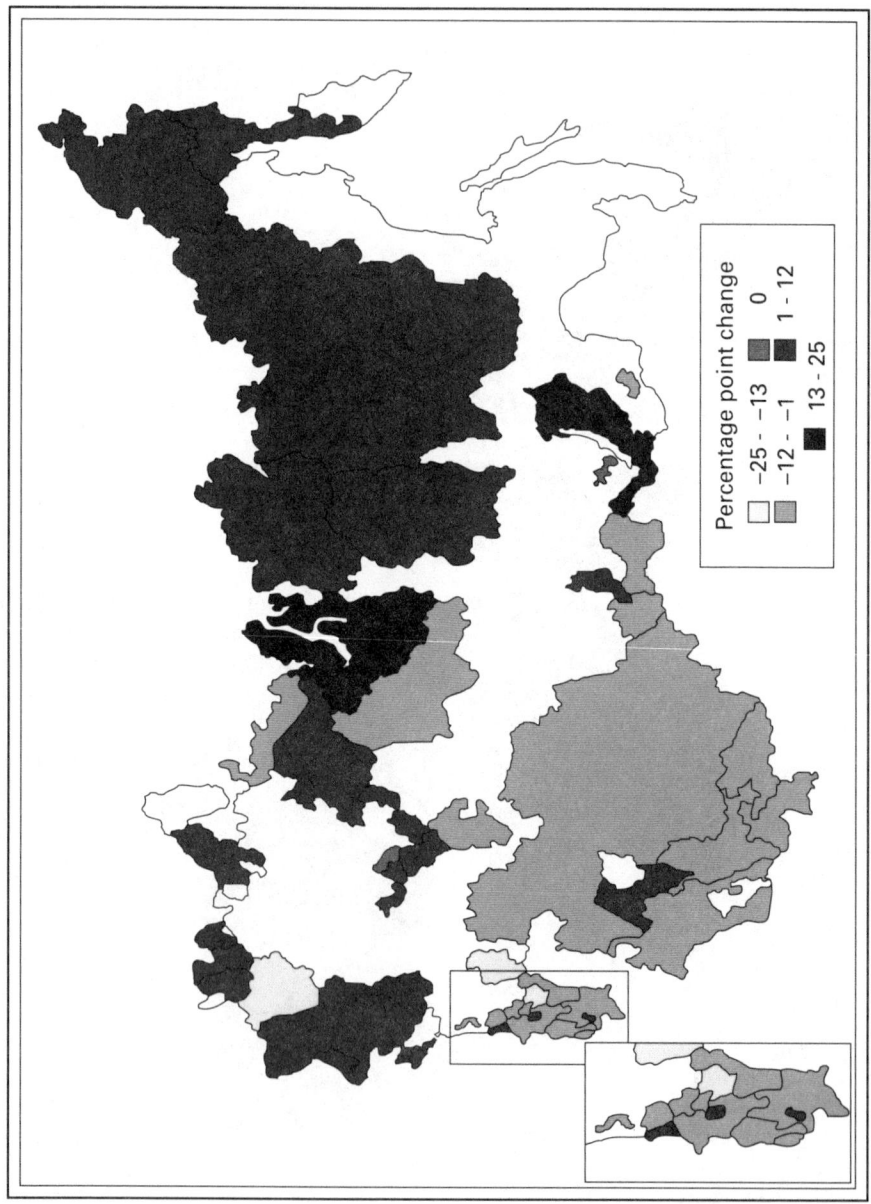

Map 4.7 Change in the Russian Proportion of the Total Population in the Non-Russian Homelands, 1959–1989

and fearful trials. On the other hand, the eastern part, which is better preserved even though it has had its share of common disasters, is where living conditions tend to be more comfortable . . . and where the high birth rate reflects exceptional vigor and probably greater confidence in the future." This study goes on to declare that the Baltic nations are doomed to physical extinction through demographic decline, while in "Central Asia and the Caucasus, ethnic consciousness and demographic vitality go hand in hand, assuring these nationalities an increasingly important place in the family of Soviet peoples" (Carrere d'Encausse 1978, 268). Given the geography of nationalism that has emerged since 1985, with the Baltic nations at the forefront of the national separatist movements while the nations of Soviet Central Asia have been relatively quiescent, it would be an understatement to say that studies such as the one cited here overemphasized the importance of demographic trends in determining the "vitality" of nations.

In contemporary Soviet Central Asia, a relatively high rate of indigenous natural increase has been compounded by Russian out-migration from the region, a reversal of a long-standing trend (Arutyunyan and Bromley 1986, 21–22; Rybakovskiy and Tarasova 1990; Goskomstat 1989b, 1990a). In Uzbekistan, Tadzhikistan, and Turkmenistan, this resulted in an absolute decline in the Russian population between 1979 and 1989, while in Kyrgyzstan and Kazakhstan the Russian population grew at a very slow rate, indicating that some of the natural increase among Russians in these two republics was offset by Russian out-migration (Goskomstat SSSR 1991b). Between 1989 and 1991, the rate of Russian out-migration increased dramatically. A net out-migration of 201,200 was registered in the four Central Asian republics from 1989 to 1991, a figure close to the net Russian out-migration from Central Asia for the entire 1979–1989 period (Table 4.2). In 1992, another 145,000 Russians emigrated from Uzbekistan, Kyrgyzstan, and Turkmenistan, and according to one estimate "300,000 of the 387,000 Russians living in Tajikistan in 1989 are reported to have left the country" (Marnie and Slater 1993, 49).

The absolute and relative declines among Russians in the non-Slavic South were not replicated in the European part of the country. Russians continued to migrate to the Baltic republics, Ukraine and Belarus', and this plus the low natural increase among the Baltic nations and the out-migration among Ukrainians and Belorussians resulted in a relative decline of indigenes in all five of these republics over the entire thirty-year period. Even so, this demographic situation has not consigned these nations to oblivion. On the contrary, the in-migration of Russians has served as a catalyst for rising national territoriality. Particularly in Estonia and Latvia, a more activated "sense of exclusiveness" regarding the demographic status of indigenes in their own homelands has been evident for much of the postwar period. According to Parming (1980, 403):

> Native resentment, especially of the Russian presence, has been identifiable since the end of the 1950s, at which time resistance to centrally dictated economic policies

because of their consequences in terms of immigration led to the purge of the leadership of the Latvian Communist Party. In more recent years, the dissatisfaction has been more bluntly expressed in a joint Estonian-Latvian *samizdat* document from 1975, which referred to the Russians as "civil garrisons" which are "an ominous tumour in the body of the Estonian and Latvian nations." Importantly, the issue of immigration is used as a pragmatic basis for demanding the restitution of pre-war sovereignty for the two republics and thus is a primary driving force behind manifestations of political nationalism.

Similarly, in the preamble of the program of RUKH (1989, 9–11), the inmigration of Russians and others and the "deportations of millions of Ukrainians" are cited as efforts by the central authorities to denationalize Ukraine. Thus interhomeland migration streams, and particularly those that had an element of force to them, served as a rationale for the Ukrainian independence movement.

During the late 1980s, all three Baltic republics attempted to gain control over interrepublic migration (e.g., FBIS 2 August 1990, 72–76). In addition, in Estonia and Latvia, and later in Moldova and Georgia, citizenship laws were drafted that would restrict membership to citizens of independent Estonia, Latvia, Moldova, and Georgia and their descendants (e.g., FBIS 27 November 1990, 80–81). This would restrict the political rights of Russians and other nonindigenes who migrated to these republics since 1940 (or in the case of Georgia since 1921)—the date of reincorporation into the USSR.[20]

In all five of these union republics except Lithuania, the rate of demographic shift in favor of Russians decreased over time (Table 4.4). Russian outmigration from Georgia was occurring between 1979 and 1988, and has increased after 1988 (Table 4.2). In the Baltics and Moldova, Russians have become net out-migrants since 1989, and the size of this net out-migration stream doubled between 1990 and 1991 in Latvia and Estonia (Kirch et al. 1992, 6). Rising indigenous nationalism in the Baltics is beginning to offset the magnet of greater economic opportunities that had been pulling Russians into the region throughout the postwar period. As national territoriality among indigenes becomes more activated and thus more overt, a more pronounced Russian outflow is likely to develop.

In Transcaucasia, due to the international conflict between Armenians and Azerbaydzhanis, the level of international mixing has declined precipitously in the past few years. Not only have Armenians and Azerbaydzhanis returned to their respective homelands by the hundreds of thousands, Russians and other nonindigenes are also leaving the region. In the Nagorno-Karabakh Autonomous Oblast itself, Armenians increased their share of the population, which

[20] Georgian nationalists also raised the possibility of establishing 1801 as the cut-off date for citizenship, since this was the year that Georgia was incorporated into the Russian Empire. See chapter 7.

had been declining dramatically due to Azerbaydzhani in-migration during the 1960s and 1970s. Indeed, it was this increasing "population pressure" of Azerbaydzhani in-migration, in addition to restrictions placed on the cultural autonomy enjoyed by Armenians, that served as catalysts for the secession demands made by the Armenians of Nagorno-Karabakh (Yamskov 1991, 139–144). Rather than leave Nagorno-Karabakh and migrate to Armenia, which would have been equated with abandoning an intimate part of the homeland, the number of Armenians in Nagorno-Karabakh actually increased dramatically during the late 1980s, even while Armenians were fleeing from other parts of Azerbaydzhan (Goskomstat SSSR 1990a, 120). The process of ethnic place-clearing or "cleansing" in Transcaucasia, as in Yugoslavia, has increased the national homogeneity of territory, while at the same time increasing international tension and conflict.

In cases similar to Nagorno-Karabakh, Abkhazia and South Ossetia have become scenes of international conflict between Georgians and Abkhazians on the one hand, and Georgians and Ossetians on the other. In each case, members of the two indigenous national communities claim the autonomous unit as their rightful homeland. Of course, for Georgians this is only part of the homeland, though it is proclaimed as an intimate, inseparable part. For Abkhazians, no other homeland territory exists, and in this sense their status is more precarious than that of the Armenians in Nagorno-Karabakh or even Ossetians in South Ossetia.

During the course of the postwar period, Georgians were migrating to Abkhazia in large numbers, and the preferential treatment afforded Abkhazians was increasingly being challenged by the Georgian plurality in Abkhazia. This "Georgian chauvinism," as proclaimed by Abkhazians, was one of the leading factors in the attempts by Abkhazians to secede from Georgia, first in 1978 with a petition to join the RSFSR (Sheehy 1978), and more recently in 1989 with a petition to become an independent union republic.[21] This was followed in 1990 by a declaration of sovereignty, which has been rejected by the Georgian Supreme Soviet. A similar declaration of sovereignty by Ossetians in the South Ossetian Autonomous Oblast was also rejected, and the autonomous unit itself was abolished by Georgia. The basis for these rejections, according to the elected president of Georgia, Zviyad Gamsakhurdia, was that the Abkhazians and Ossetians were newcomers attempting to usurp control over primordial Georgian soil.[22] In addition, the Georgian nationalist leader stated that the members of these groups were happy with their lives in Georgia, but were being manipulated by the center to rise up against the Georgian nation (Mikadze and

[21] Each of these petitions was rejected by Moscow. See chapter 7.

[22] Gamsakhurdia and other Georgian nationalists do make a distinction between Abkhazians, a supposedly primordial people of the region, and Ossetians, whose homeland is supposedly historically limited to North Ossetia. This distinction is said to be the reason for the differential treatment of Abkhazia and South Ossetia.

Shevelyov 1990, 7). However, rising anti-Georgian nativism before 1989 indicates that this is not an accurate assessment of international relations in the republic.

In Soviet Central Asia, as noted above, rapid population growth coupled with limited economic development and the resultant rise in unemployment have stimulated a rise in the out-migration of indigenes from the region. At the same time it is clear that the nativistic reactions among indigenes have also intensified in recent years. The Tadzhik attack on Armenians who were rumored to have been given preference in housing in Dushanbe, the Uzbek attack on Meskhetian Turks and Armenians for similar reasons, the clashes between Uzbeks and Kirgiz in the Osh' border region between these two republics (which was also in part a conflict over the status of this territory as part of both perceptual homelands), and recent incidents in Kazakhstan all appear to have been sparked by a situation in which the indigene's sense of exclusiveness in his or her homeland was perceived as being challenged by "outsiders." It also appears clear by these events that membership in the Islamic "brotherhood" has not reduced the threat of international conflict in the region.

Out-migration of nonindigenes has accelerated as a result of this rising anti-outsider nativism. A survey taken among those wishing to leave Tadzhikistan in 1990 indicated that fear of anti-outsider violence was the principal reason for wanting to leave (20.2 percent of respondents), followed by "the change in the linguistic situation" (11.6 percent). A "deterioration in the material conditions of life" (10.5 percent) ranked third, just above "the unsuitable climate" (8.4 percent) (FBIS 18 September 1990, 74). Surveys in Central Asia indicated that only 38 percent of Russians in Tadzhikistan and 36 percent in Uzbekistan wanted to remain, and most expressed the belief that violent interethnic conflict was likely. This belief that anti-Russian nativism was imminent was not shared by Tadzhiks and Uzbeks. Only 20 percent of Tadzhiks and Uzbeks surveyed described their relations with Russians as negative, and one-third described national relations as good (Vishnevskiy and Zayonchkovskaya 1991, 12).

The nonindigenous out-migration from Central Asia has increased dramatically since 1989 (Table 4.2), and is likely to grow more intense over time, particularly if economic conditions continue to worsen and anti-outsider sentiments continue to grow in Central Asia. Indigenes may also continue to leave the region in the face of rising unemployment in Central Asia. Overall, the "push" of nonindigenes out of Central Asia is proving stronger to date, and is resulting in the growing demographic dominance of indigenes in their respective homelands.

Within Russia itself, a number of trends are in evidence. First, in the Volga Urals region, in Karelia, and in several of the autonomous oblasts and okrugs of the east, Russian increases have been coupled with indigenous decline. In part this reflects a continuation of a long-term trend of Russian in-migration, in some of these regions going back centuries. In part, it is also apparent that some degree of indigenous out-migration has occurred over the past thirty years, resulting in the further dispersal of an already diffuse group of national communities. Finally, at least for Karelia and the Khanty-Mansi Autonomous Okrug, some degree of national reidentification of indigenes toward the Russian nation has been occurring even in the homeland. It is interesting that at the same time Karelians were declining absolutely as a result of assimilation, a Karelian People's Front was established to help preserve the national culture in Karelia. The Karelian national movement provides evidence that the very success of international integration may itself serve as a catalyst for the activation of national territoriality among the more nationally conscious indigenes. It remains to be seen whether such national front organizations will be able to "awaken" the indigenous masses.

In the east, continued in-migration of Russians, Ukrainians, Belorussians, and increasingly members of the Central Asian nations has served to dilute the already weak demographic position of the indigenous *ethnies*. Particularly in the case of the Nenets, Khanty, and Mansi, with the development of oil and natural gas reserves, a massive influx of nonindigenes has reduced the proportion of indigenes to a minimal level. This eastward movement shows no sign of abating, though a shift away from Russians and toward Ukrainians and others was apparent during the 1980s. This in-migration of Russians and other nonindigenes also appears to have sparked a rise in anti-outsider nativism, as well as a call by several of the indigenous *ethnies* for greater regional autonomy and even outright independence from Russia. It is likely that the number and intensity of international tensions and conflicts in this region will grow in the near future, although it is far from clear that the Russian Federation will face the same disintegrative processes that dismantled the USSR.

While the above group of *ethnies* are undergoing a relative (and for some an absolute) demographic decline in their respective homelands, just the opposite has occurred in the North Caucasus (Tables 4.3 and 4.4). In this region, a reconcentration of indigenes in their respective home republics occurred between 1959 and 1989, and this is especially the case for those nations whose members were deported and their ODTs abolished after World War II (e.g., Chechen, Ingush, Kalmyk, Kabardin, Balkar). This return migration stream of indigenes has been coupled increasingly with Russian out-migration, leading to a growing demographic indigenization of the home republics in the region. Clearly, forced out-migration from the national homeland led not to assimilation but to a rising sense of national self-consciousness. A relatively strong push for greater independence has been made by the indigenous elites in this region of Russia since 1991.

The goal of returning home has become the *raison d'être* of the Crimean Tatars as it was for the other deported nations before 1956. For the first time since World War II, the Crimean Tatars were recognized as a separate national community in the 1989 census, and the restoration of this official recognition presaged the restoration of their right to return to Crimea. Between 1989 and 1992, nearly 200,000 Crimean Tatars returned, and this return migration stream has caused a growing resentment against these "newcomers" among the resident Russians. Similarly, Germans are returning to the territory of the former Volga German ASSR, and this return migration stream is also causing a rising "nativism" among the Russian population currently resident there.

Since 1987, in response to rising nativism, nonindigenes have increasingly been returning to their ancestral homelands in what Soviet demographers have begun to refer to as a refugee migration stream (Rybakovskiy and Tarasova 1990). This seems a particularly apt description not only because this new wave of migration is a reaction to a fear of persecution on the basis of national identity but also because many of the "refugees" know no other home than the one they are leaving (Chervyakov et al. 1991). They may be returning to the home of their ancestors, but many have lived their entire lives in the regions from which they are fleeing. According to the 1989 census, more than half of all nonindigenes were born in their republic of residence in twelve of the fifteen union republics, and more than two-thirds of all nonindigenes were born in their republic of residence in seven of the fifteen union republics (Table 4.5). On

TABLE 4.5
Population Born in the Republic of Current Residence, 1989 (percent of indigenes, nonindigenes, and Russians)

Republic	*Indigenes*	*Nonindigenes*	*Russians*
Russia[a]	95.5	46.1	—
Ukraine	96.4	58.8	56.7
Belarus'	97.6	52.1	42.2
Moldova	98.1	64.8	52.0
Kazakhstan	95.1	65.4	66.0
Uzbekistan[a]	98.2	72.4	55.0
Kyrgyzstan	98.5	68.6	59.1
Tadzhikistan	98.5	79.5	48.1
Turkmenistan	98.9	70.5	52.0
Georgia[a]	98.8	77.2	48.3
Azerbaydzhan[a]	96.9	74.4	65.5
Armenia	78.4	69.7	26.4
Lithuania	97.8	58.5	49.7
Latvia	96.9	49.2	54.7
Estonia	95.6	38.8	42.9

Source: Statisticheskiy Komitet SNG 1993, vol. 12, 644–653.

[a] Nonindigenous percent does not include the groups with autonomous units within these republics. Including these groups would result in the following percents: Russia = 77.5 percent, Uzbekistan = 74.4 percent, Georgia = 80.5 percent, and Azerbaydzhan = 80.7 percent.

average, 63 percent of all nonindigenes were born in their republic of residence. Even a majority of Russians living outside the RSFSR were born in their republic of current residence.

The number of refugees was estimated at more than 600,000 by July 1990, including 420,000 Armenians and Azerbaydzhanis escaping from each others home republic, 63,000 Meskhetian Turks fleeing Uzbekistan, and another 100,000 leaving Baku—mainly Russians (*Argumenty i Fakty* 1990c). If we include the tens (if not hundreds) of thousands of nonindigenes emigrating from Central Asia in response to rising nativism, the more recent migration of Ossetians from Georgia, the 200,000 Crimean Tatars returning to Crimea, the growing Russian out-migration from autonomous republics such as Tuvinia, and the more than 200,000 evacuees from the Chernobyl' disaster, the number of refugees in the country must be well over two million. Russia alone had 1.3 million officially registered "refugees" and "forced migrants," and the total number of displaced persons for the entire former USSR had almost reached 3 million by mid-1993 (Schwartz 1993). This creates additional social and economic burdens in the areas of destination, and is certain to raise the level of nationalism "back home" in reaction to the mistreatment of co-nationals living outside their homelands. This situation is unlikely to improve significantly in the years ahead, and represents a potentially explosive new "national problem" facing each of the successor states.

In general, the home republics that comprised the Soviet federal system served as places toward which indigenes were attracted and from which nonindigenes were repelled. However, this demographic gravitation to or continued concentration in the homeland was occurring precisely at a time when social mobilization and international equalization were to have begun making the nation-homeland relationship, and with it the confederal structure itself, increasingly irrelevant. The lack of a correlation between socioeconomic development on the one hand, and interhomeland migration on the other, casts serious doubt on the developmentalist and internal colonial models on which solutions to the national question were built.

Two reasons for the continued attraction of indigenes toward their respective homelands are apparent. First, there is evidence of an emotional attachment to homeland that transcends more rational considerations (e.g., geographic differentials in economic opportunity). In addition, the construction of a system of national stratification which placed the indigene in a preferential position within his or her homeland but not outside it has also tended to make it rational for indigenes to remain concentrated in their homelands. Since the late 1980s, a rising "sense of exclusiveness" among indigenes toward their standing in the homeland, and with it an increase in anti-outsider nativism, has brought about a further reconcentration of nations in their respective homelands.

The international mixing that occurred in the USSR tended to serve as a catalyst for rising nativism, or an activated sense of exclusiveness among members of the indigenous nation. This is contrary to the expectation of both Marxist-Leninist and Western theorists who posited that greater international interaction would lead to rising assimilation, eventually resulting in the creation of a unified Soviet people. There do appear to be a few *ethnies* whose members are behaving according to this theory, such as the Karelians, the Khanty, and the Mansi, whose members are assimilating to the Russian nation even within their own homelands. These three *ethnies*, and perhaps a number of others such as the Mordvins, nonetheless conform to a qualifying remark made by Connor (1972, 351) in his landmark study of "nation-building" and "nation-destroying": "To be successful, the process of assimilation must be a very gradual one, one that progresses almost without visibility and awareness." Intensive interethnic mixing was occurring among these groups and Russians for centuries, clearly before the nationalization process itself. For a number of these groups, their integration with the Russian nation appears to be comparable to a process of national consolidation, rather than a process of international integration, because no national self-consciousness had developed.

For members of nations living outside the national homeland, integration occurs as an intergenerational process that favors the indigenous nation.[23] This, too, has been most successful among those nonindigenes who have lived outside their homeland for long periods of time, especially for those whose ancestors migrated to their present locations before the nationalization of the masses back home. Nevertheless, even the so-called natural assimilation of these outmigrants has served as a catalyst for rising national territoriality back home, as indigenous nationalists cite the loss of their "brethren" living outside as evidence of what is likely to happen to the entire nation if it does not control its own destiny in its own homeland.

Demographically at least, Russians have acted as the indigenous nation wherever they have lived. This has placed more pressure on the national communities whose homelands are incorporated within Russia to accommodate themselves to the Russian culture, though this does not necessarily mean a willing reidentification to the Russian nation. The additional Russification pressure among those groups whose members have achieved national self-consciousness should prove counterproductive to such international integration efforts. An example of this occurred in Yakutia, where the Yakuts protested plans to change the higher education quotas to allow more Russians to enroll in the university in Yakutsk. While this change was warranted by the demographic shift that had occurred among the potential student population, it caused a strong reaction among the indigenous Yakuts, who felt it a threat to the privileges due them in their own national homeland. A similar reaction occurred in

---

[23] This topic is discussed in detail in chapter 6.

Abkhazia, Estonia, and Latvia; demographic dilution has not resulted in "denationalization" but in rising nationalism.

Outside Russia, nations have increasingly asserted their right to control the movement of people, as well as goods and ideas, across the borders of their homelands. The desire of several of these nations to gather in their nations' members while discouraging the in-migration and encouraging the out-migration of "foreigners" has become a clear objective in the contemporary setting. This national attraction toward the homeland, of course, conforms to the belief that the homeland is the one and only place where the indigenous nation can survive and flourish (i.e., a "sense of spatial identity"). Or, as RUKH's program expressed it (1989, 28): "The actualization of the gamut of national rights of the various ethnic groups residing in Ukraine is inseparable from their comprehension of the fact that the Ukrainian nation holds the status of the historical master in the republic. Ukraine is the only territory in the world where the full-value existence and development of the Ukrainian *ethnos* are possible." Given that this sense of spatial identity, and with it a sense of exclusiveness regarding the indigene's place in the homeland, has grown exponentially since 1987, it is reasonable to predict that a return migration stream of nonindigenes to their respective homelands will grow larger in the coming years, and that the former republics' status as "nation-states" will, at least demographically, approach a reality that has not existed since the formation of the Soviet federation.

The exception to this may be in those regions bordering the homeland that nationalists continue to claim as their own. International tensions and conflicts have developed in several interrepublic border zones over the issue of nation-state delimitation. Hostilities have occurred in Transcaucasia and Moldova. Given the perception of Russian nationalists that northern Kazakhstan is part of the *rodina*, it would not be surprising to find a similar escalation of international hostilities in this region. According to Olcott (1990, 69), Russian nationalists in northeastern Kazakhstan have formed "political action committees whose goal is to get several northern rayons to secede from Kazakhstan and join Omsk oblast in the Russian republic." In Central Asia, the border zone between Kyrgyzstan and Uzbekistan has already been the site of conflict between these two groups. Border incidents have also occurred along the border between Tadzhikistan and Uzbekistan, and also between Kyrgyzstan and Tadzhikistan. In the Baltic region, Lithuanian nationalists have already laid claim to Kaliningrad Oblast as a part of their national homeland (Vol'skaya 1990, 2). Tensions have also increased between Russians and Ukrainians over the status of the border region between their home republics, as well as Crimea. More broadly, the question "What is Russia?" has become a lively topic of debate.[24]

---

[24] See chapter 7.

The potential for widespread interrepublic border disputes is depicted in a recent map produced by the U.S. State Department (Dillon 1990), and by political geographers in the USSR (*Rossiskaya Gazeta* 28 March 1991, 3; *Moscow News* 17 March 1991, 8–9; Kolosov 1992).

In conclusion, geographic mobilization has clearly not had the desired effect on international relations in the former USSR. Indeed, to a great extent it has had just the opposite of its intended effect. The reason for the failure of Marxist-Leninist (and Western) theory to predict behavior is at least partly explained by the nature of national territoriality, and the failure of Marxist theorists to grasp the subjective essence of the nationalist sense of homeland. Beyond this, geographic mobilization does not occur in a vacuum, and is itself a response to changes in the sociocultural, economic, and political conditions in the national homeland. These changes, whether described as "modernization" or simply as "development," are also responsible for the way in which international relations were shaped in the USSR. The remainder of the book examines the postwar trends in these areas.

CHAPTER FIVE

Social Mobilization and National Territoriality

THE RELATIONSHIP between social mobilization, or more generally "modernization," and national identity has been a hotly debated topic for at least the entire twentieth century. As noted above, Lenin ([1913] 1968) held that early capitalist development resulted in the creation of nations, or their consolidation. While modernization and the rise of capitalism alone cannot explain why a mass-based national consolidation was successful, the nationalization process from the nineteenth to the early twentieth century generally supports the contention that social and geographic mobilization of the masses accelerated their national consolidation (e.g., Weber 1976; Hroch 1985; Hamm 1986; Yukhneva 1984). During the postwar period, the relationship between social mobilization and national identity has generally been viewed as causal, with social and economic development acting as independent variables effecting changes in the degree of national self-consciousness (i.e., changes in the strength of intranational solidarity). On the one hand, modernization is said to cause the erasure of national self-consciousness as individuals are integrated into larger, international communities of interest (Lenin [1913] 1968; Deutsch 1953, 1966). Alternatively, social mobilization has been seen as a force resulting in the growth of intranational cohesion and international separatism (e.g., Nielsen 1985; Nagel and Olzak 1982; Olzak and Nagel 1986; Tiryakian and Nevitte 1985).

This chapter explores the nature of the relationship between social mobilization and national identity in the postwar USSR.[1] First, general theories designed to explain and predict this relationship are outlined. Second, the degree of social mobilization and international equalization in the degree of social mobility in the postwar period are examined.[2] In this analysis, distinctions between the social mobility of indigenes and nonindigenes in each national homeland are highlighted in order to assess the influence of national territoriality on the relationship between social mobilization and national identity. Finally, the chapter closes with an examination of the relationship between

---

[1] Since social mobilization was intimately connected with the sociocultural and political mobilization of nations in the USSR (i.e., the subjects of the next two chapters), we return to the relationship between social mobility and national identity in the remaining chapters of this book.

[2] Where possible, data are analyzed for national communities below the fifteen nations with union republics. However, since data are limited for national communities with autonomous units, the primary focus is on the nations with union republics.

Social Mobilization and National Identity

social mobility and international attitudes, as measured by surveys conducted in the Soviet Union from the 1960s to the 1980s.

Social Mobilization and National Identity

Research into the nature of this relationship normally treats social mobilization —or "modernization" generally—as a necessary and sufficient condition causing changes in national self-consciousness. This section discusses three of the major theoretical models which contend that social mobilization causes changes in national identity. The "diffusion-erasure" model states that increasing social mobilization leads to the disintegration of nations through a process of international integration or assimilation. The "internal colonialism/reactive ethnicity" model accepts the precepts of the diffusion-erasure model but adds that national self-consciousness has been retained in modernized societies due to the lack of international equalization in social mobilization. Finally, the "diffusion-competition" model argues that national self-consciousness is heightened during the process of social mobilization, due to the increased international competition for limited resources that results.[3]

Diffusion-Erasure

Throughout much of the twentieth century, a widely held belief has been that the increasing international social mobilization resulting from the "diffusion" of socioeconomic development would lead to the erasure of ethnonational identity through a process of international integration or assimilation (Deutsch 1953; Smith 1971). Nations were seen as backward-looking communities of belonging only, which would be supplanted by communities of interest (e.g., class) with "modernization." This diffusion-erasure model seemed quite plausible in suggesting that as "modernization" occurs, an increasing number of socially mobilized individuals come to perceive the world from a more universalistic viewpoint.[4] As these upwardly mobile individuals from different national communities come into closer contact (or so this theory contends), they come to see that their interests are not very different from one another, and indeed that they have more in common with one another than with other members of their respective national communities, where ties are more ascriptively based. As modernization proceeds, these intranational ties are increasingly eroded and replaced by those to other communities of interest (e.g., class). Social mobilization leads to the marginalization of the importance attributed to one's national identity over time. This is especially said to be the case for individuals living in an urban/industrial environment. Eventually, as the pro-

---

[3] The terms for these three models are taken from Nielsen (1985).
[4] This process would also supposedly involve the removal of a sense of homeland.

cesses of socioeconomic development diffuse and engulf the entirety of each national population, national consciousness becomes essentially meaningless, or is "erased."

Of course, this diffusion-erasure model conforms to a great extent not only with Western developmentalist theories, such as the social communication thesis of Deutsch (1953, 1966), but also with Marxism-Leninism. According to the latter, the national self-consciousness born of early capitalism was to give way to "proletarian internationalism" in late capitalist development as individual workers recognized that their needs were fulfilled by class rather than national affiliation. This is a basic tenet of Marxism, as stated in the *Communist Manifesto* of 1848 (Tucker 1978, 488):

> National differences and antagonisms between peoples are daily more and more vanishing, owing to the development of the bourgeoisie, to freedom of commerce, to the world-market, to uniformity in the mode of production and in the conditions of life corresponding thereto.
>
> The supremacy of the proletariat will cause them to vanish still faster.

This was echoed in Lenin's writings on the national question (e.g., [1913] 1968), in which he stated that as capitalism advanced, national identity would be eroded. As noted in chapter 3, as evidence he cited turn-of-the-century New York, which was seen as a melting pot in which immigrants from around the world entered, and out of which Americans emerged. New York City was not seen as unique in its capacity to assimilate foreigners to the American nation (Lenin [1913] 1975, 657): "what is taking place on a grand, international scale in New York is also to be seen in *every* big city and industrial township." Social mobilization in backward Russia was seen as the primary means through which national affiliation would be overcome.

The diffusion-erasure model has been seriously undermined by the actual experience in modernized and modernizing multinational states in the postwar world (Connor 1972). During the contemporary period a national resurgence has often coincided with increased social mobilization, while class solidarity has undergone a relative decline in importance (Nielsen 1985). Clearly, nations are not simply backward-looking communities of belonging but also forward-looking communities of interest. Two of the main alternative models developed in recent years in an effort to improve our understanding of the nature of the relationship between social mobilization and national identity are internal colonialism/reactive ethnicity and diffusion-competition.

Internal Colonialism/Reactive Ethnicity

According to this model, national self-consciousness continues to remain strong in modernized states due to the system of "internal colonialism" which normally accompanies socioeconomic development. As social mobilization proceeds, some "core" nation in the state is able to attain or retain a dominant position, at least in part through the exploitation of the so-called peripheral nations within the state. This exploitation is manifested in a "cultural division of labor" (Hechter 1975, 1978), which refers to an ethnic stratification system along socioeconomic lines that rewards the "core" and punishes the "periphery."[5] As a reaction to this exploitative situation, intranational cohesion in the periphery is maintained and peripheral nationalism develops along with modernization (Hechter 1975, 10): "To the extent that social stratification in the periphery is based on observable cultural differences, there exists the probability that the disadvantaged group will, in time, reactively assert its own culture as equal or superior to that of the relatively advantaged core. This may help it conceive of itself as a separate 'nation' and seek independence."

According to the internal colonialism model, socioeconomic inequality between nations is the key to understanding their continued existence in modernized states. The hypothetical relationship between social mobilization and national identity is that the less developed a group, the more nationally self-consciousness are its members. While Hechter (1975, 10) claimed that this thesis was "diametrically opposed" to the diffusion-erasure model described above, internal colonialism is more appropriately viewed as a corollary to diffusion-erasure. Internal colonialism accepts the overarching thesis that increasing social mobilization should lead to the erasure of national self-consciousness but adds that nations have not been "erased" because access to social mobilization has not been "diffused" equitably across nations. With international equalization and the breakdown of the "cultural division of labor," diffusion-erasure should be in evidence.

The reader should not be surprised if this model—particularly the "internal colonialism" variant elaborated by Hechter (1975)—sounds familiar. It is in essence the same explanation for the "national problem" in Russia elaborated by Lenin. As discussed in chapter 3, Lenin's nationality policies were based on the belief that international tensions and conflicts in Russia were a reaction by the non-Russian peoples to "Great Russian chauvinism" (i.e., the exploitation of a dominant core nation over the periphery). Nationality policies in the USSR were structured (in theory at least) to redress the ethnic stratification system inherited from the past.

During the postwar period, all Soviet political leaders from Khrushchev to Gorbachev proclaimed that the national problem "inherited from the past" had been "solved," implying or stating explicitly that international equalization had occurred, thus removing the basis for international antagonisms in the state. After Leonid Brezhnev declared in 1972 that equality had been achieved, the

---

[5] A more general discussion of ethnic stratification with socioeconomic development is provided in Shibutani and Kwan (1965). The relevance of this concept to the national question in the USSR is found in the works of Lewis et al. (1976) and Clem (1976, 1980).

goal of equalization was dropped from the five-year plans (Schroeder 1990, 43). However, the importance of international and interregional equalization in solving the national problem was not dropped from the rhetoric of the leadership. In the latest version of this, on the seventieth anniversary of the October Revolution Gorbachev declared (1987a, 415): "We correctly say that we have solved the national question. The revolution paved the way not only for the juridical, but also for the socio-economic equality of nations, doing an extraordinary amount for the leveling of economic, social and cultural development of all republics and regions, of all peoples."

If the central authorities proclaimed that the national problem had been solved through the equalization of nations and their homelands, the view from the "periphery" was frequently quite different. The image presented was often one of the continued exploitation of non-Russians by the central authorities and the "core" Russian nation. Indigenous elites in the less developed nations and republics complained that Moscow was not directing enough investment funds their way, and used the rhetoric of internal colonialism directly. For example, national leaders in Central Asia frequently depicted the region as the USSR's "cotton colony." Other analysts attempted to adapt the internal colonialism model to Soviet conditions. For example, Rywkin (1982, 57), following Spechler (1979), described Soviet policy toward Central Asia as "welfare colonialism," defined as "a politically opportunistic attempt to combine three diverse elements: a genuine interethnic economic equalitarianism of Leninist inspiration, a social welfarism reminiscent of the American attitudes toward its minorities, and a good deal of prudent tolerance for the increasingly numerous Muslim inhabitants in this politically sensitive geopolitical arena."

On the other hand, indigenes in the relatively more developed nations in the European part of the country also used the rhetoric of internal colonialism, and complained that Moscow was exploiting them by siphoning off the wealth generated in these republics for use in Siberia or the less developed republics (i.e., for equalization itself) (e.g., Smulders 1990). Nationalists in the developed republics argued that they would be even more developed if it were not for exploitation from the Soviet and Russian core. In this sense, the international equalization policy itself was viewed as a zero sum game in which the more developed nations perceived themselves as losers to the less developed nations in the state. This is similar to the perception of Slovenes and Croats in the former Yugoslavia (e.g., Kaiser 1990).

The question of international equalization in the USSR was the subject of a number of empirical studies during the 1970s and 1980s (e.g., Bahry and Nechemias 1981; Jones and Grupp 1984; Liebowitz 1987; Sacks 1982; Silver 1974a). The conclusions reached in these studies were mixed, though it was generally agreed that while international and interregional equalization had occurred during the postwar period according to a number of indices, equality itself had not been achieved.

A question that remains unanswered by most of these studies is the relationship between the equalization that has occurred and national identity. Regarding this question, a number of problems with the "internal colonialism" model have arisen in recent years. In several states, including the USSR, Spain, and Yugoslavia, the most developed nations lie in the periphery, and these are among the most nationalistic of groups in each state. If any doubt existed about this in the Soviet context, it has been dispelled since 1987 with the "national reawakening" among the most socially mobilized nations in the state (i.e., Estonians, Latvians, Lithuanians, Georgians, Armenians). Furthermore, the most developed socioprofessional strata are also among the most nationally conscious, according to surveys conducted in the USSR during the past two decades (Arutyunyan and Bromley 1986). Clearly, the fundamental tenets of internal colonialism that the least developed nations are the most nationalistic, and that the most developed nation in the state is the core community that has succeeded in exploiting all others, do not appear valid in several modernized multinational states, including the former USSR.

Nevertheless, since internal colonialism and variations on this theme have served as the cornerstone for understanding the relationship between social mobilization and national self-consciousness in Russia and the USSR, and since Soviet nationality policies during much of the past seventy years have been designed with this thesis in mind, this chapter examines the process of international equalization as well as social mobilization. It should be noted also that other versions of reactive ethnicity exist and are more sophisticated than internal colonialism.[6] One alternative that is particularly relevant in an assessment of continued national solidarity in modernized states is that upwardly mobile members of national communities often develop a sense of "relative deprivation" which occurs when expectations exceed an individual's or a group's capability to achieve them (Gurr 1970). A sense of relative deprivation may have been an especially important catalyst for rising nationalism in multi-homeland states such as the Soviet Union. Even if international equalization was occurring, indigenes may have continued to feel relatively deprived because they had not attained the dominance that they felt entitled to in their own homelands. In addition, even if a national community is relatively more developed than others in the state, its members may feel relatively deprived when comparing themselves to nations of other states. This appears to be the case in the Baltics, where indigenes compared their living standards to those in Scandanavia and other parts of western Europe, not with other parts of the USSR (e.g., Viksnins 1986). Finally, a sense of relative deprivation is not limited to the socioeconomic sphere, and normally includes a sociocultural and political dimension as well. The continued existence of indigenous perceptions of rel-

---

[6] Hechter's work on this relationship has also undergone modification since 1975. See, for example, Hechter and Levi (1979), Hechter et al. (1982), and Hechter (1985).

ative deprivation even during periods of socioeconomic equalization casts serious doubt on the ability of international equalization to ameliorate international relations in multihomeland states such as the USSR, let alone to solve the national problem by facilitating international integration.

Diffusion-Competition

Unlike the internal colonialism/reactive ethnicity model, diffusion-competition directly refutes the diffusion-erasure model. Here, nations are viewed as communities of interest, and heightened national consciousness is seen as an almost inherent part of modernization (e.g., Tiryakian and Nevitte 1985; Nielsen 1985). With social mobilization, larger numbers of members from each nation become urbanized, more highly educated, and come to rank the status of occupations similarly. In essence, modernization creates a more outward-looking, socially mobilized populace that is much more socioeconomically integrated than its premodern counterpart. This integration is the same "modernization effect" that led Lenin, Deutsch, and others to predict that the importance of national identity would be weakened, until eventually nations were "erased."

According to the diffusion-competition model, the opposite of this "erasure" is more likely. In multinational states, the international convergence of aspirations that occurs with social mobilization results not only in greater *interpersonal* contact and competition but also in more intense *international* competition for the limited resources in society. The reason for the maintenance of a national dimension to this competition, according to this model, is that nations in modernized states serve as interest groups that retain the loyalty of their members because they are able to provide them with a "competitive edge." Nations are viewed here as the most effective collective action groups in the state, since they are well organized and internally cohesive, and are thus able to outcompete other group affiliations, including class, for the time and energy of their members. This is particularly likely in cases where the members of one national community occupy the same territory, speak the same language, and share other cultural characteristics, and where members are present in all socio-professional strata (Nielsen 1985).

As the "cultural division of labor" breaks down and international equalization occurs, one's national identity tends to become more important as an instrument for gaining personal advancement in a highly competitive age. An increasing number of socially mobilized individuals with comparable skills, training, and so forth, begin to compete more intensely for the limited rewards of society, including high-status occupations. As interpersonal competition intensifies with equalization and social mobilization, upwardly mobile indigenes are more likely to assert that their national identity itself should be a decisive factor in determining the allocation of resources in the homeland.

Diffusion-competition may be viewed as a subsequent stage following a successful end to a period of internal colonialism. Viewed from the perspective of this model, international equalization will not only fail to solve the national problem in multinational states but will actually increase the likelihood of rising international tensions and conflict.

Diffusion-competition is more likely in multihomeland settings such as the former USSR. As indigenes become more geographically and socially mobilized, they come into greater contact with nonindigenous "outsiders," and compete with them for the resources of the homeland. Because indigenes generally feel that it is they who should be the ones to benefit from the socioeconomic development that takes place in the region claimed as their homeland, international tensions and conflicts are likely to grow along with modernization and equalization as indigenes compete more intensely with nonindigenes for the resources of the homeland. Under these conditions, social mobilization tends not to "erase" national consciousness but to activate national territoriality. Even equalization is unlikely to solve the national problem in multihomeland states, since indigenes feel they have a right to a dominant status in the homeland, and are unlikely to be satisfied as the mere equals of nonindigenes. Outside the homeland, nonindigenes are placed in a competitive disadvantage, and are more likely to respond in one of three ways: reactive ethnicity, outmigration toward their respective homelands, or acculturation and assimilation to the indigenous nation (i.e., diffusion-erasure).

While the diffusion-competition model helps to explain the continued efficacy of nations in modernized states, it is not without flaws. The more extreme versions of diffusion-competition overemphasize the "instrumentalist" nature of nations. An implicit assumption is that those nations whose leaders are unable to provide their members with a competitive edge will disappear. However, even though more national leaders have demanded sacrifices than have provided material rewards to their members, few nations have disappeared in the contemporary world. While national identity may in part result from conscious choices made by "rational actors," perceptions of genealogical and geographic connectedness rather than economic cost-benefit analyses are relatively more significant in explaining the strength of national identity (e.g., Connor 1984b). The belief that indigenes should be dominant in their ancestral homeland is more than an instrumental attempt to establish competitive advantage; it is also a reflection of a more deep-seated, emotional attitude about the "ancestral" homeland.

SOCIAL MOBILIZATION IN THE POSTWAR USSR

A great deal of social mobilization occurred in the USSR during the postwar years, even though much of this period is often characterized as one of stagnation (*zastoy*). It is also true that while equality across nations was not achieved, international equalization in the extent of urbanization, educational attainment, and occupational mobility was occurring (Jones and Grupp 1984). A number of reasons account for the lack of outright equality in the social sphere. First, at least in the early postwar period, Russians as the dominant nation in the USSR benefited inordinately from the socioeconomic development taking place. Not only was development primarily concentrated in the RSFSR; Russians also migrated to the urban/industrial centers in the non-Russian periphery to take advantage of development occurring there (Lewis et al. 1976, 146–155). Second, each indigenous nation whose homeland was officially recognized as a union republic also received preferential treatment in access to higher education and high-status occupations in their respective home republics.[7] This meant that in practice international equalization was mediated through a two-tiered system of national stratification which favored both the dominant "core" nation (i.e., Russians) throughout the state, and also the members of each indigenous nation living in their own home republics. International equalization in the country as a whole often occurred simultaneously with increasing inequality in each home republic, which was marked by an increasingly privileged status of indigenes in their respective homelands. Over time this "indigenization" became a dominant trend in the USSR (at least for those nations at the union republic level).

This section traces the degree of urbanization, educational attainment, and occupational mobility that the various nations in the USSR achieved between 1959 and 1989. Where possible, data are included on those indigenous *ethnies* whose homelands are classified as autonomous regions in the state. However, due to data limitations, the primary focus in this section is on the fifteen union republic nations.

Urbanization

Urbanization of a state's or nation's population is in general thought to be indicative of that state's or nation's socioeconomic development. In the USSR in particular, where the urban and industrial proletariat was the main beneficiary of the transition to socialism, urbanization has often been viewed as a surrogate for "modernization" (Clem 1980, 23):

> Especially for the Soviet Union, the level of urbanization is a good surrogate for "economic development," because in the USSR historically the level and the rate

---

[7] To a lesser extent, this indigenous favoritism also occurred in the autonomous regions, though here the competing claim to indigenous status between the union republic nation and the autonomous national communities diminished the extent of privileges for the autonomous groups. A hierarchy of privilege also existed among the autonomous *ethnies*. In general, national communities with autonomous republics had more autonomous rights than those with autonomous oblasts, which in turn were relatively more privileged than those with autonomous okrugs, the latter being concentrated among the peoples of Northern Siberia.

of urbanization are linked both conceptually and empirically to industrialization, the principle mechanism whereby economic development has taken place. . . . Urbanization is important as an indicator not only of economic development in the limited sense, but also of social and cultural development, because in the USSR urbanites enjoy appreciably higher living standards, better access to educational institutions, the media, services, superior health care, and so on.

Urbanization also acts to bring members from different nations into more intimate contact and more intense competition with one another. Like interhomeland migration, rural to urban migration was viewed as progressive both due to the social mobilization that occurs in cities and also due to its role in the international integration of the population. As noted above, Lenin saw the urban/industrial environment as the great facilitator of assimilation in the Russian Empire. Although much of the thinking of Lenin and the Bolsheviks changed after the October Revolution, this view of cities as melting pots did not (Ruble 1989, 405): "The projected integration of ethnic cultural identities through the creation of a unified, urban, industrial, socialist society has remained one of the central legitimation myths of the Soviet regime."

The urbanization data indicate that between 1926 and 1959 the USSR experienced rapid urbanization, increasing from 13.3 percent in 1926 to 38.2 percent in 1959 (Table 5.1). However, this urbanization was not experienced equally by all republics and nations. The Russian homeland went from the eighth most urbanized territory in 1926 to the most urbanized in 1959, and only the Komi ASSR urbanized at a faster rate during this period. In 1926 the Russians were less urbanized than the Estonians, Latvians, and Armenians. Between 1926 and 1959, Russians migrated from rural to urban areas and became more dispersed throughout the state to take advantage of the urbanization and industrialization occurring in non-Russian territories (Lewis et al. 1976, 146–155). By 1959 Russians had become the second most urbanized nation in the state (Table 5.2). Of course, this does not necessarily indicate that preference was given for development solely on a national basis. During World War II the more urbanized, developed western republics and nations were devastated, and the industrial base was further built up in Russia "behind the Urals." This no doubt contributed to the relative decline of the western republics between 1926 and 1959.

While it is true that the Russian nation benefited inordinately from the development taking place in the USSR during the Stalin era, there was also international convergence in the rate of urbanization overall. Using coefficients of variations (CVs), which measure deviation around the mean and so indicate whether there was greater convergence or equalization (smaller value) or growing divergence or inequality (larger value), it is clear that equalization occurred both among republics and national communities. In 1926 the CV for home republic urbanization was 80.3 percent. By 1959 this figure had decreased to

TABLE 5.1
Urban Population of the USSR, by Nation and Home Republic, 1926–1959 (percent)

	Home Republic			Nation		
Nation/Home Republic	1926	1959	Percentage Point Change	1926	1959	Percentage Point Change
Russian[a]	14.0	44.8	40.8	15.7	46.5	30.8
Ukrainian	13.0	33.5	20.5	6.8	28.8	22.0
Belorussian	8.6	21.1	12.5	5.3	23.1	17.8
Uzbek	17.2	28.5	11.3	13.8	17.5	3.7
Kazakh	5.6	34.3	28.7	1.3	17.7	16.4
Georgian	15.5	34.4	18.9	7.1	28.8	21.7
Azerbaydzhan	23.1	40.4	17.3	12.0	28.8	16.8
Lithuanian	11.8	24.4	12.6	7.6	21.6	14.0
Moldavian	8.5	15.2	6.7	5.8	8.0	2.2
Latvian	25.8	38.3	12.5	23.0	32.2	9.2
Kirgiz	8.3	24.1	15.8	1.1	6.5	5.4
Tadzhik	7.4	20.5	13.1	11.5	13.7	2.2
Armenian	12.1	41.0	28.9	23.8	46.3	22.5
Turkmen	7.3	29.7	22.4	0.4	16.2	15.8
Estonian	23.2	39.0	15.8	21.1	32.5	11.4
Autonomous Republics						
Karelian	6.5	34.3	27.8	1.5	16.8	15.3
Komi	0.0	41.0	41.0	1.3	18.7	17.4
Mari	0.0	18.9	18.9	0.3	6.4	6.1
Mordvin	1.4	11.6	10.2	1.6	21.2	19.6
Chuvash	2.6	18.6	16.0	1.0	14.1	13.1
Tatar	7.6	34.6	27.0	10.1	38.7	28.6
Dagestan[b]	7.3	26.8	19.5	2.7	15.0	12.3
Kabardin-Balkar[c]	0.0	27.7	27.7	0.4	9.0	8.6
Kalmyk	0.0	12.5	12.5	0.7	11.5	10.8
North Ossetian	29.8	49.8	20.0	6.0	29.3	23.3
Chechen-Ingush[c]	16.9	36.8	19.9	1.0	7.8	6.8
Bashkir	5.8	32.7	26.9	1.3	14.6	13.3
Udmurt	10.5	37.6	27.1	0.6	15.8	15.2
Buryat	11.6	26.0	14.4	0.6	10.4	9.8
Tuvin	—	20.0	—	—	5.4	—
Yakut	0.0	15.3	15.3	0.0	5.2	5.2
Abkhaz	10.7	27.1	16.4	2.6	20.0	17.4
Karakalpak	0.0	14.8	14.8	0.0	10.7	10.7
Russian	14.0	44.8	30.8	15.7	46.5	30.8

(*continued*)

TABLE 5.1 (*Continued*)

Nation/Home Republic	Home Republic			Nation		
	1926	1959	Percentage Point Change	1926	1959	Percentage Point Change
Non-Russian	11.8	31.1	19.3	9.8	26.9	17.1
Total USSR	13.3	38.2	24.9	—	—	—

Source: Clem 1980, 24–25.

Note: Table 5.1 uses the urban definition of cities of population size fifteen thousand and over, since the urban definition changed between the 1926 and 1959 census. For a discussion of census definitions of urban areas and their change over time, see Rowland 1986.

[a] The Russian homeland is defined as the RSFSR minus all autonomous republics incorporated within it.

[b] The nations included within the second set of figures under Dagestan include: Avars, Lezgins, Dargins, Kumyks, Laks, Tabasarans, Nogays, Rutuls, Tsakhurs, and Aguls.

[c] The nation category for the Kabardin-Balkar and the Chechen-Ingush rows combine the figures for both titular nations.

33.9 percent.[8] The amount of convergence was even greater for the urbanization rates across national communities—the CV declined from 117.8 percent in 1926 to 55.2 percent in 1959. Nonetheless, as is clear from both sets of statistics, "equality" across nations and homelands (i.e., CVs of 0) had not been achieved by 1959.

During the post-Stalin period, a continuing trend toward convergence in the extent of urbanization was evident between 1959 and 1979 for both home republics and nations (Tables 5.2 and 5.3; Maps 5.1 and 5.2). The coefficient of variation for republics decreased from 27.6 percent to 20.4 percent from 1959 to 1979, while the CV for nations decreased even more rapidly, from 46 percent to 33.1 percent.[9] International equalization continued during the 1980s; the coefficient of variation for nations reached 29.0 percent by 1989. However, the CV for home republics increased to 21.2 percent, indicating a growing inequality across regions in the country. This occurred primarily as a result of an extremely slow rate of urbanization among indigenes in Soviet Central Asia during the 1980s, coupled with an increasing out-migration of Russians and other nonindigenes from urban areas in the region. In addition, the international conflicts between Armenians and Azerbaydzhanis had a pronounced dampen-

---

[8] These CVs are calculated using the thirty-two national homelands listed in Table 5.1 (excluding the Tuvin ASSR and Tuvinians). The use of a percentage figure is somewhat misleading and must be treated with caution. While 0 is the minimum figure possible and indicates complete convergence (i.e., all values the same), CVs over 100 percent are possible, and there is theoretically no maximum value.

[9] Because different measures of urbanization were used for Tables 5.1 and 5.2, the urban rates and CVs for 1959 in the two tables are not the same.

TABLE 5.2
Urban Population of the USSR, by Nation and Home Republic, 1959–1989 (percent)

Nation/Home Republic	Home Republic				Nation			
	1959	1970	1979	1989	1959	1970	1979	1989
Russian	52	62	69	74	57.7	68.1	74.4	78.2
Ukrainian	46	55	61	67	39.2	48.5	55.6	62.7
Belorussian	34	43	55	65	32.4	43.7	54.7	65.1
Uzbek	34	37	41	41	21.8	24.9	29.2	31.0
Kazakh	44	50	54	57	24.1	26.7	31.6	38.7
Georgian	42	48	52	56	36.1	44.0	49.1	54.7
Azerbaydzhan	48	50	53	54	34.8	39.7	44.5	50.1
Lithuanian	39	50	61	68	35.1	46.4	57.3	65.1
Moldavian	22	32	39	47	12.9	20.4	26.8	36.0
Latvian	56	62	68	71	47.5	52.7	58.0	60.7
Kirgiz	34	37	39	38	10.8	14.6	19.6	22.2
Tadzhik	33	37	35	33	20.6	26.0	28.1	28.3
Armenian	50	59	66	68	56.6	64.8	69.7	69.9
Turkmen	46	48	48	45	25.4	31.0	32.3	33.4
Estonian	56	65	70	72	47.1	55.1	59.1	60.0
Autonomous Republics								
Karelian	63	69	78	82	30.9	44.9	55.1	62.2
Komi[a]	49	54	65	76	24.4	32.1	40.6	46.7
Mordvin	18	36	47	57	29.1	36.1	47.4	54.1
Mari	28	41	53	61	11.7	20.5	31.2	41.7
Udmurt	44	57	65	70	22.2	32.1	41.6	48.8
Chuvash	24	36	46	58	19.6	29.1	38.8	50.8
Tatar	42	52	63	73	47.2	55.0	62.8	69.0
Bashkir	38	48	57	64	19.7	26.6	36.8	51.2
Kalmyk	21	34	41	46	24.0	35.8	43.4	49.4
Chechen[b]	41	42	43	41	22.3	21.8	25.3	28.0
Kabardin[b]	40	48	58	61	14.7	23.9	37.2	44.6
Ossetian[c]	48	60	64	66	34.9	53.3	60.1	65.6
Dagestan[d]	30	35	39	44	16.3	24.0	30.8	38.4
Tuvin	29	38	43	47	9.0	17.1	22.4	31.9
Buryat[e]	35	39	50	55	16.9	24.6	34.8	42.3
Yakut	49	56	61	67	17.1	21.1	25.3	27.9
Abkhaz	37	44	47	48	27.8	34.5	40.5	48.1
Karakalpak	27	35	42	48	19.8	30.5	41.2	53.9
Other								
Jew	—	—	—	—	95.3	97.9	98.8	98.8
German	—	—	—	—	39.3	45.4	49.7	52.8

(*continued*)

TABLE 5.2 (*Continued*)

Nation/Home Republic	Home Republic				Nation			
	1959	1970	1979	1989	1959	1970	1979	1989
Pole	—	—	—	—	34.0	45.2	57.5	58.8
Bulgar	—	—	—	—	30.6	40.4	34.7	48.4
Greek	—	—	—	—	54.0	66.6	63.4	66.8
Korean	—	—	—	—	48.3	77.6	78.0	82.4

Sources: Kozlov 1982, 100; TsSU SSSR 1962, 16:20–29, 184–195; TsSU SSSR 1973, 4:20–262; TsSU SSSR 1984, 10–14; *Pravda* 1989; *Soyuz* 1990a, 1990b.

Note: Table 5.2 compares urban levels using census definitions, which remained constant between 1959 and 1989. While the census definition of urban did not change between 1959 and 1989, the criteria did vary between republics. The RSFSR had the most stringent definition of cities (12,000 plus 85 percent of the working population in nonagricultural occupations). Belorussia, Armenia, Azerbaydzhan, Estonia, Lithuania, Latvia, Uzbekistan, Kirgizia, and Kazakhstan used the same criteria. Georgia, Moldavia, Ukraine, Tadzhikistan, and Turkmenia used a somewhat less exclusive definition. The definitions for "Urban-type settlements" also varied between republics in the same way. For a description of this issue, see Rowland 1986 and Leasure and Lewis 1966.

[a] Komi percentages are for both Komi and Komi-Permyaks.

[b] Chechen homeland is the Chechen-Ingush ASSR. National urban rates are for Chechens only, since the 1979 census did not provide this information for the Ingush. The same is true for the Balkars, who share the Kabardin-Balkar ASSR.

[c] Ossetian homeland is the North Ossetian ASSR plus the South Ossetian Autonomous Oblast.

[d] Nation category under Dagestan refers to the Avar and Lezgin only, since the 1979 census provides urban data for these two nations only.

[e] Buryat homeland is the Buryat ASSR plus the Agin Buryat and Ust'-Ordyn Buryat Autonomous Okrugs. Before 1979 these were referred to as national okrugs.

ing effect on urbanization rates in both union republics, and also on the Armenian national rate.

A number of nations and homelands urbanized at a more rapid rate than the Russians or the RSFSR during the postwar period.[10] Between 1959 and 1970 ten home republics urbanized as fast or faster than the Russian homeland, while between 1970 and 1979 sixteen homelands urbanized as fast or faster. Between 1979 and 1989, however, the number of republics whose urbanization rate exceeded that of the RSFSR decreased to twelve. According to the international comparison, twelve national communities urbanized as fast or faster than the Russians between 1959 and 1970, while nineteen experienced an equal or faster rate between 1970 and 1979. Between 1979 and 1989 the urbanization rate of twenty-four of the thirty-eight national communities included in Table 5.2 exceeded the Russian rate.

[10] While definitions vary among several republics and make this change less certain (Rowland 1986), the territorial units in which definitions are the same show the same trends, indicating that real equalization in the rate of urbanization was taking place throughout the USSR.

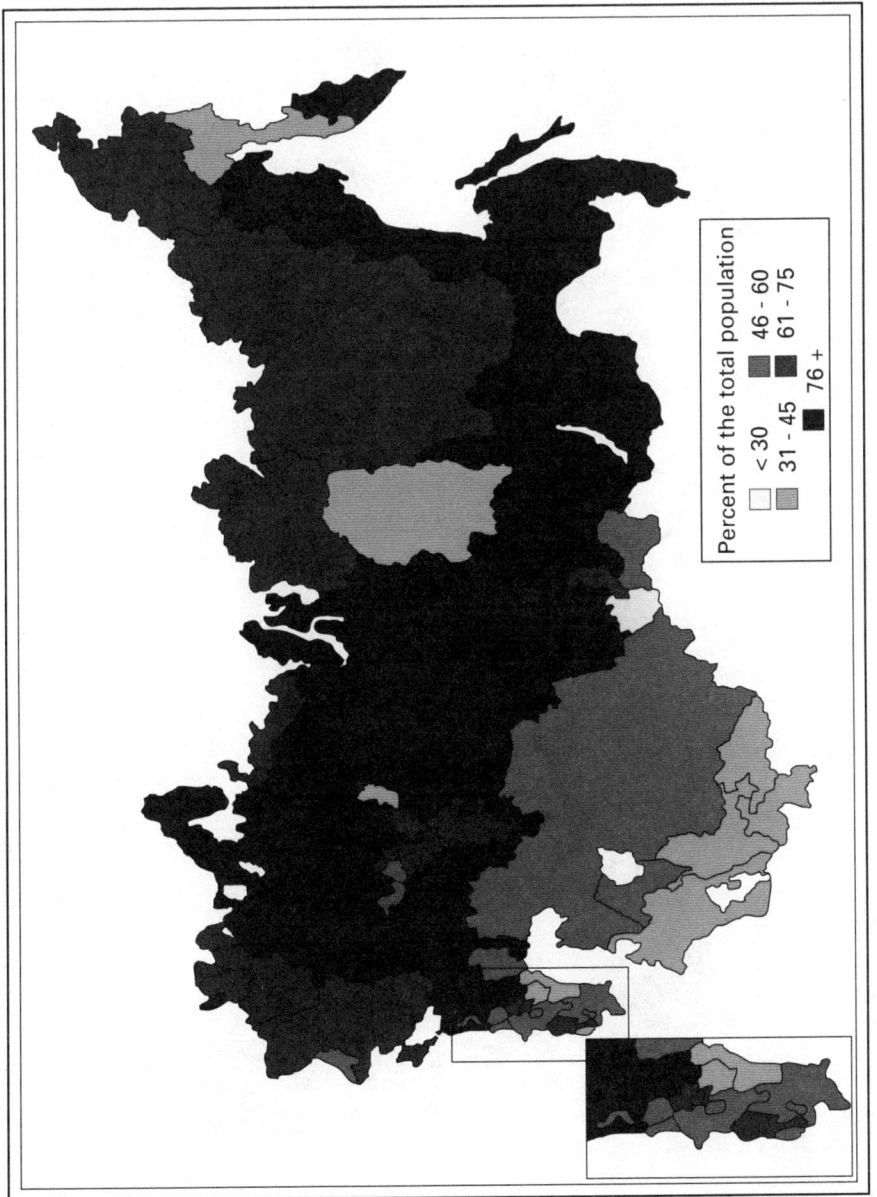

Map 5.1 Urban Percent of the Total Population, 1989

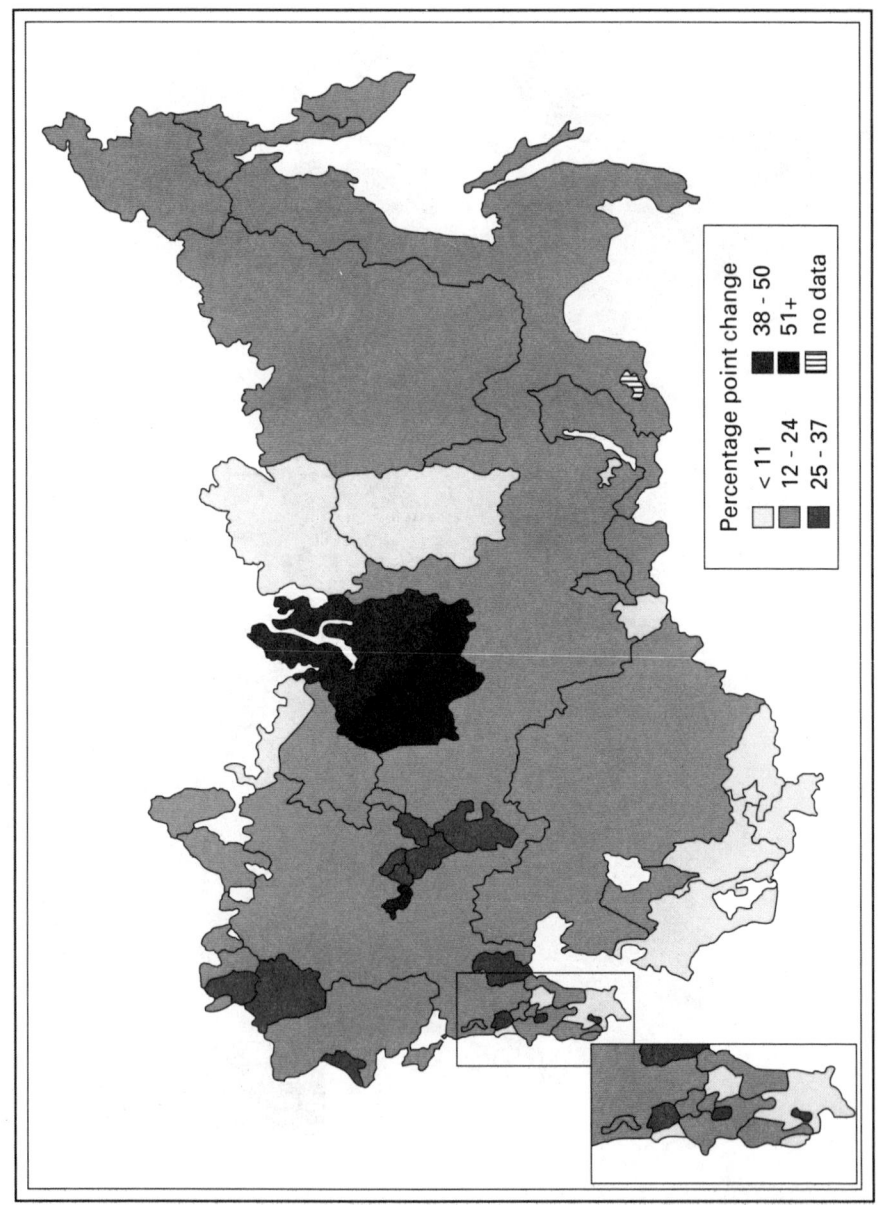

Map 5.2 Rate of Urbanization, 1959–1989

TABLE 5.3
Urbanization in the USSR, by Nation and Home Republic, 1959–1989 (average annual percentage point change)

Nation/Home Republic	Home Republic			Nation			
	1959–70	1970–79	1979–89	1959–89	1959–70	1970–79	1979–89	1959–89
Russian	0.9	0.8	0.5	0.7	0.9	0.7	0.4	0.7
Ukrainian	0.8	0.7	0.6	0.7	0.8	0.8	0.7	0.8
Belorussian	1.1	1.3	1.0	1.1	1.0	1.2	1.0	1.1
Uzbek	0.3	0.4	0.0	0.2	0.3	0.5	0.2	0.3
Kazakh	0.5	0.4	0.3	0.4	0.2	0.5	0.7	0.5
Georgian	0.5	0.4	0.4	0.5	0.7	0.6	0.6	0.6
Azerbaydzhan	0.2	0.3	0.1	0.2	0.7	0.5	0.6	0.5
Lithuanian	1.0	1.2	0.7	1.0	1.0	1.2	0.8	1.0
Moldavian	0.9	0.8	0.8	0.8	0.7	0.7	0.9	0.8
Latvian	0.5	0.7	0.3	0.5	0.5	0.6	0.3	0.4
Kirgiz	0.3	0.2	−0.1	0.1	0.3	0.6	0.3	0.4
Tadzhik	0.4	−0.2	−0.2	0.0	0.5	0.2	0.02	0.3
Armenian	0.8	0.8	0.2	0.6	0.7	0.5	0.02	0.4
Turkmen	0.2	0.0	−0.3	0.0	0.5	0.1	0.1	0.3
Estonian	0.8	0.6	0.2	0.5	0.7	0.4	0.1	0.4
Autonomous Republics								
Karelian	0.5	1.0	0.4	0.6	1.3	1.1	0.7	1.0
Komi	0.5	1.2	1.1	0.9	0.7	0.9	0.6	0.7
Mordvin	1.6	1.2	1.0	1.3	0.6	1.3	0.7	0.8
Mari	1.2	1.3	0.8	1.1	0.8	1.2	1.1	1.0
Udmurt	1.2	0.9	0.5	0.9	0.9	1.1	0.7	0.9
Chuvash	1.1	1.1	1.2	1.1	0.9	1.1	1.2	1.0

(continued)

TABLE 5.3 (Continued)

Nation/Home Republic	Home Republic				Nation			
	1959–70	1970–79	1979–89	1959–89	1959–70	1970–79	1979–89	1959–89
Tatar	0.9	1.2	1.0	1.0	0.7	0.9	0.6	0.7
Bashkir	0.9	1.0	0.7	0.9	0.6	1.1	1.4	1.1
Kalmyk	1.2	0.8	0.5	0.8	1.1	0.8	0.6	0.8
Chechen	0.1	0.1	−0.2	0.0	−0.05	0.4	0.3	0.2
Kabardin	0.7	1.1	0.3	0.7	0.8	1.5	0.7	1.0
Ossetian	1.1	0.4	0.2	0.6	1.7	0.8	0.6	1.0
Dagestan	0.5	0.4	0.5	0.5	0.7	0.8	0.8	0.7
Tuvin	0.8	0.6	0.4	0.6	0.7	0.6	1.0	0.8
Buryat	0.4	1.2	0.5	0.7	0.7	1.1	0.8	0.8
Yakut	0.6	0.6	0.6	0.6	0.4	0.5	0.3	0.4
Abkhaz	0.6	0.3	0.1	0.4	0.6	0.7	0.8	0.7
Karakalpak	0.7	0.8	0.6	0.7	1.0	1.2	1.3	1.1
Others								
Jews	—	—	—	—	0.2	0.1	0.0	0.1
German	—	—	—	—	0.6	0.5	0.3	0.5
Pole	—	—	—	—	1.0	1.4	0.1	0.8
Bulgar	—	—	—	—	0.9	−0.6	1.4	0.6
Greek	—	—	—	—	1.1	−0.4	0.3	0.1
Korean	—	—	—	—	2.7	0.04	0.4	1.1

Source: Table 5.2.

In the postwar USSR, urbanization resulted primarily in the increasing concentration of each indigenous nation in the cities of its own home republic (Table 5.4; Maps 5.3 and 5.4). Between 1959 and 1989 the shift of indigenes toward the "homeland urban" location was dramatic. Every nation and *ethnie* included in this analysis experienced an increase in the percentage of its members in this location. The international variations generally followed the contours of the federal hierarchy—union republic-level nations had the highest percentage of their membership in the homeland urban location, while autonomous okrug level *ethnies* on average had the lowest. Of course, even within each tier of the federation, substantial variation existed.

In 1989 the percentage in the homeland rural location was still greater than the percentage in the homeland urban location for six of the union republic nations, eighteen of the autonomous republic nations, and for all the autonomous oblast- and okrug-level *ethnies*. However, for most national communities, the increasing concentration in the homeland urban location was matched or exceeded by a decreasing percent in the "homeland rural" location. Clearly, the continued concentration of nations in their respective home republics discussed in chapter 4 was not an indication of indigenous immobility. The movement of indigenes from a rural, ethnically homogeneous environment to a more interethnic urban setting brought an increasing number of socially mobilized indigenes into more intense contact and competition with Russians and other nonindigenes. These were the conditions in which diffusion-competition occurred.

Urbanization was also occurring for the members of most national communities living outside their home republics (Table 5.5). The percentage of members in the "outside urban" location increased faster or decreased slower than in "outside rural" areas for all the union republic-level nations, all but two of the autonomous republic level nations, and all the autonomous oblast- and okrug-level *ethnies*. This shift in favor of the outside urban location was greater for the autonomous level groups than for the union republic-level nations. However, the outside urban location was also the place where the acculturation and assimilation of members (i.e., diffusion-erasure) was most likely to occur, and the groups whose members were least nationally self-conscious (i.e., those whose homelands are designated autonomous okrugs) were also most at risk.

An indigenization of cities was occurring along with the urbanization of indigenes, and this was working against the Russification that had occurred earlier (Table 5.6; Maps 5.3–5.6). An indigenization and "de-Russification" of cities occurred between 1959 and 1989 in all the union republics except Estonia and Latvia, and the indigenes had become demographically dominant in the cities of all union republics but Kazakhstan and Kyrgyzstan by 1989. Urban indigenization and de-Russification also occurred in all autonomous republics except Karelia and the Komi ASSR. However, in 1989 Russians still demographically outweighed indigenes in the cities of all the autonomous republics

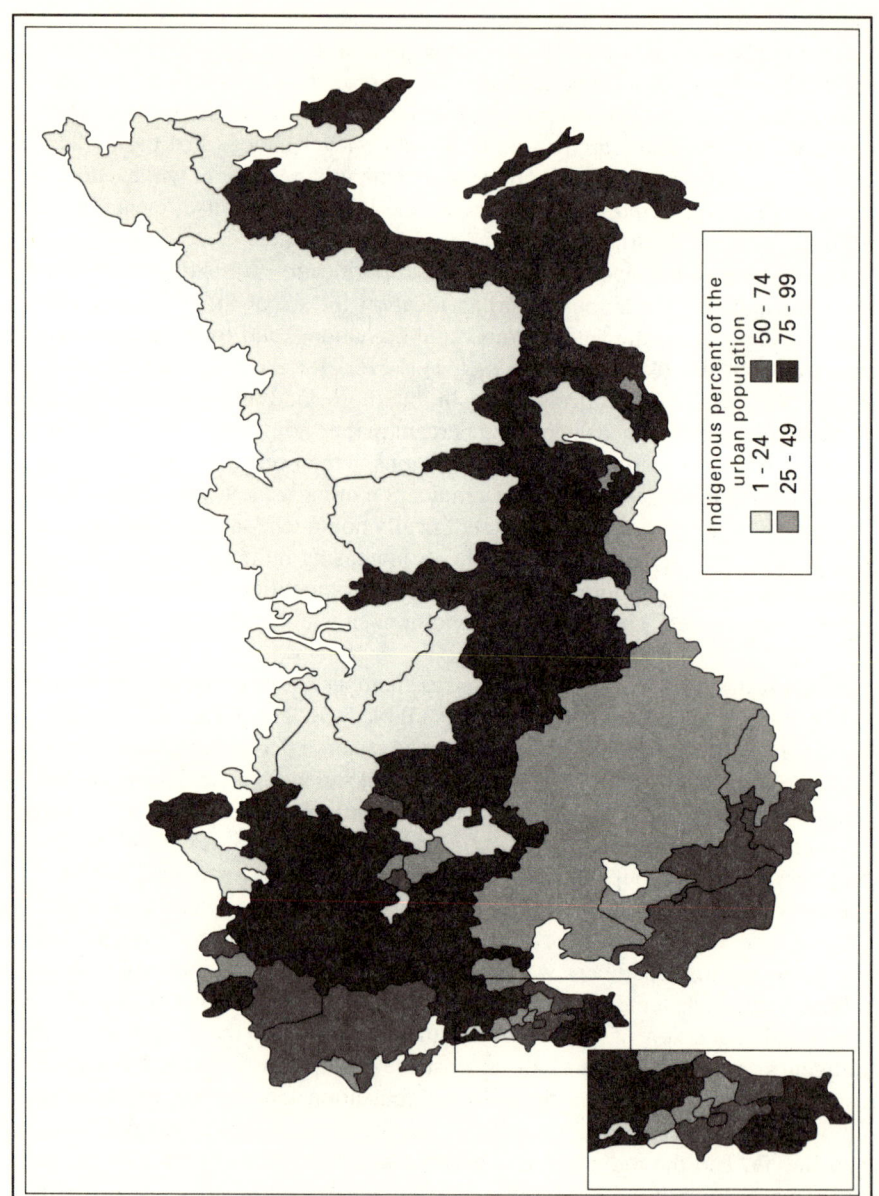

Map 5.3   Indigenous Percent of the Urban Population, 1989

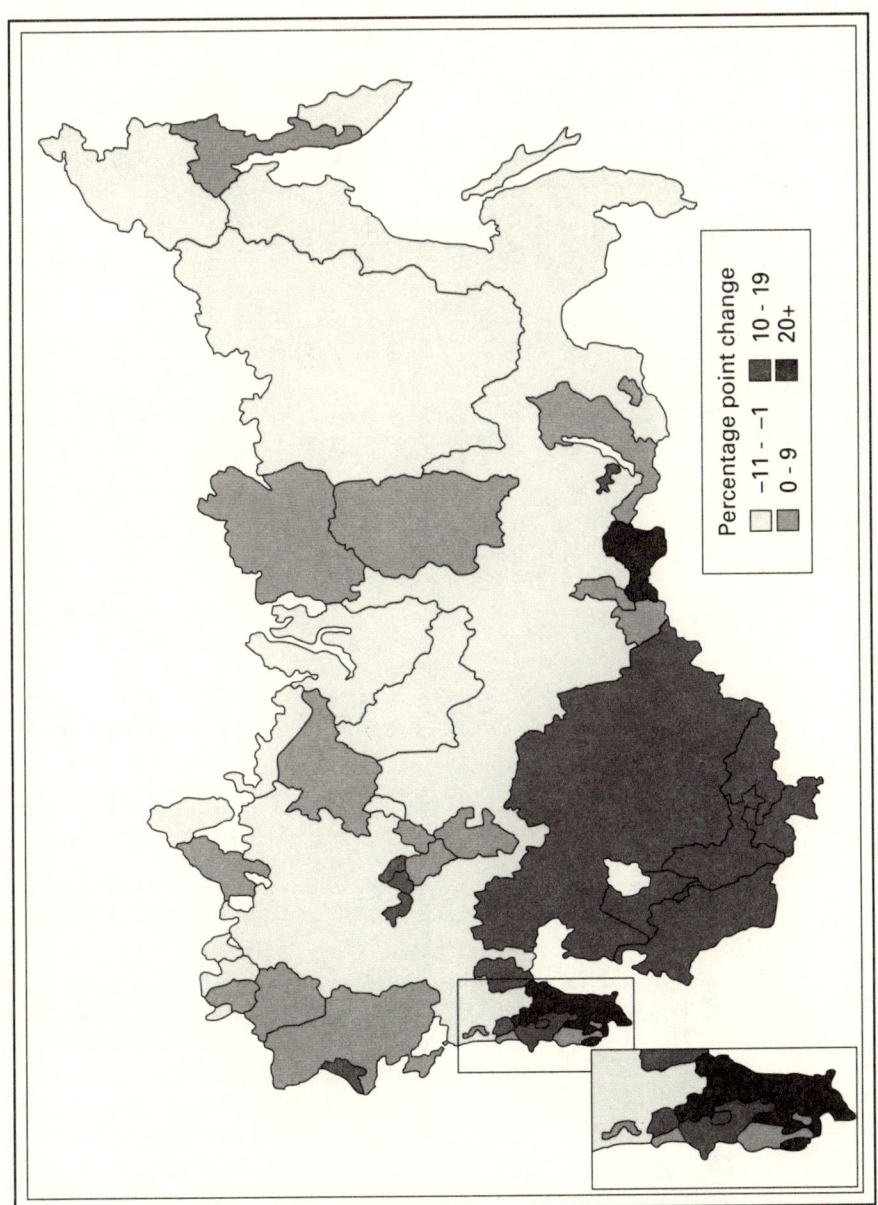

Map 5.4 Indigenization of the Urban Population, 1959–1989

TABLE 5.4
The Location of National Members in Their Home Republics, 1959–1989 (percent of total national population in homeland urban and homeland rural areas)

Nation	Homeland Urban					Homeland Rural				
	1959	1970	1979	1989	Percentage Point Change	1959	1970	1979	1989	Percentage Point Change
Union Republics										
Russian	47.1	54.8	59.5	63.3	16.2	38.7	28.7	23.1	19.2	−19.5
Ukrainian	31.6	39.7	45.7	51.1	19.5	54.7	46.9	40.5	33.6	−21.1
Belorussian	21.0	29.9	39.2	48.5	27.5	61.5	50.6	40.8	30.3	−31.2
Moldavian	8.2	14.7	20.4	27.9	19.7	77.0	70.7	64.7	55.4	−21.6
Uzbek	16.9	19.3	24.6	25.9	9.0	66.9	64.7	60.3	58.8	−8.1
Kazakh	18.7	21.1	25.0	30.8	12.1	58.4	58.9	55.7	49.5	−8.9
Kirgiz	9.5	12.8	15.9	19.2	9.7	76.9	75.7	72.6	69.0	−7.9
Tadzhik	14.7	19.5	19.3	19.8	5.1	60.5	56.8	57.9	55.4	−5.1
Turkmen	24.3	29.4	30.8	31.4	7.1	68.0	63.5	62.5	61.6	−6.4
Georgian	33.7	41.2	46.1	50.8	17.1	62.9	55.2	50.0	44.4	−18.5
Azerbaydzhan	30.8	35.6	39.6	43.1	12.3	54.0	50.6	46.4	42.6	−11.4
Armenian	29.1	38.9	45.3	46.2	17.1	26.6	23.2	20.3	20.5	−6.1
Lithuanian	31.1	43.2	54.2	61.9	30.8	61.4	50.9	40.9	33.4	−28.0
Latvian	43.3	48.5	53.2	57.0	13.7	49.4	45.3	40.2	38.1	−11.3
Estonian	42.3	50.3	54.8	55.8	13.5	48.0	41.6	38.1	38.1	−9.9
Autonomous Republics										
Bashkir	10.2	14.2	19.2	25.2	15.0	64.4	57.8	49.0	34.4	−30.0
Buryat[a]	9.9	16.5	24.2	30.2	20.3	70.8	66.2	57.5	50.8	−20.0
Avar	8.3	16.1	21.5	25.4	17.1	80.2	72.0	65.2	57.1	−23.1
Dargin	12.3	19.2	22.0	24.2	11.9	81.4	70.8	64.0	52.6	−28.8
Kumyk	29.9	37.0	39.1	38.9	9.0	59.7	52.5	49.5	43.3	−16.4

Lezgin	5.4	10.4	14.1	16.7	11.3	43.3	39.9	35.2	27.2	−16.1
Kabardin	11.3	20.8	33.8	40.1	28.8	82.2	73.8	60.5	52.9	−29.3
Balkar	11.1	23.2	45.2	48.8	37.7	69.3	63.1	44.8	34.3	−35.0
Kalmyk	12.6	29.6	36.5	41.8	29.2	48.6	50.8	46.9	42.4	−6.2
Karelian	15.9	25.7	32.3	37.2	21.3	35.3	31.9	26.4	23.0	−12.3
Komi	22.6	28.4	35.9	39.6	17.0	62.8	57.4	50.1	45.0	−17.8
Mari	4.1	7.3	13.0	17.8	13.7	51.3	42.7	36.3	30.5	−20.8
Mordvin	1.7	5.0	7.5	10.4	8.7	26.2	23.9	20.9	16.8	−9.4
Ossetian[b]	20.1	34.2	38.2	41.8	21.7	47.6	34.5	28.9	25.1	−22.5
Tatar[c]	8.0	10.0	13.0	16.8	8.8	19.1	15.9	13.0	9.7	−9.4
Tuvin	7.7	15.4	20.7	28.8	21.1	90.2	81.7	76.8	67.3	−22.9
Udmurt	14.1	19.3	25.4	29.7	15.6	62.1	49.5	41.9	36.8	−25.3
Chechen	5.3	14.8	18.2	19.2	13.9	52.9	68.2	62.7	57.5	4.6
Ingush	4.0	22.6	25.6	24.4	20.4	41.6	49.5	46.7	44.5	2.9
Chuvash	6.4	11.4	16.4	22.9	16.5	46.0	39.1	34.3	26.3	−19.7
Yakut	15.4	18.8	22.1	24.6	9.2	80.1	77.7	73.6	71.0	−9.1
Karakalpak	17.7	27.7	38.5	50.0	32.3	72.7	64.5	54.4	41.9	−30.8
Abkhaz	23.4	29.4	33.8	38.9	15.5	70.1	63.5	57.6	49.7	−20.4
Autonomous Oblasts										
Altay	5.3	6.5	7.8	8.8	3.5	78.7	77.3	75.9	74.8	−3.9
Adygey	7.5	10.4	20.6	25.5	18.0	75.3	71.2	58.8	50.9	−24.4
Khakass	12.1	14.4	22.1	27.9	15.8	73.7	67.6	58.9	50.4	−23.3
Karachay	5.9	10.9	19.0	24.9	19.0	77.4	75.2	64.3	58.1	−19.3
Cherkess	4.8	9.2	15.0	23.1	18.3	74.5	69.2	59.1	53.7	−20.8
Autonomous Okrugs										
Nenets[d]	5.3	8.8	7.8	9.8	4.5	85.2	80.5	78.4	76.2	−9.0
Evenk	0.8	1.6	1.7	2.5	1.7	13.3	11.1	10.2	9.1	−4.2
Dolgan[e]	—	5.4	4.4	5.5	0.1	—	83.7	81.4	65.6	−18.1
Koryak	1.9	12.3	12.3	15.4	13.5	79.2	66.5	59.5	55.7	−23.5

(*continued*)

TABLE 5.4 (Continued)

Nation	Homeland Urban				Homeland Rural			
	1959	1970	1979	1989	Percentage Point Change	1959	1970	1979	1989	Percentage Point Change

Nation	1959	1970	1979	1989	Percentage Point Change	1959	1970	1979	1989	Percentage Point Change
Autonomous Okrugs										
Chukchi	5.9	11.0	7.3	6.4	0.5	79.1	70.0	73.4	72.1	–7.0
Komi-Permyak	8.3	11.4	13.4	16.0	7.7	79.2	69.2	56.6	46.8	–32.4
Khanty	4.1	8.5	11.0	16.6	12.5	54.8	49.3	42.6	36.2	–18.6
Mansi	5.1	18.7	24.3	31.7	26.6	82.5	68.0	57.1	45.7	–36.8
Averages[f]										
Union Republics	26.6	32.9	38.2	42.1	15.5	57.4	52.1	47.6	43.3	–14.1
Autonomous Republics	12.1	19.9	25.9	30.1	18.0	59.0	54.2	47.7	40.9	–18.1
Autonomous Oblasts[g]	7.1	10.3	16.9	22.0	14.9	75.9	72.1	63.4	57.6	–18.3
Autonomous Okrugs	4.5	10.3	11.1	14.1	9.6	67.6	59.2	54.0	48.8	–18.8

Sources: TsSU SSSR 1962, 16 vols.; TsSU SSSR 1974, vol. 4; Goskomstat 1989d, vol. 4; Statisticheskiy Komitet SNG 1993, vol. 7, parts 1–2.

[a] The Buryat homeland figures include Buryats in the Buryat Autonomous Republic, the Agin Buryat Autonomous Okrug, and the Ust'-Ordin Buryat Autonomous Okrug.
[b] The Ossetian homeland figures include Ossetians in the North Ossetian Autonomous Republic and the South Ossetian Autonomous Oblast.
[c] The Tatar figures for 1989 include Crimean Tatars, because the Crimean Tatars were included in the Tatar totals for the 1959–79 period.
[d] The Nenets homeland figures include Nenets in the Nenets Autonomous Okrug, the Yamalo-Nenets Autonomous Okrug, and the Taymyr (Dolgano-Nenets) Autonomous Okrug.
[e] The Dolgan homeland figures include Dolgans in the Taymyr Autonomous Okrug.
[f] Averages are unweighted, with each national homeland treated as one observation.
[g] The Dolgans were excluded from the averages for Autonomous Okrugs, because there was no Dolgan figure for 1959.

TABLE 5.5
Location of National Members Outside Their Respective Home Republics, 1959–1989
(percent of national population living in outside urban and outside rural areas)

Nation	Outside Urban					Outside Rural			
	1959	1970	1979	1989	Percentage Point Change	1959	1970	1979	1989	Percentage Point Change
Union Republics										
Russian	10.6	13.2	14.4	14.8	4.2	3.6	3.3	3.1	2.7	−0.9
Ukrainian	7.6	8.8	9.9	11.6	4.0	6.1	4.6	3.9	3.7	−2.4
Belorussian	11.4	13.8	15.2	16.6	5.2	6.0	5.6	4.8	4.6	−1.4
Moldavian	4.8	5.7	6.4	8.1	3.3	10.1	8.9	8.5	8.6	−1.5
Uzbek	4.9	5.6	5.0	5.1	0.2	11.3	10.4	10.1	10.2	−1.1
Kazakh	5.3	5.7	6.8	7.9	2.6	17.5	14.4	12.5	11.8	−5.7
Kirgiz	1.3	1.8	2.1	3.0	1.7	12.3	9.7	9.4	8.8	−3.5
Tadzhik	5.9	6.5	8.7	8.5	2.6	18.9	17.2	14.1	16.3	−2.6
Turkmen	1.1	1.6	1.5	2.0	0.9	6.6	5.5	5.2	5.0	−1.6
Georgian	2.4	2.8	3.1	3.9	1.5	1.0	0.8	0.8	0.9	−0.1
Azerbaydzhan	4.0	4.1	5.0	7.0	3.0	11.1	9.7	9.0	7.3	−3.8
Armenian	27.5	25.9	24.4	23.7	−3.8	16.8	12.2	10.0	9.6	−7.2
Lithuanian	4.0	3.5	3.1	3.2	−0.8	3.5	2.4	1.8	1.5	−2.0
Latvian	4.2	4.2	4.8	3.7	−0.5	3.1	2.0	1.8	1.2	−1.9
Estonian	4.8	4.8	4.6	4.2	−0.6	5.0	3.3	2.5	1.9	−3.1
Autonomous Republics										
Bashkir	9.5	12.4	17.5	25.9	16.4	15.9	15.7	14.2	14.5	−1.4
Buryat[a]	7.0	8.1	10.6	12.1	5.1	12.3	9.3	7.7	6.9	−5.4
Avar	2.3	2.6	3.4	5.6	3.3	9.2	9.2	9.9	11.9	2.7
Dargin	3.9	3.5	3.5	6.3	2.4	2.4	6.5	10.6	16.9	14.5
Kumyk	3.1	3.3	3.9	6.9	3.8	7.3	7.2	7.6	10.8	3.5

(continued)

TABLE 5.5 (Continued)

	Outside Urban				Outside Rural			
Nation	1959	1970	1979	1989	Percentage Point Change	1959	1970	1979	1989	Percentage Point Change
Lezgin	17.8	20.1	24.2	31.3	13.5	33.5	29.7	26.5	24.9	-8.6
Kabardin	3.4	3.1	3.4	4.5	1.1	3.1	2.4	2.2	2.5	-0.6
Balkar	8.2	5.2	4.5	9.8	1.6	11.4	8.6	5.5	7.0	-4.4
Kalmyk	11.4	6.3	7.0	7.6	-3.8	27.4	13.4	9.7	8.2	-19.2
Karelian	15.1	19.1	22.8	24.9	9.8	33.8	23.2	18.5	14.8	-19.0
Komi	7.0	8.1	8.6	9.8	2.8	7.7	6.1	5.5	5.6	-2.1
Mari	7.6	13.2	18.2	23.8	16.2	37.0	36.8	32.5	27.8	-9.2
Mordvin	27.4	31.2	37.1	43.7	16.3	44.7	40.0	34.5	29.2	-15.5
Ossetian[b]	14.9	19.1	21.8	23.8	8.9	17.5	12.2	11.0	9.3	-8.2
Tatar[c]	39.2	45.0	50.0	55.0	15.8	33.7	29.1	24.0	22.5	-11.2
Tuvin	1.3	1.7	1.8	3.2	1.9	0.8	1.2	0.8	0.8	0.0
Udmurt	8.2	12.8	16.3	19.1	10.9	15.7	18.4	16.5	14.4	-1.3
Chechen	17.0	7.0	7.1	8.8	-8.2	24.7	10.0	12.0	14.5	-10.2
Ingush	34.7	16.1	15.3	16.7	-18.0	19.7	11.8	12.3	14.4	-5.3
Chuvash	13.2	17.7	22.4	27.9	14.7	34.3	31.8	27.0	22.8	-11.5
Yakut	1.7	2.3	3.2	3.3	1.6	2.8	1.3	1.1	1.0	-1.8
Karakalpak	2.1	2.8	2.7	3.9	1.8	7.5	5.1	4.4	4.2	-3.3
Abkhaz	4.3	5.2	6.7	9.2	4.9	2.1	2.0	1.9	2.3	0.2
Autonomous Oblasts										
Altay	5.4	8.3	10.4	10.5	5.1	10.7	8.0	5.9	6.0	-4.7
Adygey	7.7	11.2	13.5	16.6	8.9	9.6	7.2	7.0	6.9	-2.7
Khakass	6.9	11.3	13.0	15.4	8.5	7.3	6.7	6.0	6.4	-0.9

Karachay	5.0	5.6	6.5	8.0	3.0	11.7	8.3	10.2	9.0	-2.7
Cherkess	11.8	11.8	15.6	14.5	2.7	9.0	9.8	10.4	8.7	-0.3
Autonomous Okrugs										
Nenets[d]	3.0	4.6	7.5	8.1	5.1	6.5	6.0	6.3	6.0	-0.5
Evenk	12.5	13.7	19.8	18.3	5.8	73.5	73.6	68.4	70.2	-3.3
Dolgan[e]	—	7.4	10.3	17.1	9.7	—	3.6	3.9	11.8	8.2
Koryak	5.1	8.8	15.9	14.7	9.6	13.8	12.5	12.3	14.2	0.4
Chukchi	2.2	6.7	7.1	7.9	5.7	12.7	12.4	12.2	13.6	0.9
Komi-Permyak	6.0	11.6	19.0	24.4	18.4	6.5	7.9	11.0	12.8	6.3
Khanty	5.1	6.8	12.1	13.7	8.6	36.0	35.4	34.3	33.5	-2.5
Mansi	5.8	7.3	11.7	14.7	8.9	6.7	6.0	6.9	7.9	1.2
Averages[f]										
Union Republics	6.9	7.5	7.7	8.2	1.3	9.1	7.5	6.5	6.3	-2.8
Autonomous Republics	11.3	11.6	13.6	16.7	5.4	17.6	14.4	12.9	12.5	-5.1
Autonomous Oblasts[g]	7.4	9.6	11.8	13.0	5.6	9.7	8.0	7.9	7.4	-2.3
Autonomous Okrugs	5.7	8.5	13.3	14.5	8.8	22.2	22.0	21.6	22.6	0.4

Sources: 1959: TsSU SSSR 1962, 16 vols.; 1970: TsSU SSSR 1974, vol. 4; 1979: Goskomstat SSSR 1989d, vol. 4; 1989: Statisticheskiy Komitet SNG 1993, vol. 7, parts 1–2.

[a]The Buryat outside figures include Buryats outside the Buryat Autonomous Republic, the Agin Buryat Autonomous Okrug, and the Ust'-Ordin Buryat Autonomous Okrug.
[b]The Ossetian outside figures include Ossetians outside the North Ossetian Autonomous Republic and the South Ossetian Autonomous Oblast.
[c]The Tatar figures for 1989 include Crimean Tatars, because the Crimean Tatars were included in the Tatar totals for the 1959–79 period.
[d]The Nenets outside figures include Nenets outside the Nenets Autonomous Okrug, the Yamalo-Nenets Autonomous Okrug, and the Taymyr (Dolgano-Nenets) Autonomous Okrug.
[e]The Dolgan outside figures include Dolgans outside the Taymyr Autonomous Okrug.
[f]Averages are unweighted, with each national community treated as one observation.
[g]The Dolgans were excluded from the averages for Autonomous Okrugs, because there was no Dolgan figure for 1959.

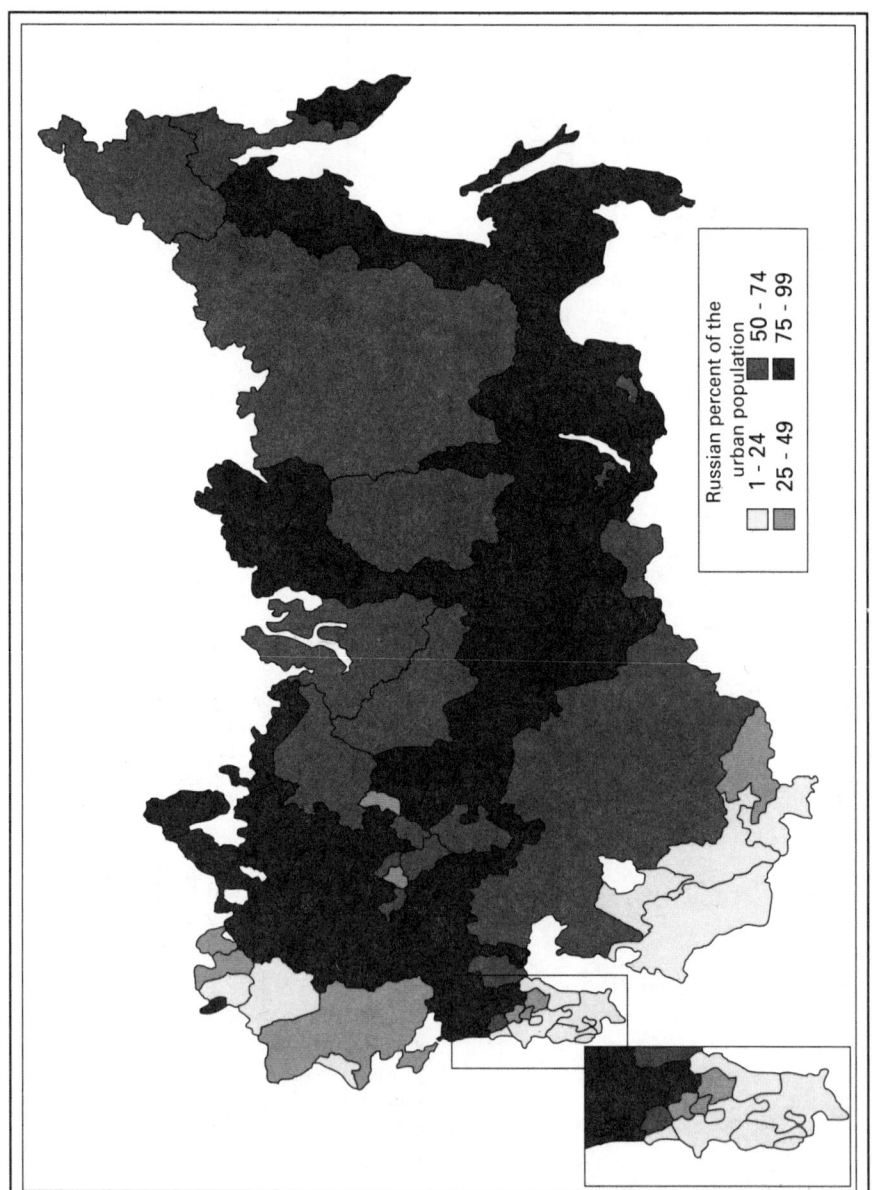

Map 5.5 Russian Percent of the Urban Population, 1989

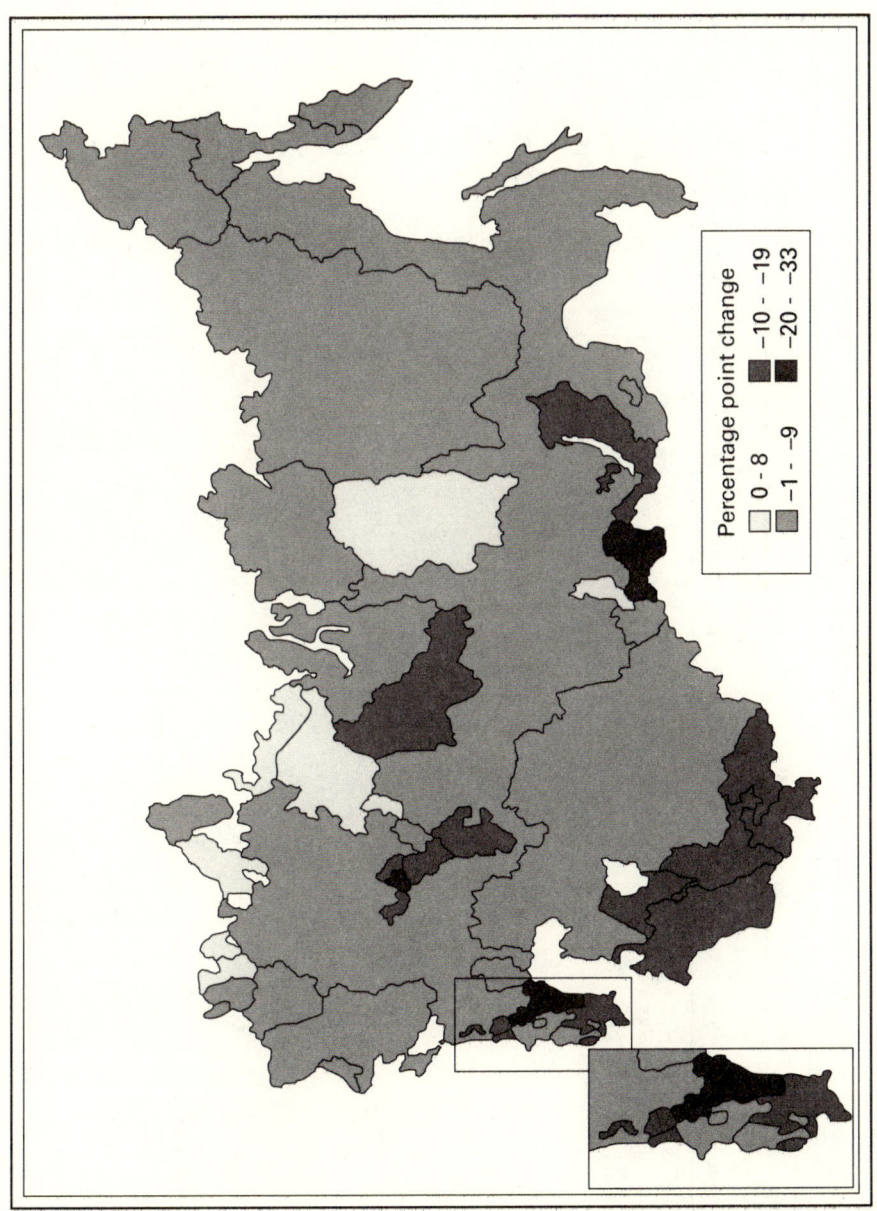

Map 5.6 Derussification of the Urban Population, 1959–1989

TABLE 5.6
National Composition of the Urban Population by Republic, 1959–1989 (percent)

Republic	Indigene				Russian			
	1959	1970	1979	1989	Percentage Point Change	1959	1970	1979	1989	Percentage Point Change

Republic	1959	1970	1979	1989	Percentage Point Change	1959	1970	1979	1989	Percentage Point Change
Union Republics										
RSFSR	87	87	86	85	−2	87	87	86	85	−2
Ukraine	62	63	64	66	4	30	30	30	29	−1
Belarus'	67	69	72	73	6	19	20	19	18	−1
Moldova	28	35	40	46	18	30	29	27	24	−6
Uzbekistan	37	41	48	54	17	33	30	25	20	−13
Kazakhstan	17	17	21	27	10	58	58	56	51	−7
Kyrgyzstan	13	17	23	30	17	52	51	46	39	−13
Tadzhikistan	32	39	43	51	19	35	30	28	22	−13
Turkmenistan	35	43	48	54	19	35	29	26	20	−15
Georgia	53	60	64	68	15	19	15	12	10	−9
Azerbaydzhan	51	61	68	77	26	25	18	14	10	−15
Armenia	92	93	95	96	4	5	4	3	2	−3
Lithuania	69	73	76	76	7	17	14	13	12	−3
Latvia	52	47	45	44	−8	34	38	40	41	7
Estonia	62	57	55	51	−11	31	34	36	39	8
Autonomous Republics										
Bashkiria	8	10	12	15	7	64	60	56	51	−13
Buryatia	8	12	15	17	9	85	83	79	75	−10
Dagestan	36	50	60	67	31	43	32	24	18	−25
Kabardin-Balkaria	17	26	36	43	26	69	60	50	44	−25

Kalmykia	35	44	45	49	15	60	49	47	56	-4
Karelia	7	8	8	8	1	73	75	76	77	4
Komi	14	15	15	14	0	59	63	65	65	6
Mari	11	16	22	26	15	76	72	68	63	-13
Mordvinia	12	17	20	22	10	82	77	75	72	-10
North Ossetia	29	40	44	49	20	55	45	41	35	-20
Tatarstan	33	37	38	42	9	61	58	56	51	-10
Tuvinia	15	25	31	41	26	80	70	64	53	-27
Udmurtia	15	17	19	20	5	74	71	70	68	-6
Chechen-Ingushetia	9	29	38	46	37	78	61	53	45	-33
Chuvashia	36	44	49	55	19	57	50	46	34	-23
Yakutia	15	15	14	13	-2	73	73	71	68	-5
Karakalpakstan[a]	22	26	31	37	15	13	9	5	3	-10
Abkhazia[b]	10	11	14	17	7	37	31	27	23	-14
Autonomous Oblasts										
Gorno-Altay	8	9	10	12	4	87	87	85	82	-5
Adygey	6	7	12	14	8	85	84	79	75	-10
Khakass	3	4	5	6	3	85	88	87	86	1
Karachay-Cherkess	10	14	20	25	15	78	73	67	60	-18
Nagorno-Karabakh[c]	75	77	75	77	2	3	2	1	2	-1
South Ossetia[d]	60	69	72	73	13	7	4	4	4	-3
Autonomous Okrugs										
Taymyr	0	1	1	2	2	83	84	83	80	-3

(continued)

TABLE 5.6
(Continued)

Republic	Indigene				Russian			
	1959	1970	1979	1989	Percentage Point Change	1959	1970	1979	1989	Percentage Point Change
Nenets	3	5	3	2	−1	76	76	77	76	0
Yamalo-Nenets	2	4	2	1	−1	65	68	70	63	−2
Ust'-Ordin	13	22	25	31	18	78	72	68	63	−15
Agin Buryat[e]	—	31	30	33	2	—	65	64	62	−3
Evenk	9	12	9	10	1	72	77	78	73	1
Komi-Permyak	55	43	48	51	−4	39	53	49	46	7
Khanty-Mansi	3	2	1	1	−2	84	81	75	66	−18
Koryak	2	9	7	9	7	82	79	78	74	−8
Chukchi	3	2	1	1	−2	78	78	76	72	−6

Sources: 1959: TsSU SSSR 1962, 16 vols.; 1970: TsSU SSSR 1974, vol. 4; 1979: Goskomstat SSSR 1989d; 1989: Statisticheskiy Komitet SNG 1993, vol. 7. The following autonomous units are located outside Russia. Figures for the titular union republic nation in which they are located were as follows:

	1959	1970	1979	1989	Percentage Point Change
[a]Karakalpakstan (Uzbeks)	24	26	25	23	−1
[b]Abkhazia (Georgians)	32	34	38	40	8
[c]Nagorno-Karabakh (Azeris)	21	20	23	20	−1
[d]South Ossetia (Georgians)	20	18	18	18	−2

except Dagestan, North Ossetia, Chechen-Ingushetia and the Chuvash ASSR in Russia, and Karakalpakstan, where Uzbeks comprised a larger share of the urban population than Karakalpaks. An indigenization of cities also occurred in all autonomous oblasts, but Russians remained demographically dominant in all but Nagorno-Karabakh and South Ossetia, two units outside the RSFSR. In each of these two autonomous oblasts, the indigenous Armenians and Ossetians comprised a greater share of the urban population than the Azerbaydzhanis and Georgians. Little indigenization of cities was apparent at the autonomous okrug-level, but a de-Russification also occurred in the urban centers of these units. Other nonindigenes were entering several of these resource-rich okrugs with development. Nonetheless, Russians retained an overwhelming presence in these cities throughout the postwar period.

The level of intensity of this international interaction varied by republic, from a low for Armenia with 96 percent of its urban population made up of Armenians in 1989 to a much greater "ethnic mosaic" or international mix in the republics of Soviet Central Asia, Moldova, Latvia, and Estonia (Table 5.6; Maps 5.3–5.6). A demographic indigenization of cities was occurring more rapidly in the Central Asian and Transcaucasian republics than in the Slavic or Baltic republics, even though the nations of the non-Slavic South remained predominantly rural. As noted above, the indigenization of Central Asian and Transcaucasian cities was occurring not only as a result of rural to urban migration of indigenes and their higher rate of natural increase relative to nonindigenes in the cities, but also due to Russian and other nonindigenous out-migration from these cities, most likely to urban areas in their respective home republics. Most striking in this regard during the 1980s was the indigenization of cities in Azerbaydzhan, which reflected not so much a massive in-migration of Azerbaydzhanis as an enormous out-migration stream of Armenians, and to a lesser extent the out-migration of Russians and other nonindigenes from the cities of Azerbaydzhan. This nonindigenous urban out-migration has continued and even accelerated since the census was taken in January 1989 (Rybakovskiy and Tarasova 1990). Urban migration data for 1989 confirm this trend (Table 5.7).

In the Baltic republics, and particularly in Latvia and Estonia, Russian in-migration into the cities of the region during the postwar period changed the ethnodemographic map of cities like Riga and Tallinn. This demographic Russification of Latvian and Estonian cities continued during 1989, albeit at a very slow pace (Table 5.7). During the late 1970s and early 1980s Russian in-migration to Lithuanian cities became relatively more intense, resulting in a slight demographic Russification in this republic. This did not continue in 1989, when Lithuanian in-migration to cities exceeded the number of Russians entering. The more intense interaction among nations in the cities of the former Baltic republics did not lead to greater international integration but rather was one of the primary catalysts leading to the national self-determination movements in the region (e.g., Kirkh et al. 1988, 34). Clearly, the demographic

TABLE 5.7
Urban Migration by Nation and Republic, 1989 (absolute number of in-, out- and net migration, in thousands)

Republic	Indigenes			Russians			Others		
	In	Out	Net	In	Out	Net	In	Out	Net
RSFSR	2750.0	2393.1	356.9	—	—	—	1054.9	883.3	171.6
Ukraine	787.4	631.3	156.1	353.8	290.8	63.0	99.9	102.2	−2.4
Belarus'	188.7	133.6	55.1	59.0	41.1	17.9	37.2	35.4	1.8
Moldova	50.5	37.6	12.9	16.0	14.0	2.0	23.5	25.3	−1.7
Uzbekistan	111.0	96.7	14.2	35.6	50.0	−14.4	64.6	106.1	−41.5
Kazakhstan	192.0	143.2	48.8	148.5	144.3	4.3	90.3	120.5	−30.2
Kyrgyzstan	38.3	28.6	9.7	20.6	20.8	−0.2	18.3	23.3	−5.0
Tadzhikistan	25.7	21.6	4.1	10.5	16.8	−6.3	16.5	27.2	−10.7
Turkmenistan	29.3	24.8	4.5	9.9	12.3	−2.4	16.3	18.8	−2.5
Georgia	30.5	20.5	10.0	7.3	10.6	−3.3	11.2	14.9	−3.7
Azerbaydzhan	135.9	47.0	88.8	8.3	20.0	−11.7	12.4	86.9	−74.6
Armenia	46.9	32.3	14.5	2.2	5.5	−3.3	1.4	6.3	−4.9
Lithuania	62.6	47.8	14.8	10.3	9.9	0.4	10.1	8.3	1.8
Latvia	21.1	20.7	0.4	18.7	17.8	0.9	8.6	11.6	−3.0
Estonia	15.0	15.8	−0.8	10.8	9.6	1.1	4.4	4.7	−0.3

Source: Goskomstat SSSR 1990b, 580–583.

Russification of Baltic cities served to activate national territoriality rather than to facilitate the "erasure" of national identity among members of the indigenous nations.

This, of course, does not mean that attaining a dominant position in the cities of one's own homeland necessarily results in quiescence. Perhaps the best example of this is Armenia, where the cities are more nationally homogeneous than in any other republic. Nationalist demonstrations in Yerevan over the status of Nagorno-Karabakh and the treatment of Armenians in Azerbaydzhan have drawn thousands of protesters, and have led to rising anti-Azerbaydzhani violence. This situation, of course, has accelerated the pace of urban indigenization in both republics (Table 5.7).

As with interhomeland migration generally, the migration of nonindigenes from the cities of another nation's homeland occurred for a variety of reasons. Geographic differentials in economic opportunity were undoubtedly important. However, as was discussed in chapter 4, the out-migration of nonindigenes at present appears more motivated by the rising anti-outsider and proindigenous nativism than by an analysis of economic costs and benefits. Since 1989, literally tens of thousands of skilled job openings in the cities are being created throughout Central Asia as a result of this rapid nonindigenous out-migration, while at the same time hundreds of thousands of unskilled rural indigenes are unemployed (see below).

Cities in the former USSR have become the chief sites of international conflict, not the melting pots envisioned by Lenin in 1913. Unlike turn-of-the-century New York and its immigrant population, urbanization has predominantly meant indigenes leaving the village and rural life and entering the cities within their own homelands. Under these conditions, this physical and socioeconomic "drawing together" (*sblizheniye*) of nations in the cities of the former Soviet Union has served as a catalyst activating national territoriality. It is in the homeland urban setting that the most extreme sense of exclusiveness among indigenes, as well as the most intense international tension between indigenes and nonindigenes, has occurred. The expectation that assimilation would accelerate with the urbanization of indigenes was clearly in error, and appears to have been the result of a basic misreading of nations as primarily backward-looking, traditional communities that would shed their primitive sense of "ethnic" and territorial belonging upon reaching the cities. Overall, urbanization, and international equalization in this measure of modernization, have occurred simultaneously with rising intranational cohesion and national separatism. This outcome, which would be predicted from the "diffusion-competition" model, appears to have been the main consequence of rising indigenous urbanization in the postwar period.

Education

As in most states, education in the USSR was viewed by the political leadership as one of the primary instruments for the political socialization of the population. In the realm of international relations within the state, the education system was seen as one of the main instruments through which the national question inherited from the past would be solved: "Education is a primary means by which a world view and a society's prevailing moral standards are formed. . . . In Soviet society, education is entirely in the hands of the state and its aim is to foster in people a feeling of internationalism" (Drobizheva 1981, 172).

In addition to the development of a universal and compulsory system of education for children of all nationalities, the state also endorsed a policy of international equalization in educational attainment as an integral part of the drawing together of nations into one Soviet people (e.g., Panachin et al. 1987, 76).[11] Education was perhaps the greatest success story in the state's effort to equalize social mobility across nations. However, as with urbanization this international convergence in the USSR overall coincided with increasing indi-

---

[11] The question of language of instruction, a critical dimension of nationality policies related to education, is discussed as part of the language and acculturation section of chapter 6.

genization of education in each home republic. Consequently, international equalization in educational attainment resulted not in rising "socialist internationalism" but rather in rising national self-consciousness and growing national separatism.

All national communities have substantially raised their level of educational attainment from that which existed a century ago. In the postwar period, universal literacy was attained, and there was an international convergence in the attainment of a basic education (i.e., primary and secondary school). According to postwar census data for higher and secondary education, in addition to rapid increases in the level of education, several nations made gains when measured against Russian educational attainment (Table 5.8). Five of the union republic nations and eighteen autonomous republic nations experienced a more rapid rate of increase than the Russians between 1959 and 1979. However, only the Georgians, Armenians, and Ossetians had higher rates of educational attainment than the Russians by 1979. The Latvians also exceeded the Russian rate in 1959 but increased at a slower rate than any other union republic or autonomous republic-level nation during the next twenty years. As a result, their rate of educational attainment had fallen below that of the Russians by 1970.[12]

The degree of international equalization in educational attainment between 1959 and 1979, as measured by coefficients of variation, was striking. The CV declined from 29.4 percent in 1959 to 10.0 percent by 1979 for the nations listed in Table 5.8. Considering that a CV of 0.0 percent would mean complete convergence (i.e., all nations with the same rate of education), the extremely low figure for 1979 across a broad spectrum of national communities whose homelands geographically span the USSR was a praiseworthy achievement.

Between 1979 and 1989 international equalization continued across nations whose homelands were designated as union republics. All fourteen non-Russian nations increased their educational attainment more rapidly than the Russians between 1979 and 1985, and Azerbaydzhanis were added to the list of nations with higher overall rates. In 1989, using a more accurate measure, the education rate of nine union republic-level nations exceeded that of the Russians. The coefficient of variation also continued to decrease for these fifteen nations, from 8.7 percent in 1979 to 7.0 percent in 1985, and to only 6.5 percent in 1989. While absolute equality was not yet achieved (and is probably an unattainable goal), this degree of international convergence represents an essential equality among nations with union republics.

At least part of the reason for the apparent equalization is demographic. The

---

[12] This slow rate of increase among Latvians was primarily due to the small proportion of the Latvian population that is in the school-aged cohorts. However, between 1979 and 1985 Russian increases in schooling were even slower than the Latvian rate of increase, resulting in a relative equalization between the two nations.

TABLE 5.8
Higher and Secondary Education (Complete and Incomplete) in the USSR
(per 1,000 population aged ten years and older, by nation)

Nation	1959	1970	1979	1985[a]	1989[b]	Percentage Point Change 1959–79	Percentage Point Change 1979–85
Union Republic							
Russian	378	508	661	709	817	28.3	4.8
Ukrainian	353	476	614	673	781	26.1	5.9
Belorussian	311	438	591	650	764	28.0	5.9
Uzbek	311	412	615	683	866	30.4	6.8
Kazakh	268	390	592	678	858	32.4	8.6
Georgian	474	578	725	784	895	25.1	5.9
Azerbaydzhan	360	424	635	725	878	27.5	9.0
Lithuanian	208	353	539	614	739	33.1	7.5
Moldavian	212	338	534	609	733	32.2	7.5
Latvian	426	488	618	696	828	19.2	7.8
Kirgiz	299	400	590	666	857	29.1	7.6
Tadzhik	299	390	565	643	843	26.6	7.8
Armenian	443	518	719	769	896	27.6	5.0
Turkmen	363	430	597	677	866	23.4	8.0
Estonian	358	462	587	661	768	22.9	7.4
Autonomous Republic							
Balkar	239	356	561	—	—	32.2	—
Bashkir	273	369	574	—	—	30.1	—
Buryat	298	427	644	—	—	34.6	—
Avar	234	308	485	—	—	25.1	—
Dargin	208	270	453	—	—	24.5	—
Kumyk	236	343	537	—	—	30.1	—
Lezgin	286	358	536	—	—	25.0	—
Ingush	162	256	514	—	—	35.2	—
Kabardin	303	417	605	—	—	30.2	—
Kalmyk	144	298	585	—	—	44.1	—
Karelian	225	338	532	—	—	30.7	—
Komi	313	412	617	—	—	30.4	—
Mari	229	329	558	—	—	32.9	—
Mordvin	210	322	509	—	—	29.9	—
Ossetian	431	515	664	—	—	23.3	—
Tatar	329	442	620	—	—	29.1	—
Tuvin	147	336	525	—	—	37.8	—
Udmurt	258	374	583	—	—	32.5	—
Chechen	110	220	491	—	—	38.1	—
Chuvash	332	424	598	—	—	26.6	—

(continued)

TABLE 5.8
Continued

Nation	1959	1970	1979	1985[a]	1989[b]	Percentage Point Change 1959–79	Percentage Point Change 1979–85
Yakut	236	374	600	—	—	36.4	—
Abkhaz	324	427	635	—	—	31.1	—
Karakalpak	252	384	593	—	—	34.1	—

Sources: 1959–79: Zinchenko, 1984, 160; 1985: *Vestnik Statistiki* 7 (1986) 67; 1989: Statisticheskiy Komitet SNG 1993, vol. 7, part 5.

[a] The 1985 data did not provide information for national communities below the union republic-level nations.

[b] The 1989 census provided eduction data for the population aged fifteen and older, making them imcompatible with the data from previous censuses. Therefore, no longitudinal comparison is possible. In addition, data for national communitities below the union republic level were not provided for the country as a whole, but only for the republic in which their autonomous units were located.

Russian nation is an older population than several of the other national communities, and has a smaller percentage of its total population in the school-aged cohorts. Increasing the rate of education, which is an age-specific process targeting the young, is relatively more difficult for the Russians as a nation, though individual Russians in the younger age cohorts may in fact be participating in the educational system to a greater extent than young members of other nations. However, international changes in educational attainment occurred too rapidly to be explained solely by international age differentials. Jones and Grupp (1984, 163), who estimated age-specific rates using census and enrollment data, concluded that "most of the non-Russian gains in educational attainment were due to greater access to education among young people." There appears to have been a conscious effort on the part of the Soviet Union to equalize international rates of educational attainment by increasing the availability of education to the formerly disadvantaged national communities. The goal of international equalization almost certainly had an impact on the rates of educational attainment in evidence.

During the 1960s and 1970s international equalization was also occurring at the higher-education level (Table 5.9). In 1959 only the Georgians, Armenians, and Ossetians (in the North Ossetian ASSR only) had higher rates than the Russians—the same three nations with higher basic education rates. In 1979 four nations had surpassed the Russian rate: Buryats joined the three previously noted. Nine nations experienced a higher percentage point increase between 1959 and 1979, and one other nation had the same rate of increase as the Russians. However, none of the *ethnies* whose homelands were designated as autonomous oblasts or okrugs had attained the higher-education level of the Russians, and those with autonomous okrugs lagged particularly far behind.

TABLE 5.9
Higher Education Rates (Complete and Incomplete) by Nation, 1959–1979 (per 1,000 population aged ten years and older)

Nation	1959			1979			Percentage Point Change		
	Total	Urban	Rural	Total	Urban	Rural	Total	Urban	Rural
Union Republic									
Russian	36	52	14	92	113	31	5.6	6.1	1.7
Ukrainian	25	47	10	70	106	23	4.5	5.9	1.3
Belorussian	22	45	10	65	98	25	4.3	5.3	1.5
Uzbek	17	44	9	58	104	38	4.1	6.0	2.9
Kazakh	21	45	13	67	119	41	4.6	7.4	2.8
Georgian	72	150	28	139	231	51	6.7	8.1	2.3
Azerbaydzhan	35	72	14	76	128	31	4.1	5.6	1.7
Lithuanian	23	53	7	74	112	24	5.1	5.9	1.7
Moldavian	9	36	6	39	86	22	3.0	5.0	1.6
Latvian	33	54	14	81	112	37	4.8	5.8	2.3
Kirgiz	21	75	14	60	143	39	3.9	6.8	2.5
Tadzhik	16	40	10	49	90	31	3.3	5.0	2.1
Armenian	52	79	19	116	151	34	6.4	7.2	1.5
Turkmen	19	40	12	51	85	34	3.2	4.5	2.2
Estonian	34	57	14	89	123	40	5.5	6.6	2.6
Autonomous Republics[a]									
Balkar	7	21	5	77	108	45	7.0	8.7	4.0
Bashkir	12	35	8	42	73	24	3.0	3.8	1.6
Buryat	31	90	19	122	216	67	9.1	12.6	4.8
Avar	10	50	6	47	105	27	3.7	5.5	2.1
Dargin	9	31	6	43	89	27	3.4	5.8	2.1
Kumyk	16	29	8	56	89	33	4.0	6.0	2.5
Lezgin	24	86	15	64	128	38	4.0	4.2	2.3
Ingush	7	47	3	42	80	18	3.5	3.3	1.5
Kabardin	16	54	10	63	113	35	4.7	5.9	2.5
Kalmyk	6	22	3	71	115	34	6.5	9.3	3.1
Karelian	11	51	7	43	63	17	3.2	1.2	1.0
Komi	22	43	14	56	94	25	3.4	5.1	1.1
Mari	10	38	7	32	61	19	2.2	2.3	1.2
Mordvin	10	18	6	33	51	19	2.3	3.3	1.3
Ossetian	44	81	25	125	167	55	8.1	8.6	3.0
Tatar	17	26	9	54	73	27	3.7	4.7	1.8
Tuvin	9	33	6	40	85	28	3.1	5.2	2.2
Udmurt	13	29	9	37	56	23	2.4	2.7	1.4
Chechen	2	14	2	27	58	17	2.5	4.4	1.5
Chuvash	16	41	11	43	73	23	2.7	3.2	1.2

(*continued*)

TABLE 5.9
Continued

Nation	1959			1979			Percentage Point Change		
	Total	Urban	Rural	Total	Urban	Rural	Total	Urban	Rural
Yakut	20	50	14	75	157	49	5.5	10.7	3.5
Karakalpak	20	49	12	63	92	43	4.3	4.3	3.1
Abkhaz	26	69	10	91	169	45	6.5	10.0	3.5
Autonomous Oblast									
Adygey	19	56	15	89	151	59	7.0	9.5	4.4
Altay	14	79	8	49	117	36	3.5	3.8	2.8
Karachay	10	41	7	75	146	53	6.5	10.5	4.6
Khakass	15	47	9	55	98	34	4.0	5.1	2.5
Cherkess	13	50	11	69	138	49	5.6	8.8	3.8
Autonomous Okrug									
Dolgan	—	—	—	22	142	15	—	—	—
Komi-Permyak	8	17	6	28	51	18	2.0	3.4	1.2
Koryak	3	10	3	14	34	8	1.1	2.4	0.5
Mansi	10	41	7	25	56	11	1.5	1.5	0.4
Nenets	2	14	1	12	59	6	1.0	4.5	0.5
Khanty	7	32	4	19	60	8	1.2	2.8	0.4
Chukchi	3	17	2	17	88	10	1.4	7.1	0.8
Evenk	11	49	9	36	96	22	2.5	5.0	1.3

Sources: TsSu SSSR 1973, 4:393–548; Goskomstat SSSR 1989d, vol. 4 (part 2, Book 2):3–125.

[a]For many of the nations, data are for the segment of the population in the home republic only, or for areas of primary residence, rather than for the entire nation. See notes attached to census tables cited above.

Because the 1989 census did not provide education data that was comparable to those found in previous censuses, this table does not include information from the most recent census. Trends in the 1980s are taken from other sources, and are discussed in the following pages. See Tables 5.10 and 5.11.

A wide gap existed between urban and rural higher-education levels; this was to be expected given that the pursuit of higher education normally involves migration to an urban area. The urban rate also increased much more rapidly than the rural rate in all cases, and this implies that, once educated, individuals tended to remain in urban areas. For those nations whose members remained predominately rural, international equalization in higher educational attainment did not occur. Fifteen groups experienced a higher rate of increase than the Russians among the urban segment of the population, and twenty-seven had a higher rate of increase among the rural members. However, because the Russians were relatively more urbanized than most other nations, only nine nations increased at a faster rate than the Russians overall.

The coefficients of variation for the higher education totals decreased from

72.2 percent in 1959 to 48.7 percent in 1979. The CV for the urban rate decreased much more slowly, from 51.5 percent in 1959 to 38.4 percent in 1979. One reason for this is that rural to urban migration was bringing a relatively less educated population to the cities and holding the overall change down. The rural CV declined even more slowly, from 55.1 percent in 1959 to 44.5 percent in 1979. Overall, international equalization in higher education occurred during the 1960s and 1970s, though "equality" was still far from being achieved. This was particularly the case when the national communities at the lower end of the federal hierarchy (i.e., those with autonomous okrugs) are included in the analysis.

More recent data on higher educational attainment indicate that international equalization continued during the 1980s. According to data on the number of students enrolled in higher-educational institutions (*VUZy*), between 1974 and 1989 the coefficient of variation declined from 38.3 percent to 29.8 percent. In addition, while in the 1974/75 school year only nine national communities exceeded the Russian rate, in the 1989/90 school year twenty nations had a higher rate than the Russians, whose rate actually declined (Table 5.10).[13] Many of those whose rate declined were among the nations with the highest educational attainment in the 1974/75 school year. The decrease among the Karelians—an exception to this general rule and one of the few national communities that is experiencing substantial international integration—may signify that it is the relatively more educated Karelians who are assimilating (i.e., diffusion-erasure).[14] The precipitous decline among the Jewish population may in part have resulted from a similar pattern of reidentification but was primarily caused by the emigration of younger, more educated Jews from the USSR.

During the postwar period, international equalization in the country as a whole occurred at the same time that the members of each indigenous nation attained a more dominant position in the educational institutions of their own home republic.[15] At the end of the 1950s a majority of the nations with union republics were underrepresented among college students in their own homelands (Ostapenko and Susokolov 1985, 47). Between 1959 and 1989 this changed dramatically, so that by the end of the 1980s only the Slavic nations

---

[13] These data should be treated with caution. First, using the total national population in the denominator is not nearly as useful for comparative purposes as is the population between the ages of eighteen and twenty-nine. The true rate of participation among Central Asian nations would be relatively higher in comparison with other nations if the latter denominator were available for use, since the southern nations have a relatively higher proportion of their populations in the younger-age cohorts. In addition, the number of participants in higher educational institutions may vary substantially from year to year, and it would be better to use a running average over a period of three or five years for trend analysis, instead of just one year. Nonetheless, while we should not make too much of any one figure in this table, the overall trends in evidence may be viewed as indicative of a continuation of the movement toward international equalization.

[14] This subject is explored in chapter 6.

[15] Unless otherwise indicated, this section deals only with nations at the union republic level.

TABLE 5.10
Students in Higher Educational Institutions at the Beginning of School Years 1974–1975 and 1989–1990, by Nation (per 10,000 national population)

Nation	1974–75	1989–90	Change
Russian	213	190	−23
Ukrainian	154	163	9
Belorussian	152	176	24
Uzbek	149	157	8
Kazakh	194	230	36
Georgian	243	274	31
Azerbaydzhan	177	172	−5
Lithuanian	196	208	12
Moldavian	112	125	13
Latvian	158	182	24
Kirgiz	176	188	12
Tadzhik	131	129	−2
Armenian	207	207	0
Turkmen	130	146	16
Estonian	176	213	37
Abkhaz	207	327	120
Balkar	286	279	−7
Bashkir	132	170	38
Buryat	396	354	−42
Peoples of Dagestan	146	173	27
Ingush	123	212	89
Kabardin	193	206	13
Kalmyk	268	304	36
Karakalpak	154	200	46
Karelian	134	106	−28
Komi (and Komi-Permyaks)	130	119	−11
Mari	100	116	16
Mordvin	102	118	16
Ossetian	253	272	19
Peoples of the North	—	113	—
Tatar	163	171	8
Tuvin	125	195	70
Udmurt	104	115	9
Chechen	87	151	64
Chuvash	110	139	29
Yakut	212	234	22
Adygey	249	241	−8
Altay	173	164	−9
Jew	389	257	−132
Karachay	247	208	−39
Khakass	175	261	86
Cherkess	279	205	−74

Sources: 1974–75: Goskomstat SSSR, 1989b, 225; 1989–90: Goskomstat SSSR, 1990a, 2.

Note: Total national populations for 1974–75 calculated on the basis of an increment added to the 1970 census figures using the formula: $\{\log (P_{1979}/P_{1970})/9 \cdot \log e\} \cdot 4.67$ years.

TABLE 5.11
Indigenous Proportion of Students Entering Higher Education, by Republic (percent)

Republic	Indigenous Percent of Students		Indigenous Percent of Population	
	1984–85	1989–90	1979	1989
RSFSR	81	80.0	82.6	81.5
Ukraine	66	66.5	73.6	72.6
Belarus'	70	70.7	79.4	77.8
Moldova	64	64.4	63.9	64.4
Uzbekistan	67	70.6	68.7	71.3
Kazakhstan	54	54.2	36.0	39.7
Kyrgyzstan	63	65.2	47.9	52.3
Tadzhikistan	61	63.0	58.8	62.2
Turkmenistan	78	78.3	68.4	71.9
Georgia	88	89.4	68.8	70.2
Azerbaydzhan	84	91.0	78.1	82.6
Armenia	98	99.1	89.7	93.3
Lithuanian	86	87.5	80.0	79.6
Latvia	51	54.2	53.7	52.0
Estonia	73	77.7	64.7	61.5

Source: See Table 5.10. The indigenous nations' proportion of the total population is reproduced here from Table 4.2.

were underrepresented in the *VUZy* of their own home republics (Table 5.11).[16] Given the dominant status supposedly reserved for the Russians in the state, this finding is quite surprising. However, it is important to note that Russians were relatively overrepresented in a number of non-Russian republics. This was particularly true in Belarus' and Ukraine, and resulted in the relative underrepresentation of indigenes in these two republics (Karklins 1984, 284). In eight of the remaining twelve republics, the indigenous nations had rates of college entry that far exceeded their proportion of the total republic population. Considering that several of these nations were predominantly rural and that a relatively larger proportion of their population was of precollege age, these figures are even more impressive, and point to the significant privileges in access to higher education that were afforded to members of the indigenous

[16] The measure used here is the ratio of the indigenous percent of students to the indigenous percent of the total population of the republic. It is what Ostapenko and Susokolov (1983, 10) label an "index of reproduction" of the indigenous intelligentsia, which is said to be optimal "when the national composition of the . . . student body of each republic corresponds to the national composition of the republic's total population" (i.e., 100 percent). A condition of underrepresentation exists when the index falls below 100, and a nation is relatively overrepresented when its index exceeds 100 percent.

nations in their respective homelands. To the extent that changes between 1984 and 1989 may be viewed as indicative of a trend in this regard, it is noteworthy that every indigenous nation except the Russians in the RSFSR retained the same rate or increased their share of the student population during the latter half of the 1980s. For Ukrainians, Belorussians, Latvians, Lithuanians, and Estonians this "indigenization" of colleges was occurring even while these indigenous nations declined as a percentage of the total population.

Access to higher-educational institutions during the postwar period was partially determined by a system of quotas originally designed to increase the prospects that less educated indigenes would gain entry (Karklins 1984).[17] This affirmative action type of program (i.e., *korenizatsiya*) was to facilitate the more rapid international equalization of educational attainment. However, two problems emerged regarding these quotas. First, official quotas appear to have been "supplemented" by informal favoritism shown indigenous candidates, so that indigenous status became one of the primary criteria for college admissions. This appears to have been particularly true in the non-Slavic south (Karklins 1984, 288–289). For example, in Kazakhstan national and even "tribal" (i.e., local or subnational ethnographic) favoritism in access to slots in the republic's higher-education institutions were uncovered in the wake of student riots in 1986 (CDSP 1987a, 10; 1987b, 13). Second, once established, indigenous quotas were difficult to reduce should changes in the national composition of the republic's population warrant it. An example of this occurred recently in Yakutia, where Russian in-migration had changed the ethnodemographic character of the population, leading to sharp national imbalances in access to higher education. For example, while Yakuts comprised only 31.1 percent of the total population, they made up 79.5 percent of the day students at Yakutsk State University in the 1985/86 school year (Bromley 1987, 2). Attempts in 1986 to shift the quotas in recognition of this new demographic situation led to Yakut student demonstrations.

According to Ostapenko and Susokolov (1985) and Arutyunyan and Bromley (1986, 76–93), indigenization of the student population during the postwar period occurred in polytechnic as well as artistic, pedagogical, and other types of *VUZy*, and this was true even in Central Asia, though indigenes here were still relatively underrepresented in the polytechnic institutions at the end of the 1970s (Lubin 1984, 112–130). This increasingly broad-based indigenization of higher education represented a trend toward a more fully developed native intelligentsia, which became increasingly capable of controlling the future of the indigenous nation and its homeland. As this occurred, the need for skilled nonindigenes was reduced. Indeed, the very presence of these outsiders, who tended to restrict indigenous access to high-status occupations,

---

[17] While several studies have noted their existence, data on these quotas are still extremely scarce.

became a serious new national problem in the non-Russian periphery (e.g., Lewis et al. 1976, 346–352). However, this does not automatically mean that those nonindigenes (and particularly Russians) who migrated to the growing urban/industrial centers in the past will voluntarily make room for the socially mobilized and increasingly educated indigenes. Instead, growing international competition for the resources of the republics, including high-status occupations, is building between the newly mobilized indigenes and the skilled nonindigenes who have become entrenched in high-status positions throughout the non-Russian periphery, with the possible exception of Georgia, Armenia, and the Baltic republics. In these republics, the indigenes had higher rates of educational attainment for a longer period of time, and nonindigenes—including Russians—entered primarily as part of the unskilled work force (e.g., Ostapenko and Susokolov 1985, 50). Even here, however, rising anti-Russian nativism was building among relatively more educated indigenes.

With education as with urbanization, international equalization was mediated through a system of national territorial discrimination, resulting not in the drawing together of more socially mobilized members of each nation but rather in the indigenization of elites throughout the country (at least for nations with union republics). This worked at cross purposes with the goals of political socialization in education, which have sought to create the conditions for an "internationalization" of the population.

Korenizatsiya policies, which established education quotas favorable to indigenes, helped accelerate the process of international equalization but also reinforced the indigenes' sense of exclusiveness regarding their status in the homeland. Rather than a *korenizatsiya* controlled from above, the process of indigenization became a *korenizatsiya* from below, which favored the indigene to the exclusion of nonindigenes. This increasing pressure for *korenizatsiya* from below is indicative of the way in which social mobilization has served as a catalyst activating national territoriality among indigenes. This more activated national territoriality has undoubtedly had an effect on the contemporary migration of nonindigenous "refugees" to their own home republics (Rybakovskiy and Tarasova 1990), and will have more far-reaching repercussions for the sociocultural, economic, and political future of nations in the former USSR.

Occupation

Changes in the occupation structure of nations provide an obvious counterpart to urbanization and education trends in any discussion of social mobility. In general, it is expected that as education levels rise and urbanization proceeds, the nation's occupation structure will also undergo a transformation from a predominantly traditional agricultural population to one with higher percentages in the secondary (manufacturing), tertiary, and quaternary (i.e., service and management) sectors, and that the latter sectors will with time assume ever greater proportions of the employed segment of the population.[18]

In addition to this overall occupational mobility, international equalization in the occupational profile of each national community was an integral part of nationality policies in the USSR. Drawing the nations of the state into the socialist sphere was to involve not only higher educational attainment and political socialization in schools but also upward mobility in employment. As with education, the goal of equalization was promoted through the use of *korenizatsiya* policies that targeted the upwardly mobile indigenes for preferential treatment (Taksanov 1989, 11). Upward occupational mobility has increased over time for each nation, and international equalization has occurred. However, international equality is still a distant goal, and given the growing unemployment in Central Asia and elsewhere, the relative gap between nations today actually appears to be increasing.

The population of the Soviet Union was rapidly transformed from a predominantly agricultural to a predominantly industrial work force. For several nations in the country, this transformation has occurred relatively recently, and a few are still predominantly agricultural (Table 5.12).

Employment trends in agriculture were mixed. While the Russians had the lowest percentage of their population engaged in agriculture in both 1959 and 1979, the percentage point differential between Russians and non-Russians declined from 31 percentage points in 1959 (24 percent compared to an average of 55 percent) to 15 percentage points by 1979 (6 percent compared to 21 percent). This "equalization" resulted primarily from the Russians having an extremely low percentage employed on the collective farm (*kolkhoz*).[19] On the other hand, the coefficient of variation in agriculture increased over time, from 31.8 percent in 1959 to 52.4 percent in 1979. All of this must be treated with caution, since a portion of the blue-collar work force was composed of state farm workers (*sovkhozniki*), which undoubtedly skews the results for both blue-collar and agricultural employment.

International equalization of blue-collar employment was evident between 1959 and 1979. Moldavians, who had the lowest percentage of their population in the blue-collar category in 1959 increased at the highest rate over the next twenty years. The Russians, who had the highest percentage in 1959, dropped to second place by 1970. Overall, while in 1959 there was a 23 percentage point difference between Russians and non-Russians (54 percent compared to an

---

[18] Although the blue-collar work force or proletariat was favored historically in the USSR, the growth in the white-collar sectors during the postwar period signifies that the desire for upward occupational mobility in socialist states did not end with the achievement of working-class status.

[19] During the past decade or so, the extent of rural depopulation in the Russian heartland is increasingly viewed as a problem by demographers (e.g., Rybakovskiy 1985, 4), economic planners, and Russian nationalists such as Solzhenitsyn (1990) who equate the Russian peasantry with the soul of the nation.

TABLE 5.12
Class Composition of Soviet Nations, 1959–1979 (percent)

Nation	Blue Collar				White Collar				Agricultural			
	1959	1970	1979	Change	1959	1970	1979	Change	1959	1970	1979	Change
Russian	54	63	63	9	22	25	31	9	24	12	6	−18
Ukrainian	34	47	56	22	13	16	23	10	52	37	22	−30
Belorussian	31	53	59	28	12	15	23	11	57	32	18	−39
Moldavian	13	32	54	41	4	7	15	11	83	61	31	−52
Uzbek	27	39	50	23	8	16	18	10	65	45	32	−33
Kazakh	43	65	64	21	16	22	28	12	40	13	8	−32
Kirgiz	22	41	56	34	8	15	20	12	70	44	24	−46
Tadzhik	18	37	55	37	8	15	15	7	74	48	30	−44
Turkmen	22	32	39	17	9	17	16	7	69	51	45	−24
Georgian	22	41	49	27	23	26	32	9	54	33	19	−35
Azerbaydzhan	34	51	58	24	15	21	23	8	51	29	19	−32
Armenian	40	60	62	22	22	25	31	9	40	15	7	−33
Lithuanian	34	52	56	22	14	18	27	13	52	30	17	−35
Latvian	46	54	58	12	19	23	28	9	35	23	14	−21
Estonian	51	57	59	8	22	25	32	10	27	18	10	−17

Source: Arutyunyan and Bromley 1986, 55.

Notes: The sum of the percentage point change for some nations does not equal zero due to rounding.

Data are available only for union republic-level nations.

The three class categories correspond to the three Soviet "classes": *Rabochiye*, *Sluzhashchiye*, and *Kolkhozniki*. However, workers on state farms (*Sovkhozniki*) are included under the blue-collar (*rabochiye*) category.

average of 31 percent), by 1979 this differential had dropped to 8 percentage points (63 percent compared to an average of 55 percent). During this twenty-year period, the coefficient of variation for blue-collar employment by nation decreased from 36.3 percent in 1959 to 10.9 percent in 1979.

An examination of white-collar employment also presents a mixed picture. While eight nations experienced a higher percentage point increase in this occupational category than the Russians between 1959 and 1979, four nations remained dominant in terms of the percentage of their populations employed in this category. The Georgians, Estonians, Armenians, and Russians can be said to be overrepresented in the white-collar occupations. In 1959 these four nations averaged 22 percent, a 10 percentage point difference from the average of the other eleven nations. In 1979, the same 10 percentage point gap remained (31.5 percent as compared to 21.5 percent). However, the coefficient of variation for white-collar employment among these fifteen nations decreased from 41.8 percent in 1959 to 25 percent in 1979, indicating a rather strong trend toward international convergence or equalization overall.

There was also international convergence in the creation and development of a highly skilled work force or national intelligentsia, not only among union republic nations but also among autonomous national communities (Table 5.13). Between 1960 and 1987 the coefficient of variation in the relative size of each nation's "intelligentsia" decreased from 86 percent in 1960 to 44 percent in 1987. However, as this convergence occurred, the Russian national rate also increased more rapidly than that of other nations. In 1960 four nations had higher rates than Russians, but by 1980 only the Jewish rate surpassed that of the Russians. This trend of more rapid expansion of the Russian elite was reversed during the 1980s. By 1987 five nations had proportionally larger intelligentsias than the Russians, although the CV showed almost no change between 1980 (46 percent) and 1987 (44 percent). A closer assessment of the data indicates that a shift in favor of non-Russian specialists was occurring throughout this period. According to trends in the rate of increase, the number of nations that exceeded the Russian rate increased from three between 1960 and 1970 (Estonian, Buryat, and Jew) to ten between 1970 and 1980 (Lithuanian, Balkar, Buryat, Kalmyk, Karakalpak, Komi, Tuvin, Adygey, Jew, and Cherkess). Between 1980 and 1987 the "intelligentsias" for twenty-four of the forty non-Russian national communities grew faster than the Russian rate.

While the amount of data available is limited even today, the trends in evidence suggest that international equalization in occupational structure was occurring during the postwar period. This of course is to be expected, given the trends in urbanization and education in evidence. Given what has already been said about the national geography of social mobility in the state, we would also expect that this international equalization in occupational mobility countrywide masks an increasing indigenization of the work force in each national homeland. The employment data available tend to support this expectation (Table

TABLE 5.13
Specialists with a Higher or Specialized Secondary Education by Nation (per 1,000)

Nation	1960	1970	1980	1987	Percentage Point Change
Russian	48	81	126	143	9.5
Ukrainian	36	65	106	125	8.9
Belorussian	33	60	105	128	9.5
Moldavian	14	29	63	82	6.8
Uzbek	16	29	53	62	4.6
Kazakh	21	38	69	95	7.4
Kirgiz	20	32	57	70	5.0
Tadzhik	17	26	46	49	3.2
Turkmen	20	61	50	62	4.2
Georgian	58	80	112	125	6.7
Azerbaydzhan	33	47	72	81	4.8
Armenian	47	65	99	118	7.1
Lithuanian	32	64	114	147	11.5
Latvian	45	74	104	129	8.4
Estonian	49	85	125	148	9.9
Autonomous Groups					
Abkhaz	28	54	88	107	7.9
Balkar	24	47	99	114	9.0
Bashkir	16	31	61	91	7.5
Buryat	35	72	119	149	11.4
Ingush	6	17	38	70	6.4
Kabardin	25	41	81	92	6.7
Kalmyk	17	39	98	144	12.7
Karakalpak	23	43	97	89	6.6
Karelian	32	58	102	124	9.2
Komi (and Komi-Permyaks)	36	59	105	126	9.0
Mari	16	27	53	79	6.3
Mordvin	15	32	66	99	8.4
Peoples of Dagestan	19	33	60	69	5.0
Ossetian	43	75	117	135	9.2
Tatar[a]	27	48	88	116	8.9
Tuvin	17	41	89	78	6.1
Udmurt	20	35	66	91	7.1
Chechen	3	12	31	43	4.0
Chuvash	24	40	75	97	7.3
Yakut	39	65	108	130	9.1
Adygey	29	58	108	137	10.8
Altay	49	77	102	112	6.3
Jew[b]	188	250	304	356	16.8

(*continued*)

TABLE 5.13
Continued

Nation	1960	1970	1980	1987	Percentage Point Change
Karachay	28	48	89	78	5.0
Khakass	25	45	89	104	7.9
Cherkess	36	65	116	128	9.2
CVs (%)	86	67	46	44	−42.0

Sources: Goskomstat SSSR 1988b, 120; TsSU SSSR 1962, vol. 16; TsSU SSSR 1974, vol. 4; TsSU SSSR 1984; Goskomstat SSSR 1989a.

Notes: Total number of specialists by nation divided by national population from relevant census.
ᵃTatar figure includes Crimean Tatars.
ᵇJewish figure includes "mountain Jews," "Georgian Jews," and "Central Asian Jews." The Jews experienced an absolute decline in the number of specialists between 1975 and 1987, but the decline in the size of the Jewish population in the country as a whole was even greater.

5.14). Between 1967 and 1987 the rate of indigenization of the blue- and white-collar work force was most rapid in the non-Slavic south, where it exceeded the rate of indigenous population growth. A growing number of reports indicate that this indigenization, especially in Central Asia, resulted at least in part from favoritism shown indigenes (e.g., CDSP 1987c, 22). Nationality policies that favored international equalization through preferential treatment of indigenes worked in concert with national territoriality to encourage indigenous elites to promote other "sons of the soil" over qualified "outsiders."

Most of the other nations with union republics remained at or near the 100 percent figure (i.e., proportional representation) throughout the period. This means that the indigenous nations were successful in gaining proportional representation but not necessarily a dominant standing in their homelands. However, because a relatively larger percentage of the indigenous than the nonindigenous population is employed on the *kolkhoz*, and also because a relatively greater proportion of the indigenous population is not of working age, even approaching occupational representation equal to the indigenous percent of the total population is probably a reflection of real indigenous overrepresentation. This is of course particularly true in the case of Central Asia, where indigenous occupational mobility and indigenization increased dramatically during the postwar period (Arutyunyan and Bromley 1986, 83). However, employment problems exist and are growing in this region of the country. At present, skilled job vacancies are increasing so rapidly as a result of nonindigenous out-migration that they cannot be filled by the number of trained indigenes, even though this number also grew substantially during the 1980s. In Kyrgyzstan, skilled labor shortages were reported to be more than 10,000 in August 1990, with estimates of rapid growth as Russians and other nonin-

TABLE 5.14
Proportional Representation of Indigenes in Blue- and White-Collar Work Force, 1967–1987; Proportional Representation of Indigenes among Directors of Enterprises and Organizations, 1989 (indigenous percent of work force/indigenous percent of republic population)

Nation	Blue- and White-Collar Work Force				Directors
	1967	1977	1987	Percentage Point Change	1989
Russian	100	100	100	0	95
Ukrainian	93	93	96	3	109
Belorussian	98	99	100	2	100
Moldavian	74	89	19	17	77
Uzbek	65	74	86	21	95
Kazakh	61	67	83	22	100
Kirgiz	59	69	79	20	105
Tadzhik	63	76	87	24	106
Turkmen	58	66	82	24	100
Georgian	96	101	103	7	127
Azerbaydzhan	80	91	94	14	113
Armenian	103	101	100	−3	107
Lithuanian	94	95	95	1	115
Latvian	95	91	92	−3	121
Estonian	99	95	95	−4	134

Sources: Goskomstat SSSR 1988b, 20; TsSU SSSR 1962, vol. 16; TsSU SSSR 1974, vol. 4; TsSU SSSR 1984; Goskomstat SSSR 1989a. Directors: Rybakovskiy and Tarasova 1990, 40.

Notes: Total number of specialists by nation divided by national population from relevant census. Figures in table are given in percent. As an example, 77.3 percent of all directors in the RSFSR in 1989 were Russian, 81.5 percent of the total population of the RSFSR was Russian, so the proportional representation of Russian directors in the RSFSR was 95 percent (77.3/81.5) · 100. The denominators for the three general ratios were the census figures for 1970, 1979, and 1989, respectively.

digenes left the cities of the republic after the nationalistic violence in Osh' Oblast (FBIS 27 August 1990, 117–118). On the other hand, unemployment levels among primarily unskilled rural indigenes were reported to be more than 80,000 in Kyrgyzstan (FBIS 27 August 1990, 117–118), 650,000 in Tadzhikistan (FBIS 18 September 1990, 73–74), and 1 million in Uzbekistan (FBIS 19 September 1990, 89–90). These figures have been increasing dramatically since 1990. Thus, while the Slavic "flight" from the cities of Central Asia in response to rising nativism is accelerating the pace of occupational indigenization at the higher end of the employment scale, an unemployment problem continues to exist among the large and growing unskilled population. This problem may actually be exacerbated by rapid Slavic out-migration, if as a consequence economic development in general is curtailed.

This problem aside, the improved standing of most indigenous nations occurred across most of the occupation sectors, and was not concentrated in the sectors of traditional indigenous dominance (i.e., health, education, state farm employment, etc.) (Goskomstat SSSR 1988b, 22–23). The indigenization of industry, the historically favored occupational sector in Soviet society, was particularly impressive during the 1970s and 1980s.[20] Given the indigenization of polytechnic *VUZy*, we may predict that this indigenization of industrial as well as sociocultural sectors will continue in the future.

There were some losers during the 1980s, and these were primarily the more developed nations. The Baltic and Slavic nations experienced decreasing dominance across a majority of occupational sectors in their respective home republics between 1977 and 1987. However, for the most part these decreases occurred in sectors where the indigenous nation was already relatively overrepresented, and this relative predominance was normally retained even after a decade of decline. Still, the relative decrease during the recent period, which was particularly widespread in the Baltic region as Russians and others migrated to the area, may help explain why it was this region rather than relatively underdeveloped Central Asia that was at the forefront of the drive for independence.

If the overall trends are somewhat equivocal, the indigenous dominance of high-status occupations is not (Table 5.14). The indigenous proportion of directors of enterprises and organizations met or exceeded the indigenous proportion of the total population in twelve of the fifteen union republics. Those nations with the greatest relative overrepresentation of directors were also those that became the most assertive of their rights to national self-determination after 1985. The discrepancy between overrepresentation among the elite and underrepresentation among the working masses was particularly apparent in Estonia and Latvia, and may be an important element in the rising national territoriality among indigenes in these two republics.

Of the three indigenous nations that were relatively underrepresented among directors, only the Uzbeks exceeded their proportional representation in the blue- and white-collar work force. The Moldavian share of directors in Moldova was far below both their percentage of the republic's population and below their noncollective work force participation rate. The other case of relative underrepresentation is the Russian nation, which is certainly counterintuitive given the status of Russians as the dominant "core" nation in the state. It may be that *korenizatsiya* in the autonomous regions of the RSFSR has favored non-

---

[20] The breakdown into eleven sectors provided in Goskomstat SSSR (1988b) is too gross for more than a general assessment of trends. For example, Sacks (1982) found that even within industry indigenes in Central Asia were concentrated in the less prestigious light sectors while Russians and other nonindigenes were primarily employed in heavy industry. According to more recent studies conducted by Taksanov (1989), Perepelkin (1987), and Shedenov et al. (1987), there continues to be an important international division of industrial labor in Central Asia.

Russian indigenes in these areas over Russians. Some evidence for this exists. For example, a survey conducted in 1967 in the Tatar ASSR indicated that intergenerational upward mobility had been greater for Tatars than for Russians across all socioprofessional categories, and particularly for the intelligentsia (Arutyunyan 1969, 136). Between 1967 and 1974–75 in three major cities of the Tatar ASSR, a strong shift toward Tatars and away from Russians was evident in white-collar employment, including the category "directors of work collectives and social and state organizations," even though Russians comprised a growing percentage of the total blue- and white-collar work force (Shkaratan 1986, 116). However, this does not appear to have occurred among the "peoples of the North" (e.g., Udalova 1989, 107). Overall, these data indicate that national stratification had become much more complex than the assumption too often made in the West that Russians are first and all others are second. Further study of the status of Russians in the RSFSR and outside is clearly warranted.

During the postwar period, upward occupational mobility was dramatic, particularly for those nations who were relatively underdeveloped in the past. This more rapid social mobility among the less developed nations resulted in an international equalization of occupational structure, although overall equality has not yet been achieved. Indeed, the downturn in economic development, along with the continued rapid population growth in Central Asia, has created a growing international employment gap during the past few years, and this is likely to grow wider in the future.

The international equalization in occupations that occurred in the USSR as a whole was brought about primarily as a result of the indigenization of the labor force in each home republic. Upward occupational mobility among indigenes was relatively more dramatic than among nonindigenes, and elite positions became more accessible to indigenes than nonindigenes during the course of the past thirty years. It has become increasingly apparent that the "cultural division of labor," which historically favored the Russians as the dominant "core" nation of the state, was being replaced not with a level playing field but rather with a new "cultural division of labor" that favored indigenes over nonindigenes. This new geography of occupational mobility indicates that indigenes have been relatively successful in pursuing a strategy of national territoriality, and that the diffusion of socioeconomic development in the country has coincided primarily with rising indigenous assertiveness rather than the erasure of national consciousness and the sovietization of the population.

Social Mobilization and International Attitudes

Following the logic of diffusion-erasure and internal colonialism, the social mobilization and international equalization that indigenes have experienced during the postwar period should have led to an improvement in international relations. If social mobilization and international equalization create the conditions for the "withering away" of nations, the more urbanized, educated, and upwardly mobile or elite members of each nation should have a more internationalist outlook than those rural, less educated, and downwardly mobile or unskilled members of the nation.

Surveys of international attitudes conducted by Soviet ethnographers and sociologists from the 1960s to the 1980s were used to test this proposition (e.g., Arutyunyan 1968, 1969, 1985; Drobizheva 1971, 1981, 1985; Susokolov 1973, 1988; Starovoytova 1976, 1987; Arutyunyan and Bromley 1986). The first such survey in the USSR was conducted in the Tatar ASSR in 1967 (Arutyunyan 1968) and measured attitudes toward national composition of the work place and family. These measures were used in subsequent surveys conducted during the 1970s and 1980s, which allows one to compare the results of the various public opinion polls on this topic across nations, republics, and over time.

In general, the results of international attitudinal surveys strongly suggest that indigenous urbanization has not been a positive factor in the disappearance of negative attitudes toward "outsiders." For example, the percentage of urban Moldavians favoring a multinational work environment in the 1970s was actually lower than the percentage for rural Moldavians (Arutyunyan and Bromley 1986, 365–366). This held true for Moldavians who had friends of another nationality, as well as for those who did not (Drobizheva 1981, 214). Among Uzbeks in Uzbekistan, an urban environment did not improve international attitudes among the more skilled blue-collar workers, and actually seems to have had a negative effect among unskilled workers (Drobizheva 1981, 200). This conforms to the more general conclusion made by Arutyunyan and Bromley (1986, 393) that an urban environment does not reduce prejudices among the less educated population, and that the "less skilled workers in cities frequently turn out to be more prejudiced than in the countryside." However, it was not only the less educated, less skilled population whose international "psychological distance" increased in the cities. For example, in the Tatar ASSR urban white-collar workers also had a less favorable opinion about international marriages than did rural white-collar workers (Drobizheva 1971). Overall, urbanization did not reduce international tensions, and in general appears to have actually exacerbated already existing "national problems" between indigenes and nonindigenes.

In general, the same may be said about the effect of education on international psychological distance. According to Drobizheva (1981, 173), "the positive effect of education on international interaction was more noticeable among those peoples for whom the 1960s and 1970s were characterized by a particularly rapid rate of growth in education." This was true for Uzbeks and Central Asian nations generally, as well as for Moldavians, and indicates the importance of the pace of social mobility in the formation of international attitudes. For Central Asians, Georgians, and Russians in Saratov Oblast, rising education led to more favorable attitudes toward an international work environment but not toward international marriage. On the other hand, in Estonia the educational level was not found to have a significant effect on international attitudes either among Estonians or among nonindigenes (Drobizheva 1981, 174–175). This indicates that education alone, as with urbanization, was not sufficient to bring about improvements in international relations. National prejudices based on traditional beliefs may be overcome by education but are, in general, replaced by growing anti-outsider sentiments as indigenes become more urbanized and educated and compete more intensely with nonindigenes for the resources of their home republics (i.e., diffusion-competition rather than diffusion-erasure is the norm for upwardly mobile indigenes).

The relationship between occupation and international attitudes is complex, varying not only across nations but also across socioprofessional categories. In general, a U-shaped curve best describes the relationship between socioprofessional group and negative international attitudes among indigenes (Arutyunyan 1968, 12). Both unskilled blue-collar workers and the intelligentsia responded more negatively to questions regarding the desirability of an international work environment and family than the more highly skilled blue-collar and lower-level white-collar workers. This held true for those indigenes who were bilingual as well as for those who knew only their own language, and for men as well as for women. International attitudes improved somewhat for unskilled workers living in a more nationally mixed environment, indicating that negative attitudes among this segment of the population were based on ethnic stereotypes that were sustained only in nationally isolated communities. However, among the upper socioprofessional strata, negative international attitudes were higher in more nationally mixed communities (Arutyunyan 1969, 138; Table 5.15), indicating that such attitudes are based not on traditional ethnic

TABLE 5.15
International Attitudes among Male Tatars, 1967 (percent)

Socioprofessional Group	Negative or Uncertain Attitude to Nonindigenous Director		Negative or Uncertain Attitude to International Marriage	
	In Mixed or Russian Towns	*In Tatar Towns*	*In Mixed or Russian Towns*	*In Tatar Towns*
Intelligentsia	8.8	6.0	17.8	10.5
White Collar	11.1	7.7	11.1	5.1
Mechanics	2.0	9.8	3.9	10.2
Unskilled Blue Collar	1.8	10.2	5.5	11.2

Source: Arutyunyan 1969, 138.

stereotypes but result from more intensive interpersonal contact and competition itself.

Summarizing the results of these surveys, Arutyunyan and Bromley (1986, 372) found that "qualified blue-collar workers of all nations have the most internationalist attitudes; these attitudes vary among the white collar workers and intelligentsias of different ethnic communities." Apparently, where interpersonal competition for high-status positions was the greatest, international attitudes were the worst. Arutyunyan and Bromley (1986, 378) go on to note that "the more individuals of each nationality are represented among the intelligentsia and skilled workers, and the higher the level of education among the population of one or another nationality, the greater the expectation and desire among them for labor advancement." As indigenous expectations rise, they become more difficult to fulfill, and a growing sense of relative deprivation becomes more likely. This suggests that even under conditions of social mobilization, international equalization, and indigenization, feelings of relative deprivation among indigenes may continue to exist so long as there are nonindigenes holding or vying for elite positions. This conclusion is supported by the results of the Tatar ASSR study, which indicated that Tatars had higher negative international attitudes than Russians even though Tatars of all socioprofessional groups had experienced more rapid upward mobility than had Russians in the autonomous republic (Arutyunyan 1969, 131). Furthermore, since job creation and investment decisions were made primarily by the central authorities in the state, feelings of relative deprivation may have existed even in relatively nationally homogeneous settings in the USSR, where indigenes felt that the Russians at the center were discriminating against them.

Even in cases where highly skilled workers were generally satisfied with their jobs and degree of social mobility, negative international attitudes were relatively high. This was particularly the case among members of the creative intelligentsia, who have a vested interest in increasing the international psychological distance between indigenes and nonindigenes (Arutyunyan and Bromley 1986, 395). More generally, the surveys conducted from 1967 through the early 1980s tended to support the diffusion-competition model among indigenes: "National self-consciousness grows along with the growth in education, culture, and a widening range of social activity. Therefore, it would be most pronounced among the intelligentsia" (Arutyunyan and Bromley 1986, 414).

The survey results for nonindigenes presented a somewhat different picture. In general, nonindigenes appear to have had a more positive international attitude than indigenes, though the level of negative attitudes was often close to the rate among indigenes, particularly for those nonindigenes who had recently migrated from their homelands to these new environs (Susokolov 1988).[21] In

---

[21] Unfortunately, the nonindigenes most often included in surveys were Russians, whose status as members of the dominant nation in the state makes it questionable whether their responses would be similar to those of other nonindigenes.

the Tatar study, the U-shaped curve evident across socioprofessional groups of Tatars was not found for the Russians, whose socioprofessional elites had the most positive international attitudes (Drobizheva 1971). A more linear relationship was also found among nonindigenes in Georgia (Arutyunyan and Bromley 1986, 366). From the evidence available, it appears that while indigenes responded to social mobility in ways that conform to the reactive ethnicity (relative deprivation) and diffusion-competition models, the responses by nonindigenes suggest that diffusion-erasure was occurring among this group, or at least among those who had lived outside their respective home republics for a long period.

Overall, however, there was little evidence that social mobilization was leading to the drawing together of nations (i.e., to greater international integration). The surveys of international attitudes cited above suggest the contrary, that international psychological distance, particularly among indigenes, was either unaffected or increased with social mobilization. The more developed nations were also those with the most negative international attitudes (e.g., Susokolov 1988, 33). In addition, the highest socioprofessional group (i.e., the intelligentsia) of each indigenous nation surveyed had among the least favorable international attitudes of any "class." And, while downward occupational mobility resulted in the most negative international attitudes, upward mobility did not necessarily result in the most positive responses (e.g., Susokolov 1988, 35). In general, the surveys of international psychological distance forced Soviet ethnographers and ethnosociologists to rethink the relationship between social mobilization and national identity (Arutyunyan and Bromley 1986, 347):

> Earlier, when peoples substantially differed in the level of socioeconomic and cultural development, it seemed that it was sufficient to overcome such differences, to liquidate national inequality—and all national problems would be solved.
>
> Now, when the past inequalities (*disproportsiya*) no longer exist, and the developed socialist nations and nationalities interact, we nonetheless have become aware that "in the process of more than one hundred nations and nationalities working and living together, new tasks in the perfection of national relations naturally arise."

According to the data presented in this chapter, the period from 1959 to 1989 was one of massive social mobility, in which all national communities participated. This certainly contradicts the depiction of much of this postwar period as one of stagnation (*zastoy*). The Soviet population as a whole, and the members of each national community for which data are available, became much more urbanized, educated, and occupationally upwardly mobile.

In addition to social mobility in general, international equalization was also in evidence, though outright equality across nations was not achieved. The geography of international equalization in the USSR was extremely important. For the most part international equalization in the country as a whole occurred as the result of the members of each indigenous nation becoming relatively more dominant in their own home republic. Thus, indigenization and growing international inequality in each homeland coincided with the process of international equalization for the country as a whole. Rather than resulting in the elimination of a "cultural division of labor" altogether, the social mobility that was occurring in the USSR during the postwar period was replacing a national stratification system that favored Russians and other highly mobilized nonindigenes with one that increasingly favored socially mobilized indigenes. The development of this new cultural division of labor helps to explain why the international equalization that was occurring was leading not to the "erasure" of national identity but rather to heightened national self-consciousness and increasing national separatism among the more socially mobilized members of each national community.

The data and analysis provided in this chapter suggest that the causal relationship between social mobilization and national consciousness depicted in the models described in the introduction must be modified to take national territoriality into account. Social mobilization is an extremely important factor in the nationalization process, as discussed in part 1. After national consolidation has occurred, social mobilization continues to serve as a catalyst activating national territoriality, since it brings upwardly mobile indigenes into more intense competition with nonindigenes for the resources of the homeland. For indigenes who continued to hold a disadvantaged status vis-à-vis nonindigenes (i.e., where socioeconomic indigenization had not taken place or had not kept pace with indigenous expectations), an outcome resembling reactive ethnicity or nativism was apparent. This may be seen as a response to a growing sense of relative deprivation, and is apparent in Central Asia, in Abkhazia and South Ossetia in Georgia, in Nagorno-Karabakh, and in Tuvinia in the RSFSR. In cases where indigenization was successful, as in the majority of union republic nations in the USSR, national separatism became a dominant trend, and was stronger in the relatively more developed nations. This may be seen as supportive of the predictions derived from the diffusion-competition model, although the nationalistic demands to become "masters of their own land" are not determined solely by an economic cost-benefit analysis.

Successful indigenization also has an effect on the relationship between social mobility and national identity among nonindigenes. For those who were dominant in the past but have now lost their competitive edge as a result of successful indigenization, a "reactive ethnicity" is likely. The rise of a reactive ethnicity among Russians living in the non-Russian periphery is clearly in evidence as anti-Russian sentiments and nativism among indigenes has grown since 1987, particularly in the non-Slavic south and the Baltic states. An increasing number of nonindigenes suffering from this "relative deprivation" have also migrated back to their original homelands. These returnees are often more nationalistic than are members who never left, and they have served to heighten nationalism and displays of national territoriality within their own homelands. This is occurring in Transcaucasia today, and is also found among the Russian "refugees" in Moscow and elsewhere.

The least support was found for diffusion-erasure, which predicts that the national problem will be solved through socioeconomic development alone. International integration or assimilation occurred in the USSR but was, in general, limited to nonindigenes who left their homelands voluntarily and lived outside for an extended period (Susokolov 1988). As is discussed in the following chapter, assimilation is an intergenerational process that has also tended to favor indigenization. However, in general, assimilation was the weakest "national process" operating in the USSR. Rising national consciousness and national separatism have been dominant trends during the postwar period.

CHAPTER SIX

The Ethnocultural Transformation of Soviet Society: Russification versus Indigenization

ETHNOCULTURAL indigenization may be defined as the attempt by members of each indigenous nation to ensure that their objective cultural characteristics retain or regain a dominant position in their homeland.[1] This aspect of national territoriality should have had an impact on the pace and direction of so-called ethnic processes in the USSR, since ethnocultural indigenization would at least in principle imply that each indigenous nation attempts to acculturate, if not assimilate, the entire population of the homeland to the indigenous language and other cultural attributes. Ethnocultural indigenization represents an attempt both to nationalize the masses in areas where national consolidation has not been completed (i.e., in the eastern and southern regions of the state), and to "renationalize" (i.e., acculturate/assimilate) nonindigenes who have already attained a national self-consciousness during a previous period. In the Soviet context, ethnocultural indigenization was a counterbalancing force to Russification outside the RSFSR, the latter of which was promoted by the state as a means of "sovietizing" the non-Russian population (e.g., Aspaturian 1968).

During the postwar period, national consolidation in each home republic continued. As discussed in part 1, nationalization proceeds with language standardization and vernacularization, as well as the social and geographic mobilization of the masses. As geographic isolation breaks down, marriages between members of different subnational ethnographic groups (i.e., intranational interethnic marriages) also become more commonplace, and this may be seen as a concrete way in which the nationalization of families occurs. At this point, children are subjected to nationalization at home as well as in school, through the mass media, and so forth. While linguistic standardization, vernac-

---

[1] As stated in chapter 1, objective characteristics of the national community include such cultural attributes as language, religion, customs, rites and rituals, dress and diet, and so forth, that members of the community share in common. For the purposes of this chapter, the focus is on language trends, both because language is frequently cited as the most important cultural characteristic of the nation, and also because it is the one with the most extensive statistical data through which trends may be analyzed. Other cultural traits are either less significant (e.g., traditional dress, diet, etc.) or more difficult to study in the Soviet context (e.g., religion), and are therefore not included in this analysis.

ularization, and universal literacy had been achieved for most of the major ethnonational communities in the state before World War II, the nationalization of families through intranational interethnic marriages was only beginning for several of these national communities, and became an intensive process only in the postwar period.

The "renationalization" process (i.e., acculturation and assimilation of non-indigenes) is normally viewed as progressing through a similar series of stages. Bilingualism is often viewed as a preliminary stage in the acculturation process, and is included in the analysis of language usage trends. Linguistic assimilation, or the adoption by one nation's members of another nation's language, is perhaps the best measure of acculturation, the first stage in the process of international integration. International marriage is seen as an intermediate stage in the assimilation process, since "internationalizing" the family holds the potential for creating an international or anational population in the future. Psychological assimilation, the final stage in the process, occurs primarily through the reidentification of children from international families, and is what Soviet ethnographers refer to as "natural assimilation" (e.g., Bromley 1969; 1983a, 237–239).[2]

The distinction between intranational consolidation and international integration may be quite vague, especially for individuals participating in these processes. The participants often lack a strong sense of national self-consciousness. On the borders between two *ethnies*, and for individuals who migrated from their homelands before nationalization, what may appear to the outside observer as international integration (whether Russification or indigenization) may in fact be more appropriately labeled national consolidation. This was certainly the case with a number of Ukrainian and Belorussian peasants living in the North Caucasus, Northern Kazakhstan, and Siberia who reidentified as Russians between 1926 and 1959, and is also a factor in Central Asia today (see below). Much of the apparent Russification among the ethnographic groups indigenous to northern Siberia, and among nonindigenes whose ancestors migrated to regions dominated by Russians in the late tsarist or early Soviet period, may also be classified as nationalization, even though nationalists "back home" often decry such reidentification as the forced assimilation of their brethren (e.g., RUKH 1989). The very act of out-migration in a multihomeland context, if that out-migration was voluntary, is likely to be engaged in by more nationally "marginal" individuals, families, and subnational ethnographic groups (i.e., those who are more willing to trade the ethnocultural benefits that accrue to members of the indigenous nation for perceived economic or other

---

[2] It is important to keep in mind that the process of assimilation is neither inexorable nor unidirectional, and caution must be exercised in treating the relationship between these measures as stages in a linear process. Nevertheless, there is clear evidence of linkage between linguistic assimilation, intermarriage, and "natural" psychological assimilation in a progression of stages (e.g., Kaiser 1988).

rewards awaiting them outside.[3] As discussed in chapter 4, a positive relationship between national marginality and out-migration was in evidence in the postwar USSR.

In this chapter, the geography of integration processes occurring between 1959 and 1989 is assessed. The assessment begins with a review of postwar language usage trends, including the changing utility of languages, linguistic assimilation, and bilingualism. This is followed by an examination of international marriage patterns in the USSR and the choice of national identity made by children from international families. These are topics that have attracted a great deal of attention, both in the West and in the USSR, and their study has been seriously biased on both sides. Western analysts and non-Russian nationalists have typically seen this process as the "unnatural" result of coercive Soviet nationality policies that have forcibly attempted to Russify the non-Russian nations. On the other hand, Soviet analysts most frequently portrayed international integration, and particularly Russification, as evidence that non-Russians were voluntarily and "naturally" amalgamating into one united "Soviet People." Although each of these positions contains an element of truth, both tell us more about the predispositions of the analysts than they do about the national processes at work in the USSR.

Since 1985 the limited extent of sovietization has become increasingly apparent. The contemporary international tensions and conflicts in the state provide striking evidence that the emergence of a Soviet people is more myth than reality. Indicative of this "new reality" is the fact that although a decade ago works on the formation of a Soviet people comprised one of the dominant themes in nationality studies in the USSR, by 1991 the term *Soviet people* itself had all but disappeared from the ethnographic literature. Russification has also been limited during the postwar period, and Western predictions of the disappearance of non-Russians through forced assimilation have been largely refuted by the latest nationalist upheavals in the state. Russification, even to the limited extent that it has occurred, has provided a catalyst for rising anti-Russian and anticommunist nationalism in several regions of the non-Russian periphery. In this sense at least, the very success of a process pointed to with pride by Soviet analysts and castigated in the West has largely proven to be counterproductive to the ultimate goal of international integration.

In general, and in contrast to the sovietization and Russification approaches of previous studies, the evidence examined in this chapter suggests that ethnocultural indigenization has been an active competitor with Russification for much of the postwar period. The geographic differentials in rates of linguistic assimilation (i.e., acculturation), intermarriage, and "natural assimilation" also

---

[3] For a discussion of the concept of ethnic or national marginality, see Gordon (1978). A discussion of migration and marginality is provided by Edwards (1986), and of the marginality of children from international parents by Burkhardt (1983). On the general concept of marginality, see Germani (1980).

support the conclusions reached in chapters 4 and 5—that geographic and social mobilization have tended to activate an indigenous "sense of exclusiveness." What we have witnessed since 1985 is a new stage in an ongoing process, a more assertive attempt to accelerate *korenizatsiya* from below. It may also be seen as a more overt attempt to indigenize the population living in the homeland, and this conforms with the expectations derived from the theory of national territoriality.

LANGUAGE USAGE TRENDS

Language is one of the most important objective characteristics of the nation. As discussed above, the standardization and vernacularization of literary languages, and the expansion of literacy in those languages, were critical processes in the nationalization of the masses occurring between 1861 and 1939. With the emergence of linguistic communities that correspond approximately to national communities, language usage becomes important both as a symbol of national identity and cohesiveness, and as an instrument used by indigenes in an effort to gain comparative advantages over nonindigenes in competition for the resources of the homeland, including high-status positions. For these reasons the functional utility of one's native language, as well as the interrelated process of linguistic assimilation, have become key ingredients in the evolution of an indigenous sense of exclusiveness toward the homeland and a critical instrument in the implementation of a strategy of national territoriality. In this section, changes in the functional utility of indigenous languages during the postwar period are examined, and the impact of this on linguistic assimilation and bilingualism, as measured in the Soviet censuses between 1959 and 1989, is assessed.[4]

As discussed in part 1, mass-based linguistic communities, like national communities, are not the primordial entities proclaimed by nationalists but rather were in the process of formation during the entire period from 1861 to 1939. The process of language standardization around a vernacular intensified during the interwar period for most of the linguistic communities in the state, in part as a result of *korenizatsiya* policies but also as a consequence of the more intensive (i.e., mass-based) geographic and social mobilization during the 1920s and 1930s. Linguistic Russification also occurred during this period, but this primarily took place as part of the mobilization of illiterate nonindigenes in Russian-dominated areas whose sense of national self-consciousness was extremely weak or nonexistent. Russification policies in the sociocultural sector

---

[4] Linguistic assimilation is measured as the change in the proportion of the national membership stating that the language of another nation is their "native" (*rodnoy*) or first language. Since 1970, Soviet censuses have also asked a question about fluency in a second language of the USSR, and responses to this question are used to measure the changing nature of bilingualism. For a discussion of these census questions, see Silver (1986).

overtook ethnocultural indigenization only in the late 1930s, and the effectiveness of new language laws favoring Russian must have been marginal before World War II.

After the 1950s, linguistic consolidation continued in several regions of the country, and particularly in the North Caucasus, Soviet Central Asia, and Siberian regions. Even today this process is by no means complete in these regions of the former USSR. Dagestan, for example, currently has twenty-seven distinct languages, twenty-one of which are without a written form. Even within the six literary languages, more than forty distinct dialects can still be identified (Tuchalayev 1988, 77).[5] The ethnolinguistic situation is no less complex in several of the more remote regions of the state, such as the Gorno-Badakhshan Autonomous Oblast in Tadzhikistan, and much of Siberia and the Far East. Linguistic consolidation, like nationalization more generally, was an ongoing process in several regions of the Soviet Union throughout the postwar period. The recency of language development contradicts the nationalists' portrayal of their native languages as both "eternal" and "natural," existing essentially unchanged from "time immemorial."

The Changing Utility of Languages

Language usage in the USSR in theory proceeded dialectically along two divergent paths. According to Guboglo (1984, 72), while each non-Russian language continued to develop, the population also became increasingly fluent in Russian, the "language of international communication." In reality, since the late 1950s the central authorities promoted Russian to a position of primacy as the lingua franca of the state which all citizens had to learn, while at the same time they undermined the utility of the non-Russian languages (e.g., Kirkwood 1991; Yagodin 1989). Russian was certainly the most favored language in the state, a status developed through numerous language laws and enshrined both in the 1977 Constitution, and more recently in the Union Treaty draft proposed by Gorbachev (FBIS 11 March 1991, 32). Russian was a required subject in all schools, while the non-Russian languages had become optional since 1958. Non-Russian student enrollments were shifting away from native language schools in favor of schools where Russian served as the language of instruction, and the native language was at most studied as a separate subject (e.g., Silver 1974b, 1978; Solchanyk 1982, 1985). In native language schools, numerous central directives called for an increase in the number of hours devoted to Russian language study (e.g., Solchanyk 1982). As recently as 1984, new education guidelines from the CPSU (1986) stated the following: "The nationality schools in the union republics will set aside an additional two to three

---

[5] On the linguistic development of the Avars, the largest national community in Dagestan, see Crisp (1985).

hours per week in grades two through eleven/twelve for Russian language study."

The availability of the native language as the language of instruction varied geographically. First, native language schools were in general geographically restricted to the home republic. In theory, if the demand was great enough, native language schools were provided regardless of location. For example, there were Uzbek-language schools outside Uzbekistan, Tatar-language schools outside the Tatar ASSR, and so forth (Guboglo 1984, 139; 1977a, 268; Chekhoyeva 1989; Appendix B). However, in the majority of cases, to live outside the home republic meant to be without the opportunity to study in one's native language, or even to study that language as a separate subject. Second, education in the native language was dominant in rural homeland areas, where indigenes generally comprised the vast majority of the population. In cities, the availability of native language schools varied according to the national composition of the population. In urban locations where the student population was multinational, instruction was normally provided in Russian, and the native language could be studied as a separate subject (e.g., Chekhoyeva 1989, 21). This was especially the case in the autonomous regions of Russia, but even in the cities of non-Russian union republics with relatively large Russian populations, the use of Russian as the language of instruction became commonplace. For example, by the 1972/73 school year in Belarus', 97.6 percent of the urban pupils were taught in Russian, and there were no schools where Belorussian was the language of instruction in Minsk (Solchanyk 1982, 37), even though Belorussians comprised 66 percent of the population in the capital (TsSU SSSR 1973, 4:200). The situation was somewhat better outside Ukraine and Belarus', but even in Frunze (Bishkek), the capital of Kyrgyzstan, 42 percent of Kirgiz children did not study in the Kirgiz language in 1988 (Yagodin 1989, 5).[6]

Finally, the availability of native language schooling varied across the autonomous structure of the Soviet federation. Members of all union republic nations had the possibility of attending native language schools through college (Appendix B). With the exception of Ukrainians and Belorussians, the number of students studying in the native language for the union republic nations expanded during the 1960s and early 1970s, and for most grew at or above the rate of indigenous population growth. During the same period, the number of pupils studying in Russian-language schools actually decreased in Uzbekistan and Azerbaydzhan, and increased more slowly than Russian population growth in all republics except Georgia (Table 6.1). This linguistic indigenization of schooling apparently corresponded with the demographic indigenization of schools discussed in chapter 5. According to surveys conducted during the 1970s and early 1980s, indigenous parents continued to favor the use of their

[6] In 1989, Kirgiz comprised 23 percent of Frunze's (Bishkek's) population, which was 56 percent Russian (Goskomstat SSSR 1991, 126).

TABLE 6.1
Number of Pupils with Russian and Native Language Instruction, 1965–1972

	Number of Pupils (1972/1965 · 100)		Population Change (1970/1959 · 100)	
Republic	NL[a]	Russian	Indigenes	Russians
Ukraine	93.8	110.4	109.4	128.7
Belarus'	85.8	128.0	114.4	141.1
Moldova	105.9	103.5	121.9	141.3
Uzbekistan	165.5	90.9	152.9	134.9
Kazakhstan	143.0	112.7	146.3	139.0
Kyrgyzstan	150.2	108.6	149.9	137.2
Tadzhikistan	159.0	123.1	152.9	130.9
Turkmenistan	153.5	107.1	153.3	119.0
Georgia	113.4	105.7	120.6	97.3
Azerbaydzhan	150.8	94.8	149.0	101.8
Armenia	128.6	113.3	127.7	117.9
Lithuania	113.7	109.6	114.6	116.0
Latvia	106.5	103.7	102.2	126.8
Estonia	101.5	107.6	101.9	139.6

Source: Guboglo 1977a, 270.
[a] NL = Native Language (i.e., Ukrainian in Ukraine).

native languages as the language of instruction, and this was particularly true for the most developed nations in the state (Table 6.2).

Still, the pressure to learn Russian in schools clearly increased during the 1970s and into the 1980s, even for the union republic nations. This was particularly true for Ukrainians and Belorussians, where there was a decrease in the number of native language schools and students in native language schools, and

TABLE 6.2
Language of Instruction Preferred by Parents (percent)

	Native Language		Russian		Depends on Class[a]	
Nation	Urban	Rural	Urban	Rural	Urban	Rural
Moldavian	60.5	78.8	25.5	12.3	14.0	8.9
Uzbek	63.4	74.0	33.8	22.9	2.8	3.1
Georgian	76.7	83.3	18.1	12.1	5.2	4.6
Estonian	83.9	82.7	3.9	3.4	12.2	13.9

Source: Arutyunyan and Bromley 1986, 306.
[a] "Depends on Class" = in younger grades, in the native language; in older grades, in Russian. A fourth category—"No Answer"—has been factored out.

a concomitant rise in the Russian-language school system (e.g., Solchanyk 1982, 1985; Sandulyak 1989). This "linguistic Russification" of schools in the non-Russian union republics, even though relatively limited, was an ongoing process, especially in the eastern cities of these two Slavic republics, and became one of the major sources of international tension (Solchanyk 1982, 33–37) and a catalyst for the activation of national territoriality in recent years. This was reflected both in the programs of the national front organizations (e.g., RUKH 1989) and also in the rash of new language laws designating the indigenous language as the official language of the republic that all nonindigenes had to learn (e.g., JPRS 1989). These laws were passed in all union republics between 1989 and 1991.

Below the union republics, the members of most national communities with autonomous republics, oblasts, and okrugs had significantly fewer opportunities to study in their native languages. According to recent information provided by Yagodin (1989, 6), Ossetians and Abkhazians in Georgia had native language instruction available through secondary schools.[7] This was among the highest level of native language instruction for national communities with autonomous units, yet this relatively privileged ethnocultural status did not prevent independence movements in these two autonomous territories. In Nagorno-Karabakh Autonomous Oblast, Armenians seeking to secede from Azerbaydzhan and become part of Armenia cited the growing restrictions on access to native language schooling as a reason for secession. However, when Moscow proposed to solve the international conflict in Nagorno-Karabakh by guaranteeing ethnocultural autonomy for the Armenians in the autonomous oblast, the offer was rejected out of hand. While ethnocultural autonomy was certainly desired by indigenes, it was clearly not the main goal motivating nationalists seeking to gain control over Nagorno-Karabakh for the Armenian nation.

In Russia, where most of the autonomous units in the state are located, a more concerted effort toward linguistic Russification of schools was made during the postwar period. There were three types of national (i.e., non-Russian) schools: (1) instruction in the native language, with Russian studied as a separate subject; (2) instruction in Russian, with the native language studied as a separate subject; and (3) instruction in both languages, normally in the native language in the younger grades with a transition to Russian afterward. Only Tatars and Bashkirs had type (1) schools available for complete secondary education, and Yakuts and Tuvins had type (1) schools through incomplete secondary education. As in the case of Abkhazians and Ossetians in Georgia, the national communities with the most extensive ethnocultural autonomy in the RSFSR are also those who are pressing most forcefully for greater sovereignty. Most other autonomous republic national communities had type (3)

[7] This does not correspond with earlier data provided by Silver (1978). See Appendix B.

schools, where instruction in the native language was available for elementary school and the transition to Russian language instruction was made by grades 2 to 3 (indigenous nationalities of Dagestan), or by grades 4 to 5 (Buryat, Komi, Mari, Mordvin, Udmurt, Chuvash ASSRs, and Khakass Autonomous Oblast). In anticipation of the shift in language of instruction, earlier grades were often conducted in both the native and Russian languages (Chekhoyeva 1989). However, the officially designated amount of native language schooling often differed from reality. For example, "In Mari ASSR native language instruction in schools has not been conducted for almost two decades" (Yagodin 1989, 5). Type (2) national schools were available for indigenes in the Kabardin-Balkar, Kalmyk, Karelian, North Ossetian, and Chechen-Ingush ASSRs, the Altay, Adygey and Karachay-Cherkess Autonomous Oblasts, and all Autonomous Okrugs (Appendix B). For most of these nationalities, there was a shift in favor of Russian language instruction by the indigenous population, though most continued to want their children to study the native language as a separate subject (e.g., Guboglo 1977a, 273–274; Crisp 1985, 154–155).

Trends in the language of publications in the USSR also indicate that Russian retained a dominant status, and even became more pervasive during the postwar period. Between 1960 and 1980 Russian language books and brochures increased from 72.7 percent to 77.8 percent of all titles and from 82 percent to 82.3 percent of all copies produced (*tirazh*). In 1988 the Russian language proportion of titles declined somewhat to 76.6 percent, but the proportion of the total number of copies published increased to 85.7 percent (Goskomstat SSSR 1989c, 369–377). This high and even increasing proportion occurred at a time when the Russian share of the total population decreased from 54.6 percent to 50.8 percent (Goskomstat SSSR 1991a, 5), making the relative dominance of Russian language publications even more pronounced.

This dominance is tempered somewhat by an examination of the publication history in each union republic, particularly when the relative proportion of each indigenous language is indexed to that nation's share of the republic's population (Table 6.3). In 1988, in addition to Russian, Estonian was also overrepresented in book titles, and Kazakh, Georgian, Lithuanian, Latvian, and Estonian were overrepresented in the share of book copies published. Between 1970 and 1988 the relative share of native language publications for all union republic-level nations in their respective homelands declined except for Lithuanians, Latvians, and Moldavians (book titles), and Russians, Lithuanians, and Latvians (copies published). With regard to journals and periodicals, all union-republic nations were relatively overrepresented in 1988 except Belorussians, Moldavians, Kirgiz, Tadzhiks, and Armenians (number of copies), while Russians, Georgians, Latvians, and Estonians were overrepresented in the number of journal titles. On average, the relative share of indigenous language journals increased between 1970 and 1988 (titles and copies), and the coefficient of variation showed convergence (i.e., equalization). This was the one publica-

TABLE 6.3
Language of Publication by Republic, 1970–1988 (Indexed Values[a]) (indigenous language percent of titles for books, journals, and newspapers)

Republic	Books			Journals			Newspapers		
	1970	1988	Percentage Point Change	1970	1988	Percentage Point Change	1970	1988	Percentage Point Change
RSFSR	112.2	111.6	−0.6	115.3	113.6	−1.7	113.0	113.1	0.1
Ukraine	51.0	29.4	−21.6	47.5	65.6	18.1	108.0	96.8	−11.2
Belarus'	24.3	17.5	−6.8	32.7	39.1	6.4	93.1	77.4	−15.7
Moldova	48.3	51.1	2.8	34.4	72.6	38.2	72.2	64.5	−7.7
Uzbekistan	67.5	61.0	−6.5	39.7	50.2	10.5	87.8	94.8	7.0
Kazakhstan	95.1	72.7	−22.4	48.1	83.1	35.0	112.3	94.5	−17.8
Kyrgyzstan	108.1	70.6	−37.5	91.3	71.1	−20.2	126.8	104.4	−22.4
Tadzhikistan	91.9	64.8	−27.1	63.5	47.6	−15.9	148.8	134.7	−14.1
Turkmenistan	99.4	54.2	−45.2	65.3	61.8	−3.5	107.0	108.2	1.2
Georgia	109.0	98.0	−11.0	110.0	118.4	8.4	128.6	124.3	−4.3
Azerbaydzhan	87.5	72.8	−14.7	86.4	61.7	−24.7	106.8	97.5	−9.3
Armenia	84.3	72.3	−12.0	82.7	65.2	−17.5	100.3	94.5	−5.8
Lithuania	80.6	90.9	10.3	87.3	92.7	5.4	101.5	97.5	−4.0
Latvia	93.9	96.4	2.5	91.3	110.4	19.1	113.8	114.4	0.6
Estonia	109.1	102.7	−6.4	109.2	108.9	−0.3	105.7	112.6	6.9
Average	84.1	71.1	−13.0	73.6	77.5	3.9	108.4	101.9	−6.5

Source: Goskomstat SSSR 1989c, 369–392.

[a]Figures represent the indigenous language percentage of total publications in each union republic indexed to the indigenous percentage of the republic's population. For example, the figures for book publications in Ukraine = (Ukrainian language percent of the titles published in Ukraine divided by the Ukrainian percentage of the total population in Ukraine) · 100. A figure over 100 represents relative overrepresentation (i.e., a higher proportion of indigenous language publications than indigenes in the homeland), and a figure under 100 represents relative underrepresentation.

tion category in which Ukrainians and Belorussians experienced a relative improvement in the share of publications in their native languages. Newspaper publication data between 1970 and 1988 indicated that the share of native language publications was at or above the indigenous share of the total homeland population for all union republic-level nations except Belorussians and Moldavians (titles), and Ukrainians, Belorussians, Kazakhs, and Moldavians (copies).

Overall, the nations whose share of the native language publications in their home republics underwent a relatively dramatic decline between 1970 and 1988 included the rapidly growing Central Asians, as well as the Ukrainians and Belorussians. For the nations of Soviet Central Asia, the relative decline is explained more by rapid population growth, which increased the indigenous share of the total population (i.e., the denominator), than by a decreasing share of publications per se. On the other hand, the relative decrease in native language publication share for Ukrainians and Belorussians in their respective homelands resulted from an actual decline in the proportion of publications rather than a change in the ethnodemographic composition of the population. It appears that for these two union republics a more concerted effort was made to promote linguistic Russification. In reaction to this, one of the first acts of Ukrainian and Belorussian nationalists was to call for a halt to this state-sponsored "denationalization" (e.g., RUKH 1989).

The proportion of native language publications in Georgia, Latvia, Lithuania, and Estonia was at, above, or only slightly below each nation's share of its home republic population throughout the 1970s and 1980s. However, the nationalists of these groups have also been outspoken regarding the threat posed by Russification and the need to protect their indigenous languages. The political elites of these nations were among the first to draft and pass new language laws designed to guarantee a dominant status for the indigenous languages in the national homelands. A perception of relative deprivation was apparent among indigenes throughout the USSR generally, without regard to the actual degree of dominance or subordination of the indigenous language to Russian. This is a clear case of the way in which the homeland, and particularly the indigene's sense of exclusiveness regarding his or her status in it, has affected nationalist perceptions and indigenous behavior toward nonindigenes in the state.

As a final consideration regarding language of publication trends, the non-Russian languages were clearly evolving into media through which non-Russian writers were more willing to express themselves. During the Stalin era, even though dozens of languages were being developed, the majority of publications were not original works but rather were translations, primarily of Russian titles. This reinforces the depiction of non-Russian language development during the interwar period as the promotion of national forms through which the socialist content of the regime could be more easily diffused. Since the 1950s, the percentage of original works in several non-Russian languages increased dramatically (e.g., Guboglo 1977c, 1984; Raun 1985). The most rapid growth in the proportion of original works occurred among the most (i.e., the Baltic) and the least (Moldavian, Central Asian) developed nations and languages. However, even for Ukrainians and Belorussians the shift in favor of original publications during the postwar period was dramatic, and by 1980 the proportion of original works exceeded half the total number of native language publications for all fourteen non-Russian union republic-level nations, and for nine of these it exceeded 75 percent (Guboglo 1984, 165–173). At least for the union republic nations, the native languages developed into more fully formed literary languages during the postwar period. This is an important qualification to the more general linguistic Russification of publications that occurred.

Beyond schooling and publications, the status of indigenous languages in the work place is also an important measure of their utility, and perhaps their future viability. Language usage on the job is also an important instrument in international competition, because the predominance of one language over another provides members of the national community most fluent in that language with a comparative advantage over others. Before 1989 learning Russian was a prerequisite for social mobility, particularly for autonomous-level nationalities and for nonindigenes living and working in urban/industrial centers outside their own home republics. According to Desheriyev and Protchenko (1968, 122; as quoted in Silver 1974b, 39), "in autonomous republics, oblasts and national okrugs (in the RSFSR), the transaction of correspondence and business in local languages in state institutions and organizations was abandoned and transferred to the Russian language." This also appears to have been the case in the eastern cities of Ukraine and Belarus', and of the urban/industrial centers of Soviet Central Asia. The status of Russian as the lingua franca of the state certainly gave Russians a comparative advantage in competition with other nonindigenes and even with indigenes in several autonomous and union republics. Furthermore, because Russian was the dominant language in the state, the geographic mobility of Russians did not necessitate their acculturation to the indigenous languages outside the RSFSR, and this undoubtedly helps to explain their relatively high rate of interhomeland migration. On the other hand, inadequate knowledge of Russian was cited as a factor in the low rate of rural to urban migration among the indigenous nations in Soviet Central Asia (Arutyunyan 1985, 30).

However, it would be a gross oversimplification to treat Russian language fluency as a universal requirement for upward mobility. First, Russian language dominance varied by economic sector, and was particularly strong in the urban/industrial sectors of the economy, where Russian workers also tended to predominate. In the so-called non-productive sectors, and particularly among the indigenous sociocultural intelligentsia, the native language tended to be the language of daily conversation (e.g., Guboglo 1984, 203). Second, Russian was more dominant in larger cities and less so in smaller urban settlements, and less still in non-Russian rural areas. For example, only 43 percent of urban Moldavians who were most fluent in Moldavian said that they most frequently conversed in Moldavian at work, while the corresponding figure for rural Moldavians was 85 percent (Guboglo 1984, 193). Finally, Russian language dominance in the blue- and white-collar sectors of the economy varied by republic. In the least developed republics, such as Moldova and the Central Asian republics, as well as in the eastern regions of Ukraine and Belarus', Russian was clearly the language of upward mobility in the cities. This linguistic Russification of the modernized work place was related to the demographic "Russianization" of the urban/industrial complex that occurred as these regions developed. Of course, this relationship also held for the autonomous regions in the RSFSR. In the more developed republics where Russians did not hold a dominant economic position, such as in Georgia and Estonia, the Russian language was not dominant in the work place.

Functionally, the Russian language became more dominant in the USSR during the postwar period, not only as the language of instruction in a growing number of non-Russian (i.e., nationality) schools but also in publications, other forms of communication, and in the urban/industrial work place. This functional expansion primarily occurred at the expense of the languages of non-Russian indigenes whose homelands were incorporated into the RSFSR as autonomous units, and also of Ukrainian and Belorussian. The real or perceived threat to the indigenous nations' standing in their own homelands that this represented served as a catalyst for the activation of national territoriality. This has become particularly apparent since the late 1980s. In this sense, the designation of Russian as the lingua franca of the USSR and its active promotion by the CPSU, like the tsarist policy of Russification before it, proved counterproductive to the ultimate goal of creating an integrated Soviet people. As is discussed in the following section, the successful acculturation of non-Russian indigenes in the USSR was extremely limited.

Linguistic Russification

Considering the privileged status that the Russian language attained in the postwar USSR, surprisingly little linguistic Russification took place during the past thirty years (Maps 6.1 and 6.2). Between 1959 and 1989 the number of non-Russians claiming Russian to be their first or native language increased from 10.2 million to 18.7 million, or from 10.8 percent to 13.3 percent of all non-Russians in the state. Almost all this linguistic Russification occurred between 1959 and 1979 (0.12 percentage points per year or 1.15 percentage points per decade); between 1979 and 1989 almost no linguistic Russification took place (0.02 percentage points per year or 0.2 percentage points for the decade) (TsSU SSSR 1962; TsSU SSSR 1973; TsSU SSSR 1984; Statis-

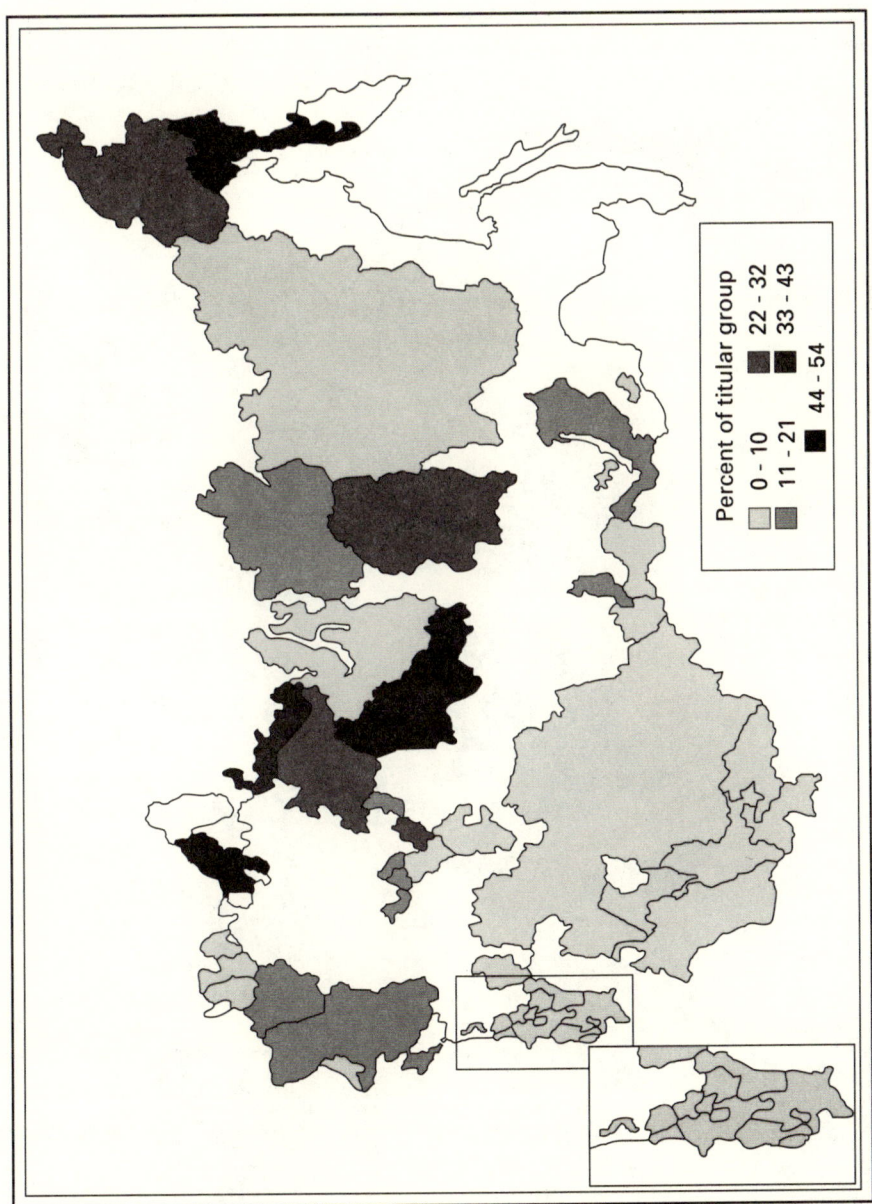

Map 6.1 Percent of Indigenes Claiming Russian as Their Native Language, 1989

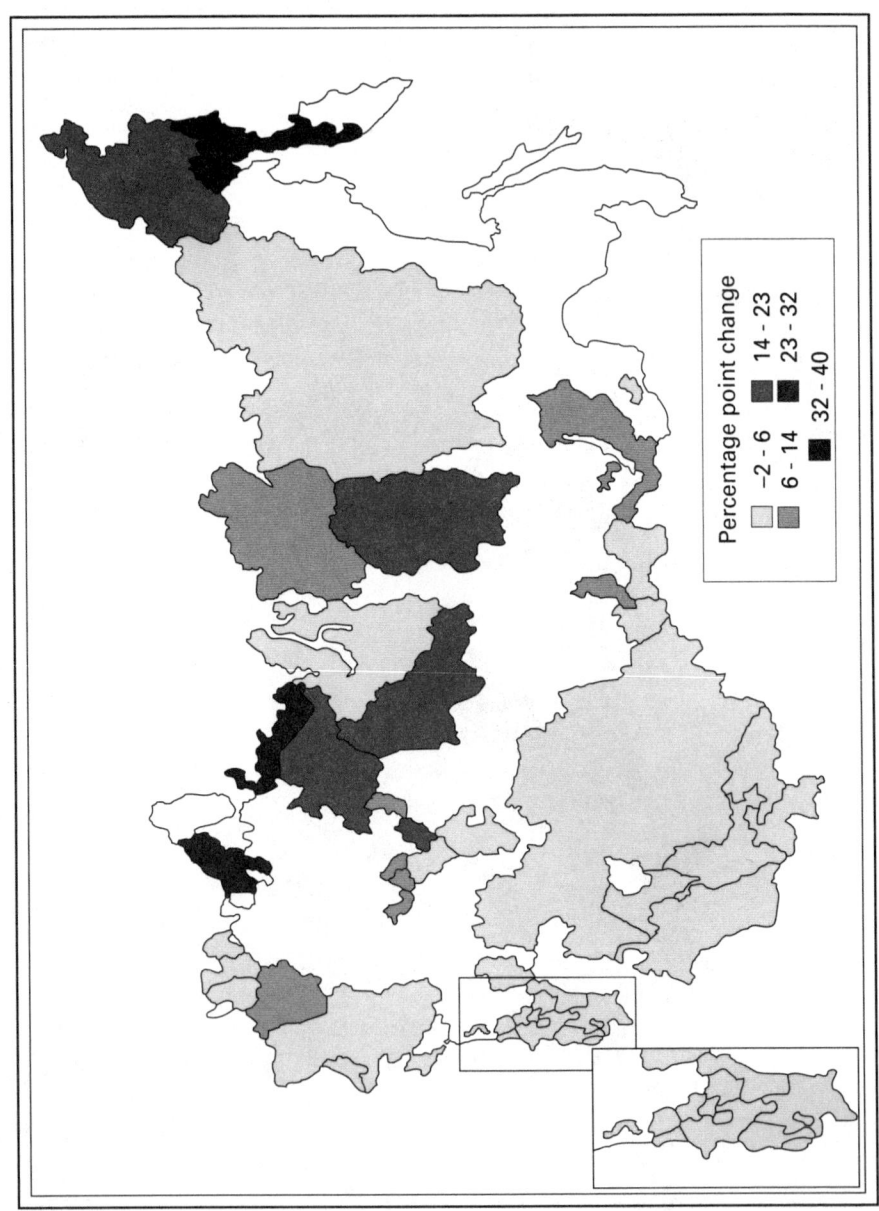

Map 6.2 Linguistic Russification of Indigenes, 1959–1989

ticheskiy Komitet SNG 1993, vol. 7, part 1). The vast majority of members of most nations in the state retained their own national languages as their language of first choice (Table 6.4). On average, only 1.7 percent of each of the fourteen non-Russian union republic-level nations experienced a linguistic shift away from the indigenous language and toward Russian between 1959 and 1989. Of course, a great deal of variance existed between these nations, with Estonians and Armenians experiencing a "de-Russification" over the entire period, Azerbaydzhanis experiencing a "de-Russification" between 1979 and 1989, and Georgians, Tadzhiks, and Turkmen experiencing no Russification during the 1980s. On the other hand, Ukrainians, Belorussians, and Moldavians experienced a much more substantial linguistic Russification between 1959 and 1989.

Among the autonomous-level national communities, linguistic Russification was more pronounced. For ASSR-level nations, only those whose homelands are located in the Northwest or the Volga-Urals region (i.e., Karelians, Komi, Mari, Mordvins, Udmurts, and Chuvash) have experienced significant linguistic Russification, and these are the groups that have interacted with local Russians intensely for a long time. Linguistic Russification for at least some members of these national communities may be more akin to a preliminary stage in the process of national consolidation than of international integration or assimilation. This is undoubtedly also the case for the Siberian peoples whose homelands are designated as autonomous okrugs and whose regions have been dominated demographically and otherwise by Russians since the eighteenth century (Bruk and Kabuzan 1982a). As noted in chapters 2 and 3, the nationalization process for most of these Siberian *ethnies* was manufactured from outside (i.e., by Moscow) during the interwar period, and the nationalization of the indigenous masses was difficult to identify before the postwar period. For members of these groups in particular, linguistic Russification may be seen as part of a process of national consolidation toward the Russian nation, rather than as the acculturation of nationally self-conscious individuals to Russian.

The "Other" category includes the largest national communities without officially designated homelands, in addition to the Jews, whose Autonomous Oblast in southern Siberia cannot be considered a national homeland. On average, these national communities appear similar to the small peoples of Siberia in the level of native language retention and linguistic Russification, although their pre-World War II Russification rates were generally higher and their postwar rate was lower. However, the average for this set of national communities is all but meaningless, since native language retention rates range from a high of 94 percent for Hungarians to a low of 14 percent for Jews.[8] In

---

[8] The linguistic assimilation of Jews and Germans during the 1970–1989 period may be more apparent than real, since the more nationally conscious members who would have been more likely to claim the native language as their first language were also those who were more likely to emigrate. Emigration has thus played a significant role in language usage shifts for these two nations.

TABLE 6.4
Native Language Retention and Linguistic Russification by Nation, 1959–1989 (percent and percentage point change)

Nation	Native Language					Russian			
	1959	1970	1979	1989	Percentage Point Change	1959	1970	1979	1989	Percentage Point Change
Union Republic Level										
Russian	99.8	99.8	99.8	99.8	0.0	99.8	99.8	99.8	99.8	0.0
Ukrainian	87.7	85.7	82.8	81.1	−6.6	12.2	14.3	17.1	18.8	6.6
Belorussian	84.2	80.6	74.2	70.9	−13.3	15.3	19.0	25.4	28.5	13.2
Uzbek	98.4	98.6	98.5	98.3	−0.1	0.5	0.5	0.6	0.7	0.2
Kazakh	98.4	98.0	97.5	97.0	−0.6	1.2	1.6	2.0	2.2	1.0
Georgian	98.6	98.4	98.3	98.2	−0.4	1.3	1.4	1.7	1.7	0.4
Azerbaydzhan	97.6	98.2	97.8	97.7	0.1	1.2	1.3	1.8	1.7	0.5
Lithuanian	97.8	97.9	97.9	97.7	−0.1	1.2	1.5	1.7	1.8	0.6
Moldavian	95.2	95.0	93.2	91.6	−3.6	3.6	4.2	6.0	7.4	3.8
Latvian	95.1	95.2	95.0	94.8	−0.3	4.6	4.6	4.8	5.0	0.4
Kirgiz	98.7	98.8	97.9	97.8	−0.9	0.3	0.3	0.5	0.6	0.3
Tadzhik	98.1	98.5	97.8	97.7	−0.4	0.5	0.6	0.8	0.8	0.3
Armenian	89.9	91.4	90.7	91.7	1.8	8.3	7.6	8.4	7.6	−0.7
Turkmen	98.9	98.9	98.7	98.5	−0.4	0.6	0.8	1.0	1.0	0.4
Estonian	95.2	95.5	95.3	95.5	0.3	4.7	4.4	4.5	4.4	−0.3
Autonomous Republic Level										
Bashkir[a]	61.9	66.2	67.0	72.3	10.4	2.6	4.5	7.1	11.2	8.6
Buryat	94.9	92.6	90.1	86.3	−8.6	5.1	7.3	9.8	13.6	8.5
Avar	97.2	97.2	97.7	97.2	0.0	0.8	1.0	1.3	1.9	1.1
Dargin	98.6	98.4	98.2	97.5	−1.1	0.9	1.2	1.4	1.9	1.0
Kumyk	98.0	98.4	98.2	97.4	−0.6	1.4	1.2	1.5	2.1	0.7
Lezgin	92.7	93.9	90.8	91.6	−1.1	3.0	3.7	4.7	4.8	1.8
Kabardin	97.9	98.0	97.9	97.2	−0.7	1.9	1.8	2.0	2.6	0.7
Balkar	97.0	97.2	96.9	93.6	−3.4	2.2	2.3	2.7	5.4	3.2
Kalmyk	91.0	91.7	91.3	90.0	−1.0	7.2	5.9	5.9	7.3	0.1

Karelian	71.3	63.0	55.6	47.8	−23.5	28.5	36.8	44.1	51.8	23.3
Komi	89.3	82.7	76.2	70.4	−18.9	10.5	17.2	23.7	29.5	19.0
Mari	95.1	91.2	86.7	80.8	−14.3	4.6	8.6	13.0	18.8	14.2
Mordvin	78.1	77.8	72.6	67.1	−11.0	21.8	22.1	27.4	32.7	10.9
Tatar[b]	92.1	89.2	85.9	83.6	−8.5	7.0	10.2	13.2	15.6	8.6
Tuvin	99.1	98.7	98.8	98.5	−0.6	0.8	1.2	1.2	1.4	0.6
Udmurt	89.1	82.6	76.4	69.6	−19.5	10.7	17.2	23.4	30.0	19.3
Chechen	98.8	98.7	98.6	98.1	−0.7	1.0	1.2	1.3	1.7	0.7
Ingush	97.9	97.4	97.4	96.9	−1.0	1.9	2.4	2.5	2.8	0.9
Chuvash	90.8	86.9	81.7	76.4	−14.4	9.0	13.0	18.1	23.3	14.3
Yakut	97.5	96.3	95.3	93.8	−3.7	2.4	3.7	4.6	6.1	3.5
Abkhaz	95.0	95.9	94.3	93.5	−1.5	3.1	3.1	4.1	4.9	1.8
Karakalpak	95.0	96.6	95.8	94.1	−0.9	0.3	0.4	0.5	1.0	0.7
Ossetian	89.1	88.6	88.2	87.0	−2.1	4.9	5.4	6.6	7.0	2.1
Autonomous Oblast Level										
Adygey	96.8	96.5	95.7	94.7	−2.1	3.2	3.4	4.2	5.1	1.9
Altay	88.5	87.2	86.4	84.3	−4.2	11.2	12.6	13.5	15.5	4.3
Karachay	96.8	98.1	97.6	96.8	0.0	1.5	1.6	2.0	2.7	1.2
Cherkess	89.7	92.0	91.4	90.4	0.7	6.7	5.4	5.9	6.3	−0.4
Khakass	86.0	83.7	80.9	76.1	−9.9	13.9	16.3	19.0	23.6	9.7
Autonomous Okrug Level										
Komi-Permyak	87.6	85.8	77.1	70.1	−17.5	12.1	14.1	22.8	29.7	17.6
Koryak	90.5	81.1	69.0	52.4	−38.1	8.9	18.2	30.6	46.4	37.5
Nenets	84.7	83.4	81.8	77.1	−7.6	5.5	9.0	14.0	18.1	12.6
Dolgan	93.9	89.8	90.0	81.7	−12.2	—	9.9	9.8	15.9	(6.0)
Khanty	77.0	68.9	67.8	60.5	−16.5	22.3	30.5	31.8	38.8	16.5
Mansi	59.2	52.4	49.5	37.1	−22.1	40.4	47.4	50.3	62.0	21.6
Chukchi	93.9	82.6	78.2	70.3	−23.6	5.7	16.9	21.2	28.3	22.6
Evenk	55.9	51.3	42.8	30.4	−15.5	8.7	16.5	20.7	28.5	19.8
Other										
Jewish[c]	21.5	17.7	14.2	14.2	−7.3	76.4	78.2	83.3	83.6	7.2
German	75.0	66.8	57.0	48.7	−26.3	24.2	32.7	42.6	50.8	26.6
Polish	45.2	32.5	29.1	30.5	−14.7	14.7	20.7	26.2	28.6	13.9

(*continued*)

TABLE 6.4
Continued

Nation	Native Language				Russian			
	1959	1970	1979	1989	Percentage Point Change	1959	1970	1979	1989	Percentage Point Change

Nation	1959	1970	1979	1989	Percentage Point Change	1959	1970	1979	1989	Percentage Point Change
Finnish	59.5	51.0	40.9	34.6	−24.9	35.7	42.5	50.3	54.6	18.9
Hungarian	97.2	96.6	95.4	93.9	−3.3	1.8	2.0	2.6	3.3	1.5
Rumanian	83.3	63.9	41.0	60.9	−22.4	2.4	3.6	4.8	5.6	3.2
Bulgarian	79.4	73.1	68.0	68.1	−11.3	18.2	24.4	29.1	28.8	10.6
Greek	41.5	39.3	38.0	44.5	3.0	46.1	49.5	56.8	51.4	5.3
Gagauz	94.0	93.6	89.3	87.5	−6.5	4.0	4.9	8.6	10.6	6.6
Korean	79.3	68.6	55.4	49.4	−29.9	20.5	31.3	44.4	50.1	29.6
Kurd	89.9	87.6	83.6	80.5	−9.4	2.9	3.8	4.8	4.5	1.6
Uygur	85.0	88.5	86.1	86.6	1.6	2.3	2.8	3.6	3.9	1.6
Gypsy	59.3	70.8	74.1	77.4	18.1	23.5	16.7	14.9	10.8	−12.7
Averages:										
Union Republics	95.6	95.4	94.4	93.9	−1.7	4.0	4.4	5.5	5.9	1.9
Autonomous Republics	91.6	90.4	88.3	86.1	−5.5	5.7	7.5	9.6	12.1	6.4
Autonomous Oblasts	91.6	91.5	90.4	88.5	−3.1	7.3	7.9	8.9	10.6	3.3
Autonomous Okrugs	80.3	74.4	69.5	60.0	−20.3	14.8	20.6	25.2	33.5	18.7
Other	70.0	65.4	59.4	59.8	−10.2	21.0	24.1	28.6	29.7	8.7

Sources: 1959: TsSU SSSR 1962, 16 vols.; 1970: TsSU SSSR 1973, vol. 4; 1979: TsSU SSSR 1984; 1989: Goskomstat SSSR 1991a.

Note: Averages are unweighted, since each national community is treated as an observation.

[a] Bashkirs not claiming Bashkir as the native language most often claimed Tatar.

[b] Tatars include Crimean Tatars, since data for this national community were not provided from 1959 to 1979. In 1989, 92.6 percent of the Crimean Tatars claimed Crimean Tatar as their native language, and 5.3 percent claimed Russian. Of all other Tatars, 83.2 percent claimed Tatar as their native language, and 16.1 percent claimed Russian.

[c] Jewish group includes Central Asian Jews, Mountain Jews, and Georgian Jews, since data were not provided for these separate communities from 1959 to 1979. In 1989, 65.1 percent of Central Asian Jews claimed the native language and 33.6 percent claimed Russian; 75.8 percent of Mountain Jews claimed the native language and 19.4 percent claimed Russian; and 90.9 percent of Georgian Jews claimed the native language compared to 8.2 percent claiming Russian. Of all other Jews, 11.1 percent claimed the native language, while 86.6 percent claimed Russian.

addition, the Gypsies actually experienced a reversal of the linguistic Russification that had occurred before 1959.[9] Several of the other groups included in this category live in regions bordering on their home states (e.g., Hungarians, Rumanians, Poles, etc.), and may continue to perceive this territory as part of their ancestral homeland. Gagauz also clearly perceive the region of Moldova where they have lived in concentrated settlements for more than two hundred years as their rightful homeland. Lacking official recognition in the federal structure of the state did not necessarily mean that national communities also lacked a "sense of homeland."

The rate of linguistic Russification did not correspond well with the international variance in the functional utility of native languages discussed above, and this was particularly true for national communities at the autonomous level in the federal hierarchy. For example, the indigenes with homelands in the North Caucasus generally had more restricted access to their native languages in school than did the national communities with homelands in the Volga-Urals region, yet the latter became much more linguistically Russified than the former.

For most non-Russians, the proportional shift away from the native language was matched almost precisely by a shift to the Russian language. The only real exception to this was the Bashkirs, a large proportion of whose members linguistically assimilated to Tatar before the war. During the postwar period, a "de-Tatarization" occurred, as Bashkirs increasingly proclaimed Bashkir to be their native language, and a smaller proportion also experienced linguistic Russification. A number of other national communities also had a relatively larger share of members who linguistically assimilated to a third language: Evenks to Yakut, Poles to Belorussian, Rumanians to Ukrainian, and Kurds to the indigenous language where their members reside. However, for the vast majority of the non-Russian population, the choice of first language was made between the language of one's own nation and the lingua franca of the state. In making their choice, the overwhelming majority of non-Russians continued to choose their own national languages first (Maps 6.3 and 6.4). Even though the functional utility of many non-Russian languages decreased during the postwar period, non-Russian indigenes strongly tended to continue claiming their own national language as their language of first choice. As is discussed below, this language selection at the time of the census was as much a vote in favor of ethnocultural indigenization and national territoriality generally as it was a functional statement about relative fluency levels.

Geographic differentials in the rate of native language retention and lin-

---

[9] As in the case of Jews and Germans, this linguistic indigenization may have also been more apparent than real, since Gypsies in the past claimed to be members of other national communities in an effort to escape persecution. During the postwar period, conditions improved for Gypsies, and increasingly members reclaimed their previously hidden national identity and language not only in the former USSR but throughout Eastern Europe (Kaiser 1988).

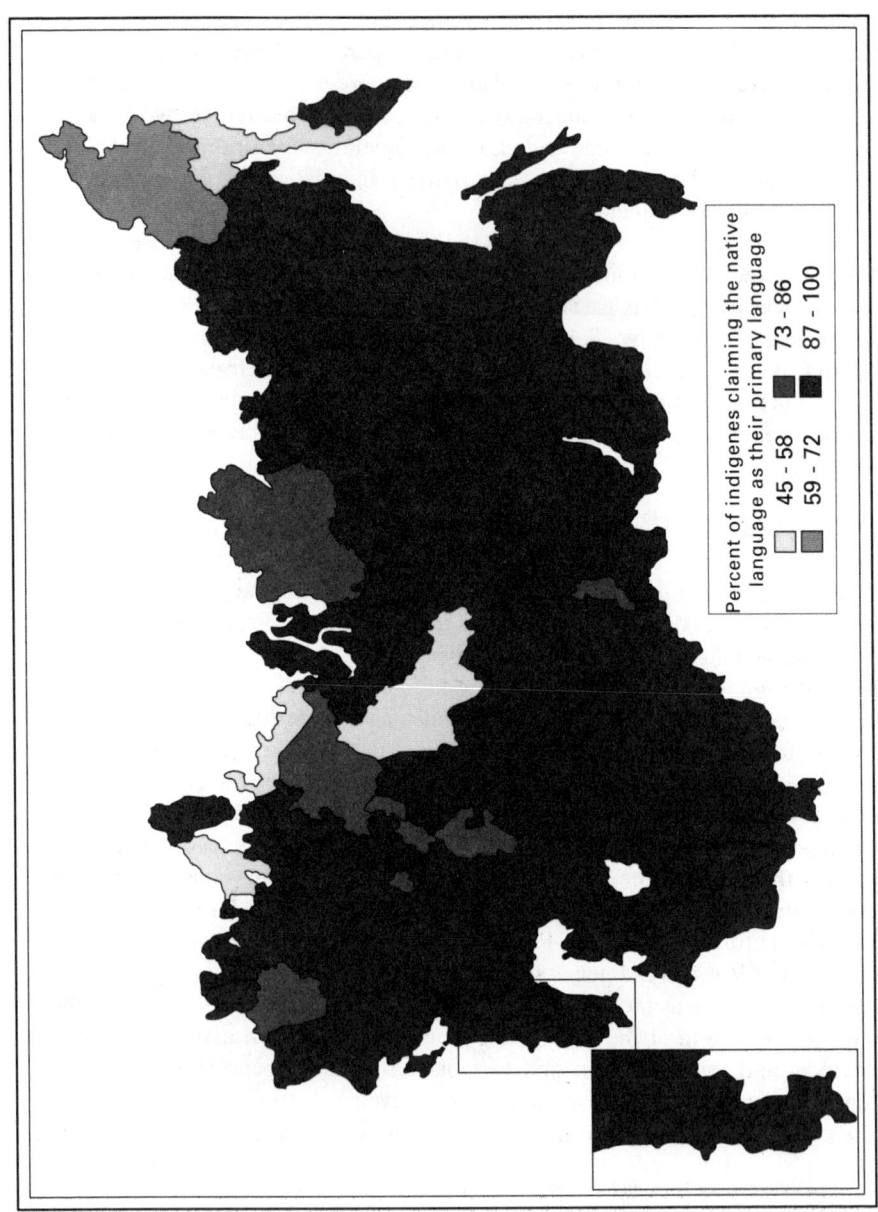

Map 6.3 Native Language Retention among Indigenes, 1989

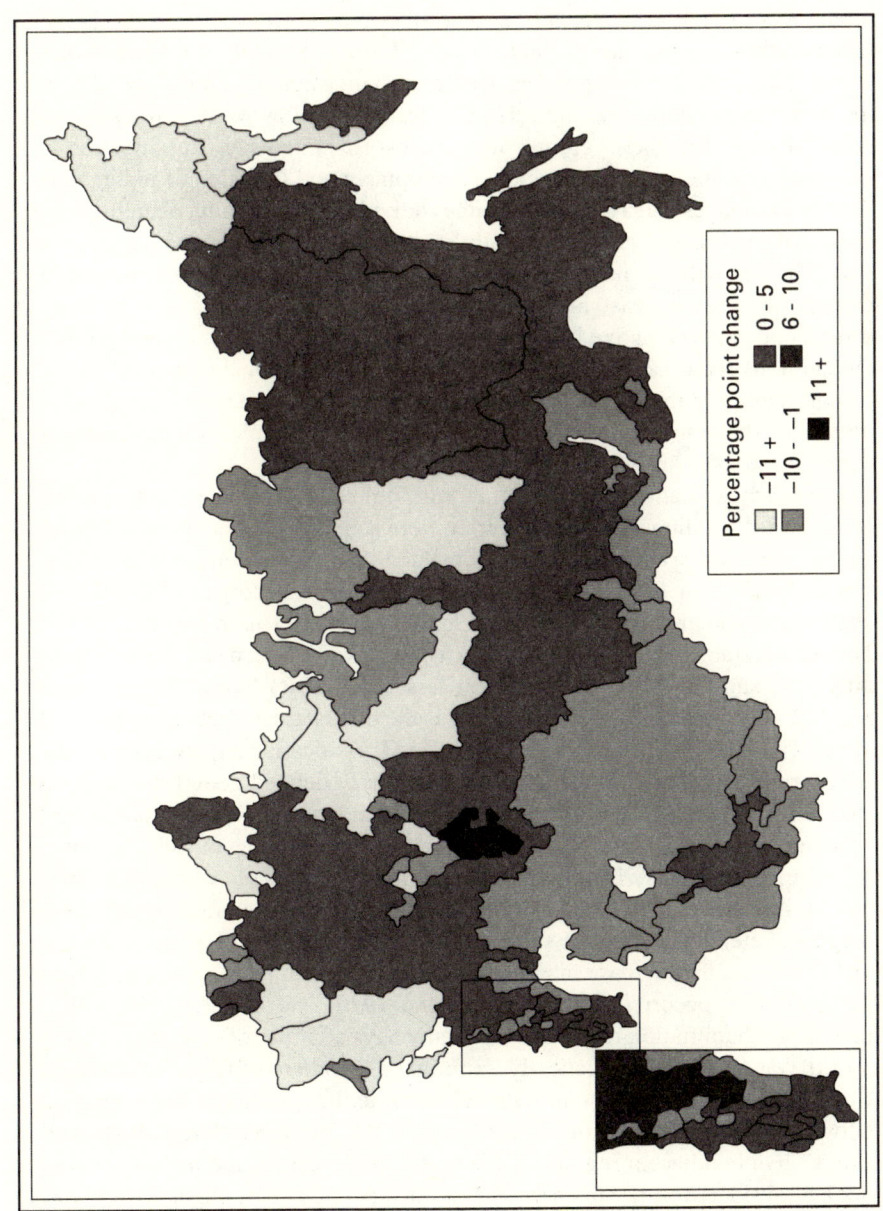

Map 6.4 Change in Native Language Retention among Indigenes, 1959–1989

guistic Russification between 1959 and 1989 were even more dramatic than international variations. First, and most generally, the rate of native language retention was almost universally higher among members living in the home republic than among those living outside (Table 6.5). Only the Khanty and Mansi, two small Siberian peoples, had lower native language retention rates in the homeland than outside, and this was true in 1959 as well as in 1989. As noted above, for these groups the process of linguistic Russification—particularly if it occurred before the development and diffusion of indigenous literary languages—may be seen by the individuals undergoing acculturation as part of a process of national consolidation, rather than international integration. That the national homeland has not been an impediment to this language change provides at least indirect evidence that this is the case. The large differential between native language retention rates among the union republic, autonomous republic, and autonomous oblast-level national communities on the one hand, and the lack of such a differential among autonomous okrug-level *ethnies* on the other, indicates that the peoples of northern Siberia have not yet experienced mass-based nationalization.

For nearly all national communities with officially designated home republics, the rate of linguistic Russification between 1959 and 1989 was higher among members living outside the homeland than those living inside (Tables 6.6 and 6.7). An increasing percentage of Uzbeks, Georgians, Azerbaydzhanis, Lithuanians, Armenians (both in the Armenian Union Republic and in Nagorno-Karabakh Autonomous Oblast), Bashkirs, Chechens, Ingush, Abkhazians, and Ossetians (in the North Ossetian ASSR) living in their home republics declared their native language as the first language between 1959 and 1989. The dual linguistic indigenization and Russification experienced by the Bashkirs that was mentioned above had a clearly defined geographic dimension, with "Bashkirization" occurring in the homeland and Russification occurring among members living outside. Among members living outside the home republic, only Avars, Dargins, Kumyks (three Dagestani national communities), Karachays, and Cherkess experienced an increase in the rate of native language retention during the thirty-year intercensal period. For the Karachay and Cherkess, the increase in native language retention rates among members living outside occurred between 1959 and 1970, and corresponded with a period of rehabilitation for at least the Karachays after their deportation during World War II. More linguistically assimilated members were returning home from exile. For the Dagestani national communities, little difference existed between members living inside and outside the home republic. Most "outsiders" live in adjacent regions of the northern Caucasus, and perhaps should not be considered as nonindigenes. The outside linguistic indigenization may also have resulted from the out-migration of members with relatively high native language retention rates.

Belorussians, Karelians, Komi, Khanty, Komi-Permyaks, Koryaks, and

TABLE 6.5
Native Language Retention Rates by Nation and Location Inside and Outside the Home Republic, 1959–1989 (percent and percentage point change)

Nation	In the Home Republic					Out of the Home Republic				
	1959	1970	1979	1989	Percentage Point Change	1959	1970	1979	1989	Percentage Point Change
Union Republic Level										
Russian	100	100	100	100	0.0	99.0	99.1	99.2	99.0	0.0
Ukrainian	93.5	91.4	89.1	87.7	−5.8	51.2	48.4	43.8	44.3	−6.9
Belorussian	93.2	90.1	83.5	80.2	−13.0	41.9	40.8	36.8	36.4	−5.5
Uzbek	98.6	98.9	98.8	98.7	0.1	97.4	97.4	96.9	96.3	−1.1
Kazakh	99.2	98.9	98.6	98.6	−0.6	95.6	94.8	92.8	90.5	−5.1
Georgian	99.5	99.4	99.4	99.7	0.2	73.4	71.4	67.3	68.6	−4.8
Azerbaydzhan	98.1	98.9	98.7	99.1	1.0	95.2	94.0	92.6	89.1	−6.1
Lithuanian	99.2	99.5	99.7	99.6	0.4	80.3	71.9	63.6	59.1	−21.2
Moldavian	98.2	97.7	96.5	95.4	−2.8	77.7	79.0	74.3	72.4	−5.3
Latvian	98.4	98.1	97.8	97.4	−1.0	53.2	51.4	55.3	44.2	−9.0
Kirgiz	99.7	99.7	99.6	99.5	−0.2	92.3	91.7	84.8	85.1	−7.2
Tadzhik	99.3	99.4	99.3	99.2	−0.1	94.6	95.6	92.8	93.1	−1.5
Armenian[a]	99.2	99.8	99.4	99.6	0.4	76.1	75.8	71.8	73.3	−2.8
Turkmen	99.5	99.3	99.2	99.2	−0.3	92.0	93.4	91.1	89.1	−2.9
Estonian	99.3	99.2	99.0	98.9	−0.4	56.6	53.5	47.1	42.6	−14.0
Autonomous Republic Level										
Bashkir	57.6	63.2	64.4	74.7	17.1	74.6	73.9	72.6	68.7	−5.9
Buryat[b]	97.2	95.8	94.1	90.6	−6.6	85.0	77.5	72.7	68.0	−17.0
Avar	99.3	99.3	99.2	98.9	−0.4	80.6	81.6	88.0	89.1	8.5
Dargin	99.2	99.1	99.0	98.9	−0.3	90.5	92.5	93.7	93.0	2.5
Kumyk	99.0	99.3	99.1	99.0	0.0	89.4	91.0	90.5	90.1	0.7
Lezgin	98.1	98.8	98.3	98.0	−0.1	87.5	88.9	83.6	86.5	−1.0

(continued)

TABLE 6.5
Continued

Nation	In the Home Republic				Out of the Home Republic			
	1959	1970	1979	1989	Percentage Point Change	1959	1970	1979	1989	Percentage Point Change
Kabardin	99.2	99.1	99.1	98.9	-0.3	78.9	79.2	77.4	74.5	-4.4
Balkar	98.9	98.8	98.6	98.4	-0.5	89.3	86.8	81.8	70.0	-19.3
Kalmyk	98.2	97.3	97.1	96.1	-2.1	79.5	68.5	62.3	57.5	-22.0
Karelian	80.9	71.7	61.8	51.5	-29.4	61.2	51.1	46.9	42.1	-19.1
Komi	93.8	86.7	80.0	74.4	-19.4	63.3	59.0	53.0	48.6	-14.7
Mari	97.8	95.8	93.7	88.4	-9.4	91.8	86.5	79.9	73.7	-18.1
Mordvin	97.3	96.2	94.3	88.5	-8.8	70.7	70.4	63.9	59.1	-11.6
Tatar	98.9	98.5	97.7	96.6	-2.3	89.5	85.9	81.8	78.4	-11.1
Tuvin	99.2	99.1	99.1	99.0	-0.2	91.9	85.0	85.9	85.6	-6.3
Udmurt	93.2	87.7	82.3	75.7	-17.5	76.2	71.4	64.4	57.7	-18.5
Chechen	99.7	99.6	99.7	99.8	0.1	97.7	94.5	94.1	92.7	-5.0
Ingush	99.4	99.3	99.4	99.6	0.2	96.6	92.4	91.9	91.1	-5.5
Chuvash	97.5	94.5	89.8	85.0	-12.5	83.4	79.1	73.4	68.1	-15.3
Yakut	98.2	97.1	96.4	95.1	-3.1	82.1	72.8	71.7	66.4	-15.7
Abkhaz	96.7	97.8	97.0	97.3	0.6	70.1	71.9	66.2	64.2	-5.9
Karakalpak	99.1	99.6	98.7	97.8	-1.3	56.4	62.0	58.9	52.1	-4.3
Ossetian[c]	95.4	98.4	98.3	98.2	2.8	70.4	67.0	67.3	64.3	-6.1
Autonomous Oblast Level										
Adygey	99.0	99.1	98.7	98.4	-0.6	85.9	84.9	83.9	82.8	-3.1
Altay	91.6	91.7	91.3	89.6	-2.0	72.5	64.0	61.7	57.7	-14.8
Karachay	99.6	99.5	99.4	99.2	-0.4	83.1	89.3	89.1	85.4	2.3
Cherkess	99.3	98.8	98.6	97.9	-1.4	53.2	67.6	70.7	65.4	12.2

Khakass	90.2	88.8	86.6	83.2	−7.0	60.6	60.5	56.8	50.5	−10.1
Armenian[a]	98.2	98.2	96.3	98.4	0.2	76.1	75.8	71.8	73.3	−2.8
Ossetian[c]	98.6	98.9	98.7	98.2	−0.4	70.4	67.0	67.3	64.3	−6.1
Autonomous Okrug Level										
Chukchi	94.6	84.9	80.5	72.7	−21.9	90.2	72.7	68.7	61.7	−28.5
Dolgan	—	91.7	93.5	90.2	(−1.5)	—	74.3	69.0	60.8	(−13.5)
Evenk	96.2	92.2	86.1	73.7	−22.5	49.3	45.3	37.0	24.8	−24.5
Khanty	74.7	63.2	64.8	55.1	−19.6	80.2	76.7	71.3	66.4	−13.8
Komi-Permyak	92.2	92.1	87.0	82.9	−9.3	54.8	59.6	53.8	48.5	−6.3
Koryak	94.8	86.2	73.1	53.5	−41.3	72.0	62.3	58.8	50.0	−22.0
Mansi	58.9	53.0	51.9	36.6	−22.3	61.1	48.2	39.0	38.8	−22.3
Nenets[d]	88.5	87.5	85.6	82.5	−6.0	48.2	49.9	54.2	44.1	−4.1
Averages:										
Union Republics	98.2	97.9	97.1	96.6	−1.6	77.0	75.7	72.2	70.3	−6.7
Autonomous Republics	95.4	94.5	92.9	91.3	−4.1	80.7	77.8	74.9	71.4	−9.3
Autonomous Oblasts	96.6	96.4	95.7	95.0	−1.6	71.7	72.7	71.6	68.5	−3.2
Autonomous Okrugs	85.7	81.4	77.8	68.4	−17.3	65.1	61.1	56.5	49.4	−15.7

Sources: 1959: TsSU SSSR 1962, 16 vols.; 1970: TsSU SSSR 1973, vol. 4; 1979: TsSU SSSR 1984; 1989: Goskomstat SSSR 1991a.

Note: Averages are unweighted.

[a] Armenians: home republic population for SSR group = those living in the Armenian SSR; home republic population for Autonomous Oblast group = those living in the Nagorno-Karabakh Autonomous Oblast. Out-of-home republic population for each group of Armenians = those living outside Armenia and Nagorno-Karabakh.

[b] Buryat home republic population includes Buryats living in the Agin Buryat Autonomous Okrug and the Ust'-Ordin Buryat Autonomous Okrug.

[c] Ossetians: ASSR home republic population = those living in the North Ossetian ASSR. Autonomous Oblast home republic population = those living in the South Ossetian Autonomous Oblast. Out of home republic population for both = those living outside the two autonomous units.

[d] Nenets: Home republic population = those living in the Nenets Autonomous Okrug, the Taymyr Autonomous Okrug, and those living in the Yamalo-Nenets Autonomous Okrug.

TABLE 6.6
Linguistic Russification of Indigenes in Homeland Urban and Rural Locations, 1959–1989 (percent of indigenes claiming Russian as the first language, and percentage point change)

Republic	Homeland Urban				Homeland Rural			
	1959	1970	1979	1989	Percentage Point Change	1959	1970	1979	1989	Percentage Point Change

Republic	1959	1970	1979	1989	Percentage Point Change	1959	1970	1979	1989	Percentage Point Change
Union Republic										
Ukraine	15.3	17.1	19.2	19.0	3.7	1.3	1.3	1.6	2.0	0.7
Belarus'	22.4	24.5	31.4	30.1	7.7	1.4	1.2	1.9	3.1	1.7
Uzbekistan	1.4	1.3	1.3	1.2	−0.2	0.1	0.1	0.1	0.1	0.0
Kazakhstan	1.8	2.7	3.0	2.5	0.7	0.4	0.5	0.7	0.6	0.2
Georgia	1.1	0.9	0.9	0.4	−0.7	0.1	0.1	0.1	0.0	−0.1
Azerbaydzhan	2.1	1.8	2.2	0.7	−1.4	0.1	0.0	0.1	0.1	0.0
Lithuania	0.3	0.3	0.3	0.3	0.0	0.0	0.1	0.1	0.1	0.1
Moldova	8.6	9.4	11.2	10.8	2.2	0.5	0.5	0.7	1.1	0.6
Latvia	2.0	2.5	2.9	3.4	1.4	1.0	1.1	1.2	1.4	0.4
Kyrgyzstan	1.2	1.3	1.3	1.0	−0.2	0.1	0.1	0.1	0.1	0.0
Tadzhikistan	1.7	1.5	1.9	1.6	−0.1	0.1	0.1	0.1	0.1	0.0
Armenia	1.3	0.3	0.7	0.3	−1.0	0.1	0.0	0.2	0.3	0.2
Turkmenistan	1.9	2.0	2.1	2.0	0.1	0.0	0.0	0.1	0.1	0.1
Estonia	1.2	1.2	1.5	1.6	0.4	0.2	0.2	0.3	0.3	0.1
Autonomous Republic										
Bashkir[a]	4.4	6.3	8.2	9.5	5.1	0.5	0.3	0.5	1.0	0.5
Buryat	11.7	13.2	14.4	18.3	6.6	1.5	2.0	2.4	4.0	2.5
Avar	3.2	2.2	2.0	1.8	−1.4	0.1	0.1	0.1	0.2	0.1
Dargin	2.8	2.7	2.5	1.8	−1.0	0.1	0.1	0.1	0.1	0.0
Kumyk	2.0	1.5	1.5	1.4	−0.6	0.2	0.1	0.2	0.2	0.0
Lezgin	7.2	4.1	3.2	2.2	−5.0	0.2	0.1	0.1	0.2	0.0

Kabardin	3.8	3.0	2.1	2.1	−1.7	0.3	0.2	0.2	0.3	0.0
Balkar	3.2	3.1	2.1	2.1	−1.1	0.5	0.3	0.4	0.3	−0.2
Kalmyk	2.5	4.0	4.5	5.5	3.0	1.6	1.9	1.6	2.3	0.7
Karelia	38.0	42.2	50.7	56.3	18.3	10.4	16.9	22.7	35.4	25.0
Komi	15.6	29.8	36.5	41.8	26.2	2.9	5.2	8.1	11.4	8.5
Mari	15.5	18.1	17.1	23.3	7.8	1.2	1.8	2.4	4.7	3.5
Mordva	21.6	16.2	17.1	23.0	1.4	1.5	1.2	1.6	4.4	2.9
North Ossetia	5.0	2.7	2.6	2.5	−2.5	0.6	0.4	0.4	0.5	−0.1
Tatar[b]	2.9	3.5	4.2	4.9	2.0	0.0	0.2	0.4	0.6	0.6
Tuvin	4.1	3.9	3.0	2.5	−1.6	0.4	0.2	0.3	0.3	−0.1
Udmurt	22.7	30.5	33.8	39.0	16.3	3.2	5.2	7.9	12.4	9.2
Chechen	1.9	2.1	1.0	0.6	−1.3	0.1	0.1	0.1	0.1	0.0
Ingush	2.8	1.7	1.1	0.7	−2.1	0.2	0.1	0.2	0.1	−0.1
Chuvash	15.6	22.0	28.0	30.5	14.9	0.7	0.7	1.6	1.4	0.7
Yakut	7.3	10.9	11.9	14.6	7.3	0.7	0.9	1.1	1.5	0.8
Karakalpak	0.5	0.4	0.4	0.6	0.1	0.0	0.0	0.1	0.1	0.1
Abkhaz	6.5	4.6	4.8	3.9	−2.6	0.5	0.3	0.6	0.6	0.1
Autonomous Oblast										
Adygey	4.9	5.0	3.4	3.4	−1.5	0.6	0.3	0.5	0.6	0.0
Altay	35.0	21.3	29.4	26.1	−8.9	6.6	7.2	6.6	8.5	1.9
Karachay	2.2	2.1	1.7	2.0	−0.2	0.3	0.2	0.3	0.2	−0.1
Cherkess	5.6	4.2	3.7	4.7	−0.9	0.4	0.2	0.2	0.2	−0.2
Khakass	21.9	24.0	24.0	26.2	4.3	7.8	8.5	9.4	11.5	3.7
Nagorno-Karabakh	7.3	4.7	8.2	2.7	−4.6	0.5	0.0	0.2	0.3	−0.2
South Ossetia	1.0	0.4	0.5	0.4	−0.6	0.1	0.1	0.1	0.2	0.1
Autonomous Okrug										
Nenets	25.6	21.9	39.1	31.0	5.4	2.0	4.1	6.2	10.9	8.9
Evenk	15.4	23.5	35.9	40.8	25.4	2.9	5.3	9.8	21.8	18.9

(*continued*)

TABLE 6.6
Continued

Republic	Homeland Urban				Homeland Rural				
	1959	1970	1979	1989	Percentage Point Change	1959	1970	1979	1989	Percentage Point Change
Dolgan	—	25.3	44.8	37.1	11.8	—	7.1	4.4	6.9	−0.2
Koryak	11.7	30.0	53.0	57.1	45.4	4.9	10.4	21.4	42.8	37.9
Chukchi	14.5	36.5	56.4	52.0	37.5	4.7	11.6	15.7	25.0	20.3
Komi-Permyak	21.9	23.3	34.9	36.2	14.3	6.1	5.3	7.8	10.6	4.5
Khanty	57.0	64.0	56.4	59.2	2.2	22.7	31.7	29.6	38.0	15.3
Mansi	55.4	71.0	66.3	76.3	20.9	40.0	40.1	40.1	54.0	14.0
Averages[c]										
Union Republics	4.5	4.8	5.7	5.4	0.9	0.4	0.4	0.5	0.7	0.3
Autonomous Republics	8.7	9.9	11.0	12.6	3.9	1.2	1.7	2.3	3.6	2.4
Autonomous Oblasts	13.9	11.3	12.4	9.4	−4.5	3.1	3.3	3.4	3.1	0.0
Autonomous Okrugs	28.8	38.6	48.9	48.7	19.9	11.9	15.5	18.7	26.3	14.4

Sources: 1959: TsSU SSSR 1962, 16 vols.; 1970: TsSU SSSR 1973, 4:20–319; 1979: Goskomstat SSSR 1989d, vol. 4; 1989: Statisticheskiy Komitet SNG 1993, vol. 7.

[a]Bashkirs not claiming Bashkir as the native language most often claimed Tatar.

[b]Tatars include Crimean Tatars, since data for this national community were not provided for 1959–79. In 1989, 92.6 percent of the Crimean Tatars claimed Crimean Tatar as their native language, and 5.3 percent claimed Russian. Of all other Tatars, 83.2 percent claimed Tatar as their native language, and 16.1 percent claimed Russian.

[c]Averages are unweighted; each national community is treated as one observation.

TABLE 6.7
Linguistic Russification of Nonindigenes in Urban and Rural Locations, 1959–1989 (percent of national members living outside the homeland claiming Russian as their first language, and percentage point change)

Nation	Outside Urban				Outside Rural			
	1959	1970	1979	1989	Percentage Point Change	1959	1970	1979	1989	Percentage Point Change

Nation	1959	1970	1979	1989	Percentage Point Change	1959	1970	1979	1989	Percentage Point Change
Union Republic Level										
Ukrainian	53.9	55.0	58.6	56.9	3.0	41.6	43.9	48.7	49.6	8.0
Belorussian	60.9	61.3	64.3	63.7	-0.6	46.1	45.8	50.1	51.7	5.6
Uzbek	3.4	3.7	4.8	5.4	2.0	0.4	0.3	0.4	0.6	0.2
Kazakh	6.7	7.5	8.0	9.2	2.5	1.6	2.3	2.9	3.6	2.0
Georgian	30.8	31.7	35.1	32.6	1.8	11.7	11.2	15.4	16.5	4.8
Azerbaydzhan	11.4	14.0	15.2	16.1	4.7	0.9	1.0	1.5	2.7	1.8
Lithuanian	20.6	29.0	36.1	37.8	17.2	8.5	13.9	18.8	23.2	14.7
Moldavian	36.3	32.8	37.3	35.7	-0.6	7.5	7.0	9.4	11.3	3.8
Latvian	54.3	52.7	46.8	55.5	1.2	31.1	31.2	30.8	42.5	11.4
Kirgiz	6.5	5.4	6.7	7.3	0.8	0.2	0.2	0.4	0.8	0.6
Tadzhik	3.2	3.9	3.5	4.3	1.1	0.3	0.3	0.4	0.5	0.2
Armenian[a]	27.0	28.2	32.2	30.3	3.3	4.8	4.3	5.9	8.5	3.7
Turkmen	12.2	10.9	14.6	12.8	0.6	0.6	0.7	0.9	1.2	0.6
Estonian	55.0	56.0	59.2	61.1	6.1	29.2	29.2	36.1	41.6	12.4
Autonomous Republic Level										
Bashkir	15.1	22.2	24.6	27.1	12.0	2.8	4.6	6.7	10.0	7.2
Buryat	27.7	34.7	36.3	38.1	10.4	7.4	11.3	14.5	19.9	12.5
Avar	16.1	18.3	18.7	18.0	1.9	1.6	1.2	1.6	2.7	1.1
Dargin	10.0	15.2	16.9	16.1	6.1	4.0	1.8	1.6	2.2	-1.8

(continued)

TABLE 6.7
Continued

Nation	Outside Urban				Outside Rural			
	1959	1970	1979	1989	Percentage Point Change	1959	1970	1979	1989	Percentage Point Change
Kumyk	16.8	17.0	17.7	15.8	−1.0	2.5	1.5	1.7	3.2	0.7
Lezgin	12.0	14.9	16.0	12.3	0.3	1.1	0.9	1.4	2.3	1.2
Kabardin	25.0	27.3	28.9	28.1	3.1	12.1	8.7	10.0	14.8	2.7
Balkar	11.0	18.1	25.3	33.4	22.4	5.5	5.8	7.8	14.1	8.6
Kalmyk	28.5	32.3	33.0	35.1	6.6	10.5	12.8	12.8	17.0	6.5
Karelian	58.5	59.1	64.3	66.6	8.1	29.7	39.8	38.4	41.4	11.7
Komi	46.6	47.4	52.9	55.5	8.9	25.0	31.7	36.6	42.0	17.0
Mari	27.9	31.0	34.7	36.7	8.8	3.4	6.6	11.1	16.0	12.6
Mordvin	49.3	47.7	50.4	50.9	1.6	16.8	15.4	20.4	25.1	8.3
Ossetian[b]	21.6	21.1	22.9	22.1	0.5	3.5	4.1	5.4	7.4	3.9
Tatar[c]	13.6	18.9	21.9	24.5	10.9	4.1	4.7	6.7	8.5	4.4
Tuvin	8.1	19.1	15.2	13.8	5.7	4.4	6.7	8.4	12.7	8.3
Udmurt	42.7	43.2	47.6	51.3	8.6	12.7	17.5	22.3	28.5	15.8
Chechen	3.1	8.3	10.0	11.9	8.8	1.4	2.7	2.8	3.3	1.9
Ingush	3.2	8.8	9.9	11.0	7.8	3.0	4.9	5.1	5.0	2.0
Chuvash	34.7	38.3	40.5	41.5	6.8	9.0	10.7	14.6	19.1	10.1
Yakut	27.5	28.8	27.6	31.7	4.2	20.5	22.6	27.9	35.5	15.5
Karakalpak	6.1	7.7	8.4	13.2	7.1	0.5	0.8	0.9	2.0	1.5
Abkhaz	21.9	25.5	28.6	29.1	7.2	10.7	10.0	13.8	16.9	6.2

Autonomous Oblast Level										
Adygey	23.7	20.7	20.3	19.7	−4.0	5.6	5.2	7.1	9.0	3.4
Altay	46.7	45.0	41.7	46.1	−0.6	15.9	24.9	30.6	33.3	17.4
Karachay	12.3	15.0	16.2	18.4	6.1	4.3	4.9	4.8	7.1	2.8
Cherkess	40.9	35.2	27.4	28.9	−12.0	15.3	6.4	9.4	10.8	−4.5
Khakass	47.9	43.2	43.9	49.4	1.5	30.1	32.3	40.5	46.0	15.9
Autonomous Okrug Level										
Nenets	34.6	41.4	46.5	54.5	19.9	21.6	31.7	38.8	39.4	17.8
Dolgan[d]	—	28.9	33.1	39.0	10.1	—	12.7	21.4	22.6	9.9
Evenk	23.9	31.9	34.4	47.2	23.3	7.1	15.1	18.0	24.0	16.9
Koryak	39.0	54.4	55.0	61.0	22.0	19.9	22.6	21.2	34.1	14.2
Chukchi	27.7	54.1	49.2	49.7	22.0	4.0	9.5	17.0	21.9	17.9
Komi-Permyak	54.7	43.9	47.9	53.3	−1.4	32.8	34.0	42.0	46.3	13.5
Khanty	51.8	49.4	56.1	53.3	1.5	13.5	17.1	18.1	23.6	10.1
Mansi	48.8	64.8	68.8	64.9	16.1	26.0	34.3	46.8	45.2	19.2
Averages[e]										
Union Republics	27.3	28.0	30.2	30.6	3.3	13.2	13.7	15.8	18.2	5.0
Autonomous Republics	22.9	26.3	28.4	29.7	6.8	8.4	9.9	11.8	15.2	6.8
Autonomous Oblasts	34.3	31.8	29.9	32.5	−1.8	14.2	14.7	18.5	21.2	7.0
Autonomous Okrugs	40.1	48.6	51.1	52.9	12.8	17.8	23.5	28.8	32.1	14.3

Sources: 1959:TsSU SSSR 1962, 16 vols.; 1970: TsSU SSSR 1973, vol. 4, 20–319; 1979: Goskomstat SSSR 1989d, vol. 4; 1989: Statisticheskiy Komitet SNG 1993, vol. 7 part 1.

[a] Armenians outside the homeland exclude those in Nagorno-Karabakh Autonomous Oblast, which is treated as part of the homeland population.
[b] Ossetians outside the homeland include those living outside both the North Ossetian ASSR and the South Ossetian Autonomous Oblast.
[c] Tatars include Crimean Tatars for 1989, because it is not possible to separate Crimean Tatars from Tatars in previous censuses.
[d] Percentage point change for Dolgans is for the period from 1970 to 1989.
[e] Averages are unweighted, with each national community treated as one observation.

Nentsy experienced a higher rate of linguistic Russification inside the home republic than outside. The higher acculturation rate inside the homeland than outside was related to a combination of factors, the most significant of which were (1) out-migration of indigenes from the homeland, which increased the proportion of native language speakers outside; (2) a relatively high rate of linguistic assimilation in the home republics; and (3) national reidentification among the more linguistically assimilated members living outside the home republic. As is discussed below, the more linguistically assimilated members living outside the home republic were also more likely to intermarry. Since the children of these international families are more likely to declare themselves Russians or members of the indigenous nation, depending on the national identity of the other spouse, the nations whose members were more linguistically assimilated outside experienced an intergenerational loss of population. In this way, the more linguistically assimilated segment of the outlying population shrank over time as a result of "natural assimilation," and the appearance of a relatively greater native language retention rate among members living outside the homeland may paradoxically signify that greater international integration or assimilation was occurring there.

Given the language trends in evidence in the postwar censuses, it is difficult to find support for the claim made by nationalists that the status of the indigenous languages in their homelands was seriously jeopardized by linguistic assimilation during the postwar period. Indeed, those nationalists pressing this claim most forcefully and demanding most vehemently that new language laws be adopted to protect the indigenous language in the homeland are often members of nations whose native language retention rates in the home republic are close to 100 percent. This holds not only for the Baltic nations, Moldavians, Georgians, and Armenians but also for the Abkhazians and Ossetians in Georgia, as well as the Armenians in Nagorno-Karabakh Autonomous Oblast. Of the union republic-level nations, only the Ukrainians and Belorussians experienced substantial linguistic Russification in the homeland during the postwar period, and for each the rate of linguistic Russification was much higher among members living outside than inside the home republic. Each of these nations also registered a slower rate of linguistic assimilation inside and out between 1979 and 1989, and this in all likelihood represented a growing national awareness among the members of each community brought about as a result of the language campaigns of RUKH and other nationalist organizations, and at the same time a decline in the status of Russians and their language. In addition, the high rates of linguistic assimilation among Lithuanians, Latvians, and Estonians living outside their respective home republics resulted from the return migration to the homeland of members who had higher native language retention rates.

In the homeland, linguistic Russification of indigenes occurred primarily in urban areas (Table 6.6). This is not surprising, since most rural areas are more nationally homogeneous, and the Russian language had a much greater functional utility in urban than in rural non-Russian areas. Still, even in the urban areas of the homeland, indigenes did not undergo extensive linguistic Russification during the postwar period. Between 1959 and 1970, twenty-three of the fifty-one national communities included in the analysis registered a decrease in the level of linguistic Russification in the cities of their home republics, and eighteen of fifty-one registered a decrease in the homeland rural areas.[10] Between 1970 and 1979 fifteen of fifty-two registered a decrease in linguistic Russification in the homeland urban areas, and four of fifty-two in the homeland rural setting. Between 1979 and 1989 twenty-six of fifty-two experienced linguistic de-Russification in the homeland urban setting, and six of fifty-two in the homeland rural setting. The greater number of national communities registering a decrease between 1959 and 1970 may have been related to the addition of a second language question in the 1970 census; given the option a number of individuals living in the homeland, and particularly in homeland urban areas, chose to reclaim their national language as the first language and downgrade Russian to the status of second language, even though these individuals were no doubt more fluent in Russian. Clearly, the designation of first language in the censuses was not necessarily a choice made on the basis of fluency level alone, and also reflected attitudes toward the native and Russian languages (e.g., Silver 1986, 1978). For example, in a survey conducted in the early 1970s, 10 percent of urban Moldavians living in Moldova stated that they were more fluent in the second language (i.e., Russian) than in the first language selected at the time of the census (i.e., Moldavian). Only 3 percent of rural Moldavians living in Moldova claimed greater fluency in the second language than in the first (Guboglo 1984, 125). Similarly, according to the results of survey data of Ukrainian children "60% of city children consider Ukrainian as the native language, in spite of the fact that in the basic spheres of life they use Russian, 40% consider two languages as native—Ukrainian and Russian" (Snezhkova 1982, 86). According to the limited information available, the gap between fluency and first language choice was greater in homeland urban areas, where the indigene's sense of exclusiveness regarding his or her status in the homeland was most seriously challenged.

For the union republic-level nations, only the Ukrainians, Belorussians, and Moldavians experienced substantial linguistic Russification in the cities of their homelands, and none of these national communities underwent significant linguistic Russification in the rural areas of their home republic. For Ukrainians and Belorussians, linguistic Russification was much more extensive in the eastern cities that remained part of the USSR between the wars and where a large proportion of the population is Russian. For all three of the nations cited above, most of the linguistic Russification occurred before 1959 (i.e., before

---

[10] This figure does not include Dolgans.

the national and linguistic consolidation of the masses), and all three experienced linguistic de-Russification between 1979 and 1989. As noted above, much of this linguistic assimilation may be more appropriately considered as linguistic consolidation, especially in the regions where Russians and other groups have mixed locally for long periods of time. Since 1959, even for the Ukrainians, Belorussians, and Moldavians, little linguistic Russification has occurred. During the 1980s, a period of rising national assertiveness and linguistic de-Russification occurred and was particularly pronounced in the cities of the homeland.

For those national communities with autonomous republics, linguistic Russification was limited for the most part to indigenes with homelands located in the northwestern and Volga-Urals regions of the RSFSR, and for most of these groups it was restricted to members living in the cities of the homelands, which were dominated demographically and otherwise by Russians. As in the case of the union republic nations, most of the linguistic Russification for those nations with the highest rates (Karelians, Maris, Mordvins, Udmurts, and Chuvashes) occurred before 1959, and the rate of acculturation was relatively limited between 1959 and 1989. Only the Komis experienced more rapid linguistic Russification after 1959 than they did before that date. For members living in the rural areas of the homeland, except for Karelians, Komis, and Udmurts, little linguistic Russification occurred during the postwar period. For the national communities with autonomous republics in the North Caucasus region, there has even been a reversal of the linguistic Russification that occurred before 1959. Finally, for the Abkhazians and Karakalpaks, whose home republics are located in Georgia and Uzbekistan, almost no linguistic assimilation respectively to Georgian or Uzbek occurred between 1959 and 1989, either among homeland urban or homeland rural segments of each nation's population.[11]

At the autonomous oblast level, only the Altays and Khakass experienced substantial linguistic Russification in their own homelands either in the cities or in the countryside, and for both of these groups this acculturation occurred before 1959, with almost no change registered in urban or rural areas of the homeland since that date. Overall, the linguistic Russification rate of the five autonomous oblast-level *ethnies* decreased in the cities of the homeland and increased only slightly in the countryside. In addition to negligible linguistic Russification, the Ossetians in the South Ossetian Autonomous Oblast experienced almost no linguistic assimilation to Georgian (1.1 percent of the homeland urban (HU) and 1.8 percent of the homeland rural (HR) population in 1989), and the Armenians in Nagorno-Karabakh experienced even less lin-

---

[11] In 1989, 1.0 percent of the homeland urban and 0.4 percent of the homeland rural Abkhaz population claimed Georgian as their first language, while 0.7 percent of the homeland urban and 2.2 percent of the homeland rural Karakalpak population claimed Uzbek as their first language (Statisticheskiy Komitet SNG 1993, vol. 7, part 2).

guistic assimilation to Azerbaydzhani (HU = 0.02 percent and HR = 0.01 percent in 1989).

Finally, for the *ethnies* of Siberia with autonomous okrugs, linguistic Russification was much more extensive in the homeland urban and rural areas. Even for these groups, much of this Russification occurred before 1959. However, it was also substantial during the postwar period, and has proceeded along with the socioeconomic development of the region and the social and geographic mobilization of indigenes. The high rate of linguistic Russification among members living in the homeland is one indication that this acculturation may be seen by the participants themselves as national consolidation.

Outside the homeland, national members living in cities and in rural areas were generally much more linguistically Russified (Table 6.7). Indeed, while linguistic Russification was often portrayed as a process coinciding with urbanization, the data available indicate that members living outside their respective homelands in rural areas acculturated to a greater extent than members living in a homeland urban setting. The homeland/outside differential in rates of acculturation was, if anything, more profound than the urban/rural differential. The only exception to this was among the autonomous okrug-level *ethnies*, whose levels in the homeland urban and outside urban locations were approximately the same by 1979. Among nonindigenes the difference between urban and rural rates of linguistic Russification was not generally as great as it was for indigenes. A third difference was that the progression of acculturation rates across levels of autonomy in the federal hierarchy that was apparent in both the homeland urban and homeland rural setting was absent among nonindigenes. The linguistic Russification rates for members of union republic-level nations living outside their homelands were generally higher than those for nonindigenous members of autonomous republic-level national communities and were only slightly lower than those for the outside homeland members of autonomous oblast-level *ethnies*. Generalizing from the geographic differentials apparent in these data, it may be said that the relatively greater degree of cultural autonomy enjoyed by indigenous members of union republic-level nations did not extend beyond the borders of the home republic. This was especially true for the Ukrainians, Belorussians, Latvians, and Estonians, and less so for the Central Asian nations whose outside members most often live in regions adjacent to the home republic.

As in the case of members living in the homeland, for the union republic-level nations most of the linguistic Russification of members living outside the home republic had occurred by 1959, and little change was registered between 1959 and 1989 in either the outside urban or rural areas. The Lithuanians were an exception to this general rule; the linguistic Russification rate among Lithuanians living in outside urban and rural areas increased relatively rapidly between 1959 and 1989. However, this resulted not from extensive new acculturation but rather from the migration of Lithuanians who had not linguistically

Russified to Lithuania, leaving a more acculturated group beyond the borders of the homeland. Latvians were also returning to their home republic, yet the percentage of linguistically Russified Latvians living outside Latvia actually declined between 1959 and 1979. The most likely explanation for this opposite trend is that the more Russified Latvians (i.e., those who had remained within the USSR during the interwar period) were being lost through intergenerational reidentification. As is discussed below, these losses were registered primarily among members living in cities outside the homeland who had intermarried. With the more rapid Latvian return migration between 1979 and 1989, the rate of linguistic Russification among members living outside Latvia increased dramatically.

Among the national communities with autonomous republics, the same differential as was noted among indigenes applies to members living outside the homeland: groups whose homelands are located in the North Caucasus had substantially lower rates of linguistic Russification than did those whose homelands are located nearer the Russian ethnocultural hearth. For a number of the North Caucasus national communities, members living outside the home republic were either living in regions adjacent to it and had lived in these "home areas" for generations or were deported from their homelands following World War II. These were not the conditions that would encourage the voluntary "drawing together" of nations. For the Volga-Urals group, while members of the Karelians, Komis, Udmurts, and so forth, living outside their respective autonomous republics generally had higher levels of linguistic Russification than those living inside, the rate of acculturation between 1959 and 1989 among those living in cities outside the home republic was frequently lower than for those living inside. However, as in the case of Latvians noted above, this was most likely the result of higher national reidentification among the children of the more acculturated members living in outside urban areas. The number of Karelians and Mordvins were declining absolutely during the entire postwar period, and the Komis, Udmurts, Maris, and Chuvash have also been identified as groups with a relatively high rate of national reidentification (Anderson and Silver 1983).

Members of the autonomous oblast-level *ethnies* living in outside urban areas experienced a "de-Russification" between 1959 and 1989, though caution must be exercised in interpreting this trend. It appears that the decreasing percentage of those claiming Russian as their native language resulted in part from out-migration of indigenes who were not already linguistically Russified and in part from intergenerational reidentification of those who had lived outside the homeland for an extended period of time. The increasing rate of linguistic Russification among outside urban Karachays resulted more from the return migration of those deported from the homeland during the 1940s than from an actual increase in acculturation.

Among the autonomous okrug-level *ethnies*, there was little apparent difference between rates of acculturation inside or outside the autonomous unit. The linguistic Russification in rural areas remained low relative to that in urban areas both inside and outside the autonomous okrugs. On moving to cities that were dominated by Russians, linguistic Russification became relatively widespread, and it was nearly as extensive in the cities of the homeland as in those outside. For this set of groups alone, the "diffusion-erasure" model appears to hold—ethnic identity was preserved in the traditional rural setting but was lost with social and geographic mobilization. However, as was noted above, the acculturation occurring among these groups may be more appropriately described as a beginning stage in the process of national consolidation than as international integration, because no mass-based nationalization had occurred.

In conclusion, using linguistic Russification as a measure of the acculturation of non-Russians toward the Russian or Soviet people, the census data during the postwar period indicates that little "progress" was made in drawing the nations and nationalities of the state together. Of course, in the area of language usage, the state also facilitated the retention of non-Russian native languages throughout this period, and this dialectical policy structure certainly offset the pressure for Russification. Nevertheless, as was discussed above, Russian was the favored language throughout the postwar period, and the USSR expanded its functional utility at the expense of the non-Russian languages. Particularly for nonindigenes, the national language was (and still is) unlikely to be very useful in their day-to-day lives. Yet the expanding utility of Russian and its enhanced status as the lingua franca during the postwar period were not matched by an equally expansive linguistic Russification of non-Russians. Most of the linguistic Russification experienced by non-Russians occurred before 1959, and in all likelihood before the national and linguistic consolidation of the illiterate, rural masses. With rising national self-consciousness in the postwar period, particularly among members living in their homelands, the rate of acculturation toward the Russian nation decreased, and during the 1980s was almost nonexistent. Even the limited linguistic Russification that occurred served as a catalyst for the activation of national territoriality, and was one of the major elements in the nationalistic demand for increasing sovereignty if not outright independence from Moscow. In this sense, the very success of acculturating non-Russians proved counterproductive to the ultimate goal of internationalizing or sovietizing the population.

Finally, spatial variations in linguistic Russification rates do not correspond well with geographic differentials in the functional utility of the Russian and indigenous languages. First, the homeland/outside differentials in the rate of linguistic Russification were generally more pronounced than the urban/rural differences, even though Russian was favored in urban/industrial centers throughout the USSR. Second, national communities with fewer opportunities to study, read publications, and use the native languages in the work place nonetheless continued to claim their native languages as their first language in censuses throughout the postwar period. National communities whose homelands are located nearer the Russian cultural hearth, even those with relatively greater access to their own national languages, underwent more extensive linguistic Russification. Yet, as noted above, the timing of this acculturation (i.e., before 1959) would suggest a process of national consolidation among members whose national consciousness was not well developed. With these geographic patterns in mind, the relationship between functional utility and linguistic assimilation appears tenuous at best.

Russian Bilingualism

The spread of Russian as a second language was extensive during the postwar period, and at least before the late 1980s societywide fluency in Russian seemed a goal within reach. The attainment of this objective was, in turn, viewed by Soviet analysts as a preliminary step along the pathway to acculturation and eventual integration into one Soviet people (Guboglo 1969, 17): "Bilingualism is a necessary (and obligatory) stage in the transition of a single individual or group of individuals from their native language to another language. Therefore, it is necessary to consider bilingualism as an important phase and as a component part of the process of linguistic assimilation." Alternatively, learning the dominant language of the state may be viewed as a necessary compromise made by socially mobilized non-Russians, and its impact on the integration process would thus be minimal (e.g., Clem 1980, 44). Considering the sense of exclusiveness felt by indigenes about their status in the homeland, it may even be the case that the need to learn Russian in order to compete for the resources of the homeland had a net negative effect on international integration. The new language laws that attempt to undermine the need for Russian as an instrument of upward mobility for indigenes in their own homelands would tend to confirm that this is the case (JPRS 1989).

Trends in Russian bilingualism between 1970 and 1989 indicate that these data must be treated with caution. A rapid expansion in the number claiming Russian language fluency occurred between 1970 and 1979, increasing from 41.8 million to 61.2 million or from 37.1 percent to 49.1 percent of the non-Russian population. The increase in Uzbekistan was particularly great, not only among Uzbeks and Karakalpaks but among the entire population, and most of the increase occurred in rural areas, where the need for Russian fluency was by all accounts minimal (Guboglo 1984, 114–115). Rumors surfaced that Rashidov, the Party First Secretary of Uzbekistan at the time, was dissatisfied with the low level of Russian bilingualism registered in the 1970 census, and that orders to improve the situation had gone out (e.g., Solchanyk 1982). Apparently, census takers in the republic followed orders too well. In 1989 a reversal of the inflated figures occurred, leading to large negative changes for Uzbeks and Karakalpaks in their respective home republics, and also for Karakalpaks (outside their ASSR), Kirgiz, Tadzhiks, Turkmen, and Kazakhs living in Uzbekistan (Table 6.8). Overall, the change in Russian bilingualism registered in the censuses between 1979 and 1989 was minimal, increasing to 68.8 million, which represented a relative decline to 48.9 percent of the total non-Russian population.

Rising levels of anti-Russian "nativism" also appear to have affected the number of indigenes claiming fluency in Russian as a second language. The Estonian decrease between 1970 and 1979, as well as the Lithuanian decrease between 1979 and 1989, should be read more as a vote against Russians in the republic or against policies of the center than as real declines in Russian language fluency. The same was probably true of the decrease among Tuvins in Tuvinia, which has become the scene of rising anti-Russian sentiments, as well as among Chechens and Ingush in their home republic.[12] For other national communities, decreasing percentages claiming Russian as a second language coincided with increasing percentages claiming it as the native language. This was particularly the case for Karelians, other Finnic groups whose homelands are located in the Volga-Urals region, the autonomous okrug *ethnies* of Siberia living in the homeland, and for the members living outside the homeland of a substantial number of national communities (Table 6.8).

Unlike trends in linguistic Russification, the adoption of Russian as a second language increased more rapidly among indigenes than nonindigenes, and among national communities with homelands at the higher end of the federal structure (i.e., union and autonomous republics). The expansion of Russian bilingualism at least between 1970 and 1979 was also greater in rural than in urban areas (Guboglo 1984, 114–115). In part, this reflects the greater level of linguistic Russification among nonindigenes and those *ethnies* with lower-ranking autonomous regions. In addition, increasing Russian fluency among indigenes, as with rising education rates, enhanced the competitive position of upwardly mobile indigenes even while it raised their sense of exclusiveness regarding the status of their ethnocultural attributes in the homeland. In this way, growing Russian fluency actually appears to have coincided with rising national assertiveness and separatism, and not the Russification of the indigenous population.

Overall, complete fluency in Russian for the entire population of the USSR appeared likely, given the trends between 1970 and 1989. However, since 1989, this has become increasingly unlikely. The adoption of language laws designed to enhance the status of the indigenous language as the lingua franca of the home republic, which all nonindigenes will be required to learn and use in the work place, in schools, and so forth, undermines the status of Russian in the non-Russian periphery (JPRS 1989). The impetus behind these laws appears to

---

[12] The Tuvinian rate of increase between 1970 and 1979 was extremely high, and the decline between 1979 and 1989 also raises questions about the accuracy of the 1979 figures.

TABLE 6.8
Russian as a Second Language by Nation and Location Inside and Outside the Home Republic, 1970–1989 (percent and percentage point change)

Nation	Inside Home Republic					Outside Home Republic				
	1970	1979	1989	Percentage Point Change 1970–79	Percentage Point Change 1979–89	1970	1979	1989	Percentage Point Change 1970–79	Percentage Point Change 1979–89
Union Republic Level										
Ukrainian	35.8	51.7	59.5	15.9	7.8	39.4	37.7	37.8	−1.7	0.1
Belorussian	56.0	62.9	60.4	6.9	−2.5	19.8	33.6	33.4	13.8	−0.2
Uzbek	13.1	52.9	22.3	39.8	−30.6	21.8	28.9	32.4	7.1	3.5
Kazakh	41.6	50.6	62.8	9.0	12.2	42.6	59.5	50.6	16.9	−8.9
Georgian	20.1	25.5	31.8	5.4	6.3	54.2	57.0	58.1	2.8	1.1
Azerbaydzhan	14.9	27.9	31.7	13.0	3.8	26.7	39.2	50.3	12.5	11.1
Lithuanian	34.8	52.2	37.4	17.4	−14.8	52.6	50.9	49.2	−1.7	−1.7
Moldavian	33.9	46.2	53.3	12.3	7.1	49.3	54.3	56.7	5.0	2.4
Latvian	45.3	58.3	65.7	13.0	7.4	42.7	34.1	39.1	−8.6	5.0
Kirgiz	19.8	28.5	36.9	8.7	8.4	13.9	36.1	22.3	22.2	−13.8
Tadzhik	16.6	27.8	30.0	11.2	2.2	11.6	35.6	20.4	24.0	−15.2
Armenian[a]	23.3	34.2	44.3	10.9	10.1	43.6	48.6	52.6	5.0	4.0
Turkmen	14.8	24.2	27.5	9.4	3.3	22.7	42.6	30.0	19.9	−12.6
Estonian	27.5	23.1	33.6	−4.4	10.5	45.2	39.9	38.2	−5.3	−1.7
Autonomous Republic Level										
Bashkir	47.9	62.5	73.9	14.6	11.4	67.2	70.2	68.8	3.0	−1.4
Buryat[b]	73.8	73.4	74.4	−0.4	1.0	32.9	65.2	62.1	32.3	−3.1
Avar	39.4	63.3	64.5	23.9	1.2	25.8	32.8	43.3	7.0	10.5
Dargin	40.8	63.4	66.1	22.6	2.7	62.6	68.3	74.4	5.7	6.1
Kumyk	56.3	72.5	74.3	16.2	1.8	67.3	73.8	75.3	6.5	1.5

Lezgin	42.5	64.3	68.2	11.8	3.9	20.7	31.2	41.8	10.5	10.6
Kabardin	71.6	77.1	78.6	5.5	1.5	68.8	70.3	66.9	1.5	-3.4
Balkar	73.9	78.4	82.4	4.5	4.0	56.6	69.0	59.7	12.4	-9.3
Kalmyk	85.3	88.5	89.7	3.2	1.2	64.0	62.0	61.7	-2.0	-0.3
Karelian	67.2	57.6	49.2	-9.6	-8.4	48.1	42.4	39.8	-5.7	-2.6
Komi	64.7	66.9	65.3	2.2	-1.6	53.7	50.0	45.2	-3.7	-4.8
Mari	66.4	77.8	75.3	11.4	-2.5	58.5	62.2	62.7	3.7	0.5
Mordvin	75.6	81.0	80.3	5.4	-0.7	61.7	59.4	55.9	-2.3	-3.5
Ossetian[c]	75.9	83.5	86.9	7.6	3.4	37.1	39.3	41.5	2.2	2.2
Tatar[d]	54.7	66.0	77.3	11.3	11.3	65.3	69.9	68.4	4.6	-1.5
Tuvin	38.0	58.9	58.3	20.9	-0.6	68.4	73.4	79.6	5.0	6.2
Udmurt	68.3	70.6	67.6	2.3	-3.0	52.2	51.6	48.9	-0.6	-2.7
Chechen	67.3	76.8	73.4	9.5	-3.4	64.1	72.6	75.9	8.5	3.3
Ingush	71.0	80.4	79.6	9.4	-0.8	71.7	77.4	80.9	5.7	3.5
Chuvash	58.3	68.1	69.2	9.8	1.1	58.4	61.2	61.1	2.8	-0.1
Yakut	40.8	55.1	65.0	14.3	9.9	64.4	66.4	61.5	2.0	-4.9
Karakalpak	9.3	44.6	19.0	35.3	-25.6	23.2	51.4	38.4	28.2	-13.0
Abkhaz	59.8	74.7	81.5	14.9	6.8	52.5	58.1	58.1	5.6	0.0
Autonomous Oblast Level										
Adygey	67.1	77.2	83.2	10.1	6.0	71.1	74.7	77.0	3.6	2.3
Altay	54.5	70.9	67.3	16.4	-3.6	56.9	57.6	54.3	0.7	-3.3
Karachay	67.7	75.9	79.7	8.2	3.8	66.9	73.7	77.1	6.8	3.4
Cherkess	71.3	73.9	78.2	2.6	4.3	65.3	57.3	70.2	-8.0	12.9
Khakass	67.9	71.8	72.4	3.9	0.6	54.7	53.3	46.7	-1.4	-6.6
Armenians[a]	17.2	31.4	55.2	14.2	23.8	43.6	48.6	52.6	5.0	4.0
Ossetians[c]	37.5	49.5	59.7	12.0	10.2	37.1	39.3	41.5	2.2	2.2
Autonomous Okrug Level										
Chukchi	59.8	60.4	61.8	0.6	1.4	54.2	64.8	59.3	10.6	-5.5
Dolgan	62.1	74.6	74.5	12.5	-0.1	60.6	62.5	46.3	1.9	-16.2

(*continued*)

TABLE 6.8
Continued

	Inside Home Republic					Outside Home Republic				
Nation	1970	1979	1989	Percentage Point Change 1970–79	Percentage Point Change 1979–89	1970	1979	1989	Percentage Point Change 1970–79	Percentage Point Change 1979–89
Evenk	73.7	74.5	65.8	0.8	−8.7	52.2	51.8	54.1	−0.4	2.3
Khanty	44.5	49.0	46.0	4.5	−3.0	53.0	57.2	55.8	4.2	−1.4
Komi-Permyak	71.4	69.6	70.2	−1.8	0.6	56.8	51.6	46.1	−5.2	−5.5
Koryak	70.0	64.6	49.0	5.4	−15.6	43.2	51.0	40.6	7.8	−10.4
Mansi	38.7	42.2	32.4	3.5	−9.8	37.8	34.0	34.5	−3.8	0.5
Nenets[e]	55.9	66.8	64.5	10.9	−2.3	48.6	54.9	44.1	6.3	−10.8
Averages:										
Union Republics	29.0	40.4	42.7	11.4	2.3	34.7	42.7	40.8	8.0	−1.9
Autonomous Republics	58.6	69.8	70.4	11.2	0.6	54.1	59.9	59.6	5.8	−0.3
Autonomous Oblasts[f]	65.7	73.9	76.2	8.2	2.3	63.0	63.3	65.1	0.3	1.8
Autonomous Okrugs	59.5	62.7	58.0	3.2	−4.7	50.8	53.5	47.6	2.7	−5.9

Sources: 1970: TsSU SSSR 1973, 4:20–319; 1979: TsSU SSSR 1984, 71–137; 1989: Goskomstat SSSR 1991a.
Note: Averages are unweighted.
[a] Armenians out of home republic exclude Armenians in Nagorno-Karabakh. The figures for this group are listed under "Autonomous Oblast."
[b] Buryat homeland figures include Buryats living in the Agin Buryat and Ust'-Ordin Buryat Autonomous Okrugs.
[c] Ossetians under ASSR: in homeland = those in North Ossetian ASSR; out of homeland = those outside North Ossetian ASSR and South Ossetian Autonomous Oblast. Ossetians in the South Ossetian Autonomous Oblast are listed under Autonomous Oblasts.
[d] Tatars include figures for the Crimean Tatars, whose members were not separated out of the 1970 or 1979 census data.
[e] Nenets in homeland include those living in the Nenets, Taymyr, and Yamalo-Nenets Autonomous Okrugs.
[f] Autonomous Oblast averages exclude figures for Ossetians in the South Ossetian Autonomous Oblast and Armenians in Nagorno-Karabakh.

have been the increasing limitations on the utility of the indigenous languages, coupled with the expansion in the proportion of indigenes claiming Russian fluency. In this sense, the expanding Russian bilingualism that occurred during the postwar period did not pave the way for further integration. Several of the language laws, and particularly those in Central Asia, recognized the continuing importance of Russian as the "language of international communication," and thereby preserved a role for Russian as a second language. Nevertheless, these laws were clearly designed to enhance the status of the indigenous language relative to Russian, and if successful they will seriously restrict Russian's role as the language of upward mobility. As was noted in chapter 4, the changing status of the indigenous language vis-à-vis Russian has been cited as a reason for Russian out-migration from the non-Russian periphery. Ethnocultural indigenization will undoubtedly enhance demographic indigenization.

The language data from the postwar censuses reveal that native language loyalty, above and beyond questions of utility and even fluency, remained strong among the vast majority of indigenes in the USSR. The designation of Russian as a second language even by indigenes who were more fluent in it than in their national language may be viewed as a political statement regarding the status of the indigenous nation and its language in the homeland. The fact that the "fluency gap" in language designation by indigenes was higher in urban areas is another indicator that rising territorial nationalism has corresponded with the social and geographic mobilization of the indigenous masses.

Linguistic Indigenization

As a final consideration, the degree to which nonindigenes have learned the indigenous language as either a first or second language is assessed.[13] First, the census data clearly show that Russians living outside the RSFSR underwent almost no linguistic assimilation toward the indigenous languages (Table 6.9). However, they increasingly claimed fluency in the indigenous language as a second language. This was particularly true in the Baltic republics, in Transcaucasia, as well as in Ukraine and Belarus'. For non-Russians living outside their homelands, a higher rate of linguistic indigenization occurred, though there was relative stagnation between 1970 and 1989. The largest increases occurred in the republics whose indigenes had become most overtly nationalistic by 1989 (i.e., Lithuania and Armenia), and the two trends were undoubtedly related. The rising percentage of non-Russian nonindigenes claiming Armenian as their native language also resulted from the out-migration of large numbers of Azerbaydzhanis, who were not linguistically assimilated to Arme-

[13] This section deals only with the fourteen non-Russian union republic nations. There has been almost no linguistic assimilation or accommodation (i.e., learning the indigenous language as a second language) toward the indigenous languages of national communities with autonomous homelands (Kaiser 1988, 277–278).

TABLE 6.9
Nonindigenes Claiming Fluency in the Indigenous Language as a First or Second Language, 1970–1989
(percent of Russians and other nonindigenes)

Republic	Russians						Non-Russians					
	First			Second			First			Second		
	1970	1989	Percentage Point Change	1970	1989	Percentage Point Change	1970	1989	Percentage Point Change	1970	1989	Percentage Point Change
Ukraine	1.5	1.6	0.1	26.0	32.8	6.8	11.4	10.0	−1.4	19.6	19.4	−0.2
Belarus'	1.5	2.2	0.7	20.6	24.5	3.9	40.4	32.4	−8.0	11.9	15.8	3.9
Moldova	0.6	0.6	0.0	13.3	11.2	−2.1	1.3	1.8	0.5	13.9	10.9	−3.0
Uzbekistan[a]	0.03	0.1	0.07	3.8	4.5	0.7	3.0	4.6	1.6	13.2	18.8	5.6
Kazakhstan	0.01	0.01	0.0	1.0	0.9	−0.1	0.4	0.7	0.3	1.4	2.1	0.7
Kyrgyzstan	0.00	0.01	0.01	1.5	1.2	−0.3	1.2	1.8	0.6	2.2	2.9	0.7
Tadzhikistan	0.02	0.05	0.03	2.4	3.5	1.1	1.3	1.1	−0.2	9.2	13.5	4.3
Turkmenistan	0.02	0.04	0.02	2.1	2.5	0.4	1.4	2.5	1.1	8.9	13.2	4.3
Georgia[b]	0.5	1.2	0.7	10.5	22.5	12.0	9.9	7.0	−2.9	11.1	19.3	8.2
Azerbaydzhan[c]	0.1	0.2	0.1	7.6	14.3	6.7	2.5	3.8	1.3	20.7	30.6	9.9
Armenia	0.5	1.4	0.9	19.0	32.2	13.2	1.8	7.2	5.4	15.8	26.9	11.1
Lithuania	2.0	4.1	2.1	30.8	33.4	2.6	3.2	4.9	1.7	13.1	17.1	4.0
Latvia	1.2	1.1	−0.1	17.1	21.1	4.0	6.3	6.4	0.1	18.1	18.3	0.2
Estonia	1.5	1.3	−0.2	12.6	13.7	1.1	7.8	7.7	−0.1	11.4	11.8	0.4
Averages	0.7	1.0	0.3	12.0	15.6	3.6	6.6	6.6	0.0	12.2	15.8	3.6

Sources: 1970: TsSU SSSR 1973, 4:20–319; 1989: Goskomstat SSSR 1991a.
Note: Averages are unweighted.
[a] Uzbekistan: Non-Russian nonindigenes exclude Karakalpaks living in the Karakalpak ASSR.
[b] Georgia: Non-Russian nonindigenes exclude Abkhazians living in the Abkhaz ASSR and Ossetians living in the South Ossetian Autonomous Oblast.
[c] Azerbaydzhan: Non-Russian nonindigenes exclude Armenians living in the Nagorno-Karabakh Autonomous Oblast.

nian. The largest decrease was registered in Belarus', which was also the republic with the highest rate of linguistic assimilation. The decrease was most likely the result of the intergenerational reidentification of Poles to the Belorussian nation. As in the case of Russians, non-Russians increasingly claimed fluency in the indigenous language as a second language. Overall, in order for nonindigenes to compete effectively for the resources of the homelands in which they live, it has become increasingly necessary for them to learn the indigenous language. Of course, with the new language laws in place, the pressure on nonindigenes to become fluent in the indigenous languages will grow in the years ahead.

In conclusion, indigenes experienced little linguistic Russification during the postwar period, even though state policies promoted Russian to a position of primacy. There was a reduction in the functional utility of the non-Russian languages, with Cyrillicization, the use of Russian loan words, spreading bilingualism, and so forth. Nevertheless, a more subjective affiliation with the indigenous language was not erased. This is clear from the continued high percentages claiming the indigenous language as the native or primary language even while fluency was shifting in favor of Russian. This tendency appears to occur with ethnocultural traits generally; the objective loss of traditional ethnocultural characteristics over time with the social and geographic mobilization of the masses has frequently coincided with a rising subjective sense of national self-consciousness among indigenes.

Geographically, this was particularly apparent in the homeland urban setting. In rural areas of the homeland, the Russian language and culture has not had as great an impact, and in these areas Russians have had to accommodate themselves to the indigenous language and culture. Outside the homeland, and particularly in urban areas, nonindigenes faced pressures to acculturate to the Russian or indigenous nations. Overall, since the vast majority of members of most nations have remained in the homeland even while they have urbanized, Russification and sovietization have had a limited impact on the population. The cities of each national homeland have become the stages for rising international tensions and conflicts as indigenes migrate to them, and not the scenes of international integration. This becomes even more apparent when the next stage in the process of assimilation—international marriage—is examined.

INTERNATIONAL MARRIAGE

International marriage has been treated by Soviet ethnographers as a more significant indicator of the potential for international integration than linguistic assimilation (e.g., Bromley 1969). This placement of international marriage in an intermediate position along the acculturation-psychological assimilation pathway is also seen in the work of Western analysts (Clem 1980, 52): "One way of substantiating the contention that true assimilation remains a distant goal is to look at the extent of interethnic marriage. . . . If anything, the degree to which individuals marry those of their own nationality (endogamy) is an even more sensitive indicator of the retention of ethnic awareness than is language loyalty."

Not surprisingly, a close correlation exists between linguistic assimilation and international marriage. For exogamy to occur, the acculturation of one or both partners has almost certainly taken place, and linguistic assimilation may be seen as a necessary though insufficient precondition for international marriage (Kaiser 1988). This relationship helps to substantiate the placement of international marriage at an intermediate position between acculturation and psychological assimilation.

International marriage is relatively more significant than linguistic assimilation for another reason. Not only is it an indicator of a reduction in the "psychological distance" between individuals from different national communities but it also creates the microenvironment within which the process of "natural assimilation" occurs, since it is the children of international families who are the main participants in this process (e.g., Bromley 1983b, 10).[14] These "internationalized" children are in turn more likely to marry internationally, resulting in an "internationalization" of the population across generations.

According to the survey data examined in chapter 5, a large and growing percentage of the population has the attitude that "nationality has no significance in marriage." In comparing these survey results with actual international marriage rates, one is struck by the lack of correspondence between the two (Table 6.10). For indigenes, rates of intermarriage are four to six times lower than the rate of positive responses to the survey question. Russians living outside the RSFSR had intermarriage rates that were 1.3 to 2.5 times lower than their rate of positive response to the survey question. Since actual intermarriage is a much more sensitive indicator of the potential for international integration than statements about attitudes toward hypothetical international marriages, we focus our attention on the data of actual intermarriage rates.

This section examines trends in international marriages and data on the national identity of children from international families. Until recently, comprehensive data on these processes were quite limited. Soviet censuses provided family data, which listed family number and size for endogamous families by nation, and also provided a total figure for international families. In addition, surveys of international marriage data were published for specific cities and rural areas during the past thirty years. While these two measures cannot be equated, mainly because international family data are cumulative over time, as opposed to the year-to-year nature of marriage statistics, the two are of course intimately related.

---

[14] The process through which children adopt a national identity or become nationally self-conscious is complex, even for children of nationally homogeneous families. For a discussion of research into the periodization of national self-consciousness in youth, see Snezhkova (1982).

TABLE 6.10
Comparison of Positive Attitudes to International Marriage (mid-1970s)[a]
with Actual Rates for Selective Nations, 1978 (percent)

	Positive Attitudes to International Marriage	Actual Rate	
		Men	Women
Uzbeks in Uzbekistan	16	4.6	3.0
Russians in Uzbekistan	44	21.5	27.3
Russians in Uzbekistan, Urban	54	21.2	26.7
Tatars in Uzbekistan, Urban	50	30.4	36.5
Moldavians in Moldavia	70	12.3	15.0
Russians in Moldavia	76	60.0	57.2
Estonians in Estonia	32	9.7	9.3
Russians in Estonia	62	24.7	29.2

Sources: International attitude surveys: Susokolov 1988; intermarriage rates: Goskomstat SSSR 1989e.
[a]Positive responses to the statement: "Nationality has no significance in marriage."

A number of studies were also published on the national identity of children from international families. The primary source of data for these studies is the nationality selected by adolescents at age sixteen, at which time internal passports were issued to all Soviet citizens. This is not a wholly satisfactory measure, since responses are, in theory, restricted to either the nationality of the father or that of the mother, and the response of "Soviet" or "no answer" was not accepted. Furthermore, one's official nationality as registered in the internal passport may differ from one's response to the question on nationality at the time of the census, since census takers are not to check documents in order to verify census answers.[15] Nonetheless, these data provide a rich source of information with which to assess the geography of international integration during the postwar period.

International Family Trends

Between 1959 and 1979 the proportion of international families in the USSR increased. This increase, however, was not experienced equally by all nations or in all republics of the country. The coefficient of variation for the urban rates increased from 35.4 percent in 1959 to 38.0 percent in 1989; the rural coefficient of variation also increased from 52.5 percent in 1959 to 54.7 percent in

---

[15] The difference between national identity in internal passports and in the census was recently analyzed through surveys of the Vepsy (Susokolov and Stepanov 1990).

1989. This indicates that the propensity to intermarry did not increase universally across homelands and national communities.

In general, international families were most common among the Slavic and Finnic nations, and among members of all nations living outside their national homelands. Regionally, there was a dichotomy of trends in the incidence of international marriage. In the non-Slavic south (i.e., Central Asia and Transcaucasia), the proportion of international families was decreasing or growing very slowly (Tables 6.11 and 6.12). At the same time, the percentage of international families in the northern and western regions of the USSR was increasing more rapidly. The regional differences in the rate of change in this measure may be explained in part by differential natural increase. Due to a greater natural increase of indigenes in the southern republics of the USSR, as well as a decline in the rate of in-migration and even a net out-migration of nonindigenes, the non-Slavic south became relatively more nationally homogeneous between 1959 and 1989. Since indigenes intermarry much less frequently than nonindigenes, the fact that indigenes are gaining proportionally in the younger age categories—where marriage most often takes place—has naturally resulted in a decreasing or slowly growing rate of exogamy. However, the decreasing rate of international families did not necessarily imply an absolute decline. Each of

TABLE 6.11
International Family Proportions in the USSR by Republic, 1959–1989 (per 1,000 families, by total, urban, and rural populations)

Republic	Total				Urban				Rural			
	1959	1970	1979	1989	1959	1970	1979	1989	1959	1970	1979	1989
USSR	103	135	149	175	151	175	181	202	58	79	92	119
Russia	83	107	120	147	108	125	132	154	56	77	93	127
Ukraine	150	197	219	253	263	296	299	317	58	78	93	122
Belarus'	110	166	201	246	237	292	295	310	56	73	92	133
Moldova	135	179	210	246	269	344	360	384	94	100	113	131
Uzbekistan	84	109	105	127	147	184	173	201	47	57	47	65
Kazakhstan	144	207	215	239	175	238	239	263	119	171	182	201
Kyrgyzstan	123	149	155	165	181	241	216	229	92	106	107	117
Tadzhikistan	89	132	130	148	167	223	231	256	55	65	59	82
Turkmenistan	84	121	123	133	149	200	199	214	25	34	33	45
Georgia	90	100	104	122	164	159	155	170	37	43	48	60
Azerbaydzhan	71	78	76	79	118	128	121	115	20	20	17	31
Armenia	32	37	40	38	50	45	49	47	14	26	22	20
Lithuania	59	96	113	128	104	149	152	157	30	46	56	70
Latvia	158	210	242	275	213	254	271	297	92	139	180	218
Estonia	100	136	158	173	142	171	186	202	51	72	90	96

Sources: 1959: Isupov 1964, 38; 1970: TsSU SSSR 1973, 272–303; 1979: Goskomstat SSSR 1989d, vol. 6, part 2, 78–117; 1989: Statisticheskiy Komitet SNG, vol. 3.

TABLE 6.12
Average Annual Percentage Point Change in the Proportion of International Families by Republic for the Total, Urban, and Rural Populations, 1959–1989

Republic	Total			Urban			Rural		
	59–70	70–79	79–89	59–70	70–79	79–89	59–70	70–79	79–89
USSR	0.29	0.16	0.26	0.22	0.07	0.21	0.19	0.14	0.27
Russia	0.22	0.14	0.27	0.15	0.08	0.22	0.19	0.18	0.34
Ukraine	0.43	0.24	0.34	0.30	0.03	0.18	0.18	0.17	0.29
Belarus'	0.51	0.39	0.45	0.50	0.03	0.15	0.15	0.21	0.41
Moldova	0.40	0.34	0.36	0.68	0.18	0.24	0.05	0.14	0.18
Uzbekistan	0.23	−0.04	0.22	0.34	−0.12	0.28	0.09	−0.11	0.18
Kazakhstan	0.57	0.09	0.24	0.57	0.01	0.24	0.47	0.12	0.19
Kyrgyzstan	0.24	0.07	0.10	0.55	−0.28	0.13	0.13	0.01	0.10
Tadzhikistan	0.39	−0.07	0.18	0.51	0.09	0.25	0.09	−0.07	0.23
Turkmenistan	0.34	0.01	0.10	0.46	−0.01	0.15	0.08	−0.01	0.12
Georgia	0.09	0.04	0.18	−0.05	−0.04	0.15	0.05	0.06	0.12
Azerbaydzhan	0.06	−0.02	0.03	0.09	−0.08	−0.06	0.00	−0.03	0.14
Armenia	0.05	0.03	−0.02	−0.05	0.04	−0.02	0.11	−0.04	−0.02
Lithuania	0.34	0.19	0.15	0.41	0.03	0.05	0.15	0.11	0.14
Latvia	0.47	0.36	0.33	0.37	0.19	0.26	0.43	0.46	0.38
Estonia	0.33	0.24	0.15	0.26	0.17	0.16	0.19	0.20	0.06

Source: Table 6.11.

the union republics that experienced a relative decline registered an increase in the absolute number of international families between 1970 and 1979.

The union republics that experienced an increase in the rate of international families were those located in the northern and western parts of the USSR. These republics generally have a greater degree of international interaction. Their populations are, on the whole, both more nationally diverse and more urbanized. As noted in chapter 4, in many of these republics the indigenous nation has experienced a slow rate of population growth in recent years, and this was especially the case in Latvia and Estonia. The rising percentage of nonindigenes in these republics set the stage for an increasing internationalization of families, which are much more common among the nonindigenous population.

In addition to these two divergent regional trends, there was clearly a difference in international family proportions between the urban and rural segments of each republic's population (Table 6.11). Again, a major cause of this differential is the different rate of international contact between the urban and rural settings. Rural regions tend to be much more nationally homogeneous than urban areas. Also, population density is much lower in the rural environment, further decreasing the possible number of international contacts. However, the rural proportion of international families actually increased faster than the urban percentage between 1970 and 1989, resulting in a convergence between town and country during this period.

The rate of change in international families underwent a dramatic decrease between 1959–70 and 1970–79 (Table 6.12). The decline in the rate of increase during the latter intercensal period in both the urban and rural areas of the country, and the fact that every republic experienced a slower rate of increase in the total during this same period, are indications that the increasing rates of educational attainment, urbanization, and upward occupational mobility among indigenes have not had the desired effect of "internationalizing" the family structure.[16] Indeed, in eleven of the fifteen republics and for the USSR as a whole, the urban rate of change was less than the rural rate between 1970 and 1979. This was dramatically different from the change registered between 1959 and 1970, when only four republics fit this description. The average annual rate of change in urban areas was lower in the latter intercensal period for all republics but Georgia and Armenia, and these two republics had among the lowest rates both in 1959 and in 1979. In five of the fifteen union republics the rate of increase in rural international families between 1970 and 1979 was greater than between 1959 and 1970.

During the 1980s, the rate of increase in international families was faster than it had been during the 1970s in nearly all the union republics. This was true for changes in the rate of international families in urban and rural areas, of the Slavic republics, Central Asia, and Georgia and Azerbaydzhan. In contrast to this, the proportion of intermarriages declined in Armenia in both urban and rural areas, and this was undoubtedly the result of the conflict over Nagorno Karabakh and the in-migration of large numbers of Armenian refugees from Azerbaydzhan. The rate of growth in the proportion of intermarriages also declined in the Baltics during the 1980s, and this does appear related to the rising level of nationalism in the region.

For an explanation of these trends, a number of changes in the demographic, social, and economic spheres are likely to have had an influence. First, as noted above, several republics became more nationally homogeneous during this period. In addition to this general demographic trend, the urbanization and urban growth of the indigenous population resulted in a demographic indigenization of cities in several union republics. Both these factors would tend to have a dampening effect on international marriage, because they were resulting in a national homogenization of the marriage pool. Beyond this, international marriage, as with acculturation and international integration generally, was partici-

---

[16] For several republics, the total rate of international families increased even though the urban and rural rates decreased. This occurred because the population overall became more urbanized, where international marriages were more commonplace. This urbanization reduced the rate of international families in the cities even while it increased the rate for the population as a whole.

pated in primarily by those more nationally marginal individuals living outside their homelands for an extended period (Bromley 1983b, 11).[17]

Overall, the rate of international families did not change substantially during the postwar period in either urban or rural areas. As in the case of linguistic assimilation, most of the "internationalization" in evidence had already occurred before World War II (i.e., before the nationalization of the masses). Even today, intermarriage between members of related ethnographic communities belonging to the same nation is much more extensive than intermarriage between members of different national communities, and in this way intermarriage facilitates the continuing process of national consolidation to a much greater extent than international integration.[18] During the past forty years, as the population became increasingly mobilized both socially and geographically, the intranational ties that bind the nations together were strengthened in the ethnocultural sphere, while the intimate "drawing together" (*sblizheniye*) of nations into one Soviet people at the level of the family was much less evident.

International Marriage Trends, 1978–1988

Recently published data make an analysis of trends in international marriages between 1978 and 1988 possible (Table 6.13). First, as in the case of linguistic assimilation, international marriage was much more likely among individuals living outside their national homelands, and especially in outlying urban areas. Second, and also in accordance with linguistic assimilation trends, international marriage rates were generally higher among members living in the outside rural than in the homeland urban setting. It may be stated that the more influential geographic factor in maintaining the endogamous barrier was residence in the national homeland, and not whether an individual resided in an urban or a rural environment. The lack of a strong positive impact by "modernization" was also apparent when comparing intermarriage rates across national communities. Estonian rates in Estonia, one of the most developed nations and republics in the USSR, were lower than Moldavian rates in Moldova, one of the least developed nations and republics in the state.[19] However, the same interaction effect found in the case of linguistic Russification did apply in the case of exogamy—the combination of outside homeland and urban residence generally resulted in the highest incidence of exogamy, while residence in homeland rural areas provided the greatest impediment to international marriage. There

---

[17] This statement again refers to the percentage entering into exogamous marriages, and not necessarily to the absolute number of such marriages concluded in a given union republic.

[18] This topic is discussed in greater detail below.

[19] Each of these two indigenous nations comprised approximately the same share of their homeland's population (Estonians = 61.5 percent of Estonia; Moldavians = 64.5 percent) (Statisticheskiy Komitet SNG 1993, vol. 7, part 2).

TABLE 6.13
International Marriage Rates by Nation and Sex, 1978–1988 (percent of total marriages by republic, total, urban, and rural)

	Total				Urban				Rural			
	Men		Women		Men		Women		Men		Women	
	1978	1988	1978	1988	1978	1988	1978	1988	1978	1988	1978	1988
Russians in:												
RSFSR	8.6	9.7	9.8	11.1	8.4	9.5	10.0	11.1	9.2	10.8	9.2	10.8
Ukraine	54.8	57.2	54.6	56.7	53.4	56.2	53.5	55.9	62.8	63.9	61.0	63.2
Belarus'	74.2	74.5	70.8	73.4	71.5	73.2	68.1	71.8	83.5	80.8	80.4	81.0
Uzbekistan	21.5	24.0	27.3	29.6	21.2	23.5	26.7	29.0	24.7	34.6	34.8	42.6
Kazakhstan	22.2	24.3	24.4	27.1	20.1	22.3	22.0	24.5	28.6	32.4	31.2	37.3
Georgia	22.5	39.6	34.5	53.2	23.7	39.4	38.0	51.7	20.0	41.6	26.1	63.1
Azerbaydzhan	19.2	24.6	34.6	40.3	20.1	25.0	35.2	40.7	4.6	16.1	26.9	31.4
Lithuania	52.3	56.5	47.4	51.7	50.5	55.4	45.8	49.0	66.5	67.2	60.6	71.3
Moldova	60.0	61.9	57.2	59.9	56.4	59.6	52.8	57.0	74.1	76.0	73.5	76.3
Latvia	34.8	37.1	35.1	37.6	32.9	35.6	33.5	35.9	46.6	48.6	45.7	50.4
Kyrgyzstan	17.7	19.4	18.8	23.0	15.7	17.7	16.9	20.9	22.3	23.6	23.2	28.2
Tadzhikistan	22.5	26.0	29.9	31.9	22.5	25.8	29.2	30.9	23.3	30.1	44.3	48.7
Turkmenistan	21.3	27.2	31.0	34.9	21.4	27.0	30.4	34.0	18.6	40.4	47.0	62.6
Estonia	24.7	24.0	29.2	27.2	23.6	23.3	27.7	26.5	43.8	34.8	51.3	39.3
Ukrainians in:												
Ukraine	20.8	20.9	21.6	22.4	29.2	26.6	30.2	28.4	9.5	9.8	10.2	10.3
RSFSR	85.7	87.9	83.5	86.8	87.9	88.9	85.5	87.5	79.4	83.6	78.1	84.1
Belarus'	92.4	90.7	90.2	89.8	92.9	91.2	91.1	90.2	91.6	88.8	87.8	88.3
Uzbekistan	89.2	91.3	89.6	91.3	89.2	91.5	89.4	91.3	89.3	87.8	91.4	91.3
Kazakhstan	75.7	81.0	75.4	80.8	79.9	83.5	79.8	83.5	69.0	75.6	68.4	74.9
Moldova	58.0	62.7	55.3	61.2	66.5	66.2	64.9	65.3	48.2	54.6	43.9	51.6
Latvia	88.1	85.5	83.9	84.0	88.1	86.4	84.3	84.7	88.3	80.4	80.8	80.7
Kyrgyzstan	71.0	84.6	71.1	84.8	74.5	86.7	77.2	87.2	67.2	81.3	62.6	80.7
Belorussians in:												
Belarus'	16.3	20.1	19.3	21.7	21.0	23.3	24.6	25.7	10.6	13.8	12.9	13.7
RSFSR	90.7	93.5	89.0	92.8	91.8	93.8	89.9	93.0	86.8	92.4	86.2	92.1
Ukraine	93.6	93.8	93.3	92.9	95.3	95.4	95.2	94.7	88.5	87.8	87.9	86.1
Kazakhstan	83.6	94.5	85.2	94.1	84.8	96.0	87.1	95.5	81.9	91.4	82.3	91.4
Latvia	81.6	84.3	84.3	85.3	83.6	84.0	85.9	84.9	74.1	85.8	78.4	87.0
Uzbeks in:												
Uzbekistan	4.6	4.3	3.0	3.3	10.3	7.6	5.9	5.8	2.6	2.7	2.0	2.1
Kazakhstan	14.6	13.9	10.3	11.4	27.5	21.8	12.9	17.8	5.1	8.3	8.8	7.0
Kyrgyzstan	5.9	11.1	4.2	8.8	10.6	14.1	6.2	8.9	2.8	9.4	3.0	8.8
Tadzhikistan	12.2	13.5	11.6	12.7	28.4	29.7	26.7	27.7	8.2	9.3	8.0	8.9
Kazakhs in:												
Kazakhstan	5.8	4.3	3.3	3.5	8.9	6.1	5.0	5.0	4.0	2.9	2.3	2.3
RSFSR	18.8	24.5	14.4	24.5	29.8	36.7	21.6	35.6	14.8	16.0	11.9	16.9
Uzbekistan	13.5	15.7	12.8	17.1	19.6	22.2	16.5	24.2	10.4	11.2	10.9	12.2

(continued)

TABLE 6.13
Continued

	Total				Urban				Rural			
	Men		Women		Men		Women		Men		Women	
	1978	1988	1978	1988	1978	1988	1978	1988	1978	1988	1978	1988
Georgians in:												
Georgia	6.4	8.5	4.0	5.5	11.4	10.6	6.5	7.1	2.5	4.8	2.2	2.7
Total[a]	17.9		9.5									
Azerbaydzhanis in:												
Azerbaydzhan	3.9	2.8	1.5	1.4	6.7	4.8	2.1	2.1	1.3	1.0	0.9	0.7
Georgia	17.1	5.2	9.9	3.4	22.0	15.2	8.5	10.8	12.5	1.8	11.0	1.0
Armenia	2.7	1.6	1.3	1.2	18.3	7.5	5.9	8.2	0.7	0.8	0.8	0.3
Lithuanians in:												
Lithuania	8.0	6.3	11.4	7.8	9.4	7.1	12.9	9.5	5.0	4.7	8.1	4.3
Total[a]	12.4		12.3									
Moldavians in:												
Moldova	12.3	14.4	15.0	16.9	26.3	24.6	31.2	29.1	7.4	7.9	9.0	8.7
Ukraine	58.5	63.2	59.3	64.4	88.1	85.8	87.2	85.1	41.5	45.9	45.6	50.6
Latvians in:												
Latvia	20.0	19.7	21.0	20.1	21.5	21.0	23.1	21.9	17.1	16.7	16.9	15.8
Total[a]	25.3		24.0									
Kirgiz in:												
Kyrgyzstan	3.0	3.7	2.4	3.0	7.8	6.3	3.5	5.3	1.8	2.9	2.1	2.3
Uzbekistan	20.9	24.1	17.7	23.3	37.8	43.2	37.8	45.6	18.9	21.0	15.3	19.6
Tadzhiks in:												
Tadzhikistan	7.4	6.6	5.3	5.6	15.5	12.0	9.8	9.5	4.6	4.6	3.9	4.1
Uzbekistan	27.6	29.0	26.2	30.2	42.8	39.8	41.9	35.5	20.8	22.8	19.2	27.5
Armenians in:												
Armenia	2.1	2.3	0.8	0.8	2.4	2.6	0.8	0.9	1.5	1.5	0.7	0.5
RSFSR	53.1	63.4	40.5	43.2	59.9	68.7	44.3	48.8	31.8	43.3	31.7	26.2
Georgia	19.6	23.7	14.9	21.7	24.3	32.7	18.9	29.9	11.8	8.1	8.5	8.1
Azerbaydzhan	12.6	16.7	11.0	17.1	15.7	20.3	14.1	21.0	2.9	3.9	1.2	3.2
Turkmens in:												
Turkmenistan	6.5	5.9	2.5	2.4	13.5	10.4	6.1	5.0	2.9	3.1	0.6	0.9
Total[a]	9.0		3.9									
Estonians in:												
Estonia	9.7	8.6	9.3	8.9	10.1	9.4	10.4	10.0	8.6	6.0	6.4	5.2
Total[a]	15.8		15.2									
Jews in:												
RSFSR	59.3	73.2	43.0	62.8	59.0	72.8	41.9	62.4	74.3	87.3	74.8	80.6
Ukraine	44.7	54.1	34.2	44.7	44.2	53.8	33.7	44.3	71.9	84.8	64.9	82.1
Belarus'	38.3	48.3	26.1	39.9	36.7	47.3	25.0	38.1	78.8	90.5	65.6	92.6

(*continued*)

TABLE 6.13 Sources (*continued*)
Source: Goskomstat SSSR 1989e, 204–321.
Notes: Caution must be exercised in treating changes in the rate of international marriage from 1978 to 1988 as a trend. The data set provides figures only for each of the two years, rather than for the entire ten-year period, and either year may include abnormally high or low figures for specific national communities in specific parts of the country.
An additional problem with the interpretation of these data is the assumption that the total number of nonindigenes living in a given republic and entering into marriage will enter into marriage in that republic. This assumption is generally valid but becomes less certain when dealing with members of nations living just beyond the borders of their homelands. Even individuals living in cities beyond the home republic have been found to return to their home villages to marry. For example, surveys of Tatars living in Leningrad reveal that some return to the villages they or their ancestors left in Tatarstan in order to find a spouse (Susokolov 1990, 131; Starovoytova 1987). However, this is by all accounts a small percentage, and in general the figures given in the table accurately reflect the geographic differences in the propensity to intermarry among the major nations in the state.
[a]"Total" figures for 1988 provided in Goskomstat SSSR 1990c, 35.

were two exceptions to this general rule. For Russians, who tended to be dominant in urban areas outside Russia, rural rates of intermarriage were generally higher than urban rates. This was also the case for Jews, who are concentrated in urban areas. Rural members of these two nations have had to accommodate themselves to the local ethnocultural setting to a greater extent than urban members, and this has resulted both in a greater degree of acculturation and intermarriage. For this reason, intermarriage between indigenes and Russians living in rural areas should not be interpreted as evidence of Russification.[20]

Overall, the differential between urban and rural rates of intermarriage was not as great as might have been predicted, and the gap between the two both inside and outside the homeland was smaller in 1988 than in 1978. Additionally, there was not a great disparity between the sexes in the propensity to intermarry. For the Slavic and Baltic nations, women tended to intermarry at or slightly above the rate for men, while for the nations of the non-Slavic south, the reverse was true. However, the gender gap in Muslim intermarriage shrank during the 1980s, which is a further signal that the traditional ethnocultural barriers to international integration have become less important over time, with rising levels of geographic and social mobilization of indigenes.[21] Neverthe-

[20] This is discussed in greater detail below, in the section on the national identity chosen by children of international families.

[21] Of course, certain aspects of ethnocultural traditions regarding marriage were retained even after significant upward mobility. For example, in surveys conducted during the 1970s, 88 percent of Uzbeks living in cities of Uzbekistan considered it necessary to ask their parents for permission to marry, while only 22 percent of Estonians living in cities of Estonia felt that parental permission was necessary. It should be noted that only 35 percent of urban Russians in Estonia agreed that parental permission was necessary, but 55 percent of urban Russians in Uzbekistan answered the question in the affirmative (Drobizheva and Susokolov 1981, 20). This indicates that the ethnocultural values

less, an indigenous barrier to international marriage was still readily apparent, and did not diminish with modernization. Endogamy is clearly not simply a consequence of geographic and demographic isolation or traditional norms but is valued even by upwardly mobile, urbanized, educated indigenes.

If attitudes toward international marriage were becoming more positive over time with rising social mobility, one would expect a higher incidence of intermarriage among younger couples. However, this was clearly not the case. Indeed, the rates of intermarriage among couples up to age twenty were among the lowest of any age cohort, and this was particularly the case for indigenes (Table 6.14). These data undermine further the already tenuous conceptual relationship between modernization and internationalization.

As in the case of international family trends between 1959 and 1989, little change in the international marriage rate was registered between 1978 and 1988 for each national community in its own homeland. For several nations, decreasing rates of intermarriage were apparent, and this was particularly true for the three Baltic nations, even though in each case their respective home republics were becoming less nationally homogeneous during this period. This occurred not only among the rural population but in the major cities of the region as well. Data from Vilnius and Kaunas in Lithuania reveal that this indigenous decline was part of a long-term indigenous trend, which was in stark contrast to the large increases in intermarriage rates experienced by Russians in these two cities (Table 6.15). The same trends were in evidence for Tbilisi between 1959 and 1988 (Susokolov 1990, 145). In addition, in twelve of fifteen cases for men and in eight of fifteen cases for women, the urban international marriage rate declined between 1978 and 1988, while in only five of fifteen cases (men) and six of fifteen cases (women) did the rural rate decrease. Only for Russians and Belorussians did the rate of international marriage increase between 1978 and 1988 for men and women in both urban and rural areas of the homeland (Table 6.16).

As was noted above, outside the homeland rates of intermarriage were generally much higher, and this was particularly true for Ukrainians and Belorussians.[22] As in the case of members living in the homeland, the change registered between 1978 and 1988 was not great for most of the national communities in most of the outlying republics. The Russian rate of intermarriage increased in every republic except Estonia, and as noted above, the Estonian rate in Estonia

---

of a region influence the behavior of nonindigenes (particularly those who have lived in the region for a long time) as well as indigenes, and lends further support to the statement made above that a process of national marginalization occurs among nonindigenes.

[22] According to Volkov (1989a, 17), Ukrainian-Russian intermarriage accounted for 44.1 percent of all international marriages in the USSR in 1979, and 42.1 percent in 1985. All other indigenous-Russian marriages accounted for only 28.9 (1979) and 29.6 percent (1985) of the total, while all other indigenous-nonindigenous marriages accounted for 17.2 (1979) and 18.4 percent (1985). All other Russian-nonindigene marriages accounted for 9.5 (1979) and 9.7 percent (1985).

TABLE 6.14
International Marriage Rates by Age and Nation, 1978–1988 (percent of marriages in each age cohort that are international)

	Age to 29		30–39		40–49		50 and Older	
	1978	1988	1978	1988	1978	1988	1978	1988
Russians in:								
RSFSR	8.9	10.1	11.8	11.7	10.9	11.6	9.6	9.8
Ukraine	54.8	57.7	55.1	55.3	54.3	55.3	52.2	53.7
Belarus'	73.1	75.3	70.8	70.0	71.0	71.4	66.4	68.6
Uzbekistan	24.8	27.2	25.2	27.4	22.4	26.8	20.3	23.1
Kazakhstan	23.3	26.6	24.7	23.7	22.9	24.1	20.7	21.8
Georgia	27.5	46.9	31.5	49.3	37.4	49.1	36.3	44.9
Azerbaydzhan	27.2	32.1	33.6	39.3	31.9	37.8	21.9	29.1
Lithuania	50.0	55.2	47.8	53.7	59.9	53.5	45.2	47.2
Moldova	60.1	63.1	55.8	57.9	51.6	57.5	50.9	49.5
Latvia	34.1	36.9	39.4	37.6	39.2	41.4	33.7	37.4
Kyrgyzstan	17.9	21.1	18.2	20.5	21.9	22.3	20.1	22.9
Tadzhikistan	27.7	28.3	23.3	33.5	18.9	30.9	21.1	25.1
Turkmenistan	26.2	31.3	27.9	34.9	32.7	31.0	20.9	22.9
Estonia	26.3	24.1	32.3	28.8	32.1	30.7	23.8	28.1
Ukrainians in:								
Ukraine	21.2	20.2	27.2	27.6	22.8	28.9	14.6	24.3
RSFSR	85.5	87.8	84.8	86.9	82.9	87.0	77.2	85.1
Belarus'	92.1	90.9	91.0	88.7	88.1	90.4	87.0	85.5
Uzbekistan	89.3	91.4	91.0	92.3	89.4	92.7	87.8	88.3
Kazakhstan	76.9	81.2	73.3	83.2	72.5	80.2	61.4	74.6
Moldova	60.6	61.1	63.7	69.0	52.6	63.8	29.3	56.7
Latvia	86.5	83.3	84.4	90.3	86.8	85.7	84.3	87.9
Kyrgyzstan	72.9	86.7	77.5	84.5	70.6	82.9	54.9	75.9
Belorussians in:								
Belarus'	17.9	20.2	22.9	24.6	19.1	26.4	9.8	19.8
RSFSR	90.6	93.5	90.0	92.8	87.7	93.0	82.4	91.2
Ukraine	93.8	93.6	95.0	94.3	95.4	95.0	83.0	89.5
Kazakhstan	85.2	94.3	84.5	96.3	81.4	92.2	92.2	93.1
Latvia	83.0	85.0	85.8	85.9	85.1	88.8	74.8	76.2
Uzbeks in:								
Uzbekistan	3.5	3.4	8.7	9.0	7.8	11.2	7.5	11.1
Kazakhstan	11.7	10.9	21.2	34.5	23.2	36.6	17.2	40.5
Kyrgyzstan	4.9	9.2	6.8	20.6	5.4	29.4	7.0	23.5
Tadzhikistan	11.3	12.2	19.6	28.7	20.2	26.2	19.0	23.2

(*continued*)

TABLE 6.14
Continued

	Age to 29		30–39		40–49		50 and Older	
	1978	*1988*	*1978*	*1988*	*1978*	*1988*	*1978*	*1988*
Kazakhs in:								
Kazakhstan	4.4	3.5	6.1	6.7	7.5	8.9	5.3	8.5
RSFSR	16.3	22.7	23.0	36.8	21.2	42.2	14.4	33.0
Uzbekistan	12.9	15.8	14.6	23.0	18.8	21.1	15.6	23.8
Georgians in:								
Georgia	4.6	6.0	5.1	8.7	9.8	13.8	15.7	14.2
Azerbaydzhanis in:								
Azerbaydzhan	4.8	1.6	4.6	4.1	7.0	9.8	6.3	11.5
Georgia	10.9	3.2	25.6	13.3	23.1	13.3	36.8	12.4
Armenia	1.5	1.0	3.1	5.2	2.5	2.6	20.0	6.6
Lithuanians in:								
Lithuania	9.4	6.4	10.0	10.5	13.9	10.0	9.4	8.2
Moldavians in:								
Moldova	14.2	14.4	21.9	24.0	16.5	26.8	5.8	19.1
Ukraine	59.6	61.7	69.5	74.5	74.1	72.9	35.1	68.0
Latvians in:								
Latvia	20.3	17.9	22.2	25.6	21.1	25.5	18.1	25.3
Kirgiz in:								
Kyrgyzstan	2.4	3.1	5.8	5.6	5.7	4.7	1.6	6.8
Uzbekistan	19.7	23.1	17.4	32.7	17.6	25.8	12.0	30.0
Tadzhiks in:								
Tadzhikistan	3.4	5.7	12.3	11.7	10.9	18.1	13.5	15.2
Uzbekistan	26.1	28.4	40.8	51.5	34.3	49.6	38.0	46.5
Armenians in:								
Armenia	1.1	1.2	3.4	2.7	6.1	4.8	2.5	4.4
RSFSR	43.5	51.4	62.4	63.8	62.7	70.6	57.6	67.9
Georgia	15.0	19.1	19.4	32.9	33.4	40.8	36.5	43.8
Azerbaydzhan	10.0	12.7	22.0	27.1	26.2	45.9	17.4	37.3
Turkmen in:								
Turkmenistan	3.8	3.3	14.0	16.7	20.7	26.9	12.7	34.4
Estonians in:								
Estonia	9.1	7.1	10.9	13.3	10.9	15.2	9.8	12.4

Source: Goskomstat SSSR 1989e.

TABLE 6.15
Intermarriage Rates for Lithuanians and Russians in Vilnius and Kaunas, 1947 and 1980 (percent and percentage point change)

	Lithuanian				Russian			
	Vilnius		Kaunas		Vilnius		Kaunas	
Date	Men	Women	Men	Women	Men	Women	Men	Women
1947	24.8	16.5	4.7	14.2	26.8	23.3	34.8	29.1
1980	19.9	20.8	4.0	5.8	51.5	49.7	56.5	53.1
Percentage Point Change	−4.9	4.3	−0.7	−8.4	24.7	26.4	21.7	24.0

Source: Susokolov 1990, 122.

also decreased. In addition, the Azerbaydzhani rate declined precipitously in Armenia and Georgia. In all three cases, the declining rate may be seen as a reflection of worsening international relations. The Armenian rate of intermarriage in Azerbaydzhan increased between 1978 and 1988, and at least on the surface this appears to contradict the relationship between international marriage rates and zones of international conflict. However, Armenian outmigration had already begun by 1988, leaving a more nationally marginal group of Armenians in Azerbaydzhan.[23] In Nagorno-Karabakh the rate of intermarriage did decline from 1.7 percent in 1974 to 0.5 percent in 1985 for Armenian men and from 0.5 percent in 1974 to 0.3 percent in 1985 for Armenian women (Susokolov 1990, 148). In addition, the Armenian increase in Azerbaydzhan overall does not signify an increase in the number of Armenian-Azerbaydzhani marriages. Unfortunately, this information was not provided. Judging by the almost nonexistent linguistic assimilation of Armenians to Azerbaydzhani, this type of intermarriage was probably minimal.

In areas where relatively large increases in the rate of intermarriage were recorded, the absolute number of those entering into marriage often declined. In the case of Jews, this undoubtedly reflected the emigration of younger, more nationally self-conscious members from the USSR to the West. The sharp increase in the rate of intermarriage among Russians in Georgia was also matched by a steep decline in the total number of Russians entering into marriage in that republic. This relationship also indicates that it was the more nationally self-conscious Russians who were migrating from Georgia (and the non-Slavic south generally), leaving behind a more nationally marginal population with a higher propensity to intermarry. The marital data for Ukrainians in Kyrgyzstan also fit this general pattern.

Using international marriage rates as a measure of the potential for interna-

[23] Later surveys revealed that more than one-third of refugee families were "international" (Chervyakov et al. 1991, 17).

TABLE 6.16
Indigenous Change in International Marriage Rates, 1978–1988
(percentage point change for each nation in its home republic)

	Men			Women		
Nation	Total	Urban	Rural	Total	Urban	Rural
Russian	1.1	1.1	1.7	1.3	1.1	1.6
Ukrainian	0.1	−2.6	0.3	0.8	−1.8	0.1
Belorussian	3.8	2.3	3.2	2.4	1.1	0.8
Moldavian	2.1	−1.7	0.5	1.9	−2.1	−0.3
Uzbek	−0.3	−2.7	0.1	0.3	−0.1	0.1
Kazakh	−1.5	−2.8	−1.1	0.2	0.0	0.0
Kirgiz	0.7	−1.5	1.1	0.6	1.8	0.2
Tadzhik	−0.8	−3.5	0.0	0.3	−0.3	0.2
Turkmen	−0.6	−3.1	0.2	−0.1	−1.1	0.3
Georgian	2.1	−0.8	2.3	1.5	0.6	0.5
Azerbaydzhan	−1.1	−1.9	−0.3	−0.1	0.0	−0.2
Armenian	0.2	0.2	0.0	0.0	0.1	−0.2
Lithuanian	−1.7	−2.3	−0.3	−3.6	−3.4	−3.8
Latvian	−0.3	−0.5	−0.4	−0.9	−1.2	−1.1
Estonian	−1.1	−0.7	−2.6	−0.4	−0.4	−1.2

Source: Goskomstat SSSR 1989e.

tional integration, we conclude that these processes: (1) did not coincide with the social and geographic mobilization of indigenes; (2) were not accelerating over time; and (3) primarily involved nonindigenes who found it necessary to integrate either with the Russian or the indigenous nation in order to fit in on another nation's homeland. Since the vast majority of members of each nation in the USSR remained in its respective homeland, the creation of a Soviet people through the concrete process of intermarriage was extremely limited. Furthermore, during the 1970s and 1980s, several nations experienced a stabilization and even a reversal of international marriage and family rates (Susokolov 1990). It is almost certain in the present environment of rising international tension and conflict between indigenes and nonindigenes that the nationalization of the family, rather than its internationalization, will become even more dominant in the future.

National Selection of Marital Partners—Case Studies

Unfortunately, the data analyzed thus far are lacking a critical dimension in the study of international relations, since they fail to provide information on the national selection of marital partners. Surveys of marriage statistics were conducted for specific urban and rural locations by Soviet ethnographers during the postwar period, and these surveys provide a data base with which to explore this dimension of international marriage. Where possible, the actual rate of intermarriage is compared with the theoretical probability of its occurrence. The theoretical probability (i.e., the likelihood that a man of nationality X will marry a women of nationality Y, based on the national composition of all men and women entering into marriage in a given locality in a given year) helps to hold constant geographic differentials in the national composition of the marriage pool, and so is more useful for comparative purposes than the actual rate of intermarriage alone.[24]

In general, the actual rate of intermarriage among indigenes was normally much lower than the theoretical probability. This was true for studies of rural areas of Kazakhstan and the Karakalpak ASSR, as well as for capital cities such as Dushanbe, Kishinev (Chisinau), and Vilnius. On the other hand, the actual rates of international marriage among nonindigenes often exceeded the theoretical probability of their occurrence. Clearly, the propensity of indigenes to marry endogamously was more than simply a reflection of ethnodemographic concentration in the homeland, just as the high intermarriage rates among nonindigenes represented more than a lack of available marriage partners from the same national community.

Several studies have examined the relationship between socioprofessional status (i.e., class) and international marriage patterns (e.g., Susokolov 1987, 1990; Susokolov and Novitskaya 1981; Arutyunyan and Bromley 1986). During the postwar period, as indigenes became more socially and geographically mobilized, socioprofessional status became a less significant factor influencing international marriage rates (Arutyunyan and Bromley 1986, 156). In their study of marriage statistics from Kishinev (Chisinau), Susokolov and Novitskaya (1981) also found little correlation between socioprofessional and ethnonational marriage patterns. They did note that during the 1950s and 1960s, a period of rapid growth in the city, the rate of nationally and socioprofessionally mixed marriages was on the rise, even though the theoretical probability for nationally and socioprofessionally homogeneous marriages increased. In the 1970s, during which time the socioeconomic and demographic growth of the city decreased and the level of social competition increased, an increase in nationally and socioprofessionally homogeneous marriages was registered. This finding supports the conclusion reached in chapter 5 that

---

[24] The theoretical probability of a specific national combination in marriage is the proportion of the number of men of a given nation entering into marriage multiplied by the proportion of the number of women of the same nation (endogamy) or another nation (exogamy) entering into marriage in a given year. For a detailed explanation of this measure and its use, see Gantskaya and Debets (1966). Since the theoretical probability assumes equal distributions and contacts between members of all nations within a given territory, it is subject to error, which is likely to become greater as the size of the territory increases. Many of the surveys comparing the theoretical probability with the actual rate have been conducted at the rayon or intracity level in an effort to minimize this problem.

"diffusion-competition" became the dominant relationship between social mobility and national identity during the postwar period, as each indigenous nation became more "modernized." However, socioprofessional status was found to be a slightly more important predictor of marital partner selection among the intelligentsia in Kishinev (Chisinau): "among specialists with higher education, Moldavians, Russians and Ukrainians were more likely to enter into marriage with representatives of the same socioprofessional group" than with members of the same nation, though the rate of both was much higher than the theoretical probability (Susokolov and Novitskaya 1981, 24).

In the Georgian capital of Tbilisi, "both social endogamy and national endogamy among specialists with higher education were above the theoretical probability." However, unlike the situation in Kishinev (Chisinau), among Georgians the level of international marriage for this elite socioprofessional group was much lower than for the remaining socioprofessional groups. This is another indication that more socially mobilized indigenes are also more nationalistic. Also, "among the working class in both cities the ethnic factor clearly prevails over the social in the selection of a marriage partner" (Arutyunyan and Bromley 1986, 161). Both national and socioprofessional endogamy among indigenes were often greater than the theoretical probability of their occurrence. From the limited evidence available, the postwar trend was toward greater indigenous endogamy. Socioprofessional endogamy became relatively less important, as a larger share of the indigenous population became more geographically and socially mobilized. The survey data reviewed below indicate that being a member of the indigenous nation itself had a dampening effect on international marriage, while nonindigenous status tended to facilitate the processes of assimilation.

INDIGENOUS INTERMARRIAGE RATES

As stated above, the actual rate of exogamy among indigenes was frequently lower than the theoretical probability of its occurrence. On the other hand, the actual rate of endogamy among indigenes was almost universally higher than the theoretical probability of its occurrence. These generalizations hold true for indigenes living in both urban and rural areas of the homeland. For example, in the rural rayons of Pavlodar Oblast in northern Kazakhstan—an area populated primarily by Russians, Ukrainians, and other non-Kazakhs—the actual rate of endogamy for Kazakhs was higher than the theoretical probability for all three rural rayons surveyed for every year between 1966 and 1979, while the theoretical probability of Kazakh-Russian marriages was higher than the actual rate of intermarriage (Kalyshev 1984, 74–75). A survey of urban areas in northern Kazakhstan also found that Kazakhs had the lowest rate of exogamy, even though the cities surveyed were not numerically dominated by members of this nation (Evstigneyev 1975, 8–12).[25]

---

[25] The survey of marriage statistics by Evstigneyev covers the period from 1940 to 1969. While a

The results of the studies on endogamy and exogamy among the indigenous population in northern Kazakhstan were comparable to those found in other regions of the USSR. Surveys conducted in Dushanbe between 1946 and 1966, the rural rayons of the Karakalpak ASSR between 1976 and 1980, the capital cities of the Baltic republics between 1945 and 1963, and in Kishinev (Chisinau) between 1950 and 1980 all indicated that the indigenous nations maintained an endogamous barrier to international integration throughout the postwar period (Kozenko and Monogarova 1971, 112–118; Tolstova 1985, 64–72; Gantskaya and Terent'yeva 1965, 1977; Susokolov and Novitskaya 1981, 14–26). Even in Ukraine and Belarus', where intermarriage with Russians was relatively extensive—particularly in the eastern regions of the republics and in the urban/industrial centers—the actual rate of indigenous intermarriage was less than the theoretical probability of its occurrence. Moreover, the trend was toward stabilization or even a decrease in the level of international marriage among indigenes during the past decade (Susokolov 1990). In the non-Russian republics, international marriage patterns among indigenes indicated a growing intranational solidarity and an increasing international segregation during the postwar period. This is quite different from either the Russification or the "internationalization" that were proclaimed as major trends of the postwar period.

Within the RSFSR, the nations and nationalities with autonomous republics, oblasts, and okrugs also evidenced a greater propensity toward endogamy within the national homeland. As with linguistic Russification, the Finno-Ugrian national communities in the Volga-Urals and northwestern regions did have higher rates of exogamy, and this primarily involved intermarriages between indigenes and Russians.[26] Within the national homeland, the Karelians, Komi, Khanty, and Mansi had particularly high rates of exogamy, and these were the national communities that were undergoing a process of international integration with Russians (Terent'yeva 1972; Susokolov 1990, 124–128). Generally higher rates of indigenous exogamy were present in the autonomous okrugs, indicating that these *ethnies* were more prone to integration. However, as noted in the case of linguistic assimilation, since a national self-consciousness was lacking among the members of these groups, this is probably more accurately labeled as national consolidation, either toward the

---

comparison of the actual rate of exogamy with its theoretical probability was not included in this study, it seems safe to say that the Kazakhs participated less than would be expected, given the multinational character of the urban population in this area. The other nation whose members intermarried at a low rate in these cities was the Ingush; this may be a reflection of the fact that the members of this nation were forcibly deported from their homeland in the northern Caucasus to this region during this period.

[26] However, because the Russians numerically dominate many of these autonomous units, it cannot be said that the actual rate of exogamy was higher than the theoretical probability of its occurrence. These studies did not provide absolute data, and so theoretical probabilities could not be calculated.

Russian nation or toward the more fully formed national communities in Siberia such as the Yakuts.[27] An intergenerational process both of consolidation among several small ethnic groups with larger indigenous national communities (e.g., Evenks toward Yakuts) and also of assimilation toward the Russian nation was occurring in this region. For the Siberian peoples, social and geographic mobilization appeared to result in the assimilation of indigenes (i.e., diffusion-erasure), and this marks these groups as distinct from most national communities in the state (Susokolov 1990, 137–138). Finally, in the North Caucasus intermarriage was particularly low among indigenes, though it was somewhat higher between related indigenous groups than between indigenes and nonindigenes. Although social and geographic mobilization was thought to hold the promise of greater consolidation between the numerous small indigenous *ethnies* in the region, intermarriage figures in Makhachkala (the capital of Dagestan) and elsewhere do not tend to support this expectation. If anything, intermarriage even between related ethnic communities in the North Caucasus underwent a decline during the 1970s and 1980s (Evstigneyev 1971, 80–85; Susokolov 1990, 150). This indicates that, in contrast to the "drawing together" of *ethnies* in Siberia and the Far East, in the Northern Caucasus each ethnic community was becoming a more fully developed nation over time.

More detailed surveys indicated that intranational intermarriage among the subnational ethnic groups was occurring, often at much higher rates than those for international marriage. For example, during the mid-1970s 23 percent of all Khakass marriages classified as endogamous were actually intranational intermarriages between members of the different subnational ethnic groups comprising the Khakass national community (i.e., Sagay, Kachin, Kyzyl', Bel'tyr, Koybal, and Shor). At the same time, international marriages accounted for 16 percent of all marriages involving Khakass men and 19 percent of all marriages involving Khakass women (Krivonogov 1980, 81–86). The subnational ethnic groups of the Mordvins (Mokshans and Erzyans), Chuvash, and Udmurts have also been undergoing a more intensive process of national consolidation, as intranational interethnic marriages have increased in frequency over time (Terent'yeva 1972). A relatively high rate of intermarriage among related *ethnies* provides evidence that national consolidation is continuing in Siberia and the Far East, as well as in Central Asia.

In selective cases, indigenes were found to intermarry at higher rates than the theoretical probability. For example, the rate of Tadzhik-Uzbek intermarriage in Dushanbe was higher than the theoretical probability of its occurrence, as was the rate of Lithuanian-Polish intermarriage in Vilnius (Kozenko and Monogarova 1971; Gantskaya and Terent'yeva 1965). In each of these instances, the nations involved were culturally similar and had interacted for an extended

---

[27] Of course, not all intermarriage was with Russians. As with linguistic assimilation patterns, Evenks were "drawing together" with the locally dominant Yakuts.

period of time. These qualifications also raise the question of whether intermarriage in these cases is "international" or whether it reflects the national consolidation in localities where members of related *ethnies* have interacted for generations.

It is often difficult to distinguish between intra- and international marriage, especially perhaps for the individuals involved. For example, in a survey of marriage patterns in the Karakalpak ASSR, it was noted that the intermarriage between Karakalpaks and other nations often occurred among subnational group members who were closely related. Karakalpak-Uzbek intermarriage was more common in the northwestern and western rayons of the autonomous republic. Here "live the Uzbek-Aral'tsy, who are ethnically close to the Karakalpaks" (Tolstova 1985, 69). Similarly, Susokolov and Novitskaya (1981, 18) conclude that "Russians and Ukrainians in Kishinev are practically not two, but one group," not only because of the ethno-cultural similarities between the two nations generally but also because the members of these national communities living in Kishinev entered from nationally mixed rayons where their ancestors had interacted and intermarried for generations, and consequently a high percentage of members of each national community is made up of children from international families. Clearly, the distinction between intranational and international marriage, like that between national consolidation and international integration generally, may be more apparent than real at the local scale, particularly for the individuals engaged in the process. For this reason, caution needs to be exercised in equating an apparent international marriage with the "internationalization" of the family.

Unfortunately, few other surveys analyze this intranational aspect of marriage patterns. National consolidation through intermarriage was generally included as part of the endogamous marriage figure. The lack of more comprehensive data at this level of analysis may correspond with the attitude expressed by Soviet ethnographers (e.g., Bromley 1983b, 9) that national consolidation processes were essentially completed by the time of the state's entry into "advanced socialism" and that international integration toward a unified Soviet people was becoming the dominant trend. However, recent surveys of the subnational ethnic communities included as part of the Russian and Tadzhik nations, as well as the survey data cited above, raise doubts that this is the case, particularly for geographically dispersed nations like the Russians and eastern *ethnies* of the RSFSR, as well as for the more remote, less developed regions of the southern tier of the former USSR, including southern Siberia, Central Asia, and the northern Caucasus. More research into the process of interethnic, intranational consolidation is clearly warranted, and if undertaken should further clarify the geographic and international variations in the degree to which the process of nationalization has been completed. This information is vital if we are to better understand and predict the development of nationalism in the successor states.

In conclusion, within the homeland endogamy prevails among indigenes. This is not simply a reflection of the national homogeneity of those entering into marriage or of the traditional ethnocultural values of the indigenous population. The endogamous barrier has been maintained by indigenes as they have become more socially and geographically mobilized; the diffusion of socioeconomic development has not resulted in the "erasure" of national solidarity among indigenes. Indeed, the limited evidence available suggests the opposite: an intensification of intermarriage between members of subnational ethnic groups over time indicates that national consolidation is at least as strong a process as international integration. Clearly, indigenes have been able not only to retain an endogamous barrier to integration with nonindigenes but also to enhance the degree of intranational cohesion during the postwar period, even though geographic and traditional sociocultural barriers have fallen.

NONINDIGENOUS INTERMARRIAGE PATTERNS

While inside the homeland indigenes retained the endogamous barrier to international integration, outside this barrier became more difficult to maintain. Small groups of dispersed individuals were much more likely to intermarry, either with Russians or with members of the locally dominant indigenous nation. However, most surveys indicated that even outside the national homeland, the rate of endogamy was often higher than would be predicted on the basis of theoretical probability. It was only among those members of nonindigenous *ethnies* who had a weakly developed sense of national self-consciousness, and particularly members whose ancestors migrated to these outlying areas before the onset of a strong mass-based nationalization, that high rates of exogamy were likely to occur. This was the segment of the nonindigenous population that has been referred to as "nationally marginal."[28] Recent surveys indicated that a relatively high percentage of indigenes who voluntarily migrated from the homeland were married to nonindigenes (Susokolov 1990, 131–133), and this implies that indigenes who chose to leave the homeland were more nationally marginal even before they left. They were further marginalized once outside the homeland, where nonindigenes were pressured to acculturate toward either the indigenous or the Russian nation in order to fit in and compete for a share of societal rewards in their new surroundings. In this way, the accelerated rate of international integration among nonindigenes was a reflection both of the more nationally marginal segment of the population that chose to migrate from the homeland and also of the way in which the national territoriality of indigenes further marginalized nonindigenes.

In the northern Kazakhstan survey cited earlier, the actual rate of Ukrainian-Russian and German-Russian intermarriage was greater than the theoretical

---

[28] While nationally marginal individuals are more likely to be found outside the homeland than inside, not all nonindigenes are nationally marginal.

probability of their occurrence (Kalyshev 1984, 75–77). The high rate of German intermarriage in Kazakhstan was in sharp contrast with the high level of German endogamy in Samara and later the Volga German ASSR, where, as early as the turn of the twentieth century, Semenov' Tyan'-Shanskiy (1901, 6:161) noted a strong tendency toward isolation among this population. With the abolition of the ASSR and the deportation and dispersal of Germans across northern Kazakhstan, as well as the mixing of Germans from different areas of settlement during World War II, this geographic and psychological isolation was disrupted, and a relatively high rate of acculturation and intermarriage with Russians occurred (Naumova 1987).[29]

The intermarriage patterns found among nonindigenes in northern Kazakhstan were reflective of general tendencies in the USSR. Belorussian-Russian intermarriage was also above the theoretical probability in Ukraine in 1969 (Chuyko 1975, 75), as was the intermarriage rate between Ukrainians and Russians in Kishinev (Chisinau) (Susokolov and Novitskaya 1981). Karelian intermarriage with Russians was particularly high in Kalinin Oblast, and this region of the RSFSR outside Karelia has been the site of national reidentification of Karelians to the Russian nation (Terent'yeva 1972, 44). Mordvinian intermarriage with Russians was also found to be particularly high outside the Mordvin ASSR. As in the case of Karelians, this was the chief cause for the absolute decline of the Mordvinian population during the postwar period, as an overwhelming majority of the children from Mordvin-Russian parents living outside the Mordvin ASSR identified themselves as Russians (Kozlov 1975, 245–246).

While exogamy outside was most often associated with Russian intermarriage, this was not always the case. As was said before, Uzbek-Tadzhik intermarriage in Dushanbe was higher than the theoretical probability. So, too, was intermarriage between Lithuanians and Poles in Vilnius. In the Bashkir ASSR, marriages between Bashkirs and Tatars were more common than those between Bashkirs and Russians. Nations whose members have been in intimate contact with one another over an extended period of time were more likely to engage in exogamy. Again, intermarriage between members of two groups who have lived in close geographic proximity for generations and share cultural values may as easily be described as intranational consolidation as international integration.

In general, those individuals residing outside the national homeland intermarried to a much greater extent than their indigenous counterparts. Even in

---

[29] This is quite distinct from the case of the Crimean Tatars and other deported nations from the northern Caucasus, who have not acculturated or intermarried to any great degree. However, it is similar to the Koreans, who were deported from the Far East to Central Asia during the 1930s. For the Germans, the more nationally self-conscious members have been seeking to emigrate to Germany. Alternatively, the older German population with roots in the Volga region has been pressing for a restoration of the Volga German ASSR.

instances where the actual rate did not exceed the theoretical probability, exogamy often involved the majority of such individuals entering into marriage. Clearly, the data on intermarriage indicate that it is the nonindigenous members of each national community who have been the population "at risk" of assimilation, either toward the dominant Russian nation or toward the indigenous nation. However, the role of international marriage in this process of international integration is not normally direct, since members of one nation who marry those of another rarely reidentify. Even for members of Siberian *ethnies*, intermarriage with Russians does not directly result in the loss of ethnic identity (Bromley and Gurvich 1987, 164). Rather, international marriage creates the conditions within which subsequent generations may reidentify ethnically. The general direction of this intergenerational process of reidentification as it occurred in the postwar USSR is the subject of the last section of this chapter.

NATURAL ASSIMILATION

Natural assimilation, defined as the voluntary reidentification of individuals from one nation to another, is most commonly associated with the selection of national identity by the children of international marriages. While "forced assimilation" has been attempted by various states throughout history, including Russia and the USSR, it is generally recognized today as futile, often resulting in rising national self-consciousness and more hostile international relations. However, the distinction between forced and voluntary decision making in the USSR and elsewhere was often a matter of degrees; the existence of a system of national stratification and national policies shaped to benefit specific nations within a given geographical region obviously made certain choices more attractive than others (Connor 1984a, 480–483). In the past, national policies tended to favor the dominant Russians in the country as a whole, and also the indigenous nations in their own respective home republics. As noted in chapter 3, during the height of the *korenizatsiya* period, children of international families tended to identify as members of the indigenous *ethnie* at least in part because of the strategic advantages enjoyed by indigenes at the time. During the postwar period, the status of being indigenous was retained and even enhanced, particularly in the sociocultural sphere, and increasingly in the economic and political sectors. Most indigenous nations strengthened their positions within their own home republics during the past forty years, and as this occurred the status of non-Russian nonindigenes (and since the late 1980s Russian nonindigenes as well) was further undermined.

In the specific context of the national identity of children from international couples, the data base from which studies are drawn is the nationality chosen for the internal passport, which was issued to every Soviet citizen at the age of sixteen. Responses were legally limited to the national identity of one of the child's parents (Terent'yeva 1969, 22).[30] In addition to these data, the results on this question from surveys of national identity are also included in the analysis.

A statistical relationship has frequently been noted between the national identity of the father and the national identity selected by children of international families.[31] However, this relationship depends both on the national identity of the parents and on the geographic context in which the international family lives. For example, in 75.8 percent of Uzbek-Russian families in Uzbekistan the children chose the national identity of the father. This was in part related to the fact that in 84.7 percent of Uzbek-Russian families the father was Uzbek; it was also related to the patriarchal orientation of Central Asian society, since in 72.3 percent of the families where the father was Russian and the mother was Uzbek, the children still chose the national identity of the father (i.e., Russian). This patriarchal tendency held true in the other Central Asian republics and in Transcaucasia, where the majority of marriages involving indigenes were between indigenous men and nonindigenous women. It was much less important in the Baltic republics and Russia. For example, in the RSFSR children selected the national identity of the father in only 28.9 percent of Uzbek-Russian families. This was more strongly related to the fact that in only 17.5 percent of the families was the father a Russian—in 95.6 percent of these families the children chose the national identity of the father. In families with an Uzbek father, only 14.7 percent chose an Uzbek identity, while 85.3 percent chose the national identity of the mother (Volkov 1989b).

When one parent was a member of the indigenous nation, children most often chose an indigenous national identity. This was one of the more universal tendencies apparent in the postwar USSR, and it reflects the continued strong attraction of an indigenous national identity even after extensive social and geographic mobilization, and an intensification of international interaction across generations. This intergenerational indigenization was most pronounced among indigenous non-Russian families. For example, 80 percent of the children from Lithuanian-Polish families in Vilnius claimed to be Lithuanian, and 79 percent of children from Latvian-Polish, Latvian-Ukrainian, and Latvian-

---

[30] In the past, children of international families were allowed to register as Russians, even if one of their parents was not a member of that nation. For example, 6.7 percent of the children from Khakass-Other (non-Russian) parents registered as Russians in the mid-1970s (Krivonogov 1980, 80). On average, 5.1 percent of children in 1979 gave responses different than the nationality of either the mother or the father, though Volkov (1989b, 9) notes that the majority of these children were from previous marriages, where the nationality of the divorced spouse was different than that of the two current parents.

[31] Snezhkova (1982, 85) found that in international families in Ukraine, boys tended to choose the nationality of the father and girls the nationality of the mother. Since boys and girls are born at about the same rate, this would tend to replace the members of each nation across generations, resulting in little natural assimilation overall. However, this more limited survey contradicts broader works that suggest a preference for a Ukrainian national identity in Ukraine (Terent'yeva 1977).

Belorussian families in Riga claimed to be Latvian (Gantskaya and Terent'yeva 1977, 481). Of course, the same high percentages were found among children of nonindigene/Russian families living in the Russian homeland. This was not only the choice of the children but also that of the parents. For example, in the majority of cases the non-Russian parents from Tatar-Russian, Armenian-Russian, and Estonian-Russian couples in Leningrad (St. Petersburg) wanted their children to select a Russian national identity (Starovoytova 1987, 98).

Even in indigenous/Russian families, children were more likely to identify as members of the indigenous nation than as Russians, though this rate was normally closer to parity. This indigenous preference held true in Kiev and other cities of Ukraine, as well as in the Baltic, Transcaucasian, and Central Asian republics (e.g., Gantskaya and Terent'yeva 1977; Arutyunyan and Bromley 1986, 171; Vinnikov 1980, 37).[32] This indigenization had a stronger negative impact on non-Russian, nonindigenous population growth but also reduced the size of the Russian population outside the RSFSR. For example, the young cohort of Russians in Kishinev (Chisinau) declined by 4 percent during the 1970s as a result of the indigenization of children from Moldavian-Russian couples (Arutyunyan and Bromley 1986, 172). So, not only did indigenes intermarry at exceedingly low rates but the intermarriage that did occur between indigenes and nonindigenes resulted in the demographic indigenization of subsequent generations. This indigenization even at the expense of the supposedly dominant Russians was widespread throughout the non-Russian periphery, though this was not the image normally conveyed by studies of the national question in the USSR.

This intergenerational indigenization held true for the nations with autonomous republics as well as for those with union republics (Arutyunyan and Bromley 1986, 171). Surveys indicated that even the small nationalities of Siberia and the Far East did not suffer losses as a result of exogamous marriages in the homeland, which were primarily with Russians. For example, about half of all children of exogamous Khakass marriages in the Khakass Autonomous Oblast registered as Khakass (Krivonogov 1980, 80). This level ensures group maintenance.[33] For Tatars in Tatarstan, children of Tatar-Russian couples chose Tatar and Russian at about an equal rate, but children of Tatar-Other couples chose Tatar more often (Busygin and Stolyarova 1988, 29). Only among the

---

[32] However, the children of Belorussian-Russian couples in Belarus' more often chose a Russian national identity, which was said to be related to a tendency for children to choose the nationality of the father and the fact that more Belorussian women marry Russian men. However, the children of Belorussian-Other (non-Russian) couples chose a Belorussian national identity more often (Kasperovich 1985, 121–122).

[33] Since only one parent is a member of the indigenous *ethnie*, a 50 percent rate of identity as a member of the indigenous nationality among children can be viewed as the replacement level. For the Khakass, about 47 percent of the children of Khakass-Russian parents identified themselves as members of the Khakass nationality, and a much higher percentage of children from Khakass-non-Russian parents identified as Khakass.

small *ethnies* of Siberia and the Far East (i.e., those indigenes at the autonomous okrug level) did intergenerational reidentification away from the indigenous *ethnie* occur. For groups such as the Khanty and Mansi, whose losses within the homeland were as great as those among members living outside, it is clear that the children of international families were not identifying themselves as members of the indigenous *ethnies*. This final stage in the process of national consolidation/international integration also sets these groups apart from the vast majority of the remaining indigenous national communities.

In marriages between nonindigenes and Russians living in the homelands of other national communities, children most often identified as Russians. For nations such as Ukrainians and Belorussians, as well as a number of Finnic nations with a long history of contact with Russians and a large proportion of their members living outside the national homeland, this resulted in an intergenerational Russification. The Russian losses resulting from indigenization mentioned above were more than compensated for by gains from this Russification of the children from Russian/nonindigenous families. For example, if the young cohort of Russians in Kishinev (Chisinau) lost 4 percent as a result of Moldavian-Russian intermarriage, it gained 3.8 percent as a result of the Russification of children from Ukrainian-Russian families in the city (Arutyunyan and Bromley 1986, 172). The Russification of children from other Russian nonindigenous families more than made up for the losses registered to Russian-Moldavian families. Overall, the Russian nation continued to grow as a result of reidentification at least through the 1970s, though the contribution of national reidentification to total growth had declined from an estimated 34 percent between 1939 and 1959 to 17 percent between 1959 and 1970 and only 16 percent between 1970 and 1979 (Bruk and Kabuzan 1982b, 13).

Using the estimating procedures adopted by Bruk and Kabuzan, we would conclude that the Russian population did not grow as a result of national reidentification during the 1980s, and if confirmed this would represent a significant shift away from the Russification of the population. Because the vast majority of Russians live in the RSFSR, and since the number of Russians living outside the RSFSR was approximately equal to the number of non-Russians living in the RSFSR, Bruk and Kabuzan (1982b) estimated that the Russian natural increase was equal to the natural increase of the total population living in the RSFSR. Using this procedure, Russian natural increase for the ten-year period from 1979 to 1988 would be approximately 8 million, which was actually greater than the total intercensal increase registered by Russians between 1979 and 1989 (7.8 million). The difference between these figures was at least in part due to the relatively crude estimating procedure used, and Topilin (1992, 32) estimated that assimilation still accounted for 11 percent of Russian population growth between 1979 and 1989. Nevertheless, the Russian population change in the last decade stands in stark contrast to previous decades, and indicates that in all likelihood a significant reduction in the number of non-Russians reidentifying as Russians occurred between 1979 and 1989.[34]

The strong preference shown by children to choose either the indigenous or Russian national identity is understandable, since Soviet society was stratified nationally so as to place Russians and indigenes in a preferential position. That the majority of children from indigenous/Russian families chose an indigenous national identity indicates that ethnocultural indigenization was a strong competitor with Russification. Russification did not pose the threat to indigenes that non-Russian nationalists and several Western analysts have claimed. Nor, for that matter, has "internationalization" been a dominant process, as Soviet ethnographers have asserted. For most nations in the USSR, indigenization has led both to the further intranational consolidation and solidarity of each indigenous nation in its own homeland, and also to the strengthening of barriers against the international integration of indigenes. At the same time, the success of indigenes in the sociocultural sphere has increased pressure on nonindigenes to accommodate themselves to the indigenous culture, or alternatively to Russian. Non-Russian nonindigenes, particularly those nonindigenes living in cities outside the homeland for extended periods, are those most likely to undergo a process of indigenization or Russification. Since most national members have remained in their respective national homelands even as they have become more socially and geographically mobilized, the process of international integration has had a limited impact on all but a few nations. Furthermore, there has been little evidence to support the contention that this internationalization has been accelerating with sociocultural and socioeconomic development. If anything, the contrary has been the case, as each indigenous nation has strengthened its own position in its own homeland over time.

During the postwar period the national consolidation of related *ethnies* continued, and reached a terminal stage with the nationalization of the masses in much of the European USSR (Bromley 1983b; Susokolov 1990). The social and geographic mobilization of increasing numbers of indigenes have coincided with the expansion of linguistic standardization, intranational interethnic intermarriage, and the "nationalization" of children from such families. National consolidation continues to be a dominant process in Siberia and the Far East, in Central Asia, and in the northern Caucasus. The national consolidation of indigenous ethnocultural characteristics is a process strengthening intranational cohesion or solidarity, and has made international integration all the more remote.

International integration has not proceeded according to the expectations of the "diffusion-erasure" model, with the exception of nationally marginal nonin-

[34] Sources for estimates: Goskomstat SSSR 1989d, 58; Goskomstat 1991a.

digenes. For these individuals, linguistic assimilation either to Russian or the indigenous language, international marriage, and the "natural" assimilation of children from international families have resulted in intergenerational reidentification toward either the Russian nation (i.e., Russification) or toward the indigenous nation (i.e., indigenization).

Russification has occurred primarily as a result of the intergenerational reidentification of children from Russian nonindigenous families, and has had an especially profound impact on several of the Finno-Ugrian national communities with homelands in the Volga-Urals and Northwest regions and that also have a large proportion of their members living outside the homeland (e.g., Karelians, Mordvins). It has also resulted in the demographic decline in the number of Ukrainians and Belorussians living outside their national homelands for extended periods. The Russification of indigenes has been limited to those small *ethnies* of Siberia and the Far East, and since the members of these groups have not attained a national self-consciousness, Russification may be seen as one form of national consolidation of the subnational *ethnies* in the region. Russification in general has occurred among groups whose members have long interacted with Russians at the local level, and are ethnoculturally related to Russians. Therefore, to some extent, much of what has been viewed as forced Russification resulting from the insidious policies of the center may be more appropriately thought of as a long-term intergenerational consolidation of nonindigenes lacking a strong national identity toward the Russian nation.

This is not to argue that state policies during the postwar period have not encouraged Russification but rather to question how effective these policies have been. Over the entire postwar period, little Russification has occurred. Acculturation to the Russian language has occurred, but it has been geographically limited to nonindigenes living and working in an urban/industrial environment or nonindigenes living and working in the Russian homeland. For indigenes, most of the linguistic Russification that has occurred preceded World War II; in the postwar USSR neither the policies favoring the Russian language as the language of upward mobility nor the social and geographic mobilization of indigenes has led to extensive linguistic Russification. Russification of indigenes has not proceeded beyond learning Russian as a second language, and as noted above, Russian bilingualism cannot be equated with acculturation (i.e., the preliminary stage in the process of international integration), let alone assimilation. Indigenous loyalty to the native language above and beyond levels of fluency indicates that while state policies may have limited access to the indigenous language, they have had little success in affecting the more subjective affiliation of indigenes toward their mother tongues. Surveys indicate that this indigenous language loyalty was found not just among rural *kolkhozniki* or unskilled *rabochiye* but also among the indigenous intelligentsia. The new language laws give political expression to this linguistic affiliation in asserting that the indigenous language must be the lingua franca of the national homeland. Of course, a privileged status for the indigenous language also provides strategic advantages for indigenes in competition with nonindigenes, and particularly with Russians. But it is not for strategic advantage alone but from a sense of exclusiveness—the belief that the indigenous nation has a right to a privileged position in its own homeland—that indigenes have remained loyal to their indigenous languages in the face of pressure to acculturate to the Russian language, and are presently reacting against the privileges afforded Russians and their language in the past.

In the past it was enough for nonindigenes to know Russian, since it was the language of upward mobility. In addition, a relatively large proportion of nonindigenes retained their own native languages. During the postwar period, linguistic indigenization has also occurred, though this has been limited to date. Since most nonindigenes are Russians, Ukrainians, or Belorussians, and since Russian was a required subject throughout the state, the linguistic Russification of nonindigenes rather than their linguistic indigenization is not surprising. State policies favoring the Russian language have had an impact in this restrictive case, limiting the ethnocultural indigenization of nonindigenes that would otherwise have occurred. Nevertheless, nonindigenes have found it increasingly necessary to learn the indigenous language, and the new language laws in the republics are likely to accelerate the process of ethnocultural indigenization. This is clearly what they are designed to do—to enhance the status of the indigenous ethnocultural attributes in the homeland as part of a strategy of national territoriality.

Indigenes have not only retained and solidified the position of their ethnocultural attributes, they have also remained highly endogamous in the homeland. Intranational marriages among indigenes exceed the theoretical probability of indigenous endogamy for almost every national community, while international marriage rates for indigenes are almost always below the theoretical probability. This endogamous barrier to the internationalization of indigenous families has been maintained not only in traditional rural settlements but also in urbanized, industrialized regions of the homeland. International marriage among indigenes, like linguistic assimilation, was a much more frequent occurrence before World War II than afterward. During the postwar period, indigenes have strengthened the ethnocultural barriers between themselves and outsiders, inhibiting or completely halting and reversing the process of international integration. Far from the creation of a Soviet people, sociocultural processes in the era of developed socialism created more fully formed nations with their own nationalistic elites in a position to take control of their homelands.

Ethnocultural indigenization has occurred through the "natural" assimilation of a majority of children from indigenous-nonindigenous families, including indigenous/Russian couples. During the 1980s national reidentification to the Russian nation apparently declined precipitously, indicating either a national resurgence for certain national communities or a declining proportion of children from international families who claimed to be Russians. In today's ethnopolitical environment, where indigenes are increasingly asserting their rights to preferential treatment in their own homelands, and where the benefits of being Russian outside the RSFSR are rapidly disappearing, both of these complementary explanations are not only possible but likely.

CHAPTER SEVEN

Political Indigenization and the Disintegration of the USSR

THE REFORM PROGRAM initiated under Gorbachev was meant to free up the creative potential of the "Soviet People" in order to revitalize the Soviet socialist economy. The creative potential unleashed by the reforms was not used for this purpose but instead was diverted to serve national territorial objectives. *Glasnost'* and democratization allowed national territoriality to become an overtly political strategy, resulting in increasingly adamant calls for decentralization of political power from the center to each indigenous nation in its own homeland. This political "separatism" initiated from below placed Gorbachev and the center in an essentially reactive position from which they were unable to escape. Over time, national separatism diffused throughout the USSR. In addition, ethnoterritorial disputes over the geographic extent of homelands and conflicts over the issue of sovereignty for the national communities whose homelands were recognized as merely autonomous or were not recognized at all in the federal hierarchy also spread rapidly throughout the state.

In the USSR, as in most multinational states, a built-in tension existed between central authorities seeking to control development for the benefit of society as a whole and indigenous elites seeking to control the allocation of homeland resources primarily for the benefit of the indigenous population. While the former often opted for nonterritorial, functional, or "vertical" political and economic structures in an effort to maintain control at the center, the latter frequently sought to enhance the decision-making authority of territorial or "horizontal" sociocultural, economic, and political institutions. This was the political geographic essence of the center-periphery relationship. In the postwar USSR, the shifting balance of forces between center and periphery was resulting in a devolution of decision-making authority to national elites in homelands (i.e., a process of political indigenization).

In assessing the process of political indigenization in the postwar USSR, the economic and political relations between center and periphery are examined.[1] First, because a long-term process of political—and indeed sociocultural and economic—indigenization and the confederalization of center-periphery rela-

---

[1] In the Soviet context, economic and political indigenization have been intimately related, since the state owned the economic resources and was responsible for economic investment allocations and decision making. For this reason, economic indigenization is subsumed under political indigenization.

tions directly contradicts the standard totalitarian model applied to the USSR, the chapter opens with a brief critique of totalitarianism. Next, the *sovnarkhozy* (regional economic councils) program initiated under Khrushchev is compared to the republican *khozraschet* (economic self-management) system and declarations of economic sovereignty that developed under Gorbachev in order to assess the process of economic decentralization and the problem of regional autarchy that emerged. This is followed by an assessment of the political indigenization that occurred during the postwar period. This section examines both the more localized international conflicts over the geographic extent of homelands, as well as the process of confederalization of political relations between center and periphery. Extensive coverage is given to the process of political indigenization since 1985, the types of international conflicts that have emerged since the late 1980s, and the prospects for a new "Commonwealth of Independent States." (CIS).

POLITICAL INDIGENIZATION AND TOTALITARIANISM

Among Western political analysts, the Soviet Union was often depicted as a totalitarian state in which political decision making was highly centralized, and in which the political center dictated almost totally the way people lived their lives. The use of the totalitarian model to describe the USSR began with the cold war in the 1950s, waned during detente in the 1970s, but was restored during the new cold war of the 1980s. In one of the more extreme statements made about the Soviet totalitarian system in recent years, Voslensky (1988, 5) defined it as "the total control by an undemocratic power over all spheres of life in society." This is little different than the basic characteristics of Soviet totalitarianism as it was depicted nearly two decades before (Meissner 1969, 74–75): "unrestricted autocracy of the party, . . . total control from above . . . and total planning, extending not only to the economic but also to the political and cultural sectors of society." Totalitarianism is also often presented as an extreme form of centralization, since political power is said to be concentrated not only at the center or "metropole" but also in the political (i.e., party) leader himself. This was explicit or implicit in much that was written about the USSR in the West, and it was undoubtedly responsible for the dominance of "Kremlinology" in political studies of the state, almost to the exclusion of what took place beyond the Kremlin walls. In order to understand the Soviet Union, according to much of this literature, one needed only to be able to read the mind of the leader. Political science debates on the explanation of events and predictions of the future bore more than a passing resemblance to astrology, frequently revolving around little more than an argument of who had a more accurate crystal ball or was more adept at long-distance mind reading.

The totalitarian model and its applicability to the Soviet Union have certainly not gone unchallenged. This model depicted the USSR as a rigid, static, and inherently fragile state—an image that was blamed for the failure of Western analysts to predict continued systemic stability under conditions of dynamic change, as had occurred during much of the postwar period (Bialer 1980, 145).[2] Totalitarianism, especially its overemphasis on the state to the exclusion of society, and its depiction of the state as unable or even unwilling to change, has also been blamed for the West's almost total unpreparedness for the reforms initiated under Gorbachev (Lewin 1988, 2–5). Clem (1988, 10–13) similarly sees the totalitarian model, coupled with "a tendency to assume the worst about the Soviet Union" as likely reasons for the failure "to anticipate . . . and to appreciate fully the pace, scope, and potential of the changes engendered by Gorbachev." The prevalence of totalitarianism in Western analyses of the USSR during the cold war of the 1950s and 1960s has also been cited as a reason for the limited research into the national question (Lapidus 1984, 557): "The totalitarian model, with its focus on the capacity of a monolithic state to bring about a well-nigh total atomization of society, left little room for explorations of the potential bases of social solidarity, including ethnicity."

The major problem with the totalitarian model, then, is that it focuses on the political core and even on the political leader of the state as the sole actors in the political system, while treating Soviet society as "atomized" and politically inert, a mere object to be manipulated. This hypercentrist and "top-down" approach to the study of the USSR was undoubtedly a more accurate description of life in the USSR during the late Stalin era (e.g., Breslauer 1986, 654–655). However, even at the height of Stalinism—as recent social histories of the period make clear—society not only existed but placed major constraints on political decision makers (e.g., Getty 1991). Furthermore, the political system itself exhibited a higher degree of local and regional influences than would be allowed for within this model. Reviewing the recent literature on political society during the interwar period, Urban and Reed (1989, 413) concluded that "the actual results in implementing regime directives in the Stalin period regularly bore no better than the faintest resemblance to the announced policy." Life, even political life, was not totally atomized and controlled from above.

Proponents of the totalitarian model have argued that "total control" through the atomization of society is more difficult under less developed conditions, and that a direct relationship exists between socioeconomic development and the ability of the state to exercise total control (e.g., Friedrich and Brzezinski 1961, 11–13). However, in the USSR the opposite appears to have been the case. During the postwar period, as noted throughout part 2, ethnodemographic and sociocultural processes often ran counter to the dictates of central planners,

---

[2] Brzezinski (1962) has defined totalitarianism as a forward-looking ideology for the institutionalization of revolution, and as such it can accommodate itself to, and actually is designed for, dynamic change. However, the issue of what happens after the revolution ends, and particularly how totalitarian regimes can cope with political countercurrents that begin to emerge in society, is not dealt with adequately even in this more dynamic depiction of the totalitarian model.

and as society developed, the totalitarian model became not more but less applicable.

The existence of a "society," indeed many societies, that influenced decision making at the center is not the only factor undermining the totalitarian model. The political and economic systems themselves underwent decentralization, which reduced the ability of the center to control the periphery. In the past, the decision-making process of "democratic centralism" may have emphasized "centralism" to the detriment of "democratic" inputs from below. However, as Soviet society became more developed and therefore more complex, it also became increasingly difficult to manage from the center. Political and economic decision-making authority (de facto if not de jure) increasingly devolved to local elites. In addition, despite the control that the center exercised over the political recruitment system (*nomenklatura*), studies of elite circulation have indicated that "the personnel system actually displayed remarkably little evidence that centralization influenced the movement of actors," and that "regionalism" proved to be "the decisive characteristic in the system of elite circulation" (Urban and Reed 1989, 417–418). Similarly, Breslauer (1986) found a process of growing local autonomy in the political system under Brezhnev. Remington (1985) also found that even in the area of public communications, which were in theory controlled from the center, the ethnoterritorial segmentation of communication channels tended to reinforce national identity. This political and economic devolution of decision-making authority gave additional content to the national-territorial structure, and made the federal system increasingly relevant in the political life of the state (Kaiser 1991). In this context at least, one can speak of the confederalization of the political system—and even of the Communist party—despite both the retention of centralized economic and political structures and the staunch opposition to any such confederalization of the Communist party by Soviet leaders from Lenin to Gorbachev (Connor 1984a; Gorbachev 1989, 44).

Since 1985 political organizations and quasi-parties have proliferated, the most successful of which have been the national fronts representing the interests of the indigenous nations. Begun as supporters of radical reform or *perestroyka*, the national movements quickly became more concerned with the rebirth of the indigenous nation and its control over the homeland than with restructuring the Soviet economy.[3] The new noncommunist, primarily nationalist parties and platforms did extremely well at the polls in the more advanced republics, and independence-oriented movements gained control in the Baltic republics,

---

[3] A number of the national front organizations that underwent this transition took names that signified their support for *perestroyka* at the outset. For example, *Sajudis*, the Lithuanian national independence movement, is Lithuanian for *perestroyka* and RUKH is a Ukrainian acronym standing for "The Popular Movement of Ukraine for Restructuring" (RUKH 1989). Similarly, the "Popular Front for the Support of Perestroyka" in Estonia became the "National Front," the organization most instrumental in the drive for Estonian independence (Taagepera 1989, 18).

Moldova, Georgia, and Armenia, while opposition "democrats" gained control in the RSFSR. Before its dissolution, the Communist party itself split in several republics, with an "orthodox" branch representing the interests of the center and a "nationalist" branch representing indigenous concerns. Even in republics where former Communist party members continue to control the presidency and the parliament, opposition national independence movements control a large number of seats in the legislature and, perhaps more important, are able to mobilize mass support in the streets.[4]

As the center-periphery relationship changed, indigenous political elites became more assertive of their self-proclaimed right to control their own nations' destinies (e.g., Beissinger 1988). This indigenous assertiveness preceded the reforms initiated by Gorbachev, as the numerous political purges for "nationalist deviations," "national exclusiveness," "localism," and so forth, demonstrate. Since 1985 national territoriality has become a much more overtly political strategy among indigenous elites. In the process the Soviet federation, in providing concrete form to the nationalistic imagery of an intimate connectivity between blood and soil and, perhaps more important, in providing a political geographic structure through which indigenes could act on their "sense of exclusiveness," itself served as a catalyst in the activation of national territoriality. Far from a transitory mechanism for resolving the national question, Soviet federalism became a means through which indigenous elites fulfilled their own national-territorial agendas.

In conclusion, the totalitarian model provides an overly simplistic depiction of the center-periphery and state-society relationships that evolved in the USSR over the course of its seventy-five-year history. Developed during the cold war in an effort to equate the new enemy (the USSR and communism) with the old (Nazi Germany and national socialism), and revived with the end of detente and the onset of a new cold war in the 1980s, totalitarianism tells us more about its proponents—past and present—than about the USSR.

Ironically, Gorbachev and his strongest supporters became the new advocates of totalitarianism during the late 1980s. The rise in international tensions and conflicts in the USSR were blamed on the Stalinist "deformation" of Marxism-Leninism, and particularly on the "command-administrative system" (e.g., Zotov 1989; Iskenderov 1989; Gorbachev 1989; Kuznetsov 1990). These criticisms of the Soviet Union's totalitarian past were used to justify the need for systemic reform (i.e., *perestroyka*) without a fundamental rejection of Marxist-Leninist ideology. As an example of this, in debates concerning the Union Treaty several authors and political elites took the position that nothing was wrong with the 1922 Union Treaty except that it was never implemented by

---

[4] Ironically, the place where the rise in national separatist movements was relatively muted was Central Asia, the region most often cited by Western analysts in the 1970s and early 1980s as the place most likely to rise against the center and secede from the USSR (e.g., Carrere d'Encausse 1978; Bennigsen 1986). This issue is discussed in detail below.

Stalin and subsequent Soviet leaders, who were more interested in amassing power at the center than in solving the national problem (e.g., Atamanchuk 1990; Nishanov 1990; Kudryatsev and Topornin 1990). Advocates of more radical change, including the nationalist elites, have also used the totalitarian model to depict the errors of the past and present. However, in this case totalitarianism is seen not only in Stalin's "deformation" of Marxism-Leninism but in the very nature of the system that Lenin initiated. Again, the varying uses to which the totalitarian model is being put tell us more about the current political climate in the successor states and the alternative visions of their future than it does about the USSR.

Economic Decentralization and the Problem of Regional Autarchy

The desirability of economic decentralization was a major subject of debate throughout the postwar period, as policymakers sought the ideal balance between the vertical ministerial and the horizontal territorial organization of the economy. As the economy grew more complex, control from the top became less and less feasible, and decision-making authority devolved to enterprise managers, as well as to political and governmental elites in localities and republics. Under Khrushchev, this de facto economic decentralization was accompanied by a radical reorganization of the economic decision-making apparatus from the vertical ministerial system to a horizontal territorial structure (i.e., the *sovnarkhozy* system). However, it soon became apparent that the problems of ministerial autarchy or "departmentalism" were quickly replaced by regional autarchy or "localism" under the new horizontal system. Under Brezhnev, a reversal in favor of the ministerial structure occurred, as the center attempted to find a balance between territorial and ministerial structures. A return to a more decentralized, territorial system of economic accountability (i.e., regional *khozraschet*) was begun under Gorbachev. Once again, economic decentralization coincided with rising regional autarchy, as indigenous nationalists pressed for greater economic sovereignty in their homelands. This section examines the relationship between economic decentralization and regional autarchy, in an effort to assess both the influence of national territoriality and political indigenization on economic processes, and also the prospects for and limitations on the formation of a new economic community.

The Sovnarkhozy *Experiment*

Decentralization of decision-making authority, especially in the economic sector, was a major part of the de-Stalinization program initiated under Khrushchev. Local soviets were activated, and the Supreme Soviet along with the so-called agencies of public self-management were revitalized in an effort to increase public "involvement and participation in the political process" (Fainsod 1965, 126). Khrushchev, like Gorbachev after 1987, appeared convinced that a loyal "Soviet People" existed and could be mobilized. Potentially the most far-reaching reform initiated under Khrushchev came in May 1957, when the vertical ministerial structure of the economy was replaced with a horizontal territorial system of 105 regional economic councils, or *sovnarkhozy*. For the most part, the *sovnarkhozy* used existing oblast, autonomous republic, and union republic boundaries. There were 70 in the RSFSR, 11 in Ukraine, 9 in Kazakhstan, 4 in Uzbekistan, and 1 for each of the other eleven union republics (Nove 1969, 97).

The ostensible purpose for the abolition of economic ministries and the creation of the *sovnarkhozy* was to put an end to ministerial autarchy or departmentalism, the tendency of each economic ministry to attempt to control all inputs needed for its own plan fulfillment, which had resulted in gross economic inefficiencies. In addition, there was "a recognition of the increasing complexity of the Soviet economy and its decision making processes" which could not be adequately handled at the center (Fainsod 1965, 126). It was also true that the strongest opposition to Khrushchev came from the central ministries, and undermining their positions to secure his own was no doubt an important factor in the decision to replace a vertical with a horizontal economic system. With the creation of the *sovnarkhozy* and the devolution of economic decision making to them, thousands of bureaucrats were transferred from Moscow to the new economic regions (Medvedev and Medvedev 1978, 83).

Almost immediately, problems arose with the new structure. Ministerial autarchy or departmentalism was replaced by territorial autarchy or localism (*mestnichestvo*), as elites in each *sovnarkhoz* attempted to use the resources at their command to satisfy the needs of their own industries and population. The reforms themselves encouraged local autarchy, because the *sovnarkhozy* continued to operate in a centrally planned environment but now lacked information about the needs of the other 104 economic regions (Nove 1969, 360). Under these conditions, the only goal that planners in each *sovnarkhoz* could fulfill was to meet their own region's needs. In addition to this systemic confusion, economic indigenization was also undoubtedly behind the rise in localism. First, many of the local economic regions, within which autarchic tendencies were displayed, were national homelands; the use of federal borders in creating the *sovnarkhozy* enhanced the likelihood that economic decentralization would coincide with rising pressures for indigenization. Second, an indigenization of political and economic elites was occurring at the same time, and increasingly it was these socially mobilized indigenes who were making the local decisions. For example, localized control of the Estonian economy, reaching 98.5 percent of all industrial output by 1959, coincided with an "Estonianization of leading party and government posts" (Raun 1987, 193–198). A similar "Georgianization" of political elites was occurring in Georgia along with the transfer of almost all economic enterprises from the center to the republic during the Khrushchev era (Suny 1989, 301–302, 314). The localism evident in the Estonian and Georgian *sovnarkhozy* and other national-territorial economic regions appeared to be largely the work of nationalist elites seeking to bring about an economic indigenization in their home republics.

Additional circumstantial evidence supports the conclusion that *mestnichestvo* was actually economic indigenization. The reorganization of *sovnarkhozy* in 1962 combined the three Baltic republics, the four Central Asian republics, and the three Transcaucasian republics into one *sovnarkhoz* each, destroying the national territorial basis of the regional economic councils that had coincided with rising economic autarchy, and at the same time introducing an international element of competition within each new *sovnarkhoz*. In addition, a Russian was placed in charge of the Central Asian *sovnarkhoz* (Nove 1969, 361). More generally, Khrushchev had relied on the centralized Communist party to guarantee against the threat of rising regional autarchy with decentralization. However, it is apparent that local party officials acted in the interests of their localities rather than in the interests of the center. The reorganization into forty-two *sovnarkhozy* in 1962 did not correspond with the regional divisions of the party, leading Nove (1969, 362) to conclude that "Khrushchev seems to have feared party officials' collusion in 'localism.' " Indigenous elites were also purged in several of the union republics between 1959 and 1963 for nationalist deviations (Hodnett 1967b, 458).

The emergence of economic indigenization with decentralization clearly contradicted the statement made in the 1961 party program that the boundaries of the republics were losing their former significance, and the statement itself may have been a signal that the experimental decentralization of decision-making authority to indigenous nationalists in homelands had failed.[5] From this point forward, a recentralization of the economic decision-making structure occurred, with the restoration of the vertical ministerial structure in 1965. However, while de jure economic decentralization was more limited during the Brezhnev era than it had been under the *sovnarkhozy* system, decision-making authority devolved de facto to enterprise managers and local political elites. In turn, these local elites were increasingly comprised of socially mobilized indigenes, chosen not according to the dictates of a centrally orchestrated *nomenklatura* system but rather through a selection procedure increasingly dominated by "regionalism" (e.g., Urban and Reed 1989; Breslauer 1986). The economic recentralization during the Brezhnev era was also limited from above, as the center attempted to combine territorial and ministerial approaches to overcome autarchic problems inherent in each (Gleason 1990a, 70). Overall, although

[5] Similarly, the center's shift in favor of artificially accelerating the pace of the unification of nations into one Soviet people at this time may be seen as an admission that the voluntary "drawing together" (*sblizheniye*) and "merger" (*sliyaniye*) were not occurring as "natural" by-products of the socialistic development of Soviet society (Connor 1984a).

economic decentralization was not a linear process throughout the postwar period, the decision-making authority of indigenous elites increased during the post-Stalin period, and this decentralization to indigenes in homelands increased the pressure from below for ever greater economic and political indigenization.

Republic Khozraschet *and Economic Sovereignty*

Under Gorbachev, the decentralization of economic decision-making authority to enterprise managers and to local and republic elites was again attempted. Regional *khozraschet* (economic self-management) was first sanctioned in the Baltic republics, Belarus', Tatarstan, Sverdlovsk, and Moscow on an experimental basis in 1989 (Schroeder 1990, 62–63). The similarities between this program and the one initiated by Khrushchev were not accidental. Proponents of republican *khozraschet* even used the *sovnarkhozy* system as a model for economic reform in the USSR (Lapidus 1989, 220). The *sovnarkhozy* system was seen by a number of Soviet economists and economic geographers as the most appropriate means of decentralizing the economy and ending the control of the ministries (Khorev 1990, 510):

> The problem of economic decentralization must be solved for the country as a whole, and it seems that we all must reflect on the most effective way to smash the omnipotence of the departments (and departmental bureaucracy along with it). In the author's opinion, there is no more effective way to do this than to switch to the path of regional comprehensive organization of socialist economics, the basis for which must be a scientifically grounded economic regionalization of the country, and a network of regional economic councils (*sovnarkhozy*), *khozraschetnyy* associations, and syndicates. . . . It has been convincingly demonstrated in recent economic studies that the USSR's economy was most efficient precisely during the time of the *sovnarkhozy*.

The consequences of this program of economic decentralization were also similar to those of the *sovnarkhozy* system. In the Baltic republics in particular, regional *khozraschet* was interpreted by nationalist elites to mean indigenous control over all economic production in the republic (i.e., economic indigenization). This was an element of *perestroyka* with which Soviet economists were totally unprepared to deal (Andreyev 1989, 60). Republican *khozraschet* gave way to declarations of economic sovereignty in numerous union and autonomous republics, despite the warning from Gorbachev at the Nineteenth Communist Party Conference in June 1988 that "any striving for national exclusiveness can lead only to economic and spiritual impoverishment" (Gorbachev 1988b, 61), and the more threatening statement made at the September 1989 Communist Party Plenum held to discuss the growing national problems facing the country (Gorbachev 1989, 30) that: "In the present circumstances, a tendency toward autarchy, an attempt by relatively prosperous republics and oblasts to isolate themselves, to fence themselves off from others, would be extraordinarily dangerous. This can only lead to very negative consequences for those who would start on such a course."

Indigenous elites increasingly claimed the right to control investment allocations from the center, to tax and spend at the republic level, and to control the utilization of the natural resources of their homelands. Indigenous elites also attempted to establish economic borders to regulate the flow of goods, to pass immigration laws to regulate the flow of people, and to gain control over financial institutions in their respective homelands (e.g., Schroeder 1991, 11). Republic elites also increasingly asserted their right to control the amount of funding collected by the center, as well as the number of economic functions controlled by central authorities. Although limits on economic sovereignty were still felt in even the most independent republics in 1989 (Dienes 1989, 260), the decentralization of the Soviet economy since 1985 had clearly outpaced anything that had been attempted before, including the *sovnarkhozy* experiment, and it was increasingly being fueled from below, not from above. That is, indigenous nationalists seeking to gain greater control over the economic resources of the homeland in order to help secure the future or destiny of the nation were successful in seizing the opportunities presented by *perestroyka* in order to reorient the reform program begun at the center toward the goals of achieving economic sovereignty in the periphery.

The concern over this economic indigenization was clearly evident in the work of Soviet economic geographers who favored decentralization, but not to the level of nations in homelands. As Khorev (1990, 513) asserted, "the very idea of republic *khozraschet* is based on a distorted principle: to divide the economy of a unified country not from an economic, but from a national-territorial criterion." Similarly, in response to an article supportive of greater economic and political sovereignty for nations in their home republics (Koroteyeva et al. 1988), Cheshko (1989, 98–99) argued that republic *khozraschet* was not the optimal path to *perestroyka*, since republics were not economically rational units, and since the demand for economic decentralization to republics was based not on economics but on a nationalistic desire to gain economic sovereignty.

Economic decentralization to indigenes seeking greater control over their own homelands can result in extreme "distortions." This was clearly evident in Yugoslavia, where decentralization without "destatization" (i.e., depoliticization) left nationalist elites in charge of economic decision making in their home republics. Each republic began to allocate economic resources for the construction of steel plants, oil refineries, and other enterprises that were not economically rational but were politically rational in the sense that most sovereign states in the world consider it vital to have an indigenous supply of such strategic materials (Kaiser 1990).

These autarchic tendencies to place economics in the service of ethnopolitical objectives are clearly in evidence in the successor states. The use of similar politically rational objectives (i.e., greater independence) in economic decision making can be expected to increase, and a number of economic analysts have already warned that decentralization without "destatization" is resulting in rising economic inefficiency as nationalists seek greater economic autarchy (e.g., Bronshteyn 1989; Granberg 1990; Cheshko 1989). The most worrisome trend for the central authorities in late 1991 was the increasing number of republics that had placed a ban on all exports. A "trade war" began between Ukraine, which refused to export agricultural commodities, and the RSFSR, which cut off fuel exports to Ukraine in retaliation (Kaslow 1991). The economic indigenization fueling these autarchic tendencies undermines the political goodwill necessary to construct a new economic agreement uniting the former union republics, even while it increases the urgency for such an economic "union treaty." The goal of economic sovereignty for nations in their homelands may even subvert other objectives currently espoused by indigenous nationalists. For example, the shale oil mining operations in Estonia and the Ignalina nuclear power plant in Lithuania were opposed by nationalists before independence as centrally controlled enterprises that pollute the homeland and endanger the survival of the nation. However, because the electricity generated by these enterprises reduces their dependency on Russian oil and gas, it is quite conceivable that these plants will continue to operate and may even be expanded in politically independent Estonia and Lithuania.

Not all nations pressured Moscow for the decentralization of economic decision making with equal vigor. The goal of economic sovereignty was most forcefully pursued in the Baltic republics, especially in Estonia and Latvia, and this was related to the perception held by indigenous nationalists throughout the region that they were held back by their association with the USSR (e.g., Smulders 1990; Girnius 1991). This perception was based not on their economic standing in the USSR, which by all accounts must be ranked at or near the most developed, but rather on a comparison with states to their west, and particularly to Finland which, like the Baltic republics, was also part of the Russian Empire that gained its independence at the time of the October Revolution but that retained its independence following World War II (e.g., Bond and Sagers 1990; McAuley 1991a). The Baltic nationalists, especially the Finnic Estonians, argued that they were as advanced as Finland during the interwar period when they were independent, and would have become at least as developed as Finland if they had retained their sovereignty. Implicit or explicit in this argument was the idea that they will become as developed as Finland once again with independence (e.g., Taagepera 1989).

The use of Finland's economic development as the basis for their demand for economic sovereignty tended to negate data which showed that the Baltic republics received more than they contributed to the Soviet economy (e.g., Granberg 1990; Schroeder 1991, 10–11; Bond and Sagers 1990, 10).[6] Except for Soviet Central Asia, the Baltic republics were the most economically dependent region in the country (Table 7.1). In 1988 all three consumed more than they produced and incurred both a domestic and foreign trade deficit. Again, except for Soviet Central Asia, the Baltic republics had the highest potential debt burden, which was more than a quarter of national income produced (NIP) in Lithuania and more than a third of NIP in Estonia. Nonetheless, the reality of economic dependency on the rest of the USSR did not dampen the pressure for economic and political sovereignty in the Baltic republics, although the need for continued economic relations with the republics to the east has been acknowledged by political elites in all three of the newly independent Baltic states.

At the other end of the spectrum, the indigenous elites of Central Asia continued to favor a relatively strong central role in economic decision making. This stance was not surprising, given the underdeveloped nature of this region's economy and its reliance on the center to redistribute wealth from the other republics to Central Asia. Like the Baltic republics, all Central Asian republics consumed more than they produced and ran both a domestic and foreign trade deficit in 1988. Except for Turkmenistan, the potential debt burden of these republics was the highest in the USSR, ranging from nearly a quarter of NIP in Uzbekistan to almost half of NIP in Kazakhstan. These republics were still being heavily subsidized by the center as of 1989 (Granberg 1990, 46–50).

Unlike the relatively developed Baltic republics, these high economic dependency figures for Central Asia coincide with low levels of socioeconomic development and declining living standards. This excessive dependency on the center had not resulted in a reorientation of investments toward Central Asian development, and if anything just the opposite occurred after 1985. The main focus of *perestroyka* was to invest in the revitalization of the industrial northwest, and to curtail expenditures on high profile, big budget items, as well as to reorient investment even more in the direction of "efficiency" and away from "equality" (Liebowitz 1991). For Central Asia, this has resulted in a rapid deterioration of economic and living conditions, with the river diversion scheme shelved and the Aral Sea problem becoming more serious, and unemployment and underemployment growing to nearly two million by 1990 (Gleason 1990b).[7] Resentment toward the center, and toward the dominant Russians living in the region, has accompanied the rise in economic problems

---

[6] It also reversed the traditional meaning of "Finlandization," since Finland now stood as a half-way house to complete independence for union republics within the USSR, rather than as an intermediate stage in the process through which the USSR was drawing formerly independent states into its orbit. The idea of Finlandization always had serious problems. For a discussion of this, see Liebowitz (1983).

[7] For a debate of the unemployment figures, see Osipov (1990) and Sagdullaev (1990).

TABLE 7.1
National Income and Trade Balances, and Potential Debt Burden,[a] 1988 (million rubles)

Republic	National Income			Trade Balance			World Prices	Potential Debt (%)
	Produced	Consumed	Balance	Domestic	Foreign	Total		
RSFSR	385,400	375,895	9,505	260	−33,588	−33,328	30,800	6.2
Ukraine	102,500	97,330	5,170	3,623	−6,551	−2,928	−2,900	0
Belarus'	26,200	23,800	2,400	4,050	−1,977	2,073	−2,100	0
Moldova	7,700	8,118	−418	−186	−837	−1,023	−2,600	18.7
Uzbekistan	20,700	23,800	−3,100	−1,667	−174	−1,841	−2,500	23.9
Kazakhstan	26,900	32,497	−5,597	−5,349	−1,906	−7,255	−6,600	47.8
Kyrgyzstan	5,000	5,998	−998	−435	−714	−1,149	−1,100	42.9
Tadzhikistan	5,000	5,680	−680	−997	−136	−1,133	−1,100	36.3
Turkmenistan	4,700	4,846	−146	−97	−187	−284	0	9.1
Georgia	10,200	9,962	238	290	−882	−592	−1,900	3.5
Azerbaydzhan	10,900	9,228	1,672	2,099	−990	1,109	−500	0
Armenia	5,800	5,105	695	−335	−775	−1,110	−1,400	7.2
Lithuania	8,900	9,812	−912	−808	−722	−1,530	−3,700	27.4
Latvia	7,000	7,478	−478	−118	−578	−696	−1,300	16.8
Estonia	4,100	4,628	−528	−332	−416	−748	−1,300	31.1

Source: Belkindas and Sagers 1990.
Notes: National income balance equals national income produced minus national income used. Negative national income balances amount to subsidies transferred from republics with positive national income balances.
Trade balances equal exports minus imports. "Domestic trade" refers to trade balances between union republics; "foreign" refers to interstate trade balances. "World prices" for trade balances were calculated using "conversion coefficients (ratios of domestic to foreign prices) for highly aggregated commodity groups," which can result in "major distortions" (Belkindas and Sagers 1990, 650).
Of course, since the prices for goods produced, consumed, and traded do not accurately reflect market conditions, it is difficult to draw firm conclusions based on these data.
For a time series analysis of "National Income Produced" and "National Income Consumed," see Bond et al. (1990, 1991).
[a]The "Potential Debt Burden" was calculated from data presented in the table. It is the sum of national income "deficit" (negative national income balance) and trade "deficit" (negative total trade balance) taken as a percentage of national income produced. Those republics with 0 figures had net surpluses for 1988.

associated with dependence on the center. With the collapse of the centralized planned economy, the economic situation in Central Asia almost certainly will worsen. This is likely to result in more frequent displays of the kind of anti-outsider nativism discussed in chapter 4. However, "reactive ethnicity" had not resulted in a growing sentiment for complete independence by the August 1991 coup. Indeed, the pressure for giving Central Asia its independence appeared to be greater outside the region. Central Asian independence was advocated by Russian nationalists (e.g., Solzhenitsyn 1990, 2), though they had done so for sociocultural, not economic reasons. Leaders of the more developed republics, including Russia, have also expressed little interest in continuing to subsidize Central Asia in the current political and economic climate. Central Asia is unlikely to receive much in the way of assistance from the new "Commonwealth of Independent States."

Except for Moldova, which also has a relatively high potential debt burden and is relatively underdeveloped, the remaining union republics (i.e., the three Slavic republics and Transcaucasia) produced more than they consumed, and except for Armenia all six had a positive domestic trade balance in 1988 (Table 7.1). Ukraine, Belarus', and Azerbaydzhan had production and trade surpluses, and Russia, Georgia, and Armenia had manageable debt burdens resulting from foreign trade deficits. Using world prices for trade, however, only Russia had a positive trade balance (Belkindas and Sagers 1990, 650).

Overall, comparing these economic indicators with the republics that were farthest along the road of independence provides convincing evidence that the declarations of economic and political sovereignty are not closely related to economic conditions. The Baltic states, Moldova, Georgia, and Armenia all face potential debt burdens, and for the Baltics and Moldova the level of debts are likely to threaten the domestic living standards of indigenes as well as nonindigenes. Belarus', Ukraine, Azerbaydzhan, and Russia have been relatively more favorably disposed toward continued participation in a renewed political confederation and an interrepublic economic community, even though their domestic economies appear relatively stronger than those that favored greater economic independence.

Within Russia, political elites in a number of autonomous units and nonautonomous oblasts have also declared their economic sovereignty. These declarations, including those made by the elites of nonautonomous oblasts that their territories comprise "free economic zones," have been made for a variety of reasons ranging from a desire for economic indigenization by non-Russians to the demand that extraction and profits from natural resources found in the nonautonomous oblasts be controlled by the local Russian population. This localist form of territoriality has become an internally divisive issue for the Russian nation, and may be cited as indirect evidence of a weakly developed "sense of homeland" and perhaps even a sign of limited national consolidation among members of the dominant nation, who have lived in specific localities far removed from the core for generations. Rising Russian localism appears to support the contention that "Russians remain an ethnically underdeveloped people in the twentieth century" (Allworth 1980, 34). In several autonomous units of Russia, where Russians are an overwhelming majority of the population, the demand for greater economic independence undoubtedly combines non-Russian indigenous national territoriality with Russian local territoriality. Should nationalism increase among Russians in these non-Russian localities—a reasonable expectation given the rising displays of nationalism in the country as a whole and the loss of dominant status by Russians in the non-Russian periphery, including the autonomous regions within Russia—this could result in growing Russian pressure for economic and political recentralization.

Conclusion

Economic reform efforts during the postwar period involved two major attempts to decentralize economic decision making, the *sovnarkhozy* system of the Khrushchev era and regional *khozraschet* under Gorbachev. Each of these decentralization efforts sparked almost immediate attempts on the part of indigenes to gain control over the economy of the homeland for the good of the indigenous nation, not of the USSR. In the first case, this led to a recentralization under Brezhnev, although enterprise managers retained greater decision-making authority, and republic elites gained greater say over economic activities on their territory over time. This occurred along with an indigenization of economic and political elites, and attempts to bring about economic indigenization in the union republics was evident even during this period of relatively high centralization. With the economic reforms under Gorbachev, indigenes pressed ever more forcefully for economic sovereignty in their homelands. Among Russians in the RSFSR, localism at the oblast level has also become apparent, indicating a relatively weak national self-consciousness and "sense of homeland" within the dominant nation. Rising national self-consciousness among the Russians is likely, and should lead to a recentralization of economic control in the nonautonomous oblasts of the RSFSR, and rising conflict in the autonomous regions between non-Russian indigenes seeking greater economic indigenization and Russian nationalists both locally and in the new Russian center.

Unlike the situation in the 1960s, the central authorities in the late 1980s were not able to carry out an economic recentralization like the one implemented under Brezhnev. Perhaps the most important reason for this was the greater degree of nationalism evident in the movement toward greater economic sovereignty at the end of the 1980s. Economic indigenization was part of the pressure from below by nationalistic indigenous elites for greater control over their own lives in their own homelands, or national territoriality, rather than an isolated consequence of economic decentralization from above. Efforts by central authorities to recentralize the economy encountered strong resistance from below, exacerbating political tensions between center and periphery.

A high degree of economic interdependence existed among the republics in the USSR. However, this economic interdependence did not necessarily inhibit indigenes in their drive for greater political independence. After all, national territoriality is not about economic well-being, even though nationalists often mythologize the past as a golden age and project this onto an independent future (Connor 1984b). The issue of "economic viability" in the determination of which nations should become independent and which should not may be a factor in discussions by outsiders but has not discouraged indigenes themselves from seeking political independence. Indeed, in an increasingly global economy, no state is "economically viable" by itself, and the recognition of smaller and smaller entities as states by the world political community provides strong counterarguments for nationalists intent on secession. Furthermore, while arguing in favor of greater political independence, most nationalists in the Baltic republics and elsewhere recognize that they will retain economic ties with the rest of the former USSR for the foreseeable future. That is, an attempt is being made to separate political sovereignty for the nation over its homeland from economic interdependence with the successor states and the rest of the world economy.[8]

Since 1989 bilateral trade agreements have been concluded between most of the former union republics (Schroeder 1991).[9] These arrangements served as an alternative way to retain economic linkages with the rest of the state, while bypassing the old center in favor of direct agreements between the republics. The "Commonwealth of Independent States" (CIS) that was established at the end of 1991 provides a potential alternative interstate mechanism for economic coordination between these economically interdependent states. However, in the current nationalistic climate, it appears unlikely that the CIS will serve as anything more than a halfway house between the USSR and the economic integration of the Soviet successor states into the capitalist world economy.

POLITICAL INDIGENIZATION AND THE DISSOLUTION OF THE USSR

As stated in the introduction to this work, national territoriality is a political strategy through which nationalists seek to gain control over the future of the nation by asserting control over the national homeland. While national territoriality was clearly in evidence throughout the postwar period, political indigenization was limited primarily to the indigenization of political elites in the national homelands. As discussed above, decision-making authority was devolving to indigenous elites in homelands for much of the postwar period. However, political power continued to be highly centralized in the country, and this unitary essence of center-republic political relations restricted the degree to which indigenes politically controlled their national homelands. After 1985, the indigenization process became much more overtly political, as nationalists pressed ever more forcefully for independence from the centralized political power structure. After the failed coup attempt in August 1991, this nationalistic dream of independence was realized, at least for those nations whose homelands were union republics. This final dimension of the indigenization process resulted in the disintegration of the state along national territorial lines.

In addition to political independence, ethnoterritorial conflicts over the geographic extent of homelands have proliferated, as neighboring indigenes seek to

---

[8] This attempt to separate political and economic sovereignty is very much in line with the structure of the contemporary world system, within which an increasingly global economy coincides with the proliferation of independent states.

[9] A large number of bilateral trade agreements and political treaties were signed between November 1990 and January 1991, at a time when central authorities moved to the "Right."

redraw the boundaries of their national territory to conform more closely either with the contemporary geographic extent of the national community or with the historical and mythological image of the "primordial" homeland. These conflicts, which occurred at a lower level of intensity throughout the Soviet period, arose to become a dominant response to the call for radical reform emanating from Moscow. These conflicts were in general localized, and therefore were not necessarily life-threatening to the future of the state.[10] However, the center's inability to manage these conflicts resulted in the further radicalization of national territorial movements, as occurred in Armenia and Moldova. Since the end of 1991 ethnoterritorial conflicts have proliferated, engulfing several of the successor states in violent confrontation with nonindigenes and indigenous minorities.

Soviet Federalism and the Drive for Independence

All states can be located somewhere along a unitary-confederal continuum according to the relative degree of political power held and exercised by central authorities on the one hand, and peripheral elites on the other. In unitary states political power is more highly centralized; national elites in homelands may be given some degree of political autonomy but are ultimately under the control of central authorities. A totalitarian state would represent the most extreme version of a unitary state, since all political power is said to be concentrated in the center and at the top of a hierarchical power structure, resulting in "total control" by ruling elites or a single all-powerful leader. Federated systems generally refer to states with political power roughly balanced between central authorities and political elites of first-order administrative units (e.g., states in the United States; union republics in the USSR), and therefore occupy the middle range of the unitary-confederal continuum. At the confederal end of this continuum, political power is held by the first-order administrative units. A central government exists and normally has some autonomous decision-making authority over a narrow range of policy issues of statewide concern, but its structure and functions are ultimately controlled by the states or republics of the system.

Confederations have been notoriously unstable in the past, and have often disintegrated into numerous national states. Beyond the confederal end of the continuum lies secession and the establishment of politically independent "nation-states," toward which nationalist elites most often aspire. This is, after

---

[10] The one possible exception to the localized nature of border conflicts is the Russian nation and the "mental map" of Mother Russia that Russian nationalists have. As discussed below, surveys indicate that for a majority of Russians inside and out of the RSFSR, homeland is defined as the entire territory of the former USSR. See also Connor (1986). Delimiting the homeland in this way clearly brings Russian claims to territory into direct conflict with all other nations whose members have declared independence from their respective homelands.

all, the ultimate objective of national territoriality. The degree of actual independence, of course, may be tempered by the participation of these sovereign nation-states in economic communities, political/military alliances, and so forth. The newly independent states in turn may adopt internal political power structures ranging from highly unitary to confederal.

According to both the original 1922 Union Treaty creating the USSR and subsequent Soviet constitutions, the union republics were voluntary participants in a confederation of sovereign states. Each of the fifteen union republics retained a number of rights which were said to guarantee their sovereign status, including their own constitutions, flags and anthems, the right to enter into foreign relations, to coin money and, perhaps most important, the right to self-determination, up to and including secession. However, although these constitutionally guaranteed rights were of symbolic importance for both the center and the republics, they were of limited utility in the day-to-day political lives of indigenes in union republics. The reality of political power relations between central authorities and "peripheral" indigenous elites throughout much of Soviet history may be described as confederal in form but unitary (though not totalitarian) in essence. This is one way of defining "Soviet federalism" (Kaiser 1991).

This is not to suggest that the Soviet Union's position along the unitary-confederal continuum remained static. Over time, the center exerted greater or lesser pressure to eliminate the confederal forms, while peripheral elites pressed for greater confederalization. According to the evidence presented throughout part 2 of this work, the idea that nationality policies crafted at the center had eliminated or were in the process of eliminating the demand by members of nations for political control over their own homelands is not supported. To the contrary, as the USSR developed, national consolidation and indigenization were underlying processes tending to increase the demand from below for a real confederalization of the state. During the postwar period, decentralization of decision-making authority, along with the indigenization of political elites in national homelands, resulted in a confederalization in center-periphery relations. After 1985, when the reform program provided a conducive environment for national territoriality to become overtly political, the indigenous pressure for political decentralization grew exponentially.

THE DEBATE OVER SOVIET FEDERALISM

Throughout the postwar period, the status of federalism in the USSR was the subject of nearly continuous debate (Hodnett 1967b; Lapidus 1984, 1989; Connor 1984a; Gleason 1990a; Remington 1985; Rajabov 1978; McAuley 1991; Kux 1990; Ebzeyeva 1982). The focus of this debate centered on the question of the transitory nature of the federal structure and on whether it had achieved the goals set for it during its creation. Chief among these political objectives was "solving the national problem" of social, economic, cultural, and political inequality inherited from tsarist Russia. As discussed in chapter 3, by equalizing the politico-juridical standing of nations in the state, Soviet federalism was to facilitate all-round international equalization. In the postwar period, international equalization became the main criterion with which to assess whether Soviet federalism had served its purpose and whether it could therefore be phased out.[11] Already by 1961, the Communist party program declared that the federal system was in the process of losing its raison d'être, since international equality had been achieved and the unification of the multinational population into "one family" had commenced (*Programma KPSS* 1961, 84). However, as noted above, this statement was clearly contradicted by the strong tendency toward economic autarchy by indigenous elites within their home republics, which occurred during the *sovnarkhozy* experiment between 1957 and 1964. While the proclamation in the 1961 party program may have reflected the view from the center of what should be, it was not an accurate statement of what international relations looked like from the periphery. The borders of national homelands had lost none of their former significance and, if anything, had become more important to the increasingly nationalized masses over time. The necessity of recentralizing the economic decision-making apparatus beginning in 1962 gives the 1961 proclamation a particularly hollow ring.

Despite this indication of Soviet federalism's failure to fulfill its mission and harmonize international relations, debates over the need for confederal forms continued throughout the 1960s and 1970s in preparation for the new constitution. Advocates of dismantling the confederal structure of the state continued to argue that Soviet federalism had outlived its usefulness, that is, that international equality and the drawing together of nations into one Soviet people had made it an anachronism at the stage of "developed socialism" (Hodnett 1967b, 462–468; Gleason 1990a, 66–72). Proponents of the continued need for the federation argued primarily that the republics were needed to guarantee international equality in the future, and thus assist in the further drawing together of nations (Hodnett 1967b, 478–479). Brezhnev himself proclaimed that the national problem inherited from the past (i.e., inequality between peoples) had been solved, but he equivocated on the implications that this had for the future of Soviet federalism. The formula used by Brezhnev was that even though the major national problem of inequality had been solved, more localized international tensions and conflicts would continue to arise as peoples interacted with one another. Soviet federalism continued to perform a role in helping to over-

---

[11] The importance of the equalization question is attested to not only by the attention of Soviet scholars and politicians but also by the numerous studies of the "equalization hypothesis" conducted in the West (e.g., Silver 1974a; Bahry and Nechemias 1981; Jones and Grupp 1984; Liebowitz 1987, 1991). Yet for all the attention paid to the equalization question, no definitive answer emerged as to whether or not international equality had been achieved. Furthermore, these studies did not address the more fundamental issue of whether or not equalization alone would solve the national problem. See chapter 5 for a detailed discussion of these issues.

come these more localized national problems (Gleason 1990a, 76; Ebzeyeva 1982, 5–7; Lapidus 1989, 212). Political theorists, such as Lepeshkin during the mid-1970s and Ebzeyeva in the early 1980s, as well as political leaders from Andropov to Gorbachev, adopted a similar approach to Soviet federalism, accepting its transitory nature but arguing in favor of its retention until the USSR—and for some the world as a whole—made the transformation from socialism to communism (Lepeshkin 1975; Ebzeyeva 1982; Gleason 1990a, 70–73). Because, in theory at least, a communist society would require neither a political party nor a government, this formulation implied that so long as a political superstructure was necessary, that structure would need to be confederal in form.

Given this official middle-of-the-road position regarding the debate over Soviet federalism, it is not surprising that the 1977 Constitution was finally adopted with virtually no change in the federal aspects of the state's structure. The preamble to the 1977 Constitution contains the statement that "a new historical community of people—the Soviet people—has come into being on the basis of the drawing together of all classes and social strata and the juridical and actual equality of all nations and nationalities and their fraternal cooperation" (CDSP 9 November 1977, 1). This seemed to signify that the need for Soviet federalism had greatly diminished if not completely disappeared. Nonetheless, the confederal structure was retained virtually in its entirety, including the right of union republics to secede. Two limitations were placed on the confederal nature of the Soviet state in 1977: the right of the union republics to their own military units, which was part of the 1936 Constitution, was not re-established in 1977; and the right to education in one's native language was also reduced to the "opportunity for school instruction in one's native tongue" (Connor 1984a, 402; CDSP 9 November 1977; Constitution 1976). In addition, central authorities were allocated the right to coordinate the foreign relations of the union republics, and this represented a limitation on the right of union republics to enter directly into foreign relations with other states (CDSP 9 November 1977, 7). Yet, the retention of the confederal structure itself, based on the voluntary union of sovereign republics that retained the right to self-determination up to and including secession, was a clear sign that "Soviet federalism" had not outlived its usefulness.

The need for retaining the confederal structure in the new constitution was an indication that the creation of a new Soviet people was more myth than reality, and indeed that pressures for political indigenization from below were having an impact on decision making at the center. Even minor attempts to remove articles favoring the indigenous nation in the republic constitutions resulted in nationalistic eruptions. The clearest example of this came in 1978, when a draft version of the new Georgian Constitution was released without a previously included statement that Georgian was the official language of the republic. This draft provoked massive demonstrations in Tbilisi and throughout the Georgian regions of the republic, finally ending in the restoration of the indigenous language clause by the central authorities in Moscow (Suny 1989, 309). Draft constitutions removing a similar language clause for Armenia and Azerbaydzhan were also rewritten in 1978 in order to restore the legal primacy of the indigenous languages in those two republics (Connor 1984a, 263). While the constitutional articles guaranteeing the sovereignty of the union republics—and by extension the indigenous nations—may have been mere form without substance, attempts by the center over time to restrict even these symbolic rights were met with more than token resistance.

The debate over sovietization and the need for confederal structures continued in the 1980s. The reforms initiated under Gorbachev seem to have been based on the existence of a Soviet people united by ideology, common economic interests, and common political objectives (Gorbachev 1986, 233). Unleashing the creative potential of this loyal citizenry through *glasnost'* and democratization was seen as the "decisive force" in the promotion of *perestroyka* that would allow the USSR to move forward out of the period of stagnation (*zastoy*) and toward a brighter communist future (Gorbachev 1986, 241; 1987b, 63).[12] This clearly did not occur. Rather than a Soviet people mobilized behind the goals of *perestroyka*, numerous nationally self-conscious communities became mobilized behind the goals of national separatism.

This nationalist reality placed the central authorities in an essentially reactive position from which they were unable to escape, while the pressure from below for a real confederalization of center-periphery relations increased exponentially (Kaiser 1991; Kux 1990). The center attempted to regain control over the pace of political decentralization, primarily through the enactment of a law on secession designed to impede the process of disintegration (*Pravda* 7 April 1990, 2; Goble 1990). When this proved ineffective, harsher measures, such as the use of economic blockades and the threat and actual use of military force, were attempted. These more extreme measures proved not only ineffective but counterproductive.

After 1990, central authorities also attempted to dictate the terms of the new relationship between center and periphery by drafting the new union treaty. Several versions of this document were published, each more confederal than its predecessor. Drafts of the new Union Treaty before the August 1991 coup reflected the confederal reality of political power relations in the USSR. The center was to retain primarily a coordinating function over issues of all-union concern, such as the economy, the environment, and foreign affairs. The union

---

[12] Gorbachev's convictions that a Soviet people existed and that most of the population felt themselves to be internationalists can be seen even as late as 1989. At the Communist Party Plenum held that year to discuss the national problems facing the state, Gorbachev (1989, 13) asserted: "We have grown up in a social atmosphere literally permeated with internationalism. Friendship of the peoples was not some kind of abstract slogan for us, but an everyday reality. Can we really forget that? Can we renounce the internationalist legacy of our revolution?"

republics, and consequently the indigenous elites in each union republic, were given control of their own political, economic, social, and cultural lives. However, a major point of contention throughout the 1990 and early 1991 negotiations was that the drafts of the new Union Treaty were being forged not by the political elites of each union republic but rather by the central authorities. Even though most of the power-sharing conditions in the drafts were acceptable, the center's control over the process was not. This dispute was finally resolved in April 1991 with the so-called 9+1 agreements, including the Slavic and Central Asian republics, Azerbaydzhan and the center. A Union Treaty binding these republics together in a confederated state was to be signed on 20 August 1991; the coup attempted on 19 August 1991 represented a desperate attempt by hard-liners at the center to avoid this confederalization and preserve the old union. However, because the Union Treaty only formalized what had already occurred in reality, the coup attempt was doomed to failure from the outset.

After the coup, the process of national separatism accelerated. The demise of the Communist party structure (though not necessarily the communist hard-liners in positions of power), the end to the Congress of Peoples Deputies, the reconstruction of the central government along confederal lines with a presidential council made up of Gorbachev and ten Union Republic Presidents (the nine republics noted above, plus Armenia), each with an equal voice, and a legislative council with an equal number of representatives from each of the ten union republics on the basis of "one nation, one vote" pluralism all reflected the new confederal reality. The Union Treaty that was to be signed before the coup was no longer confederal enough, and the process of negotiating inter-republic political and economic relations with the old center collapsed almost immediately.

The new Commonwealth of Independent States, created by Belarus', Ukraine, and Russia in December 1991 and joined almost immediately by all the former union republics except Georgia and the Baltic states, represented the culmination of these processes of decentralization and indigenization. The new center, to be located in Minsk away from the old center of power and the dominant Russian homeland, if it survives into the future, will remain extremely weak in the near future at least, performing an economic coordinating function and providing a centralized structure for the former Soviet military. Even these two functions have increasingly been called into question, with the shrinking of the ruble zone and the establishment of independent currencies in the successor states, and with the failure of Russia to gain support in the non-Russian members of the CIS for a unified military (Foye 1993). The CIS was modeled after the European Community and NATO, and is unlikely to become more than a loosely connected group of independent states in the near future. As it has turned out, Soviet federalism, far from a transitory necessity until complete unification was possible, was in reality a transitional stage on the road to national separatism and independence.

POLITICAL REPRESENTATION IN THE UNION REPUBLICS AND SUCCESSOR STATES

The question of whether members of the indigenous nation alone or the entire population of each republic should exercise this newfound political power has been at the forefront of debates since the late 1980s. The Soviet Constitution conferred "sovereign rights," including the right to secede from the USSR, to the union republics and not exclusively to members of the indigenous nations for whom the republics were named (i.e., Kazakhs in Kazakhstan, Uzbeks in Uzbekistan, Ukrainians in Ukraine, etc.). Technically, the "sovereignty" of the union republic was vested in the entire citizenry of the republic, regardless of the national identity of the individual. Yet, the right to self-determination has been proclaimed by indigenous elites as a *national* right, and the declarations of sovereignty made in 1990 were made first and foremost in the name of the indigenous nation, not of the multinational population resident in the republic. Almost all the union republic declarations are justified by the felt need to take "responsibility for the fate of the (indigenous-*RJK*) nation" (e.g., Turkmenistan: FBIS 12 September 1990, 107; Armenia: FBIS 27 August 1990b, 107; Belarus': *Argumenty i Fakty* 1990b, 1). These statements are an excellent example of an overtly displayed national territoriality on the part of indigenous political elites, in that they are seeking political sovereignty over their home republics in order to gain control over the "fate of the nation." The "equal rights" of the nonindigenous population were normally recognized in these texts, but the declarations clearly intended to make indigenes "first among equals" in the newly sovereign republics. This was true even in the case of Kazakhstan, which had about an equal number of Russians and Kazakhs at that time, although the opening clause in the declaration did also emphasize the desire to foster the "friendship of the peoples living in the republic" and only later spoke of the need to take "responsibility for the fate of the Kazakh nation" (FBIS 20 December 1990, 70). Of the union republics, only the Russian Republic's declaration of sovereignty was made without a Russian national territoriality agenda, and stated that "the RSFSR's multiethnic people are the repository of sovereignty" (FBIS 14 June 1990, 102). However, the sovereignty declaration was justified on the need to take "responsibility for the fate of Russia," which raises serious questions about the ability of non-Russian indigenes to secede from the Russian Federation and establish their own independent union republics or national states. It does appear that this declaration denies self-determination to the non-Russian nations whose homelands are located in Russia. In addition, since the question "What is Russia?" is still a major point of contention within the Russian national community, taking "responsibility for the fate of Russia" may entail going to war to retain border regions and republics. The status of these regions—and the Russian population resident in them—remains a major source of tension between Russia and its neighbors.[13]

---

[13] This topic is further discussed below.

The conflict over the question of who is sovereign is likely to become particularly acute in republics such as Kazakhstan, Kyrgyzstan, Latvia, and Estonia, where indigenes comprise less than or just more than half the population. In independent Latvia and Estonia, laws proclaiming the indigenous language to be the lingua franca of the state were followed by laws on citizenship, which provided full citizenship only to citizens of independent Latvia and Estonia and restricted access to citizenship for nonindigenes, particularly for Russians who migrated to these republics since the 1940s. In several of the nationalistic successor states, constitutions and laws on citizenship, property rights, language, and migration are being used to reconstruct the ethnic stratification system in order to secure a dominant position for members of the indigenous nation (Kaiser 1992c).[14]

Even before independence, political geographic studies of the first democratic elections to the Congress of People's Deputies found gross irregularities in electoral districts that resulted in overrepresentation for indigenes and underrepresentation for nonindigenes (Berezkin et al. 1989; Kolosov 1990; Kolosov et al. 1990). Malapportionment resulted in much smaller population districts in rural areas where indigenes predominated and larger population districts in cities where nonindigenes were concentrated. The malapportionment problem was particularly acute in Latvia, and resulted in political underrepresentation in regions where Russians were concentrated. As a result, even though Latvians made up only 52 percent of the republic's population, they comprised 78.1 percent of the deputies elected (Kolosov et al. 1990, 153–156). There was also evidence of "packing" Russians in order to dilute their voting strength in neighboring districts, a common form of gerrymandering (Kolosov 1990, 755–756).

Overall, indigenes did relatively well in gaining seats in the new parliaments at the center, in each republic, and in the local soviets (Table 7.2). Indigenes were overrepresented relative to their proportion of the total population, and the extent of this overrepresentation increased as the geographic scale decreased. In the Congress of People's Deputies, most union-republic level nations were represented at close to parity (eight were overrepresented; six were underrepresented). The major exceptions to this were Estonians and Latvians, whose level of overrepresentation was 19 and 26 percentage points, respectively. At the other end of the spectrum, Russians were the most underrepresented (11 percentage points), reflecting the multinational character of the Russian Federation and the fact that the non-Russian indigenes were relatively successful in gaining seats in the Congress of People's Deputies. According to Tishkov (1990b, 35–36), most of the non-Russian indigenous groups in the RSFSR were represented at or above their share of the total population in the legislative bodies at all three

---

[14] This process of restructuring ethnic stratification in the Soviet successor states has also occurred in the former Yugoslavia, and has been referred to as "constitutional nationalism" by Hayden (1992).

TABLE 7.2
National Composition of Total Population (TP), and Delegates to Congress of Peoples Deputies (CPD),[a] Republican Supreme Soviets (RSS), and Local Soviets (LS) (percent)

	Indigenes				Russians				Others			
Republic	TP	CPD	RSS	LS	TP	CPD	RSS	LS	TP	CPD	RSS	LS
RSFSR	82	71	78	—	82	71	78	—	18	29	22	—
Ukraine	73	69	75	86	22	27	22	10	5	4	3	4
Belarus'	78	70	74	86	13	20	20	7	9	10	7	7
Moldova	64	72	69	77	13	19	16	5	23	9	15	18
Uzbekistan	71	70	78	79	8	14	9	4	20	16	14	18
Kazakhstan	40	40	54	54	38	38	29	25	22	22	17	21
Kyrgyzstan	52	59	64	69	22	29	19	15	26	12	17	16
Tadzhikistan	62	67	75	69	8	24	8	4	30	9	17	27
Turkmenistan	72	76	74	81	10	16	15	5	18	8	11	14
Georgia	70	73	—	—	6	5	—	—	24	22	—	—
Azerbaydzhan	83	76	—	—	6	11	—	—	12	13	—	—
Armenia	93	88	—	—	2	12	—	—	5	0	—	—
Lithuania	80	85	87	—	9	5	5	—	11	10	8	—
Latvia	52	78	70	83	34	15	21	11	14	8	9	6
Estonia	62	81	77	—	30	11	20	—	8	8	3	—
+ Ave of 9[b]	63	67	70	76	19	22	18	10	19	11	12	15
+ Ave of 12[c]	66	70	73	—	17	18	15	—	17	12	12	—
+ Ave of 15[d]	69	72	—	—	16	18	—	—	16	12	—	—

Sources: Tishkov 1990a, 122–123; Tishkov 1990b, 47–49, 53–57.

Notes: Dashes (—) indicate that data were not available for these categories. Indigenes = Russians for the RSFSR. Non-Russian indigenes are included in the "Other" category.

[a] The figure for republic delegates to the CPD do not include those selected by Public Organizations.

[b] + Ave of 9 = unweighted average percents of the nine union republics for which "Local Soviet" data were available.

[c] + Ave of 12 = unweighted average percents of the twelve union republics for which "Republic Supreme Soviet" data were available. Average percents for "Russians" include the eleven non-Russian republics only.

[d] + Ave of 15 = unweighted average percents of all fifteen union republics. Average percents for "Russians" include the fourteen non-Russian republics only.

geographic scales. As in the case of sociocultural indigenization, this relative political underrepresentation of Russians in their own home republic is not what one would expect given their status as the dominant nation in the state. Outside the RSFSR, Russians were relatively overrepresented in nine of fourteen union republics. They were relatively underrepresented in the Baltic republics and Georgia, the most independence-minded of the former union republics.

In ten of the twelve union republics for which data are available, indigenes were relatively overrepresented in their republic Supreme Soviets. The two that were relatively underrepresented were the Russians and Belorussians. Russians outside the RSFSR were overrepresented in only four of the eleven union republic Supreme Soviets, while other nonindigenous national communities were overrepresented in only one of eleven. At the local soviet scale, indigenes were overrepresented in all nine of the union republics for which data were available. Russians and other nonindigenes were underrepresented at the local scale in all nine republics.

Even in cases where indigenes held a minority of seats, they were often overrepresented relative to their share of the population. For example, Kuznetsov (1990, 8) complained that Evenks represented only 27 percent of the seats in the Evenk Autonomous Okrug's legislature (Soviet of People's Deputies) and that Chukchis comprised only one-third of the representatives to the parliament in the Chukchi Autonomous Okrug. However, in 1989 Evenks were only 14 percent and Chukchis only 7 percent of their respective autonomous okrug populations. In general, indigenes gained more than a proportional share of seats to the parliaments in their homelands, and this indigenization of political representation, coupled with the decentralization of political power to nations in homelands, combined to create a potent national territorial challenge to central authorities.

This political indigenization process, which undermined equal or proportional representation, caused some Soviet analysts to advocate the elimination of the confederal structure of the state (e.g., Tishkov 1989a, 1989b). Opponents of indigenous privileges in the political sphere included nonindigenes, particularly those who previously held a privileged position (e.g., Russians outside the RSFSR), indigenous minorities who had reason to fear a rise in national chauvinism among the locally dominant indigenes (e.g., Gagauz versus Moldavians in Moldova, Abkhazians and Ossetians versus Georgians in Georgia, and Poles versus Lithuanians in Lithuania), and finally liberal democrats in Moscow who felt that any departure from equal political rights for each individual—regardless of nationality—was a move away from democracy. As an example of the latter, in arguing for greater individual freedoms and an end to special indigenous rights, Valeriy Tishkov (1989a, 1989b), the director of the Institute of Ethnology and Anthropology of the USSR Academy of Sciences, stated that (1) a special status for indigenes, which he equated with primitive aborigines, is anachronistic in the "modernized world"; (2) the division of population into indigenous (*korennoye*) and nonindigenous (*nekorennoye*) categories, and policies favoring the indigene in order to facilitate equalization, have created a new form of inequality; and (3) a Soviet people exists and sovereignty should reside with it. This argument was similar to those voiced in the 1960s and 1970s which stated that the ethnonational basis for Soviet federalism was outmoded and only hampered the further integration and well-being of the Soviet people. Tishkov also advocated replacing the system of "national territorial autonomy" with an extraterritorial "national cultural autonomy" comparable to the Austrian Marxist approach that Lenin vehemently opposed.¹⁵ The advocacy of an end to territorial divisions based on national homelands, and the treatment of these divisions as anachronistic in the developed world, clearly ignored societal processes that had been moving in the opposite direction throughout the past seventy-five years of Soviet history.

"One person, one vote" majoritarian democracy is also problematic in a multinational, multihomeland context. Majoritarian democracy may easily result in a tyranny of the majority, and this is particularly worrisome to the indigenous minorities with homelands incorporated into the home republics of larger nations (i.e., the indigenes with autonomous republics, oblasts, and okrugs, as well as those without any official recognition in the confederal structure of the state). In addition, since claims to territory are made not only on the basis of contemporary demographic extent but also and perhaps principally on the basis of a long history of residence in a given region, the use of majoritarian democracy alone in the determination of political representation is likely to create more international conflicts than it resolves. For indigenes, the perceived right to control the "fate of the nation" by controlling their homelands is not predicated on demographic strength alone. Indeed, the lack of demographic strength in regions of the homeland and the potential loss of these areas has resulted—in the successor states to both the USSR and Yugoslavia—in nationalistic attempts to regain majority status through the expulsion of ethnic others (i.e., ethnic "cleansing").¹⁶

The major alternative to majoritarian democracy is the promotion of "one nation, one vote" consociational democracy. During the late 1980s proponents of this alternative argued that the only way to save the union was to allow its member nations to exercise their right to self-determination in their own homelands, and to decide for themselves whether or not they wish to join with other nation-states in a more confederal union (Koroteyeva et al. 1988; Perepelkin and Shkaratan 1989; Kuznetsov 1990). Here, the economic and political sovereignty of indigenous *nations* rather than *republics* were viewed as the basis for a renewal of international ties and the re-integration of republics in a new confederated state. The starting point of this approach was that republics are the homelands of nations, and that indigenes need to control economic development and political decision-making in order to ensure the social reproduction of the nation in the future (i.e., in order to gain control over the fate of the nation). This gives the national homelands a mission unlike nonautonomous oblasts; the

---

[15] This topic was discussed in chapter 3. See also Connor (1984a).

[16] The drive for ethnic purification in contested areas of the homeland is not isolated to Eastern Europe and the USSR. For example, Tarzi's comparative study of state-building in the postcolonial Third World found that "whenever the state chooses to forge a collective identity on the basis of race, religion, and nationality, it produces target minorities. A mono-national integration formula in a multi-ethnic environment . . . creates victim groups subject to exclusion, segregation, expulsion, and repression" which produces refugee movements or separatism (Tarzi 1991).

latter may be as large in population or economic output, but national homelands have the additional task of orienting development to secure the future of the national community, not just providing for the social reproduction of the population (Koroteyeva et al. 1988; Perepelkin and Shkaratan 1989).[17]

Among proponents of greater sovereignty for each national community in the USSR, the question of which national communities qualified was a critical one. Galina Starovoytova, a Soviet ethnographer and member of the Congress of People's Deputies, advocated that all *ethnies* with territories represented in the federal system be given equal standing, that is, the federal system should be reconstructed as fifty-three union republics, each with the right to national self-determination up to and including secession from the state (Starovoytova 1989). "Autonomy" was seen as a Stalinist deformation of Lenin's right to national self-determination. A more moderate position was taken by Zlatopolskiy (1989), who proposed that union and autonomous republics should be recreated as equal "national states," while the autonomous oblasts and okrugs would have restricted sovereignty as "national-state formations." In an innovative article that combined elements of extraterritorial and territorial autonomy, Kuznetsov (1990) proposed a structure in which all union republics and autonomous republics would become equal republics of the federation, while autonomous oblasts and okrugs would become self-governing nationality oblasts and okrugs not subordinated to the republics. In addition, new nationality rayons, village soviets, and other units for smaller groups of peoples living in concentrated settlements would be created, similar to those that existed during the interwar period.[18] The fundamental difference of this proposal was that sovereignty would reside with national communities, not with republics (Kuznetsov 1990, 12): "The Soviet Union, in my opinion, must represent not a federation of union republics, within which autonomous republics, oblasts, and okrugs are retained but a voluntary union of equal peoples, united in republics, national oblasts, okrugs, and rayons. In the structure of the union, autonomy must not be retained in any form, except cultural. Republics, national oblasts, okrugs, and rayons, differing in name, must be equal subjects of the federation—the Soviet Union."

Each of the above proposals treated every indigenous *ethnie* as essentially equal. However, as noted throughout this work, a serious question exists regarding the national consciousness of peoples in much of the eastern part of Russia, and particularly those at the autonomous okrug level in the federal hierarchy. Furthermore, in several of these autonomous units, the indigenous "nation" is an extremely small proportion of the total population, and leaving

[17] For arguments against this, see Cheshko (1989) and Tishkov (1989b).

[18] The creation of these smaller autonomous units, which existed during the interwar period but were abolished with the 1936 Constitution, was made legal again in the new nationality policy resulting from the Party Plenum on national problems held in September 1989 (*Pravda* 24 September 1989, 2).

the demographic majority out of the political decision-making process on so fundamental an issue would be certain to create local international tensions and conflicts. A dichotomy of autonomous regions was recognized in the March 1992 draft of the Russian Constitution (*Argumenty i Fakty* 1992). All autonomous republics (i.e., ASSRs) and autonomous oblasts (except the Jewish Autonomous Oblast) were treated as equal "republics," while the status of the autonomous okrugs and the Jewish Autonomous Oblast was not upgraded (Appendix A).

An equally strident demand for self-determination has not been made by all indigenous national communities, nor have national front organizations been equally successful everywhere in mobilizing the indigenous masses behind national territorial sovereignty. A comparison of the national independence movements indicates that the nationalization of the indigenous masses continues to be highly variable across the ethnopolitical landscape, and in general is highest in the north and west and declines to the east and south. This geographic differential in the degree of national consolidation is also found in the declarations of sovereignty and independence, that are briefly examined below.

While academics and politicians in Moscow debated the future of Soviet federalism and the rights of indigenes to political and economic sovereignty, politically mobilized indigenes in the periphery were acting to secure control over their national homelands. Since 1989 declarations of sovereignty have been made by every union republic, autonomous republic, autonomous oblast, and autonomous okrug, as well as by indigenes without representation in the federal structure, such as the Gagauz in Moldova. The former deported national communities who have not yet regained their national territorial autonomy (Germans, Crimean Tatars, and Meskhetian Turks) have all made more concerted efforts to regain control over their ancestral homelands since 1989. The rash of sovereignty declaring between 1989 and 1991 gave one the impression of impending complete disintegration of the USSR along ethnoterritorial lines. However, although almost all declarations did have a strong national territoriality dimension incorporated within them, it would be incorrect to see the dozens of sovereignty declarations as equivalent expressions of a desire among indigenes everywhere for independence. The declaration made by Lithuania, which proclaimed its independence from the date of issuance—11 March 1990, was distinct from the declarations of "sovereignty" or "autonomy" made by the parliaments in a majority of the union republics, autonomous republics, oblasts, and okrugs during 1990 and into 1991, which supported greater political sovereignty in a new, more confederal union. The major distinctions in these declarations are briefly presented below.

Before the coup of August 1991, only six union republics had declared their independence or their intent to secede from the USSR, and these six refused to participate in the drafting of a new Union Treaty. However, even these more independence-minded republics cannot be seen as equally in favor of secession.

The four most developed republics and national communities in the USSR—the Baltic republics and Georgia—were most openly secessionist. Underdeveloped Moldova and landlocked, relatively impoverished Armenia—whose national elites also feel threatened by the Turkic populations fronting them to the west, south, and east—originally favored political participation in a loose confederation. Since that time, Moldavian elites under Mircha Snegur moved closer to advocating secession as an initial step to reunification with Rumania. On the other hand, Armenian officials backed away from outright political independence and after the coup agreed to participate in the new confederal councils running the central government.[19] Both Armenia and Moldova have also joined the CIS. In addition, although early on in the drive for independence there was talk of economic sovereignty and rising demands for economic autarchy, the political elites in all six of the independence-minded republics acknowledged the need for continued economic relations with the remaining union republics, and signed bilateral treaties and trade agreements with them.

The nine republics that participated in the development of a new Union Treaty were the Slavic and Central Asian republics and Azerbaydzhan. There were also major divisions within this group of republics. Before the August 1991 coup, Ukraine, Belarus', and Azerbaydzhan were internally fractured. All three had active national independence movements opposed to participation in a new Union Treaty, and the memberships of these national fronts were growing over time. However, the Supreme Soviets in all three union republics remained in the control of relatively procentrist political conservatives. In the case of Azerbaydzhan and Belarus', there was evidence of tampering with the electoral results to ensure a favorable outcome for Communist party conservatives. In Ukraine, the split was more geographic, with RUKH supporters concentrated in the more nationalistic west, and supporters of more conservative communist elites and policies concentrated in the more heavily Russified east. Since the elections in 1989 RUKH was able to rally mass support against the drafts of the Union Treaty, and this tended to radicalize the position taken by Ukraine's Supreme Soviet, whose members also began pressing for a looser form of confederation. In Belarus' and Azerbaydzhan, the national front movements were severely restricted in their ability to organize and hold mass rallies. After the failed coup, politically conservative elites in Belarus' and Azerbaydzhan attempted to join forces with the national independence movements in an effort to avoid prosecution for their pro-coup stance. Ukraine's Supreme Soviet also declared Ukrainian independence after the coup, as Communist party members sided with nationalists. This merger of Communists and nationalists, and the

---

[19] Armenia's president, Levon Ter-Petrosyan, had maintained observer status during the negotiations over a new Union Treaty between the other nine union republic presidents and Gorbachev in the so-called 9+1 talks.

"nationalizing" of communist elites in Ukraine, Belarus', and Azerbaydzhan moved national territoriality to the top of each parliament's political agenda.

The greatest irony of the independence movements during the late 1980s and early 1990s was the relative political conservatism in Soviet Central Asia and Kazakhstan. Contrary to the predictions that Central Asia was the most likely region to secede from the USSR and cause the disintegration of the state (e.g., Carrere d'Encausse 1978; Bennigsen 1986, 132), it was the region most solidly behind a relatively strong center and favored a more federal balance of power between central authorities and peripheral republics. Before the coup, declarations of sovereignty made by parliaments in the region were more procentrist than in any other group of union republics. They favored a centralized military—unlike the other union republics already discussed, and were also in favor of a stronger economic role for the center. The political elites in these republics were in basic agreement with early versions of the Union Treaty drafted by the center, which most other union republics had rejected out of hand.

The relatively more procentrist political conservatism among the Central Asian indigenous elites was reflected in the populations at large. In a survey conducted in 1989, Central Asians were found to be most confident that the Communist party acted in the interests of the public, and in general displayed more pro-regime attitudes than did the Baltic nations, Georgians, Ukrainians, or even the Russians (Mickiewicz 1990). This may, in part, help to explain the relatively weak national fronts that formed in the region. The initial programs of organizations such as *Birlik* were primarily aimed at sociocultural (e.g., language) issues, and did not represent a political challenge to the conservative Communist party elites in power (Brown 1990; *Birlik* 1989; Olcott 1990, 74).

In the post-coup political environment, the political elites in the union republics of Soviet Central Asia also declared their independence. However, these declarations did not appear to result from a strong demand from below for independence but rather represented an attempt by the political elites in the Central Asian republics—most of whom supported the coup—to escape retribution from the new anticommunist center. Given the history of dependence and the relative lack of strong national independence movements, coupled with the relative procommunist attitudes of the population, it is not surprising that these republics were most anxious to join the new Commonwealth of Independent States, once it became clear that the old center was gone. Their complete independence would undoubtedly hasten their slide into the underdeveloped Third World, which in any case may be unavoidable. This relatively procentrist stance is a far cry from the "Central Asia as Achilles Heel" scenarios popular in the West during the 1970s and early 1980s.

As the final union republic, Russia has remained the biggest question mark. While the republican leaders are clearly in favor of continued participation in a union, the actual support for confederation is more difficult to assess. As the largest republic and nation, it is doubtful that Russia and the Russians will be satisfied with the reduced status of equals with others in a confederation operating on the basis of "one nation, one vote." This may lead the Russian political elites to favor either greater centralization, such that the demographic weight of the Russian majority is taken into account, or even greater political independence, while retaining economic relations with the other union republics in an economic community. Given the size and economic assets of Russia, it is likely to retain a measure of dominance even in a loose political and economic commonwealth.

For Russia, Georgia, Moldova, Azerbaydzhan, Uzbekistan, and Tadzhikistan, there is also the potential of intrastate disintegration within the union republics, as indigenous minority elites declare their sovereignty over their national homelands. In Azerbaydzhan, Georgia, and Moldova indigenous minorities (i.e., Armenians, Abkhazians, Ossetians, Gagauz, and Russians and Ukrainians along the border between Moldova and Ukraine) have become openly secessionist in reaction to the overtly political national territoriality displayed by members of the dominant nations in these newly independent nationalistic states. This has resulted in rising international tensions and conflicts as dominant and subordinate indigenes struggle for control over territory that each claims as its rightful homeland.

Russia may itself become a loose confederation of national states, even if all autonomous units do not become independent. Nearly all the autonomous regions have declared their sovereignty, though most of these declarations call for greater sociocultural, economic, and political autonomy in the context of a renewed Russian Federation. For example, on 8 October 1990 the parliament of the Buryat ASSR declared its sovereignty as the Buryat Soviet Socialist Republic, "a sovereign multination state within the Russian Federation and the Soviet Union" (FBIS 9 October 1990, 96). The autonomous okrugs have tended to declare themselves "autonomous republics" or "autonomous oblasts" (e.g., FBIS 12 October 1990a, 112). The real challenge to the territorial integrity of Russia appears to come from the ASSRs which have declared their independence. Of these, only Tatarstan and Chechenia have announced their intent to secede from Russia; the other eighteen autonomous republics signed the Federation Treaty in March 1992. Symbolic of its announced new status, Tatarstan did not participate in the June 1991 election for president of Russia. Other ASSRs likely to follow suit include Bashkiria, Yakutia, Buryatia and Tuvinia, the latter of which has been the scene of violent conflict between Tuvinians and Russians, resulting in out-migration of Russians (Drobizheva 1991a, 12; FBIS 13 September 1990, 93–94). In reaction to the growing anti-Russian sentiments in the non-Russian homelands, Russian national self-consciousness is rising in Russia and outside the Russian homeland.[20]

---

[20] It is interesting that the explanation for continued minority ethnic self-consciousness given by

Support from local Russians for "sovereignty" was critical in several of the autonomous regions of the RSFSR. Indigenes are a minority of the total population and of the parliaments in many of these units, particularly in the autonomous okrugs. In addition, especially in the autonomous okrugs, the level of national consolidation among the indigenous *ethnies* appears minimal, making it unlikely that mass-based indigenous support for these declarations was present. In these regions, Russian localism was relatively more important in explaining the declarations of "autonomy" or "sovereignty" than was non-Russian indigenous nationalism. Other studies indicated that the deputies elected in the autonomous regions were relatively conservative (Smythe 1990; Petrov and Treyvish 1991), suggesting that support from these more reactionary political elites for sovereignty was also necessary. As the center became more "liberal," conservative Communists in the periphery sought to establish local power bases in order to isolate themselves from the changes taking place in Moscow. The interests of all three sets of elites pursuing strategies of territoriality converged in the autonomous regions of the RSFSR.

Of course, the short span of time within which the majority of these declarations of sovereignty were made indicates an external cause as well. In a federal system experiencing political and economic decentralization to first-order administrative units, the second- and third-order units can be expected to attempt to raise their standing in the federal hierarchy in an effort to ensure that local political interests are served. This has occurred even in nonautonomous oblasts of the RSFSR, where the interests of Russian localism and conservative communism alone have apparently been sufficient to overcome an overarching Russian nationalism. This sovereignty declaring by Russian localists also raises questions about the degree of national consolidation within the formerly dominant nation itself.

The specific objectives of the political elites in the autonomous regions seeking greater sovereignty are nearly as varied as the number of autonomous regions, but a few dominant themes have emerged. Both the Shatalin Plan for economic reform and the drafts of the new Union Treaty were confederal in essence but recognized only the fifteen union republics as sovereign (AN SSSR 1990; FBIS 5 September 1990, 73–74). These plans for the economic and political decentralization of the state provided little in the way of input from the national communities whose homelands were merely autonomous. The declarations of sovereignty by the autonomous regions, coming as they did at a time of intense debate over the nature of economic and political relations between central authorities and peripheral elites, may be seen as an attempt to secure a political voice in the processes of economic and political decentralization in the USSR during 1990. In the RSFSR, the sovereignty declarations were also

---

Hechter and others (i.e., "reactive ethnicity") appears to be more appropriately applied to the dominant Russians than to the non-Russian *ethnies*.

related to the negotiation of a new Russian Federal Treaty to restructure political and economic relations between the Russian central authorities and the autonomous regions (Sbornik Zakonodatel'nykh Aktov RSFSR 1991; *Argumenty i Fakty* 1990a). In particular, issues of local and indigenous control over natural resources and sociocultural issues such as language usage policies were featured items in the sovereignty declarations. The question of control over economic resources in Russia is likely to become a major issue in the near future, and may lead to a more secessionist national territoriality among indigenous nationalists in resource-rich republics such as Yakutia.

In Georgia, Azerbaydzhan, Moldova, and Lithuania, declarations of sovereignty made by indigenous minorities were related primarily to concerns over dominant-nation chauvinism. Each of these minorities was relatively procentrist, viewing the central authorities as a counterforce to rising Azerbaydzhani, Georgian, Moldavian, and Lithuanian nationalism. The center, in siding with Azerbaydzhan, disappointed the Armenians in Nagorno-Karabakh who had attempted to secede and join Armenia. In Lithuania, the Poles were unsuccessful in gaining autonomous status before Lithuanian independence. In Georgia and Moldova, declarations of sovereignty made by indigenous minorities (i.e., Abkhazians, Ossetians, Gagauz, and the Ukrainians and Russians on the left bank of the Dniester River) were rejected by the Georgian and Moldavian parliaments, and the South Ossetian Autonomous Oblast was abolished by Georgia in the process. Georgian and Moldavian nationalists claimed that these sovereignty declarations were solely the work of central authorities seeking to obstruct the Georgian and Moldavian independence movements. However, the indigenous minorities in both republics were responding in a predictable way, in that the denial of national territorial autonomy rights by Georgians and Moldavians was perceived as threatening the very existence of the minority ethnonational communities themselves. This perceived relationship between territorial control and national survival is the essence of national territoriality.

Ethnoterritorial Conflict in and among the Successor States

Beginning with 1988 in Nagorno-Karabakh Autonomous Oblast, an Armenian enclave in Azerbaydzhan that attempted to secede from Azerbaydzhan and become part of Armenia, intrarepublic and interrepublic territorial disputes have proliferated between neighboring nations over the geographic extent of their respective homelands. The number of conflicting claims to territory quadrupled between 1990 and 1992, and the number of violent international conflicts over land also escalated rapidly (Kolosov 1992; Map 7.1). The claims to territory made by nationalists are normally based on one of two justifications. First, nationalists whose members comprise a demographic majority in a given territory justify their claim to that territory on the current ethnodemographic map of the region. Second, nationalists have justified their claims to regions in

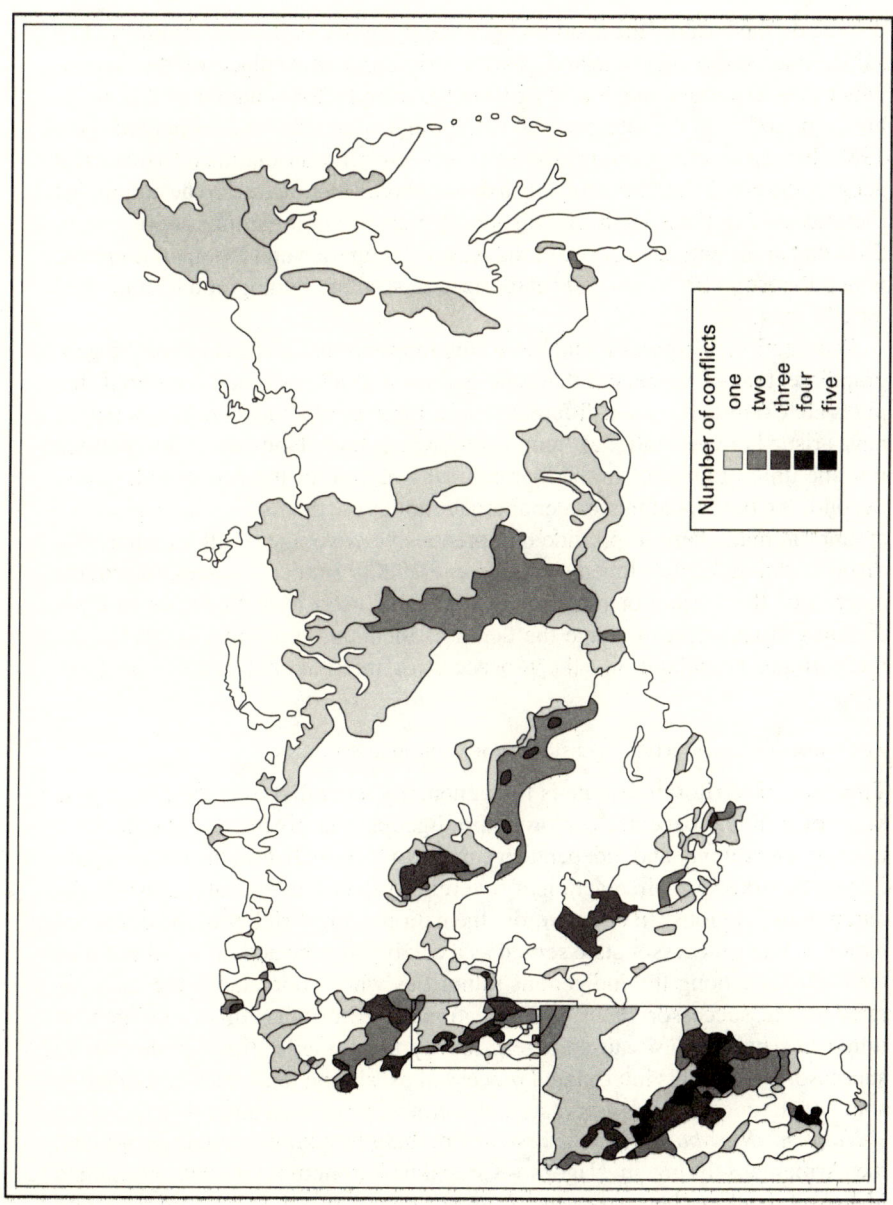

Map 7.1 Ethnoterritorial Conflicts, 1992. Based on a map produced by the Institute of Geography, Russian Academy of Sciences.

dispute on the basis of the historical geography of the national community. The subjective "sense of homeland" as the primordial birthplace of the nation, which was discussed in general terms in the introductory chapter of this book, has come to life in the international territorial disputes that have emerged since 1988. In many cases, nationalists use both a demographic claim and a historical geographic claim, and few use only a demographic justification. The nationalist rhetoric used in these territorial disputes brings to mind the international conflicts that arose with the demise of the Austro-Hungarian and Ottoman Empires, which Pearson (1983, 16–18) categorized in similar "demographic" and "historic" terms.

This section examines a number of the international conflicts over the geographic extent of homeland that emerged after 1988. National territorial disputes are examined on two different scales. First, conflicting claims to territory have arisen between national "minorities" whose homelands were incorporated into the union republics in the hierarchical structure of the Soviet federation. Second, the borders of the former union republics are themselves in dispute. No attempt is made here to provide comprehensive coverage of all the territorial disputes that have developed since the late 1980s. Rather, we seek to provide a sense of the variety or range of justifications used by nationalists in these disputes in an effort to gauge the depth of meaning attached to control over the national homeland and the prospects for international conflict management.

AUTONOMOUS "MINORITIES" VERSUS UNION REPUBLIC NATIONS

This type of territorial dispute is fundamentally a conflict over the geographic scale of political decentralization and indigenization processes. The declarations of sovereignty and independence made by nationalists at the union republic level sparked a chain reaction of sovereignty declaring by nationalists in the autonomous regions. In other words, the national territoriality of the dominant nation in each successor state served as a catalyst for the activation of national territoriality among the indigenous minorities whose homelands are incorporated in the successor states.[21] The national territoriality among indigenous minorities has in turn caused a reaction by the titular nations in the Soviet successor states. This interrelated process of escalating tensions has resulted in some of the most violent international conflicts witnessed since 1987.

Nagorno-Karabakh. In the first, and perhaps best known of these conflicts, the Armenians living in Nagorno-Karabakh Autonomous Oblast petitioned Moscow to allow their secession from Azerbaydzhan and their merger with Armenia. This petition, which was ultimately rejected by Moscow, served as a catalyst for anti-Armenian pogroms in Sumgait, Baku, and throughout the

---

[21] This diffusion of national territoriality is an excellent example of a more general tendency noted by Sack in his study of human territoriality (1986)—that territoriality exercised in one place by an individual or group often serves as a catalyst for the diffusion of territoriality to other groups and regions, and "tends to be space-filling." This topic is further discussed below.

Azerbaydzhani countryside, and equally violent anti-Azerbaydzhani reprisals in Armenia. The resulting massive refugee movements of Armenians and Azerbaydzhanis returning to their respective homelands, numbering more than 500,000 by 1990 (compared to a total population of 189,085 in Nagorno-Karabakh in 1989), provide an extreme example of the ethnic "place-clearing" function of national territoriality.[22] Armenians comprised a demographic majority in Nagorno-Karabakh at the time the petition was made, although they had declined from 84.4 percent in 1959 to 75.9 percent in 1979 (TsSU SSSR 1962, 7:53; TsSU SSSR 1984, 126). The demographic shift in favor of Azerbaydzhanis, along with restrictions placed on Armenians in the sociocultural arena and limited economic development of the autonomous oblast, were long-term processes viewed as threatening to the status of Armenians in Nagorno-Karabakh (Mirzoian 1990; Khachaturov 1988, 10). However, the Armenians claim Nagorno-Karabakh not only because Armenians are a demographic majority in the region but also because the oblast is perceived as part of Armenia's ancestral homeland (Yamskov 1991). Samvel Shahmuratian, a representative in the Armenian Supreme Soviet who spoke at the Kennan Institute in Washington, D.C. on 6 November 1990 stated that "since childhood he had been taught 'Nagorno-Karabakh is an integral part of Armenia, which was artificially separated by a six- to eight-mile corridor and unjustly placed under the jurisdiction of Azerbaijan in 1921. People there live under conditions of national oppression' " (Arslan and Shahmurtian 1990).

As a symbol of this historic claim to Nagorno-Karabakh, the Armenian name for the region—Artsakh—was adopted by nationalist leaders in Armenia, and the "reunification" of Artsakh and Armenia was proclaimed as a goal around which all Armenians should unite (FBIS 31 December 1990, 75). This may help explain why Armenians have not fled Nagorno-Karabakh with the rise in violence but have actually increased in number in this autonomous oblast. Leaving Nagorno-Karabakh is equated in the Armenian nationalist imagination with abandoning the ancestral homeland. In 1989 their percentage had increased to 76.9 percent of the population in Nagorno-Karabakh, even while it had fallen by more than 107,000 in the rest of Azerbaydzhan between 1979 and 1989, declining from 6 percent of the population to 3.6 percent (TsSU SSSR 1984, 125–126; Goskomstat SSSR 1991a, 118–121). Armenian refugees leaving other parts of Azerbaydzhan have fled to Nagorno-Karabakh, as well as to Armenia. In addition, ethnic "cleansing" of Azerbaydzhanis from Nagorno-Karabakh has occurred, further strengthening the demographic position of Armenians in the region.

Of course, Azerbaydzhani nationalists also claim Nagorno-Karabakh as the

---

[22] Sack also noted that human territoriality generally could serve a place-clearing function, and this is clearly in evidence in the case of national territoriality, not only in the Soviet successor states and Yugoslavia but more generally in multinational, multihomeland states (e.g. Kaiser 1988, 1992c; Connor 1986; Tarzi 1991).

core of their ancestral homeland which they will never relinquish. An Azerbaydzhani visitor to the Kennan Institute in 1990 argued that ethnodemographic claims to territory alone were not valid, and implied that Armenians had no historic claim to the territory (Arslan and Shahmuratian 1990). Turkic nomads migrated seasonally to Nagorno-Karabakh up to the 1930s, and during the summers comprised a majority of the population in the region. However, during the 1920s the ethnodemographic surveys and censuses that were conducted in order to delimit the federal structure were taken during the winter, when the Azerbaydzhani nomads were not in Nagorno-Karabakh. For this reason, Nagorno Karabakh is viewed by Azerbaydzhanis today as an integral part of their ancestral homeland that was unfairly "given to" the Armenians (Yamskov 1991, 134). Clearly, the conflicting historical geographies of Armenians and Azerbaydzhanis, and not ethnic demography alone, has added to the intractable nature of the territorial dispute over the status of Nagorno-Karabakh.

Georgia. A combination of demography and historical geography is also apparent in Georgia. In the Abkhazian Autonomous Republic, there has been a demographic shift toward the Georgian population from the late nineteenth century to the present day. Between 1959 and 1989 Georgians increased in number from 158,221 to 239,872, and from 39 percent to 46 percent of Abkhazia's population (TsSU SSSR 1962, 6:140; Goskomstat SSSR 1991a, 116). Abkhazians claim that this in-migration has been part of a concerted effort on the part of Georgian imperialists to dilute Abkhazian demographic strength and thus undermine Abkhazian claims to sovereignty over their ancestral homeland (Zhavoronkov and Mikadze 1990, 8). However, the Abkhazian proportion of the population has also increased during the postwar period from 15 percent in 1959 to 18 percent in 1989. Furthermore, Abkhazians have benefited from indigenization policies giving them a competitive advantage over Georgians for slots in higher education, for jobs, and for political posts. This pro-Abkhazian indigenization has caused growing resentment among the Georgians living in the autonomous republic and in Georgia generally, who have argued that they should be proportionally represented in higher education, occupations, and political posts.

The mutual antagonism between Georgians and Abkhazians is nothing new. As early as 1978 Abkhazian nationalists sent a petition to Moscow requesting the removal of Abkhazia from Georgia and its incorporation into the RSFSR (Sheehy 1978).[23] In 1989 Abkhaz nationalists declared their homeland to be a union republic independent from Georgia and equal to it in the federal structure

---

[23] This request provided early evidence that "Great Russian chauvinism" was not the only concern of minority nationalities in the USSR, and that for the indigenous minorities living outside Russia ethnic stratification that favored the dominant indigenous nations (i.e., Georgians in Georgia) was seen as a greater evil than Russian dominance in the USSR, or even in Russia.

of the USSR. This declaration was immediately rejected by the Georgian Supreme Soviet. Since 1989 a number of violent conflicts have erupted in Abkhazia over the question of Abkhazian sovereignty, and the issue of independence remains unresolved.

In a reversal of the Georgian-Abkhazian formulation, Georgian nationalists claim the South Ossetian Autonomous Oblast as part of their historic homeland over which Ossetians should have no control, even though the Ossetians comprise 66 percent of the autonomous oblast's population while the Georgians account for only 29 percent (Goskomstat SSSR 1991a, 116; Table 4.3). Georgian nationalists argue that Ossetians are newcomers attempting to assert their control over Georgian soil.[24] On the other hand, Ossetians living in Georgia claim the region as their homeland for both demographic and historical reasons. In addition to claiming the rights of a demographic majority to determine its own future, Ossetian nationalists also claim to be descendants of the Scythians who lived in the region more than twenty-five hundred years ago (Brooke 1991, A3). Ossetians have also expressed the fear that the anti-Ossetian violence experienced during the last period of Georgian independence between 1918 and 1921 would recur in a newly independent "Republic of Georgia." They appear to have been correct in this assessment; civil war erupted between Georgians and Ossetians after independence, resulting in a growing Ossetian refugee migration and an increasing number of casualties in South Ossetia.

On 11 December 1990 the Georgian Supreme Soviet not only rejected South Ossetia's declaration of sovereignty but abolished the autonomous oblast. According to the former Georgian president, Zviyad Gamsakhurdiya, the more extreme step of abolishing the autonomous oblast, rather than simply rejecting the declaration of sovereignty, was taken because the Ossetians were newcomers to the republic.[25] The Abkhazians, by contrast, were said to be a primordial people of Georgia whose autonomy was therefore inviolable (FBIS 24 December 1990, 101). However, it was not coincidental that the more extreme step of abolition was taken in South Ossetia, where the Georgians were a demographic minority, but not in Abkhazia, where Georgians make up a plurality of the local population. As the Georgian reaction to these two territorial disputes in Georgia indicates, nationalists tend to use whichever argument—demographic or historic—best serves their claims to territory in a given case.

---

[24] Georgians also argued that the declarations of sovereignty made by the minorities in the republic were actually the work of the center, which was attempting to divide and conquer the independence-minded Georgians (Mikadze and Shevelyov 1990, 7). Moldavian nationalist leaders have used a similar conspiratorial argument to deny the right of minority indigenes to self-determination. However, the demise of the USSR did not result in an end to the independence movements by the minorities in these two successor states.

[25] An additional argument given by Georgian nationalists during my stay in Tbilisi in June 1992 was that the Ossetians abolished the autonomous oblast by declaring their independence, and Georgia only nullified the declaration of independence.

Even in the case of Abkhazia, Georgian nationalists claim the territory not only because Georgians comprise a majority of the autonomous republic's population but also because the region is perceived as an integral part of the national homeland. In response to the declarations of sovereignty made by Abkhazians and Ossetians over their respective autonomous regions, Zviyad Gamsakhurdiya asserted (Mikadze and Shevelyov 1990, 7): "We'll do everything possible to prevent this territory from being taken away from Georgia. . . . In Abkhazia, 16 percent of the population wants to usurp control over vast, originally Georgian lands, claiming them as their long-standing possessions. Ossetians too have been living on the greater part of the so-called South Ossetia only since the 20th century." Given this attitude that Abkhazia is not only demographically but historically Georgian, indigenization programs and processes favoring Abkhazians in Abkhazia must be even more difficult for Georgian nationalists to tolerate. These affirmative action-type programs are unlikely to survive long in independent Georgia. The attitude of Georgian nationalists toward Abkhazia almost ensures that Abkhazians will not long be satisfied with their subordinate political status in Georgia.

The general Georgian nationalist position appears to consider the non-Georgians seeking independence as traitors to the Georgian nation, and this attitude helps to legitimize the harsh reaction against the Abkhazians and Ossetians. There is a general failure to recognize as legitimate the right to national self-determination for the Abkhazians and Ossetians. This is an ironic position for the Georgians to take, considering that their own independence was won through the use of nationalistic arguments that Georgians are a nation deserving of their own nation-state.[26] Georgian nationalists are not alone in their inability to recognize as legitimate the national self-determination movements of minorities; this appears to be a blind spot shared by dominant nations generally.

With the forcible removal of Gamsakhurdiya and his replacement by the relatively more moderate Shevardnadze, the prospects for the settlement of ethnoterritorial conflicts in the republic have improved. However, it has become increasingly clear that so long as nationalism among the Georgian masses in general remains at such a high level, moderates such as Shevardnadze are left little room to maneuver. Anyone suggesting that non-Georgians deserve territorial autonomy is perceived as a traitor to the Georgian nation. Nationalism "from below" in Georgia has tended to push political elites toward a more nationalistic position. This phenomenon is found in the other successor states as well.

Moldova. In Moldova, conflicting historical claims to homeland have emerged in the territorial dispute between Moldavians, on the one hand, and the

---

[26] The Georgian nationalist position against Abkhazian and Ossetian independence, if applied to their own independence movement, would be akin to saying that Georgian nationalists are traitors to the Russian nation or the Soviet state.

Turkic Gagauz and Slavic Russians and Ukrainians, on the other. In reaction to rising Moldavian nationalism in 1989 and 1990, evidenced by the law proclaiming Moldavian as the lingua franca of the republic, the declaration of Moldova's intention to secede from the USSR, and nationalistic support for the eventual reunification of Moldova with Rumania, the non-Moldavian Gagauz and Slavic populations declared sovereignty over the regions of the republic in which they were demographically concentrated and where their ancestors had lived (Map 7.2). In an emotional speech reacting to the declarations of sovereignty made by the Gagauz over southern Moldova and by the Slavic population over the left bank of the Dniester River, Moldavian president Mircha Snegur proclaimed (FBIS 12 October 1990b, 46, 51): "Our people have been living here for more than 2,000 years . . . this land where the remains of our ancestors rest in peace have [sic] been reshaped many times. . . . But each time the people have emerged victorious. . . . Not a single acre of our ancestors' land to satisfy the autonomous ambitions of the newcomers."

Moldavian nationalists claim historical ties to the entire region dating to the time of Roman penetration. On the other hand, the "newcomer" Gagauz nationalists assert their own historic ties to southern Moldova, where they have lived in concentrated settlements for at least the last two hundred years. Similarly, the Slavic population living concentrated on the left bank of the Dniester River adjacent to Ukraine claim the territory as "age-old Russian, Slavic land" (FBIS 16 November 1990, 80). More recently, the left bank territory currently incorporated into Moldova was not incorporated into Rumania during the interwar period, as was the rest of Moldova, but rather was part of Ukraine and the Moldavian ASSR created in the 1920s. Thus, ancient mythic history, recent events, and ethnodemography are combined to justify the declarations made in this case. A reporter from *Izvestiya* summed up this type of conflict well (FBIS 16 November 1990, 80):

> There is no peace on the banks of the Dnestr. . . . There are bitter calculations of who has lived where and for how many millennia. Historical documents are being dusted off, maps of population movements have been colored, assessments of historical events are being revised. Dacians, Goths, ancient Romans, Stephen the Great, the campaigns of Suvorov, the Russian-Turkish war, the gift of Catherine II, ancient homes, ancient townships, and so on and so forth—everything is thrown into the furnace to maintain the flames of national exclusiveness and to prove that this people alone—and no other!—have the right to this land.

Russia. The Russian presence in the autonomous regions of the Russian Federation has caused growing international tensions between the dominant Russians and the indigenous minorities, though for the most part they have not turned violent. The main exception to this has been Tuvinia, where anti-Russian sentiments escalated into violent confrontations by the fall of 1990, resulting in an out-migration of Russians from the autonomous republic sim-

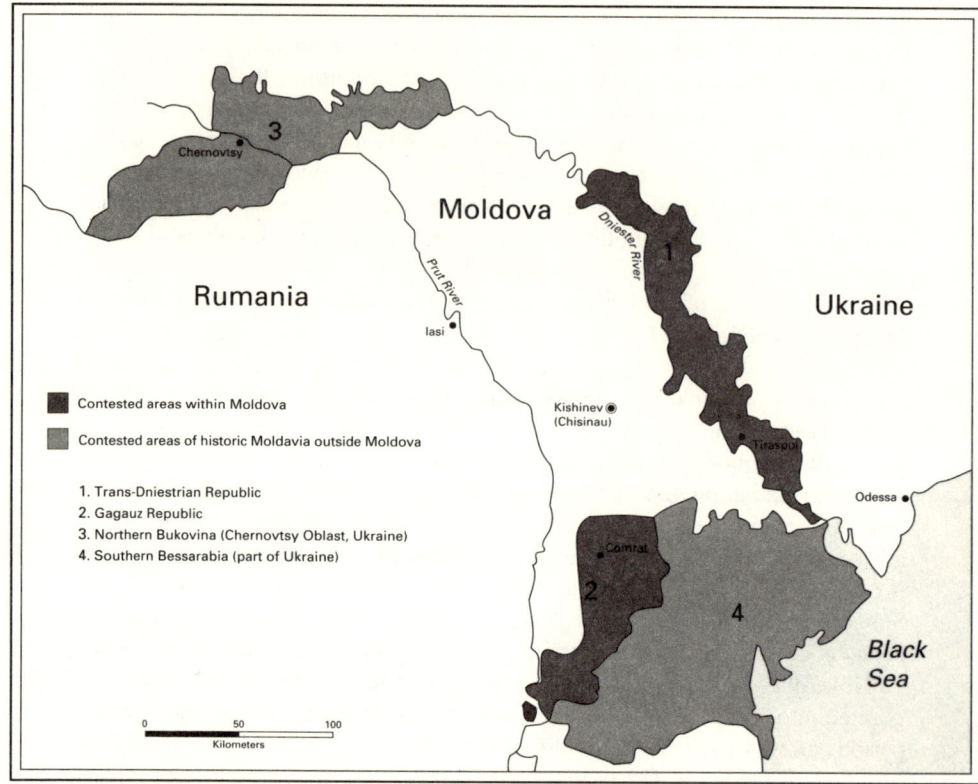

Map 7.2   Border Disputes and Territorial Conflicts, Moldova

ilar to the out-migration of Russians from Central Asia (FBIS 13 September 1990, 93–94). As noted above, the declarations of sovereignty made by these autonomous units are often supported by the local Russians, whose lack of a strong sense of national self-consciousness and sense of homeland have combined to limit the degree of international hostility that has developed within Russia. It must also be said that unlike the nationalistic leaders in Georgia, Moldova, and other republics, the political elites in Russia have been more tolerant of sovereignty declarations made in the autonomous regions of the republic, in that they have not rejected them outright. However, the draft constitution of 1992, which provided a greater political voice for the autonomous republics in the Russian Federation, also restricted the possibility of autonomous minorities seceding from the Russian Federation (*Argumenty i Fakty* 1992, 3): "The removal of part of the territory of the Russian Federation to a foreign state cannot occur without the approval of the people of the Russian Federation, expressed by way of a referendum of the RF." This is similar to the law on secession crafted by Gorbachev in an effort to regain control over the disintegration process. President Yel'tsin, although he stated in 1990 that the autonomous nations in Russia could have as much independence as they could handle, reacted against national separatism in Tatarstan and Chechen-Ingushetia (e.g., CSCE 1992). The debate in Russia's parliament over whether the name of the state should be Russia or the Russian Federation, which occurred immediately after the Federal Treaty was signed by all of the autonomous units of the state except the two mentioned above, was also a cause of growing anxiety among the non-Russians. These incidents reflect a growth in national territoriality among the Russians at the center, which is almost certain to raise the level of nationalist opposition among the non-Russians in the state.

In 1993 a renewed debate on the status of the non-Russian republics developed as part of the drafting of a new Russian constitution. While non-Russian nationalists with republics in Russia lobbied for greater sociocultural, economic, and political autonomy, the increasingly nationalistic Russians argued strenuously that each Russian oblast should have equal standing with the non-Russian republics in a federated Russia. This would provide Russians with the dominant political voice to which many Russians feel they are entitled, but would obviously subvert the consociational status of Russia as a multinational federation.

The draft constitution of July 1993 retained a statement that "calls republics 'sovereign states,' whereas the regions do not enjoy this status," and this has angered Russian nationalists (Tolz 1993). In reaction to the failure of Russian oblasts to receive equal standing with the non-Russian republics in the draft constitution, a number of Russian oblasts such as Sverdlovsk have declared themselves to be republics. On the other hand, non-Russians are unhappy about the limited sovereignty provided the republics in the draft constitution. Of particular concern for non-Russians was the absence of a right to secession (Sheehy 1993a).

This struggle over the legal status of Russians and non-Russian indigenes is certain to escalate in the coming years, and Russia faces a potential disintegrative process similar to the national separatism that resulted in the demise of the USSR. However, Russian nationalism is a much more potent force for resisting this disintegration than Soviet patriotism ever was, and the international conflicts in Russia promise to be much bloodier than those generated between Moscow and the republics during the last years of the USSR's existence.

The Deported Nationalities. A special subset of this type of territorial dispute involves national communities whose members were deported from their homelands during or following World War II and who have not been allowed to return during the postwar period. Volga Germans, Crimean Tatars, and Meskhetian Turks are the three groups whose autonomous units were not restored after Stalin's death and Khrushchev's "secret speech" of 1956.[27] For the majority of the 63,000 Meskhetian Turks who became refugees after they were forced from Uzbekistan in 1989, and for most of the remaining Meskhetian Turks living dispersed throughout the former USSR, the return to the Meskhetian homeland in southern Georgia is seen as the only acceptable future. The desire for returning to the homeland is so great that a faction has emerged which advocates that Meskhetian Turks call themselves Georgians in order to guarantee the right of return (Panesh and Yermolov 1990, 19). The majority of Crimean Tatars has also evidenced a strong desire to return to Crimea (Kiselev 1990, 9). An estimated 250,000 had voted with their feet by November 1993 (Wilson 1993, 6), creating serious housing problems and an increasingly tense situation on the island between the in-migrating "indigenous" Tatars and the resident "alien" Slavs. The Germans, whose roots over the past two hundred years were in the Volga region, but who were deported to northern Kazakhstan in a preemptive strike in September 1941, have also begun returning to their "homeland."[28]

In all three of these cases, the typical pattern of anti-outsider "nativism" has been stood on its head, as the contemporary residents in these ancestral homelands have resisted the return of the deported nations. In the cases of the former Volga German ASSR and Crimea, the mainly Slavic populations of Saratov Oblast and Crimea have argued that there is no room for the returnees. In the case of Crimea, an overwhelming majority of residents voted on 30 January 1991 to change the oblast's status to that of "autonomous republic." However, this was not a vote for the recreation of a Crimean Tatar ASSR, and the local Russians undoubtedly voted for autonomy in order to enhance their political control over the region, as well as to provide for the possibility of secession and merger with Russia should Ukraine opt for complete independence ("News Notes" March 1991, 195–196). There is also increasing pressure for the restoration of the Volga German ASSR, coming from Germans in Russia and also from Germany's political leadership. This has caused growing resentment among Russians in Saratov Oblast.

---

[27] Khrushchev's "secret speech" of 1956 acknowledged the deportation of several national communities from their respective homelands as an excess of Stalinism, and this speech paved the way for the return and full restoration of autonomous rights for most of the deported nations. However, the Meskhetian Turks, Crimean Tatars, and Volga Germans were not allowed to return home, and their autonomy was not reestablished, though their status as "outlaw nations" was changed. For a history of the deported national communities, see Kreindler (1986), Conquest (1970), Nekrich (1978), and Guboglo (1992).

[28] Kaliningrad, the former Koenigsberg region of Germany, was also proposed as a possible German autonomous unit. The thinking appeared to be that a German autonomous republic in Kaliningrad would serve as a window to the West, and particularly to German investments. This alternative appears to have been more attractive to central authorities in Moscow than to the German population, who voted to restore the Volga German ASSR in 1990 (FBIS 21 August 1990, 27–31; *Literaturnaya gazeta* 11 October 1989, 11).

In the case of the Meskhetian Turks, in addition to the demographic argument against return, Georgian nationalists deny that the Turks have a "primordial" claim to land as an indigenous group. In an interview on the subject Zviyad Gamsakhurdiya, former nationalist president of Georgia, stated (Mikadze and Shevelyov 1990, 7): "There was a time when the Turks were strangers in Georgia. Now they claim Georgian land as their own. We cannot grant their claims, because the Turks' native land is Turkey, not Georgia. Also, the lands in Meskhetia are populated by Georgians and Armenians." This nationalist intransigence on the part of the Georgian government, in addition to the opposition of local Georgians in Meskhetia, makes the return of the Meskhetian Turks doubly difficult. Without a strong center intent on resolving this issue, it is doubtful whether this return will be possible.

One additional ethnoterritorial dispute that has escalated into a bloody conflict of late has its origins in the deportations. When the Ingush were deported in 1944, part of their homeland was given to the North Ossetian Autonomous Republic (News Notes 1991). The Ingush never gave up their claim to this territory, and since 1989 have become increasingly vocal about their rights to it. This has resulted in violent clashes between the Ingush and Ossetians in North Ossetia, and the failure of Moscow to resolve the dispute in their favor has led the Ingush to contemplate declaring their independence from Russia (Sheehy 1993b). This represents a dramatic shift in favor of national separatism on the part of the Ingush, who recently separated their homeland from Chechenia because the Chechens were too independence-minded.

Autonomous "minorities," even if a demographic majority in their respective autonomous units, face serious problems as they attempt to follow a strategy of national territoriality by declaring sovereignty over their homelands. The decentralization of political and economic power to union republic-level nationalists in their home republics has, if anything, made the position of the minorities whose homelands are located in these new national states more tenuous. For this reason, many of these indigenous "minorities" advocated the retention of a stronger center that could counter the rising nationalism of the locally dominant nations. The center and the autonomous minorities found common cause in their struggle against the national territoriality of the union republic-level nations. However, the union republic-level nationalists tended to read this as Moscow's manipulation of the minorities, and thus reacted harshly to the declarations of sovereignty made by the indigenous minorities. As the center's power collapsed and that of the union republic-level nations increased, the autonomous minorities suffered the consequences of their ill-fated alliance with the center.[29]

---

[29] The nationalistic stance that Moscow was behind the minority uprisings did not end with the disintegration of the USSR. Today, nationalists in Moldova and Georgia argue that Russian imperialists have replaced the communist elites as the instigator of minority discontent in the non-Russian periphery.

BORDER DISPUTES BETWEEN THE UNION REPUBLICS

The borders of nearly all the union republics are in dispute at the present time (Map 7.1). Some of the territorial claims made are relatively straightforward. For example, Estonia and Latvia claim adjacent land in the Pskov and Leningrad oblasts of Russia that was part of independent Estonia and Latvia between the wars but was allocated to Russia after the Baltic republics were reincorporated into the USSR. Other claims involve ancient mythic histories about the contemporary nation and its ethnic origins. For example, some Lithuanian nationalists have claimed Kaliningrad Oblast, the formerly German region to the west (Koenigsburg) that was seized by the USSR at the end of World War II, as "Little Lithuania" (Gorbatov 1990, 2). This claim is based neither on recent history nor on present demographics but on the notion that the Prussians indigenous to the region were ethnically related to the Lithuanians in the Middle Ages. While the border disputes between the successor states may not be as life-threatening to the nations involved as are those between autonomous minorities and dominant indigenous nations, their resolution is nonetheless critical if the successor states are to develop good working relationships with one another.

Just as in the conflicts between autonomous minorities and union republic-level nations, the border disputes between the former union republic-level nations are based primarily on current ethnic demography and conflicting ethnic histories. Most of the border regions between union republics are national transition zones where neighboring nations merge into one another. Most of these border regions have been ethnically mixed localities "from time immemorial," and sorting out current border disputes made on the basis of who was there first or lived there longest (i.e., who is indigenous) would be a monumental task.

Borders that poorly match the geographic extent of nations have been the scenes of international conflict between the former union republics. The deportation of Armenians from Azerbaydzhan which was mentioned above was at least partially an effort at ethnic purification to reduce the demographic claim Armenians may make to a Greater Armenia. The claim to an autonomous republic made by Ukrainians and Russians living in the left bank region of the Dniester River and their claim to this region as part of a Greater Ukraine was also mentioned above. Several regions along the Moldova-Ukraine border are current points of contention (Map 7.2). Within Central Asia itself, most of the interrepublic borders poorly matched the geographic extent of national communities in the region, and this incongruity has been the primary basis for the border disputes arising between the Central Asian nations in recent years.[30] As

---

[30] In addition, Kazakhstan's claim to the Karakalpak ASSR is based both on the fact that this autonomous unit was part of Kazakhstan during the interwar period, and also on the close ethnic kinship said to exist between Kazakhs and Karakalpaks.

discussed in chapter 3, this incongruity was most likely due more to the limited information about the region and the weakly developed national identities at the time of delimitation, and less to a concerted effort to divide and conquer the Central Asians. Nevertheless, the borders as drawn in the 1920s and as modified since have been a source of international friction in the region, which is particularly intense between Tadzhiks, Uzbeks, and Kirgiz. The violent confrontation between Kirgiz and Uzbeks in Osh' Oblast (Kyrgyzstan), ostensibly over the seizure of land in an Uzbek-populated region by a Kirgiz youth group in order to build houses, was undoubtedly also a Kirgiz reaction to the call for Uzbek territorial autonomy in the region, made shortly before June 1990 by *Adolat*, a local Uzbek informal group (FBIS 9 August 1990, 89).[31] As economic conditions decline and indigenes press more forcefully for preferential treatment, border incidents such as these are likely to increase in frequency and intensity. If left unchecked, they have the potential of drawing the successor state themselves into increasingly conflictual situations, as has already occurred between Armenia and Azerbaydzhan.

The question "What is Russia?" is perhaps the most difficult issue facing the political leaders of the Soviet successor states. There appears to be a growing consensus among Russian nationalists that "Mother Russia" includes not only the Russian Republic but also northern Kazakhstan (a demographic rationale), as well as Ukraine and Belarus'. For the latter two, Ukrainians and Belorussians are themselves claimed as mere "tribes" of a greater Russian nation that was artificially divided and must today be brought back together (e.g., Solzhenitsyn 1990, 2; Solchanyk 1992). Not surprisingly, these claims have themselves caused a reaction not only among Kazakhs over the claim to northern Kazakhstan but also among Ukrainians and Belorussians, with demonstrators protesting the demotion of their nations to mere "tribes."

Surveys taken by the Institute of Ethnography indicate that the Russian population itself has undergone little change in its perception of the homeland. In the late 1970s and early 1980s, 70 percent or more of Russians living in Moscow, Kishinev, and Tashkent called the entire USSR their homeland (Drobizheva 1991a, 5).[32] In 1987 a new survey taken in Moscow indicated that 70 percent of Russians there still thought of the entire USSR as their motherland (Drobizheva 1991b, 97). These surveys and the positions of Russian nationalists indicate that " 'Russia" and the Soviet Union are indistinguishable concepts" in the minds of a significant number of Russians (Solchanyk 1992, 36). This was also reflected in a survey that found Russians about evenly split

---

[31] The call for Uzbek territorial autonomy, in turn, was made in response to a history of Kirgiz favoritism (i.e., indigenization from below) in this heavily Uzbek-populated region (FBIS 31 July 1990, 104–105; Elebayeva 1992).

[32] This did not hold true in Tallinn, the capital of Estonia, where 53 percent of Russians surveyed claimed the USSR as *rodina* and 25 percent claimed Estonia. Those with an Estonian "sense of homeland" were undoubtedly also those who favored independence in more recent surveys.

between those who viewed themselves as Russians (43 percent) and those who viewed themselves as Soviets (42 percent). However, Russians living in a foreign national environment (e.g., Tashkent) indicated that they had a feeling of homesickness (Arutyunyan 1990, 44), raising questions about the depth of emotional attachment to the entire USSR as the motherland. Nevertheless, the more expansive perception of homeland in evidence among Russians enhances the probability that international conflicts will arise in border republics such as Kazakhstan, Ukraine, Belarus', and the Baltics, where Russians live in concentrated settlements and where a Russian sense of homeland has developed over time.

The presence of large and growing numbers of Russians in neighboring union republics has been a source of international tensions from the Baltics to Central Asia for much of the postwar period, and has emerged as potentially one of the most divisive issues confronting the successor states. The "reactive ethnicity" displayed by Russians in response to their loss of privilege and to open hostility directed against them by indigenes has varied regionally. In Estonia and Latvia, Russians established "international fronts" as a reaction against the national fronts seeking independence from the USSR. Yet, a substantial number of Russians living in the region favored independence for the Baltic republics. In surveys conducted in August 1990, 41 percent of Russians in the Baltic republics favored independence, while 50 percent were opposed to secession (Gudkov 1990, 7).[33] In Ukraine, the Russian population in the eastern region of the republic was more favorably disposed toward continued participation in a federal "Union of Sovereign States" than was the western portion of the republic. The southern region known as Novorossiya during the late tsarist period and Crimea have also remained heavily populated by Russians, and for at least some local Russians this region should become part of the Russian Republic. Similarly, in the oblasts of northern Kazakhstan where Russians continue to comprise a majority, a political organization was recently founded with the goal of redrawing the union republic borders to incorporate northern Kazakhstan into Russia (Olcott 1990).

In November 1990 bilateral treaties that "acknowledge the territorial integrity" of each republic were signed between Russia and Ukraine and between Russia and Kazakhstan (FBIS 17 December 1990, 24; FBIS 11 December 1990, 73). A similar bilateral treaty, which had been delayed by the protests of Russians in Estonia, was signed between Russia and Estonia in January 1991 (FBIS 14 January 1991, 101). However, in the wake of the post-coup independence declaration made by Ukraine, Yel'tsin and his advisors once again raised the possibility of redrawing the interrepublican borders in the event that

---

[33] Caution must be exercised in reading too much into these surveys, which were taken at a time of rising nationalism. Nonetheless, Russians did vote in favor of independence in sizable numbers in the Baltic republics, and voted for independence or stayed away from the polls in Ukraine.

Ukraine or Kazakhstan gained its political independence (Clines 1991, A6).[34] After an immediate and strong reaction against what was perceived as Russian imperialism, political elites from Russia, Ukraine, and Kazakhstan reaffirmed their commitment to the territorial integrity of the republics (*New York Times* 30 August 1991, A7). Given the stance of Russian nationalists and the fact that Russian nationalism is rising among the political elites in Moscow, the border question is likely to reemerge in the years ahead, if not in Moscow, then among the Russians living in the non-Russian successor states.

CONCLUSIONS

Territorial disputes between nations over the geographic extent of homelands have emerged as one of the most significant centrifugal forces in the former USSR during the late 1980s and early 1990s. Indeed, under the present conditions it may be said that the struggle for control over the homeland has come to be equated in the minds of nationalists with the struggle for the very survival of the nation. In the perception of nationalists, to be without sovereignty in one's homeland is to be without a future. Since every region of the former USSR is claimed as homeland territory by one group over others, and since these indigenous nations have been successful in gaining competitive advantages over nonindigenes in these homeland regions through a process of indigenization, even nonindigenous groups are currently seeking some degree of national territorial autonomy. A good example of this is the Koreans in Uzbekistan, who were deported from the Soviet Far East to Central Asia in 1937. At a minority rights conference held in Leningrad (St. Petersburg) in June 1991, the Korean delegate stated that Koreans in Central Asia wanted only to preserve their ethnocultural autonomy (i.e., their survival as a separate and distinct national community). However, given the rising nativism of indigenes in the region, where all nonindigenes are increasingly being pressured to leave, the Koreans feel that their only option is to create their own autonomous republic.[35] This is an excellent example of national territoriality serving as a strategy by which nationalists seek to preserve their national community into the future by gaining control over the territory on which their members reside. This case and others like it support a general tendency of human territoriality noted by Sack (1986,

---

[34] The issue of borders emerged between Russia and the Baltic republics as the bilateral treaties were being prepared, and this was a major factor in the delay of those agreements (FBIS 21 November 1990, 76; FBIS 2 January 1991, 61). However, because Yel'tsin had endorsed Baltic independence, the borders of these three former republics were not called into question in August 1991.

[35] Having failed in their effort to establish a Korean Autonomous Republic in Uzbekistan, and faced with rapidly escalating antiforeigner nativism in Central Asia, an increasing number of Korean families have begun to emigrate to the Primor'ye region of the Russian Far East, the area from which they or their ancestors were originally deported. As in the case of the Crimean Tatars and Volga Germans, the local Russians in the Far East have not welcomed the in-migration of Koreans (Matveeva 1992).

34), that "territoriality can help engender more territoriality" and therefore "tends to be space-filling."

The national territoriality of the more nationalistic indigenes has diffused throughout the former USSR, as increasing numbers of indigenous groups and even nonindigenes have also declared their political sovereignty in an effort to gain control over the fate of the group. In the process, former *ethnies* whose members exhibited few signs of national self-consciousness have become increasingly "nationalized" as members compare their own communities and their futures to the more nationally self-conscious communities in the former USSR. The territoriality of the most nationalistic indigenes has helped set the political agenda for all groups in the former USSR, and has itself served as a catalyst in the activation of more national territoriality as a result.

During much of the postwar period, the indigenization of economic and political elites in the national homelands was an ongoing process. In part, this indigenization resulted from affirmative action-type programs that targeted members of the indigenous nations for preferential treatment. In addition, with the social mobilization and nationalization of the indigenous masses, pressure for indigenization was increasing from below. Efforts by the center to decentralize decision-making authority tended to place political power in the hands of peripheral indigenous elites who had become increasingly nationalized. The combination of these three processes—indigenization, nationalization, and decentralization—served as a potent catalyst for the rising national separatism experienced throughout the USSR during the late 1980s and early 1990s.

The process of political and economic indigenization accelerated greatly after 1987. Although, in part, this acceleration was due to the reforms initiated by the center, it is more fundamentally a reflection of the changes that have occurred in the periphery. Earlier reform programs initiated by the center were also taken over by indigenous nationalists. However, without mass-based national consolidation behind the political objectives of the indigenous elites (i.e., national territoriality), this early nationalist behavior was rather easily controlled. The first political *korenizatsiya* program initiated under Stalin during the late 1920s and early 1930s, which placed nationalized elites in positions of authority, ended with the purges of these indigenous elites for their nationalist deviations. Even the more recent *sovnarkhozy* scheme initiated by Khrushchev, which led to a sharp rise in "localism" that was particularly apparent among indigenous elites in *sovnarkhozy* that were also national homelands, was relatively easily restricted and then reversed from above. The relative ease of managing the "national question" reflected the limited degree to which the nationalization of the masses had occurred. As expected, it was relatively more difficult to restrict the decision-making authority of indigenous elites in the 1960s than it was in the 1930s. Due to the growing complexity of Soviet society, political and economic decentralization were occurring de facto, and the indigenization of elites in national homelands was proceeding apace. For these reasons, Suny (1989, 305) found that the "fall of Khrushchev in October 1964 made little difference in the national development of the Georgian republic." Similarly, Raun (1987, 219) characterized the decade following the *sovnarkhozy* experiment as "a period of consolidation of the gains made in the earlier post-Stalin years."

By the 1980s national consolidation and the pressure from below for indigenization had increased markedly. Indigenous nationalists took advantage of the changes initiated from above, as they had in the past. This time, however, the masses could be more easily mobilized behind the objectives of economic and political indigenization in the homeland. Attempts to reform the system from above quickly unleashed a revolution from below. The rapid confederalization of center-periphery relations realigned political power to conform more closely with the new political geographic realities in the state. The final phase of national territoriality—its becoming an overt strategy used by nationalists to gain political and economic sovereignty over their respective homelands—is essentially complete.

This process of indigenization, culminating in the decentralization of political power to nations in homelands, represents a solution to the national question quite unlike the one predicted by Marxism-Leninism. Soviet federalism, far from assisting in the sovietization of the population, helped to ensure against this process of internationalization. Soviet federalism has turned out to be a temporary stage in Soviet history. However, it has not served as a way station on the route to the complete unification of Soviet state and society but rather as a transitional phase on the road to national consolidation and the formation of independent national states.

In the West, research structured within the parameters of the totalitarian model also missed the fundamental changes taking place in the national communities around the country. The tendency of Western analysts to focus on policy formulations developed at the center to solve the national question, and particularly on policies that promoted the Russification of the non-Russian peoples, are reflections of the bias introduced into the study of national processes in the USSR. Not only did this lead to an underestimation of the indigenization taking place throughout the country, it also resulted in an overestimation of the degree to which the Russian nation itself could be taken as a given. Predictions of political disintegration that were made were also skewed as a result of these biases. Central Asia was mistakenly selected as the most likely candidate to initiate the dismemberment of the USSR because it was the place that contained peoples most unlike the Russian or Slavic north, and who could therefore not be assimilated. In addition, the "internal colonialism" model, which predicted that the most underdeveloped regions and nations would also be the most nationalistic, was also influential in the selection of Central Asia as the Soviet "achilles heel." However, during the late 1980s and early 1990s this region remained the most procentrist, and the most willing to participate in a renewed Soviet federation. It was the most developed nations in the state that were the most secessionist.

The solution to the old national problem (i.e., indigenization and the disintegration of the USSR along national territorial lines) has resulted in a new set of national problems. First, international disputes over the geographic extent of national homelands has become a major source of conflict since 1988. Neighboring nationalists have developed elaborate justifications for their territorial claims based both on ethnodemography of the present or the past and also on the mythic historical geography of their nations. Attempts to resolve these conflicts through the use of contemporary ethnodemography or historic justifications alone will be doomed to failure, and are likely to lead to the proliferation of violent international conflict of the type seen in Georgia. Ways of accommodating each side in these territorial disputes have yet to be found, though some combination of national territorial and national cultural autonomy holds the most promise.

Second, and related to the first new national problem, is the issue of national autonomy for indigenous minorities. Dominant indigenous nationalists are using their new political power to reconstruct an ethnic stratification system that ensures their nations the status of "first among unequals," and this has served to undermine the standing of indigenous minorities and nonindigenes in the successor states. While not every group has become equally nationalized, it is true that a general "awakening" has mobilized the members of smaller and smaller *ethnies*. The hierarchical structure of the Soviet federal system raises serious questions about the ability of these indigenous minorities to ensure that their "nations" have a future. Most indigenous minorities have declared their autonomy or sovereignty over their national homelands, and even nonindigenes living in concentrated settlements are pressing for territorial autonomy in an effort to gain control over the fate of their national communities. This has increasingly brought indigenous majorities and minorities into conflict. Indigenous minorities whose members have become nationalized over time are in principle no less deserving of national territorial sovereignty simply because their numbers are small. To ignore or reject their demands for political indigenization is to invite an escalation of international conflict and an acceleration of the disintegration process within the successor states.

Finally, the third new national problem to be resolved is the future structure of the multinational commonwealth itself. This restructuring of political and economic relations is occurring at two different geographic scales. Bilateral treaties and economic agreements between successor states have created a network of mutual international interests even while they have reinforced the political independence of each state. This process initially represented an effort by the republics to restructure their relations with one another while bypassing and undermining the political authority of the old center, which resulted in the collapse of Moscow as the "core" of the state. Second, a less successful effort to develop new economic and political union treaties that would reconstruct the center has continued. The early impetus for this reunification came from the old center itself. Since the August coup, Gorbachev lost whatever had remained of the center's ability to influence change. His vision of a renewed Soviet socialist "Union of Sovereign States" has given way to the CIS envisioned by Yel'tsin and the other two Slavic republic leaders. The new center of the CIS is powerless in and of itself, and is unlikely to serve more than a coordinating function in the region formerly known as the USSR.

CHAPTER EIGHT

Conclusions and Implications

THIS STUDY provides substantial support for the idea that the geographic restructuring of places as "ancestral" homelands has played a critical role in the formation of nations and the development of international relations in Russia and the USSR. The results of this research support the contention of Smith (1986, 161–163) that the territorialization, as well as the politicization, of *ethnies* is an essential ingredient in the development of a national self-consciousness. The development of a sense of homeland was central to the way in which national communities defined their place in the world, where they have come from as well as where their futures lie. The construction of national homelands, which was facilitated by Soviet nationality policies—including the federal structuring of the state, was particularly important for the nationalization of the masses. Once created, the particularistic image of homeland held by each nation has played a major role in shaping international relations. Indeed, the "us versus them" dichotomy that is said to underlie a national self-consciousness is replicated and reinforced in the "sense of exclusiveness" that the national membership comes to feel toward its homeland—even regions of it that most members have never visited. Since these nationalistic images of homeland are particularistic, members of neighboring nations do not carry the same mental maps of home. The conflicting homeland images and, perhaps more important, the felt need to control all the "organic" whole, provide the geographic context for the current border disputes and territorial conflicts that are being waged throughout the former USSR, Yugoslavia, Czechoslovakia, and in dozens of other multinational, multihomeland states in the world today.

Western political and sociological studies of nations and the so-called national question in the USSR have tended to focus either on group cultural attributes and their retention or on nationality policies and their impact on group identity. The significance of place has been ignored in most of these works, and this is comparable to the treatment of place as a largely irrelevant variable in political sociology generally (Agnew 1987). In large part as a result of this neglect the process of indigenization, beyond that which was provided by the center (i.e., indigenization from below or national separatism), was missed almost entirely. For example, Gleason (1990), who defined nationalism as politicized ethnicity, found no evidence of nationalist movements in the USSR. McAuley (1984) also concluded that this was the case, and found little evidence of a system-threatening national problem. Rutland (1984) also took issue with the idea that the USSR had a serious national problem, and argued that the "politics of nationality in the USSR are better understood as a mechanism of social regulation than as a vehicle for self-realisation."

These authors were by no means in the minority of studies on the national question in the USSR in their lack of attention to processes of national separatism (i.e., indigenization) occurring throughout Soviet history, and were for the most part caught completely unprepared for the rising nationalism that accompanied Gorbachev's reform program. Many analysts in the USSR and in the West explained the rise in nationalism solely as a response to the policies implemented under Gorbachev. This is stated in one of two ways. According to nationalists in the former USSR and their co-nationals living abroad, the "primordial" nations trapped within the Soviet Union are "reawakening" after a seventy-five-year period of dormancy to reclaim their proper place—both of dominance in their "ancestral" homelands and of co-equal status as "nation-states" in the world political community. On the other hand, several Soviet analysts continued to claim that the majority of people in the USSR had been successfully socialized (i.e., sovietized), and that this new nationalism was the work of a deviant few (e.g., Tishkov 1989a; 1989b). Gorbachev was clearly convinced that this was the case throughout his term as president. It was not until these analysts and central authorities were faced with the actual demise of the state that they began to recognize that nationalism had become a mass-based movement, particularly so in the most developed republics of the state.

Each of the two explanations for the recent rise of nationalism in the USSR is fundamentally flawed. As the evidence presented in this work reveals, nations are not the primordial organisms that nationalists—present and past—have depicted them to be. The vast majority of national communities with homelands in Russia and the USSR became mass-based only during the twentieth century. Far from a seventy-five-year hiatus, the Soviet period was critical in the making of nations and in the development of national territoriality in this world region. On the other hand, although nationality policies coupled with rapid socioeconomic development did help the central authorities manage the national problem confronting this multinational, multihomeland state, they were also important in the consolidation of nations and homelands in the state, which in turn became active competitors with the center for the hearts and minds of the masses. In this competition, the nation and homeland won out over the ideals of a common Soviet people and a socialist fatherland. The latter rather than the former were becoming anachronistic with the passage of time and the sociocultural, economic, and political development that occurred. As indigenes became more socially and geographically mobilized they also tended to become more nationalistic, and were increasingly pressing from below for greater sociocultural, economic, and political control over their own homelands. The evolutionary rate of change toward greater indigenization in each national republic began to accelerate and reached revolutionary proportions under Gorbachev. Nevertheless, it is important to keep in mind that the underlying tendency toward greater indigenization of life in the national homelands was present before Gorbachev. Contrary to nationalistic and Soviet depictions of the national problem in the USSR, nationalism was neither being solved through voluntary, peaceful means (i.e., sovietization), nor were nations either asleep or about to disappear under the "denationalization" policies of the Communists. The Gorbachev years and the revolutionary changes that ensued are more properly viewed as one stage in a much longer process of national separatism.

This study represents a preliminary effort to reexamine the national question in Russia and the USSR from a broad comparative perspective that brings geography back in. Such a reassessment is necessary, even critical, if we are to begin to understand why earlier theories and analyses of this question were so wrong, as well as to predict with greater certainty where nationalism is likely to take the Soviet successor states in the years ahead. It seems undeniable at this point that scholars in the West and Soviet analysts who studied nationalism in the USSR are in dire need of our own *perestroyka*.

The mutually enfolding national and territorial processes in Russia and the USSR may be unique in their details, but in general conform to national processes found in the developed west and the underdeveloped south. Socialism did not produce a unique answer to the "national question" confronting multinational, multihomeland states. The findings of this case study should therefore prove useful to the growing comparative literature on nationalism, and particularly to the still largely ignored and unexplored geographic dimension of nations and nationalism. After a summary of findings and the implications for international relations in the successor states of the former USSR, the chapter concludes with a brief comparative review of the broader significance of national territoriality.

THE MAKING OF NATIONS AND HOMELANDS IN RUSSIA AND THE USSR

The nations and homelands that currently exist in the region of the former USSR are communities of belonging and interest that have come together during the past two centuries, though nationalists throughout the region claim more primordial genealogical and geographic roots. This process of nationalization began in Russia during the eighteenth century and did not reach the final phase until the interwar period for most of the European groups. The process of mass-based national consolidation is not yet complete among indigenes in Soviet Central Asia, Siberia, and the Far East. After World War II, with the hardening of nations and homelands in the USSR, there was growing pressure from below for indigenization or national separatism, culminating in the independence movements of the late 1980s.

Prerevolutionary Nationalization

The process of national consolidation in Russia and the USSR roughly corresponds with the three stages identified by Hroch (1985): a "period of scholarly interest" (Phase A), followed by a "period of patriotic agitation" (Phase B), and finally "the rise of a mass national movement" (Phase C). The first phase describes the "ethnicization" of elites as they rediscovered their genealogical and geographic roots. The second phase marks the nationalization of elites, and with it the rise of political nationalism. The third phase identifies the formation of nations as mass-based communities of interest, which in the Russian Empire began no earlier than the late nineteenth century.

Phase A occurred in Russia during the late eighteenth and early nineteenth centuries, at least for those *ethnies* in the European part of the country. As part of this "enlightened patriotism," an emotional "sense of spatial identity" among the elites toward their homelands was readily apparent. However, at this time neither "nation" nor "homeland" was defined on an ethnic basis. Few elites felt in any way related to the peasant masses, and even those who did could not conceive of the enserfed peasantry as part of the nation. The educated elites may have viewed themselves as a nation of citizens and their homeland as the state, but the illiterate "dark masses" were viewed either as children in need of education or as subhumans in need of further evolution before they could be admitted into the national community. From the limited information available, the illiterate peasantry by and large also felt no kinship with the rural gentry and was suspicious or openly hostile to urban outsiders.

A "period of scholarly interest" began relatively early in the Baltics, in Russia and Ukraine, and in Georgia and Armenia. However, in Belorussia early research into the Belorussian language and folklore was conducted not by indigenous scholars but by Poles and Russians, who sought to prove that the Slavs of the region were part of each group's respective "nation" (Vakar 1956). Phase A "enlightened patriotism" is difficult to find in Central Asia before World War I and the October Revolution, though a "period of scholarly interest" can be identified relatively early in the nineteenth century for the Kazan' Tatars, and somewhat later for the Crimean Tatars, the Azerbaydzhanis, and the Kazakhs. The very existence of a Phase A among the small *ethnies* of the Siberian north and several other groups in the Russian east is highly dubious, and certainly did not precede the twentieth century. For several of these groups, a "period of scholarly interest" and even "patriotic agitation" appear to have been more the result of the Stalinist *korenizatsiya* policies of the 1920s and 1930s than the consequences of an indigenous process.

The imagery of a primordial nation and homeland, complete with a glorious past, was primarily the creation of nationalist elites who emerged during Phase B, a "period of patriotic agitation" that was the hallmark of romantic nationalism during the latter half of the nineteenth century. At this time, the idea of the "nation" as being bound up in the blood of the peasant masses and the soil of the homeland fundamentally redefined the community of belonging and interest. For the Russian elites, the Slavophiles and their anti-Western orientation provide one of the earliest examples of "patriotic agitators" in the Russian Empire.

For many of the other *ethnies* in the state, the transition to a Phase B nationalization of elites was a reaction to the subordinate position in which indigenous intellectuals found themselves (i.e., the ethnic stratification system that was a reflection of the colonial relations between groups at the time). Socially mobilized Latvians and Estonians found Germans in a dominant position, Lithuanians found themselves subordinated to Poles, Georgians and Azerbaydzhanis to Armenians and Russians, Ukrainians and Belorussians to Russians, Poles, and Jews. Later, Central Asians and dozens of *ethnies* in the Russian east found themselves subordinate to the dominant Russians. This subordinate position delayed for a time the onset of the nationalization process. It was often the case that these indigenous groups had developed little or no indigenous elite of their own, and upward mobility meant acculturation and assimilation to the locally dominant *ethnie*. In many of these regions, Phase B appears more as the leading edge of Phase C—"the rise of a mass national movement"—than as the conversion of an existing indigenous intelligentsia into a nationalized elite. This could only occur along with the social and geographic mobilization of the rural masses, which began for most of the *ethnies* of the Russian Empire only after 1861.

The period from 1861 to 1914 is significant as the beginning stage in the development of both a mass-based national consolidation in the Russian Empire, and also a mass-based "sense of homeland" more geographically extensive than the local region or village. The abolition of serfdom in 1861 and the subsequent increase in the rate of geographic and social mobilization of the peasantry were critical facilitators in this nationalization process. The development of transportation and communication links between town and country, rising mass literacy and education rates, and urbanization and occupational mobility were all influential in breaking down rural isolation and localism, and replacing them with the broader images of nation and homeland. The pace of mass-based national consolidation was particularly rapid in the developing northwest, while in the east and south it is difficult to find evidence that the indigenous *ethnies* had progressed to this stage in the nationalization process before 1914.

Overall, for the peasants themselves the idea of nation does not appear to have been a dominant concern before World War I and the Bolshevik Revolution. Localism, rather than nationalism, was in evidence throughout prerevolutionary Russia. This held true for the way in which peasants defined their communities of belonging and interest, as well as how they defined their homelands. Who was native and who was foreign were not determined on the basis of ethnonational identity, although clear physiographic and sociocultural distinctions of newcomers to the village were undoubtedly noted and used to label that individual as an outsider. National languages could not have been used either, since most of the peasantry was not only illiterate but spoke localized dialects that would have identified anyone from outside the local region as foreign. The definition of communities of belonging, of who was and was not a native (*rodnoy*), was determined on the basis of whether or not that individual came from the local region or village. Clearly, under these conditions "homeland" for the peasant masses was defined in local terms, not as the expansive national territories that are proclaimed by nationalists today.

This localism was beginning to give way to a broader sense of community and homeland after the abolition of serfdom, as peasants became more geographically mobile, as transportation and communication networks began to integrate them more fully into the world outside the rural village, and as they became more literate in standardized "national" languages, more educated, more urbanized, and more occupationally mobile. However, the geographic and social mobilization of the masses, particularly outside the northwestern provinces of the empire, was a process that had limited impact on the rural village and on the localist mentality of the peasantry before the October Revolution. While nationalists today speak in glowing terms of their eternal nations that have struggled to survive during the seventy-five-year communist ordeal, nations as mass-based communities of belonging and interest for the most part did not exist before 1917. The seventy-five years of communist rule was a critical period in the formation of nations and homelands in the former USSR.

The Interwar Period

During the interwar period, the more nationalized northwest gained independence and remained outside the Soviet orbit. This history of independence was extremely important in the nationalization of the masses and in the development of a sense of homeland in Estonia, Latvia, and Lithuania. It has also been used by nationalists in the Baltics since the late 1980s as a recent "golden age" on which the new states are to be founded. The fact of independence was the historic justification for the declarations of sovereignty made in 1989, although the nationalistic claim to this territory is founded on a much deeper, even primordial connection to these "ancestral" homelands. The present symbols of statehood are taken from the interwar period of independence, and proposals have been made to limit citizenship in the new states to the population living in the republics between 1918 and 1940 and their descendants. The nationalists in other republics that were outside the Russian/Soviet orbit during the interwar period (i.e., Moldova, Georgia, Azerbaydzhan, Armenia), even if it was only during the Civil War, also used this period of independence as historical justification for independence in the late 1980s.

Between the wars within the USSR, policies were designed to help manage and solve the national problem, defined by Lenin as the need to overcome a history of uneven development, colonialism, and Great Russian chauvinism. The two most important elements of these policies—the confederal form of the state and *korenizatsiya*—were key ingredients in the nationalization of the masses throughout the postrevolutionary period. In addition to these nationality policies, the geographic and social mobilization of the masses increased greatly during the interwar period, and this also accelerated mass-based national consolidation in the state.

The USSR was formally constructed as a confederation of sovereign republics in order to provide the nations of the state with political-juridical equality. The confederal units of the state, constructed for the most part on the basis of ethnic communities, helped to delimit national homelands that were for many still only vaguely perceived. Once created, the borders of the USSR helped to establish political geographic minimums for national homelands. From the interwar period forward national communities came to define the territory that was theirs as *at least* all of the land incorporated in their union or autonomous republics. Most nationalists also claim territory beyond the borders of their republics, but few if any accept the counterclaims made to "their" territory by neighboring nationalists. As a consequence of these overlapping claims to homeland, border conflicts have proliferated throughout the territory of the former USSR (*Moscow News* 17 March 1991, 8–9).

Korenizatsiya during the interwar period was a policy designed to bring about international equalization by targeting members of the indigenous nations for preferential treatment in their home republics. Coupled with the confederal structure of the state, *korenizatsiya* promoted consolidation around the "nations" whose members were given a privileged status, particularly in regions where a strong sense of national identity was lacking. In addition, *korenizatsiya* policies encouraged not only a growing "sense of spatial identity" among indigenes toward their home republics but also a "sense of exclusiveness" regarding their proper place in the national homeland. These policies helped to ensure that the national problem would become more intractable over time, even with international equalization. They also guaranteed that nationalists would use territoriality as the primary strategy in the attempt to achieve their ultimate objective—attaining control over the destiny of the nation. Nationalism in the Soviet context became the essential equivalent of national territoriality.

The social and geographic mobilization of the masses during the interwar period also furthered the nationalization process. Coupled with nationality policies, the demographic indigenization of cities, a rapid rise in literacy, and the development of literary languages for dozens of *ethnies*, rising education rates and upward occupational mobility were helping to bring about the national consolidation of the indigenous masses. Paradoxically, this was also the period of most intensive "international integration," primarily a reidentification of non-Russian nonindigenes to a Russian national identity. Most analysts in the West have interpreted this assimilation as a result of coercion from above, and to some extent this may have been true, particularly after 1938. However, those who reidentified as Russians during this period were for the most part Ukrainian and Belorussian peasants who had left their homelands before a strong sense of national self-consciousness had developed. For this reason, it seems likely that these nonindigenous peasants had never felt very Ukrainian or Belorussian, and that their "Russification" was for them as much a process of national consolidation as it was a process of international integration. Nevertheless, the loss of these members to their "primordial" nations of origin became an important historic event used by nationalists to rally the masses in favor of independence from the USSR and from the dominant Russians, who were accused of conducting a policy of forced "denationalization" (e.g., RUKH 1989).

During the 1930s it was becoming increasingly apparent that rising nationalism rather than internationalism was resulting from the nationality policies and socioeconomic development that was taking place. The purging of indigenous elites on charges of "bourgeois nationalism" was increasing throughout the decade, culminating in the Great Purge of 1937–38. However, at the same time that nationalistic indigenous elites were under attack from the center, the policy of mass-based, sociocultural *korenizatsiya*, and the nationalization of the masses that accompanied it, continued. A clear effort was made during the 1930s to distinguish between the indigenous nationalistic elites, who were seen as anticommunist deviants that the state needed to eliminate, and the indigenous masses, whose national consolidation the state continued to promote.

Nevertheless, a shift in nationality policies taking place during the 1930s increasingly favored Russians, and between 1938 and 1953 the treatment of Russians as "first among equals" became the most prominent nationality policy of the state. Coming on the heals of policies that promoted indigenization, the "Russification" and coercive antinationalist programs of the late Stalin era were counterproductive to the ultimate objective of solving the national problem, even though overt national territoriality was certainly curtailed during this period of the "Great Terror." This Stalinist "deformation" of Leninism was decried both by socialist reformers and nationalist elites during the late 1980s, and served as a catalyst in the political mobilization of the masses in favor of political decentralization and ultimately national independence.

NATIONAL TERRITORIALITY DURING THE POSTWAR PERIOD

Nations as mass-based communities of belonging and interest, and national homelands geographically more extensive than locales, have hardened only during the postwar period. For this reason, the "national problem" facing Soviet leaders during the last forty years of the state's existence was fundamentally different from the one confronting either Lenin or Stalin. Although Soviet leaders and ethnographers wrote and spoke about the "drawing together" (*sblizheniye*) of nations as the predominant national process during this period, and proclaimed that the national question had been solved through international equalization, national separatism was, if anything, becoming a more intractable problem with which the central authorities in the USSR were increasingly unable to cope.

After the completion of the nationalization process on a mass basis, the following phase was not the internationalization or "sovietization" of the population—as Soviet leaders and ethnographers predicted but rather the indigenization of life in each national homeland. This process of sociocultural, economic, and political indigenization, which may also be defined as a process of national separatism, was the dominant trend during the postwar period. The disintegration of the former USSR into independent states operated by and for the indigenous nations should be seen as the end of this much longer process of indigenization, rather than as a short-term response to the reforms initiated under Gorbachev. In this section, this indigenization process as it occurred in the postwar USSR is highlighted.

Geographic Mobilization and Nationalism

Demographically, national communities have remained highly concentrated in their respective national homelands. Out-migration, encouraged in theory by Soviet leaders and ethnographers as a way of equalizing the supply and demand for labor, and of internationalizing the population, was discouraged in reality both by the emotional attachment to homeland and by the national stratification system that had developed within the state. *Korenizatsiya* was revived as a policy after Stalin and was increasingly promoted by indigenous elites from below. This indigenization process in each homeland provided strong sociocultural, economic, and political incentives to remain at home, and equally strong disincentives for out-migration. Only Russians as the dominant nation in the state remained above this, and continued to move with relative ease from one union republic to another. A two-tiered system of national stratification thus developed, with Russians in a dominant position in the state overall but with each indigenous nation also attaining a privileged status within its own home republic. Non-Russian nonindigenes, and to a lesser extent indigenous minorities whose homelands were afforded only autonomous status in the federal hierarchy, were placed in a subordinate position within this evolving nationally stratified system. Under these conditions, it is not surprising that out-migration from the homeland was quite limited throughout the postwar period.

Since the late 1980s indigenous nationalists have begun the process of deconstructing the old national stratification system, not to replace it with democratic political institutions and a system of rewards based on merit but rather to reconstruct a new system of national stratification that reinforces the indigenous nation's dominant status in its own homeland. The rewriting of constitutions, laws on citizenship, language, property rights, and migration has been carried out by nationalistic elites with the purpose of enhancing the status of the indigenous nation as "first among unequals." In the process, the status of Russians and other nonindigenes in the non-Russian periphery has declined precipitously. In this more nationalistic environment, as indigenes assert more forcefully their right to a dominant status in their "ancestral" homelands, nonindigenes have been made to feel increasingly unwelcome. One response has been nonindigenous out-migration, which has increased dramatically since 1987, particularly in the regions of violent international confrontation (i.e., Transcaucasia and Central Asia). The out-migration of nonindigenes whose families may have lived in the same village for generations and who thus know no other "home" has been accurately described by Soviet demographers as refugee migration (Rybakovskiy and Tarasova 1990). In some regions of the former USSR, such as Transcaucasia, forcible ethnic purification or "cleansing" of homeland regions is clearly in evidence. Those who are emigrating cite rising anti-outsider "nativism" on the part of indigenes and the growing fear of persecution for being members of nonindigenous nations or indigenous minorities as their principal reasons for wishing to leave. In addition, in this new overtly nationalistic environment, nonindigenes find themselves increasingly unable to compete with indigenes. The size of this refugee migration stream has reached nearly three million to date and is likely to continue growing in the near future. The declining status and increasingly hostile treatment of Russians and other nonindigenes living outside their home republics has already begun to sour relations between the successor states, and is certain to undermine the ability of the political elites in each independent state to reconstruct a working relationship within the framework of a new Commonwealth of Independent States (CIS). The status of Russians living outside Russia, and the impact of their situation on Russian nationalism "back home," have become especially critical issues that will determine to a great extent the future prospects for the CIS.

The out-migration of indigenes from their homelands is currently impeded by rising nationalism in the Soviet successor states. The psychological and sociocultural barriers to leaving the homeland and living on another nation's turf that have held nations in place have been supplemented by rising national territoriality among indigenes, displayed as anti-immigrant nativism and acts of violence. In addition, political barriers, such as new immigration and language laws, are becoming more serious impediments to movement outside one's homeland. Finally, economic collapse may be somewhat worse in Soviet Central Asia than in Russia but is occurring in all of the successor states. The geographic differentials in economic opportunity do not create the conditions for a redistribution of nations away from their respective homelands and, if anything, encourage a further reconcentration.

The serious economic decline is raising the attractiveness of emigration from the former USSR to the West. This is particularly true for members of those nations with homelands outside the former USSR, such as Germans and Jews, although Jewish emigration is impeded by declining economic conditions and the unstable political situation in Israel. In addition, Germans from the East are often treated as "foreigners" once they arrive in Germany, even though they are officially considered part of the nation. Germany has attempted to keep the Germans of the former USSR in place. The potential emigration of Russians also appears to be rising, along with their declining status, particularly among the young Russians living in the non-Russian successor states. Nevertheless, the predicted massive Slavic emigration to the West is unlikely, and the reconcentration of nations in homelands is more likely.

As an alternative to out-migration, nationalists living outside the borders of their respective home republics but in regions considered to be part of their "ancestral" homeland are laying claim to these territories. Indigenous national territoriality has engendered a reactive national territoriality among nonindigenes, particularly those living across the border from their formal home republic (e.g., Armenians in Nagorno Karabakh, Tadzhiks in Uzbekistan, Uzbeks in Tadzhikistan and Kyrgyzstan, Russians in northern Kazakhstan and in eastern Ukraine, and Russians and Ukrainians in eastern Moldova). International tensions are found along almost every segment of border between the former union republics. This is not surprising, given the fact that the confederal structure of the state established the minimum geographic extent of each national homeland, which does not often coincide with the more geographically expansive claims made by nationalists. These national territorial conflicts are also certain to undermine the ability of the political elites in each successor state to work together in the CIS.

Indigenous minorities with only autonomous status for their homelands or with no officially recognized homeland are in some ways placed in a more precarious position than nonindigenes, since they have no other homeland in the country toward which to emigrate. A reactive national territoriality has been rising among these minorities as well, resulting in declarations of sovereignty over their homelands and attempts to secede from the union republics in which their homelands are incorporated. Members who may have lived beyond the borders of the autonomous territories in the past have also begun a homeward movement since the late 1980s, particularly in regions of open hostility such as Georgia and Azerbaydzhan.

The primary result of all this movement has been the reconcentration of nations in homelands and a growing national segregation generally, in a nationalistic version of the general "place-clearing function" of territoriality noted by Sack (1986, 33). This demographic indigenization is certain to continue, as nonindigenes move to their respective home republics. Nationalists will also attempt to make border adjustments to the former republics in the name of ethnonational "purification" of the homeland or the recovery of "ancestral" lands, but territorial transfers are likely to create as many new "national problems" as they solve. Even though nations have remained highly concentrated in their respective home republics, it is difficult to conceive of a future in which the multinational successor states are transformed into ethnically pure nation-states, with each political unit containing one and only one nation and homeland. In 1989, 43.4 million members of the fifteen union republic-level nations lived outside their respective home republics, and the more than a hundred other national communities with members resident in the state add another 27.8 million nonindigenes and indigenous minorities with which the successor states will have to deal (Goskomstat SSSR 1991a). Unless indigenous nationalists are able to make a place at the table for nonindigenes who may have lived in the same city or village for generations—and thus consider this place to be their home, and also for indigenous minorities whose "autonomous" homelands are incorporated within the former union republics, international conflict will continue to escalate, and the CIS itself will be stillborn. The focus of future research on the national question in the former USSR must address ways of resolving international territorial disputes short of violent confrontation.

Social Mobilization and Nationalism

As noted above, Soviet leaders and ethnographers looked to socioeconomic development and international equalization to solve the "national problem" inherited from the Russian Empire. Lenin's theoretical works addressing this issue offered a combination of "developmentalism" (i.e., diffusion-erasure) and "internal colonialism" to explain the existence of nations and to provide solutions to the problems associated with their interaction in the multinational Russian Empire. Although the Soviet Union was never an economic superpower, rapid economic development and social mobilization were occurring throughout the interwar and much of the postwar periods. In addition, international equalization was occurring in the rate of educational attainment, occupational mobility, and urbanization—the three measures of social mobilization used in this study. If the socioeconomic prescription for solving the national problem had been accurate, improvements in international relations in the state should have become readily apparent, as loyalty to nation and homeland were supplanted by loyalty to still broader communities of belonging—international Soviet society and the socialist fatherland. However, proclamations by Soviet leaders and ethnographers aside, the "national problem" had not been solved, nor had it even become less significant over the course of time. During the seventy-five-year history of the USSR, the social mobilization and equalization of indigenous masses has coincided not with their internationalization but rather with their national consolidation and rising nationalism. This relationship between socioeconomic development and national consciousness is supportive of the "diffusion-competition" model as elaborated by Nielsen (1985).

The Soviet case provides further evidence against both "developmentalism" and "internal colonialism," the two models on which the nationality policies of the USSR were based.

The social mobilization that occurred in the USSR, and the nationalization of the masses that corresponded with it, did not reduce the importance of place, but it did change the geographic scale from rural localities to broader national homelands. The social mobilization of indigenes, and their equalization with nonindigenes, brought them into closer contact and competition with nonindigenous "outsiders" for the resources of the homeland, including high-status occupations. This process of "modernization" in and of itself would probably have been sufficient to serve as a catalyst in the activation of national territoriality among upwardly mobile indigenes. Nationality policies favoring indigenous upward mobility ensured that national territoriality would be the outcome of socioeconomic development. International equalization in the country as a whole coincided with a system of indigenous privilege in each home republic, reinforcing the perception among indigenes that they and they alone should be socially, culturally, economically, and politically dominant in their own homelands. The geographic context in which social mobilization and international equalization occurred in the USSR created a new national problem—a system of national stratification with indigenous elites in a privileged position in their home republics, who used this position to press for further indigenous concessions from the center (i.e., indigenization from below). The combination of nationalization and indigenization with socioeconomic development was making the centralized nature of political and economic power in the multinational, multihomeland USSR increasingly anachronistic as the state became more modernized.

Sovietization, Russification, or Indigenization?

The national dialectic predicting the sovietization of the masses with social mobilization and international equalization has not come to pass. The process of national consolidation was recognized by Soviet ethnographers, who talked of a national "flowering" (*rastsvet*) that accompanied socioeconomic development. However, according to the national dialectic, national consolidation was essentially complete, and was giving way to the internationalization of the population. This international "drawing together" (*sblizheniye*) was said to be creating a Soviet People, whose loyalty was primarily owed to the socialist fatherland, even while they still considered themselves members of national communities. The "synthesis" resulting from this dialectical process was variously defined as the "merger" (*sliyaniye*) of nations, implying an actual end to national communities, or the unity (*yedinstvo*) of the population into one Soviet citizenry, which still retained some ethnocultural differences. In almost all the writing on "national processes," the trend line indicated that the consolidation of nations and homelands was essentially complete, that nations were drawing closer together, and that it was only a matter of time before they either disappeared entirely or were supplanted by more important communities of belonging (i.e., Soviet society, the communist world, the international proletariat, etc.). Few, if any, predicted the "synthesis" that has actually emerged from this process—rising national separatism.

THE LIMITS OF SOVIETIZATION

Since 1987 the idea of a new "Soviet People" has declined in stature from one of the most researched topics in Soviet ethnographic studies to barely a footnote. This is not to say that no elements of the Soviet socialist ideal have become part of the sociocultural outlook of the population. Egalitarianism and communalism—each of which preceded the Bolshevik Revolution in the Russian countryside—are likely to survive and to impede attempts to convert the planned socialist economy into a capitalist system. There is also a segment of the population that, in all likelihood, feels itself more Soviet than Russian or Ukrainian or Kazakh or any other national identity. For example, it seems clear that Gorbachev was and remains a committed socialist and internationalist, as Lenin was before him. This appears to have contributed to Gorbachev's disastrous misreading of the national problem in the USSR. It is also likely that at least a proportion of the children from nationally mixed marriages—particularly if they are the second or third generation of "international" children—feel themselves to be more Soviet than nationalist. This appears especially likely for children whose parents are both nonindigenes. Of course, individuals may feel both Soviet and national at the same time, and while these two forms of identity have come into conflict at least for members of the non-Russian nations in the state, this does not mean that they will necessarily conflict in the future. Perhaps more important, since Russians served as the dominant nation and culture through which sovietization was promoted, no necessary conflict exists between a Russian nationalist and a Soviet socialist identity. In a recent survey, nearly as many Russians considered themselves Soviets (42 percent) as Russians (43 percent) (Solchanyk 1992, 34). Similarly, a significant number of Russians identify the entire USSR as their homeland. One of the most important new national questions emerging with the collapse of the USSR is the effect that disintegration is having on Russians' sense of national self-consciousness and on their mental map of the Russian homeland. This issue, along with the dramatic transformation of Russians in the non-Russian periphery from dominant group to subordinate minority, need much more attention than they have received to date.

The Soviet ideal has not yet expired, and will reemerge in the successor states. Nevertheless, the ideological belief in a Soviet People that was evolving to supplant the nation as the primary focus of each citizen's identity and loyalty was clearly misguided. The nationalization of the indigenous masses, not their sovietization, was the dominant "national process" occurring over the past seventy-five years. For this reason, there is little cause for concern that a socialist or communist counterrevolution will occur in the former USSR. On the contrary, the real concern in the West and in the successor states should be the rapid move to the Right of nationalist movements.

MUSLIM NATIONALISM?

While Soviet leaders and ethnographers wrote of a Soviet People that was about to eclipse the nations of the state, Western analysts focused their attention either on the survival and expansion of a traditional supranational "homo-Islamicus" in opposition to a "homo-Sovieticus," or alternatively on the Russification of non-Russians. The idea that a Muslim "nation" existed as the primary form of loyalty among the more than forty national communities whose members at one time claimed Islam as their principal religion and whose homelands geographically span the USSR, that this Muslim "nation" was growing rapidly and would soon overtake the dominant Russians as the largest "nation" in the USSR, and that this "nation" strongly opposed communism and represented the greatest threat to the Soviet state was primarily the creation of Alexander Bennigsen (e.g., 1971, 1979, 1986). Although Islam is certainly important in the lives of the believers, little evidence exists that all Muslims in the former USSR share a sense of supranational self-consciousness that supersedes their separate national or even local levels of identity. On the contrary, the sociocultural trends in evidence strongly suggest that nationalization of the Muslim masses toward separate Uzbek, Kazakh, Kirgiz, Tadzhik, Azerbaydzhani, Tatar, and so on, nations has been the dominant "national process" at work among these groups. A lack of geographic mobility has existed throughout all the Muslim territories, the language usage patterns indicate a strong loyalty to the national language, and intermarriage rates are extremely low for Muslims not only with the "infidels" from the north but also with members of other Muslim nations (Kaiser 1992a). Consolidation of each national community in its respective homeland has predominated, and has even resulted in the "de-Tatarization" of Bashkirs during the postwar period.

As the results of this study indicate, the Muslims of the former USSR do not represent a nation of more than fifty million members, immune to the forces of modernization and on the verge of an Islamic fundamentalist revolution. In addition, the rate of population growth in Central Asia is not an asset or a sign of national vitality but is a problem that is undermining the ability of nations in the region to recover economically and environmentally from the socialist policies of the past. Finally, since 1987, the Muslims of Central Asia were not at the forefront of nationalist opposition to Soviet rule, which was predicted by the "homo-Islamicus" school (Bennigsen 1986; Carrere d'Encausse 1979). On the contrary, the region was the most procentrist of any group of republics in the USSR. Ironically, the pressure for the separation of Central Asia from the rest of the former USSR appears to be stronger among nationalist elites in the Slavic states, who have declared their unwillingness to continue subsidizing these economic dependencies.

The lack of Muslim nationalism in the region does not mean that all is well in Central Asia. The region is suffering more than most from economic and environmental collapse. This is serving as a catalyst for a violent form of anti-outsider nativism, which is being directed by indigenes against nonindigenes without regard to whether the outsider is Muslim or not. This violent manifestation of national territoriality is certain to grow along with the region's slide into the underdeveloped South.

THE LIMITS OF RUSSIFICATION

As this study indicates, the postwar focus on Russification in studies of the national question also appears to have been misguided. Most of the Russification in the state occurred during the interwar period, before a strong sense of national self-consciousness among the masses had developed. Since the 1950s, even though the Russian language and culture retained their primacy throughout the state, the rate of Russification of the population decreased appreciably, and was primarily occurring among nonindigenes. The only exception to this was the *ethnies* of northern Siberia, who were undergoing a process of Russification inside the homeland as well as outside. For these groups, whose members have not experienced extensive nationalization, Russification appears more comparable to a process of national consolidation than international integration. The same was undoubtedly also true for at least some of the nonindigenes who had lived outside their respective homelands all their lives, and were perhaps the second or third generation to live in these outlying areas. Particularly if their ancestors migrated from the homeland before their nationalization, these individuals were likely to have had a weakly developed sense of national self-consciousness. What appeared to outside observers as international integration was more likely to be perceived as national consolidation by those individuals participating in the process.

Among indigenous members of nations in the USSR, little linguistic Russification occurred during the postwar period, and since the majority of each nation's population has remained concentrated in its respective home republic, overall Russification in the postwar period has been quite limited. Most non-Russians claimed knowledge of Russian only as a second language, even though this ranking often did not correspond with the relative level of fluency between indigenous and Russian languages. The secondary status of Russian was clearly a nationalistic statement made by indigenes who were expressing their attitude about the standing that their own language and culture should have in their national homelands. The new language laws proclaiming the indigenous language to be the lingua franca of the republic that all nonindigenes must learn was an even clearer statement to this effect.

For the most part, Russification did not proceed beyond linguistic assimilation, a preliminary stage in the process of international integration. International marriages with Russians did increase with urbanization and higher levels of international interaction. As in the case of linguistic Russification, the nonindigenous population engaged most actively in intermarriage with Russians, while the indigenous rate of intermarriage was consistently below the theoretical probability of its occurrence. As a result of intermarriage, nonindigenes were losing adherents through the "natural" assimilation of children from international families. Nonindigenous non-Russians lost out through "natural" assimilation both to the Russian and to the indigenous nations. Children from Russian-indigenous families most often identified as members of the indigenous nation, resulting in an indigenization of Russians over time, not in the Russification of indigenes. The "denationalization" of indigenes through a process of Russification was extremely limited in the postwar USSR.

Overall, before the 1980s the Russian nation was growing as a result of assimilation, primarily through the "natural" assimilation of nonindigenes, although the rate of increase attributed to reidentification was much lower in the postwar period than it had been during the interwar period (Bruk and Kabuzan 1982b). Between 1979 and 1989, using the same measure as Bruk and Kabuzan used to calculate reidentification up to 1979, it appears as though the Russian nation actually lost as a result of a net reidentification away from Russian and toward non-Russian national identities. Topilin (1992) estimated that the Russian nation continued to grow as a result of national reidentification between 1979 and 1989, but at a much slower rate than in previous decades. This was most likely a reflection of the declining status of Russians in the non-Russian periphery during the late 1980s. Children of international families with one Russian parent and the other a member of the indigenous nation who identified themselves as Russians in the past were less likely to do so in an era where indigenous nationalism and anti-Russian sentiments were on the rise. This dramatic shift away from Russification is a powerful indicator of the precipitous decline in status suffered by Russians in the non-Russian periphery, even as early as January 1989 (i.e., the date of the last census). In turn, the declining status of Russians outside Russia has become a potent catalyst for rising Russian nationalism "back home."

ETHNOCULTURAL INDIGENIZATION

During the postwar period, ethnocultural indigenization was an active competitor with Russification. National consolidation continued in those regions of the state where a mass-based national consciousness was still weakly developed. The indigenous language and culture were also promoted by upwardly mobile indigenes, who were becoming more numerous and more nationalistic over time. Only the small Siberian peoples of the north and a few Finnic groups, such as the Karelians whose members have long histories of close interaction with Russians (i.e., beginning long before the nationalization process), appear to be losing adherents through Russification in their homelands.

Rising national consciousness itself was responsible for the retention and promotion of the indigenous language, particularly in the face of rising pressure from above to learn Russian. In this sense, the Russification that was promoted by the central authorities in the state appears to have been counterproductive. Since the late 1980s the language laws passed in nearly every union and autonomous republic proclaimed the indigenous language to be the official language of the republic that all citizens of the republic will be expected to learn. These language laws, even those that accepted the Russian language as the language of international communication, established the indigenous language in each former republic as both a symbol of and an instrument for the ethnocultural domination of indigenes in their homelands.

The pressure on nonindigenes to acculturate to the indigenous nation or to leave for "home" (the latter is undoubtedly favored by indigenous nationalists) has grown enormously since the late 1980s. Ethnocultural indigenization is likely to continue and to promote the process of demographic indigenization discussed above. However, the successor states are unlikely to solve their own national problems through the assimilation or expulsion of all nonindigenes and indigenous minorities. As noted above, there were a total of 71.2 million nonindigenes and indigenous minorities in January 1989, and most lived in areas that they had come to consider as home. Some accommodation of the nonindigenous and indigenous minority languages and cultures will be necessary in order to defuse the international tensions and conflicts that have escalated since 1987.

Finally, it will be necessary to reexamine the way in which indigenous status is defined in the successor states. The majority of those currently classified as nonindigenes have no other home to go to, and feel themselves to be indigenous in the place they happen to reside. If nations are recognized not as primordial organisms rooted to a particular place but rather as modern communities of belonging and interest, then an individual or group should be able to establish indigenous status as a result of more recent residence in an area. Nationalistic arguments based on historic myths should not be allowed to deny an individual or group the land that they have lived on for the last three or four generations, since nations as mass-based communities do not extend into the past much beyond that point. Unfortunately, with nationalists in charge of the process of change, a redefinition of who is indigenous, and therefore deserving of preferential or at least equal treatment with all other indigenes, is unlikely to occur in the near future.

Political Indigenization and the Future of the CIS

As noted above, policies designed to solve the national problem in the USSR—the confederal form adopted by the state and *korenizatsiya*—structured the evolution of international relations in the USSR, and were even important elements in the emergence of a mass-based national consciousness and sense of homeland. The confederal structure of the state began as mere form and was in theory a political geographic instrument used to consolidate power and to help solve the national problem. As such, the confederated state was seen as a temporary structure that would give way to a unitary state and a unified society. In theory, as the USSR developed and as the population was sovietized, the confederal structure of the state was becoming less significant. This was certainly the image projected in the 1961 Communist party program and in anniversary speeches by the party leaders throughout the postwar period. However, far from fading in significance, the confederal borders of the state were taking on a national reality that they had not had before. A sense of homeland that was at least coextensive with the officially delimited territory was growing, along with a growing sense of national self-consciousness among the indigenous masses.

During the postwar period, along with the geographic and social mobilization of the masses, indigenous elites were growing in number and pressing the center more forcefully from below for greater rights and privileges in their own "ancestral" homelands. This pressure for indigenization from below created a new national problem with which the center was increasingly unable to cope. While central authorities spoke of the unification of republics and peoples that was making the confederal form increasingly unnecessary, an increasing number of indigenous nationalists were being created who felt that the unitary essence of political power in the state was the real problem. Only a real confederalization of center-periphery relations would satisfy the national territoriality ambitions of an increasing number of indigenous nationalists.

With the reforms initiated under Gorbachev, this is precisely what occurred. Political power was increasingly exercised by nationalists in their homelands, who were willing and able to mobilize the indigenous masses behind the goals of national self-determination. Almost immediately, indigenous nationalists seized control of the pace and direction of the reforms, placing Gorbachev and the center in the unenviable position of reacting to initiatives from below rather than directing change from above. The center attempted to regain control over the pace of confederalization through the passage of a "law on secession" and the redrafting of the Union Treaty, but these efforts were largely ignored by indigenous nationalists intent on independence for their nations and homelands. The confederal structure of the state did serve as a transitional device, not as a stopping point on the road to complete unification but rather as a jumping-off point for complete independence. In the near future at least, indigenous nationalists in each successor state are unlikely to cede much political power to the Commonwealth of Independent States.

The disintegration of the USSR has generally been applauded in the West as the end of totalitarianism and the birth of democracy in the region. Our tendency to contrast communism with freedom and democracy is no doubt responsible for the general optimism that accompanied the revolutionary changes in the former USSR. However, it is necessary to sound a note of caution. The "totalitarian model" not only blinded us to the societal changes taking place that ultimately brought about the demise of the USSR. It has also tended to blind us as to the motivations of those who are currently in charge of the successor states. We need to keep in mind that nationalists have won political control over their homelands, and that these nationalists will not necessarily act democratically in the pursuit of their national territorial agendas. This national territoriality was clearly in evidence in the declarations of sovereignty and independence made since 1989, which were proclaimed with the goal of securing control over the fate of the indigenous nation, and not in the name of the multinational population that lives in the republic. The recent events in Georgia also provide strong evidence that nationalism rather than democracy was the mobilizing force behind the demise of the USSR. With an ethnically "pure" nation-state standing as the political geographic ideal of indigenous nationalists, dictatorial rulers intolerant of nonindigenes and indigenous minorities rather than democratic leaders supportive of multinational pluralism are more likely to emerge in the successor states.

The major conflict that has begun to develop in the Soviet successor states pits indigenous nationalists who claim the right to determine for themselves their own future in their own homelands (i.e., national territoriality) against nonindigenes and indigenous minorities who seek the right to a political voice. Indigenes whose nations enjoy a demographic majority in the homeland favor one person, one vote majoritarian democracy, while nationalists in the minority advocate the development of more consociational or pluralistic political systems based on a one nation, one vote principle. Of course, nations with demographic majorities in their own national states can all too easily become tyrannical, even within majoritarian democratic political structures. We have already seen this in the case of Georgia, and it is likely to become a more serious problem in Russia. On the other hand, allowing national minorities an equal political voice no matter how small the group undermines the principle of equal representation and may actually encourage the further politicization and territorialization of groups whose members had been acculturating and assimilating in the past. At the level of the interstate CIS, the Russians as a demographic majority with 145 million members may not be satisfied for long if they are afforded only co-equal status with nations as small as the Kirgiz, with only 2.5 million members. The best of all possible worlds would combine the two approaches to manage political conflicts that emerge as a consequence of national territoriality, by allowing for a great deal of national autonomy for indigenous minorities in their own homelands while preserving the political interests of the dominant nation in each successor state through majoritarian democratic institutions.

Because the USSR was created as a hierarchy of autonomies, this structuring of homelands has led to conflicts not only over the placement of borders between the former union republics but also between nationalists who claim all the territory within their union republic and nationalists who claim the territory of autonomous units within that union republic as their homelands (e.g., Azerbaydzhanis versus Armenians over Nagorno-Karabakh, Ossetians, and Abkhazians versus Georgians). Without a relatively neutral center to mediate these international disputes, they are likely to grow in frequency and intensity in the years ahead. Moscow is not likely to be accepted as neutral in these disputes, and if Minsk (i.e., the CIS) cannot serve this function, the United Nations or another interstate organization will be needed to fill the void.

For indigenous minorities, some recognition of their own claim to a region of the state as their homeland must be made. If national self-consciousness and indigenous status are the criteria used to justify the demand for independent statehood, then it is difficult to deny states to indigenous groups whose members feel nationally self-conscious, even if their homelands were only designated as "autonomous" within the old confederal structure. For nonindigenes without a sense of homeland toward the region in which they live, national cultural autonomy, or at least the right to preserve their own ethnocultural heritage, must be respected. Barring these concessions to nonindigenes and indigenous minorities, international tensions and conflicts will escalate, and the prospects for economic recovery and political compromise will diminish.

Unfortunately, few nationalists are willing to compromise on the territorial issue, and the tendency of indigenous majorities to deny minorities the right to territorial autonomy has itself served as a catalyst in the activation of national territoriality among these minorities. Smaller and smaller groups are making declarations of sovereignty and independence in reaction to the rising nationalism and anti-"outsider" nativism of the dominant nations in each state. This national territoriality diffusion process appears to confirm a general tendency noted by Sack (1986: 34), that "territoriality can help engender more territoriality" and thus "tends to be space-filling." Even groups such as the Koreans in Soviet Central Asia, with no strong sense of homeland toward the local region in which they live, feel that they need to gain political control over this territory through the creation of autonomous republics in order to ensure that their ethnocultural identity will be preserved in an increasingly nationalistic environment.

Is it possible to decouple the objective of nationalism or national territoriality—controlling the fate of the nation—from the primary means used to achieve this objective—gaining control over the "ancestral" homeland? Proposals reminiscent of the Austrian Marxist—"national cultural" or "extraterritorial" autonomy have surfaced in the former USSR, and may hold promise for stabilizing relations between indigenes and nonindigenes, the latter of whom can expect ethnocultural support from the national membership in their "home" republics. This may even lessen the border conflicts between the former union republics, and would improve the prospects for the CIS. Of course, this still leaves the problem of indigenous minorities with no other homeland to turn to for support, whose members feel a sense of homeland toward the place they live and nowhere else. For these indigenous minorities, some degree of "national territorial autonomy" must be provided if international conflict is to be minimized.

The results of this research leave one decidedly pessimistic about the prospects for decoupling the nationalist objective of controlling the nation's destiny from the territorial means used to achieve it. The primary message of this study is that a sense of homeland has developed along with a sense of national self-consciousness in the former USSR, and that national homelands have actually become more significant over the course of time. Indeed, for most nationalists, little or no distinction is made between control of homeland and control of the national destiny. Under these circumstances, attempts to strip nations of a privileged standing in their homelands will itself serve as a catalyst for rising nationalism and exacerbate still further international tensions and conflicts.

At present, national territoriality is the dominant political force mobilizing indigenous elites and masses alike to restructure the political geography of the former USSR into independent nation-states where the future of the "primordial" nations will not only be secured but will also be glorious. As we noted above, the other side of the national territorial equation is written by nationalists in equally stark terms: the indigenous nations that fail to gain complete control over their "ancestral" homelands will perish. Under these circumstances, compromise on the national territorial problems facing the successor states is unlikely, since those willing to discuss the possibility of trading land for peace are branded as traitors to the nation.

The future of the CIS does not look promising. Attempts by nationalists in the successor states to restructure national stratification to secure a dominant political, economic, and sociocultural standing for indigenes will increase the level of international discord. Russian nationalism is on the rise, particularly in response to the anti-Russian sentiments and the declining status of Russians in the non-Russian states. Russian political elites have also begun to proclaim Russia, rather than the CIS, as the legitimate successor to the USSR, and the dominance asserted by Russians is raising serious concerns in the non-Russian successor states. The CIS is unlikely to survive this process of national territoriality.

A geographic approach to the study of nationalism in the former USSR provides convincing evidence that place has lost none of its significance over the course of time. With socioeconomic development and the formation of nations as mass-based communities of belonging and interest, more expansive homelands replaced locales as the geographic scale of belonging. The creation of national republics in the Soviet confederal structure helped give form to what were at the time more vaguely defined mental images of home. *Korenizatsiya* policies targeting indigenes for preferential treatment in their home republics but not outside furthered the development of indigenous nations and a sense of homeland that at minimum included all the territory in the home republic. Although the Soviet political elites often thought of the national republics as empty containers within which the national problem would be solved, these national homelands took on a reality that challenged, and eventually undermined, the existence of the multinational, multihomeland USSR itself. Once created in the imaginations of the national membership, the "ancestral" homelands have become the focus of nationalist loyalty, and have structured the way in which members of nations behave toward one another and toward the political center. The geographic context in which socioeconomic development has occurred and nationality policies have been implemented almost guaranteed that the national problem would not only become more intractable over time, but that nationalism would become the essential equivalent of national territoriality in the former USSR.

The failure to recognize the importance of the geographic context in which nations are formed and interact, both by policymakers in the Soviet Union and by analysts in the West more generally, has resulted in serious misconceptions about the nature of nationalism in the USSR and the prospects for solving or at least managing the "national problem." This study, which emphasizes this neglected though extremely important topic, is one of the first serious steps in an effort to bring geography back into the study of nations and nationalism in this world region. A better understanding of the nation-homeland bond and national territoriality is critical, for as events over the past few years in the Soviet Union and elsewhere (e.g., Yugoslavia) have demonstrated, the desire to control life in the homeland is one of the most powerful motivating forces driving indigenous nationalists today. It is hoped that this study will provide a framework both for more detailed studies of particular national communities in the successor states of the former USSR and for more comparative interstate and international works on the geography of nationalism in the world today.

The Significance of National Territoriality in Comparative Studies of Nationalism

The national territoriality that ultimately led to the disintegration of the USSR is not unique to that place. The nationalization and indigenization processes that occurred in Russia and the USSR are comparable to trends in evidence in other multinational, multihomeland states, and particularly those of the developed west. The attempt made by nationalists to control the "ancestral" homeland in order to gain control over the fate of the nation is a nearly ubiquitous feature of the political geographic landscape (e.g., Anderson 1988; Smith 1986; Connor 1986). The results of this study provide strong evidence that the geography of nationalism in the socialist USSR conforms to the general experiences of national and territorial formation in the world political system. In this section, this literature is reviewed and the findings of this study are placed in a broader comparative context.

A majority of states in the world political system are multinational, multihomeland states, and as such are confronted with national problems similar to those which the political elites in the USSR attempted to resolve. One-fifth of the states in North and South America fall into this category, while one-third of the European states, two-thirds of the Asian states, and three-quarters of the African states incorporate more than one ethnonational community and its self-perceived homeland.[1] Given the lack of congruence between political state and national homeland, which is particularly apparent in the new states created following decolonization in Asia and Africa, the potential utility of national territoriality as a general framework with which to analyze "ethnic" separatism outside the Soviet context is vast. A preliminary assessment is offered below.

The most directly comparable case studies are Yugoslavia and Czechoslovakia, not only because both were multinational, multihomeland socialist state but also because each adopted the Leninist-Stalinist federal model for solving their national problems (Kaiser 1988). In addition, indigenization programs and regional equalization policies were implemented in an effort to overcome the interethnic and interregional inequality that was thought to lie behind the national problems confronting each state (Kaiser 1990, 1994). As in the case of the USSR, in both Yugoslavia and Czechoslovakia indigenization policies were supplemented in Slovakia and the non-Serbian home republics by indigenization from below, as the growing number of indigenous elites in each republic sought to gain a dominant standing for the indigenous nation in its respective homeland. Yugoslavia became a confederation of essentially sovereign nation-states by the mid-1970s, although this did little to dampen the national territorial aspirations of both the most (i.e., Slovenia and Croatia) and the least (i.e., Albanians in Kosovo) developed national communities in the state. Similarly, economic and political equalization between the Czech Republic and Slovakia coincided with rising Slovak nationalism after 1968 (Kaiser 1988; Connor 1984b), further supporting the contention that "diffusion-competition" rather than "diffusion-erasure" or "internal colonialism" is the model that best predicts the relationship between socioeconomic development and national self-consciousness for members of the indigenous nation.

[1] This categorization of states considered nation-states to be those with the indigenous nation comprising 90 percent or more of the population. In addition, states with multinational immigrant populations (primarily in the Americas) and with multinational populations with only one homeland were also differentiated. For the world as a whole, 50 percent fell into the multinational, multihomeland category, 21 percent into the nation-state category, 23 percent into the multinational immigrant category, and 6 percent into the multinational, one homeland category. The ethnic data base used for this compilation was provided in Bruk (1986).

Since 1989 each state has disintegrated along national territorial lines. In each, the process of disintegration was facilitated by the federal structure that was originally created in order to solve the national problem. In addition, the new national states created have begun the process of structuring and reinforcing the ethnic stratification system to ensure a dominant position for the indigenous nation in a process that Hayden (1992) has aptly named "constitutional nationalism." Reacting to their new status as a minority in foreign lands, the Serbs of Croatia and Bosnia have attempted to seize control of self-proclaimed home regions, with the assistance of the Serbian government and the former Yugoslav army. The ethnic "cleansing" program currently under way is part of this effort, and is likely to expand to include Kosovo, a region populated primarily by Albanians but which Serbian nationalists proclaim as the birthplace of the Serbian nation.

The attempts by nationalists to clear places claimed as part of the homeland of ethnic others is comparable to the ethnic purification and demographic indigenization in evidence in the Soviet successor states, and particularly in Transcaucasia. The reactive Serbian nationalism in Bosnia and Croatia is of particular concern not only because of the devastating local consequences but also because the potential exists for a similarly tragic response by the Russians living in the non-Russian successor states. A similar effort at ethnic purification will likely occur in southern Slovakia, in eastern Rumania, and in northern Serbia, a region where Magyars are concentrated. This will almost certainly result in the rise of an irredentist movement among the Magyars in the region who will seek "reunification" with Hungary. Slovenia and the Czech Republic have avoided this fate of internal ethnoterritorial conflict not because the indigenous nations are more civilized or more modern, as some analysts have suggested, but because their homelands are more nationally homogeneous.

In the developed west, several multinational, multihomeland states are confronted with national separatism, though all movements are not equally strong (Gourevitch 1979; Orridge 1982; Orridge and Williams 1982; Zariski 1989). The Quebecois movement in Canada, the Basque and Catalonian movements in Spain, the Scottish and Welsh nationalism in Great Britain (not to mention the conflict in Northern Ireland), the tension between Flemish and Walloonian nations in Belgium, and the Breton and Corsican movements in France all indicate that the most developed states in Europe have not overcome their own national problems, even though for the most part they have had a much longer time to work them out. National territoriality in Western Europe has become more apparent during the postwar period, and to a great degree this increase in nationalism is comparable to the processes in evidence in the USSR.

In each of these states, the state idea was structured with a single nation in mind, peripheralizing the remaining national communities in each state. Economic development in the peripheral regions, even when it has brought equalization or relatively greater prosperity to the peripheral nations, has not dampened nationalism, and has, if anything, heightened both national self-consciousness and a nationalistic sense of exclusiveness toward the homeland. Indeed, Nielsen's elaboration of a general theory of "diffusion-competition" (1985) resulted from his comparative study of socioeconomic development and national identity in Western Europe, and particularly in Belgium (Nielsen 1980). As in the case of Russia and the USSR, the salience of indigenous national identity increases with socioeconomic development and equalization, as an increasing number of indigenes comes to compete for the resources of the homeland with socially mobilized outsiders. This is the case not only in Belgium but in Spain and Canada (Pi-Sunyer 1985, 270; Laczko 1986). Modernization, and even equalization, will not solve national problems.

Beyond economics, a similar set of demographic, ethnocultural and political catalysts are also in evidence. The in-migration of Castilians to the Basque homeland (*Euskadi*), of French to Corsica, and of English to Wales served as a catalyst for a rising sense of exclusiveness among the indigenes (Zariski 1989, 261–262; Conversi 1990, 62). The immigration of guestworkers and foreigners from former colonies, and the more recent wave of refugees from Eastern Europe, coupled with economic recession, have also sparked a rise in anti-outsider nativism among dominant nations (e.g., Germans, French, and English). The status of the indigenous ethnocultural attributes in the homeland, and particularly language, has also been a potent catalyst for the activation of national territoriality in Belgium, Spain, and Canada. This is particularly the case in homelands where the indigenous ethnocultural attributes are in decline, which is viewed as a threat to the security of the nation and its future viability. As in the USSR, the acculturation of minority nations toward dominant groups that has occurred has been to the great extent counterproductive, in that protecting the status of indigenous ethnocultural attributes has served to energize national separatist movements. This has been particularly the case in Belgium (Murphy 1988; Nielsen 1980), Canada, and Spain.

Finally, political parties have been formed by each of the national minorities, and have rallied support for greater territorial autonomy and outright independence for the nation in its homeland. The success of these parties has been quite variable both across groups and over time. However, minority nationalists throughout the developed west have been successful in winning a greater degree of political autonomy in their respective homelands over time. Whether they will be satisfied with a more confederal status and remain part of the multinational, multihomeland states or seek outright independence remains to be seen, though the successful use of national territoriality in the USSR and Eastern Europe has added new energy to the national independence cause in several of these states.

The creation of a European Community (EC) and the coming together of a "United States of Europe" is seen by some as a process that is counter to the disintegration that occurred in the USSR. However, this is an overly simplistic assessment of trends in Europe. First, the prospects for a federal "United States of Europe" appear extremely remote, since few of the EC states are willing to cede real political power to the European Community. Second, this assessment misses the important point that minority nationalists in the EC states favor a stronger European center as a way of gaining greater independence from the dominant cores of their multinational, multihomeland states. For example, both Scottish and Basque nationalists favor a stronger EC as a way to weaken the political ties that bind them, respectively, to Great Britain and Spain. This appears to be comparable to the minority nationalists' position in the USSR during the late 1980s and early 1990s, who favored a relatively stronger center to counter the growing strength of the locally dominant nations.

In Western Europe, the growing demands for territorial autonomy by the indigenous minorities have been accommodated to a greater extent than they were in the USSR. Political decentralization during the 1970s and 1980s in Spain, Belgium, Canada, and Great Britain has allowed for greater indigenous control in *Euskadi*, Catalonia, Wallonia, Flanders, Quebec, Scotland, and Wales. More recently, political decentralization in France has provided a greater measure of home rule for Brittany and Corsica. Of course, Switzerland has been relatively stable because it has allowed for a great deal of territorial autonomy within each canton, which accommodated the national territorial ambitions of indigenes in the state. It is also significant that Switzerland was created before the nationalization process, which allowed for a more successful integration of the population toward a Swiss identity.

The greater degree to which national territoriality has been accommodated in the developed west has not solved the national problems facing the multinational, multihomeland states in the region, though it has lent these states a greater degree of legitimacy than that which existed in the USSR. Separatist movements continue to challenge the legitimacy of each of these states, even though outright independence has not yet occurred. The national territorial challenges in the developed west provide strong evidence that national homelands have become even more significant over time and with "modernization."

The degree to which nationalism in the underdeveloped South is comparable to national territoriality in the developed North has been a subject of debate for many years. The main argument against comparing "ethnic" separatism in Africa and Asia to nationalism in Europe is that fully formed nations do not exist in the Third World (i.e., nationalization has not yet and may never occur). The assumption in much of this literature is that the nations of Europe are truly ancient, while the peoples of Africa and Asia are for the most part tribes that have not yet undergone the transition to ethnic groups, let alone nations.

Second, the states themselves for the most part gained independence only in the postwar period, and the colonial status of the region itself is said to distinguish the communities in the region from those that came into being in the North. In the new states created following decolonization, nation-building was to occur with independence and development. National consolidation would reconstruct the multiethnic or multitribal colonies as nation-states. That this nationalization has not yet occurred is thought to result from continued underdevelopment coupled with the lack of adequate time.

As a counter to this argument, the results of this study indicate that national consolidation in Europe (including Russia and the USSR) is not as ancient a process as it is typically depicted to be. In addition, the idea that development would erase ethnic identity and replace it with a national identity whose geographic extent would conform to state boundaries has not occurred in the developed North, and there is little reason to expect that additional time will recreate the multiethnic states of Africa and Asia into nation-states. The assumption that "ethnic" separatism in the Third World is a form of primitive tribalism distinct from the nationalism experienced in the developed world also appears tainted by a good deal of Eurocentrism, if not actual racism.

This is not to argue that no differences exist between national territoriality in Europe and the USSR on the one hand, and Asia and Africa on the other. Clearly, nationalization processes are not yet complete, and ethnic fragmentation is generally greater in the Third World than in the developed North. However, it seems more appropriate to compare ethnic separatism in Asia and Africa with the national territoriality found in Europe and the former USSR first in order to assess the degree of similarity or divergence of trends rather than to assume a difference that might or might not exist.

Separatism in Africa and Asia does appear to conform to the expectations derived from national territoriality. First, indigenous nationalists out of power in both the USSR and the developed West have used the rhetoric of colonial exploitation, and have presented national separatism as decolonization. While the reality may have been quite different, the semantics of decolonization nationalism in the developed North were comparable to those in Africa and Asia. In the underdeveloped South, after decolonization and independence, the political elites in most states in the region attempted to reconstruct a system of ethnic stratification that would favor their own domination over other ethnic communities in the state (Horowitz 1985). Apparently little effort was made toward nation-building through the political, economic, and sociocultural incorporation and enfranchisement of all indigenous *ethnies* in the states. This state-building process through ethnic exclusion created "target minorities" who have responded by emigrating or, if the group out of power is geographically concentrated, by attempting to secede (Tarzi 1991). This subsequent stage in the process of decolonization appears similar to what is occurring in several Soviet successor states today.

The in-migration of ethnic outsiders into the homeland has also been one of the major catalysts for rising anti-outsider nativism, and of separatist movements (Horowitz 1985; Weiner 1978). The finding by Horowitz (1985, 263) that "Government-supported colonization schemes that bring ethnic strangers into the region are uniformly regarded as plots to overwhelm the existing majority in the region by weight of numbers" is comparable to the Baltic nationalist reaction to the Russian in-migration that occurred during the postwar period. Social mobilization among indigenes in their own homelands has tended to coincide with a rising sense of exclusiveness, and appears to conform to the prediction that ethnic solidarity among indigenes becomes more, not less salient, with socioeconomic development (Ayoade 1986). In addition, the development of the homeland by indigenes has frequently coincided with growing demands for indigenous political control over this territory (Cobbah 1988). The socioeconomically developed nations of the Third World, particularly those locked out of political power, are also among the most active in the pursuit of national independence (e.g., Sikhs of India, Tamils of Sri Lanka). In addition, while "backward groups in backward regions" are more frequently secessionist, these secessionist movements are not necessarily driven by economic considerations (Horowitz 1985, 259): "Economic interest may act either as an accelerator or a brake on separatism. Yet, among the most frequent and precocious secessionists—backward groups in backward regions—economic loss or gain plays the smallest role, ethnic anxiety the largest."

The acculturation and assimilation that has occurred frequently serves as a catalyst activating separatist movements in Asia and Africa. The threat that this poses to group survival has been found to be as great an underlying source of ethnic conflict as is interhomeland migration (Horowitz 1985, 263). Indigenous elites also appear similar in their desire to gain politically dominant positions in their homelands, and when the pathway to such territorial autonomy is blocked, separatism has also been the result.

National territoriality as developed in this study provides a geographic framework for the study of national separatism in the developed and underdeveloped worlds that has been for the most part lacking. The tendency in much of the literature on nations and nationalism has been to focus on ethnocultural attributes (i.e., nations as primordial organisms) or economic status (i.e., nations as interest groups), and to treat these as causal agents explaining both national identity and the rise and fall of nationalist movements. This is clearly an oversimplification of the nature of nations and the context in which nationalization occurs. Reformulating the definition of nations as communities of belonging and interest whose members seek to control their homelands in order to secure their future (i.e., national territoriality) not only helps bring geography back into the study of nations and nationalism but also places economic, demographic, and sociocultural trends in their proper perspective. Viewing these as catalysts for the activation of national territoriality, and reexamining the empirical record for evidence of indigenization (i.e., national separatism) in national homelands, will enrich our understanding of the complex social processes through which nations are made and within which they interact with one another.

The geography of nationalism in Russia and the USSR is comparable to the experience in other world regions. More detailed comparative studies of nationalism in the USSR and other multinational, multihomeland states are clearly warranted, and will provide a deeper understanding of nationalism outside the USSR; alternatively, the geography of nationalism as it has developed in the First and Third Worlds will enhance our understanding of nationalism in Russia and the USSR, and of what lies ahead in the successor states.

APPENDIX A

Evolution of the Soviet Federal System

Federal Unit	Date of Creation	Previous Status (month/year)	Status as of 1 January 1993
USSR			Abolished
RSFSR	January 1918		Rossiya, Russian Federation, member of CIS
Bashkir ASSR	March 1919		Republic of Bashkortostan
Buryat ASSR	May 1923	Autonomous Oblast, 1/22–5/23	Republic of Buryatia, seeks reunification with the Agin Buryat and Ust'-Ordin Buryat Autonomous Okrugs
Dagestan ASSR	January 1921		Republic of Dagestan
Kabardin-Balkar ASSR	December 1923	Autonomous Oblast, 1/22–12/23; Became Kabardin ASSR with deportation of Balkars, 4/44; restored 1957	Republic of Kabardino-Balkaria
Kalmyk ASSR	October 1935	Autonomous Oblast, 11/20–10/35; Abolished with deportation of Kalmyks, 12/43; restored 1957	Republic of Kalmykia
Karelian ASSR	June 1923	Autonomous Labor Commune, 6/20–6/23; Karelo-Finnish SSR, 3/40–1956	Republic of Karelia
Komi ASSR	December 1936	Autonomous Oblast, 8/21–12/36	Komi Republic
Mari ASSR	December 1936	Autonomous Oblast, 12/20–12/36	Mari El Republic
Mordvinian ASSR	December 1934	Autonomous Oblast, 1/30–12/34	Republic of Mordvinia
North Ossetian ASSR	December 1936	Autonomous Oblast, 7/24–12/36	Republic of North Ossetia, seeks reunification with South Ossetia (Georgia)

(*continued*)

Federal Unit	Date of Creation	Previous Status (month/year)	Status as of 1 January 1993
Tatar ASSR	May 1920		Republic of Tatarstan, seeks full independence and bilateral treaty relationship with Russia
Tuvin ASSR	October 1961	Autonomous Oblast, 10/44–10/61	Republic of Tuva
Udmurt ASSR	December 1934	Autonomous Oblast, 11/20–12/34	Republic of Udmurtia
Chechen-Ingush ASSR	December 1936	Chechen Autonomous Oblast, 11/22–12/36	Republic of Chechenia, seeks full independence from Russia
		Ingush Autonomous Oblast, 7/24–12/36 Abolished with deportation of Chechens and Ingush 2/44; restored 1957	Republic of Ingushetia, seeks restoration of Ingush territory currently incorporated within North Ossetia
Chuvash ASSR	April 1925	Autonomous Oblast, 6/20–4/25	Republic of Chuvashia
Yakut ASSR	April 1922		Republic of Sakha (Yakutia)
Volga German ASSR	1923	Autonomous Labor Commune, 10/18–1923 Abolished with deportation of Germans, 9/41; has yet to be restored	
Crimean ASSR	1921	Abolished with deportation of Crimean Tatars, 5/44; restored 1/91	Republic of Crimea (Ukraine)
Adygey Autonomous Oblast	July 1922		Republic of Adygea
Gorno-Altay Autonomous Oblast	June 1922	Formerly Oyrot Autonomous Oblast	Republic of Gorno-Altay
Evrey (Jewish) Autonomous Oblast	May 1934		Jewish Autonomous Oblast

(*continued*)

Appendix A · 411

Federal Unit	Date of Creation	Previous Status (month/year)	Status as of 1 January 1993
Karachay-Cherkess Autonomous Oblast	January 1922	Became Cherkess Autonomous Oblast after deportation of Karachay, 10/43; restored 1957	Republic of Karachay-Cherkessia
Khakass Autonomous Oblast	October 1930		Republic of Khakassia
Nenets Autonomous Okrug	1929		Nenets Autonomous Okrug
Yamalo-Nenets Autonomous Okrug	December 1930		Yamalo-Nenets Autonomous Okrug
Taymyr Autonomous Okrug	December 1930		Taymyr Autonomous Okrug
Khanty-Mansi Autonomous Okrug	December 1930	Formerly Ostyko-Vogul' NO	Khanty-Mansi Autonomous Okrug
Evenk Autonomous Okrug	December 1930		Evenk Autonomous Okrug
Vitimo-Olykmin Nationality Okrug	December 1930	Abolished 1936	
Okhotsko Evenk Nationality Okrug	December 1930	Abolished 1936	
Koryak Autonomous Okrug	December 1930		Koryak Autonomous Okrug
Chukchi Autonomous Okrug	December 1930		Chukchi Autonomous Okrug
Komi-Permyak Autonomous Okrug	February 1925		Komi-Permyak Autonomous Okrug
Agin-Buryat Autonomous Okrug	September 1937	Formerly part of Buryat ASSR	Agin-Buryat Autonomous Okrug

(*continued*)

Federal Unit	Date of Creation	Previous Status (month/year)	Status as of 1 January 1993
Ust'-Ordyn Buryat Autonomous Okrug	September 1937	Formerly part of Buryat ASSR	Ust'-Ordin Buryat Autonomous Okrug
Ukraine SSR Crimean Oblast	December 1917	West Ukraine added 10/39	Ukraine, member of CIS Republic of Crimea
Belorussian SSR	January 1919	West Belorussia added 10/39	Republic of Belarus', member of CIS
Estonian SSR	July 1940	Baltic republics independent through interwar period; returned as part of Hitler-Stalin Pact	Republic of Estonia
Latvian SSR	August 1940		Republic of Latvia
Lithuanian SSR	July 1940		Republic of Lithuania
Moldavian SSR	August 1940	Moldavian ASSR part of Ukraine created 10/24; union republic created with return of Bessarabia	Republic of Moldova, member of CIS; self-declared Gagauz and Trans-Dniestrian Republics seek independence from Moldova
Georgian SSR[a]	February 1921	Independent from 1918 to 2/21	Republic of Georgia
Abkhaz ASSR	March 1921		Republic of Abkhazia, seeks independence from Georgia
Adzhar ASSR	June 1921		Republic of Ajaria
South-Ossetian Autonomous Oblast	May 1922		Declared independence from Georgia and intention to unite with North Ossetia, territory was abolished by the Georgian Parliament
Armenian SSR[a]	November 1920	Independent from 1918 to 11/20	Republic of Armenia, member of CIS; seeks to unite with Nagorno-Karabakh
Azerbaydzhan SSR[a]	April 1920	Independent from 1918 to 5/20	Republic of Azerbaijan
Nakhichevan ASSR	February 1924	Autonomous Oblast, 7/23–2/24	Republic of Naxchivan

(continued)

Federal Unit	Date of Creation	Previous Status (month/year)	Status as of 1 January 1993
Nagorno-Karabakh Autonomous Oblast	July 1923		Declared independence from Azerbaijan, seeks to unite with Armenia
Kazakh SSR	December 1936	Kirgiz (Kazakh) ASSR, 8/20; part of RSFSR	Republic of Kazakhstan, member of CIS
Kirgiz SSR	December 1936	Kara-Kirgiz Autonomous Oblast, 10/24 Kirgiz ASSR, 2/26–1936; part of RSFSR	Republic of Kyrgyzstan, member of CIS
Uzbek SSR[b]	October 1924		Republic of Uzbekistan, member of CIS
Karakalpak ASSR	March 1932	Autonomous Oblast in Kazakh ASSR, 5/25–3/32	Republic of Karakalpakstan
Turkmen SSR[b]	October 1924		Republic of Turkmenistan, member of CIS
Tadzhik SSR[b]	December 1929	Tadzhik ASSR, 10/24–6/29; part of Uzbek SSR	Republic of Tajikistan, member of CIS
Gorno-Badakhshan Autonomous Oblast	January 1925		Badakhshon Autonomous Viloyat

Sources: Informatsionno-Statisticheskiy Otdel pri Prezidiume Verkhovnogo Soveta SSSR 1954; Kozlov 1977a; Gurvich 1987; Kolarz 1969, 122–123. For deportation information: Kreindler 1986. Information for column 4: United States Department of State (1992; 1992/1993).

Notes: Autonomous Okrugs were originally called Nationality Okrugs. In addition to the four tiers of territorial autonomy delineated above, approximately 5,300 Nationality Soviets and 250 Nationality Rayons existed for smaller peoples or minorities living in concentrated areas, including Russian settlements outside the RSFSR. These were created from the mid-1920s to the early 1930s, and were abolished at the time of the 1936 Constitution.

[a]The three Transcaucasian republics were part of the Transcaucasian Soviet Federated Socialist Republic (TCSFSR) between 1922 and 1936.

[b]The Central Asian republics of Uzbekistan, Turkmenistan, Kyrgyzstan, and Tadzhikistan were formed from Turkestan, the Bukharan, and Khorezm People's Soviet Republics, which were abolished after 1924. Parts of the territory from Turkestan populated by Kazakhs were added to the Kazakh ASSR.

APPENDIX B

Native Language Instruction in the USSR

GRADE LEVEL OF NATIVE LANGUAGE INSTRUCTION IN THE USSR
(MAXIMUM = 10 YEARS, COMPLETE SECONDARY EDUCATION)*

Nation	1960	1969	1980
UNION REPUBLIC			
Ukrainian	10	10	10
Belorussian	10	10	10
Uzbek	10	10	10
Kazakh	10	10	10
Georgian	10	10	10
Azerbaydzhan	10	10	10
Lithuanian	10	10	10
Moldavian	10	10	10
Latvian	10	10	10
Kirgiz	10	10	10
Tadzhik	10	10	10
Armenian	10	10	10
Turkmen	10	10	10
Estonian	10	10	10
AUTONOMOUS REPUBLIC			
Abkhaz	4	4	—
Karakalpak	10	9	—

*For union republic nations, native language universities are also normally available in the homeland.

NATIVE LANGUAGE INSTRUCTION IN THE RSFSR

Nation	1958[a]	1960[b]	1969[b]	1972[a]	1980[c]
AUTONOMOUS REPUBLIC					
Avar	4	4	0	1	2 or 3
Dargin	4	4	0	2	2 or 3
Kumyk	4	3	0	2	2 or 3
Lezgin	4	4	0	2	2 or 3
Bashkir	10	10	10	10	10
Buryat	7	6	6	6	4 or 5

(*continued*)

Native Language Instruction in the RSFSR (*continued*)

Nation	1958[a]	1960[b]	1969[b]	1972[a]	1980[c]
Kabardin	4	4	0	0	0
Balkar	4	2	0	0	0
Kalmyk	4	2	0	0	0
Karelian	—	0	0	—	0
Komi	7	4	1	3	4 or 5
Mari	7	4	1	3	4 or 5
Mordvin	7	4	3	3	4 or 5
Ossetian	4	4	0	0	0
Tatar	10	10	10	10	10
Tuvin	7	7	8	7	8
Udmurt	7	4	2	3	4 or 5
Chechen	4	0	0	0	0
Ingush	4	1	0	0	0
Chuvash	7	7	4	4	4 or 5
Yakut	7	7	6	8	8
Autonomous Oblast					
Altay	4	6	4	3	—
Adygey	4	4	2	0	—
Karachay	4	0	0	0	0
Cherkess	4	—	—	0	0
Khakass	4	4	0	3	4 or 5
Autonomous Okrug					
Komi-Permyak	7	4	1	3	—
Mansi	—	—	—	0	0
Nenets	2	—	—	0	0
Khanty	2	—	—	0	0
Chukchi	2	—	—	0	0
Evenk	2	—	—	0	0
Koryak	2	—	—	—	0
Other					
Armenian	10	—	—	10	—
Azerbaydzhan	10	—	—	2	—
Kazakh	10	—	—	10	—
Turkmen	4	—	—	—	—
German	—	—	—	0	0
Korean	7	—	—	—	—

Sources: [a]1958, 1972: Compilations of Soviet authors as cited in Silver 1974b, 33–34; [b]1960, 1969: Silver 1978, 258–259; [c]1980: Guboglo 1984, 134–136.

Notes: The Silver estimates for 1960 and 1969 reflect the grade level at which textbooks in mathematics and the natural sciences were published. It appears that, in general, the Guboglo figures for the end of the 1970s and beginning of the 1980s (column headed by "1980") track better with the Soviet data for 1958 and 1972 than with Silver's estimates, although the two sets of earlier figures do not diverge significantly.

Languages of Instruction Other Than the Native and Russian Languages (1960s and early 1970s)

Republic	Language of Instruction
Ukraine	Moldavian, Hungarian, Polish
Uzbekistan	Tadzhik, Turkmen, Kazakh, Karakalpak, Kirgiz
Kazakhstan	Uzbek, Tadzhik, Korean, Uygur
Georgia	Abkhaz, Azerbaydzhan, Armenian, Ossetian
Azerbaydzhan	Armenian, Georgian
Kyrgyzstan	Uzbek, Tadzhik
Tadzhikistan	Uzbek, Turkmen, Kirgiz, Kazakh
Armenia	Azerbaydzhan
Turkmenistan	Uzbek, Kazakh

Source: Guboglo 1977a, 268.

Note: No information was available from this or other sources on additional languages of instruction in the Baltic republics, Moldavia, or Belorussia. Their exclusion from this table does not necessarily mean that no other languages of instruction were present.

Bibliography

Agnew, John. 1984. Place and political behaviour: The geography of Scottish nationalism. *Political Geography Quarterly* 3:191–206.
———. 1987. *Place and politics: The geographical mediation of state and society*. Boston: Allen & Unwin.
Akiner, Shirin. 1983. *Islamic peoples of the Soviet Union*. London: Kegan Paul International.
Alekseyev, V., and A. Moskovskiy. 1980. Razvitiye rabochego klassa v Sibiri v period stroitel'stva sostializma." In *Formirovaniye i razvitiye mnogonatsional'nogo rabochego klassa SSSR v period stroitel'stva sotsializma (1921–1937 gg.)*, 123–134. Tbilisi: Metsniyereba.
Allworth, Edward. 1980. Ambiguities in Russian group identity and leadership in the USSR. In *Ethnic Russia in the USSR*, edited by E. Allworth, 17–38. New York: Pergamon.
———. 1973. Regeneration in Central Asia. In *The nationality question in Soviet Central Asia*, edited by Edward Allworth, 3–18. New York: Praeger.
Allworth, Edward, ed. 1971. *Soviet nationality problems*. New York: Columbia University Press.
———. 1973. *The nationality question in Soviet Central Asia*. New York: Praeger.
———. 1980. *Ethnic Russia in the USSR*. New York: Pergamon.
Alstadt-Mirhadi, Audrey. 1986. Baku: Transformation of a Muslim town. In *The city in late imperial Russia*, edited by Michael Hamm, 283–318. Bloomington: Indiana University Press.
AN SSSR. 1990. *Novyy soyuznyy dogovor: Poiski resheniy*. Moskva: Institut Gosudarstva i Prava, Akademiya Nauk SSSR.
Anderson, Barbara. 1980. *Internal migration during modernization in late nineteenth-century Russia*. Princeton: Princeton University Press.
Anderson, Barbara, and Brian Silver. 1983a. Measuring shifts in ethnic identity and native language among non-Russians in the USSR. *Demography* 20:461–490.
———. 1983a. Socio-demographic consequences of World War II on the non-Russian nationalities of the USSR. Paper presented at the conference: "The Impact of World War II on the Soviet Union." Baton Rouge: Louisiana State University, April 25–26.
Anderson, Benedict. 1983. *Imagined communities: Reflections on the origin and spread of nationalism*. London: Verso.
Anderson, J. 1988. Nationalist ideology and territory. In *Nationalism, self-determination and political geography*, edited by R. Johnston, D. Knight, and E. Kofman, 18–39. London: Croom Helm.
Ardrey, Robert. 1966. *The territorial imperative: A personal inquiry into the animal origins of property and nations*. New York: Dell.
Andreyev, V. 1989. Ob ekonomicheskoy samostoyatel'nosti respublik. *Kommunist* (12):59–65.
Argumenty i Fakty. 1992. Konstitutsiya Rossiyskoy Federatsii (proyekt), no. 12 (special issue).

———. 1990a. Konstitutsiya Rossiyskoy Federatsii (proyekt), no. 47 (special issue).

———. 1990b. Deklaratsiya Verkhovnogo Soveta Belorusskoy Sovetskoy Sotsialisticheskoy Respubliki o Gosudarstvennom Suverenitete Belorusskoy Sovetskoy Sotsialisticheskoy Respubliki (31):1–2.

———. 1990c. Bezhentsy v ozhidanii (#28).

Armstrong, John. 1982. *Nations before nationalism*. Chapel Hill: University of North Carolina Press.

Arslan, A., and S. Shahmurtian. 1990. Armenia and Azerbaijan. *Meeting Report* (Kennan Institute) 8, no. 3.

Arutyunyan, Yu. 1968. Opyt sotsial'no-etnicheskogo issledovaniya. *Sovetskaya Etnografiya* (#4):3–13.

———. 1969. Konkretno-sotsiologicheskoye issledovaniye natsional'nykh otnosheniy. *Voprosy Filosofii* (#12):129–139.

———. 1972. Izmeneniye sotsial'noy struktury sovetskikh natsiy. *Istoriya SSSR* (#4): 3–20.

———. 1985. Natsional'nyye osobennosti sotsial'nogo razvitiya. *Sotsiologicheskiye Issledovaniya* (#3):28–35.

———. 1990. Sotsial'no-kul'turnoye razvitiye i natsional'noye samosoznaniye. *Sotsiologicheskiye Issledovaniya* (#7):42–49.

Arutyunyan, Yu., and Yu. Bromley, eds. 1986. *Sotsial'no-kul'turnyy oblik sovetskikh natsiy*. Moskva: Nauka.

Aspaturian, Vernon. 1968. The non-Russian nationalities. In *Prospects for Soviet society*, edited by A. Kassof, 143–198. New York: Praeger.

Atamanchuk, G. 1990. A new treaty—is it only a matter of powers? *Soyuz* (#30):4 (cited in *FBIS Soviet daily reports* 14 August 1990 [157]:28–31).

Atkin, Muriel. 1992. Religious, national, and other identities in Central Asia. In *Muslims in Central Asia: Expressions of identity and change*, edited by Jo-Ann Gross, 46–77. Durham, N.C.: Duke University Press.

———. 1993. Tajikistan: Ancient heritage, new politics. In *Nations and politics in the Soviet successor states*, edited by Ian Bremmer and Ray Taras, 361–383. Cambridge: Cambridge University Press.

Ayoade, John. 1986. Ethnic politics in Nigeria: A conceptual reformulation. In *Ethnicity, politics and development*, edited by D. Thompson and D. Ronen, 105–118. Boulder: Lynne Rienner.

Bahry, Donna, and Carol Nechemias. 1981. Half full or half empty?: The debate over Soviet regional equality. *Slavic Review* 40:366–383.

Balabanov, S., and E. Shvetsova. 1987. Gosudarstvennaya politika upravleniya razvitiyem narodnostey severa. In *Problemy sovremennogo sotsial'nogo razvitiya narodnostey severa*, edited by V. Boykopp, 28–36. Novosibirsk: Nauka.

Banac, Ivo, and Frank Sysyn, eds. 1986. Concepts of nationhood in early modern eastern Europe. *Harvard Ukrainian studies* 10, nos. 3/4 (special issue).

Bassin, Mark. 1991. Russia between Europe and Asia: The ideological construction of geographical space. *Slavic Review* 50:1–17.

Baumann, Robert. 1987. Subject nationalities in the military service of imperial Russia: The case of the Bashkirs. *Slavic Review* 46:489–502.

Becker, Seymour. 1973. National consciousness and the politics of the Bukhara People's

Conciliar Republic. In *The nationality question in Soviet Central Asia*, edited by E. Allworth, 159–167. New York: Praeger.

Beissinger, Mark. 1988. Ethnicity, the personnel weapon, and neo-imperial integration: Ukrainian and RSFSR provincial party officials compared. *Studies in Comparative Communism* 21:71–85.

Belkindas, Misha, and Matthew Sagers. 1990. A preliminary analysis of economic relations among union republics of the USSR: 1970–1988. *Soviet Geography* 31:629–656.

Bennigsen, Alexandre. 1971. Islamic, or local consciousness among Soviet nationalities? In *Soviet nationality problems*, edited by Edward Allworth, 168–182. New York: Columbia University Press.

———. 1979. Several nations or one people? Ethnic consciousness among Soviet Central Asian muslims. *Survey* 24:51–64.

———. 1986. Soviet minority nationalism in historical perspective. In *The last empire: Nationality and the Soviet future*, edited by Robert Conquest, 131–150. Stanford, Calif.: Hoover Institution Press.

Berezkin, A., et al. 1989. The geography of the 1989 elections of People's Deputies of the USSR (preliminary results). *Soviet Geography* 30:607–634.

Bialer, Seweryn. 1980. *Stalin's successors*. Cambridge: Cambridge University Press.

Birlik. 1989. Uzbek Popular Front. *Central Asia and Caucasus Chronicle* (#6):4–7.

Blaut, James. 1987. *The national question: Decolonising the theory of nationalism*. London: Zed.

Bohac, Rodney. 1991. Everyday forms of resistance: Serf opposition to gentry exactions, 1800–1861. In *Peasant economy, culture, and politics of European Russia, 1800–1921*, edited by Esther Kingston-Mann and Timothy Mixter, 236–260. Princeton, N.J.: Princeton University Press.

Bolmenkova, L. 1988. *Internatsionalizm v deystvii*. Moskva: Mysl'.

Bond, Andrew, and Matthew Sagers. 1990. Adoption of law on economic autonomy for the Baltic republics and the example of Estonia: A comment. *Soviet Geography* 31:1–10.

Bond, Andrew, Misha Belkindas, and Andrey Treyvish. 1990. Economic development trends in the USSR, 1970–1988: Part I (production and productivity). *Soviet Geography* 31:705–731.

———. 1991. Economic development trends in the USSR, 1970–1988: Part 2 (consumption, investment, and income redistribution). *Soviet Geography* 32:1–57.

Borg, J. 1989. "As Eastern Europe goes, so goes . . . Guam?" *Washington Post* 16 December.

Borzykh, N. 1984. Mezhnatsional'nyye braki v SSSR v seredine 1930-x godov. *Sovetskaya Etnografiya* (#3):101–112.

Bradley, Joseph. 1986. Moscow: From big village to metropolis. In *The city in late imperial Russia*, edited by Michael Hamm, 9–42. Bloomington: Indiana University Press.

Braker, Hans. 1971. The Muslim revival in Russia. In *Russia enters the twentieth century 1894–1917*, edited by Erwin Oberlander et al., 182–198. New York: Schocken Books.

Breslauer, George. 1986. Provincial party leaders' demand articulation and the nature of center-periphery relations in the USSR. *Slavic Review* 45:650–672.

Breuilly, John. 1982. *Nationalism and the state*. Manchester, England: Manchester University Press.
Bromley, Yu. 1969. Etnos i endogamy. *Sovetskaya Etnografiya* (#6):84–91.
———. 1981. Osnovnyye vidy istoriko-kul'turnykh obshchnostey i tendentsii ikh dinamiki. *Sovetskaya Etnografiya* (#1):10–23.
———. 1983a. *Ocherki teorii etnosa*. Moskva: Nauka.
———. 1983b. Etnograficheskoye izucheniye sovremennykh natsional'nykh protsessov v SSSR. *Sovetskaya Etnografiya* (#2):4–14.
———. 1987. National processes in the USSR—achievements and problems. *Current Digest of the Soviet Press* 39 (7):1–3.
Bromley, Yu., ed. 1977. *Sovremennyye etnicheskiye protsessy v SSSR*. 2d ed. Moskva: Nauka.
Bromly, Yu., and I. Gurvich. 1987. Sovremennyye etnokul'turnyye protsessy u narodnostey kraynego severa. In *Problemy sovremennogo sotsial'nogo razvitiya narodnostey severa*, 159–168. Novosibirsk: Nauka (Sibirskoye otdeleniye).
Bronshteyn, M. 1989. Regional'nyy khozraschet: nuzhny trezvost' i dokazatel'nost'. *Kommunist* (#5):60–64.
Brooke, James. 1991. As centralized rule wanes, ethnic tension rises anew in Soviet Georgia. *New York Times* (2 October):A3.
Brooks, Jeffrey. 1985. *When Russia learned to read*. Princeton, N.J.: Princeton University Press.
Brown, Bess. 1990. The role of public groups in perestroika in Central Asia. *Report on the USSR (Radio Liberty)* (26 January):20–25.
Bruk, S. 1986. *Naseleniye mira: etnodemograficheskiy spravochnik*. Moskva: Nauka.
Bruk, S., and V. Kabuzan. 1980. Dinamika i etnicheskiy sostav naseleniya Rossii v epokhy imperializma (konets XIX v.—1917 g.). *Istoriya SSSR* (#3):74–93.
———. 1981. Chislennost' i rasseleniye Ukrainskogo etnosa v XVIII—nachalye XX v. *Sovetskaya Etnografiya* (#5):15–31.
———. 1982a. Dinamika chislennosti i rasseleniya Russkogo etnosa (1678–1917 gg.). *Sovetskaya Etnografiya* (#4):9–25.
———. 1982b. Dinamika chislennosti i rasseleniya Russkikh posle velikoy oktyabr'skoy sotsialisticheskoy revolyutsii. *Sovetskaya Etnografiya* (#5):3–21.
Brzezinski, Zbigniew. 1962. *Ideology and power in Soviet politics*. New York: Praeger.
Burds, Jeffrey. 1991. The social control of peasant labor in Russia: The response of village communes to labor migration in the Central Industrial Region, 1861–1905. In *Peasant economy, culture, and politics of European Russia, 1800–1921*, edited by Esther Kingston-Mann and Timothy Mixter, 52–100. Princeton, N.J.: Princeton University Press.
Burkhardt, William. 1983. Institutional barriers, marginality, and adaptation among the American-Japanese mixed bloods in Japan. *Journal of Asian Studies* 42:519–544.
Bushnell, John. 1990. Peasants in uniform: The tsarist army as a peasant society. In *The world of the Russian peasant: Post-emancipation culture and society*, edited by Ben Eklof and Stephen Frank, 101–114. Boston: Unwin Hyman.
Busygin, E., and G. Stolyarova. 1988. Kul'turno-bytovyye protsessy v natsional'no-smeshannykh sem'yakh. *Sovetskaya Etnografiya* (#3):27–36.
Carlisle, Donald. 1991. Uzbekistan and the Uzbeks. *Problems of Communism* 40 (5):23–44.

Carrere d'Encausse, Helene. 1979. *Decline of an empire: The Soviet Socialist Republics in revolt*. New York: Harper & Row.
Carter, Stephen. 1990. *Russian nationalism: Yesterday, today, tomorrow*. London: Pinter.
CDSP. 9 November 1977. The new USSR Constitution. *Current Digest of the Soviet Press* 29 (41):1–13.
———. 1987a. More repercussions of Alma-Ata riots. *Current Digest of the Soviet Press* 39 (2):8–11.
———. 1987b. Probing the roots of Kazakhstan's troubles. *Current Digest of the Soviet Press* 39 (5):13–15.
———. 1987c. Our moral values: Only friendship does good. *Current Digest of the Soviet Press* 39 (20):22–23.
Chekhoyeva, S. 1989. Yazykovaya situatsiya v natsional'nykh shkolakh RSFSR. *Sovetskaya Pedagogika* (#6):19–23.
Chervyakov, V., V. Shapiro, and F. Sheregi. 1991. *Mezhnatsional'nyye konflikty i problemy bezhentsev*. 2 parts. Moskva: Institut Sotsiologii.
Cheshko, S. 1989. Ekonomicheskiy suverenitet i natsional'nyy vopros. *Kommunist* (#2):97–105.
Chew, Allen. 1970. *An atlas of Russian history: Eleven centuries of changing borders*. Rev. ed. New Haven: Yale University Press.
Chistov, K. 1977a. Osnovnyye tipy dukhovnoy kul'tury narodov predrevolyutsionnoy Rossii. In *Sovremennyye etnicheskiye protsessy v SSSR*, edited by Yu. Bromley, 321–334. Moskva: Nauka.
———. 1977b. Dukhovnaya kul'tura i protsessy etnicheskoy konsolidatsii narodov SSSR. In *Sovremennyye etnicheskiye protsessy v SSSR*, edited by Yu. Bromley, 349–365. Moskva: Nauka.
Christian, David. 1991. The black and the gold seals: Popular protests against the liquor trade on the eve of emancipation. In *Peasant economy, culture, and politics of European Russia, 1800–1921*, edited by Esther Kingston-Mann and Timothy Mixter, 261–293. Princeton, N.J.: Princeton University Press.
Chuyko, L. 1975. *Braki i razvody*. Moskva: Statistika.
Clem, Ralph. 1976. The changing geography of Soviet nationalities and its socio-economic correlates: 1926–1970. Ph.D. dissertation, Columbia University, New York.
———. 1980. The ethnic dimension of the Soviet Union, parts I and II. In *Contemporary Soviet Society: Sociological perspectives*, edited by Jerry Pankhurst and Michael Sacks, 11–62. New York: Praeger.
———. 1988. Perestroika: The social context of reform in the Soviet Union. In *Gorbachev's new thinking*, edited by Ronald Liebowitz, 9–22. Cambridge: Ballinger.
———. 1992. The frontier and colonialism in Russian and Soviet Central Asia. In *Geographical perspectives on Soviet Central Asia*, edited by Robert Lewis, 19–36. London: Routledge.
Clem, Ralph, ed. 1986. *Research guide to the Russian and Soviet censuses*. Ithaca: Cornell University Press.
Clines, Francis. 1991. New vote promised. *New York Times* (27 August):A1+.
Cobbah, Josiah. 1988. Toward a geography of peace in Africa: Redefining sub-state self-determination rights. In *Nationalism, self-determination and political geography*, edited by R. Johnston et al., 70–86. London: Croom Helm.

Connor, Walker. 1967. Self-determination: The new phase. *World Politics* 20:30–53.
———. 1972. Nation-building or nation-destroying? *World Politics* 24:319–355.
———. 1978. A nation is a nation, is a state, is an ethnic group is a . . . *Ethnic and Racial Studies* 1:377–400.
———. 1984a. *The national question in Marxist-Leninist theory and strategy*. Princeton, N.J.: Princeton University Press.
———. 1984b. Eco- or ethno-nationalism? *Ethnic and Racial Studies* 7:342–359.
———. 1986. The impact of homelands upon diasporas. In *Modern diasporas in international politics*, edited by Gabriel Sheffer, 16–45. London: Croom Helm.
———. 1990. When is a nation? *Ethnic and Racial Studies* 13:92–103.
Conolly, Violet. 1971. The "nationalities question" in the last phase of tsardom. In *Russia enters the twentieth century 1894–1917*, edited by Erwin Oberlander et al., 152–181. New York: Schocken Books.
Constitution. 1976. *Constitution (Fundamental Law) of the Union of Soviet Socialist Republics*. Moscow: Progress.
Conquest, Robert. 1967. *Soviet nationalities policy in practice*. New York: Praeger.
———. 1968. *The great terror: Stalin's purges of the thirties*. New York: Collier.
———. 1970. *The nation killers*. New York: Macmillan.
Conversi, Daniele. 1990. Language or race? The choice of core values in the development of Catalan and Basque nationalisms. *Ethnic and Racial Studies* 13:50–70.
Corrsin, Stephen. 1990. Language use in cultural and political change in pre-1914 Warsaw: Poles, Jews, and Russification. *The Slavonic and East European Review* 68:69–90.
CPSU. 1986. Concerning the further optimization of general secondary education for young people and the improvement of conditions of work in the general education school. *The Soviet Review* 27:44–59.
Crisp, Simon. 1985. The formation and development of literary Avar. In *Sociolinguistic perspectives on Soviet national languages*, edited by Isabelle Kreindler, 143–162. Berlin: Mouton de Gruyter.
CSCE. 1992. *Report on the Tatarstan referendum on sovereignty*. U.S. Commission on Security and Cooperation in Europe. April 14.
Curtiss, John. 1968. The peasant and the army. In *The peasant in nineteenth-century Russia*, edited by Wayne Vucinich, 108–132. Stanford: Stanford University Press.
Dal', Vladimir. 1881. Otechestvo and rodina. *Tolkovyy slovar' zhivago Velikoruskago yazyka*. St. Petersburg: M. O. Vol'fa.
Demko, George. 1969. *The Russian colonization of Kazakhstan 1896–1916*. Bloomington: Indiana University Press.
Desheriyev, Yu., and I. Protchenko. 1968. *Razvitiye yazykov narodov SSSR v Sovetskuyu epokhu*. Moskva: Nauka.
Deutsch, Karl. 1953. *Nationalism and social communication*. Cambridge: MIT Press.
———. 1966. Nationalism and social communication. In *An Inquiry into the foundations of nationality*. 2d ed. Cambridge: MIT Press.
Dienes, Leslie. 1989. Perestroyka and the Slavic Regions. *Soviet Economy* 5:251–275.
Dillon, Leo. 1990. Ethnicity and political boundaries in the Soviet Union. Map 0858. Washington, D.C.: Office of the Geographer, U.S. Department of State.
Dixon, Simon. 1990. The Russians: The dominant nationality. In *The nationalities question in the Soviet Union*, edited by Graham Smith, 21–37. London: Longman.

Donnelly, Alton. 1968. *The Russian conquest of Bashkiria 1552–1740*. New Haven and London: Yale University Press.

Drobizheva, L. 1971. Sotsial'no-kul'turnyye osobennosti lichnosti i natsional'nyye ustanovki. *Sovetskaya Etnografiya* (#3):3–15.

———. 1977. Vyravnivaniye urovnya kul'turnogo razvitiya narodov SSSR. In *Sovremennyye etnicheskiye protsessy v SSSR*, edited by Yu. Bromley, 334–349. Moskva: Nauka.

———. 1981. *Dukhovnaya obshchnost' narodov SSSR*. Moskva: Mysl'.

———. 1985. Natsional'noye samosoznaniye: baza formirovaniya i sotsial'no-kul'turnyye stimuly razvitiya. *Sovetskaya Etnografiya* (#5):3–16.

———. 1991a. Etnicheskoye samosoznaniye Russkikh v sovremennykh usloviyakh: ideologiya i praktika. *Sovetskaya Etnografiya* (#1):3–13.

———. 1991b. The role of the intelligentsia in developing national consciousness among the peoples of the USSR under perestroika. *Ethnic and Racial Studies* 14:87–99.

Drobizheva, L., and A. Susokolov. 1981. Mezhetnicheskiye otnosheniya i etnokul'turnyye protsessy. *Sovetskaya Etnografiya* (#2):11–22.

Dunlop, John. 1983. *The faces of contemporary Russian nationalism*. Princeton, N.J.: Princeton University Press.

Dzyuba, Ivan. 1970. *Internationalism or Russification?* 2d ed. London: Weidenfeld and Nicolson.

Ebzeyeva, S. 1982. Sovetskaya federatsiya na etape zrelogo sotsializma. *Sovetskoye Gosudarstvo i Pravo* (#7):3–10.

Edwards, David. 1986. Marginality and migration: Cultural dimensions of the Afghan refugee problem. *International Migration Review* 20:313–325.

Eklof, Ben. 1986. *Russian peasant schools: Officialdom, village culture, and popular pedagogy, 1861–1914*. Berkeley: University of California Press.

———. 1990. Peasants and schools. In *The world of the Russian peasant: Postemancipation culture and society*, edited by Ben Eklof and Stephen Frank, 115–132. Boston: Unwin Hyman.

Eklof, Ben, and Stephen Frank, eds. 1990. *The world of the Russian peasant: Postemancipation culture and society*. Boston: Unwin Hyman.

Elebayeva, Aynur. 1992. The Osh incident: Problems for research. *Post-Soviet Geography* 33:78–88.

Emerson, Rupert. 1960. *From empire to nation: The rise and self-assertion of Asian and African peoples*. Boston: Beacon Press.

Emmons, Terence. 1968. The peasant and the emancipation. In *The peasant in nineteenth-century Russia*, edited by Wayne Vucinich, 41–71. Stanford: Stanford University Press.

Enloe, Cynthia. 1973. *Ethnic conflict and political development*. Boston: Little, Brown and Company.

Evstigneyev, Yu. 1971. National'no-smeshannyye braki v Makhachkale. *Sovetskaya Etnografiya* (#4):80–85.

———. 1975. Interethnic marriages in some cities of northern Kazakhstan. *Soviet Sociology* 13 (3):3–16.

Fainsod, Merle. 1965. *How Russia is ruled*. Rev. ed. Cambridge: Harvard University Press.

Fanger, Donald. 1968. The peasant in literature. In *The peasant in nineteenth-century Russia*, edited by Wayne Vucinich, 231–262. Stanford: Stanford University Press.

FBIS. 14 June 1990. Text of sovereignty declaration published (RSFSR). *Soviet Daily Reports* (115):102–103.

———. 31 July 1990. Reportage on interethnic tension in Osh Oblast. *Soviet Daily Reports* (147):104–106.

———. 2 August 1990. Estonian 'law on immigration' published. *Soviet Daily Reports* (149):72–76.

———. 9 August 1990. Uzbek, Kirghiz writers discuss Osh events. *Soviet Daily Reports* (154):88–91.

———. 21 August 1990. Statehood for Soviet Germans viewed. *Soviet Daily Reports* (162):28–31.

———. 27 August 1990. Armenian declaration of independence published. *Soviet Daily Reports* (166):106–107.

———. 27 August 1990. Kirghizia's sovereignty future analyzed. *Soviet Daily Reports* (166):117–118.

———. 5 September 1990. Synopsis of Shatalin group economic program. *Soviet Daily Reports* (172):69–74.

———. 12 September 1990. Declaration of Turkmen sovereignty published. *Soviet Daily Reports* (177):107–108.

———. 13 September 1990. Threats, violence reported in Tuva conflict. *Soviet Daily Reports* (178):93–94.

———. 18 September 1990. Tajikistan tension 'shows no sign of abating'. *Soviet Daily Reports* (181):73–74.

———. 19 September 1990. *Soviet Daily Reports* (182):89–90.

———. 9 October 1990. Buryat Autonomous Republic declares sovereignty. *Soviet Daily Reports* (195):96–97.

———. 12 October 1990c. Moldavian nationalism sparks Russian backlash. *Soviet Daily Reports* (198-S):58–61.

———. 12 October 1990a. Koryak Autonomous Soviet Republic proclaimed; Komi-Permyak Okrug becomes Autonomous Oblast. *Soviet Daily Reports* (198):112.

———. 12 October 1990b. Snegur addresses Moldavian Supreme Soviet. *Soviet Daily Reports* (198-S):45–51.

———. 16 November 1990. Paper views intransigent attitudes. *Soviet Daily Reports* (222):78–83.

———. 21 November 1990. Yeltsin discusses Ukraine treaty at session. *Soviet Daily Reports* (225):72–78.

———. 27 November 1990. Citizenship bill promulgated (Moldova). *Soviet Daily Reports* (228):80–81.

———. 11 December 1990. Russian-Kazakh treaty signed in Moscow. *Soviet Daily Reports* (238):73–74.

———. 17 December 1990. Treaty between RSFSR, Ukrainian SSR. *Soviet Daily Reports* (242-S):23–25.

———. 20 December 1990. Kazakh declaration on state sovereignty. *Soviet Daily Reports* (245):70–72.

———. 24 December 1990. Gamsakhurdia views South Ossetia, citizenship. *Soviet Daily Reports* (247):100–101.

---. 31 December 1990. Ter-Petrosyan new year message praises unity. *Soviet Daily Reports* (251):75.

---. 14 January 1991. Russian-Estonian governments sign agreement. *Soviet Daily Reports* (009):110.

---. 11 March 1991. Revised draft union treaty published. *Soviet Daily Reports* (047):28–33.

Fierman, William. 1985. Language development in Soviet Uzbekistan. In *Sociolinguistic perspectives on Soviet national languages: Their past, present and future*, edited by Isabelle Kreindler, 205–233. Berlin: Mouton de Gruyter.

Foye, Stephen. 1993. CIS joint command abolished. *RFE/RL Daily Report* no. 112 (16 June).

Friedrich, Carl, and Brzezinski, Zbigniew. 1961. *Totalitarian dictatorship and autocracy*. New York: Praeger.

Gans, Herbert. 1979. Symbolic ethnicity: The future of ethnic groups and cultures in America. *Ethnic and Racial Studies* 2:1–20.

Gantskaya, O. 1977. Obshchiye tendenstii etnosotsial'nogo razvitiya brachno-semeynykh otnosheniy. In *Sovremennyye etnicheskiye protsessy v SSSR*, edited by Yu. Bromley, 433–460. Moskva: Nauka.

Gantskaya, O., and G. Debets. 1966. O graficheskom izobrazhenii rezul'tatov statisticheskogo obsledovaniya mezhnatsional'nykh brakov. *Sovetskaya Etnografiya* (#3):109–118.

Gantskaya, O., and L. Terent'yeva. 1965. Etnograficheskiye issledovaniya natsional'nykh protsessov v Pribaltike. *Sovetskaya Etnografiya* (#3):3–19.

---. 1977. Mezhnatsional'nyye braki i ikh rol' v etnicheskikh protsessakh. In *Sovremennyye etnicheskiye protsessy v SSSR*, edited by Yu. Bromley, 460–483. Moskva: Nauka.

Gardanov, V., B. Dolgikh, and T. Zhdanko. 1961. Osnovnyye napravleniya etnicheskikh protsessov u narodov SSSR. *Sovetskaya Etnografiya* (#4):9–29.

Gellner, E. 1983. *Nations and nationalism*. Ithaca: Cornell University Press.

Germani, Gino. 1980. *Marginality*. New Brunswick, N.J.: Transaction Books.

Getty, J. Arch. 1991. State and society under Stalin. *Slavic Review* 50:18–35.

Girnius, K. 1991. Baltic states opt for independence. In *Soviet federalism: Nationalism and decentralisation*, edited by Alastair McAuley, 160–177. Leicester and London: Leicester University Press.

Gleason, Gregory. 1990a. *Federalism and nationalism: The struggle for republican rights in the USSR*. Boulder: Westview Press.

---. 1990b. Marketization and migration: The politics of cotton in Central Asia. *Journal of Soviet Nationalities* 1 (2): 66–98.

Goble, Paul. 1990. Gorbachev, secession, and the fate of reform. *Report on the USSR (Radio Liberty)* 2 (17):1–2.

Gold, John. 1982. Territoriality and human spatial behaviour. *Progress in Human Geography* 6:44–67.

Gorbachev, Mikhael. 1986. Politicheskiy doklad Tsentral'nogo Komiteta KPSS XXVII S'ezdu Kommunisticheskoy Partii Sovetskogo Soyuza. In M. S. Gorbachev, *Izbrannyye rechi i stat'i*, vol. 3, 180–280. Moskva: Politizdat, 1987.

---. 1987a. Oktyabr' i perestroyka: revolyutsiya prodolzhaetsya. In M. S. Gorbachev, *Izbrannyye rechi i stat'i*, vol. 5, 386–436. Moskva: Politizdat, 1988.

———. 1987b. *Perestroika: New thinking for our country and the world*. New York: Harper & Row.

———. 1988a. *Perestroyka i novoye myshleniye dlya nashey strany i dlya vsego mira*. Moskva: Politizdat.

———. 1988b. O khode realizatsii resheniy XXVII S'ezda KPSS i zadachakh po uglubleniyu perestroyki. In *Materialy XIX Vsesoyuznoy Konferentsii Kommunisticheskoy Partii Sovetskogo Soyuza*, 3–89. Moskva: Politizdat.

———. 1989. O natsional'noy politike partii v sovremennykh usloviyakh. *Doklad i zaklyuchitel'noye slovo na Plenume TsK KPSS 19, 20 Sentyabrya 1989 goda*. Moskva: Politizdat.

Gorbatov, A. 1990. Bol'shiye plany vokrug "Maloy Litvy." *Pravda* (22 March):2.

Gordon, Milton. 1978. *Human nature, class, and ethnicity*. New York: Oxford University Press.

Goskomstat SSSR (Gosudarstvennyy Komitet SSSR po Statistike). 1987. *Narodnoye khozyaystvo SSSR za 70 let*. Moskva: Finansy i Statistika.

———. 1988a. *Slovari natsional'nostey i yazykov*. Moskva: Goskomstat SSSR.

———. 1988b. *Trud v SSSR: statisticheskiy sbornik*. Moskva: Finansy i Statistika.

———. 1989a. *Natsional'nyy sostav naseleniya*. Moskva: Finansy i Statistika.

———. 1989b. Naseleniye. *Statisticheskiy Press-Bulleten'* (#4):49–79.

———. 1989c. *Narodnoye obrazovaniye i kul'tura v SSSR: statisticheskiy sbornik*. Moskva: Finansy i Statistika.

———. 1989d. *Itogi vsesoyuznoy perepisi naseleniya 1979 goda*, 10 volumes. Moskva: Goskmostat SSSR.

———. 1989e. *Naseleniye SSSR 1988: statisticheskiy ezhegodnik*. Moskva: Finansy i Statistika.

———. 1990a. *Natsional'nyy sostav naseleniya SSSR: po dannym vsesoyuznoy perepisi naseleniya 1989 g*. Moskva: Finansy i Statistika.

———. 1990b. *Demograficheskiy ezhegodnik SSSR, 1990*. Moskva: Finansy i Statistika.

———. 1990c. *Narodnoye khozyaystvo SSSR v 1989 godu*. Moskva: Finansy i Statistika.

———. 1990d. Sostav studentov vysshikh uchebnykh zavedeniy po korennym natsional'nostyam na nachalo 1989/90 uchebnogo goda. *Press Vypusk* (#105).

———. 1991a. *Natsional'nyy sostav naseleniya SSSR: po dannym vsesoyuznoy perepisi naseleniya 1989 g*. Moskva: Finansy i Statistika.

———. 1991b. *Narodnoye khozyaystvo SSSR v 1990 g*. Moskva: Finansy i Statistika.

Gottmann, J. 1973. *The significance of territory*. Charlottesville: University Press of Virginia.

Gourevitch, Peter. 1979. The reemergence of "peripheral nationalisms." *Comparative Study of Society and History* 21:303–322.

Grabowicz, George. 1982. *The poet as mythmaker: A study of symbolic meaning in Taras Shevchenko*. Cambridge: Harvard University Press.

———. 1989. Province to nation: Nineteenth century Ukrainian literature as a paradigm of the national revival. *Canadian Review of Studies in Nationalism* 16:117–132.

Granberg, A. 1990. The economic mechanism of inter-republic and inter-regional relations. *Soviet Review* 31 (5):38–54.

Greenfeld, Liah. 1990. The closing of the Russian mind. *The New Republic* (5 February):30–34.
Guboglo, M. 1969. O vliyanii rasseleniya na yazykovyye protsessy. *Sovetskaya Etnografiya* (#5):16–30.
———. 1972. Razvitiye mnogonatsional'noy sovetskoy pechati v 1917–1940 gg. *Istoriya SSSR* (#6):121–132.
———. 1984. *Sovremennyye etnoyazykovyye protsessy v SSSR*. Moskva: Nauka.
———. 1977a. Razvitiye obshchestvennykh funktsiy yazykov narodov SSSR v sfere shkol'nogo obrazovaniya. In *Sovremennyye etnicheskiye protsessy v SSSR*, edited by Yu. Bromley, 260–275. Moskva: Nauka.
———. 1977b. Vzaimodeystviye yazykov narodov SSSR i razvitiye dvuyazychiya. In *Sovremennyye etnicheskiye protsessy v SSSR*, edited by Yu. Bromley, 294–315. Moskva: Nauka.
———. 1977c. Razvitiye obshchestvennykh funktsiy yazykov narodov SSSR v sfere pechati. In *Sovremennyye etnicheskiye protsessy v SSSR*, edited by Yu. Bromley, 275–284. Moskva: Nauka.
———. 1992. *Deportatsii narodov SSSR (1930-e–1950-e gody)*. Moskva: Institut Etnologii i Antropologii.
Gudkov, Lev. 1990. Russkiye v respublikakh. *Moskovskiye Novosti* (#41):7.
Gumilev, L. 1990. *Ethnogenesis and the biosphere*. Moscow: Progress.
Gurr, Ted. 1970. *Why men rebel*. Princeton, N.J.: Princeton University Press.
Gurvich, I. 1972. Sovremennyye napravleniya etnicheskikh protsessov v SSSR. *Sovetskaya Etnografiya* (#4):16–33.
———. 1980. Polveka avtonomii narodnostey severa SSSR." *Sovetskaya Etnografiya* (#6):3–17.
———. 1987. *Etnicheskoye razvitiye narodnostey severa v sovetskiy period*. Moskva: Nauka.
Gurvich, I., and Ch. Taksami. 1985. Sotsial'nyye funktsii yazykov narodnostey severa i dal'nego vostoka SSSR v sovetskiy period. *Sovetskaya Etnografiya* (#2):54–63.
Guthier, Steven. 1977. The Belorussians: National identification and assimilation, 1897–1970. Part 1, 1897–1939. *Soviet Studies* 29:37–61.
Hamm, Michael, ed. 1986. *The city in late imperial Russia*. Bloomington: Indiana University Press.
Hammer, Darrell. 1988. Glasnost' and "the Russian idea." In *Russian nationalism today*. Radio Liberty Research Bulletin, 19 December (special edition).
Hanaway, Jr., William. 1973. Farsi, the vatan, and the millat in Bukhara. In *The nationality question in Soviet Central Asia*, edited by Edward Allworth, 143–150. New York: Praeger.
Hayden, Robert. 1992. Constitutional nationalism in the formerly Yugoslav republics. *Slavic Review* 51 (4):654–673.
Hechter, Michael. 1975. *Internal colonialism: The Celtic fringe in British national development, 1536–1966*. Berkeley: University of California Press.
———. 1976. Ethnicity and industrialization: On the proliferation of the cultural division of labor. *Ethnicity* 3:214–224.
———. 1978. Group formation and the cultural division of labor. *American Journal of Sociology* 82:293–318.
———. 1985. Internal colonialism revisited. In *New nationalisms of the developed*

west, edited by Edward Tiryakian and Ronald Rogowski, 17–26. Boston: Allen & Unwin.
Hechter, Michael, and Margaret Levi. 1979. The comparative analysis of ethnoregional movements. *Ethnic and Racial Studies* 2:260–274.
Hechter, Michael et al. 1982. A theory of ethnic collective action. *International Migration Review* 16:412–434.
Henriksson, Anders. 1986. Riga: Growth, conflict, and the limitations of good government, 1850–1914. In *The city in late imperial Russia*, edited by Michael Hamm, 177–208. Bloomington: Indiana University Press.
Hewitt, George. 1985. Georgian: A noble past, a secure future. In *Sociolinguistic perspectives on Soviet national languages: Their past, present and future*, edited by Isabelle Kreindler, 163–179. Berlin: Mouton de Gruyter.
Hobsbawm, Eric. 1983. Mass-produced traditions: Europe, 1870–1914. In *The invention of tradition*, edited by Eric Hobsbawm and Terence Ranger, 263–307. Cambridge: Cambridge University Press.
———. 1990. *Nations and nationalism since 1780*. Cambridge: Cambridge University Press.
Hobsbawm, Eric, and Terence Ranger, eds. 1983. *The invention of tradition*. Cambridge: Cambridge University Press.
Hodnett, Grey. 1967a. What's in a nation? *Problems of Communism* 16 (5):2–15.
———. 1967b. The debate over Soviet federalism. *Soviet Studies* 18:458–481.
Hoffmann, David. 1991. Movement to Moscow: Patterns of peasant in-migration during the First Five-Year Plan. *Slavic Review* 50:847–857.
Horowitz, Donald. 1981. Patterns of ethnic separatism. *Comparative Study of Society and History* 23:165–195.
———. 1985. *Ethnic groups in conflict*. Berkeley: University of California Press.
Hovannisian, Richard. 1983. Caucasian Armenia between imperial and Soviet rule: The interlude of national independence. In *Transcaucasia: Nationalism and social change*, edited by Ronald Suny, 259–292. Ann Arbor: The University of Michigan Slavic Publications.
Hroch, Miroslav. 1985. *Social preconditions of national revival in Europe*. Cambridge: Cambridge University Press.
Hrushevsky, Michael. 1970. *A history of Ukraine*. Hamden: Archon Books.
Ikhilov, M. 1965. K voprosu o natsional'noy konsolidatsii narodov Dagestana. *Sovetskaya Etnografiya* (#6):92–101.
Informatsionno-Statisticheskiy Otdel pri Prezidiume Verkhovnogo Soveta SSSR. 1954. *Administrativno-territorial' noye Deleniye Soyuznykh Respublik na Marta 1954 goda*. Moskva: Izvestiya Sovetov Deputatov Trudyashchikhsya SSSR.
Inorodtsy. 1894. *Entsiklopedicheskiy slovar'*, vol. 13, 224–225. St. Petersburg.
Isayev, M. 1979. *Yazykovoye stroitel'stvo v SSSR*. Moskva: Nauka.
Iskenderov, A. 1989. Natsional'nyy vopros i mezhnatsional'nyye otnosheniya v SSSR: istoriya i sovremennost' (vstupitel'noye slovo). *Voprosy Istorii* (#5):3–97.
Isupov, A. 1964. *Natsional'nyy sostav naseleniya SSSR*. Moskva: Statistika.
Ivanov, V. 1989. *Istoricheskaya mysl' v Rossii XVIII-serediny XIX v. o narodakh severo-vostoka Azii*. Moskva: Nauka.
Izmaylov, A., and M. Kolmakova. 1980. Stanovleniye i razvitiye sovetskoy natsio-

nal'noy shkoly. In *Ocherki istorii shkoly i pedagogicheskoy mysli narodov SSSR 1917–1941 gg.*, 141–176. Moskva: Pedagogika.
Izvestiya. 24 November 1990. Soyuznyy dogovor.
Johnson, Robert. 1990. Peasant and proletariat: migration, family patterns, and regional loyalties. In *The world of the Russian peasant: Post-emancipation culture and society*, edited by Ben Eklof and Stephen Franks, 81–100. Boston: Unwin Hyman.
Johnston, R., D. Knight, and E. Kofman, eds. 1988. *Nationalism, self-determination and political geography*. London: Croom Helm.
Jones, Ellen. 1985. *Red army and society: A sociology of the Soviet military*. Boston: Allen & Unwin.
Jones, Ellen, and Fred Grupp. 1984. Modernization and ethnic equalization in the USSR. *Soviet Studies* 36:159–184.
———. 1987. *Modernization, value change and fertility in the Soviet Union*. London: Cambridge University Press.
JPRS. 1989. Republic language legislation. *JPRS-UPA (Soviet Union: Political Affairs)* 63 (5 December).
Kaiser, Robert. 1988. National territoriality in multinational, multi-homeland states: A comparative study of the Soviet Union, Yugoslavia and Czechoslovakia. Ph.D. dissertation, Columbia University, New York.
———. 1990. The equalization dilemma in Yugoslavia. *Geoforum* 21:261–276.
———. 1991. Nationalism: the challenge to Soviet federalism. In *The Soviet Union: A new regional geography?*, edited by Michael Bradshaw, 39–65. London: Belhaven.
———. 1992a. Nations and homelands in Soviet Central Asia. In *Geographical perspectives on Soviet Central Asia*, edited by Robert Lewis, 279–312. London: Routledge.
———. 1992b. Social mobilization in Soviet Central Asia. In *Geographical perspectives on Soviet Central Asia*, edited by Robert Lewis, 251–278. London: Routledge.
———. 1992c. National territoriality and demographic indigenization in the non-Russian periphery. Contribution to the panel on patterns of disintegration in the former Soviet Union. *Post-Soviet Geography* 33:347–404.
———. 1994. Czechoslovakia: The disintegration of a binational state. In *Federalism: The multiethnic challenge*, edited by Graham Smith. London: Longman (forthcoming).
Kalyshev, A. 1984. Mezhnatsional'nyye braki v sel'skikh rayonakh Kazakhstana. *Sovetskaya Etnografiya* (#2):71–77.
Kamm, Henry. 1992. Crimean Tatars, exiled by Stalin, return home. *New York Times* (8 February):4.
Karamzin, Nicholas. 1802. On the love of the fatherland and national pride. In *Russian intellectual history; an anthology*, edited by Marc Raeff, 107–112. New York: Harcourt, Brace & World, 1966.
———. 1811. A memoir on ancient and modern Russia (extract). In *A documentary history of Russian thought from enlightenment to Marxism*, edited by W. Leatherbarrow and D. Offord, 32–41. Ann Arbor, Mich.: Ardis.
Karklins, Rasma. 1984. Ethnic politics and access to higher education: The Soviet case. *Comparative Politics* 16:277–294.

Karpovich, Vladimir. 1986. *On Lenin's work "Critical remarks on the national question."* Moscow: Novosti Press.
Kaslow, Amy. 1991. Soviets face sharp food shortages. *The Christian Science Monitor* (30 September):3.
Kasperovich, Galina. 1985. *Migratsiya naseleniya v goroda i etnicheskiye protsessy.* Minsk: Nauka i Tekhnika.
Kaymarazov, G. 1988. *Formirovaniye sotsialisticheskoy intelligentsii na severnom Kavkaze.* Moskva: Nauka.
Khachaturov, K. 1988. Fruits of complacency and inaction. *Moscow News* (#12):10.
Khomich, L. 1980. Yamalo-Nenetskiy Avtonomnyy Okrug (k 50-letiyu obrazovaniya). *Sovetskaya Etnografiya* (#6):67–77.
Khorev, B. 1990. Economic decentralization and regionalism. *Soviet Geography* 31:509–516.
King, Robert. 1973. *Minorities under communism.* Cambridge: Harvard University Press.
Kingston-Mann, Esther. 1991. Breaking the silence: An introduction. In *Peasant economy, culture, and politics of European Russia, 1800–1921*, edited by Esther Kingston-Mann and Timothy Mixter, 3–20. Princeton, N.J.: Princeton University Press.
Kingston-Mann, Esther, and Timothy Mixter, eds. 1991. *Peasant economy, culture, and politics of European Russia, 1800–1921.* Princeton: Princeton University Press.
Kirch, Aksel, Marika Kirch, and Tarmo Tuisk. 1992. *The non-Estonian population today and tomorrow: A sociological overview.* Tallinn: Estonian Science Foundation.
Kirkh, A. et al. 1988. Etnosotsial'naya differentsiatsiya gorodskogo naseleniya Estonii. *Sotsiologicheskiye Issledovaniya* (#3):30–35.
Kirkwood, Michael. 1991. Glasnost', "the national question" and Soviet language policy. *Soviet Studies* 43:61–81.
Kir'yanchuk, V., and V. Podkolzin. 1990. Perestroyka and the economic region in state management and planning. *Soviet Geography* 31:366–374.
Kiselev, V. 1990. Deportirovannyye. Samozakhvatchiki. Chto dal'she. *Moskovskiye Novosti* (#45):8–9.
Knight, David. 1982. Identity and territory: Geographical perspectives on nationalism and regionalism. *Annals of the Association of American Geographers* 72:514–531.
———. 1988. Self-determination for indigenous peoples: The context for change. In *Nationalism, self-determination and political geography*, edited by R. Johnston et al., 117–134. London: Croom Helm.
Kohn, Hans. 1945. *The idea of nationalism: A study in its origins and background.* New York: Macmillan.
Kohut, Zenon. 1986. The development of a Little Russian identity and Ukrainian nationbuilding. *Harvard Ukrainian Studies* 10:559–576.
Kolarz, Walter. 1969. *The peoples of the Soviet far east.* Hamden: Archon.
Kolosov, V. 1990. The geography of elections of USSR People's Deputies by national-territorial districts and the nationalities issue. *Soviet Geography* 31:753–766.
———. 1992. *Ethno-territorial conflicts and boundaries in the former Soviet Union.* England: University of Durham.
Kolosov, V., N. Petrov, and L. Smirnyagin. 1990. *Vesna 89: geografiya i anatomiya parlamentskikh vyborov.* Moskva: Progress.

Konstantinov, F. 1985. *Kommunizm i natsii*. Moskva: Nauka.
Korel', L., V. Tapilina, and V. Trofimov. 1988. *Migratsiya i zhilishche*. Novosibirsk: Nauka (Sibirskoye Otdeleniye).
Koroteyeva, V., L. Perepelkin, and O. Shkaratan. 1988. Ot byurokraticheskogo tsentralizma k ekonomicheskoy integratsii suverennykh respublik. *Kommunist* (#15):22–33.
Kostinskiy, Grigoriy. 1990. Regional preferences and concepts of Soviet youth. *Soviet Geography* 31:732–752.
Kozenko, A., and L. Monogarova. 1971. Statisticheskoye izucheniye pokazateley odnonatsional'noy i smeshannoy brachnosti v Dushanbe. *Sovetskaya Etnografiya* (#6):112–118.
Kozlov, V. 1971. Etnos i territoriya. *Sovetskaya Etnografiya* (#6):89–100.
———. 1975. *National'nosti SSSR: etnograficheskiy obzor*. Moskva: Statistika.
———. 1977a. Natsional'no-gosudarstvennoye stroitel'stvo i razvitiye etnicheskikh protsessov v SSSR. In *Sovremennyye etnicheskiye protsessy v SSSR*, edited by Yu. Bromley, 87–104. Moskva: Nauka.
———. 1977b. Izmeneniya v rasselenii i urbanizatsiya narodov SSSR kak usloviya i faktory etnicheskikh protsessov. In *Sovremennyye etnicheskiye protsessy v SSSR*, edited by Yu. Bromley, 137–158. Moskva: Nauka.
———. 1977c. Etnicheskiye protsessy i dinamika chislennosti narodov SSSR. In *Sovremennyye etnicheskiye protsessy v SSSR*, edited by Yu. Bromley, 484–499. Moskva: Nauka.
———. 1982. *Natsional'nosti SSSR*. 2d ed. Moskva: Finansy i Statistika.
Kramer, Jane. 1972. *Unsettling Europe*. New York: Random House.
Krawchenko, Bohdan. 1985. *Social change and national consciousness in twentieth century Ukraine*. New York: St. Martin's Press.
Kreindler, Isabelle. 1985. The Mordvinian languages: A survival saga. In *Sociolinguistic perspectives on Soviet national languages: Their past, present and future*, edited by Isabelle Kreindler, 237–264. Berlin: Mouton de Gruyter.
———. 1986. The Soviet deported nationalities: A summary and an update. *Soviet Studies* 38:387–405.
Kreindler, Isabelle, ed. 1985. *Sociolinguistic perspectives on Soviet national languages: Their past, present and future*. Berlin: Mouton de Gruyter.
Kristof, Ladis. 1967a. The geopolitical image of the fatherland: The case of Russia. *The Western Political Quarterly* (1967):941–954.
———. 1967b. The state-idea, the national idea and the image of the fatherland. *Orbis* 11:238–255.
Krivonogov, V. 1980. Mezhetnicheskiye braki u Khakasov v sovremennyy period. *Sovetskaya Etnografiya* (#3):73–86.
Kryukov, M. 1986. Eshche raz ob istoricheskikh tipakh etnicheskikh obshchnostey. *Sovetskaya Etnografiya* (#3):58–69.
Kudryavtsev, V., and B. Topornin. 1990. What kind of new union treaty should we have? *Izvestiya* (19 June):3. (Also cited in FBIS *Soviet Daily Reports* 2 July 1990 (127):25–28).
Kushner, P. 1951. *Etnicheskiye territorii i etnicheskiye granitsy*. Moskva: Akademii Nauk SSSR.
Kux, Stephan. 1990. Soviet federalism. *Problems of Communism* 39 (2):1–20.

Kuzeyev, R., V. Babenko, and N. Moiseyeva. 1988. Osobennosti etnonatsional'nogo razvitiya narodov Volgo-Ural'skoy istoriko-etnograficheskoy oblasti za gody Sovetskoy vlasti. *Sovetskaya Etnografiya* (#1):3–15.

Kuznetsov, A. 1990. Avtonomiya ili samoupravleniye? *Sovetskaya Etnografiya* (#2):3–14.

Laczko, Leslie. 1986. On the dynamics of linguistic cleavage in Quebec: A test of alternative hypotheses. *International Journal of Sociology and Social Policy* 6:39–60.

Lapidus, Gail. 1989. Gorbachev and the "national question": Restructuring the Soviet federation. *Soviet Economy* 5:201–250.

———. 1984. Ethnonationalism and political stability: The Soviet case. *World Politics* 36:555–580.

Latvijas Republikas Valsts Statistikas Komiteja (RVSK). 1990. *Latvijas skaitlos 1989 goda*. Riga: Latvijas RSVK.

Lazzerini, Edward. 1985. Crimean Tatar: The fate of a severed tongue. In *Sociolinguistic perspectives on Soviet national languages*, edited by Isabelle Kreindler, 109–124. Berlin: Mouton de Gruyter.

Leasure, J. William, and Robert Lewis. 1966. *Population changes in Russia and the USSR: A set of comparable territorial units* (Social Science Monograph series). San Diego, Calif.: San Diego State College Press.

———. 1967. Internal migration in the USSR: 1897–1926. *Demography* 4:479–496.

———. 1968. Internal migration in Russia in the late nineteenth century. *Slavic Review* 27:375–394.

Lee, Everett. 1966. A theory of migration. *Demography* 3:47–57.

Lenin, V. [1913] 1968. Critical remarks on the national question. In *National liberation, socialism and imperialism, selected writings by V. I. Lenin*, 12–44. New York: International.

———. [1913b] 1975. Two cultures in every national culture. In *The Lenin anthology*, edited by Robert Tucker, 654–658. New York: W. W. Norton.

———. [1914] 1968. The right of nations to self-determination. In *National liberation, socialism and imperialism, selected writings by V. I. Lenin*, 45–104. New York: International.

———. [1916] 1968. The discussion on self-determination summed up. In *National liberation, socialism and imperialism, selected writings by V. I. Lenin*, 125–164. New York: International.

———. [1918] 1975. The chief task of our day. In *The Lenin anthology*, edited by Robert Tucker, 433–437. New York: W. W. Norton.

———. [1920] 1975. Theses on the national and colonial questions. In *The Lenin anthology*, edited by Robert Tucker, 619–625. New York: W. W. Norton.

———. [1922] 1975. The question of nationalities or "autonomization." In *The Lenin anthology*, edited by Robert Tucker, 719–724. New York: W. W. Norton.

Lepeshkin, A. 1975. Sovetskiy federalizm v period razvitogo sotsializma. *Sovetskoye Gosudarstvo i Pravo* (#8):3–12.

Lewin, Moshe. 1988. *The Gorbachev phenomenon: A historical interpretation*. Berkeley: University of California Press.

Lewis, Robert. 1984. The universality of demographic processes in the USSR. In *Geographical studies on the Soviet Union*, edited by George Demko and Roland

Fuchs, 109–130. University of Chicago, Department of Geography, Research Paper No. 211.

———. 1987. Soviet demographic policy: How comprehensive, how effective? In *Soviet geographic studies in our time*, edited by Lutz Holzner and Jeane Knapp, 23–50. The University of Wisconsin—Milwaukee, College of Letters and Science.

Lewis, Robert, Richard Rowland, and Ralph Clem. 1976. *Nationality and population change in Russia and the USSR*. New York: Praeger.

Lewis, Robert, and Richard Rowland. 1979. *Population redistribution in the USSR*. New York: Praeger.

Libardian, Gerard. 1983. Revolution and liberation in the 1892 and 1907 programs of the Dashnaktsutiun. In *Transcaucasia: Nationalism and social change*, edited by Ronald Suny, 185–196. Ann Arbor, Mich.: The University of Michigan Slavic Publications.

Liber, George. 1989. Urban growth and ethnic change in the Ukrainian SSR, 1923–1933. *Soviet Studies* 41:574–591.

Liebowitz, Ronald. 1983. Finlandization: An analysis of the Soviet Union's "domination" of Finland. *Political Geography Quarterly* 2:275–287.

———. 1986. Education and literacy data in Russian and Soviet censuses. In *Research guide to the Russian and Soviet censuses*, edited by Ralph Clem, 155–170. Ithaca: Cornell University Press.

———. 1987. Soviet investment strategy: A further test of the "equalization hypothesis." *Annals of the Association of American Geographers* 77:396–407.

———. 1991. Spatial inequality under Gorbachev. In *The Soviet Union: A new regional geography?*, edited by Michael Bradshaw, 15–38. London: Belhaven Press.

Linz, Juan. 1985. From primordialism to nationalism. In *New nationalisms of the developed west*, edited by Edward Tiryakian and Ronald Rogowski, 203–253. Boston: Allen & Unwin.

Literaturnaya gazeta. 11 October 1989. Nemetskaya avtonomiya: Gde? Kogda? Kak? (41):11.

Long, Larry. 1988. *Migration and residential mobility in the United States*. New York: Russell Sage Foundation.

Longworth, Philip. 1990. Historians and nationalism. *The Slavonic and East European Review* 68:100–105.

Lorimer, Frank. 1946. *The population of the Soviet Union*. Geneva: League of Nations.

Lubin, Nancy. 1984. *Labour and nationality in Soviet Central Asia*. Princeton, N.J.: Princeton University Press.

Magosci, Paul. 1978. *The shaping of a national identity: Subcarpathian Rus', 1848–1948*. Cambridge: Harvard University Press.

Makarova, G. 1987. *Narodnyy Komissariat po Delam Natsional'nostey RSFSR 1917–1923 gg. istoricheskiy ocherk*. Moskva: Nauka.

Maksimov, G. 1976. Povyshenniye urovnya obrazovznniya naseleniya SSSR. In *Vsesoyuznaya perepis' naseleniya 1970 goda: sbornik statey*, edited by G. Maksimov, 181–193. Moskva: Statistika.

Marker, Gary. 1990. Literacy and literacy texts in Muscovy: A reconsideration. *Slavic Review* 49:74–89.

Marnie, Sheila, and Wendy Slater. 1993. Russia's refugees. *RFE/RL Research Report* 2, no. 37 (17 September):46–53.

Matley, Ian. 1973. Ethnic groups of the Bukharan State ca. 1920 and the question of nationality. In *The nationality question in Soviet Central Asia*, edited by E. Allworth, 134–142. New York: Praeger.

Matveeva, E. 1992. Locals say no to Korean autonomy in the Maritime Territory. *Moscow News* (#38):5.

McAuley, Alastair. 1991a. Economic constraints on devolution: The Lithuanian case. In *Soviet federalism: Nationalism and decentralisation*, edited by Alastair McAuley, 178–195. Leicester and London: Leicester University Press.

McAuley, A., ed. 1991b. *Soviet federalism: Nationalism and decentralisation*. Leicester and London: Leicester University Press.

McAuley, Mary. 1984. Nationalism and the Soviet multi-ethnic state. In *The state in Socialist society*, edited by Neil Harding, 179–210. Albany: The State University of New York Press.

Medvedev, Roy, and Zhores Medvedev. 1978. *Khrushchev: The years in power*. New York: W. W. Norton.

Meissner, Boris. 1969. Totalitarian rule and social change. In *Dilemmas of change in Soviet politics*, edited by Zbigniew Brzezinski, 73–88. New York: Columbia University Press.

Mickiewicz, Ellen. 1990. Ethnicity and support: Findings from a Soviet-American public opinion poll. *Journal of Soviet Nationalities* 1:140–147.

Mikadze, Akaky, and Vladimir Shevelyov. 1990. Zviad Gamsakhurdia: We have tolerated separatists too long. *Moscow News* (#48):7.

Mironov, Boris. 1990. The Russian peasant commune after the reforms of the 1860s. In *The world of the Russian peasant: Post-emancipation culture and society*, edited by Ben Eklof and Stephen Franks, 7–44. Boston: Unwin Hyman.

Mirzoian, V. 1990. Nagornyi Karabakh: Statistical considerations. *Soviet Anthropology and Archeology* 29 (2):12–33.

Mitchneck, Beth. 1991. Geographical and economic determinants of interregional migration in the USSR, 1968–1985. *Soviet Geography* 32:168–189.

Mitrofanova, A. 1980. Nekotoryye voprosy razvitiya rabochego klassa Rossiskoy Federatsii. In *Formirovaniye i razvitiye mnogonatsional'nogo rabochego klassa SSSR v period stroitel'stva sotsializma (1921–1937 gg.)*, 102–122. Tbilisi: Metsniyereba.

Monogarova, L. 1980. Evolutsiya natsional'nogo samosoznaniya Pripamirskikh narodnostey. In *Etnicheskiye protsessy u natsional'nykh grupp Sredney Azii i Kazakhstana*, edited by R. Dzharylgasinova and L. Tolstova, 125–135. Moskva: Nauka.

Moscow News. 17 March 1991. A map of unrest in the USSR. (#11):8–9.

Mosse, George. 1975. *The nationalization of the masses: Political symbolism and mass movements in Germany from the Napoleonic Wars through the Third Reich*. New York: Howard Fertig.

Murphy, Alexander. 1988. Evolving regionalism in linguistically divided Belgium. In *Nationalism, self-determination and political geography*, edited by R. Johnston et al., 135–150. London: Croom Helm.

———. 1990. Historical justifications for territorial claims. *Annals of the Association of American Geographers* 80:531–548.

———. 1991. Regions as social constructs: The gap between theory and practice. *Progress in Human Geography* 15:22–35.

Myl'nikov, A. 1989. Administrativno-politicheskaya sistema. In *Cheshskaya natsiya na zaklyuchitel' nom etape formirovaniya*, edited by V. Freydzon, 35–46. Moskva: Nauka.

Nagel, Joane, and Susan Olzak. 1982. Ethnic mobilization in new and old states. *Social Problems* 30 (2):127–143.

Nairn, T. 1977. *The break-up of Britain: Crisis and neo-nationalism*. London: NLB.

Naumova, O. 1987. Natsional'no-smeshannyye sem'i u Nemtsev Kazakhstana. *Sovetskaya Etnografiya* (#6):91–100.

Nekrich, Alexandre. 1978. *The punished peoples*. New York: W. W. Norton.

Netting, Anthony. 1967. Russian liberalism. The years of promise. 1842–1855. Ph.D. dissertation, Columbia University, New York.

New York Times. 30 August 1991. Statement on unity from Kiev, A7.

"News Notes." March 1991. Crimean region votes for autonomous status. *Soviet Geography* 32:195–197.

"News Notes." 1991. Checheno-Ingushetia: Background to current unrest. *Soviet Geography* 32 (December):701–706.

Nielsen, Francois. 1980. The Flemish movement in Belgium after World War II: A dynamic analysis. *American Sociological Review* 45:76–94.

———. 1985. Toward a theory of ethnic solidarity in modern societies. *American Sociological Review* 50:133–149.

Nishanov, R. 1990. R. Nishanov news conference. *Izvestiya* (22 December):10; also cited in FBIS *Soviet Daily Reports* 31 December (251):33.

Nissman, David. 1993. Turkmenistan: Searching for a national identity. In *Nations and politics in the Soviet successor states*, edited by Ian Bremmer and Ray Taras, 384–397. Cambridge: Cambridge University Press.

Nove, Alec. 1969. *An economic history of the U.S.S.R.* Middlesex, England: Penguin.

Oberlander, Erwin, George Katkov, Nikolaus Poppe, and George von Rauch, eds. *Russia enters the twentieth century 1894–1917*. New York: Schocken.

Olcott, Martha. 1985. The politics of language reform in Kazakhstan. In *Sociolinguistic perspectives on Soviet national languages*, edited by Isabelle Kreindler, 183–204. Berlin: Mouton de Gruyter.

———. 1987. *The Kazakhs*. Stanford: Hoover Institution Press.

———. 1990. Perestroyka in Kazakhstan. *Problems of Communism* 39 (4):65–77.

———. 1993. Kazakhstan: A republic of minorities. In *Nations and politics in the Soviet successor states*, edited by Ian Bremmer and Ray Taras, 313–330. Cambridge: Cambridge University Press.

Olzak, Susan, and Joane Nagel, eds. 1986. *Competitive ethnic relations*. Orlando: Academic Press.

Orridge, Andrew. 1982. Separatist and autonomist nationalisms. The struture of regional loyalties in the modern state. In *National separatism*, edited by Colin Williams, 43–74. Cardiff: University of Wales Press.

Orridge, A., and C. Williams. 1982. Autonomist nationalism: A theoretical framework for spatial variations in its genesis and development. *Political Geography Quarterly* 1:19–39.

Osipov, O. 1990. Unemployment: Myths and reality. Is there work for all in Uzbekistan? *Journal of Soviet Nationalities* 1 (2):130–145.

Osipov, V. 1990. Thoughts on the Russian question. Paper presented at the Kennan Institute for Advanced Russian Studies, Washington, D.C. 3 April.

Ostapenko, I. 1980. Rol' promyshlennykh rayonov strany v podgotovke kvalifitsirovannykh kadrov dlya respublik Sredney Azii i Kazakhstana. In *Formirovaniye i razvitiye mnogonatsional'nogo rabochego klassa SSSR v period stroitel'stva sotsializma (1921–1937 gg.)*, 87–101. Tbilisi: Metsniyereba.

Ostapenko, L., and A. Susokolov. 1983. Etnosotsial'nyye osobennosti vosproizvodstva intelligentsii. *Sotsiologicheskiye Issledovaniya* (#1):10–16.

———. 1985. Dinamika natsional'nogo sostava studenchestva soyuznykh respublik v poslevoennyye gody. *Sovetskaya Etnografiya* (#2):46–54.

Panachin, F. et al. 1987. *Ocherki istorii shkoly i pedagogicheskoy mysli narodov SSSR, 1961–1986*. Moskva: Pedagogika.

Panesh, E., and L. Yermolov. 1990. Turki-Meskhetintsy. *Sovetskaya Etnografiya* (#1):16–24.

Pankhurst, Jerry, and Michael Sacks, eds. 1980. *Contemporary Soviet society: Sociological perspectives*. New York: Praeger.

Panyutich, V. 1990. *Sotsial'no-ekonomicheskoye razvitiye Belorusskoy derevni v 1861–1900 gg*. Minsk: Navuka i Tekhnika.

Parming, Tonu. 1980. Population processes and the nationality issue in the Soviet Baltic. *Soviet Studies* 32:398–414.

Pearson, Raymond. 1983. *National minorities in Eastern Europe, 1848–1945*. London: Macmillam.

Perepelkin, L. 1987. K voprosy ob etnokul'turnykh faktorakh trudovoy deyatel'nosti rabotnika sovremennoy promyshlennosti. *Sovetskaya Etnografiya* (#2):83–88.

Perepelkin, L., and O. Shkaratan. 1989. Ekonomicheskiy suverenitet respublik i puti razvitiya narodov. *Sovetskaya Etnografiya* (#4):32–48.

Perrie, Maureen. 1990. The Russian peasant movement of 1905–7: Its social composition and revolutionary significance. In *The world of the Russian peasant: Postemancipation culture and society*, edited by Ben Eklof and Stephen Franks, 193–218. Boston: Unwin Hyman.

Petro, N. 1987. "The project of the century": A case study of Russian national dissent. *Studies in Comparative Communism* 20:235–252.

Petrov, Nikolay, and Andrey Treyvish. 1991. Vseyu li Rus'yu vybirayut prezidenta Vseya Rusi? *Nezavisimaya Gazeta* (6 June):2.

Petrovich, Michael. 1968. The peasant in nineteenth century historiography. In *The peasant in nineteenth-century Russia*, edited by Wayne Vucinich, 191–230. Stanford: Stanford University Press.

Pipes, Richard. 1968. *The formation of the Soviet Union: Communism and nationalism, 1917–1923*. Rev. ed. New York: Atheneum.

———. 1974. *Karamzin's memoir on ancient and modern Russia*. New York: Atheneum.

Pi-Sunyer, Oriol. 1985. Catalan nationalism: Some theoretical and historical considerations. In *New nationalisms of the developed west*, edited by Edward Tiryakian and Ronald Rogowski, 254–276. Boston: Allen & Unwin.

Pletsch, Carl. 1979. "The socialist nation of the German Democratic Republic" or the asymmetry in nation and ideology between the two Germanies. *Comparative Study of Society and History* 21:323–345.

Plotnieks, Andris. 1991. Evolution of the Soviet federation and the independence of

Latvia. In *Soviet federalism: Nationalism and decentralisation*, edited by Alastair McAuley, 134–148. Leicester and London: Leicester University Press.

Poppe, Nikolaus. 1971. The economic and cultural development of Siberia. In *Russia enters the twentieth century 1894–1917*, edited by Erwin Oberlander et al., 138–151. New York: Schocken.

Portugali, J. 1988. Nationalism, social theory and the Israeli/Palestinian case. In *Nationalism, self-determination and political geography*, edited by R. Johnston, D. Knight, and E. Kofman, 151–165. London: Croom Helm.

Pravda. 28 April 1989. O predvaritel'nykh itogakh vsesoyuznoy perepisi naseleniya 1989 goda.

———. 24 September 1989. Natsional'naya politika partii v sovremennykh usloviyakh.

———. 7 April 1990. Zakon Soyuza Sovetskikh Sotsialisticheskikh Respublik o poryadke resheniya voprosov, svyazannykh s vykhodom soyuznoy respubliki iz SSSR.

Programma KPSS. 1961. Programma Kommunisticheskoy Partii Sovetskogo Soyuza. *Kommunist* (#16):20–101.

Radishchev, Alexandre. 1789. A discourse on what it means to be a son of the fatherland. In *A documentary history of Russian thought from enlightenment to Marxism*, edited by W. Leatherbarrow and D. Offord, 18–24. Ann Arbor, Mich.: Ardis.

Raeff, Marc. 1971. Patterns of Russian imperial policy toward the nationalities. In *Soviet nationality problems*, edited by Edward Allworth, 22–42. New York: Columbia University Press.

Rajabov, S. 1978. Geographical factors and certain problems of federalism in the USSR. *International Social Science Journal* 30 (1):88–97.

Rakowska-Harmstone, Teresa. 1970. *Russia and nationalism in Central Asia: The case of Tadzhikistan*. Baltimore: Johns Hopkins Press.

Ramet, Pedro. 1984. *Nationalism and federalism in Yugoslavia, 1963–1983*. Bloomington: Indiana University Press.

Rashin, A. 1956. *Naseleniye Rossii za 100 let (1811–1913)*. Moskva: Gosstatizdat.

Raun, Toivo. 1985. Language development and policy in Estonia. In *Sociolinguistic perspectives on Soviet national languages*, edited by Isabelle Kreindler, 13–35. Berlin: Mouton de Gruyter.

———. 1987. *Estonia and the Estonians*. Stanford: Hoover Institution Press.

Remington, Thomas. 1985. Federalism and segmented communication in the USSR. *Publius* 15 (Fall):113–132.

Riasanovsky, Nicholas. 1968. Afterword: The problem of the peasant. In *The peasant in nineteenth century Russia*, edited by W. Vucinich, 263–284. Stanford: Stanford University Press.

———. 1969. *Nicholas I and official nationality in Russia, 1825–1855*. Berkeley: University of California Press.

———. 1976. *A parting of ways: Government and the educated public in Russia 1801–1855*. Oxford: Clarendon Press.

Robinson, Geroid. 1932. *Rural Russia under the old regime*. London: Longmans, Green.

Rodionov, A., and V. Muntyan. 1990. Poisk putey resheniya natsional'nykh problem v pervyye gody Sovetskoy vlasti (1917–1923 gg.). *Sovetskaya Etnografiya* (#3):31–43.

Rogger, Hans. 1960. *National consciousness in eighteenth century Russia*. Cambridge, Mass: Harvard University Press.

———. 1983. *Russia in the age of modernization and revolution 1881–1917*. London: Longman.

Rorlich, Azade-Ayse. 1986. *The Volga Tatars: A profile in national resilience*. Stanford: Hoover Institution Press.

Rossiskaya Gazeta. 28 March 1991. Chuma na vashi domy! Territorial'no-etnicheskiye konflikt i ikh prichiny.

Rothchild, Donald. 1986. Hegemonial exchange: An alternative model for managing conflict in middle Africa. In *Ethnicity, politics, and development*, edited by Dennis Thompson and Dov Ronen, 65–104. Boulder: Lynne Rienner.

Rowland, Richard. 1986. Urbanization and migration data in Russian and Soviet censuses. In *Research guide to the Russian and Soviet censuses*, edited by Ralph Clem, 113–130. Ithaca: Cornell University Press.

Rozyeva, N. 1980. Razvitiye natsional'noy shkoly v SSSR. In *Ocherki istorii shkoly i pedagogicheskoy mysli narodov SSSR 1917–1941 gg.*, 329–349. Moskva: Pedagogika.

Ruble, Blair. 1989. Ethnicity and Soviet cities. *Soviet Studies* 41:401–414.

RUKH. 1989. *RUKH program and charter*. Ellicott City, Md.: Smoloskyp.

Russia TsSK (Tsentral'nyy Statisticheskiy Komitet'). 1897. *Pervaya vseobshchaya perepis' naseleniya Rossiskoy Imperii, 1897 g.*. 89 volumes.

———. 1906. *Ezhegodnik' Rossiy 1905 g.* St. Petersburg: Tsentral'nyy Statisticheskiy Komitet'.

———. 1912. *Statisticheskiy ezhegodnik' Rossiy 1911*. St. Petersburg: Tsentral'nyy Statisticheskiy Komitet'.

———. 1915. *Statisticheskiy ezhegodnik' Rossiy 1911*. St. Petersburg: Tsentral'nyy Statisticheskiy Komitet'.

Russian Nationalism Today. 1988. *Radio Liberty Research Bulletin* (19 December) (special edition).

Rutland, Peter. 1984. The "nationality problem" and the Soviet state. In *The state in socialist society*, edited by Neil Harding, 150–178. Albany: The State University of New York Press.

Rybakovskiy, L. 1985. Aktual'nyye problemy migratsii i ikh klassifikatsiya. In *Sovremennyye problemy migratsii*, edited by V. Tomin et al., 3–13. Moskva: Mysl'.

———. 1987. *Migratsiya naseleniya: prognozy, faktory, politika*. Moskva: Nauka.

Rybakovskiy, L., and V. Tarasova. 1989. Sovremennyye problemy migratsii naseleniya SSSR. *Istoriya SSSR* (#2):68–81.

———. 1990. Migratsionnyye protsessy v SSSR: novyye yavleniya. *Sotsiologicheskiye Issledovaniya* (#7):32–42.

Rywkin, Michael. 1982. *Moscow's Muslim challenge: Soviet Central Asia*. Armonk, N.Y.: M. E. Sharpe.

Sack, Robert. 1983. Human territoriality: A theory. *Annals of the Association of American Geographers* 73:55–74.

———. 1986. *Human territoriality: its theory and history*. Cambridge: Cambridge University Press.

Sacks, Michael. 1982. *Work and equality in Soviet society*. New York: Praeger.

Sagdullaev, Namaz. 1990. Where is myth and where is reality (response to Osipov article). *Journal of Soviet Nationalities* 1 (2):146–156.
Salikov, R., I. Kopylov, and E. Yusupov. 1987. *Natsional'nyye protsessy v SSSR*. Moskva: Nauka.
Sandulyak, L. 1989. Comments included in discussion: "Sud'by natsional'nykh kul'tur, yazyka i narodnogo obrazovaniya." *Sovetskaya Pedagogika* (#9):11–20.
Sbornik Zakonodatel'nykh Aktov RSFSR. 1991. *Sbornik zakonodatel'nykh aktov RSFSR o gosudarstvennom suverenitete, soyuznom dogovore i referendume*. Moskva: Sovetskaya Rossiya.
Schroeder, Gertrude. 1991. Perestroyka in the aftermath of 1990. *Soviet Economy* 7 (1):3–13.
———. 1990. Nationalities and the Soviet Economy. In *The nationalities factor in Soviet politics and society*, edited by Lubomyr Hajda and Mark Beissinger, 43–71. Boulder: Westview Press.
Schwartz, Lee. 1986. Regional population redistribution and national homelands in the USSR. Ph.D. dissertation, Columbia University, New York.
———. 1990. Regional population redistribution and national homelands in the USSR. In *Soviet nationality policies: Ruling ethnic groups in the USSR*, edited by Henry Huttenbach, 121–161. London: Mansell.
———. 1993. Refugee flows in the former Soviet Union: Policies and prospects. Paper presented at the annual meeting of the Association of American Geographers, Atlanta, Georgia, 9 April.
Seliverstov, Vyacheslav. 1991. Inter-republican interactions in the Soviet Union. In *Soviet federalism: Nationalism and decentralisation*, edited by Alastair McAuley, 111–127. Leicester and London: Leicester University Press.
Semenov' Tyan'-Shanskiy, Veniamin, ed. 1899–1914. *Rossiya. Polnoye geograficheskoye opisaniye nashego otechestva*. 11 vols. S. Peterburg': A. F. Devriyen.
Seregny, Scott. 1991. Peasants and politics: Peasant unions during the 1905 Revolution. In *Peasant economy, culture, and politics of European Russia, 1800–1921*, edited by Esther Kingston-Mann and Timothy Mixter, 341–377. Princeton, N.J.: Princeton University Press.
Seton-Watson, Hugh. 1956. *The decline of Imperial Russia 1855–1914*. New York: Praeger.
———. 1977. *Nations and states: An enquiry into the origins of nations and the politics of nationalism*. Boulder: Westview.
Shafarevich, Igor. 1989. Rusofobiya. *Nash Sovremennik* (#6):167–192.
Shafer, Boyd. 1972. *Faces of nationalism: New realities and old myths*. New York: Harcourt Brace Jovanovich.
Shanin, T. 1989. Ethnicity in the Soviet Union: Analytical perceptions and political strategies. *Comparative Study of Society and History* 31:409–438.
Shedenov, U. et al. 1987. Rasseleniye i etnosotsial'nyye protsessy v sovremennom Kazakhstane. In *NTR i natsional'nyye protsessy*, edited by O. Shkaratan, 144–154. Moskva: Nauka.
Sheehy, Ann. 1978. Recent events in Abkhazia mirror the complexities of national relations in the USSR. *Radio Liberty Research Reports* 141/78 (June 26).
———. 1989. 1989 census data on internal migration in the USSR. *Radio Liberty Report on the USSR* (10 November):7–9.

———. 1993a. Regions object to higher status of republics. *RFE/RL Daily Report* no. 120 (28 June).

———. 1993b. Ingushetia to declare independence? *RFE/RL Daily Report* no. 143 (20 July).

Shibutani, T., and K. Kwan. 1965. *Ethnic stratification: A comparative approach.* New York: Macmillan.

Shkaratan, O. 1986. Etnosotsial'naya struktura naseleniya gorodov Tatarskoy ASSR. In *Etnosotsial'nyye problemy goroda*, edited by O. Shkaratan, 112–125. Moskva: Nauka.

Shoup, Paul. 1968. *Communism and the Yugoslav national question.* New York: Columbia University Press.

Silver, Brian. 1974a. Levels of sociocultural development among Soviet nationalities: A partial test of the equalization hypothesis. *American Political Science Review* 68:1618–1637.

———. 1974b. The status of national minority languages in Soviet education: An assessment of recent changes. *Soviet Studies* 26:28–40.

———. 1974c. Social mobilization and the Russification of Soviet nationalities. *American Political Science Review* 68:45–66.

———. 1978. Language policy and the linguistic Russification of Soviet nationalities. In *Soviet nationality policies and practices*, edited by Jeremy Azrael, 250–306. New York: Praeger.

———. 1986. The ethnic and language dimensions in Russian and Soviet censuses. In *Research guide to the Russian and Soviet censuses*, edited by Ralph Clem, 70–97. Ithaca: Cornell University Press.

Smith, Anthony. 1971. *Theories of nationalism.* London: Duckworth.

———. 1981. States and homelands: The social and geopolitical implications of national territory. *Millennium: Journal of International Studies* 10 (3):187–202.

———. 1986. *The ethnic origins of nations.* Oxford: Basil Blackwell.

———. 1988. The myth of the "modern nation" and the myths of nations. *Ethnic and Racial Studies* 11:1–26.

Smith, Graham. 1989. Gorbachev's greatest challenge: Perestroika and the national question. *Political Geography Quarterly* 8:7–20.

———. 1990. Nationalities policy from Lenin to Gorbachev. In *The nationalities question in the Soviet Union*, edited by Graham Smith, 1–20. London: Longman.

Smith, Michael. 1991. The politics of linguistics in Central Asia: Then and now. Paper presented at the Southern Conference on Slavic Studies, Savanna, Georgia, March 21–23.

Smulders, Modris. 1990. *Who owes whom? Mutual economic accounts between Latvia and the USSR, 1940–1990.* Riga: The Economic Reform Commission of the Council of Ministers of the Republic of Latvia.

Smythe, Regina. 1990. Ideological vs. regional cleavages: Do the radicals control the RSFSR Parliament? *Journal of Soviet Nationalities* 1 (3):112–157.

Snezhkova, I. 1982. K probleme izucheniya etnicheskogo samosoznaniya u detey i yunoshestva. *Sovetskaya Etnografiya* (#1):80–88.

Soja, Edward. 1971. *The political organization of space.* Washington, D.C.: Association of American Geographers (Resource Paper No. 8).

Sokolova, Z. 1961. O nekotorykh etnicheskikh protsessakh, protekayushchikh u

Sel'kupov, Khantov i Evenkov Tomskoy Oblasti. *Sovetskaya Etnografiya* (#3):45–52.
Solchanyk, Roman. 1982. Russian language and Soviet politics. *Soviet Studies* 34:23–42.
———. 1985. Language politics in the Ukraine. In *Sociolinguistic perspectives on Soviet national languages: Their past, present and future*, edited by Isabelle Kreindler, 57–105. Berlin: Mouton de Gruyter.
———. 1992. Ukraine, the (former) center, Russia, and "Russia." *Studies in Comparative Communism* 25:31–45.
Solzhenitsyn, A. 1990. Kak nam obustroit' Rossiyu. *Komsomol'skaya Pravda* July (special issue).
Soyuz. 1990a. Nas 285,761,976 chelovek, i vse my zhivem v odnoy strane. *Soyuz* (#32).
———. 1990b. Narody SSSR: sel'skoye naseleniye. *Soyuz* (#39):15–16.
Spechler, Dina. 1990. Russian nationalism and Soviet politics. In *The nationalities factor in Soviet politics and society*, edited by Lubomyr Hajda and Mark Beissinger, 281–304. Boulder: Westview.
Spechler, Martin. 1979. Regional development in the USSR, 1958–78. In *Soviet Economy in a time of change*. Vol. 1. Joint Economic Committee, United States Congress. Washington, D.C.: U.S. Government Printing Office.
Stalin, J. [1913] 1934. Marxism and the national question. In *Marxism and the national and colonial questions*, 3–61. New York: International.
———. [1917] 1934. Report on the national question. In *Marxism and the national and colonial questions*, 62–67. New York: International.
———. [1920] 1934. The policy of the Soviet government on the national question in Russia. In *Marxism and the national and colonial questions*, 78–87. New York: International.
———. [1922] 1934. The amalgamation of the Soviet republics. In *Marxism and the national and colonial questions*, 120–136. New York: International.
———. [1923] 1934. Report on national factors in party and state development. In *Marxism and the national and colonial questions*, 147–171. New York: International.
———. [1925] 1934. The political tasks of the university of the peoples of the East. In *Marxism and the national and colonial questions*, 206–220. New York: International.
———. 1926. Extract from a letter to Comrade Kaganovich and other members of the Central Committee of the Communist Party of the Ukraine. In *Marxism and the national and colonial questions*, 229–231. New York: International.
———. 1930. Deviations on the national question. In *Marxism and the national and colonial questions*, 256–262. New York: International.
———. 1934. Deviations towards nationalism. In *Marxism and the national and colonial questions*, 267–268. New York: International.
Starovoytova, Galina. 1976. K issledovaniyu etnopsikhologii gorodskikh zhiteley. *Sovetskaya Etnografiya* (#3):45–56.
———. 1987. *Etnicheskaya gruppa v sovremennom Sovetskom gorode*. Leningrad: Nauka.
———. 1989. Soviet legislator discusses nationality issues. *Meeting Report* (Kennan Institute) (27 November).

———. 1990. Vse dobroye zhivo v Russkom narode. *Nabat* (#4).
Statisticheskiy Komitet SNG (Sodruzhestva Nezavisimykh Gosudarstv). 1992. Napravleniya i prichiny migratsii naseleniya. *Statisticheskiy Bulleten'* no. 14 (October):127–135.
———. 1993. *Itogi vsesoyuznoy perepisi naseleniya 1989 goda.* 12 vols. Minneapolis, Minn.: Eastview Press.
Steiner, Eugen. 1973. *The Slovak dilemma.* Cambridge: Cambridge University Press.
Straus, Kenneth. 1990. The new peasant-recruits on the shop floor: Social conflict and adaptation, 1929–1935. Paper presented at the Annual Meeting of the American Association for the Advancement of Slavic Studies, Washington, D.C., October 18–21.
Suny, Ronald. 1986. Tiflis: Crucible of ethnic politics, 1860–1905. In *The city in late Imperial Russia*, edited by Michael Hamm, 249–282. Bloomington: Indiana University Press.
———. 1989. *The making of the Georgian nation.* Bloomington: Indiana University Press.
Suny, Ronald, ed. 1983. *Transcaucasia: Nationalism and social change.* Ann Arbor: University of Michigan Slavic Publications.
Susokolov, A. 1973. Neposredstvennoye mezhetnicheskoye obshcheniye i ustanovki na mezhlichnostnyye kontakty. *Sovetskaya Etnografiya* (#5):73–78.
———. 1987. *Mezhnatsional'nyye braki v SSSR.* Moskva: Mysl'.
———. 1988. Etnosi pered vyborom. *Sotsiologicheskiye Issledovaniya* (#6):32–40.
———. 1990. *Natsional'no-smeshannyye braki i sem'i v SSSR: chast' 1.* Moskva: Institut Etnografii, AN SSSR.
Susokolov, A., and A. Novitskaya. 1981. Etnicheskaya i sotsial'no-professional'naya gomogennost' brakov. *Sovetskaya Etnografiya* (#6):14–26.
Susokolov, A., and V. Stepanov. 1990. Malochislennyy etnos: voprosy national'noy i sotsial'noy politiki. *Sovetskaya Etnografiya* (#5):34–47.
Swietochowski, Tadeusz. 1983. National consciousness and political orientations in Azerbaijan, 1905–1920. In *Transcaucasia: Nationalism and social change*, edited by Ronald Suny, 209–232. Ann Arbor: University of Michigan Slavic Publications.
———. 1991. The politics of literary language and the rise of national identity in Russian Azerbaijan before 1920. *Ethnic and Racial Studies* 14:55–63.
Symmons-Symonolewicz, K. 1985. The concept of nationhood: Toward a theoretical clarification. *Canadian Review of Studies in Nationalism* 12:215–222.
Szporluk, Roman. 1980. History and Russian ethnocentrism. In *Ethnic Russia in the USSR*, edited by E. Allworth, 41–54. New York: Pergamon.
Taagepera, Rein. 1989. Estonia's road to independence. *Problems of Communism* 38 (6):11–26.
Taksanov, A. 1989. *Perestroyka i nekotoryye problemy razvitiya natsional'nykh kadrov industrial'nogo rabochego klassa.* Tashkent: Fan.
Tankayev, S. 1985. *Dialektika dvukh tendentsiy v bytu sotsialisticheskikh natsiy.* Alma Ata: Kazakhstan.
Tarzi, Shah. 1991. The nation-state, victim groups and refugees. *Ethnic and Racial Studies* 14:441–452.
Taylor, Peter. 1985. *Political geography: World-economy, nation-state and locality.* London: Longman.

Tazbir, Janusz. 1986. Polish national consciousness in the sixteenth to the eighteenth century. *Harvard Ukrainian Studies* 10:316–335.
Terent'yeva, L. 1969. Opredeleniye svoyey natsional'noy prinadlezhnosti podrostkami v national'no-smeshannykh sem'yakh. *Sovetskaya Etnografiya* (#3):20–30.
———. 1972. Nekotoryye storony etnicheskikh protsessov v Povolzh'ye, Priural'ye i na Evropeyskom Severe SSSR. *Sovetskaya Etnografiya* (#6):38–51.
Thalheim, Karl. 1971. Russia's economic development. In *Russia enters the twentieth century 1894–1917*, edited by Erwin Oberlander et al., 85–110. New York: Schocken.
Thompson, Dennis, and Dov Ronen, eds. 1986. *Ethnicity, politics and development*. Boulder: Lynne Rienner.
Tillett, Lowell. 1969. *The great friendship: Soviet historians on the non-Russian nationalities*. Chapel Hill: University of North Carolina Press.
Tiryakian, Edward, and Neil Nevitte. 1985. Nationalism and modernity. In *New nationalisms of the developed west*, edited by Edward Tiryakian and Ronald Rogowski, 57–86. Boston: Allen & Unwin.
Tiryakian, E., and R. Rogowski, eds. 1985. *New nationalisms of the developed west*. Boston: Allen & Unwin.
Tishkov, V. 1989a. O kontseptsii perestroyki mezhnatsional'nykh otnosheniy v SSSR. *Sovetskaya Etnografiya* (#1):73–89.
———. 1989b. Narody i gosudarstvo. *Kommunist* (#1):49–59.
———. 1990a. An assembly of nations or an all-union parliament? *Journal of Soviet Nationalities* 1 (1):101–127.
———. 1990b. Ethnicity and power in the republics of the USSR. *Journal of Soviet Nationalities* 1 (3):33–66.
Tolstova, L. 1985. Natsional'no-smeshannyye braki u sel'skogo naseleniya Karakalpakskoy ASSR. *Sovetskaya Etnografiya* (#3):64–72.
Tolz, Vera. 1993. Republics and regions unhappy about draft constitution. *RFE/RL Daily Report* no. 113 (13 July).
Topilin, Anatoliy. 1992. Vliyaniye migratsii na etnonatsional'nuyu strukturu. *Sotsiologicheskiye Issledovaniya* (#7):31–43.
Torsvik, Per, ed. 1981. *Mobilization, center-periphery structures and nation-building*. Bergen: Universitetsforlaget.
Troynitsky, Nicolas, ed. 1905. *Obshchiy svod' po imperii rezul'tatov' razrabotki dannykh' pervoy vseobshchey perepisi naseleniya*. 2 vols. St. Petersburg: Tsentral'nyy Statisticheskiy Komitet'.
TsSU (Tsentral'noye Statisticheskoye Upravleniye pri Sovete Ministrov) SSSR. 1928. *Vsesoyuznaya perepis' naseleniya 17 Dekabrya 1926*, kratkiye svodki. Vol. 7: Vozrast i Gramotnost' Naseleniya SSSR. Moskva: TsSU SSSR.
———. 1929. *Vsesoyuznaya perepis' naseleniya 1926 goda*. 56 vols.
———. 1959. *Slovari natsional'nostey i yazykov*. Moskva: Gosstatizdat.
———. 1962. *Itogi vsesoyuznoy perepisi naseleniya 1959 goda*. 16 vols. Moskva: Gosstatizdat.
———. 1969. *Slovari natsional'nostey i yazykov*. Moskva: Statistika.
———. 1973. *Itogi vsesoyusnoy perepisi naseleniya 1970 goda*. 7 vols. Moskva: Statistika.

———. 1977. *Narodnoye obrazovaniye, nauka i kul'tura v SSSR: statisticheskiy sbornik.* Moskva: Statistika.

———. 1984. *Chislennost' i sostav naseleniya SSSR: po dannym vsesoyuznoy perepisi naseleniya 1979 goda.* Moskva: Finansy i Statistika.

Tuan, Yi-Fu. 1977. *Space and place: The perspective of experience.* Minneapolis: University of Minnesota Press.

Tuchalayev, S. 1988. Obucheniye shestiletnikh detey v Dagestane. *Sovetskaya Pedagogika* (#2):77–81.

Tucker, Robert, ed. 1975. *The Lenin anthology.* New York: W. W. Norton.

———. 1978. *The Marx-Engels reader.* 2d ed. New York: W. W. Norton.

Udalova, I. 1989. Izmeneniye chislennosti i sostav intelligentsii narodnostey severa (na primere Nanaytsev). In *Narody Sibiri na sovremennom etape*, edited by V. Shmakov, 100–113. Novosibirsk: Nauka.

United States Department of State. 1992. Name changes in the former Soviet Union. *Geographic Notes* 2 (2):25–29.

United States Department of State. 1992/1993. Map: Administrative divisions of Russia. *Geographic Notes* 2 (4):17–19.

Urban, Michael, and Russell Reed. 1989. Regionalism in a systems perspective: Explaining elite circulation in a Soviet republic. *Slavic Review* 48:413–431.

Vakar, Nicholas. 1956. *Belorussia: The making of a nation.* Cambridge: Harvard University Press.

van den Berghe, P. 1981. *The ethnic phenomenon.* New York: Elsevier.

Vestnik Statistiki. 1986. Statisticheskiye Materialy. *Vestnik Statistiki* (#7):67–80.

Viksnins, George. 1986. The Latvian economy: Change under Gorbachev? *Journal of Baltic Studies* 17 (3): 238–255.

Vinnikov, Ya. 1980. Natsional'nyye i etnograficheskiye gruppy Sredney Azii po dannym etnicheskoy statistiki. In *Etnicheskiye protsessy u natsional'nykh grupp Sredney Azii i Kazakhstana*, edited by R. Dzharylgasinova and L. Tolstova, 11–42. Moskva: Nauka.

Vinogradov, V., ed. 1968. *Yazyki narodov v pyati tomakh.* Leningrad: Nauka.

Vishnevskiy, A., and Zh. Zayonchkovskaya. 1991. *Migratsiya iz SSSR: chetvertaya volna.* Moskva: Tsentr Demografii i Ekologii Cheloveka.

Vodarskiy, Ya. 1973. *Naseleniye Rossii za 400 let (XVI-nachalo XX vv).* Moskva: Prosveshcheniye.

Volkov, A. 1989a. Etnicheski smeshannyye sem'i v SSSR: dinamika i sostav. *Vestnik Statistiki* (#7):12–22.

———. 1989b. Etnicheski smeshannyye sem'i v SSSR: dinamika i sostav (natsional'nost' detey v etnicheski smeshennykh sem'yakh). *Vestnik Statistiki* (#8):4–24.

Vol'skaya, O. 1990. Bol'shiye plany vokrug "Maloy Litvy." *Pravda* (22 March):2.

Voslensky, Michael. 1988. The Soviet system: Historical and theoretical evaluation. In *The Soviet Union and the challenge of the future* (vol. 1), edited by Alexander Shtromas and Morton Kaplan, 3–12. New York: Paragon House.

Vucinich, Wayne, ed. 1968. *The peasant in nineteenth-century Russia.* Stanford: Stanford University Press.

Walicki, Andrzej. 1975. *The Slavophile controversy.* Oxford: Clarendon.

---. 1979. *A history of Russian thought from enlightenment to Marxism.* Stanford: Stanford University Press.
Watters, Francis. 1968. The peasant and the village commune. In *The peasant in nineteenth-century Russia,* edited by Wayne Vucinich, 133–157. Stanford: Stanford University Press.
Weber, Eugen. 1976. *Peasants into Frenchmen: The modernization of rural France, 1870–1914.* Stanford: Stanford University Press.
Weiner, Myron. 1978. *Sons of the soil: Migration and ethnic conflict in India.* Princeton, N.J.: Princeton University Press.
Wexler, Paul. 1985. Belorussification, Russification and Polonization. Trends in the Belorussian language 1890–1982. In *Sociolinguistic perspectives on Soviet national languages: Their past, present and future,* edited by Isabelle Kreindler, 37–56. Berlin: Mouton de Gruyter.
Wheatcroft, Stephen. 1990. More light on the scale of repression and excess mortality in the Soviet Union in the 1930s. *Soviet Studies* 42:355–367.
---. 1991. Crises and the condition of the peasantry in late imperial Russia. In *Peasant economy, culture, and politics of European Russia, 1800–1921,* edited by Esther Kingston-Mann and Timothy Mixter, 128–172. Princeton, N.J.: Princeton University Press.
White, P. 1985. What is nationality? *Canadian Review of Studies in Nationalism* 12:1–23.
Whittaker, Cynthia. 1984. *The origins of modern Russian education.* Dekalb: Northern Illinois University Press.
Willetts, Harry. 1971. The agrarian problem. In *Russia enters the twentieth century 1894–1917,* edited by Erwin Oberlander et al., 111–137. New York: Schocken.
Williams, Colin, ed. 1982. *National separatism.* Cardiff: University of Wales Press.
---. 1986. The question of national congruence. In *A world in crisis? Geographical perspectives,* edited by R. Johnston and P. Taylor, 196–230. Oxford: Basil Blackwell.
Williams, Colin, and Anthony Smith. 1983. The national construction of social space. *Progress in Human Geography* 7:502–518.
Williams, C., and E. Kofman, eds. 1989. *Community conflict, partition and nationalism.* London: Routledge.
Wilson, Andrew. 1993. Crimea's political cauldron. *RFE/RL Research Report* 2, no. 45 (12 November):1–8.
Wixman, Ronald. 1984. *The peoples of the USSR: An ethnographic handbook.* Armonk, N.Y.: M. E. Sharpe.
Wolfe, Bertram. 1964. *Three who made a revolution.* Rev. ed. New York: Delta.
Yagodin, G. 1989. Sovershenstvovaniye mezhnatsional'nykh otnosheniy i shkola. *Sovetskaya Pedagogika* (#8):3–11.
Yamskov, A. 1991. Nagorny Karabakh: Causes of the conflict and ways to solve it. In *National processes in the USSR: Problems and trends,* edited by V. Tishkov, 129–160. Moscow: Nauka Publishers.
Yaney, George. 1982. *The urge to mobilize: Agrarian reform in Russia, 1861–1930.* Urbana: University of Illinois Press.
Yukhneva, Nataliya. 1984. *Etnicheskiy sostav i etnosotsial'naya struktura naseleniya Peterburga.* Leningrad: Nauka.

Zariski, Raphael. 1989. Ethnic extremism among ethnoterritorial minorities in western Europe. *Comparative Politics* 21:253–272.

Zaslavsky, Victor, and Yuri Luryi. 1979. The passport system in the USSR and changes in Soviet society. *Soviet Union* 6 (2):137–153.

Zelnick, Reginald. 1968. The peasant and the factory. In *The peasant in nineteenth-century Russia*, edited by Wayne Vucinich, 158–190. Stanford: Stanford University Press.

Zeymal', E. 1988. Narodnosti i ikh yazyki pri sotsialisme. *Kommunist* (#15):64–72.

Zhavoronkov, G., and A. Mikadze. 1990. Kak uberech' Abkhaziyu? *Moskovskiye Novosti* (#46):8.

Zhdanko, T. 1972. Natsional'no-gosudarstvennoye razmezhevaniye i protsessy etnicheskogo razvitiya u narodov Sredney Asii. *Sovetskaya Etnografiya* (#5):13–29.

———. 1977. Etnicheskiye obshchnosti i etnicheskiye protsessy v dorevolyutsionnoy Rossii. In *Sovremennyye etnicheskiye protsessy v SSSR*, edited by Yu. Bromley, 36–86. Moskva: Nauka.

Zinchenko, I. P. 1984. Natsional'nyy sostav naseleniya SSSR. In *Vsesoyuznaya perepis' naseleniya 1979 goda: sbornik statyey*, edited by A. A. Isupov and N. Z. Shvartser, 150–162. Moskva: Finansy i Statistika.

Zlatopolskiy, D. 1989. The national statehood of the union republics: Certain vital problems. *Sovetskoye Gosudarstvo i Pravo* (#4):12–20 (as cited in JPRS-UPA-89-013-L, 28 July 1989, pp. 1–7).

Zotov, V. 1989. Natsional'nyy vopros: deformatsii proshlogo. *Kommunist* (#3):79–89.

Zubaida, Sami. 1989. Nations: Old and new. Comments on Anthony D. Smith's "The myth of the 'modern nation' and the myths of nations." *Ethnic and Racial Studies* 12:329–339.

Index

Abkhazia, 178, 189; Abkhazian claims to, 362; Abkhazian privileges in, 183, 362, 364; Georgian claims to, 364; Georgian migration to, 177–78, 183, 362; reactive ethnicity in, 248, 362–64. *See also* autonomous republics; Georgia
Abkhazians, 177–78, 183, 257, 272, 282, 284, 358, 362–64
acculturation, 8–10, 26, 27, 40, 62, 103, 295; and assimilation, 295–96, 322; and bilingualism, 251, 288, 322; as a catalyst for national territoriality, 9, 27, 40–41, 89, 403, 406; and ethnocultural indigenization, 250; and the functional utility of languages, 287–88; of indigenes, 262; linguistic assimilation as, 39n, 41, 62n, 251–52, 394; and national territoriality, 282; among non-indigenes, 140, 209, 250–51, 285–88
Adzhars, 136. *See also* Georgia
Adygey, 238. *See also* North Caucasus
Adygey Autonomous Oblast, 258. *See also* autonomous oblasts; North Caucasus
Africa, comparability of national territoriality in, 404–6
agricultural work force, 236. *See also* peasantry
Albanians, 401–2. *See also* Yugoslavia
Altay Autonomous Oblast, 258. *See also* autonomous oblasts; Siberia
Altays, 284. *See also* Siberia; *ethnie*
Andropov, 344
Armenia: anti-Azerbaydzhani violence in, 224, 361; and the Commonwealth of Independent States, 354; declaration of independence in, 354, 383; demographic indigenization of the cities in, 122; economic health of, 337–38; education in, 129; Greater, 370; international interaction in the cities of, 223; international family rates in, 300; international marriages in, 308; the language debate in, 40; legal status of language in, 345; linguistic indigenization in, 293; native language publications in, 258–60; national separatism in, 329, 354; nationalist demonstrations in the cities of,

224; and the new Union Treaty, 354n; occupational mobility in, 81; refugees in, 361; and the Transcaucasian Federal Republic, 109; urbanization in, 202–4. *See also* Transcaucasia; union republics
Armenian-Azerbaydzhani War of 1905, 82
Armenians: 159n, 238; in Azerbaydzhan, 257, 300, 356, 370; de-Russification among, 265; and the dispute over Nagorno-Karabakh, 156, 182, 257, 300, 358, 360–62, 388; educational attainment of, 226; and their "gravitation" toward Armenia, 119, 166, 182; international marriages among, 308; linguistic indigenization among, 272, 282; as the locally dominant group in Transcaucasia, 65, 81–82, 119, 382; in Nagorno-Karabakh, 171, 182–83, 223, 257, 282, 284, 358, 360–62, 388; and the nationalization of elites, 36, 39, 381; and the nationalization of the masses, 82; "natural" assimilation among, 319; urbanization among, 202–4
Asia, comparability of national territoriality in, 404–6
assimilation: 8–10, 20, 24–27, 65, 97–98, 101, 103, 106, 107, 115, 119, 140–141, 188, 295; and acculturation, 295–96, 322; as a catalyst for national territoriality, 24, 26, 146–47, 185, 188, 315, 385, 406; as a communist objective, 151–52; and diffusion-erasure, 249; and ethnocultural indigenization, 250; and federalization, 138; forced, 143, 252, 317; and geographic mobility, 152, 313; and indigenization, 126, 130, 138, 146, 164, 249, 251, 320, 394; and international equalization, 145; international marriage and, 251–52, 282, 295–317, 393–94; linguistic, 8–9, 39, 39n, 42, 251–53, 282–88, 293, 295–96; and migration, 165–66, 170, 185, 199–200, 251–52; national marginality and, 251; national stratification and, 317; and nationalization, 146, 188, 251, 265, 313, 316–17; "natural," 141, 164, 186–88, 235, 251–52, 282, 296, 317–24, 318n, 394; of

assimilation (cont.)
  nonindigenes, 25, 62–63, 119–21, 140–43, 146, 164, 186–88, 209, 235, 249–51, 285–88, 311, 315, 317–18, 384–85, 395; psychological, 251; Red Army as an agent of, 144; reverse, 164–65; and Russification, 138–47, 151, 171, 188, 251–52, 285–87, 317, 393–94; and social mobilization, 192, 247, 313; into (one) Soviet people, 138, 146, 152, 252; and urbanization, 96, 192–93, 200; voluntary, 252
attitudinal surveys, international. *See* international attitudes, surveys of
autarchy, 326, 330, 354; and indigenization, 331–35; ministerial, 326, 331; regional, 326, 330–38
autonomization, 100, 151. *See also* Stalin
autonomous oblasts, 110, 228; declarations of sovereignty in, 356–58; delimitation of, 110; indigenization of cities in, 223; international marriage in, 312; and linguistic Russification, 265, 284–85, 286; as national-state formations, 352; native language retention in, 269–72; native language schools in, 257–58; Russian-language schools in, 257–58; Russians in, 171, 178; status of, 352–53; titular minority status in, 171, 178; as union republics, 352
autonomous okrugs, 228; declarations of sovereignty in, 356–58; delimitation of, 157; de-Russification of cities in, 223; and diffusion-erasure, 287, 313; indigenization of cities in, 223; international marriages in, 312; linguistic Russification in, 265, 272, 285, 286–87; as national-state formations, 352; native language retention in, 269–72; native language schools in, 257–58; "natural" assimilation in, 319–20; nonindigenous in-migration to, 223; Russian-language schools in, 257–58; Russians in, 171, 178, 223; status of, 352–53; titular minority status in, 171, 178; as union republics, 352. *See also* nationality okrugs; Siberia
autonomous republics: declarations of sovereignty in, 356–58; delimitation of, 110; demographic indigenization of, 171–72, 177–78; indigenization of cities in, 209, 223; indigenous concentration in, 119–20; international marriages in, 312; and linguistic Russification, 265, 284, 286; as national states, 352; native language retention in, 269–72; native language schools in, 257–58; "natural" assimilation in, 319; political indigenization in, 134; of Russia, 110; 119–20, 353; Russian-language schools in, 257–58; Russians in, 178, 209, 223; of Turkestan, 110; as union republics, 352
Avars, 254n, 272. *See also* Dagestan; North Caucasus
Azerbaydzhan: anti-Armenian pogroms in, 360–61; Armenians in, 257, 300, 356, 370; Armenian dominance of the cities in, 82; economic health of, 337–38; demographic indigenization of the cities in, 65, 122–23; education in, 129; international marriages in, 308; intrastate disintegration in, 356; legal status of language in, 345; national independence movement in, 354, 383; and the new Union Treaty, 346, 354; nonindigenous urban out-migration from, 223; out-migration of Armenians from the cities of, 182–83, 223; refugees in, 361; Russian-language schools in, 255; separatism among indigenous minorities in, 356; and the Transcaucasian Federal Republic, 109; urbanization in, 202–4; vernacularization in, 42. *See also* Transcaucasia; union republics
Azerbaydzhani language, linguistic assimilation to, 285
Azerbaydzhanis, 82, 159n, anti-Armenian sentiments among, 82, 119; and the Armenian-Azerbaydzhani War of 1905, 82; Armenian violence against, 224, 361; in the cities of Nagorno-Karabakh, 223; and their concentration in Azerbaydzhan, 119, 182; de-Russification among, 265; and their dispersal from Azerbaydzhan, 119; and the dispute over Nagorno-Karabakh, 156, 182–83, 257, 300, 358, 360–62, 388; and their in-migration to Nagorno-Karabakh, 183; international marriage rates among, 308; and irredentism, 158; linguistic indigenization among, 272; and the nationalization of elites, 36, 39, 381–82; and their return migration to Azerbaydzhan, 166, 293–94
Azeris. *See* Azerbaydzhanis

Balkars, 165, 185, 238. *See also* deported nations; North Caucasus

Baltic guberniyas, 76, 80. *See also* Estland; Kurland; Lifland
Baltics: border disputes in, 156, 189, 370; and the Commonwealth of Independent States, 346; declarations of independence in, 354; demographic indigenization of the cities in, 223; demographic Russification and national self-determination movements in, 181, 223; demographic Russification of the cities in, 223; economic dependency in, 336; economic sovereignty in, 335; emancipation in, 49; German domination in, 39, 49, 65, 80, 382; and indigenization of high status occupations, 242; international family rates in, 300; international marriages in, 304–5, 312; linguistic indigenization in, 293; literacy in, 66n, 67; national separatism in, 181, 328; native language publications in, 261; native language retention in, 282; "natural" assimilation in, 318–19; natural increase among indigenes in, 181; potential debt burden in, 336; reactive ethnicity in, 248; Russian migration from, 166; Russian migration to, 181. *See also* Estonia; Latvia; Lithuania
Bashkir ASSR. *See* Bashkiria
Bashkiria, 112, 316, 356
Bashkirs, 67, 257, 269, 272, 316, 392
Basques, 402–4
Belarus', 157, 262; and *Adradzhen'ne*, 14n; and the Commonwealth of Independent States, 346; demographic indigenization of cities in, 65, 122; economic health of, 337–38; education in, 129; emancipation in, 49; international marriage rates in, 141, 312; national independence movement in, 354; and the new Union Treaty, 354; occupational mobility in, 81; as a part of the Russian Motherland, 42, 170, 371; regional *khozraschet* in, 333; Russian language schools in, 255–57; Russian migration to, 181. *See also* Slavic republics; union republics
Belgium, 402–4
Belorussia. *See* Belarus'
Belorussian language: and linguistic indigenization in, 293–95; publications in, 128; native language publications in, 258–60; native language schools in, 255–56; and Russification, 42, 126; and its status in Belorussia, 126, 255; and the stigma attached to vernacular, 41–42
Belorussians: and their "gravitation" to Belorussia, 117, 119, 167–68; international marriage rates among, 141, 305, 316; linguistic de-Russification among, 284; localism among, 40; and their migration from Belorussia, 166–67, 181; and the nationalization of elites, 37, 39, 381–82; "natural" assimilation among, 319–20; occupational mobility among, 81; political underrepresentation among, 349; Polonization, Russification, and nationalism among, 85; Russification of, 119, 143, 251, 265, 272, 282–83, 285, 320, 322, 384–85; as a "tribe" of the Russian nation, 371
Belorussification: of cities in Belorussia, 124; demographic, 119; of Poles, 295
Bessarabia, 42, 67. *See also* Moldova, Rumania
bilateral treaties, 340, 372–73, 376
bilingualism: and acculturation, 322; and anti-Russian nativism, 289; and the functional utility of indigenous languages, 252–53, 322; and linguistic Russification, 288–89; and the new language laws, 289, 293; as a preliminary stage in the acculturation process, 251, 288; and rising national separatism, 289; Russian, 288–93, 322, 393; and social mobilization, 288–89
Birlik, 355
Birobidzhan, 103. *See also* Jewish Autonomous Oblast
border disputes, 156, 189–90, 353, 356, 358, 364–65, 370–73, 388. *See also* ethnoterritorial conflicts
Bosnia, 401
Bretons, 402
Brezhnev: on the drawing together of nations, 152, 343; economic recentralization under, 332, 339; on international equalization in the USSR, 194–45, 343; on the need for federalism, 343–44
Brittany, 404
Bukhara, 110. *See also* Central Asia; Turkestan
Bukharans, 135. *See also* Central Asians
Buryatia, 258, 356. *See also* autonomous republics; Siberia
Buryats: 238, emigration of, 120; national self-consciousness of, 58; and a rising sense of exclusiveness toward Buryatia, 58

Canada, 402–4
Castilians, 403
Catalans, 402, 404
Catalonia, 404
center-periphery relations: 325; confederalization of, 345, 375, 396; and decentralization in the postwar USSR, 325, 328–40; and the new Union Treaty debates, 345–46
Central Asia, 57, 262, 316; border disputes in, 156, 189, 370–71; and the Commonwealth of Independent States, 355; debt burden in, 336; declarations of independence in, 355; declarations of sovereignty in, 355; demographic indigenization of the cities in, 223; demographic Russification, 76, 119, 124; deteriorating economic and environmental conditions in, 336–38, 393; and the disintegration of the USSR, 375–76; divide and rule in, 110, 371; economic dependency in, 336–38; education in, 72, 129, 234; ethnographic differentiation in, 110, 135, 157; formation of republics in, 110, 156; geographic immobility and localism in, 51, 65, 82, 135; independence of, 337–38; indigenization of the work force in, 131–32, 240; industrialization in, 76, 120; internal colonialism in, 195; international attitude surveys in, 184, 244–45; international family rates in, 298–300; international interaction in the cities of, 223; international marriage in, 142, 304; intranational marriage rates in, 313; Islamic primary schools in, 72; language development in, 127, 254; literacy in, 67; migration to, 53–57, 119; national separatist movements in, 329n; native language publications in, 260–61; the nationalization of elites in, 36, 39, 381–82; the nationalization of the masses in, 82, 110, 142, 313–14, 321; nativism in, 166, 170, 184, 248, 337, 393; "natural" assimilation in; 318–19; new language laws in, 293; and the new Union Treaty, 346, 354–55; pan-Islamic sentiments in, 110, 184; pan-Turkic sentiments in, 110; political conservatism in, 355, 376; potential debt burden in, 336; rapid natural increase in, 164, 178, 181; Russian migration from, 166, 170, 181, 184, 241; unemployment in, 236, 241, 336; urbanization in, 202; welfare colonialism in, 195. *See also* Kazakhstan; Kyrgyzstan; Tadzhikistan; Turkestan; Turkmenistan; union republics; Uzbekistan

Central Asians: and their attitudes toward the Communist party, 355; and their dispersal from Central Asia, 162, 178, 184; international attitudes among, 244–45; linguistic Russification among, 285; political conservatism among, 355
centralization: of economic system, 332, 339; Lenin on, 99–101, 107, 328; of political power, 100–101, 325; and totalitarianism, 326, 341
Chechenia, 356. *See also* autonomous republics; North Caucasus
Chechen-Ingushestia, 177, 177n, 223, 258, 367. *See also* autonomous republics; North Caucasus
Chechens, 159, 185, 272, Russian bilingualism among, 289. *See also* deported nations; North Caucasus
Cherkess, 238, 272. *See also* North Caucasus
Chisinau, 310, 311, 312, 314, 316, 319, 320. *See also* Moldova
Chukchi, 157, 171, 350. *See also* Siberia; ethnies
Chukchi Autonomous Okrug, 350. *See also* autonomous okrugs; Siberia
Church Slavonic, 35–36. *See also* language; Russian language
Chuvash: intranational marriage among, 313; linguistic Russification of the, 265, 284, 286; Russification of, 286
Chuvash ASSR, 132, 223, 258. *See also* autonomous republics; Volga-Urals
citizenship laws, 182, 348
coefficients of variation (CVs), 121, 200, 202, 226, 230–31, 236, 238, 258, 297
collective farm (*kolkhoz*), 236
collectivization, 95, 113, 115; and *dekulakization*, 115, 123; and excess mortality in Kazakhstan, 119; geographic mobility during, 113, 122; and nationalization, 120, 145; and urbanization, 122
Commonwealth of Independent States, 326, 338, 340, 346, 353–56, 377, 387–89, 396–99
communism, 397; and assimilation, 151–52; and its attainment, 152; and nationalism, 134
Communist party: attitudes toward, 355; confederalization of, 328–29; and declarations

of sovereignty, 357; destruction of, 346; and economic indigenization, 332; indigenization of, 132; and national independence movements, 329, 354–55
confederal structure: 27, 107, 269, 343–45, 350, 384, 396, 398, 409–13; of Czechoslovakia, 401; of the Communist party, 328–29; and the delimitation of republics and autonomous units, 99, 104, 107–10, 151, 156–57; and national territoriality, 329; and nationalization, 151; transitory nature of, 342–43, 350, 375, 396; of Russia, 356, 367; of the USSR, 107–13, 147, 151, 154; of Yugoslavia, 401
confederalization, 28, 325–26, 328–29, 342, 345–46, 351, 375, 396, 403
confederation, 107, 113, 152, 341, 353–56, 401; in form, unitary in essence, 112–13, 151, 342–44, 384, 396; and secession, 341–42, 345–46, 351
Congress of Peoples Deputies, 346, 348; and the gerrymandering of electoral districts, 348; and the malapportionment of electoral districts, 348
conscious peasantry. *See* peasantry, conscious
Constitution, 342; of 1924, 112; of 1936, 109, 109n, 113; of 1977, 254, 343–44; of Russia, 366–67
Corsica, 404
Corsicans, 402–3
Council of Nationalities, 112
Crimea: declaration of sovereignty in, 368; territorial dispute over, 189, 353, 368, 372
Crimean Tatar language, vernacularization of, 42
Crimean Tatars, 185–86, 367–69; and their claim to Crimea, 353; international marriage among, 316n; nationalization of elites, 36, 381; and their return migration to Crimea, 185–86, 368. *See also* deported nations
Croatia, 401–2
Cyrillicization of linguistic scripts, 127, 295; and Russification, 139
Czech Republic, 401–2
Czechoslovakia, comparability of national territoriality in, 401–2

Dagestan, 137, 177n, 223, 254, 258, 272, 313. *See also* North Caucasus

Dargins, 272. *See also* Dagestan; North Caucasus
debt burden, potential, 336–38
decentralization, economic, 326, 328, 330–40, 357, 374; from below, 334, 374; and indigenization, 331–32, 334–35, 339, 342, 374–75; political, 325, 328, 342, 357, 374, 404
decolonization, 401, 404–5
dekulakization, 115, 123. *See also* collectivization
democracy, 347–58, 396–97; "one nation, one vote" consociational, 351, 397; "one person, one vote" majoritarian, 351, 397
democratic centralism, 328. *See also* Communist party; Lenin; Marxism-Leninism; Stalin
democratization, 325, 345
demographic indigenization. *See* indigenization, demographic
denationalization, xvii-xviii, 9, 20, 24, 26, 83n, 95, 96, 101, 144, 182, 189, 191–93, 260, 380, 385, 389, 394. *See also* assimilation
deported nations, 316n, 353, 367–69
de-Russification, 124, 135, 209, 223, 265, 284, 320–21. *See also* indigenization
de-Stalinization, 330, 368n. *See also* Khrushchev
developmentalism, 159, 187, 193, 389–90. *See also* diffusion erasure; modernization thesis
diffusion-competition, 192, 197–98, 209, 248, 311, 389, 401, 403; and international attitudes of indigenes, 245–47; and international equalization, 197–98; and national separatism, 248; and nationalism, 25; among upwardly mobile indigenes, 245–46; and urbanization, 200
diffusion-erasure, 192–93, 243, 249, 321–22, 401; among autonomous-okrug *ethnies*, 287, 313; and internal colonialism, 194; and international attitudes, 244–45; among nonindigenes, 198, 209, 247, 321–22; among upwardly mobile indigenes, 245–46. *See also* developmentalism; modernization thesis
disintegration, 345, 356, 358, 364–67, 369, 375–76. *See also* border disputes; ethnoterritorial conflict; national independence movements; national separatism

divide and rule, 110, 112, 371
Dniester River, 358, 365. See also Moldova
druzhba narodov, 31
Dushanbe, 310, 312, 313, 316. See also Tadzhikistan

Eastern Europe, 403
economic decentralization. See decentralization, economic
economic interdependence, 336; and economic viability, 337–40; and nativism, 337; and political independence, 339–40. See also debt burden, potential
economic sovereignty. See sovereignty, economic
education, 72, 129, 226, 234; attitude of the peasantry toward, 73–74; attitude of the tsars toward, 72; in the Caucasus, 72; in Central Asia and Kazakhstan, 72, 129, 234; and the development of indigenous intelligentsias, 234; in European Russia, 72; in Georgia, 129, 226; and indigenization, 125–29, 225–26, 231–35; and international age differentials, 228; international attitudes and, 244–45; international equalization in, 129–30, 225–31, 228, 389; and literacy, 71; and national self-consciousness, 226; and national separatism, 226; and the nationalization of the masses in prerevolutionary Russia, 71–75, 87, 382; in the native language, 128–29, 254–58, 414–16; under Nicholas I, 72; and occupational mobility, 235; and political socialization, 225; quotas, 234; regional variation in, 72–73; religious, 72–73; secular, 72; for serfs, 71–72; in Siberia, 72; and social mobilization, 71–72, 225–35; as a solution to the national problem, 225; universal and compulsory system of, 128, 225; and urbanization, 230–31. See also literacy
emancipation, 33, 47–50, 59–60; in the Baltic guberniyas, 49; in Belorussia, 49; in Congress Poland, 49; impoverishment resulting from, 48; and literacy, 66; in Lithuania, 49; and nationalization, 47, 49, 382; and occupational mobility, 75; and peasant mobilization, 48; in Russia, 49; in Transcaucasia, 49; in Ukraine, 49
emigration, 119–20, 387–88, 405

endogamy, 296, 301, 305, 311–12, 315, 323
English, the, 403
enlightened patriotism, 33–37; defined, 34; the definition of homeland during, 35; and the emotional attachment to homeland, 35; as the ethnicization of elites, 33, 35–36; as the first phase of nationalization, 33–34; 380–81; among non-Russians, 36–37; and the Russian language debate, 36. See also nationalization
Estland, 49, 51, 67. See also Baltics
Estonia, 19, 21, 53, 75, 94; autarchic tendencies in, 335; bilateral treaties with, 372–73; citizenship laws in, 182, 348; demographic Russification of the cities in, 209, 223; economic sovereignty in, 335; independence and nationalization in, 383; the indigenization of cities in, 65; indigenization of high-status occupations in, 242; international attitudes in, 245; international family rates in, 299; international interaction in the cities of, 223; international marriage rates in, 301, 304n, 305–6; National Front of, 328n; national self-consciousness in, 53; nativism in, 170, 181–82; occupational mobility in, 80; political indigenization in, 348; potential debt burden in, 336; regional *khozraschet* in, 333; Russian inmigration and national territoriality in, 181–82, 189; Russian out-migration from, 166; territorial claims made by, 370. See also Baltics; union republics
Estonian language: and linguistic standardization in Estonia, 126; publications, 258; retention, 282; and its status in independent Estonia, 126, 348
Estonianization, 331
Estonians: 238; de-Russification among, 265; international attitudes among, 245; and the nationalization of elites, 36, 37, 39, 381–82; "natural" assimilation among, 319; political overrepresentation among, 348–49; and their return migration to Estonia, 166; Russian bilingualism among, 289; Russification of, 63, 285; upward mobility among, 80. See also Baltics
Estophiles, 37
ethnic "cleansing," 183, 351, 351n, 361, 387, 402. See also indigenization, demographic
ethnic group, 3. See also *ethnie*

ethnic reidentification, 117, 119, 140, 142. *See also* assimilation
"ethnic" separatism. *See* national separatism
ethnic stratification. *See* national stratification
ethnicism, eastern, 14–15
ethnicity, 4; politicized, 3, 378
ethnicization: 33; of elites in tsarist Russia, 35, 36. *See also* enlightened patriotism; nationalization of elites
ethnie, 6, 14, 28, 34, 35n, 36, 37, 39, 40, 44, 65, 68–69, 71, 73, 80, 109–10, 111, 115, 126, 135, 137, 142, 171, 171n, 312–15, 320, 322, 374, 378
ethnocultural indigenization. *See* indigenization, ethnocultural
ethnographic differentiation, 44–45, 110, 135–36, 157. *See also* nationalization
ethnolinguistic identity, 45, 89
ethnoterritorial conflict, 183, 189, 325, 340–41, 353, 356, 358–78, 384, 388, 397–400. *See also* border disputes; international conflicts
Eurocentrism, 405
European Community, 403–4
Euskadi, 403–4
Evenk Autonomous Okrug, 350. *See also* autonomous okrug; Siberia
Evenks, 142, 157, 269, 313, 350. *See also ethnies*; Siberia
exogamy, 296, 298, 301, 311–12, 315, 316–17. *See also* international marriage

Far East, 254, 313, 316n, 319–20, 321, 322
fatherland, 35, 44, 83, 100, 138–39. *See also* homeland
federal hierarchy, 109, 199n, 269, 285, 325, 352, 357; and demographic indigenization, 178; and ethnoterritorial disputes, 325, 376; and the hierarchy of privilege among indigenes, 169, 255–56; and urbanization, 209. *See also* confederal structure
federal structure. *See* confederal structure
Federal Treaty of Russia, 358, 367
federalism: and centralism, 100–101; and the colonial question, 100; Lenin's views on, 99–101, 151, 375, 383–84; and the national problem, 342–43, 375; and national territorial autonomy, 95, 99–101; Soviet, 342–46, 375
federalization: 27, 101; and assimilation, 138; and a developing sense of homeland, 135–37, 156, 269, 378, 396; and international equalization, 115, 124, 342–46; and nationalization, 120, 124, 134–35, 137, 144. *See also* confederalization
Finland, 52–53, 75, 80, 94, 335–36
Finlandization, 336n
Finno-Ugrian national communities, 312, 320, 322
Flanders, 404
Flemish, 402
formation of the USSR: 107–13; as a confederation, 112–13; as a federation, 113, 151; and *Narkomnats*, 108; as a unitary state, 112–13; the use of ethnodemographic data in the, 108; and variation in the level of autonomy, 109, 199n. *See also* confederal structure, federal hierarchy
France, 402, 404
free economic zones, 338. *See also* sovereignty, economic
French, 403

Gagauz, 353, 356, 358, 365. *See also* Moldova
Gamsakhurdiya, 363–64, 369. *See also* Georgia; Georgians
Gaspraly, Ismail, and the development of a pan-Turkic language, 42
gastarbeiter. *See* guestworkers
geographic mobility, 51, 65, 82, 135; and assimilation, 152, 313; during collectivization, 113, 122; ease of, 50–51; and indigenous concentration in homelands, 115–21, 158–70; and industrialization, 113, 122; and the internal passport system, 124; and international marriages, 141, 301, 304–5, 309, 311, 315; and national self-consciousness, 50–66, 152; and nationalization, 50–51, 53, 87, 113, 115, 191, 250, 382, 384–85; and national territoriality, 23, 190, 386–89; of the peasantry, 47–60, 95, 113, 115, 124; restrictions on, 189; of Russians, 53n; of Slavic peasants, 53; of Ukrainians, 53n. *See also* migration, urbanization
Georgia, 21, 30; Armenian dominance in the cities of 65, 81, 119; citizenship laws in, 182; and the Commonwealth of Independent States, 346, 354; declaration of independence in, 354, 383; demographic Russification of the cities in, 122; eco-

454 · Index

Georgia (cont.)
nomic health of, 337–38; education in, 129; and ethnoterritorial conflict in Abkhazia and South Ossetia, 183, 356, 358, 362–64, 397; indigenization of the cities in, 65; international attitudes in, 247; international family rates in, 300; international marriages in, 308; intrastate disintegration in, 356, 362–64; and the status of Meskhetian Turks, 369; national separatism in, 329; occupational mobility in, 81; political indigenization in, 134; and the Transcaucasian Federal Republic, 109, 134. See also Transcaucasia; union republics

Georgian language: the language debate in, 40; linguistic assimilation to, 284; literacy in, 67; native language publications in, 258–60; as the official language of Georgia, 344–45; retention, 282; Russian-language schools in, 255; and its standardization, 127; stigma attached to vernacular, 41

Georgianization, 115, 119, 331–32

Georgians, 238; and anti-Armenian sentiments, 65, 81, 119; in the cities of South Ossetia, 223; and (their) demographic domination of Abkhazia, 177–78, 183, 362; educational attainment of, 226; ethnographic differentiation of, 136; international attitudes among, 245; linguistic indigenization among, 272; linguistic Russification among, 265; and national territoriality, 137, 362–64; and the nationalization of elites, 36, 37, 39, 381–82

Germanization, 39, 41, 65

Germans: anti-foreigner nativism among, 403; as a deported nation, 353, 367–69; emigration of, 387–88; and Estophiles, 37; international marriage among, 315–16; linguistic Russification of, 265n; as a locally dominant group, 39, 49, 65, 80, 382; and the Volga German ASSR, 186, 316, 353, 368. See also deported nations

gerrymandering, 348

glasnost', 325, 345

Gorbachev, 328, 377, 396; on the existence of a Soviet people, 152, 325, 345, 345n, 379; on international equalization in the USSR, 194–95; and national separatism, 325–26, 345, 379–80, 386; reform programs of, 325, 345; and regional *khozraschet*, 330, 333–38; on solving the national problem, 195; on Soviet federalism, 344; as a Soviet man, 391; on totalitarianism, 329; as a Westernizer, 39n

Gorno-Badakhshan Autonomous Oblast, 254. See also autonomous oblasts, Tadzhikistan

Great Britain, 402, 404

guestworkers, 24, 403

Gypsies, 269, 269n

hegemonial exchange, 132

homelands, xvii–xviii, 3; autarchic tendencies in, 331; definitions of, 45; demographic claims to, 19, 154, 341, 351, 358–73, 376; emotional attachment to, 18, 35, 168, 187, 198, 385; as an empty container, 5, 103, 105, 147, 168, 400; and enlightened patriotism, 35; ethnoterritorial disputes over, 325, 340–41, 356, 358–73, 376–77, 378, 384, 388; as a factor in international conflict, 106; and federalization, 135–37, 156, 269, 378, 396; as the geographic cradle of the nation, 10, 15, 18, 39, 360; geographic extent of, 18–19, 53, 86, 156; historic claims to, 18–19, 154, 341, 351, 360–73, 376; home republics as, 115, 154, 156–58; indigenization of life in, 29, 124–25, 159, 187, 386; and indigenization policies, 124–25, 137, 144, 151, 169, 199, 234, 240, 374, 378–79, 384, 400; and indigenous status, 39–40, 169, 199, 255–56, 373, 395; as locality, 16, 47, 52–53, 86, 94; as a mediator between social mobilization and national self-consciousness, 25; migration from, 152–53, 159–62, 164–68, 178, 181, 184, 200, 261, 386–87; national gravitation to, 115–21, 158–70, 182, 187, 209, 388; and national self-consciousness, 10, 15–22, 86, 378; and national territoriality, 18, 21–22, 32, 40, 80, 83–85, 88, 125, 188, 340, 397, 399–400; as a nationalist invention, 10, 17, 382–83; and nationalization, 17, 83, 88, 94, 198, 380–83; native language retention in, 270–72, 282, 322–23; political control of, 340; and primordialism, 17–18, 341; reconcentration of indigenes in, 166, 170, 181, 185–87, 293–94, 368; and romanticism, 83, 382; Russian meaning of, 42, 58, 84, 117, 138–39, 169–70, 189, 371; a sense of exclusiveness toward, 21–22, 32, 40, 49, 85–86, 120, 125, 134, 137, 145, 154–55, 187–89, 198; a sense of spatial identity with, 18, 32, 40, 84, 189, 380–81; as a social construct, 10, 156; as the state, 83, 139, 381; and sovietization, 152; Stalin's misunderstanding of, 103, 107, 115, 147; subjective sense of, 10, 16, 83, 86, 103, 144–45, 147, 168, 360, 378, 382, 399–400; as a tangible attribute of nations, 7; three phases in the making of, 83. *See also* home republics

home republics, 145; and demographic strength of indigenes in, 178; indigenous dispersal from, 162; as geographic minima of homelands, 115, 154, 156–58, 384, 388, 400; as guarantors of international equality, 115, 187; increasing inequality in, 199; and their loss of significance, 152, 159, 162, 187; national "gravitation" to, 115–21, 158–70, 187, 209; as nationally homogeneous places, 115, 151; urbanization of, 202–8. *See also* homelands; autonomous oblasts; autonomous okrugs; autonomous republics; union republics; confederal structure; federalism

Hungarians, 265, 269
Hungary, 402

iconography, 9, 9n, 38, 138
independence, declarations of, 337–40, 353–56, 365, 367, 383. *See also* national independence movements
independence, and nationalism, 94–95
indigenes, 24–27; acculturation of, 262; diffusion-competition among, 245–46; diffusion-erasure among, 245–46; endogamy among, 323; inferior status of, 39–40, 242; international marriages among, 301, 305, 310–15, 323, 394; linguistic Russification among, 172–82; and their migration to the cities in their homelands, 63–66, 80, 123, 209; national separatism among, 356, 358; native language retention among, 272–83; political overrepresentation among, 347–50; preferential treatment of, 169, 199, 255–56, 373, 395; and reactive ethnicity, 40, 57, 184, 247–48, 395; and their reconcentration in homelands, 187; relative deprivation among, 246–47, 260; Russians as, 188, 371–72; Russian bilingualism among, 289; Russification of, 171, 322, 394; social mobilization of, 68, 130, 170; urbanization of, 63–66, 121–22, 170, 209

indigenization: as acculturation, 250; and assimilation, 126, 130, 138, 146, 164, 249–51, 317, 320, 394; and autarchic tendencies, 331–35; of cities, 63–66, 80, 122–23, 124, 209, 223–24; of the Communist party, 132; and confederalization, 342, 375; and decentralization, 331–32, 334–35, 339, 342, 374–75; demographic, 24, 61, 120–22, 171–72, 177–78, 185, 293, 395; and the development of national cultural forms, 125; and education, 125–29, 225–26, 231–35; of elites, 235, 374; ethnocultural, 26, 125, 127–29, 137, 164n, 250, 252–53, 269, 293, 323, 394–95; from below, 125, 374–75, 378, 386, 390, 396; and geographic differentials in preferential treatment, 169; of high-status occupations, 242–43; of industry, 242; intergenerational, 318–19; and interhomeland migration, 159, 168–69; and international equalization, 106, 124–35, 145, 199, 234–36, 240–43, 248, 384, 389–90; and international marriage, 142, 164; Lenin's views on, 124, 383–84; of life in homelands, 29, 124–25, 159, 187, 386; linguistic, 125–28, 139, 254–56, 272, 282, 293–95, 323; and literacy, 125–26; and national segregation, 151; and national self-consciousness, 105, 125, 130; national separatism as, 29, 378–79, 386; and national territorial autonomy, 125; and nationalization, 124–35, 250; and "natural" assimilation, 317–19; of nonindigenes, 142, 164, 248, 251, 318–19, 322–23; and occupational mobility, 236, 242–44; opposition to, 350–51; as a policy of "affirmative action" in homelands, 105, 107, 124–35, 137, 144, 151, 169, 199, 234, 240, 323, 374, 378–79, 384, 390, 400; political, 27–28, 125, 129, 132–35, 137, 325, 330, 333, 340–77, 395–400; in the Red Army, 132–33; of Russians, 394; and Russification, 127, 137–38, 250–51, 320–21, 394; and a sense of exclusiveness, 137, 384; and social mobilization, 248; socioeconomic, 25–26, 89n, 125, 130–32, 325n, 331–40; and sovietization, 126, 137, 243, 386; Stalinist policy of, 37, 95, 105–7, 121, 124–35,

indigenization (*cont.*)
374, 384; as territorial response, 28–29, 32; urbanization and, 209, 223; and the vernacularization of literary languages, 126–28; of the work force, 80–81, 130–32, 238–43. *See also* nationalization
industrial work force, 75–76, 120, 236–41; demographic indigenization of, 80–81, 130–32, 238–43; international attitudes of, 245–46; international equalization in, 236–38; as *otkhodniki*, 48, 59n, 60, 76, 78; and ties to the rural villages, 76; and *zemlyachestvo*, 76
industrialization, 75–76, 113, 120, 122
Ingush, 154, 159, 185, 272, 312n, 369; Russian bilingualism among, 289. *See also* deported nations; North Caucasus
inorodtsy, 57
internal colonialism, 49, 57–58, 96–97, 106, 187, 191, 193–97, 389–90, 401; as a corollary to diffusion-erasure, 194; and a "cultural division of labor," 194, 243, 248; in the developed republics of the USSR, 195; and international attitudes, 243–45; and international inequality, 194–97; and national self-consciousness, 191, 193–97; and national stratification, 194, 248; in the underdeveloped regions of the USSR, 195, 375; and welfare colonialism, 195. *See also* reactive ethnicity; relative deprivation
internal passports, 124, 165, 297, 317, 318n
international attitudes: and diffusion-competition, 245–47; and diffusion-erasure, 244–45; of downwardly mobile members, 244; and education, 244–45; of elites, 244; among indigenous blue-collar workers, 245–46; among indigenous intelligentsias, 245; and internal colonialism, 243–45; and international equalization, 243–44; and international marriage, 296; and migration, 246; toward nationally mixed families, 244–45; toward a nationally mixed work place, 244–45; among nonindigenes, 246–47; toward nonindigenes, 244; and occupational mobility, 245–46; and social mobilization, 243–47; surveys of, 244–47; urbanization and, 244
international conflict management, 360, 389, 397–98
international conflicts, 106, 308, 326, 360, 370, 376, 389, 398–99. *See also* border disputes; ethnoterritorial conflict
international equality: in educational attainment, 225–26; home republics as guarantors of, 115, 187; and internal colonialism, 194–97; lack of, 195, 198–99, 202, 231, 236, 243, 247
international equalization, 191, 193–97, 247, 343; in agricultural employment, 236; and assimilation, 145; and continued relative deprivation among indigenes, 196–97; in the development of a national intelligentsia, 238–39; and diffusion-competition, 197–98; and diffusion-erasure, 194–97; and equality, 195, 199, 202; in educational attainment, 129–30, 225–31, 389; federalization and, 115, 124, 342–46; the geography of, 247–48; and growing interrepublic inequality, 199; through indigenization, 106, 124–35, 145, 199, 234–36, 240–43, 248, 384, 389–90; in industrial employment, 236–38; and international attitudes, 243–44; Lenin on the need for, 97, 124, 194, 383–84, 389; in literacy, 129, as a means of solving the national problem, 96–98, 124, 144–45, 152, 187, 194–96, 198, 247, 385–86, 389; as measured by coefficients of variation, 121, 200, 202, 226, 230–31, 236, 238, 258, 297; and national separatism, 225, 248; and national stratification, 199, 248; and national territoriality, 146, 187, 225, 240, 390; and nationalization, 144, 390; and occupational mobility, 236, 238–43, 389; in the postwar USSR, 152, 194, 199; in the rate of urbanization, 121, 200–204, 389; and relative deprivation, 196–97; and social mobilization, 199, 225–26, 389; Stalin on the need for, 144; in white-collar employment, 238; as a zero-sum game, 195
international families, 296–301; attitudes toward, 244–45
international integration. *See* assimilation
international marriage, 137, 140–42, 301–17; and assimilation, 251–52, 282, 295–317, 393–94; gender differentiation in, 304–5; among indigenes, 301, 305, 310–15, 323, 394; and indigenization, 142, 164; and interhomeland migration, 164; and international attitudes, 296; and international conflict, 308; and intranational marriages,

313–14; and linguistic assimilation, 282, 296; and national self-consciousness, 315; and nationalization, 137, 142, 250–51, 312–16, 321; and "natural" assimilation, 164, 251, 296, 317; among nonindigenes, 141–42, 164, 297, 299, 304, 304n, 305–6, 309–10, 315–17, 316n, 394; among Russians, 141–42, 304–5, 305n, 308, 311–12, 314–16; and Russification, 142, 304, 312; and social mobilization, 301, 304–5, 309–11, 315; theoretical probability of, 310; and urbanization, 141, 298–30. *See also* acculturation; assimilation
irredentas, 157–58. *See also* border disputes; ethnoterritorial conflict
irredentism, 157–58, 402. *See also* national separatism; nationalism; secession
Islam, 110, 184, 392–93; and education in the Russian Empire, 72–73; and the nationalization of elites in Central Asia, 36, 39; and the nationalization of the Muslim masses, 82, 110, 392; and the vernacularization of literary languages, 42
Islamicization, 73

jadidism, 42, 73
Jewish Autonomous Oblast, 103, 353. *See also* autonomous oblasts; Birobidzhan
Jews, 67, 231, 238, 265, 304, 308, 382, 387–88

Kabardin-Balkar ASSR, 177n, 258. *See also* autonomous republics; North Caucasus
Kabardins, 185. *See also* deported nations; North Caucasus
Kalinin Oblast, 316
Kaliningrad Oblast, 368n, 370
Kalmyk ASSR, 178, 258. *See also* autonomous republics
Kalmyks, 159, 185, 238. *See also* deported nations
Karachay-Cherkess Autonomous Oblast, 258. *See also* autonomous oblasts; North Caucasus
Karachays, 272, 286. *See also* deported nations; North Caucasus
Karakalpaks, 177, 223, 238, 284, 288–89, 314. *See also* Central Asians; Uzbeks
Karakalpakstan, 177–78, 178n, 223, 310, 312, 314, 370n. *See also* Central Asia; Uzbekistan

Karamzin, Nicholas, 35
Karelia, 120, 184–5, 209, 258, 316. *See also* autonomous republics
Karelian People's Front, 185. *See also* national independence movements
Karelians: and (their) "gravitation" to Karelia, 120; international marriages among, 312, 316; Russification of, 120, 171, 185, 188, 231, 265, 272, 282, 284, 286, 289, 312, 316, 322, 394. *See also* Finno-Ugrian national communities
Kaunas, 305. *See also* Lithuania
Kazakhstan: 58; bilateral treaties with, 372–73; border disputes in, 189, 388; demographic Russification of cities in, 65, 209; declaration of sovereignty in, 347–48; demographic Russification of northern, 82, 154; education in, 72, 129, 234; excess mortality in, 119; indigenization of higher education in, 234; indigenization of the work force in, 131–32; international marriage in, 310, 311–12, 315–16; literacy in, 67; native language publications in, 258–60; as part of the Russian homeland, 154, 170, 371; political conservatism in, 355; potential debt burden in, 336; Russian loss of plurality status in, 178; Russian outmigration from, 181; school attendance in, 72; territorial claims made by, 370; vernacularization in, 42. *See also* Central Asia
Kazakhs: 57, 159n, and their dispersal from Kazakhstan, 119; emigration of, 119; excess mortality among, 119; international marriages among, 311–12; nationalization of elites, 36, 381; nationalization of the masses, 82; reidentification of, 119; Russian bilingualism among, 289; and their sense of exclusiveness toward Kazakhstan, 154, 155; and their urbanization, 121–22. *See also* Central Asians
Kazan', 73. *See also* Tatarstan
Kazan' Tatars. *See* Tatars
Khakass, 154, 284, 313, 319, 319n. *See also ethnie*; Siberia
Khakass Autonomous Oblast, 258, 319. *See also* autonomous oblasts; Siberia
Khanty: 142, 157, 171; international marriages among, 312; "natural" assimilation among, 320; Russification of, 185, 188, 272, 282, 312. *See also ethnie*; Siberia

Khanty-Mansi Autonomous Okrug, 171, 185. *See also* autonomous okrugs; Siberia

Khorezm, 110. *See also* Central Asia; Turkestan

Khrushchev: on the attainment of communism, 152; on the deported nations, 368, 368n; and de-Stalinization, 330, 368n; on the drawing together of nations, 152; on international equalization in the USSR, 152, 194; and the *sovnarkhozy* experiment, 330–33, 374–75

Kiev, 319. *See also* Ukraine

Kipchaks, 136–37. *See also* Central Asians

Kirgiz, 119, 159n, 184; Russian bilingualism among, 289. *See also* Central Asians

Kirgizia. *See* Kyrgyzstan

Kishinev. *See* Chisinau

Komi, 238; international marriages among, 312; linguistic Russification of the, 265, 272, 282, 284, 286; Russification of, 286, 312. *See also* Finno-Ugrian national communities

Komi ASSR, 178, 209, 258. *See also* autonomous republics; Volga-Urals

Komi-Permyaks, 154, 171, 272, 282. *See also ethnies*; Siberia

Koreans, 316n, 373, 398. *See also* deported nations

korenizatsiya. *See* indigenization

Koryak Autonomous Okrug, 129; Siberia Koryaks, 171, 272, 282. *See also* autonomous okrugs; *ethnie*; Siberia

Kosovo, 401–2

Kumyks, 272. *See also* Dagestan; North Caucasus

Kurds, 269

Kurland, 49, 51. *See also* Baltics

Kyrgyzstan: border disputes in, 189, 371; demographic Russification of the cities in, 122, 209; international marriage in, 308; native language publications in, 258–60; native language schools in, 255; nativism in, 170; political indigenization and representation in, 348; Russian language schools in, 255; Russian out-migration from, 181, 240–41; unemployment in, 241. *See also* Central Asia

language: and acculturation, 251, 287–88; and bilingualism, 252, 288–93, 322, 393; Church Slavonic, 35–36; and enlightened patriotism, 35–36; and indigenization policies, 125–28, 139, 254–55; of instruction in schools, 128–29, 139, 254–58, 414–16; as an instrument in international competition, 9, 253, 323; laws, 126, 257, 260, 282, 288, 289, 293, 295, 322–23, 348, 365, 395; legal status of, 126, 138, 254, 261–62, 344–45; and linguistic indigenization, 125–28, 139, 255–56, 272, 282, 293–95; as a link between elites and masses, 36, 40; and literacy, 67, 125–29, 253; as a modern nationalist invention, 7, 10; and nationalization, 35–36, 126, 250, 253–53, 321; as an objective characteristic of nations, 6, 250n, 253; pan-Turkic, 42; policies, 8–9, 27, 287, 322; of publication, 127–28, 258–61; retention of native, 265–83, 322–23; Russian, 35–36, 67, 128, 138–39, 254–55, 257–62, 283, 288–93, 295, 322–23, 393, 395; and script used, 127, 295; standardization of, 35–36, 70–71, 87, 125–27, 139n, 250, 253–54, 321; as a symbol of national identity, 9, 253, 323; usage on the job, 261; utility of, 252–53, 261–62, 283, 287, 295, 322; vernacularization of, 35–36, 40–42, 87, 125–27, 253. *See also* literacy

Latinization of linguistic scripts, 127

Latvia, 19, 21, 94; citizenship laws in, 182, 348; demographic Russification of the cities in, 209, 223; economic sovereignty in, 335; gerrymandering of electoral districts in, 348; independence and nationalization in, 383; indigenization of the cities in, 65; indigenization of high-status occupations in, 242; international family rates in, 299; international interaction in the cities of, 223; malapportionment of electoral districts in, 348; nativism in, 170, 181–82; occupational mobility in, 80; political indigenization in, 348; Russian in-migration and national territoriality in, 181–82, 189; Russian out-migration from, 166; territorial claims made by, 370. *See also* Baltics; union republics

Latvian language: and linguistic standardization in Latvia, 126; literacy in, 67; native language publications in, 258–60; retention, 282; and its status in independent Latvia, 126

Latvians: educational attainment of, 226; the

lack of elites among, 39; and the nationalization of elites, 39, 381–82; "natural" assimilation among, 318–19; political overrepresentation among, 348–49; and their return migration to Latvia, 166, 286; Russification of, 63, 285–86; upward mobility among, 80; urbanization and nationalization among, 65

Lenin, 96, on centralism, 99–101, 107, 328; on the delimitation of autonomous territories, 99, 151; on federalism, 99–101, 151, 375, 383–84; and "Great Russian chauvinism," 194, 383–84; and indigenization, 124, 383–84; on international equalization, 97, 124, 194, 383–84, 389; on modernization and denationalization, 96, 192–93, 389; on national cultural autonomy, 101; on the national problem facing Russia, 96, 383–84; on national territorial autonomy, 98–100; on nations and capitalism, 96; on the right to national self-determination, 97–98, 104, 106, 113, 352, 364; on the role of elites from oppressed and oppressor nations, 97; and totalitarianism, 330; on urbanization and assimilation, 96, 192–93, 200. *See also* Marxism-Leninism; national problem; Stalin

Leningrad. *See* St. Petersburg

Leningrad Oblast, 370

Lifland, 49, 51, 67. *See also* Baltics

linguistic assimilation. *See* assimilation, linguistic

linguistic indigenization. *See* indigenization, linguistic

linguistic particularism, 42

literacy, 66–69; in the Baltic guberniyas, 66n, 67; in Bessarabia, 67; in Central Asia, 67; in the cities, 67; and education, 71, and emancipation, 66; and equalization, 129; in European Russia, 66; outside European Russia, 67; in indigenous languages, 125–29, 253; in Kazakhstan, 67; in Lithuania, 67; and nationalization, 67–68, 87, 95, 251, 253, 382; among non-European indigenes, 67; among peasants, 66–67; in prerevolutionary Russia, 66–71; regional variation in, 67–68, 129; and rural to urban migration, 59; in the Russian language, 67, 69; and Russification, 69, 87; and social mobilization, 66–71; in standardized languages, 70, 87, 128–29; in Ufa, 67; universal, 226; and vernacularization, 67. *See also* education

Lithuania, 21, 94, autarchic tendencies in, 335; declaration of independence in, 353–54; demographic indigenization of the cities in, 223; demographic Russification of the cities in, 223; emancipation in, 49; independence and nationalization in, 383; international marriage in, 305; potential debt burden in, 336; Russian out-migration from, 166; territorial claims made by, 370

Lithuanian language: and linguistic indigenization in Lithuania, 293; and linguistic standardization in Lithuania, 126; literacy in, 67; publications in, 258–60; retention, 282; and its status in independent Lithuania, 126

Lithuanians, 238; international marriages among, 313, 316; linguistic indigenization among, 272; linguistic Russification of, 285–86; and the nationalization of elites, 36, 37, 39, 381–82; "natural" assimilation among, 318; and their return migration to Lithuania, 166, 285–86; Russian bilingualism among, 289

locale, 5, 30, 39

localism, 16–17, 35, 39, 40, 45, 47, 51–53, 75, 79, 86–88, 94, 115, 145, 331–32; and the collectivization of agriculture, 95, 115; as a contender with nationalism and sovietization, 115; and economic indigenization, 331; and the lack of standardized languages, 70–71, 87; among peasants, 44–45, 47, 52, 60–61, 70–71, 83, 85–88, 115, 382–83; Russian, 338–39, 356–57, 366; under the *sovnarkhozy* system, 326, 330–33

location, 5, 29, 32, 39

Magyar Creed, 23

Magyars, 402

Makhachkala, 313. *See also* Dagestan; North Caucasus

Malorossiya, 42. *See also* Ukraine

Mansi, 171, international marriages among, 312; "natural" assimilation among, 320; Russification of, 185, 188, 272, 312. *See also ethnie*; Siberia

marginality, 30

Mari: linguistic Russification of the, 265, 284, 286; Russification of, 286. *See also* Finno-Ugrian national communities

Mari ASSR, 132, 258. *See also* autonomous republics; Volga-Urals
Marxism-Leninism: as developmentalism, 193; and national self-consciousness, 193; and the totalitarian model, 329–30. *See also* communism; Communist party; Lenin; Stalin
Meskhetia, 369. *See also* Georgia
Meskhetian Turks, 184, 187, 353, 367–69. *See also* deported nations
mestnichestvo, 331–32. *See also* localism
migration, 53–57, 119; and the activation of national territoriality, 24–25; 57, 153, 170, 181–82, 189, 224, 387, 405; affect of social mobilization on, 59, 168; to areas of labor deficit, 165; from areas of labor surplus, 165; 59; and assimilation, 165–66, 170, 185, 199–200, 251–52; eastward, 53–54; and emotional attachment to homeland, 168, 386; forced, 159, 185; of guestworkers, 24, 403; intrahomeland, 159; interhomeland, 117, 119–22, 152–53, 159–62, 164–71, 178, 181–82, 184–85, 189, 200, 209, 223, 261, 365, 386–87; and the internal passport system, 124, 165; and international attitudes, 246; and international marriage, 164; and literacy, 59; and national "gravitation" to the homeland, 117, 119–20, 158–70, 182, 386–88; and national "marginality," 164, 251, 315; and national self-consciousness, 57, 86, 164, 170, 185; and national separatism, 153, 183, 405; and nationalization, 24–25, 57–59, 85–86; and nativism, 166, 170, 184, 224, 248–49, 386–87, 405; of nonindigenes, 53–58, 153, 159, 182, 184–85; policies, 54, 165, 387; and population pressure in the west, 56; a rational-choice model of, 169–70; refugee, 186–87, 249, 361, 363, 368, 387, 403; in response to geographic differentials in economic opportunity, 158–59, 224; in response to "life-cycle events," 158; in response to "push" and "pull" factors, 159n; new restrictions on, 189; return, 17, 56, 166, 170, 181–82, 184–87, 223–24, 240–42, 248–49, 285–86, 293–94, 387–88; rural-rural, 51–58; rural-urban, 59–66, 80, 121–23, 168, 200, 209, 261; seasonal, 48, 59n, 60; to Siberia, 53–57, 85, 166, 171; and social mobilization, 59, 168; and transportation, 51. *See also* geographic mobility

military conscription, 78; and nationalization in prerevolutionary Russia, 79–80; reforms to, 79
Minsk, 346. *See also* Belarus'
modernization thesis, 45. *See also* developmentalism; diffusion-erasure
Moldavian ASSR, 365. *See also* autonomous republics; Ukraine
Moldavians, 67, 238; and the creation of national identity, 157–58; international attitudes among, 244–45; international marriage among, 311; and the lack of a literary language prior to World War I, 42; linguistic de-Russification among, 284; linguistic Russification of, 265, 283; Russian language fluency among, 262, 283. *See also* Rumanians
Moldova, 67, 157, 157n, 262; border disputes in, 156, 189, 353, 356, 358, 364–65, 370, 388; citizenship laws in, 182; and the Commonwealth of Independent States, 354; declaration of independence in, 354, 365, 383; indigenous underrepresentation in high-status occupations in, 242; international attitudes in, 244–45; international interaction in the cities of, 223; international marriage rates in, 301; intrastate disintegration in, 356, 358, 364–65; national separatism in, 329; native language publications in, 258–61; new language law in, 365; potential debt burden in, 338; and reunification with Rumania, 157–58, 354, 365; Russian out-migration from, 166; separatism among indigenous minorities in, 356, 358. *See also* Rumania; union republics
Mordvinia, 258, 316. *See also* autonomous republics; Volga-Urals
Mordvins: intranational marriages among, 313, 316; Russification of, 120, 143, 188, 265, 284, 286, 316, 322. *See also* Finno-Ugrian national communities
Muslims, 304; and nationalism, 392–93; as a unified nation, 392. *See also* Islam; pan-Islamic consciousness

Nagorno-Karabakh, 156, 170–71, 182–83, 223–24, 248, 257, 282, 284–85, 300, 308, 358, 360–62. *See also* Armenia; Azerbaydzhan; ethnoterritorial conflicts
Narkomnats, 104, 108, 112. *See also* Stalin
narod, 36, 45, 46, 49, 58, 62, 79, 88–89, 136

narodnost', 136
nation-state, 4, 14n, 28, 85, 89, 97, 98, 99, 113, 145, 189, 342, 379, 389, 397, 405
national consolidation. *See* nationalization
national cultural autonomy, 95, 101–4, 350–51, 376, 398–99
national front organizations. *See* national independence movements
national independence movements, 328–29, 328n, 329n, 354–55, 374, 388. *See also* national separatism
national marginality, 164, 192, 251–52, 252n, 301, 308, 315, 321–22, 393
national problem, 26, 27, 29, 31, 32, 95, 105–6, 113, 170, 187, 234–35, 376, 378–80; "class essence" of, 106; and education, 225; Lenin on the, 96, 383–84; mass based, 147; modernization, equalization, and the, 96–98, 124, 144–45, 152, 187, 194–96, 198, 247, 385–86, 389; and national stratification, 194n; territorial and extraterritorial approaches to solving the, 95, 98–103, 105, 107, 144–46, 342–44, 350–51, 376, 398–99; Stalin on the, 102–3; and totalitarianism, 327, 375–76; urbanization and the, 244
national question. *See* national problem
national reidentification. *See* assimilation
national self-consciousness, 10–22, 24, 30, 34, 47, 57–58, 103, 188, 249, 398; and the delimitation of autonomous units, 108; as a dialogue between past and future, 21; and its diffusion to the rural countryside, 77, 88; educational attainment and, 226; erasure of, 192–93, 243, 249, 321–22, 401; in Estonia, 53; in Finland, 53; and forced assimilation, 317; and forced outmigration, 185; and geographic mobilization, 50–66, 152; and indigenization policies, 105, 125, 130; and interhomeland migration, 164, 170, 185; and internal colonialism, 191, 193–97; and international marriage, 315; among the masses, 47, 87, 191; and "modernization," xvii, 25, 45, 152, 191–98; and natural increase, 181; political legitimacy of, 132; politicization of *ethnies* and, 378; as a reaction to nonindigenous in-migration, 57, 86; and reidentification, 143, 146; among Russians, 58; as a sense of common destiny, 10, 20–22; as a sense of common geographic origins, 15–19; and a sense of exclusiveness toward the homeland, 86, 378; as a sense of shared ancestry, 10–14; and social mobilization, 66, 152, 191–98, 226, 248, 295; territorialization of *ethnies* and, 378; variation in the intensity of, 30; and urbanization, 65, 86; among youth, 296n
national self-determination, 19, 94, 97, 170, 242, 347, 397–98; and the delimitation of autonomous units in the USSR, 107–9; the right to, 97–98, 104, 106, 113, 352, 364; as secession, 97–98, 102, 104, 351–52
national separatism, 3, 20, 26, 28–29, 32, 95, 101n, 181, 249, 328–29, 354, 374, 385–86, 401–7; and the August 1991 coup, 346; and bilingualism, 289; and diffusion-competition, 248; and the Gorbachev reforms, 325–26, 345, 379–80, 386; as indigenization, 29, 378–79, 386; among indigenous minorities, 356, 358; and international equalization, 225, 248; and migration, 153, 183, 405; and modernization, 191; rising education and, 226; in the successor states, 356; as the synthesis of the national dialectic, 391; and urbanization, 225
national stratification, 26, 34, 35n, 39–40, 80, 81, 96–97, 106, 115, 124, 144, 187, 243; and assimilation, 317; and a "cultural division of labor," 194, 248; as an impediment to nationalization, 120; and internal colonialism, 194, 194n; and international equalization, 199, 248; and nationalization, 120; and Soviet nationality policies, 194; in the successor states, 348, 386–87, 399, 402; a two-tiered system of, 199, 243, 386
national territorial autonomy, 98–102, 103, 104–5, 350–51, 358; and federalism in the USSR, 95, 99–101; and indigenization, 125; for indigenous minorities, 397–99; Lenin's views on, 98–100; as a means of solving the national problem, 95, 107, 144–45, 376, 398–99; among nonindigenes, 373–74; Stalin's views on, 103–4, 105
national territoriality, 16, as an activated political strategy, 22, 28, 32, 325, 329, 340; and its activation, 22–28, 93, 224, 257, 262, 287; in Africa and Asia, 404–6; and assimilation, 146–47, 185, 188, 315, 385, 406; in the Baltic guberniyas, 80; catalysts

462 · Index

national territoriality (cont.)
for the activation of, 9, 23–24, 27, 40–41, 89, 185, 188, 225, 235, 262, 360, 374, 398, 403, 406; confederal structure and, 329; control over economic and political decision-making and, 24, 27, 330–40; in Czechoslovakia, 401–2; and declarations of sovereignty, 347, 360, 397; as an end in itself, 23, 398–99; ethnic place-clearing function of, 361, 388; and ethnocultural indigenization, 250, 269; geographic mobility and, 23, 190, 386–89; as indigenization from below, 125, 374–75, 378, 386, 390, 396; and the indigenization of education, 235; and indigenization policies, 105, 107, 124–35, 240, 323, 390; among indigenous minorities, 360, 376; as innate response, 18, 22; and interhomeland migration, 24–25, 57, 153, 170, 181–82, 189, 224, 387, 405; and international equalization, 146, 187, 225, 240, 390; first language choice and, 269; as a latent feeling, 22, 32; and linguistic assimilation, 282; and localism, 86–87; migration and, 24–25, 57, 153, 405; and national marginality, 315; as nationalism, 22–23, 384, 400; among nonindigenes, 373–74, 398; among non-Russians, 85, 137, 362–64; and occupational mobility, 242–43; political legitimacy of, 132; Russian in-migration as a catalyst for, 181–82, 189, 224; Russian nationalism as a catalyst for, 85, 89, 367; and Russification, 95, 125, 224, 257, 262, 287; and secession, 341–42, 397; as a sense of exclusiveness, 21–22, 32, 40, 49, 80, 83–85, 88, 125, 188, 340, 397, 399–400; as a sense of spatial identity, 18, 32, 40, 88; and its significance for comparative studies of nationalism, 380, 400–407; social mobilization and, 24–25, 187, 198, 235, 248, 390, 405–6; Soviet federalism and, 329; as a special case of human territoriality, 22, 88; state-sponsored assimilation and, 24, 26; in the underdeveloped South, 404; and uneven development, 27; urbanization and, 224–25; in Western Europe and Canada, 402–4; and World War I, 94; in Yugoslavia, 401–2

nationalism: age of, 3; bourgeois, 31; in cities, 59, 66; and communism, 134; diffusion-competition theory of, 25; as a contender with localism and sovietization, 115; decolonization, 405; definitions of, 3–4, 23; as deviant behavior, 153, 379; as eastern ethnicism, 14–15; geographic studies of, 4–5; and the Gorbachev reforms, 379; and independence during the interwar period, 94–95; as loyalty to the nation, 3; Muslim, 392–393; as national territoriality, 22–23, 384, 400; and nationalist movements, 4; and the nation-state ideal, 4, 397; non-Russian, 89, 105–6, 252; peripheral, 194; as a political geographic doctrine, 4; and political indigenization, 134; as politicized ethnicity, 3, 378; reactive, 58; romantic, 36–38, 45–46, 85, 144; Russian, 17, 34, 39, 58, 84–85, 89, 105–6, 154, 338–39, 356–57, 367, 394, 399; as western territorialism, 14–15. See also national separatism; national territoriality

nationalist parties, 328–29. See also national independence movements

nationality okrugs, 109, 137. See also autonomous okrugs

nationality policies, 94–105, 124–25, 144–47, 170–71, 240, 252, 378, 385; and assimilation, 143, 252, 317; and internal colonialism, 193–97; and nationalization, 95–96, 105, 115, 124; and Stalinist deformations of, 106–7, 112n, 144, 153, 329, 352, 385. See also Brezhnev; Communist party; Gorbachev; Khrushchev; Lenin; Marxism-Leninism; Stalin

nationality rayons, 109–10, 137, 143, 352, 352n. See also federal hierarchy

nationality soviets, 109–10, 137, 143, 352, 352n. See also federal hierarchy

nationalization: and assimilation, 146, 188, 251, 265, 313, 316–17; and collectivization, 120, 145; and the confederal structure of the USSR, 151; and education, 71–75, 87, 382; of elites, 12–13, 16, 33, 34–43, 64–65, 87, 145, 381–82; and emancipation of serfs, 47, 49, 382; and ethnocultural indigenization, 250; enlightened patriotism and, 33–37, 380–81; of families, 250–51, 309, 321; and federalization, 120, 124, 134–35, 137, 144; geographic differentials in the timing of, 51; geographic and ethnographic limitations of, 13–14, 45; and geographic mobilization, 50–51, 53, 87,

113, 115, 191, 250, 382, 384–85; and independence movements, 374, 383; and indigenization policies, 124–35; and intermarriage, 137, 142, 250–51, 312–16, 321; and international equalization, 144, 390; and the language debate, 35–36; and linguistic standardization, 126, 250, 253–54, 321; and literacy, 67–68, 87, 95, 251, 253, 382; of the masses, 13, 33, 43–93, 95, 110, 113, 115, 126, 137–38, 142, 144–45, 147, 188, 191, 250, 265, 313–14, 321, 353, 357, 374, 378, 381–85, 391–92; military conscription and, 79–80; and "modernization," xvii, 33, 45, 59, 95, 191–98; and multiple levels of identity, 31; and the myth of shared ancestry, 11; and national stratification, 120; and nationality policies, 95–96, 105, 115, 124; patriotic agitation and, 33, 37–43, 71, 381; of the peasantry, 43–44, 49, 86, 115, 123, 382; the (three) phases of, 33, 380; as a process of horizontal consolidation and vertical incorporation, 11, 33; in reaction to the in-migration of nonindigenes, 24–25, 57–58, 85–86; and the role of rural teachers, 43, 75; and romanticism, 37–38, 381; and rural to urban migration, 59; and Russification, 251, 393; and a sense of homeland, 17, 83, 88, 94, 198, 380–83; and social mobilization, 66–83, 87, 95, 115, 191–98, 248, 250, 382, 384–85, 389–90; and the Soviet censuses, 136; Stalin and, 37, 381; and transportation, 50, 382; of "tribes" in the underdeveloped South, 404–5; and urbanization, 64–66, 87, 124, 382; and vernacularization, 36, 40, 87, 250, 253; and World War I, 94, 108; and *zemlyachestvo*, 61

nations, 94; as collective action groups, 197; as collections of citizens, 35, 381; as communities of belonging, 6, 192–93; as communities of interest, 6, 20–21, 192–93, 197; "core," 194; definitions of, 5–22, 29–30, 380–81, 406; as extended families, 12; as imagined communities, 11–12; the instrumentalist dimension of, 6, 10, 20, 198; Marxist-Leninist definitions of, 96; and national self-consciousness, 10; objective characteristics of, 6–10, 250n, 253, 295; oppressed, 97; as oppressor, 97, 105; peasants as the core of, 38, 45, 88, 381; "peripheral," 194; proletarianization of, 131;

the primordial dimension of, 6, 10, 12, 17, 18, 20, 379; the "reawakening" of, 12–13, 379; socialist, 31; sovereignty of, 347, 351–52; Stalin's definition of, 8, 102–3; the subjective dimension of, 10–22, 295; and union republics, 112; urbanization of, 200–225

native language schools, 128–29, 254–58, 414–16; in cities, 255; outside the homeland, 254–55; in rural areas, 255; Russian language study in, 254. *See also* education; language

nativism, 24, 115, 153, 166, 170, 180–82, 184–88, 224, 248, 337, 368, 387, 393, 398, 403, 405; and deteriorating economic conditions, 337; and migration, 166, 170, 184, 224, 248–49, 386–87, 405; and Russian bilingualism, 289; among socially mobilized indigenes, 235

natsional'nost', 136

natsiya, 136

"natural" assimilation. *See* assimilation, "natural"

natural increase: geographic differentials in, 117, 164, 178, 298; and national self-consciousness, 181; as a sign of "biological vitality," 178–79

Nenets, 171, 185, 272, 282. *See also ethnie*; Siberia

nomenklatura system, 328, 332

nonindigenes, 24; accommodation of, 395; acculturation of, 140, 209, 250–51, 285–88; and (their) assimilation, 25, 62–63, 119–21, 140–43, 146, 164, 188, 209, 249–51, 285–88, 311, 315, 317–18, 384–85, 395; diffusion-erasure among, 198, 209, 247, 321–22; disadvantageous position of, 159, 169, 248, 386; indigenization of, 142, 164, 248, 251, 318–19, 322–23; indigenous reaction against, 40, 57, 184, 247–48, 395; in-migration of, 53–58, 153, 159, 185; international attitudes among, 246–47; and international marriage, 141–42, 164, 297, 299, 304, 304n, 305–6, 309–10, 315–17, 316n, 394; linguistic indigenization of, 293–95, 323; linguistic Russification of, 251, 269, 272–82, 285–88, 323, 393–94; and their migration from Central Asia, 184; national marginality of, 315, 393; national stratification favoring, 80; national territoriality among, 373–74,

nonindigenes (*cont.*)
398; native language retention among, 272–82; native language schooling for, 254–55; "natural" assimilation of, 318, 394; political rights of, 347, 389; reactive ethnicity among, 198, 248–49; as refugees, 186–87, 235; and their return "home," 186–87, 223–24, 248–49, 387; Russian bilingualism among, 289; Russification of, 140, 146, 251, 253, 269, 272–82, 285–88, 321–23, 384–85, 393–94

non-Russian languages: fluency in, 283; and linguistic indigenization, 255–56, 272–82, 293–95, 323; literacy in, 67–68; and the new language laws, 126, 257, 260, 282, 288, 289, 293, 295, 322–23, 348, 365, 395; original publications in, 261; restrictions in the use of, 42, 69, 254, 269, 287, 293, 295

non-Slavic South, 166, 181, 223, 240, 248, 298, 304, 308. *See also* Central Asia; Transcaucasia

North Caucasus, 57, 58, 65, 251; demographic indigenization in, 185; demographic Russification in, 76, 117, 120; deported nations from, 316n; international marriage in, 313; language standardization in, 254; linguistic Russification in, 269, 284, 286; nationalization in, 314, 321; Russian out-migration from, 185

North Ossetia, 223, 258, 369. *See also* North Caucasus; South Ossetia

Novorossiya, 76, 372; demographic Russification in, 76. *See also* Ukraine

occupational mobility: in Armenia, 81; in Belorussia, 81; education and, 235; emancipation and, 75; in Estonia, 80; in Finland, 80; in Georgia, 81; and the indigenization of high-status occupations, 242–43; and indigenization policies, 236, 242–44; industrialization and, 75; and international attitudes, 245–46; international equalization and, 236, 238–43, 389; in Latvia, 80; and limited employment opportunities, 78; and national territoriality, 242–43; in Poland, 80; in prerevolutionary Russia, 75–83; and reactive ethnicity, 80–81; and social mobilization, 235–43; in Ukraine, 81, 130; urbanization and, 75, 235. *See also* social mobilization

Official Nationality, 35, 44, 45, 72
officially delimited territories (ODTs), 154, 156–58. *See also* confederal structure; federal hierarchy; home republics
Osh' Oblast, 184, 241, 371. *See also* border disputes; ethnoterritorial conflict; Kyrgyzstan; Uzbekistan
Ossetians, 171, 183, 223, 226, 257, 282, 284, 358, 363–64, 369. *See also* border disputes; ethnoterritorial conflict; Georgia; North Caucasus; North Ossetia; South Ossetia
otechestvo. *See* fatherland
otkhod (temporary labor migration), 48, 59n, 60, 76, 78. *See also* migration; urbanization
otkhodnichestvo, 48, 59n, 60, 76, 78, 123
otkhodniki, 60, 76. *See also* peasantry

pan-Islamic consciousness, 110, 184. *See also* Central Asia; Islam; Muslims; Turkestan
pan-Turkic consciousness, 110, 184. *See also* Turkestan; Central Asia
Pavlodar Oblast, 311
peasantry: and anti-elite sentiments, 44, 46–47; and anti-outsider sentiments, 44, 83, 86, 88, 381–82; aspirations for upward mobility among, 77–78; and its attitudes toward education, 73–74; and collectivization, 95, 113, 115, 122–23; conscious, 43, 47, 75n, 76, 79, 88; as the core of the nation, 38, 45, 88, 381; elite attitudes toward, 43–45, 47, 381; emancipation of, 47–50; ethnographic distinctions among, 44–45; the geographic mobilization of, 47–60, 95, 113, 115, 124; and literacy, 66–67; localism among, 44–45, 47, 52, 60–61, 70–71, 83, 85–88, 115, 382–83; nationalization of, 43–44, 49, 86, 115, 123, 382; and *otkhodnichestvo*, 48, 59n, 60, 76, 78, 123; a sense of homeland among, 86, 382; the social mobilization of, 47, 59, 115; and urbanization, 59–60; and *zemlyachestvo*, 61, 66, 76, 87, 123
peoples of the north: and the development of literary languages, 126; linguistic Russification of the, 265, 270–72, 289; and the nationalization of elites, 37, 381–82; and the nationalization of the masses, 126, 137;

Russification of, 394–95. See also *ethnie*; Siberia
perestroyka, 152–53, 325, 333–34, 336, 345, and national front organizations, 328, 328n. See also Gorbachev
Poland, 49, 76, 80, 86, 94
Poles, 269, 313, 316, 318, 381–82; Belorussification of, 295
Polish dominance, in Lithuania and Belorussia, 39, 41, 65; and nationalization in Belorussia, 37
Polish uprising of 1863, 49, 78n
political decentralization. See decentralization, political
political independence. See independence, political
political representation, 347–50. See also democracy; democratization; indigenization; national territoriality; successor states
political socialization, 225. See also indigenization; nationalization; Russification; sovietization
Polonization, 37, 41, 65, 85
popular literature, and nationalization, 67–68
primordialism, 17–18, 341. See also nationalism; nations
proletarian internationalism, 109, 130, 193. See also communism; Communist party; Lenin; Marxism-Leninism; Stalin
Pskov Oblast, 370
psychological distance, 244. See also international attitudes
purges, 134, 137–38, 143, 145

Quebec, 404
Quebecois, 402

Radishchev, Alexandre, 35, 43–44
rastsvet, 26, 97, 390
reactive ethnicity, 40, 41, 58, 80, 193, 196, 356n, 394, 399; among indigenes, 40, 57, 184, 247–48, 363–64, 395; among nonindigenes, 198, 248–49; and occupational mobility, 80–81; among Russians, 41–42, 85, 89, 248, 252, 260, 356–57, 372. See also internal colonialism
Red Army: as an agent of assimilation, 144; and indigenization policies, 132–33; national-territorial units in, 132–33, 144

refugees, 186–87, 361, 363, 368, 387, 403. See also migration
regional *khozraschet*, 326, 330–39; and economic indigenization, 333, 339; and economic sovereignty, 326, 330, 333–40; and the *sovnarkhozy* system, 333. See also Gorbachev, Khrushchev
regionalism, 328, 332
relative deprivation, 25, 27, 40, 47, 77–80, 113, 196–97; among indigenes, 246–48, 260; and international equalization, 196–97; and the nationalization of the masses in prerevolutionary Russia, 79, 82; among nonindigenes, 248; and upward mobility, 246. See also internal colonialism; reactive ethnicity
Riga, 319. See also Latvia
rodina, 35, 45, 85, 86, 169–70. See also homelands
romanticism, 36–38, 45–46, 83, 85, 144, 382; and emancipation of serfs, 47; and the nationalization process, 37–38, 381
RSFSR. See Russia
RUKH, 18, 83n, 189, 282, 328n, 354. See also national independence movements; Ukraine
Rumania, 42, 157–58, 354, 365, 402. See also Moldova
Rumanians, 42, 269. See also Moldavians
Russia: autarchic tendencies in, 335; bilateral treaties with, 372–73; border disputes with, 370, 371–73, 388; and the Commonwealth of Independent States, 346, 355–56; as a confederation of national states, 356, 367; declarations of sovereignty in, 347, 366; draft constitution of, 366–67; eastern *ethnies* of, 109, 137, 157, 171, 178, 223, 228, 253, 257–58, 265, 269–72, 285–87, 289, 312–14, 317, 319–20, 322, 381; economic health of, 337–38; education in, 71–75, 87, 382; emancipation in, 49; as the homeland image of the state, 139; indigenization of the work force in, 132; indigenous underrepresentation in high-status occupations in, 242; international marriage in, 312; intrastate disintegration in, 356, 365–67; Russian localism in, 356–57, 366; Russian perceptions of, 17, 42, 55, 58, 84–85, 117, 138, 154, 169–70, 189, 341, 371–72, 391; "natural" assimila-

Russsia (*cont.*)
  tion in, 318; new Federal Treaty in, 358, 367; and Rossiya, 85, 139; rural depopulation in, 236n; and the socialist fatherland, 138–9, 169–70; urbanization in, 59–66, 200, 204
Russian imperialism, 369n, 371, 373. *See also* Russian nationalism
Russian language: and bilingualism, 288–93, 322, 393; debate over, 35–36; fluency in, 262, 283, 393; functional utility of, 262, 283, 287, 295; as the language of international communication, 139, 254, 293, 395; as the language of upward mobility, 139, 261–62, 288–89, 293, 322–23; as the lingua franca of the state, 138, 254, 261–62; literacy in, 67, 69; obligatory study of, 139, 254; publications, 258–61; and Russification, 69, 87, 262, 322; schooling in, 128, 139, 254–58; as a second language, 283, 322
Russian nationalism: as a catalyst for rising non-Russian national territoriality, 85, 89, 367; and the geographic expansion of Russia, 58, 84–85, 154; the importance of the ancestral homeland to, 17, 34, 39, 154; v. local nationalism, 104–5; and localism, 338–39, 356–57; and pressure for economic and political recentralization, 338; as a reaction to the declining status of Russians, 394, 399; and a sense of exclusiveness toward Russia, 85. *See also* national territoriality; nationalism; Russian imperialism
Russianization, 115, 138, 262. *See also* Russification; sovietization
Russian-ness, 35, 36, 58, 68, 138, 338, territorial view of, 83
Russians: and their attitudes toward independence, 372; and bilingualism in the non-Russian languages, 293; educational attainment of, 72–74, 226; and their emigration, 388; ethnographic differentiation of, 135; favored status of, 26, 34, 35n, 39, 65, 80, 106, 144, 151, 169–70, 194–95, 199–200, 261, 322, 382, 386; as indigenes throughout the USSR, 188, 371–72; indigenization of, 394; international attitudes among, 245–47, 246n; international marriage among, 141–42, 304–5, 305n, 308, 311–12, 314–16; linguistic assimilation among, 293; localism among, 338–39, 357, 366; and migration to the non-Russian republics, 53n, 117, 119–22, 170, 181–82, 189; and migration to the non-Russian autonomous units of Russia, 120, 171, 178, 184–85, 209, 223, 365; national self-consciousness among, 58, 338–39, 357, 366; national territoriality among, 367; and the nationalization of elites, 35n, 35–39, 381; and the nationalization of the masses, 43–93, 314, 357; "natural" assimilation among, 317–21; in non-Russian republics, 117, 178, 372; as the oppressor nation, 97, 105; and perception of homeland, 42, 58, 84, 117, 138, 154, 169–70, 341n, 371–72, 391; political underrepresentation among, 348–49; reactive ethnicity among, 248, 356–57, 372; refugees, 249, 387; and return migration to Russia, 166, 170, 181, 184, 240–41, 248–49, 293, 387–88; as Soviet people, 372, 391; status of, 243; territorial claims made by, 371–72; urbanization of, 121, 200, 204
Russification, 8n, 9, 26, 34, 39, 41–42, 61–63, 65, 69, 76, 81, 87, 102, 117, 119–20, 127, 143, 251, 265, 272, 282–83, 285–86, 319–20, 322, 384–85; and the activation of national territoriality, 95, 125, 224, 257, 262, 287; and assimilation, 138–47, 151, 171, 188, 251–52, 285–87, 317, 393–95; as a counterproductive policy, 63, 95, 143, 188, 252, 287, 322–23, 385, 395; of cities, 62, 170, 200, 204, 209, 223; demographic, 65, 76, 82, 117, 119–20, 122, 124, 154, 181, 209, 223, 285; and de-Russification, 124, 135, 223, 265, 284, 320–21; as an end in itself, 139, 145; of indigenes in autonomous okrugs, 171, 322, 394; and indigenization, 127, 137–38, 250–51, 320–21, 394; and international marriage, 142, 304, 312; linguistic, 135, 138–39, 172–82, 251, 253–54, 257, 262–89, 295, 323, 393–95; and national self-determination movements, 181, 223; and nationalization, 251, 393; as "natural" assimilation, 320, 322, 394; of nonindigenes throughout the USSR, 140, 146, 251, 253, 269, 272–82, 285–88, 321–23, 384–85, 393–94; of non-Russians in Russia, 117, 120, 140, 143, 171, 185, 188, 231, 265, 272, 282, 284, 286, 289, 312, 316, 322,

394; and reactive ethnicity among non-Russians, 41–42, 85, 89, 248, 252, 260, 356–57, 372; of schools, 257; as sovietization, 137–38, 250, 252; Stalin and, 95, 107, 144, 151; of Ukrainians, 85, 117, 142, 251, 265, 283, 285, 320, 322, 384–85; and urbanization, 62, 62n, 170, 282–87

St. Petersburg, 39, 59, 60, 61, 62n, 63, industrialization in, 76; and its influence on the nationalization of non-Russian elites, 37, 64–65; literacy in, 67; Russification in, 61–63, 319

Sajudis, 328. *See also* Lithuania; national independence movements

Samara, 316

Saratov Oblast, 245, 368

sblizheniye, 26, 97, 146, 152, 225, 301, 332n, 385, 390. *See also* acculturation; Soviet people; sovietization

Scotland, 404

Scottish people, 402, 404

secession, 97–98, 102, 104, 106, 341–42, 351–52, 397, 405–6; and confederalization, 341–42, 345–46, 351; law on, 345, 396. *See also* disintegration; national independence movements; national separatism; national territoriality; nationalism

Sel'kups, 142

sense of place, 5, 16, 30, 32, 39

Serbs, 402

serfdom, abolition of, 47–50. *See also* emancipation; peasantry

Shatalin Plan, 357. *See also* economic interdependence; sovereignty

Shevardnadze, 364. *See also* Georgia

Siberia, 103, 104, 129, 142, 157, 251, 253, 265; autonomous okrug *ethnies* of, 109, 137, 157, 171, 178, 223, 228, 253, 257–58, 265, 269–72, 285–87, 289, 312–14, 317, 319–20, 322, 381; education in, 72; industrialization in, 76, 120; labor deficit in, 166; language standardization in, 253; migration to, 53–57, 85, 166, 171; nationalization in, 321; as part of Russia's perceptual homeland, 17, 84–85; return migration from, 17, 56; as Utopia, 17, 55, 84

Slavic republics: demographic indigenization of the cities in, 223; indigenous dominance of occupational sectors in, 242; international family rates in, 300; and the new Union Treaty, 346, 354. *See also* Belarus'; Russia; Ukraine

Slavophiles, 36, 38, 45, 144, 381

Slavophilism: and "Mother Russia," 84; and the Russian nation, 38–39; and Shafarevich, 39n. *See also* romanticism; Russian nationalism

sliyaniye, 26, 97, 152, 332n, 390. *See also* assimilation; sovietization

Slovakia, 401–2

Slovenia, 401–2

Snegur, 365. *See also* border disputes; ethnoterritorial conflict; Moldova

social mobilization: and assimilation, 192, 247, 313; and diffusion-competition, 197–98, 245–48; and diffusion-erasure, 192–93, 245–46, 389; education and, 71–72, 225–35; and fertility, 164; of indigenes, 68, 130, 170; and indigenization, 248; and international attitudes, 243–47; and international equalization, 199, 225–26, 389; and international marriage, 301, 304–5, 309–11, 315; literacy and, 66–71; and migration to cities, 59, 168; and national marginality, 192; and national self-consciousness, 66, 152, 191–98, 226, 248, 295; and national territoriality, 24–25, 187, 198, 235, 248, 390, 405–6; and nationalization of the masses, 66–83, 87, 95, 115, 191–98, 248, 250, 382, 384–85, 389–90; and nativism, 235; occupational mobility and, 235–43; in the postwar USSR, 198–249; of the peasantry, 47, 59, 115; and Russian bilingualism, 288–89; and a sense of homeland, 66; and sovietization, 152, 170, 243, 390; and urbanization, 199–225

South Ossetia, 171, 223, 284; abolition of, 183–84, 358, 363; declaration of sovereignty in, 183, 363–64; Georgian claims to, 363–64; Georgians in, 223; Ossetian claims to, 363–64; reactive ethnicity in, 248, 363–64. *See also* disintegration; ethnoterritorial conflict; Georgia; Georgians; North Ossetia; Ossetians

sovereignty: for autonomous nations and *ethnies*, 352, 356–58, 369, 376, 388; declarations of, 183, 347–48, 353–55, 357, 360, 362–73, 397; economic, 326, 330, 333–40, 340n; of nations, 347, 351–52; politi-

sovereignty (*cont.*)
cal, 325, 339–340, 340n; and the strength of the domestic economy, 336–38; of union republics, 113, 342, 345–46, 347–52. *See also* confederal structure; disintegration; national independence movements; national self-determination
Soviet federalism. *See* federalism, Soviet
Soviet people, 26, 31, 105, 107, 137, 138, 142, 146, 152, 170, 188, 225, 252, 262, 288, 301, 309, 323, 325, 331, 332n, 343–45, 350–51, 372, 379, 390–92. *See also* assimilation; Russification; sovietization
sovietization, 8n, 31n, 105, 123, 151–52, 252, 295, 379–80, 390–92; as a contender with nationalism and localism, 115; Gorbachev on, 152–53, 379; as an impediment to Russian nationalization, 138; and indigenization, 126, 137, 243, 386; through Russification, 137–38, 250, 252; and social mobilization, 152, 170, 243, 390; and Soviet federalism, 343–45, 375. *See also* assimilation; Russification; sovietization
sovnarkhozy, 326, 330–33, 339, 374–75; the delimitation of, 331; and localism, 331. *See also* decentralization; Khrushchev
Spain, 402–4
Stalin, 8; and "autonomization" of the USSR, 100, 151; and the Constitution of 1936, 109, 109n, 113; and (his) definition of nations, 8, 102–3; and the deformation of Marxism-Leninism, 106–7, 112n, 144, 153, 329, 352, 385; on the delimitation of autonomous units, 104; and forced migration, 159; and "Great Russian chauvinism," 103, 105–6, 144, 200; and indigenization policies, 37, 95, 105–7, 121, 124–35, 374, 388; and international equalization, 144; and "local" (non-Russian) nationalism, 105–6; and the meaning of homeland, 103, 107, 115, 147; and *Narkomnats*, 104, 108, 112; on national-cultural autonomy, 103–4; on the national problem, 102–3; on national territorial autonomy, 103–4, 105; and nationalization, 37, 381; and the proletarianization of nations, 131; publications under, 260; on the right to national self-determination, 104, 106; on the right to secession, 104, 106; and Russification, 95, 107, 144, 151; and totalitarianism, 327;

and the Union Treaty of 1922, 107, 110, 112–13, 329–30
state farm (*sovkhoz*), 236
states, categorization of, 401, 401n. *See also* nation-states
successor states, national separatism in, 356; national stratification in, 348, 386–87, 399, 402; political representation in, 347–58
Sverdlovsk, 333
Switzerland, 404

Tadzhikistan: border disputes in, 189, 371, 388; demographic Russification of the cities in, 122; intrastate disintegration in, 356; language standardization in, 254; native language publications in, 258–60; nativism in, 170, 184; Russian out-migration from, 181, 184; unemployment in, 241. *See also* Central Asia; successor states
Tadzhiks, 121, 136, 159n, 184; and their "gravitation" to Tadzhikistan, 119; international marriage among, 313, 316; linguistic Russification among, 265; and their perception of interethnic relations, 184; Russian bilingualism among, 289. *See also* Central Asians
Tatar ASSR. *See* Tatarstan
Tatar language (Kazan'): schooling in, 255, 257; vernacularization of, 42
Tatars (Kazan'): and (their) dispersal from Tatarstan, 110; and (their) "gravitation" to Tatarstan, 120; international attitudes among, 245–47; international marriages among, 316; and the nationalization of elites, 36, 381; and the nationalization of the masses, 82; "natural" assimilation among, 319
Tatarstan: declaration of independence in, 356, 367; divide and rule in, 112; indigenization of high-status occupations in, 243; indigenization of the work force in, 132; international attitudinal surveys in, 244–47; "natural" assimilation in, 319; regional *khozraschet* in, 333. *See also* autonomous republics; Volga-Urals
Tbilisi, 311, 344. *See also* Georgia
territorial claims, 370–72. *See also* border disputes; ethnoterritorial conflict; international conflicts
territoriality, 18, 22–23, 28, 88, 360n, 361n, 373–74, 388, 398; and the compartmental-

ization of human interaction in space, 18n, 28; indigenous, 80; as a sense of exclusiveness, 18n, 21–22, 80; as a sense of spatial identity, 18. *See also* homeland; national territoriality
totalitarianism, 326–30, 396–97; and centralization, 326, 341; critiques of, 326–27; and Kremlinology, 326; and socioeconomic development, 327–28; during the Stalin era, 327; and studies of the national problem, 327, 375–76. *See also* Communist party; confederal structure; Stalin; unitary-confederal continuum
"tribalism," 405
"tribes," 371, 404–5
Transcaucasia, 82, 249, Armenian dominance in, 65, 81, 119, 382; border disputes in, 156, 189; demographic indigenization of the cities in, 223; "ethnic cleansing" in, 183, 387, 402; international family rates in, 298; linguistic indigenization in, 293; national segregation in, 182; "natural" assimilation in, 319; nonindigenous migration from, 182; Russian migration from, 166, 182; and the Transcaucasian Federal Republic (TCSFSR), 107–9, 112, 134. *See also* Armenia; Azerbaydzhan; Georgia
Transcaucasian Federal Republic (TCSFSR), 107–9, 112, 134. *See also* Transcaucasia
Turkestan, 82, 110, 135. *See also* Central Asia
Turkic languages: and the Arabic script, 127; and the Cyrillic script, 127; and the Latin script, 127. *See also* pan-Turkic consciousness
Turkmen, 159n, linguistic Russification among, 265; and their "gravitation" to Turkmenistan, 119; Russian bilingualism among, 289. *See also* Central Asians
Turkmenistan: demographic indigenization of the cities in, 122; potential debt burden in, 336; Russian out-migration from, 181. *See also* Central Asia
Tuvinia, 248, 289, 356, 365–66. *See also* autonomous republics; ethnoterritorial conflicts; Siberia
Tuvins, 238, 257, Russian bilingualism among, 289, 289n

Udmurtia, 258. *See also* autonomous republics; Volga-Urals

Udmurts: intranational marriages among, 313; linguistic Russification of the, 265, 284, 286; Russification of, 286. *See also* Finno-Ugrian national communities
Ufa, 67. *See also* Bashkiria
Ukraine, 18, 157, 262, autarchic tendencies in, 335; bilateral treaties with, 372–73; border disputes in, 156, 189, 370, 388; and the Commonwealth of Independent States, 346; economic health of, 337–38; Greater, 370; indigenization of cities in, 65, 122, 124; indigenization of the work force in, 130–31; international marriage in, 312, 316; as *Malorossiya*, 42; national independence movement in, 354; "natural" assimilation in, 318n, 319; and the new Union Treaty, 354; occupational mobility in, 81, 130; as part of the Russian homeland, 170, 371; Russian in-migration and national territoriality in, 181–82, 189; Russian-language schools in, 256–57; Russian migration to, 117, 181. *See also* Slavic republics
Ukrainian language: development and Russification, 42; and linguistic indigenization, 126, 293; policies against the use of, 42; publications in, 259–61; schooling in, 129, 255–56; and the stigma attached to vernacular, 41
Ukrainianization, 65, 115, 122, 124, 126, 130
Ukrainians: excess mortality among, 121; and their geographic concentration in Ukraine, 117, 167–68; international marriage rates among, 305, 305n, 308, 311–12, 314–16; the lack of elites among, 40; limitations in occupational mobility among, 81; linguistic de-Russification among, 284; and their migration from Ukraine, 53n, 166–67, 181; and the nationalization of elites, 36, 39, 381–82; "natural" assimilation among, 318–20; Russification among, 85, 117, 142, 251, 265, 283, 285, 320, 322, 384–85; as a "tribe" of the Russian nation, 371; and urbanization, 121
underdeveloped South, comparability of national territoriality in, 404
unemployment, 236, 241, 336
uneven development, 27, 383. *See also* internal colonialism
union republics: autonomous units as, 352; bilateral trade agreements among, 340,

470 · Index

union republics (*cont.*)
372–73, 376; border disputes between, 156, 189–90, 353, 370–73, 388; of Central Asia, 110; demographic strength of indigenes in, 178; disintegration of, 345, 356, 358, 364–67, 369, 375–76; formation of, 99, 104, 107–10; indigenization and national territoriality in, 137, 369; international family rates in, 296–301; new language laws in, 126, 257, 260, 282, 288–89, 293, 295, 322–23, 348, 365, 395; for nations, 112; native language retention in, 269–82; native language schools in, 255–57; political representation in, 347–58; Russian-language schools in, 255–57; Russians in, 53n, 117, 119–22, 170, 178, 181–82, 189, 372; sovereign rights of, 113, 342, 345–46, 347–52. *See also* successor states

Union of Sovereign States, 377

Union Treaty, of 1922, 107, 110, 112, 113, 329–30, 342; new, 254, 329, 345–46, 353–55, 357, 396. *See also* confederal structure; Gorbachev; Stalin

unitary-confederal continuum, 112–13, 341–42. *See also* confederal structure; confederalization; Soviet federalism

United States of Europe. *See* European Community

upward mobility, 76, 77–78, 80–81, 131–32, 246–47. *See also* occupational mobility; social mobilization

urbanization: and assimilation, 96, 192–93, 200; and collectivization, 122; and the de-Russification of cities, 209, 223; and diffusion-competition, 200; and education, 230–31; equalization in the rate of, 121, 200–204; of home republics, 202–8; and its impact on the peasantry, 59–60; of indigenes, 63–66, 121–22, 170, 209; and the indigenization of cities, 63–66, 80, 122–24, 209, 223–24; and international attitudes, 244; international and interrepublic equalization in the rate of, 121, 200–204, 389; and international marriages, 141, 298–30; during the interwar period, 121–24, 200; as a measure of geographic and social mobilization, 121, 153, 199–200; and the national problem, 244; and national self-consciousness, 65, 86; and national separatism, 225; and national territoriality, 224–25; and nationalization, 64–66, 87, 124, 382; of nations, 200–225; and occupational mobility, 75, 235; in prerevolutionary Russia, 59–66; and rural-urban migration, 59–66, 80, 121–23, 168, 200, 209, 261; Russian rate of, 121, 200, 204; and Russification, 62, 62n, 170, 282–87; in the RSFSR, 200, 204; and social mobilization, 199–225; as a surrogate for modernization, 199–200; and *zemlyachestvo*, 61, 66, 87, 123. *See also* geographic mobility; migration; social mobilization

Uzbek language: linguistic assimilation to, 284; schooling in, 255

Uzbekistan, 140, and Birlik, 355; border disputes in, 189, 371, 388; demographic Russification of the cities in, 122; indigenous underrepresentation in high-status occupations in, 242; indigenization of the work force in, 131–32; international attitudes in, 244; intrastate disintegration in, 356; nativism in, 184, 368; "natural" assimilation in, 318; political indigenization in, 134; potential debt burden in, 336; Russian bilingualism in, 288–89; Russian-language schools in, 255; Russian out-migration from, 181, 184; unemployment in, 241. *See also* Central Asia; successor states

Uzbeks, 119, 121, 136, 159n, 184, and the demographic Uzbekization of Karakalpakstan, 177–78, 223; international attitudes among, 244–45; international marriages among, 313, 314, 316; as locally dominant group in Turkestan, 110; "natural" assimilation among, 318; and perceptions of interethnic relations, 184; reidentification of Kazakhs and Turkmen as, 140; Russian bilingualism among, 288–89

vernacularization, 35–36, 40–42, 67, 71, 87, and indigenization, 125–28; as a link between elites and masses, 36; and literacy, 67; among the Muslim *ethnies*, 42; and nationalization, 36, 40, 87, 250, 253; of the non-Russian languages, 40–42; of the Russian language, 35–36. *See also* language; literacy; nationalization

Vilnius, 305, 310, 313, 316, 318. *See also* Lithuania

Volga German ASSR, 186, 316, 353, 368

Volga Tatars. *See* Tatars
Volga Urals, 269, 284, 286, 289, 312, 322

Wales, 404
Wallonia, 404
Walloonians, 402, 404
welfare colonialism, 195. *See also* internal colonialism
Welsh, 402–3
Western Europe, comparability of national territoriality in, 402–4
western territorialism, 14–15. *See also* nationalismnationalim
Westernism, 38
Westernizers: and (their) attitude toward the peasantry, 44, 45; Gorbachev as a, 39n; and the Russian nation, 38. *See also* Russian nationalism; Slavophiles
World War I: and national territoriality, 94; and nationalization, 94, 108
white-collar work force, 238; international attitudes of, 245–46. *See also* occupational mobility; social mobilization; upward mobility

Yagnobs, 136. *See also* Tadzhikistan; Tadzhiks
Yakutia, 170, 188, 234, 356, 358. *See also* autonomous republics; Siberia
Yakuts: national self-consciousness of, 58, 188, 313; native language schooling for, 257; and a rising sense of exclusiveness toward Yakutia, 58, 188. *See also* Siberia
Yamalo-Nenets Autonomous Okrug, 171. *See also* autonomous okrugs; Siberia
Yel'tsin, 367, 372–73, 377
Yerevan, nationalist demonstrations in, 224. *See also* Armenia; ethnoterritorial conflicts
Yugoslavia, comparability of national territoriality in, 401–2

zemlyachestvo, 61, 76; and the impact of urbanization, 61, 66, 87, 123. *See also* localism; migration; peasantry
zemlyaki, 61. *See also* peasantry
zero-sum game, 195

Ethno-National Communities of the USSR

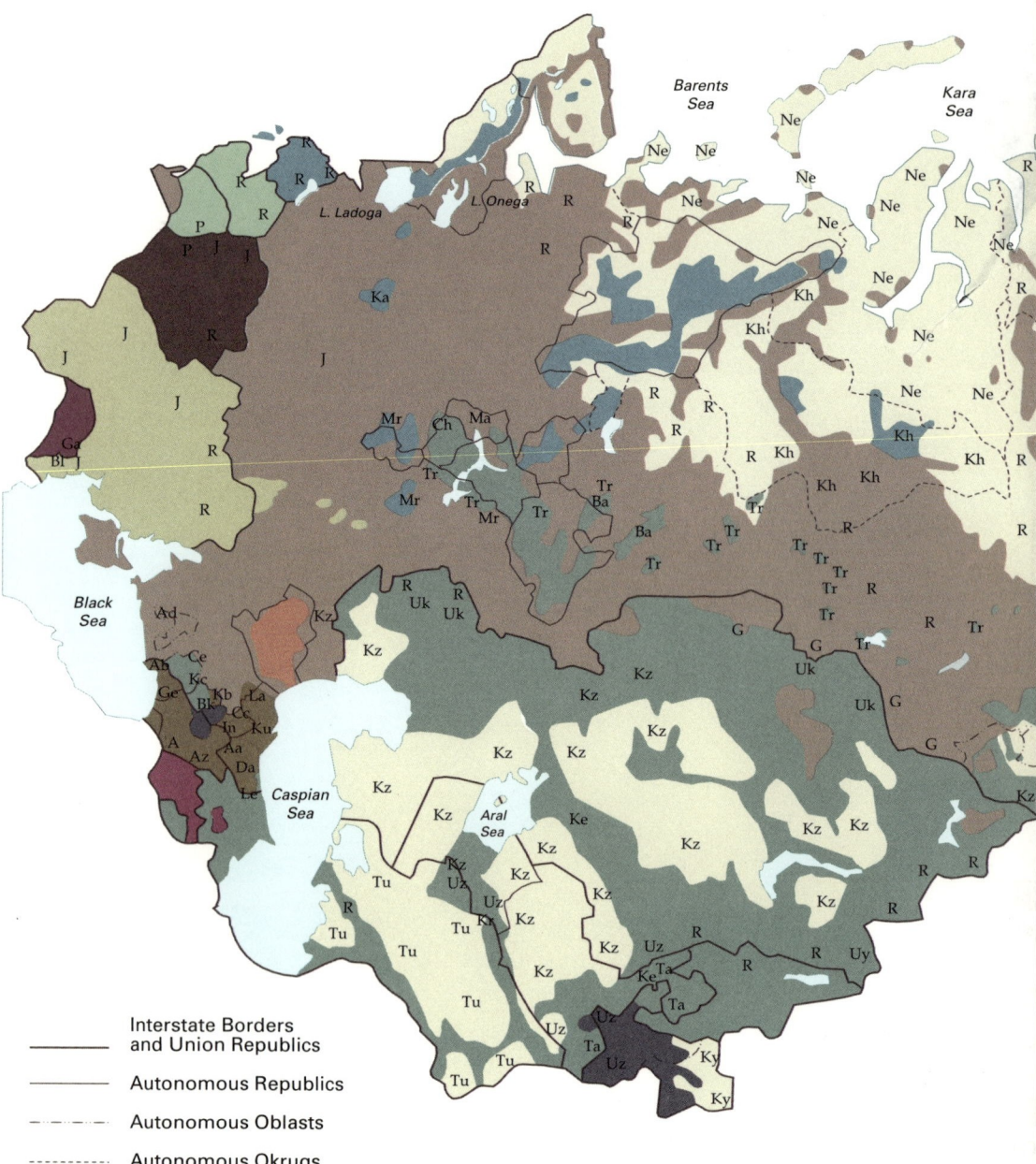

Interstate Borders and Union Republics
Autonomous Republics
Autonomous Oblasts
Autonomous Okrugs

* Only the largest national communities listed here. See the map key for complete information